Worship, Music, and Interpretation

McMaster Divinity College Press
McMaster General Studies Series, Volume 16

"Wendy J. Porter has offered the church an unusual perspective of the interchange between worship, music and interpretation in the life of Christian worship over time. Porter is successful in interweaving her findings into an insightful contribution to help alleviate the common tendency to bifurcate areas of study. Porter's scholarly and mature work should be read by every serious practitioner of musical worship."

—**Constance Cherry**, professor emeritus, Indiana Wesleyan University

"Wendy Porter's essays are a wonderful gift to the church. Deeply rooted in biblical text and the history of worship through music, she offers a series of important probes that remind us of the importance and challenges of music in worship. All who are engaged in leading and planning worship need to read and reflect on these important papers."

—**David Firth**, tutor in Old Testament, Trinity College Bristol

"Understanding contemporary worship is difficult for contemporary people because you can't read the label from inside the bottle. In this collection, Dr. Wendy Porter uses her skills as a musicologist and liturgical historian to lead readers outside the bottle, deftly exploring how music has interpreted and expressed the Christian faith. Page after page shines fresh light that will help scholars, students, and practitioners of Christian worship."

—**Dr. Matthew Westerholm**, professor of church music & worship, Southern Baptist Theological Seminary

"Porter's *Worship, Music, and Interpretation* brings together thirty years of scholarship. Her essays—which address music and texts set to music from Old Testament times to the twenty-first century—draw attention to the complex diversity of Christian musical expression while highlighting continuous functions of "contemporary" composers of every generation. Highly recommended!"

—JOSHUA A. WAGGENER, professor of church music and worship, Southwestern Baptist Theological Seminary

Worship, Music, and Interpretation

Exploratory Essays

WENDY J. PORTER

☙PICKWICK *Publications* · Eugene, Oregon

WORSHIP, MUSIC, AND INTERPRETATION
Exploratory Essays

McMaster General Studies Series, Volume 16
McMaster Divinity College Press

Copyright © 2024 Wendy J. Porter. All rights reserved. Except for brief quotations in critical publications or reviews, no part of this book may be reproduced in any manner without prior written permission from the publisher. Write: Permissions, Wipf and Stock Publishers, 199 W. 8th Ave., Suite 3, Eugene, OR 97401.

Pickwick Publications
An Imprint of Wipf and Stock Publishers
199 W. 8th Ave., Suite 3
Eugene, OR 97401

McMaster Divinity College Press
1280 Main Street West
Hamilton, ON, Canada L8S 4K1

www.wipfandstock.com

PAPERBACK ISBN: 979-8-3852-2330-5
HARDCOVER ISBN: 979-8-3852-2331-2
EBOOK ISBN: 979-8-3852-2332-9

McMaster General Studies Series
ISSN 2564-4408 (Print)
ISSN 2564-4416 (Ebook)

Cataloguing-in-Publication data:

Names: Porter, Wendy J.

Title: Worship, Music, and Interpretation : Exploratory Essays / Wendy J. Porter.

Description: Eugene, OR: Pickwick Publications, 2024 | McMaster General Studies Series 16 | Includes bibliographical references and index.

Identifiers: ISBN 979-8-3852-2330-5 (paperback) | ISBN 979-8-3852-2331-2 (hardcover) | ISBN 979-8-3852-2332-9 (ebook)

Subjects: LCSH: Worship—History—Early church | Liturgies, Early Christian.

Classification: BV6 .P67 2024 (paperback) | BV6 (ebook)

VERSION NUMBER 09/27/24

Cover Image: No. 1, "Psalm 24" (from the Five Smooth Stones series, Watercolour with FIMO) by James Tughan (tughansemaphore.ca)

Contents

Lists of Tables and Figures | vii
Preface | ix

    1   An Introduction to Worship, Music, and Interpretation | 1

Part One: Music and Interpretation in the Early Church

    2   Liturgical and Musical Interpretation | 17

    3   Music and the Early Church | 37

    4   Creeds and Hymns in the Early Church | 54

    5   A Word about Women, Music, and Sensuality in the Early Church | 72

    6   Ekphonetic Notation in Liturgical Manuscripts | 98

    7   Is Early Christian Music Jewish or Greco-Roman? | 109

    8   Romanos Melodus and the Ancient Christian Musical Tradition | 136

Part Two: Musical Traditions and Interpretations

    9   The Composer as Interpreter of the Bible | 155

    10   Resurrection in the Western Wind Credos of Taverner, Sheppard, and Tye | 187

CONTENTS

11 Images of Christ in Credos of Bach, Beethoven, and Stravinsky | 200

12 Sacred Music at the Turn of the Millennia | 226

13 Contemporary Worship Songs and Suffering | 249

14 Christian Worship and the Toronto Blessing | 269

15 William Byrd, Reformation Liturgy, and Contemporary Worship | 290

Part Three: The Past and Present of Music and Worship

16 New Songs in Biblical and Christian History | 323

17 Theological Reflections on the History of Christian Worship | 356

Modern Authors Index | 413
Ancient Sources Index | 421

Lists of Tables and Figures

Table 1. Songs with reference to Pain and Suffering | 253
Figure 1. Placement of the *Crucifixus* in the Credo by Time Signature | 206
Figure 2. Placement of the *Crucifixus* in the Credo by Key | 207

Preface

THE ESSAYS IN THIS volume have, for the most part, been written over a number of years and for a variety of purposes.¹ In one essay that is new, chapter 16, on the notion of the contemporary worship song, I examine the Old and New Testaments for evidence for the call for a "new song" in biblical worship, trace some of the major innovations in Christian music, and then mention some implications for contemporary Christian music. This essay follows from some of my earlier work on the history of music from the ancient world to the present, here with emphasis upon the biblical writings.

    I am pleased to be able to republish all of the other essays by acknowledging their previous publication. All of the essays retain the heart of their original publication, and although I have not attempted to bring them entirely up to date, I have made slight revisions throughout. However, for many, if not most of them, because of the subject matter involved, there has been relatively little published since their initial appearance. In a number of the chapters, where possible and necessary, I have referred to significant recent publications. I have also made changes to ensure that the essays fit together to form a coherent whole on the topic of sacred music and its interpretation, especially as that interpretation has been seen through the ages, from the ancient to the modern world. I have provided transliteration of Greek words for those unfamiliar with it (apart from in chapters 8 and 9, when dealing with Greek editions of papyri).

    1. Most of these papers were presented at conferences revolving around a specific theme and my presentations usually included segments of musical recordings or displayed images of ancient documents that I could annotate, none of which can be included here.

One of the distinctives of this volume is that it contains scholarly work in the areas of musicology and worship studies that addresses topics from ancient times to the present. Those who address this range of topics are relatively few, I realize, but I have enjoyed the opportunity to bring together a range of skills and interests, from my practice as a contemporary worship musician with several published CDs, from classical music training, from research in ancient studies relating to music and some pertaining to Greek, and from my own PhD research in musicology, as well as an ongoing practice of theological reflection on the nature of Christian worship past and present to be able to address some of these issues. I am not a master of all the intricacies of these subjects, but I have attempted to explore and weave their subject matter together, and out of these various pieces, to present a cohesive whole that a range of readers may benefit from my studies of sacred music through the ages.

The essays that have been previously published appeared in the following places, and I hereby acknowledge their previous publication and my use of them here:

- Chapter 2: "Liturgical Interpretation." In *Dictionary of Biblical Criticism and Interpretation*, edited by Stanley E. Porter, 206–10. London: Routledge, 2007; and "Music and Interpretation." In *Dictionary of Biblical Criticism and Interpretation*, edited by Stanley E. Porter, 230–35. London: Routledge, 2007.

- Chapter 3: "Music." In *Dictionary of New Testament Background*, edited by Craig A. Evans and Stanley E. Porter, 711–19. Downers Grove, IL: InterVarsity Press, 2000.

- Chapter 4: "Creeds and Hymns." In *Dictionary of New Testament Background*, edited by Craig A. Evans and Stanley E. Porter, 231–38. Downers Grove, IL: InterVarsity Press, 2000.

- Chapter 5: "λαλέω: A Word about Women, Music, and Sensuality in the Early Church." In *Religion and Sexuality*, edited by Michael A. Hayes, Wendy J. Porter, and David Tombs, 101–24. Studies in Theology and Sexuality 2. Roehampton Institute London Papers 4. Sheffield: Sheffield Academic, 1998.

- Chapter 6: "The Use of Ekphonetic Notation in Vienna New Testament Manuscripts." In *Akten des 23. Internationalen Papyrologenkongresses, Wien, 22.–28. Juli 2001*, edited by Bernhard Palme,

581–85. Vienna: Österreichische Akademie der Wissenschaften, 2007.

- Chapter 7: "Misguided Missals: Is Early Christian Music Jewish or Is It Graeco-Roman?" In *Christian-Jewish Relations through the Centuries*, edited by Stanley E. Porter and Brook W. R. Pearson, 202–27. Roehampton Institute London Papers 6. Sheffield: Sheffield Academic, 2000.

- Chapter 8: Porter, Wendy J., and Stanley E. Porter. "P.Vindob. G 26225: A New Romanos Melodus Papyrus in the Vienna Collection." *Jahrbuch der Österreichischen Byzantinistik* 52 (2002) 135–48 (with plate).

- Chapter 9: "The Composer of Sacred Music as an Interpreter of the Bible." In *Borders, Boundaries and the Bible*, edited by Martin O'Kane, 126–53. JSOT Supplement Series 313. Sheffield: Sheffield Academic, 2002.

- Chapter 10: "Musical-Textual Relationships regarding Resurrection in the Western Wind Settings of the Creed by John Taverner, John Sheppard and Christopher Tye." In *Resurrection*, edited by Stanley E. Porter, Michael A. Hayes, and David Tombs, 275–87. Roehampton Institute London Papers 5. Sheffield: Sheffield Academic, 1999.

- Chapter 11: "Bach, Beethoven and Stravinsky Masses: Images of Christ in the Credo." In *Images of Christ: Ancient and Modern*, edited by Stanley E. Porter, Michael A. Hayes, and David Tombs, 375–98. Roehampton Institute London Papers 2. Sheffield: Sheffield Academic, 1996.

- Chapter 12: "Sacred Music at the Turn of the Millennia." In *Faith in the Millennium*, edited by Stanley E. Porter, Michael A. Hayes, and David Tombs, 423–44. Roehampton Institute London Papers 7. Sheffield: Sheffield Academic, 2001.

- Chapter 13: "Trading My Sorrows: Worshiping God in the Darkness—The Expression of Pain and Suffering in Contemporary Worship Music." In *The Message in the Music: Studying Contemporary Praise and Worship*, edited by Robert Woods and Brian Walrath, 76–91. Nashville: Abingdon, 2007.

- Chapter 14: "The Worship of the Toronto Blessing?" In *The Toronto Blessing—or Is It?*, edited by Stanley E. Porter and Philip J. Richter, 104–30. London: Darton, Longman and Todd, 1995.

- Chapter 15: "William Byrd and the Musical Reshaping of Liturgy in Reformation England: Insights for Worship in a Post-Christian Context." In *The Reformation: Past Voices, Current Implications*, edited by Steven M. Studebaker and Gordon L. Heath, 152–82. McMaster General Studies Series 13. Eugene, OR: Pickwick, 2021.

- Chapter 16: N/A

- Chapter 17: "A Historical Journey of Theological Reflection on Christian Worship." In *Rediscovering Worship: Past, Present, and Future*, edited by Wendy J. Porter, 176–231. McMaster New Testament Studies. Eugene, OR: Pickwick, 2015.

—Wendy J. Porter
McMaster Divinity College, Hamilton, ON, Canada

1

An Introduction to Worship, Music, and Interpretation

THE CHRISTIAN CHURCH HAS in many ways, throughout the rich length of its history, placed music at the centre of its worship. This music may take various forms, from the formal music of highly liturgical settings to the more informal music of contemporary Christian music. Nevertheless, music has enjoyed a continuous role within the Christian church, from its roots in the Old Testament until the present. The essays within this volume richly illustrate the history of the important place of music within the Christian church throughout its expansive history, beginning especially within the New Testament up to its various contemporary forms of expression. This long and varied history manifests a wide range of musical forms and types. Some of these are direct reflections of the music that was contemporary at the time and in that context, while at other times the musical forms diverge and are developed in unique expressions. In any case, music has been an integral part of the worship of the Christian church from the start to where we are now.

This wide and rich tradition of ecclesial music may and should be examined for its musical merits and the theological insights that it may prompt or provoke. These may be appreciated in numerous ways, as musical adaptations and innovations within varied musical contexts and settings and as forms of expression of the Christian worshipping ethos. At various times within the history of the development of the Christian musical tradition, specific composers or song writers emerge in their engagement in writing music for the Christian church. Some of these musicians have been completely devoted to this kind of writing for the church, and their music can be appreciated for advancing forms of musical worship. Others of these musicians have also composed music for contexts outside of the Christian church as secular composers. At times such a distinction is easy to make, while at other times such a distinction is virtually impossible because the intersection and intertwining of sacred and secular is so inextricably woven. Musicians who have composed for both the Christian church and the world outside of the church have contributions to be recognized as we examine the Christian musical tradition, as essays within this volume exemplify.

Most importantly, however, is the major focus of this volume on the function and purpose of sacred music. Contemporary music of the twenty-first century is often seen as a form of entertainment for those who hear it. Vast numbers of musical compositions are written, performed, recorded, and distributed with the primary, if not only, purpose of entertaining its listeners, whether this is in the live concert hall or through various forms of recorded media. Although music continues to play an important part in the worship of the contemporary Christian church, the restructuring of the liturgy—one might say its downgrading of formalization—has led to music taking a less central role in the worship experience, so that, even if it is often referred to as "worship," music is often seen and characterized as a form of Christian entertainment that prepares for, responds to, or frames other elements of the liturgy.

The purpose of this volume, however, is not primarily to assess the musical merits of the music of the Christian church or to assess its value as entertainment, even if a form of sacred entertainment, but to see the role of music as interpretation. Music has been used throughout the history of the Christian church as a form of interpretation of the Christian experience. The focus of this interpretation has often been on the Scriptures of the church, and we will see in a number of essays how Christian music has interpreted the Scriptures for those engaged in Christian worship. Such instances of interpretation begin within the Bible itself and are continued through to the present contemporary church. The history of Christian worship has been for its music to interpret its sacred writings to those who participate in this worship, as I show in various ways in virtually every chapter within this volume. What frequently surprises me is that relatively few participants in Christian worship seem to appreciate that their experience of Scripture is often mediated to them by their musical liturgy or the role and function of music, including the use of particular musical selections, within their Christian worship. However,

Christian music through the ages has engaged in much more than simply interpretation of Scripture, as important and central as this has been to its experience. The interpretive function of music within Christian worship has extended beyond the Scriptures to a variety of Christian expression. These forms of expression include sermons, credal statements, and other elements of the Christian liturgy.

The question that emerges, if we recognize the importance of music as interpretation within Christian experience, is how it is that music performs this act of interpretation. This is not an easy question to answer, because the means of interpretation vary across a number of factors. They vary according to time period, with various types and means of interpretation being used in specific periods within Christian history, dependent upon wider cultural factors such as the forms of music and liturgy and worship that are current at the time. These modes of interpretation also vary according to the contours of musical expression. As the chapters in this volume illustrate, there are numerous ways in which music has taken shape within the church, and so the approach to interpretation within these expressions of music must also vary according to the musical norms. Some of these are incredibly complex and tax the most highly accomplished musicians while others are less complex and more suited to lay performance. Nevertheless, they all reflect perspectives on Christian experience. Finally, it is noteworthy that various composers have chosen to engage in their interpretation of the Christian Scriptures and experience on the basis of personal factors, influenced by their own musical and liturgical contexts. This is not a quality that pertains only to the present day. Several chapters in this volume reflect the varying ways in which composers, even from similar eras, engage in unique interpretations through music.

This volume is divided into three major parts, following this opening introductory chapter, and concluding with a major essay that theologically reflects upon the musical worship life of the church through its history. Part One is concerned with music and interpretation primarily of the early church and consists of seven chapters. Chapter 2 sets the stage for the rest of the volume by introducing the notion of liturgical and musical interpretation of Scripture and of the Christian tradition. In the first half of the chapter the notion of liturgy is introduced, focusing upon the Eucharist, but then expanded to include a number of other early Christian liturgical texts. I emphasize throughout how much these liturgical texts are expressions of Scripture and Scripture-like interpretation. The second half of the chapter deals with musical interpretation of Scripture, as evidenced in a number of Christian musical texts, beginning with the earliest Christian hymn of the third century and ending with the late twentieth-century *ikonic* writing of John Tavener. I return to a number of the musical examples that I introduce here in subsequent chapters for fuller exposition, but here I attempt merely to show how interpretation is fundamental to music and liturgy.

Chapter 3 is specifically on music in the early church. By music, here I mean some of the details and definitions of music within the early Christian community. The chapter is divided into three substantive sections. The first treats voices and instruments. One might think that the question of ancient singing and its instrumental accompaniment is relatively straightforward, or at least discoverable from the ancient sources. That is not the case. Here I discuss the question of singing style and of substance, including what Paul means when he speaks of "psalms, hymns, and spiritual songs" (Eph 5:19; Col 3:16), which I refer to in a later chapter, as well as the relation of early Christian music to psalmody, and what role musical instruments did or did not have in the early church. There are no easy answers to any of these questions. In the second section, I discuss the sources and traditions of music. These include the challenges of written sources such as the third-century Christian hymn found in the papyrus, P.Oxy. XV 1786, and I refer to this significant and unique document at various places throughout this volume. I also consider the importance of oral sources. In the third section, I discuss the origins and influences of early Christian music, such as the temple, synagogue, or Greco-Roman world and practice. This chapter leaves as many unanswered questions as it answers but provides the scope of consideration for speaking about music in the early church.

In chapter 4, I treat creeds and hymns in the early church. Creeds and hymns are directly related to music, as they are often distinguished by features that call forth poetic or musical means of production, although we know nothing of how this took place. In this chapter, I begin with a definition of a hymn or creedal statement, a topic of surprisingly widespread debate in contemporary scholarship. It is not altogether clear what these are, whether they can be distinguished, and whether the New Testament contains any of them. I then identify various approaches to this material that include source criticism, form criticism, functionalist studies, and musical and liturgical studies. I offer a brief treatment of the major hymnic or creedal passages within the New Testament, ranging from the canticles in Luke's Gospel through the Pauline and Petrine letters to the book of Revelation. Much more could be said about any of these passages, but this survey provides a means of identifying their major formal characteristics and their theological significance within their respective contexts.

Chapter 5 examines a notoriously problematic couple of verses, 1 Cor 14:34–35, a passage that seems to prohibit women from speaking in church. There have been many different solutions proposed for this verse that appear to be so non-egalitarian. These include proposals that the verses are an interpolation or that there are some kinds of obvious disruptions by the women involved. However, rather than addressing the problem from the traditional standpoints, I choose to address the question by investigating some little-explored possibilities related to music. I examine the meaning of the word λαλέω (*laleō*), which is often simply translated as "speak." I instead examine a number of contexts where this word seems to indicate speaking in a prophetic way that possibly appealed to pagan religious practice. I also investigate the word αὐλός (*aulos*), which is usually mistakenly translated as "flute," when it indicated a reedpipe more closely resembling the double-reed oboe. This instrument was considered the most sensual of instruments in the ancient Greco-Roman world. When these two factors are taken into consideration, new light is shed on this old problematic passage, by suggesting that the problem in Corinth may have been with women who were engaging in ecstatic, sensual prophecy that was unfitting within the Christian context.

Chapter 6, although short by comparison with several others, introduces some material that is almost certainly unfamiliar to many New Testament scholars and contemporary musicians: *ekphonetic* notation. Ekphonetic notation comprises the diacritical marks that were placed upon manuscripts that contained the scriptural readings—inserted at the time of copying or often later—to indicate how they were to be intoned within a liturgical context. By drawing upon the edition of New Testament Greek papyri and parchment documents that I edited with Stanley Porter, I trace the development of diacritical marks from punctuation in the earliest manuscripts to full sets of ekphonetic markings in later manuscripts. I then pay special attention to the features of one particular manuscript, a tenth-century parchment that contains ekphonetic markings on three of four extant pericopes. Besides the interesting question raised by the fact that one of the four pericopes is not ekphonetically marked at all, I indicate the major musical-rhetorical intonational patterns that suggest how this manuscript was used within the liturgy of the early church. The development of such notation raises questions about the growth and development of the early church, its biblical and musical tradition, and the question of what constitutes music in relation to the church's developing worship practices.

Much of the dispute over early Christian music revolves around determining its sources. There are two major positions—that the music originated in Jewish worship or that the music is dependent upon Greco-Roman sources, which is discussed in chapter 7. The majority of New Testament scholars may be unaware of the complexities of the problem in terms of the lack of evidence upon which to make a decision, and as a result, simply posit Jewish origins of Christian worship in the synagogue and/or the temple. Those outside of New Testament studies, and in particular musicologists, are themselves divided upon this question. There are those who argue for the Jewish side of the equation and those who argue for the Greco-Roman, sometimes in strongly worded and even vociferous arguments with and responses to each other. In this chapter, I survey the major positions of the two sides and conclude that the musical influences were assuredly complex and originated in both Jewish and Greco-Roman musical traditions. As an example to illustrate the complexity, I examine scholarly opinion on the first early Christian musical manuscript, P.Oxy. XV 1786, dated to the third century. This document itself, which has been subject to varied interpretation, illustrates the complexity of the origins of Christian music in both Jewish and Greco-Roman sources.

Chapter 8 is more technical than many of the other chapters in this volume, as it presents an edition of a fragmentary papyrus of the sixth-century Christian poet Romanos Melodus. In this edition, co-authored with Stanley Porter, we present an introduction to Romanos Melodus, a diplomatic text of this fragmentary papyrus, a reading edition, and then a reconstruction of that portion of his canticle. When we published this papyrus fragment, it was one of only four known to be from Romanos Melodus and the first one to be identified as his at the time of publication (others were published prior to confirmation that they were of Romanos Melodus and then confirmed later). However, rather than just being an exercise in textual criticism and reconstruction, the process of examining the papyrus offers insights into both the poet and the tradition of which he was a part. His *kontakia* were versified sermons set to music, and so they give evidence of the musical and sermonic traditions of the developing Christian church, especially as that church was developing various strands within the East. Romanos Melodus combines both Greek and Syriac elements into his versified sermons, with this one posing several problems that illustrate his formative place within the Christian musical and theological tradition.

Part Two of this volume is concerned with the Christian church and its musical traditions and interpretations, with emphasis on musicians of the Reformation period and later. Whereas Part One was concerned with music of the early church and even the ancient world, Part Two deals with an established Christian church and its treatment of its musical tradition. The first chapter of this section, Chapter 9, develops and supports the notion of the composer as a biblical interpreter. I use five examples in this chapter to illustrate this point. As a transition from Part One to Part Two, I include two early church examples before I turn to three later ones. The first example is the early Christian hymn in 1 Tim 3:16 and the second is a brief return to the first Christian hymn with musical notation, P.Oxy. XV 1786. Even though the authors of these hymns are subject to dispute, if they are known at all, they nevertheless illustrate interpretation of the texts that they present. The first interprets the life of Jesus Christ, while the second, the Oxyrhynchus fragment, has been subject to continuing debate over its text but offers some theological interpretation. The three subsequent examples include a responsory of John Sheppard as a transitional Reformation composer, a motet of Johann Sebastian Bach from the eighteenth century, and a motet of Francis Poulenc from the twentieth. These three varied composers all illustrate what is also seen in the first two examples—the composers take their scriptural texts and musically interpret them in various ways to emphasize and highlight certain features of the text. These examples, representative of the larger Christian music tradition, illustrate the continuing tradition of biblical interpretation by composers from its earliest times to the present.

In chapter 10, I offer a brief look at how three major sixteenth-century English composers, John Taverner, John Sheppard, and Christopher Tye, interpret two sections of the Latin creed in their musical setting of the *Western Wind* mass. The traditional thought is that the creed was fixed in form, but these three composers, even though they were composing at roughly similar times, engaged in a variety of means to interpret their text through musical means. The *Western Wind* melody provided the basis for their musical interpretation, a tune famously attributed to Henry VIII, but these composers altered both the music and formal text to present their differing interpretations of resurrection. I note in particular that whereas they emphasize both Jesus' resurrection and the resurrection of the dead, they, and especially Tye, place special focus upon the resurrection of the dead. The approach that I use in this chapter is more fully developed and illustrated in my book, *Early English Composers and the Credo*, in which I illustrate how these three composers, along with Thomas Tallis and William Byrd, interpret the entire Latin creed through musical and textual means to emphasize particular passages in ways that bring theological meaning to the forefront.

In chapter 11, I continue the pattern of previous chapters by discussing three more composers as interpreters of musical texts. This chapter focuses upon three masses by three well-known composers, although two of them are not well known for their sacred music. I examine the Credos in J. S. Bach's *Mass in B Minor*, Ludwig Beethoven's *Missa Solemnis*, and Igor Stravinsky's *Mass*. That is, I attempt to see how each composer establishes his image of Christ as depicted within their setting of the Credo. Bach drew on some of his previous works to create this monumental work of devotion. He utilizes a number of musical features—such as structure, tempo, and key among others—to emphasize the incarnation within his Mass. In contrast, Beethoven, who is not known for his sacred music and wrote only this one Mass, creates a work that is very modern in its emphasis—by means of similar musical techniques—on the humanness of Christ. In the third selection, Stravinsky, who is also not known for his sacred music but who wrote this Mass after a return to the Russian Orthodox Church and in reaction to works that he believed did not reflect proper piety, creates an *ikonic* portrait of Christ that does not emphasize any particular feature. The image of Christ is central to each rendition of the Mass, but each of these composers emphasizes a different dimension within the Credo.

In chapter 12, I return to the kind of study that I offered in chapter 9, as a transition to the second part of this volume. In chapter 9, I present five examples to help make the transition from the music of the Bible and the early church to the developed Christian musical tradition. In chapter 12, I present three examples, each one marking an important temporal point in the history and development of Christian music. The first example returns to the New Testament itself, this time to Phil 2:5–11, a passage that may well be one of the early Christian hymns, whether Paul wrote it himself or he already knew it from early Christian worshipping communities. This is an example from the beginning of the Christian millennium. The second example returns to the ekphonetically annotated text that I described and discussed in chapter 6. This document from the tenth century offers a window into Christian worship at the transition between the two millennia of Christianity. The text is from the Gospel of John, with three of the four pericopes containing ekphonetic notation. In this extended analysis, I go into more detail by describing the musical-rhetorical movements indicated by the major notational symbols. The third and final example is a musical setting of John's Gospel by the contemporary composer John Tavener (not to be confused with John Taverner from the sixteenth century). Tavener writes from within the Orthodox tradition, and hence his setting of major episodes from within John's Gospel traces the account of the life of Jesus by creating individual *ikonic* portraits of him. The text and the music are simple and sparse. They reveal both the interpretive features of the Orthodox tradition, but, more than that, Tavener's interpretation of John's Gospel. There is a sense in which Tavener's setting provides a close to the second millennium by pointing both to the future of Christian music and reinforcing its past tradition of being based upon the Bible, even if being interpretive.

Chapter 13 provides an analysis of contemporary worship songs on the topic of pain and suffering. This chapter, although it focuses upon one particular topic and a pre-set list of songs with which I was provided, offers an example of how to evaluate contemporary music for those who choose music for corporate Christian worship. I examine the 77 most frequently sung contemporary Christian worship songs on the CCLI (Christian Copyright Licensing International) list at the time according to three levels: the *lyrics*, what I call the *lyric-music interchange*, and the *context*. Lyrics are crucial to a song, and one must move beyond the individual words alone to evaluate the overall contribution of the lyrics. The lyric-music interchange addresses the very important factor of how the words of the text are supported by or countered by the music itself. There must be an appropriate interchange for each to be successful. The final consideration, and arguably the most important, is the context. Even if one has good lyrics and a supportive lyric-music interchange, the song being considered must be appropriate for a given context in which it is to be used. It must be appropriate for the leader, the musicians, and, most importantly, for the congregation singing the song. On the basis of my study of the 77 songs, I narrow the list down to ten songs—and single out two for special comment—that appropriately represent the topic of pain and suffering, that I might have chosen to use for the context of Christian worship at the time, and that still speak to the process in the present.

About twenty-five years ago, a movement swept through a number of churches of various denominations called the Toronto Blessing. Originating in the Toronto Airport Vineyard, this movement spread quickly throughout North America and the United Kingdom, especially but not exclusively in charismatic churches. The reactions were varied but almost invariably strong on all sides. In this chapter, I assess worship in the Toronto Blessing as evidenced in churches in London, England, by evaluating it through several criteria. The first concerns worship itself and whether it is Christ-centred. The second concerns four major church traditions: baptistic, charismatic, evangelical, and sacramental. The third involves personal observation of the Toronto Blessing in English churches in light of the two criteria above. I suggest that in the contexts that I observed, the Toronto Blessing did not appear to have a strong biblical foundation in the work of Christ and was not apparently in keeping with other relevant church traditions. The dynamic thrust of the Toronto Blessing itself has now essentially faded, but as similar movements emerge, claiming to provide a unique experience of God that others have missed, this chapter provides some guidelines for evaluating such a movement on the basis of its practice in relation to the Bible and the traditions of the Christian church.

In chapter 15, perhaps surprising in its position in this collection, I discuss the music of William Byrd, one of England's greatest composers and one who negotiated the difficult era of transition from Catholicism to Protestantism, while remaining a Roman Catholic. Even though Byrd flourished during that difficult time we call the Reformation, in particular in sixteenth-century England with its sectarian conflicts, I suggest that the atmosphere in England during this time probably seemed much more post-Christian than Christian in many respects, at least to Byrd. He contended with his own form of worship wars, ones that pitted his musical and religious sentiments against the newly instituted forms of musical expression that originated with the continental Reformation. As a result, Byrd had to adapt in creative and sometimes even covert ways that led to surprising innovations, including songs written for very small gatherings of Christian worshipers, that may help us to understand musical worship in a contemporary post-Christian context, and provide us with some timely insights, challenges, and guidelines.

Part Three concludes and summarizes what has been presented above, but in a way that attempts to extend the discussion beyond the confines of this volume. Although I have at times made some general comments, especially in the opening chapters, about the background to the development of Christian music and liturgy, much of this volume includes specialized and focused studies upon specific eras, individual composers, and individual works. I realize that much more could be said about each one, but in each instance where I have attempted such a study, I have tried to show the significance of the individual or text for music and worship within the Christian tradition. These studies have sometimes spanned a range of eras, even the entire two millennia of the Christian era, but most of them have attempted to develop the common theme that Christian thought regarding music and worship, and especially how the Christian church has engaged in interpreting Scripture and its various traditions through the unlikely arena of its music and worship, has been at the heart of the development of the Christian church throughout its history. Some of these studies have been mere sketches, while others have offered a more technical discussion. Those within the field of Christian theology who are not musicians or liturgical specialists may find some of these surprising or challenging. However, in this concluding part, I offer two survey chapters that change the tone and style of presentation to offer in single chapters broad overviews of music and worship.

In chapter 16, which I developed for a guest professorship presentation but did not previously publish, I develop further some of the insights that I have gained in the course of studying contemporary worship and music from the standpoint of a trained musician and musicologist. The notion of a contemporary worship song probably brings to the minds of most people the music of the last thirty or forty years or so, or perhaps just the last decade. In this essay, I first review passages in the Old Testament where there is a common refrain to sing a *new song* of worship. I trace the range of references in the Old Testament to music and worship, focusing upon how those who enter into worship are called to bring new songs to the experience. I then turn to the New Testament, and again trace the references to music and worship in the New Testament. There is a range of passages where the various people involved are called to worship with their own form of a new song. In other words, the history of biblical worship is the call to bring a *new song* to the Lord. Worship music throughout the Bible is always called upon to be contemporary or relevant within its immediate context. I then turn to the history of worship music, beginning with the early church. The initial evidence is sparse but even its early stages reveal that this worship through music was new and contemporary. There are a number of anonymous and many more well-known composers of church music throughout the history of the church, but few of them are ever referred to as composers of "contemporary worship music." I contend that this is exactly what they were, as they composed new songs for the worship of their ecclesial communities. In the final major section, rather than seeing a disjunction with what we more typically call contemporary worship music, I see continuity in a number of important composers who continue the tradition of creating contemporary worship songs, new songs for the church.

In the final chapter, I focus upon the third of the sections surveyed in the previous chapter and offer in a single chapter an overview of the two millennia of the Christian church and how it has treated the subject of worship. By worship, and for the purpose of this chapter's survey, I include a range of elements such as liturgy and sacraments, but especially music. I use the metaphor of Christian worship as a journey, and I divide this journey into six periods spanning the last two-thousand years. I describe major events within the broader church in its context in the world for each period, as well as individual centuries within them, and then draw attention to significant features in the worship and worship music of the church. As a result, I make a number of correlations with individual chapters that I presented above, but in so doing I am calling the Christian church, and in particular those who are responsible for the elements of its worship, to re-examine where we have been in our history, where we are in our current practice, and where we should cast our vision for the future. The Christian church began with musical and liturgical acts that were part of developing an entire worshiping community. It is in our best interests as those involved in the continuing life of the church to investigate our past experiences of musical worship and liturgy, to learn from these, and to offer constructive proposals for our continuing lives as worshiping people.

Music and worship have been integrated in biblical communities from the earliest evidence of the Old Testament, through the New Testament and church history, right to the present. In this collection of essays, I attempt to trace the history of their relationship. Rather than concentrating upon a particular period or individual composers—although I do offer several focused and specialized studies in this volume—my purpose here is to weave together an account of the importance of music and worship as a major contributing factor, including a major interpretive component, within the life of the Christian church.

Part One

Music and Interpretation
in the Early Church

2

Liturgical and Musical Interpretation

INTRODUCTION

This chapter introduces the foundational nature and scope of musical and liturgical interpretation throughout the history of the Christian church, beginning with the Bible, both Old and New Testaments, and proceeding through into the life of the church. Both music and the liturgy itself provide explicit means that reveal ways in which the church has engaged in interpretation of its experience, even if this is done in varying ways. In this chapter, I wish to highlight some of those important moments in the life of the Christian church when musical and liturgical interpretation has occurred. The purpose here is not to illustrate a particular way in which liturgy or music should be used to interpret, but to show that throughout the history of the Christian tradition such interpretive acts have occurred, especially in significant and fundamental liturgical and musical expressions. Music and liturgy are inextricably intertwined throughout the history of the Christian church, and it is very difficult to separate the two, as they are often linked in ways that illustrate their interdependence. Nevertheless, for the sake of discussion, I first discuss liturgical interpretation of Scripture, beginning with the Eucharist, and then turn to musical interpretation.

LITURGICAL INTERPRETATION

The term "liturgy" comes from the Greek verb, λειτουργέω (*leitourgeō*) with three meanings that have some bearing for this discussion: (a) at Athens, it was to serve public office at one's own cost; (b) to perform public duties or to serve the state; or (c) to serve a master, to perform religious service, or to minister. In the Eastern church, "liturgy" refers specifically to the Eucharist (Communion or Lord's Table); in the Western church, "liturgy" frequently includes the entire scope of the Christian service of worship. Yet, throughout the centuries of the Christian church, it is the texts and actions of the liturgy surrounding the Eucharist, Lord's Table, or Communion that have been the most important elements of the liturgy, even if much more is involved.

Exodus 12:6–8 and 12:24–27 describe the events and observance of the Passover in the Old Testament. The Gospel accounts place Jesus and the disciples in preparation for the Passover in the first instance of his blessing and sharing of the bread and wine with his disciples (Mark 14:12–26; Matt 26:17–30; Luke 22:7–22). Other passages that speak about the breaking of bread and the manner in which one should partake of the Lord's Supper include 1 Cor 10:16–17, 21; 11:20–29; and Acts 2:42, 46.

In the Western sense of the word, many (and arguably most or even all) churches that do not think of themselves as liturgical do in fact have a liturgy. The form of their worship, the familiar words that are used, the order in which the service proceeds, and how Communion or the Lord's Supper is observed are all part of this liturgy. This becomes evident in a church that tries to change elements of its non-liturgy and meets with resistance from some of its members. In other words, all churches observe some form of liturgy that must be recognized and taken into account when speaking of Christian worship.

Furthermore, every liturgy, in some way, interprets the Bible—although not all liturgies do it consciously or explicitly. This chapter will illustrate how such liturgical interpretation of Scripture occurs in early liturgical forms. Since the earliest records of the early church participating in the Lord's Supper (e.g., Didache, Justin Martyr, and Hippolytus), the actions, words, objects, and order of the proceedings have all played a part in interpreting the New Testament account and its Old Testament background. As the Christian church grew and spread, various interpretations of the New Testament accounts emphasized different elements as important, which was reflected in their liturgies. As some interpretations were thought to be heretical, church leaders assembled in several councils to deal with these supposedly deviant interpretations and to prevent their spreading through the formalization of doctrinal statements in creeds.

Sources and Documents

Before turning to the forms of expression of early liturgies and their interpretation of Scripture, I examine the sources of these early liturgies. The earliest document that gives some indication of how the early church observed the Lord's Supper and how its service of worship took place is the Didache (9–10; 14; late first or early second century). In Did. 9, instructions are given on how to observe the thanksgiving meal (literally, "Eucharist"). The cup is treated first, with a prayer of thanksgiving included in the document. The fragment of bread is then prayed over, distributed, and eaten, and then another fairly lengthy prayer of thanks follows the eating of the bread, "when you have had enough to eat."

The first known writer that discusses the Lord's Supper is Justin Martyr (ca. 100–165) in his First Apology (ca. 155), which was written to Emperor Antoninus Pius, and then, later, in his Dialogue with Trypho the Jew. We know from Justin Martyr's account that the early church celebrated the Eucharist each Sunday. It began with Scripture reading, included a sermon by the president of the gathering, and had intercessions that finished with the kiss of peace. Bread, wine, and water were brought to the president, who offered a prayer of thanksgiving for them. About sixty years later comes the first text of the eucharistic prayer, found in Hippolytus's The Apostolic Tradition (ca. 200). Although the original Greek text has not been found, and the version only exists in a composite of fifth-century Latin, with several other translations, it is clear that there was a prayer of thanksgiving, and the bread and wine were offered in memory of Christ's death and resurrection.

By the eleventh century, this liturgy, in its Roman form, had greatly expanded to include the following components: introit (antiphon and psalm verses); *Kyrie eleison*; *Gloria in excelsis Deo*; reading of an epistle; gradual (response); alleluia; sequence; reading of a Gospel; *Credo*; offertory (antiphon and prayer); preface; *Sanctus and Benedictus*; canon of the mass (that is, the eucharistic prayer); the Lord's Prayer; a versicle and response (*pax*); *Agnus Dei*; rite of peace; communion of the priest (with communion antiphon); post-communion (prayer); and the dismissal (*Ite, missa est*).[1]

---

1. Harper, *Forms and Orders*.

PART ONE: MUSIC AND INTERPRETATION IN THE EARLY CHURCH

Shifting Liturgies

Ancient liturgies are often grouped and studied in *families*, tracing the development of ancient liturgies, that is, the earliest Christian liturgies, toward their more recognizable forms today. These ancient families would include such liturgies as the Alexandrian (leading to Ethiopic and Coptic); West Syrian (leading to Syrian Orthodox, Maronite, Malankarese); East Syrian (leading to Assyro-Chaldean, Mar Thoma, and Malabarese, as well as Armenian); Armenian (leading to Armenian Apostolic and Armenian Catholic); Basil/Chrysostom or Byzantine (leading to Orthodox, Ukrainian Catholic, Melkite); Roman (leading to Roman Catholic); North African; and Gallican, Celtic, Mozarabic, and Ambrosian leading to Toledo Cathedral, Spain, and the Milan Archdiocese, Italy.[2]

Later liturgies, stemming initially from the period of the Reformation, include a variety of ecclesial traditions. Some of the most easily recognizable consist of the following: Lutheran (leading to Evangelical Lutheran); Reformed (leading to Presbyterian); Anglican (leading to Episcopal); Anabaptist (leading to Mennonite); then Quaker (leading to Friends); Separatist and Puritan (leading to some Baptist, Congregationalist, other Free Church, and United Church of Christ); Methodist (leading to United Methodist); Frontier or Revival (leading to Southern Baptist and numerous others); and Pentecostal (leading to Assemblies of God) among a variety of others.

Each of these groups and the subsequent developments both within them and away from them involves interpretation of Scripture in the way each enacts and understands church practice, church texts and documents, church theology, etc. This chapter attempts to capture the fundamental place of scriptural interpretation in these liturgies.

As the early church grew, spread, and developed in numerous ways, it also began to deteriorate in various ways. Several by-now famous individuals became highly disillusioned with the corruption within the developed and formalized Roman Catholic Church, and these individuals desired, in some cases, radical reforms from within the church, or, in others, complete distancing from the church as it was currently known. These individuals became new interpreters of the Bible and, in many cases, wrote the documents that formed the new shape of the particular church with which they were associated. These include a surprisingly large number of important figures in Protestant church history: Martin

---

2. Jones et al., eds., *Study of Liturgy*; White, *Introduction to Christian Worship*.

Luther (*Formula missae*, 1523; *Deutsche Messe*, 1526); Ulrich Zwingli (the Zwingli Liturgy: *Liturgy of the Word*, 1525, *Action or Use of the Lord's Supper*, 1525); Martin Bucer (the Strassburg Liturgy; *Psalter, with Complete Church Practice*, 1539); John Calvin (*The Form of Church Prayers*, 1545 [Strassburg], 1542 [Geneva]); Thomas Cranmer (The First and Second Prayer Books of King Edward VI, The English Rite: *The Booke of the Common Prayer*, 1549; *The Book of Common Prayer*, 1552); John Knox (*The Forme of Prayers*, 1556); the Puritans (*A Booke of the Forme of Common Prayers*, 1586). Later, the Westminster Directory (*A Directory for the Publique Worship of God*, 1644), Richard Baxter's Savoy Liturgy (*The Reformation of the Liturgy*, 1661), and John Wesley's outline for Methodist worship (*The Sunday Service of the Methodists in North America*, 1784) all became fundamental documents for various strains of the Christian church and their subsequent liturgies. Each of the above clearly interprets the Bible in some way by outlining those practices and texts that would be retained and those that would be abandoned or destroyed. In some cases, the writer or interpreter explained the changes in detail; in others, the writer simply introduced and enforced them.

Liturgical Texts

The eucharistic prayer or canon of the Mass, also known as the ἀναφορά (*anaphora*) or the prayer of consecration, comes from the Greek verb ἀναφέρω (anapherō); "I carry up; I offer up [in sacrifice])." The oldest name for this prayer is, in fact, εὐχαριστία (*eucharistia*; "thanksgiving"). This prayer, during which the bread and wine are consecrated in the Mass or Eucharist, is the most solemn part of the Eucharist. Jesus' prayers over meals are thought to include the blessing (בְּרָכָה) and the thanksgiving (הוֹדָיָה or תּוֹדָה) of Jewish prayers, and this is echoed in the eucharistic prayer.

There does not seem to be an Urtext, or one single text, of this prayer from the earliest days of the church, but there are several similar prayers. The early eucharistic prayer begins with what is known as the *Sursum corda*, an introductory dialogue. The priest begins, "Lift up your hearts," and the people respond, "We lift them up unto the Lord." Hippolytus's *Apostolic Tradition* includes the following: (Priest) "The Lord be with you all"; (People) "and with thy spirit"; (Priest) "Lift up your hearts"; (People) "We lift them up unto the Lord"; (Priest) "Let us give thanks unto the Lord"; (People) "It is meet and right to do so"; and the same canons include: "This is the body of Christ," with the response, "Amen"; and "This is the blood of Christ," with the response, "Amen."[3]

The later *Apostolic Constitutions* tell us that, following this, the eucharistic prayer contains a thanksgiving; narrative of the institution (the account of the Lord's Supper as found in the Synoptic Gospels and 1 Cor 11:23–26, thus putting Scripture at the centre of the eucharistic prayer); anamnesis ("remembrance"); epiclesis ("invocation"); and a concluding doxology (words expressing praise or glory to God, usually in trinitarian form, e.g., Lesser Doxology, "Glory be to the Father and to the Son and to the Holy Spirit . . ."). Almost all anaphoras or eucharistic prayers of historic rites contain these basic categories and in this order. Exceptions include the mid-fourth-century Egyptian Anaphora of St. Serapion (within which the narrative on institution and anamnesis are conflated) and the East Syrian Anaphora of the Holy Apostles Addai and Mari which is now missing the institution narrative.

There are a number of other early Christian liturgical texts that are based upon and function as interpretations of Scripture. Another text used regularly in the liturgy includes the Magnificat, which is directly taken from the New Testament. This is known as Mary's prayer in Luke 1:46–55 and has parallels to Hannah's prayer in 1 Sam 2:1–10. This is one of the few Marian texts taken directly from the Bible. The Paternoster or the Lord's Prayer comes directly from Matthew's Gospel where Jesus gives instructions on prayer (Matt 5:9–13). As early as the Didache, there are admonitions to pray this scriptural prayer, "as the Lord commanded in his gospel."[4] The *Benedictus dominus* ("Blessed be the Lord") is Zechariah's prayer of prophecy from Luke 1:68–79. The *Nunc dimittis* ("Lord, now lettest thou thy servant depart") is Simeon's prayer and blessing from Luke 2:29–32.

The texts of the Ordinary of the Mass include the *Kyrie eleison, Gloria, Credo, Sanctus with Benedictus,* and *Agnus Dei*. These texts are the ones most often set to music through the centuries by the greatest composers. Apart from the *Credo*, they were assembled between the fourth and eighth centuries for the celebration or observance of mass in the Christian church. The *Credo* was not formally incorporated as a standard text within the mass until the eleventh century. Several of these texts are

---

3. Hippolytus, *Trad. Ap.*
4. Did. 8:2.

from the Bible, but not all, although they may be perceived as such by those who have heard them regularly in their liturgical setting.

I treat each of these sections of the Ordinary to note their scriptural interpretation. The *Kyrie* is not exactly Scripture. The three lines of this text—*Kyrie eleison* ("Lord, have mercy"); *Christe eleison* ("Christ, have mercy"); *Kyrie eleison* ("Lord, have mercy")—have generally remained in Greek even throughout the centuries of Latin observance of the mass. The original form of this petition possibly had more to do with honouring a king and worshipping a sun-god than with calling upon Christ to have mercy. Nonetheless, this response, originally used in the liturgy to follow a litany, has become an oft-repeated prayer of the church, and expresses very simply the essence of a petition heard so often in the Psalms, but also in the Gospels, such as is spoken by the blind man in Matt 9:27.

The *Gloria in excelsis Deo* ("Glory to God in the highest") is known as the Greater Doxology. It is a composite of Scripture passages and other nonbiblical phrases. Luke 2:14, from the birth narrative, contains some of its phrases, "Glory to God in the highest, and on earth peace among people with whom he is well pleased." John 1:29 (ESV), where John is speaking to Jesus, contains the exclamation, "Behold, the Lamb of God, who takes away the sin of the world!" Other sections of the *Gloria* are not specifically drawn from Scripture, although they use Scripture-like language.

The *Credo in unum deum* ("I believe in one God") originated in an attempt to preserve a *right* interpretation of biblical doctrines. Later concerns about accuracy and heresies led to the revisions that occurred in the councils of the fourth and fifth centuries. This text is not technically a biblical text at all, but from its conception, it attempts to interpret and present the most important tenets and facts of Scripture relevant to the believer. There are four main sections to this *Credo* text: the first expresses belief in God; the second expresses belief in the Lord Jesus Christ; the third expresses belief in the Holy Spirit; and the final section expresses belief in the holy catholic church. Composers throughout the history of the Christian church, including some of its most important, have used their musical settings of this, and other, liturgical texts to highlight those features that they deemed most important or outlined them in such a way as to present a certain view of them.[5]

---

5. See Porter, *Early English Composers and the Credo*, where I examine how John Taverner, Christopher Tye, Thomas Tallis, John Sheppard, and William Byrd interpreted the Latin Creed through their various settings. See also chapter 10 below in this volume for a specific study of this topic.

Part One: Music and Interpretation in the Early Church

The *Sanctus* is from Isa 6:3, which is part of Isaiah's vision of the Lord: "Holy, holy, holy is the Lord of hosts; the whole earth is full of his glory" (ESV). Revelation 4:8 also uses this threefold statement, where the four living creatures never cease to say, "Holy, holy, holy, is the Lord God, the Almighty, who was and who is and who is to come" (NASB).

The *Benedictus qui venit* ("Blessed is he who comes") was removed from the *Sanctus* during the Reformation. The statement suggested Christ's presence in the elements of the Eucharist, so it was removed by some over disputes over the nature of what transpires in the Eucharist. Where the *Benedictus* is included with the *Sanctus*, it is clearly indicated in the title of the section, signifying the theological importance of this combination. *Benedictus qui venit* is from the triumphal entry of Jesus into Jerusalem in Matthew's Gospel: "Hosanna to the Son of David; Blessed is he who comes in the name of the Lord; Hosanna in the highest!" (Matt 21:9, NIV). Other relevant passages for this text are Luke 19:38 ("Blessed is the King who comes in the name of the Lord; peace in heaven and glory in the highest," NIV); and Ps 118:26 ("Blessed is the one who comes in the name of the Lord," NIV). The text of the *Benedictus* is a complex set of biblical interpretations.

The *Agnus Dei* ("Lamb of God") consists of three lines: "Lamb of God, that takes away the sin of the world, have mercy upon us. Lamb of God, that takes away the sin of the world, have mercy upon us. Lamb of God, that takes away the sin of the world, grant us peace." The biblical background to the first section of each of these three lines is in John 1:29 ("Behold, the Lamb of God who takes away the sin of the world!" NIV). The phrase "have mercy upon us" is not strictly biblical in its wording, although Matt 18:33 does instruct the one who has been forgiven a debt to have mercy on a fellow slave, "even as I [Jesus] had mercy on you." Again, as with the *Kyrie* (see above), the phrase reiterated here expresses the heart of a petition, such as one encounters in the Psalms or Lamentations. The final phrase of this tripartite plea, "grant us peace," was a later addition, when the prayer began to also accompany the kiss of peace that followed the breaking of the bread. Again, it is not strictly biblical in its wording. Scripture talks about granting life and loving kindness (Job 10:12), salvation (Ps 85:7), and the desire of the righteous (Prov 10:24). However, in the Old Testament, we encounter the blessing, "The Lord bless you, and keep you; the Lord make his face shine upon you and be gracious to you; the Lord lift up his countenance on you and give you peace" (Num 6:24–26, ESV). In the New Testament, after Jesus' resurrection, Jesus stands in the midst of the disciples and says, "Peace be with you," and then again, "Peace be with you; as the Father has sent me, I also send you." Eight days later, Jesus appears once more to the disciples and begins, "Peace be with you." The *Agnus Dei* text is clearly allusive and written with scriptural resonances.

Antiphons to Mary, such as *Alma redemptoris mater* ("Kind mother of the redeemer"), *Ave regina caelorum* ("Hail, O queen of heaven"), *Regina Caeli* ("Queen of heaven"), and *Salve regina* ("Hail, O queen") are not Scripture texts but do in fact interpret Scripture with Mary as the object of worship and are thereby part of the scriptural interpretive tradition.

The *Te Deum laudamus* ("We praise thee, O God") is another text that is not technically drawn from Scripture itself and is more like an extemporaneous prayer. This prayer of praise begins by addressing God, the Father everlasting, whom all the earth worships. About halfway through the prayer, it shifts to address Christ specifically: "Thou art the King of glory O Christ. Thou art the everlasting Son of the Father." This shift in subject is maintained to the end of the prayer. The very last line of this prayer also shifts person, in that the language throughout the prayer is "we"; only in the last line does it shift to "me": "O Lord, in thee have I trusted, let me never be confounded."

Summary of Liturgical Interpretation

From the earliest known records of the celebration or observance of the Lord's Supper, the church in all its manifestations has been involved in interpreting the New Testament accounts of it. This has taken place through those Scripture passages which are enshrined in the liturgy; the collage of Scripture and nonscriptural passages that are juxtaposed in other texts of the liturgy; the order and priorities of both specific actions and words in the liturgy; and even the musical settings used for certain set texts of the liturgy—all are a part of how the liturgy has been used to interpret Scripture, whether intended or not, or explicit or not.

MUSICAL INTERPRETATION

After introducing the importance of liturgical interpretation of Scripture in the above section, it is appropriate to turn to the similar role of musical interpretation of Scripture within the Christian church. Whereas there are those who might more easily concede the role of interpretation of Scripture within the liturgy, there are perhaps some who have not recognized the role of music in such interpretation throughout the history of the church.

The composer of sacred music, to some degree in every century since the beginning of the Christian church, has interpreted the Bible and other liturgical texts through the musical-textual interrelationships of these compositions. These works shed light on the history of interpretation of the Bible at the time of their composition, as well as influencing how Scripture is perceived within Christian worship and liturgy. Whether composers altered biblical and theological passages, juxtaposed biblical passages, used nonbiblical texts to provide commentary on biblical ones, or specifically set individual words or phrases in a way that influences one's view of the larger text, each presents a particular view of the biblical passage and is itself an interpretation of it. In this section, I selectively focus upon a few significant examples of musical interpretation of scriptural and other liturgical texts throughout Christian history.

Third-Century Christian Hymn

An anonymous Christian hymn, the first to be found with accompanying musical notation, is dated to the latter part of the third century. This Greek musical fragment, P.Oxy. XV 1786, was found written on the back of a papyrus account for corn, in Oxyrhynchus, Egypt.

This early Christian hymn provides interesting evidence of early biblical interpretation through music. Fragments torn away from the manuscript and sections that are simply missing mean that we do not know the full extent of this work. We do know that this musical work draws not only on the Old Testament, but also on the New, as well as incorporating some extra-biblical ideas regarding cosmic worship and more developed trinitarian notions.[6] The fact that the hymn was written down may suggest that it had been known previously, for the passing on of music was largely by means of oral tradition and this would have been the means to preserve the hymn. In that case, it may represent biblical as well as theological interpretation from the second or early third century; if the hymn was a new composition, it may represent slightly later interpretation.

Hunt and Jones, who published this early Christian fragment of papyri that was earlier discovered by Grenfell and Hunt, summarize the hymn, saying, "Creation at large is called upon to join in a chorus of praise to Father, Son, and Holy Spirit, and the concluding passage is the

---

6. See Cosgrove, *Ancient Christian Hymn*, 37–63.

usual ascription of power and glory to the 'only giver of all good gifts.'"[7] (One question that comes to mind is, "Was it the 'usual ascription' at the time or only later with extended use?") The doxology at the end of this hymn fragment shows an integration of Old Testament-like sections within it, while placed clearly within the new Christian tradition, as the shift from terms like "Lord" to "Father, Son, and Holy Spirit" indicates. An integration of psalm passages, language that sounds like Revelation, and echoes of classical Greek hymns (e.g., Cleanthes, *Hymn to Zeus*) result in a hymn that synthesizes and reinterprets earlier documents in an unprecedented way.

Tenth-Century New Testament Lectionary

One Greek parchment codex that I have examined contains the lectionary passages from John 6:71—7:46. Its ekphonetic or musical-rhetorical notation and other markings give interpretive clues as to the musical presentation of this scriptural passage in a liturgical setting.[8] The surviving four folios (or eight pages) include headings that divide the units according to a liturgical calendar.

Ekphonetic notation varies from manuscript to manuscript, even where the pericopes are the same—here the liturgical hand provides clues to interpretation of this biblical passage.[9] Scholars think the signs represent melodies or melodic formulae, passed down through oral tradition.[10] In this portion of the lectionary, the text is divided into four pericopes or scenarios, with only three of the four notated ekphonetically. The indication is that three of the four pericopes of this manuscript were used liturgically, while the fourth was not, for a reason not clear at this point.

Although ekphonetic notation is still not entirely understood, nor the actual sounds that it represents, it is clear that the notation represents

---

7. Hunt and Jones, "1786. Christian Hymn." Cf. West, "Analecta Musica"; Werner, "Music"; Pöhlmann and West, eds., *Documents of Ancient Greek Music*, 190-94; and most recently, Cosgrove, *Ancient Christian Hymn*. I return to this passage for further discussion in chapters 7 and 9 and refer to it in others.

8. This codex is located at the Austrian National Library (Suppl. Gr. 121), and its Gregory-Aland numbering is 0105 (see Gregory, *Textkritik*, 3:1066-74; Hunger and Hannick, *Katalog*, 208; Porter and Porter, eds., *New Testament Greek Papyri and Parchments*). Cf. chapter 6 below where I discuss this in more detail.

9. Wellesz, *History*, 256; Tillyard, *Handbook*, 13.

10. Velimirović, *Byzantine* Elements, 61-67.

a specific interpretive plan for each passage as a whole. Single words or groups of two words often are given specific emphases. It is evident that the interpreter was involved in very close readings of the text; it seems to be understood that the person delivering these musical readings would accurately interpret and deliver the text according to the ekphonetic notation that indicated rising and falling intonation and the like for musical and rhetorical purposes.

Sixteenth-Century Responsory by Sheppard

The choice of texts plays a role in musical interpretation of the Bible, such as the responsory of English composer John Sheppard (ca. 1515–1558). The Latin text, *Verbum caro factum est* ("The Word was made flesh"), a six-part respond-motet for Christmas Day, is one such choice.[11]

Verbum caro factum est comes from two New Testament passages: John 1:14 ("The word was made flesh and dwelt among us, and we beheld his glory, as of the only Son of the Father, full of grace and truth") and John 1:1 ("In the beginning was the Word, and the Word was with God, and the Word was God") combined with the Lesser Doxology, "Glory be to the Father and to the Son and to the Holy Spirit." Although the doxology is not technically Scripture, in most musical-liturgical settings, it is treated as Scripture and has a scriptural sound to it.

Prior to the sixteenth century, responsory settings were limited to a very small number of texts.[12] Sheppard, using a new distribution of polyphony and plainchant between the parts, reshapes and, essentially, reinterprets these texts. The form of the responsory and the pattern of repetition in the text emphasizes the last phrase of John 1:14, and juxtaposes others, which gives increasing attention to the second and third parts of this verse, each time it is repeated with its variations. Increasing prominence is given to the penultimate phrase, "full of grace," and even more prominence to the final repetitive phrase, "of truth." In the second setting, the conflated text now reads: "In the beginning was the word and the word was with God and the word was God/we beheld his glory as of the only Son of the Father." In the last section, "and we beheld his

---

11. This is located at the Christ Church Library of the University of Oxford (Mus. 979–83 [No. 144]) (see Hofman and Morehen, eds., *Latin Music*). In chapter 10 of this volume, I discuss another text treated by Sheppard as well as John Taverner and Christopher Tye. See also Porter, *Early English Composers and the Credo*, ch. 5.

12. Doe, "Latin Polyphony," 93–94.

glory as of the only Son of the Father/full of grace and truth" now reads "Glory be to the Father and to the Son and to the Holy Spirit/full of grace and truth." This draws attention back to John 1:14 and suggests that it is fundamental to the other two texts. Sheppard has taken a liturgical practice and applied it to a text that had not been set polyphonically in this way. In doing so, he presents a new liturgical perspective on this New Testament text.

Eighteenth-Century Motet by Bach

Johann Sebastian Bach (1685–1750) frequently interprets biblical passages through his music, whether they are his settings of passions, masses, or his own cantatas, chorales, or motets, while some would even include his instrumental music. Bach's notations in his Bible give evidence of his interest in interpreting it. One example is how he juxtaposes two verses from Rom 8 (vv. 26–27) with a hymn from Martin Luther (*Komm, Heiliger Geist, Herre Gott*, 1524) in his motet, *Der Geist hilft unser Schwachheit auf* ("The Spirit helps us in our weakness," BWV 226).[13] He uses this setting to interpret the Lord's nearness in the time of death and mourning, clearly articulating the feeling of sorrow, and contrasting this with the secure calm of the Holy Spirit's presence with the grieving believer.

The use of chromatic notes, the tritone, and minor seconds all help to express the anguish of the text. As the biblical text shifts from the personal dimension and suffering to the "mind of the Spirit" and "God's will," the musical writing becomes more straightforward and spacious.

The third section is the briefest. It brings the listener back to Luther's familiar hymn, in the familiar style of the Lutheran chorale. The verse, appropriate to the situation, speaks of help from the Holy Spirit—in keeping with the earlier Romans text—and of preparation for death, finding the grave a door or portal to God in heaven, and to life immortal. The concluding "Halleluja, halleluja" at this point is oddly fitting and provides a victorious if brief conclusion to the work. Bach's setting of two verses in Romans and their transition to Luther's hymn takes one on a journey through suffering and pain towards the mind of God and ultimately becomes a hymn that speaks of life immortal.

---

13. See chapter 11 below for further examination of Bach alongside Beethoven and Stravinsky in their masses.

PART ONE: MUSIC AND INTERPRETATION IN THE EARLY CHURCH

Nineteenth-Century Mass by Beethoven

The *Missa Solemnis* of Ludwig van Beethoven (1770–827) clearly depicts one aspect of the Christ figure that has never been so evident before—the humanity of Christ. While the standard *Credo* text always has the phrase *et homo factus est* ("and was made man"), Beethoven treats this statement in a new way. His division of the text, use of tempos, keys, and their interrelationships, attention to certain words and ideas in the various sections, and integration and contrast of soloists and chorus, all clearly interpret this phrase in an unprecedented way.[14]

Beethoven marks out fifteen independent sections in the text of the *Credo*. In doing this, he isolates phrases that Bach, for instance, does not, such as the separation of *et homo factus est* from its preceding *et incarnatus est* ("and was incarnate"). This gives deliberate emphasis to the role of Jesus becoming human. Part of Beethoven's genius is in the ambiguity about the central focus of his *Credo*: is it three or four sections? If three, *et homo factus est* is in the middle of the three. If four, then if *crucifixus* is central by intention, the symmetrical balance does not fully support this arrangement. The question relates partly to the passage that follows immediately after *crucifixus: et resurrexit*. In some ways *et resurrexit* seems to belong to the previous group and in some ways to the following group. It is unlikely that this ambiguity is unintentional.

The interaction and contrast of soloists with chorus clearly directs attention to the human image presented in *et incarnatus, et homo*, and *crucifixus*. The four soloists begin with a semispoken style, while the chorus enters *pianissimo*, also in a semispoken style of chant, creating a sense of underlying mystery that reinforces the inexplicable concept of how God could become human. From a quiet and intense chant section, the tenor emerges from the choir on the same note that the upper voices have been chanting. As the music abruptly changes from archaic mode into D major, the tenor moves up a tone to begin in earnest the full phrase, *et homo factus est*. In this shift, the sudden and rather unexpected change from minor chord to major (*tierce de picardie*) creates a dramatic transition from suppressed tension to bold release. The tenor line presents *et homo factus est* as though utterly thrilled to discover that he is human and truly alive. Beethoven fleshes out the Christ image by filling in the depth of his humanity. Indeed, his Christ figure seems to live and breathe, and even seems quite modern.

14. See chapter 11.

Twentieth-Century Motet by Poulenc

Although Francis Poulenc (1899–1962) is sometimes characterized as sentimental and nostalgic,[15] his *Tenebrae factae sunt* ("It became dark") is anything but these.[16] This third of four motets is deeply expressive—it seems to place the listener right at the crucifixion and gives a vivid and profoundly moving interpretation of that event.

The text is the key to this powerful motet, a standard text for Holy Week. Poulenc's is by no means a standard musical interpretation of it, however. *Tenebrae factae sunt* is a composite of the four Gospel accounts of the crucifixion: "It became dark when the Jews had crucified Jesus, and around the ninth hour Jesus exclaimed in a loud voice: 'My God, why have you forsaken me?' and with inclined head he gave up the spirit. Crying out, Jesus with a loud voice said, 'Father, into your hands I commend my spirit,' and with inclined head, he gave up the spirit."

The first phrase is paraphrased from the three Synoptic Gospel accounts (Matt 27:45; Mark 15:33; Luke 23:44), although they do not state, "it became dark when the Jews had crucified Jesus," but say that it became dark. The second portion of the text follows Matt 27:46 and Mark 15:34 closely. The next section comes from John 19:30, Matt 27:50, and the final lines from Luke 23:46.

Poulenc mixes old with new in this work, bringing about a metamorphosis of the text and scene. The first muted notes of the motet give an impression of darkness and foreboding, setting the scene of the crucifixion. It is poignant that, in Jesus' exclamation "in a loud voice, 'My God, my God, why have you forsaken me?'" it is only the first two words that are sung in that "loud voice." The rest are quiet, as though Jesus has used all the breath he can muster to speak the first two words. Their echo is much like the sound of a desperate, dying, and forsaken man: "MY GOD ... my God ... why have you forsaken me ... ?" Poulenc's choice of upper voices and notes on *Deus meus* ("My God") further suggests a strained sound, one that cannot be sustained and must subside. This suggestion of physical fatigue, pain, effort, and rejection is Poulenc's interpretation of Jesus' final moments on the cross.[17]

---

15. Mellers, *Man and his Music*, 227.
16. See chapter 9.
17. Hengel, *Cross*, 93–185.

Part One: Music and Interpretation in the Early Church

Twentieth-Century Mass by Stravinsky

Igor Stravinsky (1882–1971) had moved far from his *Rite of Spring* ballet of 1911 by the time he composed the *Mass* in the mid-1940s.[18] He wrote the mass for liturgical use, not concert performance,[19] one of his few uncommissioned works, suggesting genuine piety.

Within this short *Mass*, Stravinsky uses classical symmetry as a formal arch, with the longest movement being the *Credo*. He chose Latin,[20] although his native Russian would have been a natural choice, his having rejoined the Russian Orthodox Church in the late 1920s. Stravinsky's pragmatic reason was that Russian Orthodoxy did not allow for musical instruments in its services, which he was not prepared to forgo. Written for children's and men's voices—Stravinsky expressed the belief that women's voices were too passionate for liturgical chant—the liturgical nature of the setting is evident throughout.[21]

Stravinsky's Christ image in the *Credo* is somewhat two-dimensional and symbolic, certainly not sentimental in any way. The *Credo* is scored for voices in semi-chant, and, in fact, the setting is one long and practically unbroken chant. The unusual instrumentation of oboes, *cor anglais* (English horn), bassoons, trumpets, and trombones creates a sound not unlike an organ. The dynamic range is narrow, and the vocal range limited, with few dramatic effects or ornamentation.[22] There are no soloists in the *Credo*—no one individual emerges in this section at all. Attention is focused on the function of the text, and, as a result, his mass creates an image of Christ that is almost featureless and flat. There is no sense of emotion to suggest the warmth of a living Christ. The image is a symbolic one that does not seem intended to display a natural lifelikeness or an ethereal otherworldliness but is simply functional.[23] This setting of the mass has an element of timelessness.[24] Stravinsky seems to have been trying to transcend normal temporal boundaries, and in some ways to present the mass in the tradition of the great icon painters of the Orthodox Church.

---

18. For more extended discussion of this example, see chapter 11.
19. Stravinsky and Craft, *Igor Stravinsky*, 76.
20. Amy, "Aspects," 196.
21. Craft, ed., *Stravinsky*, 246–47.
22. Siohan, *Stravinsky*, 129; Druskin, *Igor Stravinsky*, 26.
23. White, *Stravinsky*, 447; Walsh, *Music*, 193.
24. White, *Stravinsky*, 100.

LITURGICAL AND MUSICAL INTERPRETATION

Twentieth-Century Musical Ikons by Tavener

The choral work, "We Shall See Him as He Is" by John Tavener (1944–2013), represents the continuing musical and liturgical need to reinterpret biblical passages.[25] Tavener uses Byzantine musical idioms and some theological ideas of the Eastern Christian church, and brings them to an unusually receptive Western Christian church. He attempts to present visual symbols and forms of ritual through his music, using ancient chant formulae and the terminology of "ikons."[26] These ikons reflect his interest in the iconography of the Greek Orthodox Church. Tavener's musical settings are sometimes deceptively simple, often extreme in vocal and instrumental range, with minute changes in orchestration, ornamentation, or dynamics, and little development in the classical sense. The music is static and ritualistic. The idea of mosaic also exists in his musical timbres and in the compilation of the text.

Mother Thekla of the Greek Orthodox Church is the compiler and arranger of the text for this work. The New Testament images are not exactly rewritten, but the text is reductionistic, even minimalistic. While appearing at first to come from John's Gospel, the text conflates three books that tradition attributes to the same author, but which have very different styles of writing and very different roles in the New Testament: John's Gospel, the First Epistle of John, and Revelation or the Apocalypse of John. John is the perceived author and main character of this musical work. The interesting merging of texts is observed in the two phrases that form the refrain. The first, the title of this work, "we shall see him as he is" (1 John 3:2), is combined with the second phrase of the refrain, "Amen, come Lord Jesus," from the penultimate verse in Rev 22:20. The refrain is sung in Greek throughout the piece until the very last line of the work, where it is in English. The words outline a portrait without filling in the details.

The work is set out in eleven "ikons" or pericopes from John's Gospel. An example of the abbreviated form of text is found in "Ikon 1": "I heard: Before time was. Time within. Time beyond. Created. Uncreated. Bodiless Body."[27] In a stylized way, Tavener provides insight into the twentieth-century penchant to reread and reinterpret old texts, rearranging them in new kaleidoscopic ways.

---

25. For more extended discussion of this example, see chapter 12 below.
26. Burn, "Liner Notes," 3.
27. See John 1:1–4 and 1 John 1:1–2.

Part One: Music and Interpretation in the Early Church

Summary of Musical Interpretation

While having merely touched on these works, and each is only representative of a much larger body of works, it is evident that each one unveils and interprets unique facets of the scriptural text through its musical setting. The works reveal composers in the role of interpreter of the Bible. Although the composition of sacred music in recent years has been seen as less creative than that of writing music for its own sake, in fact, the composer, in writing sacred music, has had the unique opportunity of engaging intellectually with Scripture at a theological level by composing a musical work that recreates the text in some new form. In this new form, the composer sets out for performance and for evaluation a personal or collective interpretation of the biblical text.

CONCLUSION

This chapter introduces the essence of this volume by illustrating a number of features: the interconnectedness of liturgy, worship, and music; the role of interpretation throughout all of these; the importance of Scripture in the developing liturgical and musical forms of the Christian church; and the varied means by which such scriptural interpretation occurs. There is much more that could be said about each of the examples explicated above—and in several of the subsequent chapters I return to the same composers and some of the same works to provide more detailed discussion—but the purpose here is not to exhaust each example but to make the point strongly and well that sacred music as part of Christian experience, such as liturgy, has served as a form of scriptural interpretation throughout the history of and in varying ways within the Christian church. Chapters that follow illustrate this major point or expand and develop it in varying ways in more detail.

REFERENCES AND FURTHER READING

Amy, Gilbert. "Aspects of the Religious Music of Igor Stravinsky." In *Confronting Stravinsky: Man, Musician, and Modernist*, edited by Jann Pasler, 195–206. Berkeley: University of California Press, 1986.

Burn, Andrew. "Liner Notes." In *We Shall See Him as He Is* by John Tavener. Performed by BBC Welsh Symphony Orchestra. Directed by Richard Hickox. CD Recording. Colchester, UK: Chandos, 1992.

Cosgrove, Charles. H. *An Ancient Christian Hymn with Musical Notation: Papyrus Oxyrhynchus 1786. Text and Commentary*. Studien und Texte zu Antike und Christentum 65. Tübingen: Mohr Siebeck, 2011.

Craft, Robert, ed. *Stravinsky: Selected Correspondence. Vol. I*. London: Faber and Faber, 1982.

Doe, Paul. "Latin Polyphony under Henry VIII." *Proceedings of the Royal Musical Association* 95 (1968) 81–96.

Druskin, Mikhail. *Igor Stravinsky: His Life, Works and Views*. Translated by M. Cooper. Cambridge: Cambridge University Press, 1983.

Gregory, Caspar René. *Textkritik des Neuen Testaments*. 3 vols. Leipzig: Teubner, 1909.

Harper, John. *The Forms and Orders of Western Liturgy from the Tenth to the Eighteenth Century*. Oxford: Clarendon, 1991.

Hengel, Martin. *The Cross of the Son of God*. Translated by J. Bowden. London: SCM, 1986.

Hofman, May, and John Morehen, eds. *Latin Music in British Sources c. 1485—c. 1610*. Early English Church Music Supplementary 2. London: Stainer and Bell, 1987.

Hunger, Herbert, and Christian Hannick. *Katalog der Griechischen Handschriften der Osterreichischen Nationalbibliothek*: Part 4. Vienna: Österreichischen Nationalbibliothek, 1994.

Hunt, Arthur S., and H. Stuart Jones. "1786. Christian Hymn with Musical Notation." In *The Oxyrhynchus Papyri XV*, edited by Bernard P. Grenfell and Arthur S. Hunt, 21–25. Egypt Exploration Society Graeco-Roman Memoirs. London: Egypt Exploration Fund, 1922.

Jones, Cheslyn, Geoffrey Wainwright, and Edward Yarnold, SJ, eds. *The Study of Liturgy*. London: SPCK, 1978.

Mellers, Wilfred H. *Man and his Music: The Story of Musical Experience in the West— Romanticism and the Twentieth Century*. Volume 4. London: Barrie and Rockliff, 1962.

Pöhlmann, Egert, and Martin L. West, eds. *Documents of Ancient Greek Music*. Oxford: Clarendon, 2001.

Porter, Stanley E., and Wendy J. Porter, eds. *New Testament Greek Papyri and Parchments: New Editions*. Mitteilungen aus der Papyrussammlung der Österreichischen Nationalbibliothek (Papyrus Erzherzog Rainer) Neue Serie XXIX, XXX. Folge (MPER XXIX, XXX). Berlin: de Gruyter, 2008.

Porter, Wendy J. *Early English Composers and the Credo: Emphasis as Interpretation in Sixteenth-Century Music*. Routledge Research in Music Series. London: Routledge, 2022.

Siohan, Robert. *Stravinsky*. Translated by Eric W. White. London: Calder and Boyars, 1965.

Stravinsky, Igor, and Robert Craft. *Igor Stravinsky: Expositions and Developments*. London: Faber and Faber, 1962.

Tillyard, Henry J. W. *Handbook of the Middle Byzantine Musical Notation*. Monumenta Musicae Byzantinae Subsidia 1/1. Copenhagen: Levin and Mundsgaard, 1935.

Velimirović, Miloš. M. *Byzantine Elements in Early Slavic Chant*. Monumenta Musicae Byzantinae Subsidia 4. Copenhagen: Munksgaard, 1960.

Walsh, Stephen. *The Music of Stravinsky*. Oxford: Clarendon, 1993.

Wellesz, Egon. *A History of Byzantine Music and Hymnography*. 2nd ed. Oxford: Clarendon, 1961.

Werner, Eric. "Music." In *The Interpreter's Dictionary of the Bible*, edited by George Arthur Buttrick, 3:457–69. 4 vols. Nashville: Abingdon, 1962.

Part One: Music and Interpretation in the Early Church

West, Martin L. "Analecta Musica." *Zeitschrift für Papyrologie and Epigraphik* 92 (1992) 1–54.
White, Eric W. *Stravinsky: The Composer and his Works*. London: Faber and Faber, 1979.
White, James F. *Introduction to Christian Worship*. 3rd ed. Nashville: Abingdon, 2000.

3

Music and the Early Church

INTRODUCTION

INVESTIGATION OF THE MUSIC of the early church has traditionally drawn on the efforts of liturgical scholars, musicologists, and historians, as well as biblical scholars, in attempting to find out what the music of the earliest Christian church consisted of and its possible origins. There are still many questions to be answered, and perhaps many questions yet to be asked. This chapter attempts to address the questions for which we currently have few answers.

The distance of time and culture makes the task of identifying or reconstructing the musical fibre of the early Christian church particularly elusive. While interest in the subject is rising and investigation of it is increasingly sophisticated, essential features of this music remain largely unknown to us. For instance, what did the music sound like? What melodies did it use? Was the music Jewish or something else? These most basic questions and others like them form the basis of scholarly discussion about music in the early Christian church, for even elementary characteristics of the music remain somewhat of a mystery. Essays on this topic frequently begin by saying that the early Christian church was a singing church, but what that means is hard to define, as we will see in this chapter.

The sources of information on the subject of music in the early Christian church are limited. Some possible sources require much lateral thinking in order to interpret the possible relevance they may have for the subject, and this is one area in which comparative musicology has played a necessary and significant role. Musical texts are likely preserved in the Bible and in other related literature, but how they were used is unclear. In that sense, discussion of music in the early church is also a discussion of how music interacted with, or interpreted, the Bible.

Finally, scholarly discussion about the music of the early Christian church inevitably turns to the question of backgrounds and influences; that is, based on the religious and cultural backgrounds against which the early Christian church was set and within which it thrived, determining which of these influenced its music is a major question. As a result, in this chapter, I discuss three major topics: the voices and instruments of the early church, the sources and traditions of its music, and the origins of and influences upon this music.

VOICES AND INSTRUMENTS

The most essential element of music—that is, to experience it, either by hearing it or by participating in it—is what we know the least about when it comes to the music of the early Christian church. The kind of singing, the descriptive terms that were used, and the use of musical instruments all merit attention.

Singing with One Voice

Johannes Quasten's classic work on the music and worship found in pagan and Christian antiquity devotes some discussion to the kind of singing that was likely in the early Christian church.[1] He writes, "the ideal of early Christian singing was unity or monophony,"[2] and this thought is based in part on some of the church fathers' use of the term "one voice," which is seen to be an indication of singing in unison. For instance, Clement of Rome (ca. 96 CE) states: "Let us, therefore, gathered together in concord by conscience, cry out earnestly to him as if with one voice, so that we might come to share in his great and glorious promises."[3] Later, Eusebius of Caesarea (ca. 260–340 CE) uses similar language to describe Christian singing.[4] Eric Werner also writes that "the ideal of the early Church was, according to the Apostolic literature, the κοινωνία [*koinonia*] i.e., the

---

1. Quasten, *Music and Worship*, 66–72.
2. Quasten, *Music and Worship*, 68.
3. See no. 20 in McKinnon, ed., *Music in Early Christian Literature*, 18.
4. See no. 206 in McKinnon, ed., *Music in Early Christian Literature*, 97–98. See also Quasten, *Music and Worship*, for further examples and discussion.

congregation singing in unison."[5] Even Paul is thought by some to support this view, where he writes, "so that with one heart and mouth you may glorify the God and Father of our Lord Jesus Christ" (Rom 15:5–6, NIV).

Most scholars also think that singing was unaccompanied, although the surest evidence for this view comes generally from later third- and fourth-century documents, not from the first century. Quasten, for instance, points out that, in Rev 5:8, John speaks of a "new song" and that he "expressly mentions that it is accompanied by the music of the cithara,"[6] thus at least implying the use of accompanied singing.

Psalms, Hymns, and Spiritual Songs

Perspectives on these three terms, "psalms, hymns, and spiritual songs" (Eph 5:19; Col 3:16), ranged widely over the twentieth century and into the twenty-first. From a musicological perspective, Egon Wellesz, a leading musicologist of the Byzantine era, proposed that the terms were specific in meaning. He defined psalmody as "the cantillation of the Jewish psalms and of the canticles and doxologies modeled on them," hymns as "songs of praise of a syllabic type, i.e. each syllable is sung to one or two notes of melody," and spiritual songs as "Alleluias and other chants of a jubilant or ecstatic character, richly ornamented."[7] It is thought that Wellesz's distinctions are typical of later Christian chant but not necessarily of early Christian chant,[8] and it has also been argued linguistically that the three words seem to be at least contextual synonyms.[9] Wellesz was aware of the view that the three words are synonyms but suggests that "the individuality of psalm, hymn, and spiritual song is obvious to the student of comparative liturgiology."[10] At this point, therefore, it remains unknown exactly what musical form may have been meant by any of these three terms, if any, although it is possible that Wellesz's proposal was too easily dismissed by biblical scholars.

---

5. Werner, "Conflict," 431.
6. Quasten, *Music and Worship*, 72.
7. Wellesz, "Early Christian Music," 2.
8. See Smith, "First-Century Christian Singing."
9. See Meeks, *First Urban Christians*, 144.
10. Wellesz, *History of Byzantine Music*, 33–34.

Part One: Music and Interpretation in the Early Church

Psalmody

Paul Bradshaw, from a liturgist's point of view, comments on psalmody as follows:

> Liturgical and musical historians have tended to assert confidently that psalmody was a standard part of the early synagogue . . . There is, however, an almost total lack of documentary evidence for the inclusion of psalms in synagogue worship . . . While the *Hallel* seems to have been taken over into the domestic Passover meal at an early date, and apparently also into the festal synagogue liturgy, the first mention of the adoption of the daily psalms in the synagogue is not until the eighth century.[11]

Most scholars think that the Jewish psalmody of the synagogue is what the first Christians sang, and as the earliest Christians were Jews, it is reasonable to think that Jewish psalmody was the basis of their music. Evidence of psalmody in the Christian church is cited from writers in the first centuries outside of the Jewish tradition who describe psalmody as an unusual form of music, while writers from within the Jewish tradition find nothing exceptional about it—which suggests that it is familiar to them. The logic seems reasonable.

However, if Bradshaw's assessment is correct, it is difficult to know what role psalmody played in early Christian services. Justin Martyr (ca. 100–165 CE), for instance, gives a detailed description of a eucharistic service at Rome but makes no mention of music or psalm singing.[12] His description may not be representative of the first century or of other locations and gatherings. Nonetheless, psalmody seems to have played some role in the early church, for it is mentioned in later writers, both Jewish and Christian, although it may not have had a large established role until one or two centuries after Jesus Christ. Philo's detailed description of an evening gathering of the Therapeutae is often considered an indication of musical practices in religious gatherings of the time of the New Testament and is thought also to shed light on early Christian gatherings.[13] James W. McKinnon suggests,

---

11. Bradshaw, "Search," 22–23. See also McKinnon, "On the Question of Psalmody"; Smith, "Ancient Synagogue."

12. Apel, *Gregorian Chant*, 65–66.

13. Philo, *Contempl.* 10.80–81.

[in] Judaism the psalmody that accompanied sacrifice in the late Temple was music in the fullest sense, but the psalms recited in the synagogues, and in the early Christian gatherings as well, were more scripture than song. They were no doubt recited with some sort of cantillation, but so was all scripture; it would take several centuries in each of the religions before psalmody became music in a self-conscious sense.[14]

Another area of the church gatherings where music may have been fostered was at the common meals. For instance, the Synoptic Gospel accounts of the Last Supper (Matt 26:30; Mark 14:26) mention that Jesus and his disciples sang a hymn before they went out, which event is thought by many scholars to be an allusion to singing the Psalms of the Jewish *Hallel*. Similarly, several second- and third-century accounts describe psalmody as a part of common Christian meals.[15]

Musical Instruments

It is commonly thought that musical instruments were banned from the early church on account of their worldly nature. Some scholars believe that instruments were banned throughout the first century; others, that they were banned after the destruction of the temple as a way of expressing disapproval. Of the Jews, Werner says,

> Rabbinic sources explain the strict prohibition of any instrumental music in the Synagogue as an expression of mourning for the loss of the Temple and land, but the present writer has been able to show that a certain animosity against all instrumental music existed well before the fall of the Temple . . . It seems that this enmity towards instrumental music was a defense against the musical and orgiastic mystery cults in which Syrian and Mesopotamian Jews not infrequently participated . . . The primitive Christian community held the same view, as we know from apostolic and post-apostolic literature: instrumental music was thought unfit for religious services.[16]

However, McKinnon's search of early rabbinical writings and other contemporaneous literature has found no support for the idea that

---

14. McKinnon, "Early Western Civilization," 10.

15. McKinnon, ed., *Music in Early Christian Literature*, 9.

16. Werner, "The Music of Post-Biblical Judaism," 315. See also Werner, "Conflict," 468.

instruments were banned in the synagogue, but also no evidence that musical instruments were ever employed in the ancient synagogue. As a result, he observes that the central element of the service, the simple declamation of Scripture, had no call for the use of instruments in any case.[17] McKinnon further clarifies the position of some of the church fathers regarding their ostensibly being against musical instruments:

> Music historians have tended to assume . . . that ecclesiastical authorities consciously strove to maintain their music free from incursion of musical instruments. There is little evidence of this in the sources however. What one observes there are two separate phenomena: a consistent condemnation of instruments . . . and an ecclesiastical psalmody obviously free of instrumental involvement . . . The truth remains that the polemic against musical instruments and the vocal performance of early Christian psalmody were—for whatever reasons—unrelated in the minds of the church fathers.[18]

Summary

This discussion shows that questions regarding the use of voices and instruments in the early church are not easily answered, as on virtually every question—the nature of singing, what was sung, the use of Psalms, and the role of musical instruments—the evidence is incomplete and often later, and the opinions both ancient and modern often mixed. In other words, the role of voices and instruments in the music of the early church is far from certain, even in relation to its use within the Jewish synagogue of the time.

SOURCES AND TRADITIONS OF MUSIC

There are a variety of sources and traditions regarding music in the early church, but the evidence is necessarily limited and subject to divergent interpretations.

Written Sources

Written sources that may be relevant to studying music in the early Christian church are very diverse and spread far and wide. How to

---

17. McKinnon, "Exclusion"; "On the Question of Psalmody."
18. McKinnon, ed., *Music in Early Christian Literature*, 3.

determine which are truly relevant and what they can tell us is the difficulty. Ordered somewhat chronologically, some of the varied sources that are used are: the Old Testament;[19] ancient writings and musical artifacts of ancient cultures;[20] ancient Greek literature on musical subjects or literature that incorporates either written music or texts that are written to be sung;[21] the Apocrypha (intertestamental literature); the New Testament;[22] the apocryphal New Testament books; musical fragments from around the time of Christ;[23] the Dead Sea Scrolls;[24] letters;[25] later collections of hymns;[26] writings of the church fathers;[27] written records of later liturgical practices; frescoes and funerary sculptures that depict musical scenes;[28] Jewish writings such as the Talmud and Mishnah;[29] and later chant books and other liturgical books that preserve the ancient rites of branches of the Christian church.[30] I cannot discuss all of these in this chapter, but I highlight some of their contributions and limitations.

Each of these sources poses numerous difficulties. One would think that the New Testament would be the most authoritative source on music in the early Christian church, but where music is referred to at all, there are more questions than certainties as to what is meant. New Testament passages worth considering are not primarily about music but include incidental references. They include the parallel passages mentioned above about Jesus and his disciples having sung a hymn before going to the Mount of Olives (Matt 26:30; Mark 14:26); Paul and Silas praying and singing hymns in prison at midnight (Acts 16:25); Paul's discourse on praying and singing both with the spirit and with the mind (1 Cor 14:15); his reference to having a hymn as part of one's contribution to

---

19. Sendrey, *Music in Ancient Israel*; Smith, "Musical Aspects."

20. E.g., Sachs, *Rise of Music*; Farmer, "Music of Ancient Egypt"; Farmer, "Music of Ancient Mesopotamia"; Galpin, *Music of the Sumerians*.

21. Henderson, "Ancient Greek Music."

22. Smith, "Musical Aspects."

23. E.g., West, "Analecta Musica."

24. Werner, "Musical Aspects."

25. van Beeck, "Worship."

26. Wellesz, *History of Byzantine Music*.

27. McKinnon, "Meaning of the Patristic Polemic"; McKinnon, ed., *Music in Early Christian Literature*.

28. Quasten, *Music and Worship*.

29. Werner, *Sacred Bridge*.

30. Wellesz, *Eastern Elements*.

Part One: Music and Interpretation in the Early Church

the strengthening of the church (1 Cor 14:26); his reference to Psalms, hymns, and spiritual songs (Eph 5:19; Col 3:16); a comment in the book of James on the appropriateness of singing songs of praise when one is happy (Jas 5:13); and instances of singing a new song, singing in a loud voice, and singing the song of Moses (Rev 5:9, 12; 14:3; 15:3).

Similarly, there are limited references to musical instruments in the New Testament, but some that are mentioned are the Greek αὐλός (aulos) (thought by some to be equivalent to the Roman *tibiae*, although the modern equivalent is the oboe),[31] harp, kithara, lyre, pipe, and timbrel.[32] These each have a long history preceding the time of the New Testament and can be found in various forms in ancient cultures.[33] New Testament references to playing musical instruments or to the instruments themselves are found in the pericope where Jesus finds αὐλός players in attendance over a dead girl (Matt 9:23–24); parallel Synoptic passages that quote a children's ditty sung in the marketplace that mentions playing the αὐλός (Matt 11:16–17; Luke 7:32); music and dancing in the home of the prodigal son (Luke 15:25); the clanging gong and noisy cymbals mentioned in Paul's discourse on love in 1 Cor 13;[34] Paul's discussion about using intelligible words, comparing instruments such as the αὐλός, harp, and trumpet that require delineation of notes in order to know the melody (αὐλός, harp) or to recognize a call to battle (trumpet; 1 Cor 14:7–9);[35] and a declaration that harpists and musicians, flute players and trumpeters will not be heard again (Rev 18:22). One notices again that there is no systematic treatment of musical instruments in this collection of passages.

Other musical references are found in the Apocrypha in such books as Judith and Maccabees. Acts of John (first century) mentions the playing of the αὐλός and dancing in relation to hymn singing.[36] The Old

---

31. See McKinnon, "Early Western Civilization," 7; Scott, "Roman Music." Again, this is not a "flute," as is typically described in many New Testament sources (e.g., BDAG).

32. See Sachs, *History*; Sadie, ed., *New Grove Dictionary*; Werner, "Musical Instruments," 369–76.

33. See, e.g., Schlesinger, *Greek Aulos*; McKinnon and Anderson, "Aulos"; Wulstan, "Tuning"; and West, "Babylonian Musical Notation."

34. See Werner, "If I Speak in the Tongues of Men," who argues that Paul detested musical instruments.

35. See also chapter 5.

36. Apel, *Gregorian Chant*, 39.

Testament is replete with musical references, as well as several quotations of canticles.[37] The book of Psalms in the Old Testament is thought by many to be the musical texts that were used by early Christians.[38] Depictions of musical scenes that are thought to take place near to the time of Christ give some insight into musical practices of the time, sometimes related to certain cult activities and religious rites.[39] Musical fragments that show notation of some of the music in the centuries surrounding the time of Jesus Christ may contain insights into the kind of music used by early Christians.[40]

Although some of these sources are particularly relevant for early Christian music, it is rare that they can provide conclusive evidence on an issue. For example, the fragmentary notated Christian hymn found on the papyrus at Oxyrhynchus (P.Oxy. XV 1786), first published in 1922, is still one of the most significant finds pertaining to the music of early Christianity, yet there is no consensus as to what it tells us or whether it is representative of music of the third-century Christian church or earlier.[41] On its discovery and publication it was thought to show close ties with Greek culture and religion, in particular because of its Greek musical notation.[42] It also has been argued that the hymn is a failed attempt to apply Greek notation to a Christian hymn.[43] Recent study, however, has again shown aspects of the Greek hypothesis to have merit.[44]

---

37. Smith, "Musical Aspects."
38. Smith, "Which Psalms."
39. Quasten, *Music and Worship*.

40. West, "Analecta Musica." For some examples of ancient but undated Jewish melodies, see Davison and Apel, eds., *Historical Anthology*, 8. For a transcription of the Greek "First Delphic Hymn" (ca. 138 BCE) and of Mesomedes's "Hymn to the Sun" (ca. 130 CE) as well as "Seikilos Song" (first century CE), see Davison and Apel, eds., *Historical Anthology*, 9–10.

41. Hunt and Jones, "1786. Christian Hymn." I treat this hymn in more detail in chapter 9 and refer to elsewhere throughout this volume.

42. See early discussions in Hunt and Jones, "1786. Christian Hymn"; Abert, "Ein neu entdeckter früchristlicher Hymnus"; Reinach, *La Musique Grecque*; more recently, Pöhlmann, ed., *Denkmäler Altgriechischer Musik*; see also Werner, "Music"; Wellesz, *History of Byzantine Music*, 156; Pöhlmann and West, eds., *Documents*, 190–94; Cosgrove, *Ancient Christian Hymn*, who provides a history of research (esp. 1–11).

43. Holleman, "Oxyrhynchus Papyrus 1786."
44. West, "Analecta Musica"; Cosgrove, *Ancient Christian Hymn*.

Part One: Music and Interpretation in the Early Church

Oral Tradition

Some scholars think that certain Jewish oral traditions that have been handed down through the centuries may have changed very little and hence constitute a source for early Christian music. If this is true, it makes it possible that the singing of some isolated Jewish communities may preserve ancient forms of Jewish psalmody[45] and therefore reflect psalmody of the earliest churches in Christianity. Abraham Z. Idelsohn's transcriptions and recordings of Jewish music in the first two decades of the twentieth century were based in part on this premise. The real sound of the music of antiquity is hidden in the past, yet hints of it may exist and be reconstructed from formulaic patterns of notes that have been woven into the various oral traditions of the Jews.[46] The inherent difficulty in this historical-reproductive approach is that historical threads must be connected over very long periods of time, and move backwards in time, in order to show that melodies and musical patterns of the Jews were taken over by the early Christian church. Such threads are easily severed.

Similar connections must be made[47] in order to show that the early church's musical roots exist in the traditional music of branches of the Christian church that have retained the most ancient forms of liturgy, such as may be found in Syrian church music.[48] In this regard, comparative musicology has attempted to analyze ancient musical traditions that are thought to be preserved in various languages and cultural settings, which include not only Syrian but also Georgian,[49] Armenian,[50] and Byzantine,[51] as well as branches of Judaism,[52] to identify common roots and to determine the chronology of their development.[53] There are many difficulties to be worked out in tracing oral tradition back to its most primitive sources—specifically, the lack of written records—but it is becoming recognized that new approaches must be developed in this regard.

---

45. Idelsohn, *Jewish Music*, followed by Werner, *Sacred Bridge*.
46. See Werner, "Common Ground."
47. E.g., Wellesz, *Eastern Elements*.
48. See, e.g., Husmann, "Syrian Church Music."
49. Jeffery, "Earliest Christian Chant Repertory."
50. Hannick, "Armenian Rite"; Hannick, "Christian Church."
51. Strunk, *Essays*, 151–64.
52. E.g., Werner, "Common Ground."
53. See Sendrey, *Music in Ancient Israel*; Werner, *Sacred Bridge*; Jeffery, "Earliest Christian Chant Repertory." For discussion in general on oral tradition, see Treitler, "Homer and Gregory."

ORIGINS AND INFLUENCES

The discussion above of sources and traditions leads directly back to the question that has dominated discussions about music of the early Christian church—the question of origins and influences. Is the music Jewish? Is it Greek? Or is it a combination of these and other influences?[54]

The twentieth century saw a tremendous increase in scholarly writings on Jewish origins of the music of the early Christian church. These include the groundbreaking work in comparative musicology by Idelsohn, which showed links between the music of isolated Jewish communities that are thought to preserve Jewish chant from before the rise of the Christian church.[55] Similarly, the work of Wellesz and Werner represents a vast field of study in musical and liturgical origins, particularly Jewish.[56] It is no surprise to find Jewish origins in the musical traditions of the Christian church. As Roger Beckwith, the biblical scholar, states, "At its origin, Christianity was a Jewish religion. Jesus Christ was a Jew, and his first followers were Jews."[57] It is equally unsurprising, however, to find influences of the Greco-Roman multicultural environment within which the Christian church was situated. Some of these are discussed below.

The Influence of the Jewish Temple

The Jewish temple is frequently cited as being highly influential on the music of the early Christian church. The difficulty with this position is that the temple music was formal music, performed by professional musicians. There seems to be little reason to think that this music had much influence on the early church, partly because Christianity only began in the early thirties and the temple was destroyed in 70 CE, and partly because the early church was not a formal or formalized institution. The earliest church consisted of small, informal gatherings, while the temple was a highly regularized formal institution, therefore allowing for little direct influence. Nonetheless, the early church may have incorporated the cantillation of Scripture,[58] which is something that would have been learned originally through the formal training and traditions of the temple.

---

54. This topic is discussed in more detail in chapter 7.

55. However, cf. Hucke, "Toward a New Historical View," 438–39.

56. Wellesz, *Eastern Elements*; Werner, *Sacred Bridge*. There are numerous other publications by both Wellesz and Werner, and others.

57. Beckwith, "Jewish Background," 39.

58. E.g., Maxwell, *Outline*, 2; Werner, "Music of Post-Biblical Judaism."

PART ONE: MUSIC AND INTERPRETATION IN THE EARLY CHURCH

Werner writes that both cantillation and psalmody directly influenced the early Christian church: "Not only are these two elements, the core of the ancient musical liturgy, common to both Synagogue and Church, they also are by far the best preserved and most authentic features."[59]

The Influence of the Synagogue

Two common assumptions regarding the continuity of practices in the Jewish synagogue and the early Christian church have come under recent scrutiny. The first is that the liturgy of the Jewish synagogue was carried over directly into the Christian church.[60] The New Testament scholar Ralph Martin, for instance, writes, "Christianity entered into the inheritance of an already existing pattern of worship, provided by the Temple ritual and synagogue Liturgy."[61] The New Testament makes clear that Jesus frequently attended and taught in the synagogue on the sabbath (Luke 4:15–16), as did Paul (Acts 17:2), so it is reasonable to think that the synagogue's liturgical practices were carried on in the early church. But there are difficulties with this seemingly straightforward view, focused particularly on institutional differences.

The synagogue in the first century seems to have been known as a place of study, as a place of prayer,[62] and also as a place where discussions and certain kinds of general business took place. However, current research on the first-century synagogue recognizes several unsolved problems. There is some question as to the exact nature of the synagogue, even as to its formal existence before the destruction of the temple in 70 CE,[63] and recent liturgical scholarship has found little evidence of an established synagogue liturgy. Bradshaw, in an article of a similar title as his later book, questions the confidence Christian liturgical scholars place on the sure foundations of Jewish liturgical research by pointing out that Jewish scholars are not nearly so certain of a single *Urtext* of this liturgy as has been thought.[64] The idea of a single pattern from which all

---

59. Werner, "Conflict," 438; but on cantillation, cf. McKinnon, "Early Western Civilization," 10.

60. E.g., Dugmore, *Influence*; Dix, *Shape of the Liturgy*.

61. Martin, *Worship*, 19.

62. But cf. McKinnon, "On the Question of Psalmody."

63. van der Horst, "Was the Synagogue a Place of Worship before 70 CE?"; Bradshaw, *Search*. See the review of discussion in McKay, "Ancient Synagogues."

64. Bradshaw, "Search."

later liturgical practices and documents evolved has been found to be unlikely; more likely is that there has always been more than one pattern, even from the earliest days.

The outcome of the discussion on the liturgy of the synagogue will have repercussions on the second assumption: that there was a continuing tradition of music from the Jewish synagogue to the early church.[65] Here again difficulties have been encountered. There is doubt, for instance, regarding the role that formal psalmody had in the synagogue of the first century, particularly if there was no formal liturgy.[66] McKinnon's observation is that there seems to have been no singing in the synagogue.

However, none of this denies the influence of Judaism on the early church but suggests that it may not have occurred in the manner that is commonly thought, for it is not only the formal liturgy and formal psalmody of the synagogue that may have influenced the Christian church. For instance, musical practices such as psalmody were also a part of the family observance of religious life. The most significant Jewish influence may have been through the music that was a part of Christian family meals.[67]

The Influence of the Greco-Roman World

It has been mentioned above that, in the earlier part of the twentieth century, the discovery of P.Oxy. XV 1786 contributed to the idea that early Christian music was highly influenced by Greek music. Later, scholars questioned whether the single papyrus fragment represented a tradition or whether it was a single deviation from that tradition.[68] More recent investigation suggests that a complete move away from the former possibility may have been premature.[69]

However, a less compartmentalized view acknowledges that Jewish religion and culture were highly significant components of the early music of Christianity but also recognizes the influence of the surrounding

---

65. Dix, *Shape of the Liturgy*; Martin, *Worship*, 45.

66. Smith, "Ancient Synagogue"; McKinnon, "On the Question of Psalmody"; Bradshaw, *Search*; see some acknowledgment from Martin, *Worship*, 41, who says, "we admit that there is some doubt as to the extent to which the singing of divine praises had developed in the Palestinian synagogues of the first century"; cf. Dix, *Shape of the Liturgy*.

67. E.g., Smith, "First-Century Christian Singing."

68. Holleman, "Oxyrhynchus Papyrus 1786."

69. West, "Texts with Musical Notation."

Greco-Roman culture, a confluence of religious and cultural ingredients that may have combined both contemporary and ancient practices. The position that acknowledges a combination of influences has untidy edges and non-discrete boundaries, but it is the most consistent with the multicultural environment in which Christianity first began, as well as the fact that Christianity had some things in common with Judaism while it held other things directly in conflict with Judaism. This is the direction in studies of early Christian music that may bring us closest to its origins.

CONCLUSION

The assessment of the evidence above recognizes that there is much that we do not and, barring the unforeseen, cannot know about the origins of music in the early church. There is a wide variety of incidental evidence to be considered, but how one interprets this evidence in relation to the early church is far from clear. As a result, the situation within the early church is susceptible to a variety of hypotheses. I believe that the most plausible explanation is that the musical origins of the early church were multi-faceted and reflected the complex cultural and situational heritage of Christianity as it developed from within Judaism but within the Greco-Roman world.

REFERENCES AND FURTHER READING

Abert, Hermann. "Ein neu entdeckter früchristlicher Hymnus mit antiken Musiknoten." *Zeitschrift für Musikwissenschaft* 4 (1921–1922) 524–29.

Apel, Willi. *Gregorian Chant*. Bloomington: Indiana University Press, 1958.

Bauer, Walter, et al. *Greek–English Lexicon of the New Testament and Other Early Christian Literature*. 3rd ed. Chicago: University of Chicago Press, 2000. (BDAG)

Beckwith, Roger T. "The Jewish Background to Christian Worship." In *The Study of Liturgy*, edited by Cheslyn Jones, Geoffrey Wainwright, and Edward Yarnold, 39–51. London: SPCK, 1983 [1978].

Beeck, Frans Jozef van. "The Worship of Christians in Pliny's Letter." *Studia Liturgica* 18 (1988) 121–31.

Bradshaw, Paul F. "The Search for the Origins of Christian Liturgy: Some Methodological Reflections." *Studia Liturgica* 17 (1987) 26–34.

Cosgrove, Charles H. *An Ancient Christian Hymn with Musical Notation: Papyrus Oxyrhynchus 1786. Text and Commentary*. Studien und Texte zu Antike und Christentum 65. Tübingen: Mohr Siebeck, 2011.

Davison, Archibald T., and Willi Apel, eds. *Historical Anthology of Music: Oriental, Medieval and Renaissance Music*. Rev. ed. Cambridge, MA: Harvard University Press, 1977.

Dix, Gregory. *The Shape of the Liturgy*. Westminster: Dacre, 1954.

Dugmore, Clifford W. *The Influence of the Synagogue upon the Divine Office*. London: Faith, 1964 [1944].

Farmer, Henry G. "The Music of Ancient Egypt." In *Ancient and Oriental Music*, edited by Egon Wellesz, 255–82. Oxford: Oxford University Press, 1966 [1957].

———. "The Music of Ancient Mesopotamia." In *Ancient and Oriental Music*, edited by Egon Wellesz, 228–54. Oxford: Oxford University Press, 1966 [1957].

Galpin, Francis W. *The Music of the Sumerians and their Immediate Successors the Babylonians and Assyrians*. Cambridge: Cambridge University Press, 1937.

Hannick, Christian. "Armenian Rite, Music of the." In *The New Grove Dictionary of Music and Musicians*, edited by Stanley Sadie, 1:596–99. 20 vols. 2nd ed. New York: Grove, 2001.

———. "Christian Church, Music of the Early." In *The New Grove Dictionary of Music and Musicians*, edited by Stanley Sadie, 4:363–71. 20 vols. 2nd ed. New York: Grove, 2001.

Henderson, Isobel. "Ancient Greek Music." In *Ancient and Oriental Music*, edited by Egon Wellesz, 336–403. New Oxford History of Music 1. London: Oxford University Press, 1966 [1957].

———. "The Oxyrhynchus Papyrus 1786 and the Relationship between Ancient Greek and Early Christian Music." *Vigiliae Christianae* 26 (1972) 1–17.

Horst, Pieter W. van der. "Was the Synagogue a Place of Worship before 70 CE?" In *Jews, Christians, and Polytheists in the Ancient Synagogue: Cultural Interaction During the Greco-Roman Period*, edited by Steven Fine, 18–43. London: Routledge, 1999.

Hucke, Helmut. "Toward a New Historical View of Gregorian Chant." *Journal of the American Musicological Society* 33 (1980) 437–67.

Hunt, Arthur S., and H. Stuart Jones. "1786. Christian Hymn with Musical Notation." In *The Oxyrhynchus Papyri XV*, edited by Bernard P. Grenfell and Arthur S. Hunt, 21–25. Egypt Exploration Society Graeco-Roman Memoirs. London: Egypt Exploration Fund, 1922.

Husmann, Heinrich. "Syrian Church Music." In *The New Grove Dictionary of Music and Musicians*, edited by Stanley Sadie, 18:472–81. 20 vols. 2nd ed. New York: Grove, 2001.

Idelsohn, Abraham Z. *Jewish Music in its Historical Development*. New York: Schocken, 1967 [1929].

Jeffery, Peter. "The Earliest Christian Chant Repertory Recovered: The Georgian Witnesses to Jerusalem Chant." *Journal of the American Musicological Society* 47 (1994) 1–38.

Martin, Ralph P. *Worship in the Early Church*. 2nd ed. Grand Rapids: Eerdmans, 1978.

Maxwell, William D. *An Outline of Christian Worship: Its Developments and Forms*. London: Oxford University Press, 1965 [1936].

McKay, Heather A. "Ancient Synagogues: The Continuing Dialectic between Two Major Views." *Currents in Research: Biblical Studies* 6 (1998) 103–42.

McKinnon, James W. "Early Western Civilization." In *Antiquity and the Middle Ages: From Ancient Greece to the Fifteenth Century*, edited by James W. McKinnon, 1–44. Man and Music. Basingstoke, UK: Macmillan, 1990.

———. "The Exclusion of Musical Instruments from the Ancient Synagogue." *Proceedings of the Royal Musical Association* 106 (1979–1980) 77–87.

———. "The Meaning of the Patristic Polemic against Musical Instruments." *Current Musicology* 1 (1965) 69–82.

Part One: Music and Interpretation in the Early Church

———. "On the Question of Psalmody in the Ancient Synagogue." *Early Music History* 6 (1986) 159–91.
McKinnon, James W., ed. *Music in Early Christian Literature*. Cambridge Studies in the Literature of Music. Cambridge: Cambridge University Press, 1987.
McKinnon, James W., and Robert Anderson. "Aulos." In *New Grove Dictionary of Musical Instruments*, edited by Stanley Sadie, 1:85–87. London: Macmillan, 1984.
Meeks, Wayne A. *The First Urban Christians: The Social World of the Apostle Paul*. New Haven: Yale University Press, 1983.
Pöhlmann, Egert, ed. *Denkmäler Altgriechischer Musik: Sammlung, Übertragung und Erläuterung aller Fragmente und Fälschungen*. Nürnberg: Verlag Hans Carl, 1970.
Pöhlmann, Egert, and Martin L. West, eds. *Documents of Ancient Greek Music*. Oxford: Clarendon, 2001.
Quasten, Johannes. *Music and Worship in Pagan and Christian Antiquity*. 2nd ed. Washington, DC: National Association of Pastoral Musicians, 1980.
Reinach, Théodore. *La Musique Grecque*. Les introuvables. Paris: Editions d'Aujourd'hui, 1926.
Sachs, Curt. *The History of Musical Instruments*. New York: Norton, 1940.
———. *The Rise of Music in the Ancient World East and West*. New York: Norton, 1943.
Sadie, Stanley, ed. *The New Grove Dictionary of Musical Instruments*. New York: Macmillan, 1984.
Schlesinger, Kathleen. *The Greek Aulos: A Study of Mechanism and of Its Relation to the Modal. System of Ancient Greek Music*. London: Methuen, 1939.
Scott, J. E. "Roman Music." In *Ancient and Oriental Music*, edited by Egon Wellesz, 404–20. New Oxford History of Music 1. London: Oxford University Press, 1966 [1957].
Sendrey, Alfred. *Music in Ancient Israel*. New York: Philosophical Library, 1969.
Smith, John A. "The Ancient Synagogue, the Early Church and Singing." *Music & Letters* 65 (1984) 1–16.
———. "First-Century Christian Singing and its Relationship to Contemporary Jewish Religious Song." *Music & Letters* 75 (1994) 1–15.
———. "Musical Aspects of Old Testament Canticles in their Biblical Setting." *Early Music History* 17 (1998) 221–64.
———. "Which Psalms Were Sung in the Temple?" *Music & Letters* 71 (1990) 167–86.
Strunk, W. Oliver. *Essays on Music in the Byzantine World*. New York: Norton, 1977.
Treitler, Leo. "Homer and Gregory: The Transmission of Epic Poetry and Plainchant." *Musical Quarterly* 40 (1974) 333–72.
Wellesz, Egon. "Early Christian Music." In *Early Medieval Music up to 1300*, edited by Dom Anselm Hughes, 1–13. New Oxford History of Music 2. Rev. ed. London: Oxford University Press, 1955.
———. *Eastern Elements in Western Chant: Studies in the Early History of Ecclesiastical Music*. Copenhagen: Ejnar Munksgaard, 1967 [1947].
———. *A History of Byzantine Music and Hymnography*. 2nd ed. Oxford: Clarendon, 1998 [1961].
Werner, Eric. "The Common Ground in the Chant of Church and Synagogue." In *Three Ages of Musical Thought: Essays on Ethics and Aesthetics*, 3–15. New York: Da Capo, 1981.
———. "The Conflict between Hellenism and Judaism in the Music of the Early Christian Church." *Hebrew Union College Annual* 20 (1947) 407–70.

———. "'If I Speak in the Tongues of Men . . .': St. Paul's Attitude to Music." *Journal of the American Musicological Society* 13 (1960) 18–23.

———. "Music." In *Interpreter's Dictionary of the Bible*, edited by George Arthur Buttrick et al., 3:457. 4 vols. New York: Abingdon, 1962.

———. "The Music of Post-Biblical Judaism." In *Ancient and Oriental Music*, edited by Egon Wellesz, 313–35. New Oxford History of Music 1. London: Oxford University Press, 1966 [1957].

———. "Musical Aspects of the Dead Sea Scrolls." *Musical Quarterly* 43 (1957) 21–37.

———. "Musical Instruments." In *Interpreter's Dictionary of the Bible*, edited by George Arthur Buttrick et al., 3:349–76. 4 vols. New York, Abingdon, 1962.

———. *The Sacred Bridge: The Interdependence of Liturgy and Music in Synagogue and Church During the First Millennium*. 2 vols. New York: Columbia University Press, 1959; New York: Ktav, 1984.

West, Martin L. "Analecta Musica." *Zeitschrift für Papyrologie und Epigraphik* 92 (1992) 1–54.

———. "The Babylonian Musical Notation and the Hurrian Melodic Texts." *Music & Letters* 75 (1994) 161–79.

———. "Texts with Musical Notation." In *Oxyrhynchus Papyri LXV*, edited by Michael W. Haslam et al., 81–102. Egypt Exploration Society Graeco-Roman Memoirs 85. London: Egypt Exploration Society, 1998.

Wulstan, David. "The Tuning of the Babylonian Harp." *Iraq* 30 (1968) 215–28.

4

Creeds and Hymns in the Early Church

INTRODUCTION

Hymnic and creedal statements—which as we shall see have many elements in common with music—are thought to have played a significant role in the development of the Christian church, and hence require inclusion in any discussion of the musical and liturgical foundations of the church. Fragments of these hymnic and creedal statements and references to others are thought to be found in the New Testament and merit further discussion. In this chapter, I will begin with an important definition of terms, then discuss various approaches to the materials related to hymns and creeds, examine some of the hymns and creeds found within early Christianity, and then finally discuss other references to hymns and creeds. The scope of the potential material for discussion is surprisingly large, so I can only address some of the major high points.

DEFINITION OF TERMS

The writing of what are often called hymns has a long history. For instance, the Greek word ὕμνος (*humnos*, "hymn") was used for many centuries in Greek classical culture before Christianity's inception. At least since the time of Homer, a hymn was a song of adoration to a god.[1] Performance of a hymn addressed to a god was the focus of competitions in the ancient world, which probably includes the second-century BCE paean to Apollo, known as the First Delphic Hymn, that calls upon the

---

1. Allen and Sikes, *Homeric Hymns*.

Muse to sing a song to Apollo.[2] Later examples include the well-known Cleanthes's *Hymn to Zeus*, which calls upon the god who directs the world to be praised.[3]

Biblical psalms that are considered hymns are those that express adoration to God,[4] and the language of some New Testament hymnic passages is reminiscent of hymns found either in the Hebrew Bible or in the Greek Septuagint. However, the kind of language found in Old Testament psalms/hymns is common also to some ancient Assyrian and Sumerian hymns.[5] The third-century Christian hymn, P.Oxy. XV 1786, which is probably a mix of both Hellenistic and Jewish influences within the Greek musical tradition, also shows a use of language similar to that of these various predecessors.[6]

Christian and non-Christian hymns have much in common. Sometimes it is the context that distinguishes New Testament hymns from pagan hymns, and sometimes it is the language, such as the use of terms like "the God of Israel" and certainly references to Christ. Many New Testament hymns and creedal statements are also distinct from those found in the Old Testament in that they are Christological.[7]

The earliest Christians' perspective on what constituted the hymn seems to have been fairly broad. Eric Werner writes that "early Christianity frequently referred indiscriminately to all sung praises as hymns"[8] and that the "difficulty lies chiefly in the ambiguous term *hymnos*, since Biblical pieces like the canticles, as well as post-Biblical spontaneous utterances and Apocryphal compositions were all termed hymns."[9] Augustine's often cited definition is "Hymns are praises of God with song . . . If there be praise, and it is not of God, it is not a hymn; if there

---

2. Henderson, "Ancient Greek Music," 363. See also West, *Ancient Greek Music*, 14–21.

3. von Arnim, ed., *Stoicorum veterum fragmenta*, 121–23.

4. Cumming, *Assyrian and Hebrew Hymns*, 18.

5. See, e.g., Cumming, *Assyrian and Hebrew Hymns*; Vanderburgh, *Sumerian Hymns*.

6. See Hunt and Jones, "1786. Christian Hymn"; Pöhlmann and West, eds., *Documents*, 190–94; and Cosgrove, *Ancient Christian Hymn*. See also references throughout this volume.

7. Although see Hengel, *Between Jesus and Paul*, 86, who refers to Ps 110 as Christological.

8. Werner, *Sacred Bridge*, 1:207.

9. Werner, "Conflict," 434.

be praise, and praise of God, and it is not sung, it is not a hymn. If it is to be a hymn, therefore, it must have three things: praise, and that of God, and song."[10]

Since the early part of the twentieth century there have been increasing numbers of studies on hymns and creeds in the New Testament, although the distinctions between the two are often a matter for debate.[11] Hymnic or creedal passages are often formally identified, for instance, on the basis of heightened poetical language or structure, uncharacteristic vocabulary, or the formulaic use of introductory phrases such as πιστὸς ὁ λόγος (*pistis ho logos*, "this is a faithful saying"; e.g., 2 Tim 2:11–13) or ὁμολογουμένως (*homologoumenōs*, "undeniably"; e.g., 1 Tim 3:16), a relative pronoun, such as ὅς (*hos*, "who"; e.g., Phil 2:6–11; Col 1:15–20), or the connective ὅτι (*hoti*, "that"; e.g., Rom 10:9; 1 Cor 15:3–5). Eduard Norden mixes content and form when he distinguishes three basic kinds of hymn, one addressed to God, one about God, and one based on the relative clause ("who") or participle that introduces it.[12] Ralph P. Martin tends toward the criterion of content when he says that scholars look for passages that have "a lyrical quality and rhythmic style, an unusual vocabulary . . . some distinctive piece of Christian doctrine."[13] Frequently the definitions used are fairly general and mixed, although each hymnic passage is usually thought to have a poetic quality that contributes to its distinctiveness within its larger biblical context.

The threefold reference in the New Testament to "psalms, hymns, and spiritual songs" (Eph 5:19; Col 3:16) has raised the obvious question as to what distinctions there are between these three terms. Most scholars think there is none. However, Egon Wellesz's view should perhaps be reconsidered. He musically differentiates psalms as referring to psalmody or the cantillation of Jewish psalms (combining some features of speaking as well as of singing), hymns as more syllabic songs of praise, and spiritual songs as jubilant or ecstatic chants and alleluias.[14] This proposal makes sense of the use of the three different words as descriptive of distinct,

---

10. See no. 360 in McKinnon, ed., *Music in Early Christian Literature*, 158.

11. Meeks, *First Urban Christians*, 144. See Longenecker, *New Wine*, who takes an expansive view of the subject.

12. Norden, *Agnostos Theos*, 143–76. Cf. Deichgräber, *Gotteshymnus und*, esp. 11–21.

13. Martin, *Worship*, 48.

14. Wellesz, "Early Christian Music," 2; Wellesz, *History of Byzantine Music*, 33–34.

even if not greatly different, types of music. Other New Testament references to hymns include the parallel verses in Matt 26:30 and Mark 14:26 ("when they had sung a hymn"; commonly thought to refer to the *Hallel* [Pss 113–18]), the hymns that Paul and Silas were singing at midnight in prison (Acts 16:25), and the kind of hymn a Corinthian brings "when you come together" (1 Cor 14:26). These references, unfortunately, are not systematically discussed within the New Testament itself.

Creedal formulas are statements that succinctly sum up the basic beliefs of the Christian faith.[15] It has long been thought that the earliest and most essential statement of Christian belief is found in the brief creedal statement "Jesus is Lord" (Rom 10:9). Creedal formulas are also frequently associated with baptism; however, while several New Testament creeds are clearly derived from the context of baptism, the liturgical context of others is unknown. Creedal phrases or related concepts include the following instances: "Jesus is the Christ/the Christ is Jesus" (Mark 8:29; Acts 17:3; 18:5; 1 John 5:1); "Jesus the Son of God" (Acts 9:20); "Jesus (Christ) is Lord" (Acts 10:36; 11:20; Rom 10:9); "Jesus Christ our Lord" (Rom 1:3–4); "Jesus is the Son of God" (1 John 4:15); "Jesus Christ has come in the flesh" (1 John 4:2); the significance of the death of Christ (1 John 2:2); the oneness of God (Jas 2:19); formal doxology (Rom 16:25–27; Jude 24–25); creedal formula centred on the resurrection of Christ (1 Cor 15:3–5); observing the Lord's Supper as proclaiming Christ's death (1 Cor 11:26); two-article affirmation of "one God, the Father . . . one Lord, Jesus Christ" (1 Cor 8:6); three-article affirmation of Father, Son and Holy Spirit (Matt 28:19; 2 Cor 13:13); creed-like phrases (1 Tim 1:17; 6:15–16); statements opening with "faithful is the saying" (1 Tim 1:15);[16] and an anti-docetic creedal formulation (Phil 2:5–11, but generally regarded as a hymn). A later creedal formula is found in the well-known acronym ΙΧΘΥΣ (*ichthus*, "Jesus Christ, Son of God, Saviour").[17]

Categorizing the passages as hymnic or creedal, as has already been noted, is not without its difficulties. Basic distinctions have been made, but frequently texts will fall in more than one category, and there are numerous differences of opinion regarding categorization. Some hymns are direct quotations from the Hebrew Bible/Old Testament (e.g., 1 Pet 2:6–8), while others are based more on the Greek Old Testament, the

---

15. Leith, "Creeds."
16. See Knight, *Faithful Sayings*.
17. Ι (Ἰησοῦς, "Jesus"); Χ (Χριστός, "Christ"); Θ (Θεοῦ, "[of] God"); Υ (Υἱός, "Son"); Σ (Σωτήρ, "Saviour")

Septuagint (such as Luke 1:46–55). Some of the texts are highly poetic (e.g., 1 Tim 3:16), while some are basic creedal statements (e.g., Mark 8:29; Rom 10:9). Some are thought to be baptismal (e.g., Titus 3:4–7). Some are doxological in nature (e.g., 1 Tim 6:15–16; Rev 4:8) and some are Christological (e.g., Phil 2:5–11; Col 1:15–20). Some have binary parallel structures (e.g., 1 Cor 8:6), and some have ternary parallel structures (e.g., Eph 5:14). There are, in fact, numerous passages that may be considered hymnic or creedal within the New Testament, depending upon how these categories are defined.[18] In other words, whether large or small, there are numerous passages within the New Testament that raise the question of whether they are hymnic or creedal.

APPROACHES TO THE MATERIAL

In response to the relative abundance of passages to consider, there are several different approaches that have been and may be applied to interpreting these kinds of passages. I refer to several of them here to show their various contributions to interpretation of the passages themselves.

Source-Critical Studies

The beginning of source-critical studies of these passages began especially with the form-critical work of Norden that pointed to certain passages originating in earlier sources.[19] Norden noticed that there was a higher level of writing in certain brief passages and suggested that this may be because the verses came from a source other than that particular writer. Source-critical studies have often focused on the Jewish backgrounds to these passages. The structure of the passages themselves is thought to give

---

18. I have attempted here a relatively complete list for the sake of inclusion and the possibility of further examination for those interested: Matt 28:19; Mark 8:29; Luke 1:46–55, 68–79; 2:14, 29–32; John 1:1–16; Acts 4:24–30 (or 24, 26); 5:42; 9:20, 22; 10:36; 11:20; 17:3; 18:5, 28; 22:6; Rom 1:3–4; 3:13–18, 24–26; 9:33; 10:9–10; 11:33–36; 16:25–27; 1 Cor 5:4; 8:6; 11:26; 12:3; 13:14; 15:3–5; 2 Cor 1:3–4; 5:18–21; 11:12–15; 13:13; Eph 1:3–14; 2:12–19 (or 14, 16); 4:4–9/10; 5:14; Phil 2:5 (or 6)–11; Col 1:15–20 (12–14); 2:8, 9–15 (or 13–15); 1 Tim 1:15, 17; 3:16; 6:12, 15–16; 2 Tim 1:8–10; 2:11–13; Titus 3:4–7; Heb 1:3; Jas 2:19; 4:12; 1 Pet 1:3–5 (or 3–12), 18–21 (or 20); 2:6–7/8 (or 4–8); 2:21–25 (or 21–22); 3:18–22 (or 18); 1 John 2:2, 22; 4:2,10, 15; 5:1, 5; Jude 24–25; Rev 1:4–8; 4:8, 11; 5:9–10, 12, 13; 7:10, 12; 11:15, 17–18; 12:10–12; 14:3; 15:3–4; 16:5–7; 19:1–2, 3, 5; 19:6–8; 22:17 (or seven antiphonal units: 4:8–11; 5:9–14; 7:9–12; 11:15–18; 16:5–7; 19:1–2, 3, 5; 19:14, 5–8). See Aune, *Revelation 1–5*, 315.

19. Norden, *Agnostos Theos*, 143–76. See also Sanders, *New Testament Christological Hymns*.

indications of their original language, giving rise to the notion of retroverting or translating them back into their original language (for example, Aramaic) for the purpose of study. Some of the hymnic passages, such as the canticles found in Luke, are obviously paraphrased from or rendered in the style of the Hebrew or Greek Old Testament. It has also been suggested that the Greek sources of some passages were written and used by the earliest church gatherings, for example, the church at Antioch.[20] Some scholars have more recently included the possibility of the biblical author writing these passages, though perhaps in an elevated style.[21]

Form-Critical Studies

Related to source-critical studies, as noted above, features of these passages have been important in attempts to distinguish different forms. For instance, what may seem at first like a simple question—whether the possible hymnic or creedal passage in 1 Tim 3:16 consists of two groups of three lines or three groups of two lines—has been the subject of a long debate that has not reached a consensus.[22] Each passage has a history of its own regarding the scholarly view of its structure and form. Passages of high contention also include Col 1:15–20 and Phil 2:5–11, usually over the number and arrangement of stanzas.

Functionalist Studies

A fundamental issue that has been the subject of more recent discussion is how these passages function within the New Testament contexts. Stephen E. Fowl concentrates this approach on several possible hymns in Paul's writings (Phil 2:5–11; Col 1:15–20; 1 Tim 3:16).[23] Fowl suggests that isolating the definition, source, and form of a hymn may be of less importance than how it functions in its present New Testament context. The fact that Paul does not call these passages hymns suggests that it is an unimportant distinction for his purpose, which is to develop his point or to present his case within the context of the letter.

---

20. Gundry, "Form, Meaning and Background," 221–22.
21. E.g., Wright, "Ἁρπαγμός."
22. Gundry, "Form, Meaning and Background."
23. Fowl, *Story of Christ*.

PART ONE: MUSIC AND INTERPRETATION IN THE EARLY CHURCH

Musical and Liturgical Studies

In attempting to reconstruct the musical and liturgical world of the New Testament and the early church, scholars are dependent on isolated and fragmentary references to musical and liturgical practice, as we have seen in chapter 2 above. Some scholars contend that the early church took over the practices of the Jewish synagogue, while others believe that psalmody, for instance, was not widely used in early Christian liturgy. Nonetheless, there is a steadily increasing body of knowledge about the sacred music and the liturgy of the early Christian church, with ongoing attempts to find more clues as to its earliest history.[24] The use of such data to understand the early church in its worship is the focus of musical and liturgical studies.

Having mentioned the body of data and several ways to interpret these materials, I now turn to several examples of hymns and creeds.

A CLOSER LOOK AT SOME HYMNS AND CREEDS

There are numerous examples that one might bring forward for consideration. In this survey, I identify some possibilities from throughout the New Testament that would probably be recognized by many if not most scholars as hymns or at least passages that draw attention to themselves through their language.[25]

Luke 1:46–55

The Magnificat, which begins "My soul magnifies the Lord," is thought to be in the line of traditional Jewish psalmody.[26] Joseph A. Fitzmyer considers it to be much like other "'hymns of praise' among the canonical psalms," such as Ps 136.[27] The language of the Magnificat, or Mary's song, seems to rely on the Greek Septuagint, however, with little evidence of the song having existed previously in Hebrew or Aramaic. Fitzmyer calls it "a

---

24. See, e.g., Bradshaw, *Search*; Holleman, "Early Christian Liturgical Music"; Jeffery, "Earliest Christian Chant Repertory"; McKinnon, "On the Question of Psalmody"; Quasten, *Music and Worship*; Smith, "First-Century Christian Singing"; Smith, *Musical Aspects*; Werner, *Sacred Bridge*.

25. For recent research on most of the passages that follow, see Gordley, *New Testament Christological Hymns*.

26. Farris, *Hymns*, 116.

27. Fitzmyer, *Gospel according to Luke I—IX*, 359.

mosaic of OT expressions drawn from the LXX."[28] The Jewish thought, rather than Christian, suggests an author other than the Lukan author.[29] Some textual variants associated with this hymn have the name Elizabeth instead of Mary, although the attribution to Mary is generally upheld; whether this means that she wrote the song is debatable. A text that has some similarities to Mary's song is 1 Sam 2:1–10, the song of Hannah, thought by many scholars to be the main influence on the Lukan passage. Stephen Farris writes that the hymn "displays . . . the characteristic structure of the declarative psalm of praise," which means that it begins with praise and then gives the reasons for that praise.[30] He thinks that attempts to divide the hymn into strophes, which have variously resulted in proposals of two, three, or four strophes, are unnecessary and contends that the hymn fits within the "consistent promise–fulfillment–praise progression in Luke 1–2,"[31] thereby fulfilling the function of Luke's narrative to show this progression.

John 1:1–18 (or 1:1–16)

Scholars are not agreed on whether the prologue to John's Gospel, "In the beginning was the Word," is a hymn. Those who say it is point out the uses of parallelism and chiasm, for instance, that elevate the language from prose to poetry. Some split the passage into sections of verses that may represent an earlier hymn, with authorial insertions of polemical and explanatory prose.[32] However, D. A. Carson suggests that the prologue to the Fourth Gospel may not be drawn from a source but that it was written in its entirety by the author, an opinion he bases on the similarity of the writing style of the prologue to that of the rest of the Gospel, as well as the close correspondence of the material to the rest of the book.[33] This relates to its function as well, for Carson notes that the prologue is essential and integral to the rest of the book. A more developed functional analysis is provided by Stanley Porter, in comparison with other types of criticism mentioned above.[34] Musically, Carl Krael-

---

28. Fitzmyer, *Gospel according to Luke I—IX*, 359.
29. Marshall, *Gospel of Luke*, 79.
30. Farris, *Hymns*, 114.
31. Farris, *Hymns*, 112.
32. Dunn, *Unity and Diversity*, 137.
33. Carson, *Gospel according to John*, 112.
34. Porter, *John*, 89–119.

ing and Lucetta Mowry believe that this passage suggests a combination of Jewish and Greek musical characteristics.[35]

Romans 10:9

This creedal statement, "That if you confess with your mouth, 'Jesus is Lord,' and believe in your heart that God raised him from the dead, you will be saved," is thought by many to contain the earliest baptismal confession of faith: "Jesus is Lord." James Dunn writes that it "is clearly a public confession of a solemn nature" and that Paul is citing a creedal formula that is well established.[36] Discussions about the use of the word *Lord* attempt to determine whether this word would have been perceived with Jewish overtones because of its common use in the Septuagint, where it is frequently used to replace the Hebrew, Yahweh, or understood in its contemporary usage in the Greco-Roman world, where it is a word addressed to one held in high esteem.

1 Corinthians 15:3–5

First Corinthians 15:3–5 is one of the main New Testament creedal statements, the essence of which is Christ died, was buried, was raised, and was seen.[37] Martin clearly sees the characteristics of a "credal formulary" in these verses:

> The four-fold "that" introduces each member of the creed ... The vocabulary is unusual, containing some rare terms and expressions which Paul never employs again. The preface to the section informs us that Paul "received" what follows in his next sentences as part of his instruction ... now in turn, he transmits ... to the Corinthian Church what he has received as a sacred tradition.[38]

Although there are many arguments for a Semitic source and the passage shows dependence on Isa 53, the form in the New Testament is a Greek composition.[39] Hans Conzelmann says the passage is clearly two double statements: in the first statement, "he died, he was buried," and in

---

35. Kraeling and Mowry, "Music in the Bible," 309.
36. Dunn, *Romans 9–16*, 606.
37. See Schweizer's comparison with 1 Tim 3:16 in "Two New Testament Creeds."
38. Martin, *Worship*, 57–58.
39. Conzelmann, *1 Corinthians*.

the second, "he was raised, he appeared." Others find an essentially three-part statement: Christ died, was buried, and was raised from the dead.

Ephesians 5:14

This hymnic fragment reads "Therefore, it is said, 'Wake up, O sleeper, rise from the dead, and Christ will shine upon you.'" The rhythm of the language and the two introductory phrases both indicate the distinctiveness of the passage. Whether it is an earlier Christian hymn or one written by Paul himself, two Old Testament references that seem to have influenced the passage are Isa 26:19 and 60:1, 2. From the first passage there is the influence of the rhythmic pattern and the use of the three concepts of rise, waken, and the dead. From the second comes the contrast of light and darkness.[40] Some consider the form of this hymn to be ternary, although the first two are a couplet of parallel imperative statements, while the third is a responding statement. The function of this hymn seems to be calling the nonbeliever to believe and is thought to have been used in a baptismal context.

Philippians 2:6-11

This passage is widely acknowledged as an early Christian hymn.[41] Fowl states that "in calling these passages hymns we are using a term that is the construction of a later, critical community, and not a straightforward translation of ὕμνος in either its specific or generic sense."[42] Nevertheless, most would agree that the writing style of these six verses is distinctly different from the preceding and following verses. As a result, many scholars think that this passage is a quotation by Paul of a work written earlier than the writing of the epistle.[43] However, Pauline authorship is gaining ground.[44] The Philippian hymn may stand at the forefront of Christological hymns of the Christian church, providing a template for Christian theology and hymn writing that reflects a ternary pattern:

---

40. O'Brien, *Letter to the Ephesians*.

41. See Deichgräber, *Gotteshymnus und Christushymnus*, 118–33. But see Fee, "Philippians 2:5–11," 30. For recent research on this passage, see Fewster, "The Philippians 'Christ Hymn.'" This passage is treated in more detail in chapter 12 below.

42. Fowl, *Story of Christ*, 33.

43. Martin, *Hymn of Christ*, xxxiv.

44. Fee, "Philippians 2:5–11"; Gundry, "Style and Substance," 288; Silva, *Philippians*, 92–93; Martin, *Hymn of Christ*, 42–62; Wright, "Ἁρπαγμός," 352.

Christ's preexistence, his incarnation and death on a cross, and his resurrection and ultimate exaltation.[45]

Fowl's discussion of hymns as exemplars suggests that Paul uses the Philippian passage to offer a solution to the Christian community that was being persecuted.[46] Musically speaking, Kraeling and Mowry think the hymn exemplifies a mixture of features: "As read in the original Greek the lyric ... has a regularity of construction hardly to be imitated in translation ... The absence of parallelism, the brevity and equality of the lines and the stanza-form shows that we are dealing here with a composition even more remote from Jewish psalmody. The lyric is in fact a hymn to Christ as κύριος or Lord, and hence quite out of keeping with Jewish tradition. Yet the rhythm is not quantitative but accentual, with three beats to the line, which suggests that it must have been sung in oriental fashion and not in one of the Greek modes."[47]

Colossians 1:15–20

This Christological passage, which begins "he is the image of the invisible God," uses exalted language to declare the supremacy of Christ in creation and in redemption.[48] The use of an introductory relative clause ὅς ἐστιν (*hos estin*, "who is"), a style that suggests a strophic arrangement, the use of rhetorical devices, and distinct language are all considered indications that this is a traditional hymn,[49] and the majority of New Testament scholars probably see this as a pre-Pauline hymn.[50] Various proposals as to sources or influences on this passage include Jewish circles influenced by Greek ideas, Gnosticism, rabbinic Judaism, and Hellenistic Judaism. Paul Achtemeier and others, however, maintain that claims that the hymn is non-Pauline do not hold up and that it is much more likely that Paul wrote the hymn, whether prior to the writing of the epistle or at the time, for the passage is central to the work, not a disjunctive leap.[51] As to its form, many scholars agree that the passage consists of two strophes but disagree as to where the second strophe begins. The hymn may

---

45. Contra Dunn, *Christology in the Making*, 114–25.
46. Fowl, *Story of Christ*, 93.
47. Kraeling and Mowry, "Music in the Bible," 309.
48. See Deichgräber, *Gotteshymnus und Christushymnus*, 143–55.
49. O'Brien, *Colossians, Philemon*.
50. See discussion in Cannon, *Use of Traditional Materials*.
51. Achtemeier, "Omne Verbum Sonat."

have been used against the Colossian heresy by emphasizing that even the cosmic powers are subject to Christ: Christ was first in creation; now through his resurrection, he is first in everything. Ernst Käsemann, however, discusses it in terms of a primitive Christian baptismal liturgy.[52]

1 Timothy 3:16

Traditionally Paul the apostle has been thought to be the author of 1 Timothy, although many scholars now think that the letter is pseudepigraphal and was written later than the time of Paul, with proposals ranging from the end of the first century to as late as mid-second century.[53] There is a similar lack of consensus regarding who wrote the specific passage found in 1 Tim 3:16, which begins "Who was manifested in flesh..." Since the beginning of the twentieth century, the view that has found increasing acceptance is that the writer of 1 Timothy quotes an early Christian hymn or creed.[54] The use of ὁμολογουμένως (*homologoumenōs*, "undeniably") in the introductory phrase is thought to be an indicator of this hymnic passage, as is the use of the relative pronoun ὅς (*hos*, "who").[55]

In Martin's outline of the characteristics of a creed compared with those that define a hymn,[56] 1 Tim 3:16 fits with some of his criteria of a creed, but in more cases with those of a hymn. The verse uses a different style of writing that sets it apart from the rest of the letter. The writing is compact—a total of eighteen Greek words in six lines. The content, however, of these six lines is expansive, summarizing six events in which Christ is central. The use of six verbs in the passive voice is a means by which Christ is understood to be the grammatical subject of each clause. The fact that this hymn was placed within the letter provides an insight into the author's view of the story of Christ, as well as how he saw it functioning within the larger context of the letter. In its bold Christology, the hymn addresses asceticism in the church,[57] as well as negative speech

---

52. Käsemann, "A Primitive Christian Baptismal Liturgy," 149–61.

53. Guthrie, *New Testament Introduction*, 623–24. This passage is treated in more detail in chapter 9 below.

54. Norden, *Agnostos Theos*, 250–63; Deichgräber, *Gotteshymnus und Christushymnus*, 133–37. Cf. Fowl, *Story of Christ*, 37–45.

55. But see Marshall, *Pastoral Epistles*, 523.

56. Martin, "Aspects of Worship," 14–17.

57. Fowl, *Story of Christ*, 154–74.

among its members.⁵⁸ The succinct and poetical nature of the words of the hymn is particularly apparent in its parallel Greek form with its six passive verbs, a factor that suggests musical and liturgical use.

1 Peter 3:18–22

The beginning of this creedal hymn states "For Christ died for our sins once for all, the righteous for the unrighteous, to bring you to God. He was put to death in the body but made alive by the Spirit." Of the full passage, Leonhard Goppelt says that "nowhere else are so many aspects of the second article of the Apostles' Creed found in a preliminary stage of development."⁵⁹ But, although both traditional creedal and hymnic elements are used, Peter H. Davids writes, "arguments for a hymnic structure in part or all of this passage are not yet convincing."⁶⁰ Achtemeier suggests that failed attempts to reconstruct an original hymn or creedal statement are because this passage only alludes to familiar traditions without taking over their original form.⁶¹ He identifies some of the more important linguistic features that point to the use of earlier traditions or materials as the use of ὅτι (*hoti*, "that"), ἵνα (*hina*, "so that"), ὅς (*hos*, "who"), parallel phrases, reference to the exaltation of Christ, a threefold statement that Christ died, was made alive, and ascended into heaven, and the use of ἅπαξ λεγόμενα (*hapax legomena*, "words appearing once"). It is thought that the context for this passage is a baptismal setting, but Frank L. Cross proposed that it is baptism within the paschal liturgy, noting that "as far back as our evidence takes us, the Paschal Liturgy has been for Christians a regular occasion for baptism."⁶²

Revelation 4:8

The hymn found in this verse, "Holy, holy, holy, Lord God Almighty, who was, and is, and is to come," bears a resemblance to Isa 6:3 ("Holy, holy, holy is the Lord Almighty; the whole earth is full of his glory").⁶³ The first name of God in Rev 4:8 is "Lord God Almighty," which seems to be

---

58. Guthrie, *Pastoral Epistles*, 42–43.
59. Goppelt, *Commentary on I Peter*, 247.
60. Davids, *First Epistle of Peter*, 134–35.
61. Achtemeier, *1 Peter*, 242.
62. Cross, *1 Peter*, 28.
63. The latter is known as the *Tersanctus* ("Thrice Holy") found in Eastern liturgies.

used because of its frequent use in the Septuagint, while the second name of God, the one "who was, and is, and is to come," has been thought to be drawn from the Hebrew Old Testament and Jewish exegetical tradition.[64]

This wording for God is also, however, a familiar description found in Greco-Roman literature.[65] David E. Aune contends that John depended on two main influences in writing the hymns found in Revelation: Jewish traditions regarding the heavenly liturgy and the court ceremonial practices of Hellenists and Romans to sing hymns and shout acclamations to the emperor.[66] The context of this verse has been thought to be directly related to the liturgy of the early church or Jewish synagogue. Gregory Beale argues that the passage does not indicate what the liturgical patterns were but is meant to be the pattern after which the church shapes its worship.

Revelation 5:12

This doxological hymn, rather than describing attributes of God, lists those things that the Lamb is worthy to receive: "Worthy is the Lamb, who was slain, to receive power and wealth and wisdom and strength and honor and glory and praise." These are of the highest order and by rights belong only to God, but it is clearly shown that now they are also transferred to Jesus Christ, the Lamb. Lists similar to the one found here can be found in 1 Chr 29:11 and in the Greek version of Dan 2:37 but also in writings such as Philo (*Ebr.* 75).

OTHER REFERENCES TO HYMNS AND CREEDS

It is not only the New Testament that contains such passages. There are hymnic or creedal passages and references to others in contemporary literature outside the New Testament, but only brief reference can be made to them here. Early references to hymns are found in the well-known letters of Pliny the Younger to the emperor Trajan,[67] and mention of primitive Greek hymns is found in the *Apostolic Constitutions* (fourth century), examples of which are appended to Codex Alexandrinus (fifth century) and are expanded forms of the greater doxology, "Glory to God in the

---

64. Beale, *Book of Revelation*, 332.
65. E.g., Plato, *Tim.* 37E (see Aune, *Revelation 1–5*).
66. Aune, *Revelation 1–5*, 316.
67. Pliny the Younger's *Ep. Tra.* was written ca. 107–15 CE. For some discussion, see van Beeck, "Worship of Christians."

highest." The lesser doxology, *Doxa Patri* (identical with the Latin *Gloria Patri*) "Glory be to the Father, and to the Son, and to the Holy Spirit: as it was in the beginning, is now, and ever shall be, world without end. Amen," was in use in Rome already by the time of Clement, about 91 CE.[68]

CONCLUSION

This discussion of hymns and creeds of the early Christian church shows that there is not a lack of evidence for discussion. In fact, if we are to consider the entire range of material, we see that the New Testament is laced with hymnic or creedal passages. More importantly, however, is the fact that there are major and significant passages within the New Testament that have characteristics of being hymns or creeds. These hymns or creeds are usually thought to have originated within an earlier period in the Christian church but are used by the biblical author to reflect a particular theological point or argumentative strategy within the biblical book. By studying such passages, we see that the early church used not only music in the more formal sense, but used passages that had distinctly musical and similar characteristics as an important part of its ritual, liturgy, and communication.

REFERENCES AND FURTHER READING

Achtemeier, Paul J. *1 Peter: A Commentary on First Peter*. Hermeneia. Minneapolis: Fortress, 1996.

———. "Omne Verbum Sonat: The New Testament and the Oral Environment of Late Western Antiquity." *Journal of Biblical Literature* 109 (1990) 3–27.

Allen, Thomas W., and Edward Ernest Sikes. *The Homeric Hymns*. London: Macmillan, 1904.

Arnim, Hans Friedrich August von, ed. *Stoicorum veterum fragmenta: Vol. 1*. Stuttgart: Stutgardiae In aedibus B.G. Tuebneri, 1964.

Aune, David E. *Revelation 1–5*. Word Biblical Commentary 52A. Dallas: Word, 1997.

Beale, Gregory K. *The Book of Revelation: A Commentary on the Greek Text*. New International Greek Testament Commentary. Grand Rapids: Eerdmans, 1999.

Beek, Frans Jozef van. "The Worship of Christians in Pliny's Letter." *Studia Liturgica* 18 (1988) 121–31.

Bradshaw, Paul F. *The Search for the Origins of Christian Worship: Sources and Methods for the Study of Early Liturgy*. Oxford: Oxford University Press, 1992.

Cannon, George E. *The Use of Traditional Materials in Colossians*. Macon, GA: Mercer University Press, 1983.

Carson, Donald A. *The Gospel according to John*. Leicester: InterVarsity, 1991.

Conzelmann, Hans. *1 Corinthians*. Hermeneia. Philadelphia: Fortress, 1975.

---

68. Bichsel, "Hymns, Early Christian."

Cosgrove, Charles H. *An Ancient Christian Hymn with Musical Notation: Papyrus Oxyrhynchus 1786. Text and Commentary*. Studien und Texte zu Antike und Christentum 65. Tübingen: Mohr Siebeck, 2011.

Cross, Frank L. *1 Peter: A Paschal Liturgy*. New York: Morehouse-Gorham, 1954.

Cumming, Charles Gordon. *The Assyrian and Hebrew Hymns of Praise*. Columbia University Oriental Studies 12. New York: AMS, 1966 [1934].

Davids, Peter H. *The First Epistle of Peter*. New International Commentary of the New Testament. Grand Rapids: Eerdmans, 1990.

Deichgräber, Reinhard. *Gotteshymnus und Christushymnus in der frühen Christenheit: Untersuchungen zu Form, Sprache und Stil der frühchristlichen Hymen*. Studien zur Umwelt des Neuen Testaments 5. Göttingen: Vandenhoeck & Ruprecht, 1967.

Dunn, James D. G. *Christology in the Making: A New Testament Inquiry into the Origins of the Doctrine of the Incarnation*. 2nd ed. Grand Rapids: Eerdmans, 1989.

———. *Romans 9–16*. Word Biblical Commentary 38B. Dallas: Word, 1988.

———. *Unity and Diversity in the New Testament: An Inquiry into the Character of Earliest Christianity*. Philadelphia: Westminster, 1977.

Farris, Stephen. *The Hymns of Luke's Infancy Narratives: Their Origin, Meaning and Significance*. Journal for the Study of the New Testament Supplement Series 9. Sheffield: Sheffield Academic, 1985.

Fee, Gordon D. "Philippians 2:5–11: Hymn or Exalted Pauline Prose?" *Bulletin for Biblical Research* 2 (1992) 29–46.

Fewster, Gregory P. "The Philippians 'Christ Hymn': Trends in Critical Scholarship." *Currents in Biblical Research* 13 (2015) 191–206.

Fitzmyer, Joseph A. *The Gospel according to Luke I—IX*. Anchor Bible 28. Garden City, NY: Doubleday, 1981.

Fowl, Stephen E. *The Story of Christ in the Ethics of Paul: An Analysis of the Function of the Hymnic Material in the Pauline Corpus*. Journal for the Study of the New Testament Supplement Series 36. Sheffield: JSOT, 1990.

Goppelt, Leonhard. *A Commentary on I Peter*. Grand Rapids: Eerdmans, 1993.

Gordley, Matthew E. *New Testament Christological Hymns: Exploring Texts, Contexts, and Significance*. Downers Grove, IL: InterVarsity, 2018.

Gundry, Robert H. "The Form, Meaning and Background of the Hymn Quoted in 1 Timothy 3:16." In *Apostolic History and the Gospel: Biblical and Historical Essays Presented to F. F. Bruce*, edited by W. Ward Gasque and Ralph P. Martin, 203–22. Exeter: Paternoster, 1970.

———. "Style and Substance in 'The Myth of God Incarnate' according to Philippians 2:6–11." In *Crossing the Boundaries: Essays in Biblical Interpretation in Honour of Michael D. Goulder*, edited by Stanley E. Porter, Paul Joyce, and David E. Orton, 271–93. Leiden: Brill, 1994.

Guthrie, Donald. *New Testament Introduction*. Rev. ed. Downers Grove, IL: InterVarsity, 1970.

———. *The Pastoral Epistles: An Introduction and Commentary*. Rev. ed. Tyndale New Testament Commentaries. Grand Rapids: Eerdmans, 1990.

Henderson, Isobel. "Ancient Greek Music." In *Ancient and Oriental Music*, edited by Egon Wellesz, 336–403. New Oxford History of Music 1. London: Oxford University Press, 1966 [1957].

Hengel, Martin. *Between Jesus and Paul: Studies in the Earliest History of Christianity*. London: SCM, 1983.

PART ONE: MUSIC AND INTERPRETATION IN THE EARLY CHURCH

Holleman, A. W. J. "Early Christian Liturgical Music." *Studia Liturgica* 8 (1971) 185–92.

Hunt, Arthur S., and H. Stuart Jones. "1786. Christian Hymn with Musical Notation." In *The Oxyrhynchus Papyri XV*, edited by Bernard P. Grenfell and Arthur S. Hunt, 21–25. Egypt Exploration Society Graeco-Roman Memoirs. London: Egypt Exploration Fund, 1922.

Jeffery, Peter. "The Earliest Christian Chant Repertory Recovered: The Georgian Witnesses to Jerusalem Chant." *Journal of the American Musicological Society* 47 (1994) 1–38.

Käsemann, Ernst. "A Primitive Christian Baptismal Liturgy." In *Essays on New Testament Themes*, 149–61. Philadelphia: Fortress, 1964.

Knight, George W., III. *The Faithful Sayings in the Pastoral Letters*. Kampen: Kok, 1968.

Kraeling, Carl H., and Lucetta Mowry. "Music in the Bible." In *Ancient and Oriental Music*, edited by Egon Wellesz, 283–312. New Oxford History of Music 1. Lonodon: Oxford University Press, 1966 [1957].

Leith, John H. "Creeds, Early Christian." In *Anchor Bible Dictionary*, edited by David Noel Freedman, 1:203–6. 6 vols. New York: Doubleday, 1992.

Longenecker, Richard N. *New Wine into Fresh Wineskins: Contextualizing the Early Christian Confessions*. Peabody, MA: Hendrickson, 1999.

Marshall, I. Howard. *The Gospel of Luke*. New International Greek Testament Commentary 3. Grand Rapids: Eerdmans, 1978.

———. *The Pastoral Epistles*. International Critical Commentary. Edinburgh: T. & T. Clark, 1999.

Martin, Ralph P. "Aspects of Worship in the New Testament Church." *Vox Evangelica* 2 (1963) 6–32.

———. *A Hymn of Christ: Philippians 2:5–11 in Recent Interpretation and in the Setting of Early Christian Worship*. Downers Grove, IL: InterVarsity Press, 1997. Originally published as *Carmen Christi: Philippians 2:5–11 in Recent Interpretation and in the Setting of Early Christian Worship*. Society for New Testament Studies Monograph Series 4. 1967. Reprint, Grand Rapids: Eerdmans, 1983.

———. *Worship in the Early Church*. 2nd ed. Grand Rapids: Eerdmans, 1978.

McKinnon, James W. "On the Question of Psalmody in the Ancient Synagogue." *Early Music History* 6 (1986) 159–91.

McKinnon, James W., ed. *Music in Early Christian Literature*. Cambridge Studies in the Literature of Music. Cambridge: Cambridge University Press, 1987.

Meeks, Wayne A. *The First Urban Christians: The Social World of the Apostle Paul*. New Haven: Yale University Press, 1983.

Norden, Eduard. *Agnostos Theos: Untersuchungen zur Formengeschichte religiöser Rede*. 1913. Reprint, Darmstadt: Wissenschaftliche Buchgesellschaft, 1956.

O'Brien, Peter T. *Colossians, Philemon*. Word Biblical Commentary 44. Waco, TX: Word, 1982.

———. *The Letter to the Ephesians*. Pillar New Testament Commentary. Grand Rapids: Eerdmans, 1999.

Pöhlmann, Egert, and Martin L. West, eds. *Documents of Ancient Greek Music*. Oxford: Clarendon, 2001.

Porter, Stanley E. *John, his Gospel, and Jesus: In Pursuit of the Johannine Voice*. Grand Rapids: Eerdmans, 2015.

Quasten, Johannes. *Music and Worship in Pagan and Christian Antiquity*. 2nd ed. Washington, DC: National Association of Pastoral Musicians, 1980.

Sanders, Jack T. *The New Testament Christological Hymns: Their Historical Religious Background*. Society for New Testament Studies Monograph Series 15. Cambridge: Cambridge University Press, 1971.

Schweizer, Eduard. "Two New Testament Creeds Compared." In *Issues in New Testament Interpretation: Essays in Honor of Otto A. Piper*, edited by William Klassen and Graydon F. Snyder, 166–77. London: SCM, 1962.

Silva, Moisés. *Philippians*. Baker Exegetical Commentary on the New Testament. 2nd ed. Grand Rapids: Baker, 2005.

Smith, John A. "First-Century Christian Singing and its Relationship to Contemporary Jewish Religious Song." *Music & Letters* 75 (1994) 1–15.

Smith, William Sheppard. *Musical Aspects of the New Testament*. Amsterdam: W. Ten Have, 1962.

Vanderburgh, Frederick Augustus. *Sumerian Hymns from Cuneiform Texts in the British Museum: Transliteration, Translation and Commentary*. Contributions to Oriental History and Philosophy 1. New York: AMS, 1966 [1908].

Wellesz, Egon. "Early Christian Music." In *Early Medieval Music up to 1300*, edited by Dom Anselm Hughes, 1–13. New Oxford History of Music 2. Rev. ed. London: Oxford University Press, 1955.

———. *A History of Byzantine Music and Hymnography*. 2nd ed. Oxford: Clarendon, 1998 [1961].

Werner, Eric. "The Conflict between Hellenism and Judaism in the Music of the Early Christian Church." *Hebrew Union College Annual* 20 (1947) 407–70.

———. *The Sacred Bridge: The Interdependence of Liturgy and Music in Synagogue and Church During the First Millennium*. 2 vols. New York: Columbia University Press, 1959; New York: Ktav, 1984.

West, Martin L. *Ancient Greek Music*. Oxford: Clarendon, 1992.

Wright, N. T. "Ἁρπαγμός and the Meaning of Philippians 2:5–11." *The Journal of Theological Studies* 37 (1986) 321–52. Republished in revised form in Wright, *The Climax of the Covenant: Christ and the Law in Pauline Theology*, 56–98. Edinburgh: T. & T. Clark, 1991.

5

A Word about Women, Music, and Sensuality in the Early Church

αἱ γυναῖκες ἐν ταῖς ἐκκλησίας σιγάτωσαν (*hai gunaikes en tais ekklēsias sigatōsan*). οὐ γὰρ ἐπιτρέπεται αὐταῖς λαλεῖν (*ou gar epitrepetai autais lalein*), ἀλλὰ ὑποτασσέσθωσαν, καθὼς καὶ ὁ νόμος λέγει (*alla hupotassesthōsan, kathōs kai ho nomos legei*). εἰ δέ τι μαθεῖν θέλουσιν, ἐν οἴκῳ τοὺς ἰδίους ἄνδρας ἐπερωτάτωσαν (*ei de ti mathein thelousin, en oikō tous idious andras eperōtatōsan*). αἰσχρὸν γάρ ἐστιν γυναικὶ λαλεῖν ἐν ἐκκλησίᾳ (*aischron gar estin gunaiki lalein en ekklēsia*).

Let the women keep silent in the churches; for they are not permitted to speak, but let them subject themselves, just as the Law also says. And if they desire to learn anything, let them ask their own husbands at home; for it is improper for a woman to speak in church (1 Cor 14:34–35, NASB).

PROBLEMS WITH PAUL'S STATEMENT

PAUL'S STATEMENT IN 1 Cor 14:34–35 seems almost consciously designed to inflame the modern woman and to confound commentators of all generations. However, I do not intend to pursue the typical, popular avenue of arguing that Paul was a misogynist or to suggest that Paul's letters of the first century are or should be sensitive to twenty-first century gender issues. It is generally agreed that women and men were not treated as equals in many areas of life in New Testament times, and the evidence shows that most women did not have an equal voice in Greek and Roman culture (although they are clearly represented in the New Testament as being the ones who supported Jesus' ministry). Nevertheless, Paul's statement in 1 Cor 14:34–35 still strikes the hearer as being categorical and even exclusive: "Let the women keep silent in the churches; for they are not permitted to speak." The question I am interested in pursuing is this—what were these women really doing that merited such a strong statement?

There are three main problems that commentators must deal with in these two verses in 1 Cor 14:34–35. The first is the inconsistency of these two verses with 1 Cor 11:5 related to women's roles in the church. First Corinthians 14:34–35 states that women are not permitted to speak in the church, while 1 Cor 11:5 discusses what is appropriate for women to wear when they are *praying* and *prophesying* in the church. Those who are already convinced of the inconsistency of Paul's writing, or of the low regard that he had for women, find plenty here to support their case. Obviously, something appears inconsistent in these two statements. The second problem is the abruptness of vv. 34–35 within 1 Cor 14. These two verses seem to appear without introduction in a discourse on speaking in tongues and prophesying, and then disappear in the same abrupt manner; the preceding verse and the verse that follows these two verses do not seem to fit together. The third problem is some confusion about Paul's use of the word λαλέω (*laleō*) and what it really means in this context. It seems to be a simple word, but the sense is confusing in these two verses. These three problems all centre on the nature of the disruption that these women were apparently creating, and whom Paul was really addressing. There is some dispute about who the women were, based on the translation of the word γυναῖκες (*gunaikes*), which could be translated "women" or "wives." The reference to men is often translated "husbands," which implies "wives." The disruption seems to be that the "wives," if that is the right term, were shaming their husbands publicly by arguing loudly with them about certain issues. But is this translation correct, and does it justify the strong language that Paul uses in these verses?

Solutions that have been proposed by commentators do not adequately deal with the problems; they tend to downplay certain issues or ignore them entirely. I will survey and evaluate some of the proposed solutions, and then discuss several unresolved problems and further questions in understanding Paul's statement, especially in the light of the culture of the period and Paul's specific use of the language.

Part One: Music and Interpretation in the Early Church

A SURVEY OF THE STANDARD SOLUTIONS

I begin with a survey of the standard solutions that one might find especially among New Testament commentators on First Corinthians.

Modern Commentators on 1 Cor 14:34–35

An examination of proposals and supposed or posited solutions by modern commentators shows that for the most part these interpretive problems remain unresolved. Modern commentators can be categorized under three major proposed solutions.

The Inconsistency of 1 Cor 14:34–35 with 1 Cor 11:5

Is it possible that, in the course of writing the letter, Paul simply changed his mind about the status of women speaking in the church? Most scholars do not conclude this, so answers must be found to resolve the inconsistency. Archibald Robertson and Alfred Plummer suggest that 1 Cor 11:5 ("women who prophesy . . .") may simply be hypothetical, meaning, if a woman were to prophesy, here is something she should do. This reading of the text alleviates the necessity of trying to explain the contradiction of 14:34–35 with the earlier passage, as the first one is presented as purely hypothetical; however, this argument is unconvincing.[1] Reginald St John Parry judges there to be a simple solution regarding the inconsistency between Paul's statement in 1 Cor 11:5 and 14:34: in chapter 11 "he [Paul] is dealing with the dress of women, and gives rules which extend beyond the case of women when praying or prophesying. Here [14:34] he is dealing definitely with the question whether women are to speak (whether with "tongues" or in prophesying) and forbids it."[2] So, Parry's argument is that 11:5 is simply a response to the larger question about whether women should wear a veil, but 14:34 is a response to the specific issue about whether women should speak. He sidesteps the issue of the inconsistency by asserting that it is *not* inconsistent.[3] More common

---

1. Robertson and Plummer, *Critical and Exegetical Commentary on the First Epistle of St. Paul to the Corinthians*, 324–25.

2. Parry, *First Epistle of Paul the Apostle to the Corinthians*, 210 (noted also by Garland, *1 Corinthians*, 665).

3. Parry does point out, however, the understanding that each woman had a husband or a male member of the family to whom she belonged, in the convention of the times, which is important to gaining insight into the culture. See the text (No. 16) in Lewis, *Documents*, 65, which refers to Babatha's husband who served as her

in later commentaries is the idea that women can prophesy but are not allowed to interpret or are not allowed to judge the prophecy of their own husband; the text does not seem to support this view.[4]

The Abruptness of vv. 34–35 within 1 Cor 14

Commentators have attempted numerous ways of resolving the problem of how 1 Cor 14:34–35 fits into the context of the surrounding verses. One of the difficulties lies in the gender of the word μόνους (*monous*) in v. 36. The word μόνους which is masculine accusative plural, could be used to refer to a group of people that is all male or a group that is a mixture of female and male, but not a group that is all female. If the group was all female, the word should in this case be μόνας (*monas*). The shift in gender is hard to account for in this passage. James Moffatt believes that, in an earlier version of this text, vv. 34–35 were placed after v. 40, which solves the problem of the interruptive element of these verses in the context of the surrounding verses but, as he himself admits, does not address the issue of the apparent contradiction of this statement with Paul's earlier statement about women prophesying in church.[5]

One way of dealing with these verses is simply to conclude that they do not belong in the passage at all. For example, Hans Conzelmann basically dismisses them from 1 Cor 14 by saying, "This self-contained section upsets the context; it interrupts the theme of prophecy and spoils the flow of thought."[6] Ironically, Paul may be dealing with this very situation in the church—that of prophecy being interrupted and the context being upset. Another solution to the problem of vv. 34–35 is that these verses are marginalia, an addition by a scribe, or reflect some kind of well-known saying of the time that Paul for some reason decided to incorporate. Charles H. Talbert says that Paul's statement could be a quotation of the Corinthian stance on women participating in the church. If this were the case, several of the accompanying problems with these verses are solved: (1) Paul's position in these verses no longer disagrees

---

transactional guardian. But this may not accurately reflect the position of women in the early church; for a different viewpoint, see Stark, *Rise of Christianity*, 95–128 (note that the chapter to which I refer in Stark's book is a revised form of his article, "Reconstructing").

4. Forbes, *Prophecy and Inspired Speech*, 272.

5. Moffatt, *First Epistle of Paul to the Corinthians*, 231. For recent discussion, see Payne, *Man and Woman*, 217–67; and Payne, "Vaticanus."

6. Conzelmann, *1 Corinthians*, 246.

with his earlier statement about women prophesying in church, because it does not reflect his own stance; (2) The lack of agreement in gender is plausibly resolved. If vv. 34–35 were an interpolation, then the lack of agreement in gender would not create quite the same problem, although there is still some question as to whom Paul is addressing in regard to this interpolation; (3) The suggestion of a quotation regarding the Corinthian stance on women could also account for the sharp, sarcastic tone of the words in v. 36, in that they would be a response to what Paul evidently views as an untenable position.[7] However, these verses lack the kind of wording that typically introduces quotations (such as elements of diatribe, quotation formulas, etc.). One must be cautious not to be seen to be solving biblical difficulties by simply removing everything that does not fit or cannot be explained, which is an unsatisfactory solution.

Paul's Use of ΛΑΛΕΩ

The scholarly consensus leans towards the idea that the women in the Corinthian church were arguing, loudly, with their husbands during the gathering at the church. Henry Leighton Goudge takes only a few lines to comment that the women were *undoubtedly* interrupting the assembly, agreeing that there were women with the gift of prophecy, some perhaps with the gift of tongues. Goudge thinks that, although these were not the women that Paul was specifically addressing, he would have forbidden the women to exercise these gifts publicly in the church.[8] Arthur Penrhyn Stanley also dismisses these troublesome verses quite summarily: "Women, it would seem from the Apostle's allusion to the practice in xi. 5, and prohibition of it in xiv. 34, 35, had felt themselves entitled to speak. The Apostle rests his prohibition on the general ground of the subordination of women to their natural instructors, their husbands."[9] William Orr and James Walther suggest that γυναῖκες (*gunaikes*) should really be translated "wives," not "women," and the resultant interpretation is that the wives were embarrassing their husbands in public conversations or contradictions.[10] Paul's solution to the problem of this disturbance is to forbid the women to talk in church—they must wait to ask questions

---

7. Talbert, *Reading Corinthians*, 92–94. For strong response against Talbert and similar arguments, see Watson and Culy, *Quoting Corinthians*, 124–37.

8. Goudge, *First Epistle to the Corinthians*, 130.

9. Stanley, *Epistles of St Paul to the Corinthians*, 279.

10. Orr and Walther, *1 Corinthians*, 312.

of their husbands at home. Somehow, even if honour and shame are an important part of the culture, embarrassment does not seem like the fundamental issue that would bring Paul to this forceful statement. Craig Blomberg approaches these verses from a modern equal rights perspective and tries to eliminate the category of "all" in order to exonerate "all" women from the blame of being a disturbance; at the same time, he points out that some of the less cultured men could well have been an equal disturbance in the church.[11] But, even though Blomberg may be right about the situation—that is, probably not "all" women were creating a disturbance and possibly "some" men were contributing to the disturbance—is the issue really to try to read twenty-first century egalitarianism into first-century writings? On the other hand, if Paul actually was saying something quite different, then Blomberg's defense of women is an unnecessary attempt to redeem Paul. If Paul did indeed categorically say that all women were not to speak in church, then, from a twenty-first century perspective, his statement seems indefensible—but then so do those of many other writers from 2,000 years ago, and even from more recent times. Evidence of the latter can be found in Charles Hodge's comments, which reveal some interesting perceptions about women in the church. He says that the word αἰσχρόν (aischron), which is used to describe the woman who speaks in the church, properly means "ugly, deformed." Hodge extrapolates: "As the peculiar power and usefulness of women depend on their being the objects of admiration and affection, any thing which tends to excite the opposite sentiments should for that reason be avoided."[12] As insightful as Hodge may have been into the role of women in the church, he and most commentators have not accounted for the sexual connotations of this word αἰσχρόν (aischron) or renderings of it, such as "obscene."

As a result, scholars have recognized the need to go back to lexical and contextual investigation of the word λαλέω (laleō)[13] although the precedent of earlier commentators seems too strong for some later ones to stray far from the common opinions. Blomberg gives the gloss that the women were "chattering,"[14] as do many other commentators, but there is

11. Blomberg, *1 Corinthians*, 280–81.

12. Hodge, *First Epistle to the Corinthians*, 305.

13. See Thiselton, *First Epistle to the Corinthians*, 1150.

14. Blomberg, *1 Corinthians*, 280. See LSJ 872, where the editors say that λαλέω (laleō) in classical literature usually means "chatter, babble." But this is not necessarily its meaning in later Hellenistic times, including in this passage in the New Testament,

reason to think that Paul is not using this meaning, as I will show further below. Blomberg points out a feature of the use of λαλέω (*laleō*) in this passage: "'speak,' in twenty of the twenty-one appearances of this verb in this chapter outside of vv. 34–35, refers either directly or by analogy to one of four very particular kinds of speech: tongues, their interpretation, prophecy or its evaluation."[15] Kevin Quast contributes a further observation on this subject: "In these two verses, Paul uses the general term in Greek for talking: *lalein*. In contrast to *legein*, which always refers to the [sic] meaningful speech, *lalein* can refer simply to the sounds produced by people, animals, and even inanimate objects."[16] Although this kind of distinction is not always made in the New Testament, there is reason to believe that the categories can be maintained in some cases. Few commentators deal with Paul's extended usage of the word λαλέω (*laleō*) over λέγω (*legō*) in this chapter, but it may be a key to understanding Paul's multi-faceted use of the word λαλέω (*laleō*) in this context. Paul specifically describes the necessity of distinct sounds so that the "tune can be understood" (v. 7); it would seem logical that he would choose distinct words with particular care so that their meaning can be clearly understood. It is somewhat ironic that in this very chapter about sounds and words being clear or unclear, understood or not understood, there should be so much confusion as to what Paul means. C. K. Barrett argues that λαλέω (*laleō*) would not be used in the sense of "chatter" when it had been used as "prophesy" in the earlier part of the chapter.[17] However, if Paul had introduced a new context for the word earlier in the chapter in order to draw on it later, this argument would no longer apply.

In vv. 34–35, the word λαλέω (*laleō*) lacks specific qualifiers, while, in most of the rest of the chapter, it has specific qualifiers (see discussion below). Gordon Fee provides some interesting thoughts for further consideration, although perhaps not in the direction that he had intended. He says that the use of the verb in vv. 34 and 35 is unique, and attributes a certain meaning to this usage:

> If authentic, this unqualified use of the verb seems to tell against the probability that only *a single* form of speech is being

as indicated by Thiselton, *First Epistle to the Corinthians*, 1157.

15. Blomberg, *1 Corinthians*, 281. Blomberg's numbers are not quite correct, for outside of vv. 34 and 35, which has two instances, there are not 21 but 22 uses of the verb λαλέω (*laleō*). The total in this chapter is 24.

16. Quast, *Reading the Corinthian Correspondence*, 86.

17. Barrett, *Commentary on the First Epistle to the Corinthians*, 332.

prohibited. Elsewhere Paul has said "speak in *tongues*" when that is in view, and when he means "discern" he says "discern," not "speak". . . . [T]he plain sense of the sentence is an absolute prohibition of all speaking in the assembly.[18]

Fee's suggestion is that the natural outcome of his statement is that indeed women should be silent in the church in all respects; however, introducing the unique use of this verb only points out the possibility that the word in this unqualified context means something different than the other uses of the word, not necessarily that it is a later gloss, as Fee suggests.

Unresolved Problems

The result of these various solutions and interpretations of the passage is that the same problems still remain. The inconsistency of the two passages in 1 Corinthians is not resolved, the question of the abruptness of vv. 34–35 in the section is not answered, and Paul's use of λαλέω (*laleō*, "to speak") is not satisfactorily explained—all of which leaves one still uncertain as to the nature of the disruption in the Corinthian church.

However, there are a number of issues that are not even addressed by many of the commentators. These have to do with the context of the growth of the early church, the status and role of women both in the surrounding culture and within the church, and the context of prophecy in the church.

A CLOSER LOOK AT THE CONTEXT OF THE EARLY CHURCH

In this section, I turn from the usual issues that are discussed in commentaries and related works regarding 1 Cor 14:34–35 and turn to some neglected issues that merit attention.

Issues that Need to Be Addressed

The above-mentioned solutions to the problems with Paul's statement mainly deal with twenty-first century issues that relate to the difficulty

---

18. Fee, *First Epistle to the Corinthians*, 707, a passage that appears to have been deleted in the revised edition of the commentary, when Fee relegates treatment of 1 Cor 14:34–35 to a two-page text-critical discussion (see Fee, *First Epistle to the Corinthians* [rev. ed.], 780–81).

PART ONE: MUSIC AND INTERPRETATION IN THE EARLY CHURCH

of interpretation and application to a present-day context. But if one can look at these verses, as well as what is known or can be reasonably conjectured about the cultural and religious context of the early church, without the somewhat crippling result of forcing the words to necessarily fit a present-day situation, it is possible to get a different view of the situation that these verses may address. I address three issues before attempting a proposed solution.

WOMEN AND PROPHECY IN THE BIBLE

The first issue is women and prophecy in the Bible. Some commentators seem to neglect evidence from the Old Testament that women could take an active role in prophecy as prophets. The Old Testament has several references to women prophesying (Ezek 13:17 ["daughters of your people who prophesy"]; Joel 2:28 ["Your sons and daughters will prophesy"]; Exod 15:20 ["Then Miriam the prophetess, Aaron's sister"]; Judg 4:4 ["a prophetess, the wife of Lappidoth"]; and Isa 8:3 [I "went to the prophetess"]). The examples are of women being considered as prophets in the context of a group of people prophesying, as well as of individual women who are called "prophetess." Whatever the exact behaviour of these women, it can be seen that there was a category of women whose role, at least in part, was that of prophesying. There are also several references in the New Testament to women prophesying (Acts 12:9 ["four unmarried daughters who prophesied"]; Acts 2:17 ["Your sons and daughters will prophesy"]; Luke 2:36 ["a prophetess, Anna, the daughter of Phanuel"]), including 1 Cor 11:5 ("But every woman ... while praying or prophesying"). None of these references, including 1 Cor 11:5, prohibits women from this role, and yet discussions about the inconsistency of 1 Cor 14:34-35 with 1 Cor 11:5 often centre on the idea that Paul contradicts himself by saying in one section that a woman should be doing something and in another that a woman should not be doing that same thing. But several issues are not addressed by these comments. First, 1 Cor 11:5 does not say anything about a woman "not prophesying." Secondly, these women may have been prophesying somewhere other than "in the church." Paul's statement in 1 Cor 14:34-35 seems to refer specifically to location "in the church." Thirdly, the verbs used in 11:5 are προσεύχομαι (*proseuchomai*, "to pray") and προφητεύω (*prophēteuō*, "to prophesy"); the word used in 14:34 is λαλέω (*laleō*), which may suggest something entirely different in this context. If Paul meant to refer to the same situation, the clearest means of doing that would have been to use the same language, but he does not.

The Role of Women in the Rise of Christianity

From the perspective of a sociologist, Rodney Stark offers an insightful and instructive view of how crucial women were to the rise of Christianity.[19] He suggests not only that women had a major role in the churches, but also that they were the large proportion of its first members and highly instrumental in bringing their husbands and families into the church and ultimately to the Christian faith.

Stark provides observations from a social-scientific perspective on women's involvement in the rise of Christianity. His research in this area casts an interesting light on the problem being discussed here. One statement sets the stage for further observations:

> Amidst contemporary denunciations of Christianity as patriarchal and sexist, it easily is forgotten that the early church was so especially attractive to women that in 370 the emperor Valentinian issued a written order to Pope Darnasus I requiring that Christian missionaries cease calling at the homes of pagan women . . . because within the Christian subculture women enjoyed far higher status than did women in the Greco-Roman world at large.[20]

Stark suggests that because of Christianity's stance against infanticide (especially related to female infants) and abortion, women were thus accorded a higher status within the church; this would have resulted in a higher recruitment of women, because it would be attractive to women to join this new kind of culture. In contrast, in the Greco-Roman world, "men greatly outnumbered women."[21] Stark thinks that the Christian community was very different from the surrounding culture in ratios of men to women, and that the number of converts to Christianity would

---

19. Stark, *Rise of Christianity*, 95–128.

20. Stark, *Rise of Christianity*, 95. Roman marriage had changed from *cum manu*, where the wife was under the power of her husband, to *sine manu*, where the wife remained under the control of her *paterfamilias*, rather than under her husband.

21. See, e.g., Cassius Dio, *Hist. rom.* 54.16.2, who says, "since among the nobility there were far more males than females, he [Augustus] allowed all who wished, except the senators, to marry freedwomen, and ordered that their offspring should be held legitimate."

have been predominantly women.²² He takes the example of the book of Romans where Paul sends personal greetings to fifteen women and eighteen men, and concludes that, in a culture where men would normally outrank women in such things as prominent positions in the church, the quite high number of women suggests that there was a predominantly female congregation to merit this ratio. These newly converted women may well have been involved in the church without their husbands, although there is evidence that some women brought their husbands to a conversion of some description, which Stark calls secondary conversion.²³

In conjunction with this, there may have been a much higher toleration for "exogenous marriages" than is currently thought. There were more women than men in the church, so obviously there was a shortage of potential husbands. The idea that husbands were consecrated through their wives, generally thought to refer to wives who were converted to Christianity after being married,²⁴ may in fact refer to women who converted before marrying (1 Cor 7:14).

Insights into 1 Cor 14:34–35 from the Church Fathers

Several of the church fathers make comments that perhaps shed light on the situation of the early church. Cyril of Jerusalem (ca. 315–86) finds Paul's statement particularly useful in supporting his own position: that women should be *seen* in church, that they should be *seen to be pious* in church, but that they should certainly not be heard in church. He says,

> The men, then, ought to sit and occupy themselves with some useful book: let one read and another listen. If there is no book, let one pray and another say something of benefit. The assembly of virgins, however, should be gathered together, quietly reciting psalms or reading, so that their lips move, but the ears of others do not hear—Nor I do not permit that a woman speak in the Church (1 Cor 14:34). And the married woman should do likewise; she should pray and move her lips, while not allowing her voice to be heard (*Procatechesis* XIV; PG XXXIH, 356).²⁵

---

22. Stark, *Rise of Christianity*, 100.

23. Part of Stark's social-scientific data to substantiate these kinds of claims is present-day research in new religious movements, where often the women of a given culture are the first to be converted to the new religion/faith.

24. See Porter, "Holiness, Sanctification," for a survey of various views.

25. See no. 154 in McKinnon, ed., *Music in Early Christian Literature*, 75–76.

Jerome (341–420) also appears to agree fully with this reading of Paul's statement; he uses it as support for his position that everyone knows that women who sing psalms to the Lord should be doing it in their own rooms at home:

> Indeed your liberality is so great, that to win favor among your Amazons you write in another place, "Women ought also to have knowledge of the law"; while the Apostle teaches that women must be silent in the church, and if there is something they do not know, they ought to ask their husbands at home (1 Cor 14:34–35). Nor is it enough for you to have given knowledge of the Scriptures to your army, but you must be regaled with their voices and songs, for you add in a title, "That women ought also to sing psalms to the Lord." But who does not know that women are to sing psalms in their chambers, away from the company of men and the crowded assembly? But you in truth grant what is not permitted, so that, with the support of their master, they flaunt what they ought to do modestly and without any witness (*Dialogus contra pelagianos* 1.25; *PL* XXIII, 519).[26]

The tone and construction of this passage of Jerome is almost laughable, but it does indicate the status of women's voices, at least in Jerome's opinion: they are not to be heard in song.

Ambrose (ca. 339–97), on the other hand, contradicted the current opinion and interpretation of Paul's same statement, saying that it would be acceptable for women to join in the singing of psalms in the church. This, however, does not clarify whether Ambrose meant that the women were only allowed to use their voices to *sing*—in this case, psalms—but not to *speak* in any way, or whether they simply were not allowed to participate in any other kind of *singing* apart from the singing of psalms. In either case, these statements reflect the current state of church affairs at the time, and music apparently was a major issue. As Ambrose states,

> The Apostle admonishes women to be silent in church, yet they do well to join in a psalm; this is gratifying for all ages and fitting for both sexes. Old men ignore the stiffness of age to sing [a psalm], and melancholy veterans echo it in the joy of their hearts; young men sing one without the bane of lust, as do adolescents without threat from their insecure age or the temptation of sensual pleasure; even young women sing psalms with no loss of wifely decency, and girls sing a hymn to God

---

26. See no. 334 in McKinnon, ed., *Music in Early Christian Literature*, 145.

with sweet and supple voice while maintaining decorum and suffering no lapse of modesty . . . (*Explanatio psalmi* 9; *PL* XIV, 924–45; *CSEL* LXIV, 7–8).[27]

Ambrose seems to interpret Paul's words as not forbidding the singing of psalms in the church, which means he did not consider Paul's words to prohibit all forms of utterances. Whether he thinks that Paul's words are related to speaking only, to some kind of ecstatic or prophetic utterance, or to something else completely is unclear. He does give some insight into the thinking of the time that there is something about the power of singing such that it could lead people morally astray, and a woman to lose her "wifely decency."

Possible Clues to a New Solution

I turn now to some of the possible means of a solution to the problem of understanding this passage. There are several items that are of interest in trying to discover possible solutions to the difficulties raised by 1 Cor 14:34–35, and which are not often dealt with by commentators for one reason or another. But if one can look at these verses in the context of the New Testament world and early Christianity—without trying to force them into a twenty-first century context and application—interesting possibilities are raised.

Women and Pagan Religion

There were numerous religious cults being practiced in the period of the New Testament writings. Many of these included public spectacles, involving social, political, and even ecstatic dimensions, many of them including women. The practice and celebration of the Dionysian, Mythraic, and Isiac (pertaining to Isis), various mystery cults, and other cult groups that sprang up were a distinct element of the culture of the Greco-Roman world that still had an influence in the time of the New Testament.[28]

---

27. See no. 276 in McKinnon, ed., *Music in Early Christian Literature*, 126–27.

28. Angus, *Religious Quests*, esp. 19–46, 76–92; Beard and Crawford, *Rome*, 25–39; Taylor, *Roman Society*, 73–89; Witt, *Isis*, esp. 255–68; Meyer, ed., *Ancient Mysteries*. Some New Testament scholars also acknowledge the role of these pagan religions and cults in the surrounding culture of the early church (see Theissen, *Psychological Aspects*, 271–91, 302–3). With Witherington and others, one can question Delphic influence on 1 Cor 14. But that does not mean that other religious practices of the Greco-Roman world cannot inform our understanding, as will be seen below. See Witherington, *Conflict and Community*, 274–90.

A WORD ABOUT WOMEN, MUSIC, AND SENSUALITY IN THE EARLY CHURCH

Strong negative associations connected with the high involvement of women as leaders of these festivities[29] (as well as numerous female deities who were the objects of worship) may well have had an effect on the early church. It is difficult to imagine that the activities and nature of celebrations such as these did not affect the New Testament church, or at least some of its members, in some way. It is more curious that commentators and writers on the subject of such verses as 1 Cor 14:34–35 do not raise this at least as a possibility, since it has been clearly seen that the Isis cult was firmly established and practiced at Corinth, as well as in other cities Paul encountered in his journeys.[30] Instead, these verses are read as though they were written for an isolated and almost hermetically sealed environment, one that did not come into contact with the surrounding religious world. Yet a main subject of 1 Cor 14 is that of a person who speaks in tongues with no one to interpret, and who is thus thought of as a barbarian. This language is highly suggestive of a variety of possible outside influences, especially those associated with various forms of emotive behavior, perhaps related to other religious practices.

Associations of the Verb ΛΑΛΕΩ with Music

The problematic verse for commentators in relation to 1 Cor 14:34–35 seems to be 1 Cor 11:5, where Paul states, "And every woman who prays or prophesies with her head uncovered dishonors her head—it is just as though her head were shaved" (NIV). As mentioned above, the Greek word used in this verse is not λαλέω (*laleō*) but προφητεύουσα (*prophēteuousa*). If Paul, in 1 Cor 14:34–35, were referring specifically to the same activity of women as in 1 Cor 11:5, it would be reasonable to think that he would have used the same word, thus clarifying that this indeed is the activity to which he now refers. However, he uses the word λαλέω (*laleō*) and we are left to define the sense in which he uses it. Paul's two uses of λαλέω (*laleō*) in 1 Cor 14:34–35 could mean "chatter," as many commentators have suggested,[31] and yet the verb does not seem

---

29. Kiefer, *Sexual Life in Ancient Rome*, 118–20.

30. Witt, *Isis*, 255–68.

31. Albert Debrunner notes that in the classical period, the meaning in the *compound forms* of the word λαλέω (*laleō*) is "to prattle" or "to babble." Not one of the twenty-four forms of λαλέω used in this chapter is a compound form (i.e., forms with a prefix). However, other writers seem to say that the common meaning in Greco-Roman times *is* "chatter" (see above) (see "λέγω, λόγος, ῥῆμα, λαλέω," 4:76). The latest English edition of Bauer says of λαλέω (*laleō*) that in classical Greek the word usually

to mean that in any other of the twenty-two uses in the chapter. In some respects, this chapter is not so much about speaking in tongues as it is about clarity, orderliness, and understanding.

It is possible that Paul has chosen the word λαλέω (*laleō*) to provide a comparison on several levels. In vv. 7 and 8 he introduces musical imagery, pointing out the similarity of meaningless speech to the playing of instruments—as Paul describes them—with meaningless sounds, sounds that are tuneless, unless there is a distinction in the notes. In v. 9, he describes the necessity of using the tongue and involving the mind to communicate, and here λαλέω (*laleō*) is used somewhat differently than its use in any of the preceding verses, being most closely connected with vv. 34–35. Interestingly, the two uses of the verb in vv. 34 and 35 do not have qualifiers, such as, to speak "in tongues"; their usage stands out from that of others in the chapter, a factor infrequently addressed by commentators.[32] Of the various uses of the verb λαλέω (*laleō*) in this chapter, several are connected with some sort of description of the speaking, that is, "speaking in tongues" or "to speak five words with the mind." Several do not have a description but name a specific recipient, and a couple have the sense of expressed content.[33] The instances that do not fit within these categories relate to each other by lacking a means of expression, or by lacking a comprehending recipient: v. 9 has two uses of the verb, with the sense of being understood by no one: (1) "how will it be known what is spoken?"; (2) "for you will be speaking into the air"; v. 11 uses the verb twice to refer to a lack of comprehension as that of a barbarian. In a similar manner, vv. 34 and 35 each use the word in the context of a lack of the right or place to express something. Paul apparently intends by his patterned use of the verb that some connecting sense be given to these related uses.

It seems reasonable to think that Paul may also have introduced musical imagery in vv. 7–15 in order to refer back to it in vv. 34–35. Certainly, Paul's layout and language of 1 Corinthians 14 allow for several interesting conceptual connections. First, in v. 7, Paul asks the question: "Even in the case of lifeless things that make sounds, such as the flute or harp, how will anyone know what tune is being played unless there is a

---

means "chatter, babble" (see BDAG 582–83).

32. Cf. Fee, *First Epistle to the Corinthians*, 707.

33. Means/manner: 1 Cor 14:2a, 4, 5a, b, 6a, 13, 18, 19, 23, 27, 39; recipient: 1 Cor 14:2b, 3, 6b, 21, 28; expressed content: 1 Cor 14:2c, 29. Cf. Blomberg, *1 Corinthians*, 281, for a similar observation.

distinction in the notes?" Here Paul introduces two musical instruments, the first being the αὐλός (*aulos*), often translated "flute" but more like the oboe,[34] and the second being the κιθάρα (*kithara*, "harp" or "lyre"; note the κιθάρα [*kithara*] is not a wind instrument, so is not as germane to the context of this discussion).[35] Paul is the only writer in the New Testament who uses the word αὐλός (*aulos*) as a noun to refer to the actual instrument, not to the act of playing the instrument (αὐλέω [*auleō*]) or to the one who plays the instrument (αὐλήτης [*aulētēs*]).

The verb λαλέω (*laleō*) is often used in association with production of a variety of sounds, including musical ones. The common usage of λαλέω (*laleō*) in Greek from all periods is with regard to production of human speech. There are other uses that are worth noting for this discussion, however, many of them in the Greek of the New Testament. With reference to inanimate things, the verb can mean "sound, give forth sounds or tones which form a kind of speech," such as in Rev 10:4a, καὶ ὅτε ἐλάλησαν αἱ ἑπτὰ βρονταί (*kai hote elalēsan hai hepta brontai*, "and when the seven peals of thunder had spoken") and v. 4b, Σφράγισον ἃ ἐλάλησαν αἱ ἑπτὰ βρονταί, καὶ μὴ αὐτὰ γράψῃς (*sphragison ha elalēsan hai hepta brontai, kai mē auta grapsēs*, "seal up the things which the seven peals of thunder have spoken"). Verse 3 also uses this form of the word: ἐλάλησαν αἱ ἑπτὰ βρονταὶ τὰς ἑαυτῶν φωνάς (*elalēsan hai hepta brontai tas heautōn phōnas*, "the seven peals of thunder uttered [spoke] their voices").[36] There is an association of λαλέω (*laleō*) and Paul's

---

34. McKinnon and Anderson define the αὐλός (*aulos*) as a "Greek reed instrument. It was the most important ancient Greek instrument; the name is often mistranslated 'flute' in modern sources. It is classified as a reedpipe" ("Aulos," 85). The mistranslation they refer to also appears in numerous versions of the Bible. The more appropriate present-day instrument to equate it with would be the oboe. However, according to Michaelides, the αὐλός (*aulos*) was a generic designation of various wind instruments (especially the reed-blown ones) used by the Greeks and the verb αὐλεῖν (*aulein*), which is to play the αὐλός (*aulos*) "was often used in the sense of playing any wind instrument" (Michaelides, *Music of Ancient Greece*, 46). Contra BDAG 151 which retains the traditional translation as "flute."

35. The αὐλός (*aulos*) and the κιθάρα (*kithara*) are instruments that are commonly referred to in combination by writers outside of the New Testament. The only other writer in the New Testament who uses forms of the word κιθάρα (*kithara*), whether as a noun or otherwise, is the writer of Revelation. Forms of the word are used six times in four verses in Revelation, once in connection with αὐλός (*aulos*), in Rev 18:22. The only other New Testament usage is the one being dealt with here, that is, Paul's use of it in 1 Cor 14:7. For pictures of these instruments from ancient artifacts, see Zschietzschmann, *Hellas and Rome*, 249, 250, 255.

36. By extension, this sounding can focus on particular kinds of things that make

second-mentioned instrument, the κιθάρα (*kithara*), in Achilles Tatius, in a discourse on the water talking: "if you wish to hear the water talking, open your ears and wait a little . . . the water sings like a lyre" (τὸ ῥεῦμα δὲ ὡς κιθάρα λαλεῖ [*to hreuma de hōs kithara lalei*]).[37] This combination of λαλέω (*laleō*) and musical instruments is also one that Pseudo-Aristotle uses. In fact, the association of the word λαλέω (*laleō*) and αὐλός (*aulos*) in Pseudo-Aristotle's *De audibilibus* is unique enough to suggest at least a reference to Pseudo-Aristotle on the part of Paul. Conceptually, the thought that is presented in Paul strikingly resonates with that of Pseudo-Aristotle. In conjunction with his discussion of how sounds appear to come from the source of their production but are only heard when they fall on our hearing, Pseudo-Aristotle uses the αὐλός (*aulos*) as one of his examples, combining the musical instrument and λαλέω (*laleō*) in the same context:

> ὅταν γάρ τις λαβὼν κέραμον ἢ αὐλὸν ἢ σάλπιγγα, προσθείς τε ἑτέρῳ πρὸς τὴν ἀκοήν, διὰ τούτων λαλῇ (*hotan gar tis labōn keramon ē salpinga, prosthesis te heterō pros tēn akoēn, dia toutōn lalē*, ". . . for whenever someone, taking a pitcher or a reedpipe or a trumpet, and putting it near another person in order to hear, talks through these things . . .")[38]

In 1 Cor 14:7, Paul introduces musical instruments, including the αὐλός (*aulos*), and continues the thought in vv. 9–11, where he talks about uttering clear speech, rather than that of a barbarian. These verses have a noticeable similarity with Pseudo-Aristotle's description of sounds and "talking" through an αὐλός (*aulos*). Further, Paul writes, "how will anyone know what tune is being played unless there is a distinction in the notes?"; Pseudo-Aristotle writes, "But voices appear clear in proportion to the accuracy of the articulation. For unless there is perfect articulation the voices cannot be clear."[39] Although some have argued that Paul did not know the classical writings, Evelyn B. Howell makes a compelling

---

noise, such as musical instruments. The verb can refer to inanimate objects, such as musical instruments, that are "spoken into," such as the αὐλός (*aulos*).

37. Achilles Tatius, *Leuc. Clit.* 2.14.8 (Gaselee, Loeb Classical Library). Note that what the Loeb Classical Library translates as "sings as a lyre" are the familiar words ὡς κιθάρα λαλει (*hōs kithra lalei*).

38. Ps.-Aristotle, [*Aud.*] 801a.29–30 (Translated here by Stanley E. Porter).

39. Ps.-Aristotle, [*Aud.*] 801b.1–2 (Hett, Loeb Classical Library).

case for Paul's use of, even quotation of, classical writers including Aristotle or Pseudo-Aristotle.[40]

It may be significant that 1 Cor 14:34 and 35, which do not otherwise fit within the pattern of usage in 1 Cor 14, use the verb in a way that more closely fits the pattern of its earlier usage in vv. 9, 11.

Not only does Paul use the word αὐλός (*aulos*) as a noun in this unique way in the New Testament, he uses it in connection with another word that is used infrequently in the New Testament—the word φθόγγος (*phthongos*), meaning "voice, sound, tone." James Hope Moulton and George Milligan give it the gloss "utterance, sound," citing several papyri in support of this usage,[41] while LSJ defines it as "distinct sound." Paul is the only writer who uses the word φθόγγος (*phthongos*) in the New Testament: as well as in 1 Cor 14:7, he uses it in a quotation of Ps 19:4 in Rom 10:18. Pseudo-Aristotle uses the word in *De audibilibus*: σαθεῖς δὲ μάλιστα αἱ φωναὶ γίνονται παρὰ τὴν ἀκρίβειαν τὴν τῶν φθόγγων (*satheis de malista hai phōnai ginontai para tēn akribeian tēn tōn phthongōn*, "but voices appear clear in proportion to the accuracy of the articulation")[42] for which one may read also "distinct sound" or "tones." Again, Paul's use of this word in its context is at least reminiscent of Pseudo-Aristotle: "if they do not produce a distinction in the tones." In any case, this independent usage of φθόγγος (*phthongos*) in the New Testament is unique to Paul. Perhaps Paul's reason for using it is to further define the meaning of his use of λαλέω (*laleō*).

First Corinthians 14:9 has a twist to it that is not represented in any other verse, other than its relation to the preceding vv. 7 and 8, which refer to the playing of musical instruments: Paul says, "unless you utter by (through) the tongue (διὰ τῆς γλώσσης [*dia tēs glōssēs*]) speech that is clear, how will it be known what is spoken? For you will be speaking into the air." This use of "by the tongue" with the preposition and article to describe speech is unparalleled in this chapter. Paul's previous and following uses of the word "tongue" are in the context of speaking "in *a* tongue" (γλώσσῃ [*glōssē*]) or "in tongues" (γλώσσαις [*glōssais*]) without the preposition or article, rather than the use of the tongue to delineate and articulate clear speech. This suggests that Paul in v. 9 is referring

---

40. Howell, "St. Paul." It is unfortunate that Howell does not deal with musical subjects because certainly there is the possibility that Paul is at least referring to Pseudo-Aristotle's work in 1 Cor 14.

41. Moulton and Milligan, *Vocabulary*, 667.

42. Ps.-Aristotle, [*Aud.*] 801b.1–2 (Hett, Loeb Classical Library).

to the production of sound or some kind of production of sound other than speaking in a normal way. This could imply some kind of musical *means* of expression, such as a form of wailing, or vocal sounds other than words, that could be disturbing in pitch, sound, or connotation. It could also suggest a wind instrument, which requires use of the tongue.

The ΑΥΛΟΣ (*aulos*): Instrument of Prophecy and of Sensuality?

Were these women who were creating the "disturbance" incorporating vocal and instrumental sounds into some form of ecstatic or prophetic utterance? One instrument in particular has been associated at various times with prophecy, sexuality, and pagan practices—the αὐλός (*aulos*). Music in the New Testament is hard to define and virtually impossible to trace. There has been a consensus that the early church was very limited in its use of music, particularly instrumental music. However, this is an argument based mostly on the New Testament's silence on the subject and on some knowledge of Jewish practices at the time. It is also important to realize that these women were not necessarily, nor even likely, Jewish women. Paul's use of λαλέω (*laleō*) in 1 Cor 14:34–35, in conjunction with musical imagery, suggests that it is appropriate to explore briefly the possible associations of this imagery, including possible sensual and ecstatic associations connected with ancient worship.

References in the Septuagint to the Αὐλός (*aulos*)

The Septuagint—the Greek form of the Old Testament that would have been used by most early Christians—refers to the αὐλός (*aulos*) several times. The Greek form of 1 Sam 10:5 refers to four instruments. This verse occurs in a series of instructions that Samuel has received from God, and which he is giving to Saul, the newly anointed king. Samuel tells Saul that he (Saul) will go to Gibeah of God, where there is a Philistine outpost. As he approaches the town, he will "meet a procession of prophets coming down from the high place with a harp, tambourine, *flute* [better: "reedpipe"] and a lyre before them, and they will be prophesying" (καὶ ἀπαντήσεις χορῷ προφητῶν καταβαινόντων ἐκ τῆς Βαμά, καὶ ἔμπροσθεν αὐτῶν νάβαλ καὶ τύμπανον καὶ αὐλὸς καὶ κινύρα, καὶ αὐτοὶ προφητεύοντες [*kai apantēseis chorō prophētōn katabainontōn ek tēs*

A WORD ABOUT WOMEN, MUSIC, AND SENSUALITY IN THE EARLY CHURCH

bama, kai emprosthen autōn nabal kai tumpanon kai aulos kai kinura, kai autoi prophēteuontes]).

The "song of the vineyard" in Isa 5:12 includes the instruments κιθάρας (kitharas), ψαλτηρίου (psaltēriou), τυμπάνων (tumpanōn), and αὐλῶν (aulōn), and in translation, the verse reads: "They have harps and lyres at their banquets, tambourines and *flutes* [reedpipes] and wine, but they have no regard for the deeds of the Lord, no respect for the work of his hands." This verse follows a verse of woe to those who are overly occupied with the pursuit of drinks and who drink too much of it "till they are inflamed." Notice the conjunction of musical instruments and wine in the context of excess at the banquet. Later in Isa 30:29, the αὐλός (aulos) is referred to on its own: "You will have songs as in the night when you keep the festival; And gladness of heart as when one marches to the *flute* [reedpipe], To go to the mountain of the Lord, to the Rock of Israel." Here we see that the "flute" as it is called here, the αὐλός (aulos) is associated with the life of excess and is the accompanying instrument of a journey to the mountain of the Lord.

The Αὐλός (aulos) as a Sensual Instrument

In the Classical period, according to McKinnon, "The Greek word 'mousike' embraces not only the tonal phenomenon but also the text that is set and even the accompanying dance."[43] If this is still true in the context of the Hellenistic age, the accompanying connotations of various aspects of music would be a possible hindrance to worship in the church, and there would be a reason for banning "mousike" from the church. The αὐλός (aulos) as a musical instrument appears twice in Homer's *Iliad*. In the first reference, Homer says that Agamemnon "marvelled at the many fires that burned before the face of Rios, and at the sound of flutes [reedpipes; αὐλῶν (aulōn)] and pipes, and the din of men" (10:12–13).[44] In the second, after victory, "young men were whirling in the dance, and in their midst flutes [reedpipes; αὐλοί (auloi)] and lyres sounded continually."[45] Giovanni Comotti speaks of Plato's low opinion of the αὐλός (aulos) because it can be played in all the harmoniae, but Comotti goes on to say "that the aulos would have met with Plato's disapproval simply because

---

43. McKinnon, "Early Western Civilization," 3.
44. Homer, *Il*. 10.12–13 (Murray, Loeb Classical Library).
45. Homer, *Il*. 18.495 (Murray, Loeb Classical Library).

of the psychagogic and orgiastic nature of its sound, which was not conducive to equilibrium and calm, but rather, disturbed the listener and excited the irrational part of the soul."[46] In writing of the religious music of ancient Egypt during Greco-Roman times, Farmer says that there was a continuing importance placed on music in the temples. At Armant, in Roman times,

> The flute or reed-pipe was certainly still attached to the service of Amen, and Apuleius and Claudian both testify to its presence in the temple. Of course it was the emblem of fertility . . . Herodotus also affirms that at the festival of Osiris they had processions, the women carrying images preceded by an *aulos* player (reed-piper).[47]

In Henry Farmer's summary of Herodotus's account, the αὐλός (*aulos*) player leads "the semi-hysterical multitude. Some of the women jingled their sistra in frenzied excitement, while others, in greater abandon, exposed themselves."[48] Farmer agrees that the *aulos* "has ever been considered the sexual instrument *par excellence*."[49]

McKinnon concludes his investigation with the claim that music was thought unsuitable for the "higher" religions, such as Christianity:

> Students of ancient religion will readily recognize this phenomenon [Elisha falling into a trance whenever a minstrel played] of musically inspired prophecy as one that was common enough in antiquity to leave etymological traces in several languages; to cite only the Latin, "praecinere" means both to prophesy and to play the aulos, and "carmen" means both a magical charm and a song. There is present here at least a hint of a much broader hypothesis—that all the musical accoutrements of ancient religion have no place in the higher religions like Judaism, Christianity and Islam. In addition to musically inspired prophecy, one must cite the even more widespread phenomenon of orgiastic dance, in the most extreme manifestations of which the participants were driven by the music of pipe and drum to acts of self-mutilation or the dismemberment of a live creature. And there is of course the most common of all such cultic activity, animal sacrifice, which appears always to have been accompanied by

---

46. Comotti, *Music in Greek and Roman Culture*, 70.
47. Farmer, "Music of Ancient Egypt," 261.
48. Farmer, "Music of Ancient Egypt," 262.
49. Farmer, "Music of Ancient Egypt," 262.

instrumental music in the various religions of the Mediterranean basin. The function of this music is difficult to define, no doubt because it was perceived differently as sacrifice itself took on different meanings throughout the centuries, ranging from the feeding of some fearsome demigod to the act of praise and thanksgiving performed in the Temple of Jerusalem.[50]

McKinnon suggests that religions that focus on "the word" or "the book"—such as a canon of sacred writings like the Bible—view themselves as having to "purge" themselves of these old associations.[51]

Paul's Use of ΑΙΣΧΡΟΣ (*AISCHROS*)

If these kinds of connotations were still prevalent in the time of the early church, and if 1 Cor 14:34–35 possibly refers to such practices, then Paul's use of the strong word αἰσχρός (*aischros*) is quite understandable. This word is used four times in the Pauline letters: (1) 1 Cor 11:6 ("but if it is *disgraceful* for a woman to have her hair cut off or have her head shaved, let her cover her head"); (2) 1 Cor 14:35 ("for it is *improper* for a woman to speak in church"); (3) Eph 5:11–12 ("And do not participate in the unfruitful deeds of darkness, but instead even expose them; for it is *disgraceful* even to speak of the things which are done by them in secret"); and (4) Tit 1:10–11 ("For there are many rebellious men, empty talkers and deceivers, especially those of the circumcision, who must be silenced because they are upsetting whole families, teaching things they should not teach, for the sake of *sordid* gain").

The word is used in similarly strong contexts in other Greek writers. For example, Aristotle uses a related word αἰσχρολογία (*aischrologia*) in *Nicomachean Ethics*, where he speaks of comparing the old and modern comedies: "the earlier dramatists found their fun in *obscenity*, the moderns prefer innuendo, which marks a great advance in decorum."[52] Moulton and Milligan, using the papyri and non-literary sources to inform their understanding of αἰσχρός (*aischros*), cite a reference from the collection of papyri in Berlin (BGU IV.1024.7.20) "where a judge says to a scoundrel ἀπέσφα[ξ]ας γυναῖκα, Λιόδιμε, αἰσχρῶς (*apespha[ks]as gunaika, Liodime, aischrōs*)": "You cut the throat of a woman, Diodymius,

---

50. McKinnon, "Early Western Civilization," 9–10.
51. McKinnon, "Early Western Civilization," 9.
52. Aristotle, *Eth. nic.* 4.8.6 (Rackham, Loeb Classical Library).

shamefully."[53] Further to this, Moulton and Milligan say, "The word is not common, and is peculiar to Paul" in the New Testament. However, Paul uses other forms of the same word, such as αἰσχρότης (*aischrotēs*) in Eph 5:4 ("*filthiness* and silly talk, or coarse jesting, which are not fitting"); and αἰσχρολογίαν (*aischrologian*) in Col 3:8 ("put them all aside: anger, wrath, malice, slander, and *abusive speech* from your mouth"). Here, Moulton and Milligan say the adjective αἰσχρολογία (*aischrologia*) "is generally associated with foul or filthy rather than abusive speaking in Col 3:8." The LSJ gives this word the gloss "foul language, obscenity." Stephen C. Barton refers to its powerful social connotations.[54] The evidence points towards a much stronger sense than translators of the Bible and commentators have commonly given it. With this understanding, Paul apparently used this word specifically because of the abhorrent or repellent nature of these women's actions in the Corinthian church; for instance, "it is abhorrent that a woman should behave in this manner in church."

CONCLUSION: WOMEN, MUSIC, AND SENSUALITY IN 1 COR 14:34–35?

An investigation of who the women of 1 Cor 14:34–35 were, and the nature of the disturbance that Paul addresses, should take greater cognizance of Paul's language and its possible relation to the social and religious context that Paul is addressing. The troublesome women may not have had a long history of being in a church and may not have been versed in the ways and beliefs of the church. If Stark's suggestions in this matter are correct, women may have become involved in the church in an attempt to achieve the higher status accorded to women in this new Christianity, which status was not available to them elsewhere. These women may have become involved in the church without necessarily being converts to Christianity or may have brought with them practices and beliefs from the pagan world or other religions. Even if these women were part of the church, they may have had husbands who were not converted, or who were not actively involved in the church.

What were the practices that Paul is strongly resisting? The women who were creating a disturbance may have been actively involved not only in prophecy, which may have been acceptable, but may have been prophesying in a manner that represented secular or pagan religious

---

53. Moulton and Milligan, *Vocabulary of the Greek Testament*, 14–15.
54. Barton, "Paul's Sense of Place."

practice, including invoking music as an element of the prophetic/ecstatic experience. New to the Christian church, as virtually everyone was in the first century, these women may have unwittingly brought intrusive and secular habits with them—elements that were antagonistic to the spirit of Christianity, reminders of pagan sacrifices or orgiastic festivals—incorporating them in meetings where people actively prophesied and spoke in tongues. This may not have seemed that unusual to them. They may have come with a previous understanding of ecstatic experiences and their accompanying musical elements, bringing with them various associated sexual connotations and pagan elements of non-Christian or non-church ceremonies or celebrations. These women may have influenced the playing of a prophetic instrument, perhaps the αὐλός (*aulos*), which had many negative associations with pagan cults and sexuality. Perhaps the fact that Paul suggested that those women who wished to learn something should ask the men in their own households was not so that men could explain theological issues, but so that women would be reminded of the disturbing sensuality of their musical/prophetic utterances. In a culture where, at least later, proper musical practice was associated with "virgins" and it was seen as unsuitable for women to be singing in public, let alone making some other kind of musical utterance with the voice or with an instrument, the possible problems it was creating for men in the congregation other than the women's husbands (or other than their *own* husbands) may have been construed as overtly sexual.

REFERENCES AND FURTHER READING

Angus, Samuel. *The Religious Quests of the Graeco-Roman World: A Study in the Historical Background of Early Christianity*. London: John Murray, 1929.

Barrett, Charles Kingsley. *A Commentary on the First Epistle to the Corinthians*. 2nd ed. Black's New Testament Commentaries. London: Adam and Charles Black, 1971.

Barton, Stephen C. "Paul's Sense of Place: An Anthropological Approach to Community Formation in Corinth." *New Testament Studies* 32 (1986) 229–46.

Bauer, Walter, et al. *Greek–English Lexicon of the New Testament and Other Early Christian Literature*. 3rd ed. Chicago: University of Chicago Press, 2000. (BDAG)

Beard, Mary, and Michael Crawford. *Rome in the Late Republic*. London: Duckworth, 1989 [1985].

Blomberg, Craig L. *1 Corinthians*. New International Version Application Commentary. Grand Rapids: Zondervan, 1994.

Comotti, Giovanni. *Music in Greek and Roman Culture*. Translated by Rosaria V. Munson. Baltimore: Johns Hopkins University Press, 1989.

Conzelmann, Hans. *1 Corinthians*. Hermeneia. Philadelphia: Fortress, 1975.

Part One: Music and Interpretation in the Early Church

Debrunner, Albert. "λέγω, λόγος, ῥῆμα, λαλέω." In *Theological Dictionary of the New Testament*, edited by Gerhard Kittel and Gerhard Friedrich, translated by Geoffrey W. Bromiley, 4:76. 10 vols. Grand Rapids: Eerdmans, 1964–1976.

Farmer, Henry G. "The Music of Ancient Egypt." In *Ancient and Oriental Music*, edited by Egon Wellesz, 255–82. Oxford: Oxford University Press, 1966 [1957].

Fee, Gordon D. *The First Epistle to the Corinthians*. New International Commentary of the New Testament. Grand Rapids: Eerdmans, 1987. Rev. ed., 2014.

Forbes, Christopher. *Prophecy and Inspired Speech: In Early Christianity and its Hellenistic Environment*. 1995. Reprint, Peabody, MA: Hendrickson, 1997.

Garland, David E. *1 Corinthians*. Baker Exegetical Commentary on the New Testament. Grand Rapids: Baker Academic, 2003.

Goudge, Henry Leighton. *The First Epistle to the Corinthians*. Westminster Commentaries. London: Methuen, 1903.

Hodge, Charles. *The First Epistle to the Corinthians*. 5th ed. London: The Banner of Truth Trust, 1958.

Howell, Evelyn B. "St. Paul and the Greek World." *Greece & Rome* 11 (1964) 7–29.

Kiefer, Otto. *Sexual Life in Ancient Rome*. London: Routledge and Kegan Paul, 1956 [1934].

Lewis, Naphtali. *The Documents from the Bar Kokhba Period in the Cave of Letters: Greek Papyri*. Jerusalem: Israel Exploration Society, Hebrew University of Jerusalem and the Shrine of the Book, 1989.

Henry George Liddell, Robert Scott, and Henry Stuart Jones. *A Greek-English Lexicon*. 9th ed. Oxford: Clarendon, 1996. (LSJ)

McKinnon, James W. "Early Western Civilization." In *Antiquity and the Middle Ages: From Ancient Greece to the Fifteenth Century*, edited by James W. McKinnon, 1–44. Man and Music. Basingstoke, UK: Macmillan, 1990.

McKinnon, James W., ed. *Music in Early Christian Literature*. Cambridge Studies in the Literature of Music. Cambridge: Cambridge University Press, 1987.

McKinnon, James W., and Robert Anderson. "Aulos." In *New Grove Dictionary of Musical Instruments*, edited by Stanley Sadie, 1:85–87. London: Macmillan, 1984.

Meyer, Marvin W., ed. *The Ancient Mysteries: A Sourcebook—Sacred Text of the Mystery Religions of the Ancient Mediterranean World*. San Francisco: Harper and Row, 1987.

Michaelides, Solon. *The Music of Ancient Greece: An Encyclopedia*. London: Faber and Faber, 1978.

Moffatt, James. *The First Epistle of Paul to the Corinthians*. Moffatt New Testament Commentary. London: Hodder and Stoughton, 1938.

Moulton, James Hope, and George Milligan. *Vocabulary of the Greek Testament: Illustrated from the Papyri and Other Non-Literary Sources*. London: Hodder and Stoughton, 1914–1929.

Orr, William F., and James A. Walther. *1 Corinthians: A New Translation*. Anchor Bible 32. Garden City, NY: Doubleday, 1976.

Parry, Reginald St John. *The First Epistle of Paul the Apostle to the Corinthians*. Cambridge: Cambridge University Press, 1916.

Payne, Philip Barton. *Man and Woman, One in Christ: An Exegetical and Theological Study of Paul's Letters*. Grand Rapids: Zondervan, 2005.

———. "Vaticanus Distigme-obelos Symbols Marking Added Text, including 1 Corinthians 14:34–35." *New Testament Studies* 63 (2017) 604–25.

Porter, Stanley E. "Holiness, Sanctification." In *Dictionary of Paul and his Letters*, edited by Gerald F. Hawthorne, Ralph P. Martin, and Daniel G. Reid, 400–401. Downers Grove, IL: InterVarsity, 1993.

Quast, Kevin. *Reading the Corinthian Correspondence: An Introduction*. New York: Paulist, 1994.

Robertson, Archibald, and Alfred Plummer. *A Critical and Exegetical Commentary on the First Epistle of St. Paul to the Corinthians*. 2nd ed. International Critical Commentary 32. Edinburgh: T. & T. Clark, 1978.

Stark, Rodney. "Reconstructing the Rise of Christianity: The Role of Women." *Sociology of Religion* 56 (1995) 229–44.

———. *The Rise of Christianity: A Sociologist Reconsiders History*. Princeton: Princeton University Press, 1996.

Stanley, Arthur Penrhyn. *The Epistles of St. Paul to the Corinthians*. 5th ed. London: John Murray, 1882.

Talbert, Charles H. *Reading Corinthians: A Literary and Theological Commentary on 1 and 2 Corinthians*. New York: Crossroad, 1989.

Taylor, David. *Roman Society*. Inside the Ancient World. London: Macmillan, 1980.

Theissen, Gerd. *Psychological Aspects of Pauline Theology*. Translated by John P. Galvin. Philadelphia: Fortress, 1987.

Thiselton, Anthony C. *The First Epistle to the Corinthians*. New International Greek Testament Commentary. Grand Rapids: Eerdmans, 2000.

Watson, Edward W., and Martin M. Culy. *Quoting Corinthians: Identifying Slogans and Quotations in 1 Corinthians*. Eugene, OR: Pickwick, 2018.

Witherington, Ben, III. *Conflict and Community in Corinth: A Socio-Rhetorical Commentary on 1 and 2 Corinthians*. Grand Rapids: Eerdmans, 1995.

Witt, Reginald Eldred. *Isis in the Ancient World*. Baltimore: Johns Hopkins University Press, 1997 [1971].

Zschietzschmann, Willy. *Hellas and Rome: The Classical World in Pictures*. London: Zwemmer, 1959.

6

Ekphonetic Notation in Liturgical Manuscripts

INTRODUCTION

SEVERAL YEARS AGO, I was hunting through the shelves of the library of the Institute for Classical Studies in London and came across a book that I was delighted to find because it is not always readily available. It was Carsten Høeg's book on ekphonetic notation.[1] The book was published in 1935 and I noted that the library had received this copy into their collection within a year or two of its publication. As this work is one of, if not the, most important discussions of this topic, I was surprised to discover that the pages of this book were completely uncut. I went to the circulation desk to ask what the library's policy was on uncut books, and the busy librarian in response asked if I would mind taking a letter-opener and cutting the pages open myself, which I did with pleasure but also with some trepidation. But the evidence of these uncut pages suggests that in well over sixty years from the time of publication until my cutting it, this particular copy of the book had never been used.

I mention this episode because the subject of the book, ekphonetic notation, is surely one of the clearest indicators we have in determining whether or not a particular New Testament manuscript has ever been used by the Christian church, even if monographs about it have not. The combination of the various marks of punctuation with the musical-rhetorical symbols that are called ekphonetic notation must be considered as

---

1. Høeg, *La Notation Ekphonétique*. Cf. also Wellesz, *History of Byzantine Music*, 284–300, whose system I largely follow.

clues left on the document itself that suggest its living use in the church in some liturgical context, and even provide some clues as to its liturgical and even theological interpretation.

WHAT IS EKPHONETIC NOTATION?

The documents that I bring into the discussion of ekphonetic notation are drawn from the Greek New Testament papyri and parchments of the Austrian National Library collection in Vienna, dating from about the fourth to the tenth centuries. Although only two of these are clearly notated ekphonetically, it is instructive to look at the larger collection and make some observations on the general development we can see in the various kinds and levels of markings in these manuscripts.[2]

New Testament scholars unfortunately tend to have little first-hand knowledge of these documents and, as a result, they overlook the significance or are even unaware of the existence of the markings and notations that are an integral part of some of these papyri and parchments, which can provide various levels of information about these New Testament sources from the first millennium after Jesus Christ.

Part of the problem is that punctuation and the more formalized symbols of ekphonetic notation are frequently omitted in published editions of these manuscripts. As a result, New Testament scholars—and others—can remain totally unaware of this level of notation in these manuscripts.[3] The fact that ekphonetic symbols may be added by a second or even third hand could suggest that they are peripheral, but, to the contrary, these markings are a clear indication that the document was used—or at the very least, prepared for use—in the developing life of the Christian church.

Manuscripts that have no punctuation and no ekphonetic notation tell us little about how that text was perceived or presented. As punctuation over time increasingly appears in the original hand, in such things as dots at the ends of phrases or sentences, we get at least a glimpse of how the phrasing and syntax were understood by the scribe who added them or as reflecting an already existing tradition witnessed in the document that he was transcribing. As the manuscripts increasingly move towards the more specific symbols of ekphonetic notation and increased

---

2. Porter and Porter, eds., *New Testament Greek Papyri and Parchments*.

3. Yes, one can look at photographs, but these can be difficult to decipher, even for those who know the significance of the notation.

punctuation and prosodic marks, so we get a clearer glimpse of how the New Testament passages were understood and presented. Because of these various factors, in our editions of the Greek New Testament Papyri and Parchments of the Vienna collection, Stanley Porter and I have tried to represent and comment upon these layers of markings in the manuscripts wherever they are decipherable. Sometimes the ink of these marks or symbols has faded more than that of the words of the text, and sometimes the marks are oddly placed. We are pleased that the plates for all these manuscript pages and fragments were made available in the original publication. The fact that these New Testament documents of the Vienna collection are gathered for the first time in our edition means that New Testament scholars and others now have an opportunity to freely examine and compare these manuscripts. I think it becomes evident that it is more than the words themselves which are valuable here. Two of the later manuscripts of this collection clearly present the interpretive aspect of ekphonetic notation (see discussion below).[4]

Unfortunately, this shorthand notation cannot provide us with the full aural spectrum of sounds that it represents, but the growth of notation seems to have followed a pattern. At first, there are the markings of breathing, accent, and perhaps intonation, often in the original hand. As these documents are increasingly handled by a second or third person, with markings of breathing, accent or intonation, and punctuation, and then the more specific symbols of ekphonetic notation being added, we find the phrases of the text are delineated in smaller and more subordinate units. Pericopes often similar to those we still delineate in the New Testament are articulated by ekphonetic markings within these texts.

It is easy for musicologists to dismiss the notion that these markings represent music, or that they are musical indications, and this of course raises the larger question—what is music? Is music only represented by the traditional notation of music as we see it gathered in the recent Oxford University Publication by Egert Pöhlmann and Martin West?[5] Is it only the formal hymns? Or does it also include these shorthand symbols found in New Testament manuscripts? Professor Edwin Judge observed

---

4. See, e.g., Hannick, "Les Lectionnaires Grecs."

5. Pöhlmann and West, eds., *Documents*. For background to the discussion of Greek music, see such works as the following: Reinach, *La Musique Grecque*; Georgiades, *Musik und Rhythmus*; Gamberini, *La Parola*; Comotti, *Music in Greek and Roman Culture*; Barker, ed., *Greek Musical Writings 1*; West, *Ancient Greek Music*; Landels, *Music in Ancient Greece and Rome*. See also Mathiesen, *Bibliography of Sources*.

in conversation that Denise Jourdan-Hemmerdinger's proposal from years ago has never been adequately responded to, where she suggests that various dots written above letters may be musical notation and stem from Semitic influence.[6] Eric Werner also has contributed numerous arguments on possible Semitic influence on later notation, although he relies heavily on quite late Hebrew manuscripts.[7] It is notable that Pöhlmann and West completely pass over Jourdan-Hemmerdinger's proposal but also fail to include any mention of Werner who interprets such documents as P.Oxy. XV 1786,[8] the early Christian hymn, very differently than West.[9] This third-century papyrus, of course, raises many other questions. For instance, why is it that a biblical-sounding text as in P.Oxy. XV 1786 can be notated as a hymn, but strictly biblical text such as we are discussing in this chapter does not use the specific musical symbols at the level of syllables, but rather, uses ekphonetic notation which is written at the level of phrases of text. Does this prove that the latter is not music? If so, perhaps our definition needs expanding. Even familiarity with the symbols of figured bass in baroque music, or even the modern-day chord charts of popular music—where the musical chords and structure are presented only as chord and bass-note letter-names above lines of text—should remind us that shorthand in music is a common technique. Even today, without knowledge of what a chord chart code represents, it means little; with an understanding of the system, it represents the musical setting of that text.

The paired ekphonetic symbols of *oxeia, bareia, apostrophos, kremaste,* and *kentemata,* and the coupling of *oxeia* with *teleia,* to name some of these symbols, are generally found encompassing phrases of text, with one symbol placed at the beginning of the phrase and one at the end. More importantly, they work together to outline larger discourses. In our eighth- or ninth-century parchment page of Matt 28,[10] these

---

6. Jourdan-Hemmerdinger, "Nouveaux Fragments Musicaux sur Papyrus."

7. Werner, *Sacred Bridge*; "Oldest Sources," 225–26.

8. Hunt and Jones, "1786. Christian Hymn"; and most recently Cosgrove, *Ancient Christian Hymn,* who is in greater sympathy with West. See also Mountford, "Greek Music"; "Cairo Musical Fragment."

9. See some discussion of this in chapter 9 below, as well as chapter 7. On his own translation of the text, see Werner, "Music," 466.

10. Porter and Porter, eds., *New Testament Greek Papyri and Parchments,* Objekt 24 (Tafel XXII). This parchment has not apparently been previously published. Cf. Hunger and Hannick, *Katalog,* 181. The biblical text consists of Matt 28:5–19.

ekphonetic symbols appear to be somewhat irregular. This may be due to the darkness of the page, which makes the reading a bit difficult, and further fading of these markings. Our tenth-century parchment pages of John 7,[11] however, are much clearer to read and the system of notation is more obviously consistent. We clearly see such symbols as the *kathiste* encompassing narrative phrases, or *bareia* or *kremaste* on certain sections of emphasis.

SOME DEVELOPMENTS OF EKPHONETIC NOTATION

Let me briefly trace in the Vienna Greek New Testament manuscripts of the first millennium the development of ekphonetic symbols. What we observe is a gradual but progressive inclusion of a larger and more frequent range of markings.

Of the fourth-century manuscripts that use some form of punctuation, or other marks, all use the raised dot, some use double dots and the low dot, some use the spiritus asper and diaeresis, as well as diastrophe to separate the palatal sounds of two side-by-side kappas, and some introduce a few other less distinguishable marks, possibly of accentuation.[12]

The fifth-century manuscripts use raised dots with frequency, while some use medial, low, or double dots; marks for rough breathing and diaeresis are found; and some diacritical marks are used that may indicate accent or intonation, sometimes in combination with the end of a unit.[13]

---

11. Porter and Porter, eds., *New Testament Greek Papyri and Parchments*, Objekt 40 (Tafel XXXV–XXXVIII). Hunger and Hannick, *Katalog*, 208. The biblical text consists of John 6:71—7:46. For some discussion of this manuscript, see chapter 12 below.

12. E.g., see Porter and Porter, eds., *New Testament Greek Papyri and Parchments*, Objekt 23 (Tafel XXI) (058 [G 39782; Matt 18]: raised dot, double dot, diple, diaeresis on omega and upsilon); Objekt 26 (Tafel XXIII, XXIV) (0214 [G 29300; Mark 8]: raised dot, low dot); Objekt 28 (Tafel XXI) (059 [G 39779; Mark 15]: raised dot, diastrophe, diaeresis); Objekt 27 (Tafel XXI) (0215 [G 36112; Mark 8]: raised dot, medial dot, staurogram); Objekt 31 (Tafel XXVI) (0181 [G 39778; Luke 9, 10]: raised dot, diaeresis, few other marks of accentuation); Objekt 48 (Tafel XLIII) (0221 [G 19890; Roma 5, 6]: raised dot, rough breathing, possibly a circumflex).

13. E.g., see Porter and Porter, eds., *New Testament Greek Papyri and Parchments*, Objekt 25 (Tafel XXIII, XXIV) (0213 [G 1384; Mark 3]: raised dot); Objekt 35 (Tafel XXX) (0182 [G 39781; Luke 19]: raised dot, only few other diacriticals, with function difficult to determine other than unit boundaries); Objekt 43 (Tafel XLI) (0216 [G 3081; John 8, 9]: medial dot, few diacriticals); Objekt 44 (Tafel XL) (0217 [G 39212; John 11, 12]: raised dot, low dot, comma [apostrophe?], diaeresis, rough breathing? accents or intonation marks).

Eleven of the sixth-century manuscripts have numerous prosodic marks, which may indicate accent, intonation, unit endings, and possibly, in some cases, all of these, especially at the end of a section.[14]

In the seventh-century manuscripts, we see one that has many diacritical marks and the distinctive use of the teleia.[15] Of the eighth- and ninth-century manuscripts, the one of greatest significance that I have already mentioned is Objekt 24 in our collection (Suppl. Gr. 106; Tafel XXII). This single page of a parchment codex contains Matt 28:5–19. The text at the top of the page begins with an angel appearing to the women at Jesus' empty tomb with the message that Jesus is alive. A full range of ekphonetic symbols is found in this passage, although many are indistinguishable. It is interesting to note also the strokes that delineate the foreign words Γαλιλαίαν (Galilaian) and μαθηταῖς (mathētais).

---

14. E.g., see Porter and Porter, eds., *New Testament Greek Papyri and Parchments*, Objekt 22 (Tafel XX) (0237 [K 8023; Matt 15]: raised dots); Objekt 29 (Tafel XXIII, XXIV) (0184 [K 8662; Mark 15]: raised dots, diaeresis, ekthesis); Objekt 32 (Tafel XXVII) (0190=070 [K 9007; Luke 10]: raised dots, many prosodic marks [intonation or breathing], other diacritical marks/grave-like mark, possibly apostrophe [completion of a word or unit], possibly more than one hand. It also includes demarcation of the Hebrew name Μαριάμ [Mariam]); Objekt 33 (Tafel XXVIII) (0191=070 [K 9031; Luke 12]: diaeresis, grave mark, apostrophe, circumflex-like mark [but inconsistent], raised punctuation); Objekt 36 (Tafel XXXI) (0179=070 [K 2700; Luke 21]: raised dot, double dot, line, diaeresis, apostrophe [this fragment has fewer marks than others belonging to 070]); Objekt 37 (Tafel XXXII, XXXIII) (Theologische Gr 31; purple parchment codex; Luke 24): raised dot, acute, grave, single dot above letter (not indicated by Tischendorf). Objekt 41 (Tafel XXXIX, XL) (0180=070 [K 15; John 7]: medial dot, double dot, diaeresis, short stroke, other diacritical marks = units of division or intonation? [here the number and type is more restricted than some others belonging to 070]); Objekt 50 (Tafel XLII) (0222 [G 29299; 1 Cor 9]: raised dot, diaeresis, numerous other diacritical marks in a second hand); Objekt 51 (Tafel XLIV) (0223 [G 3073; 2 Cor 1, 2]: hand 1 [diaeresis, double dot, low dot, raised dot]; hand 2 [imprecise marks, acute, circumflex, grave, linking of οὗ οὗ [ou ou], rough breathing, wavy diacritical over οὗ [ou], raised dot]); Objekt 53 (Tafel XLV, XLVI) (0225 [G 19802; 2 Cor 5, 6, 8]: raised dot, low dot, double dot, diaeresis over υ, spiritus asper/rough breathing).

15. Objekt 54 (Tafel XLIV) (0183 [G 39785; 1 Thess 3, 4]: raised dot, medial stroke, comma [apostrophe?], diaeresis, rough breathing, many other diacriticals, some fill spaces, others correct original hand, use of teleia). See also, however, Objekt 20 (Tafel XVII, XIX; G 39784 [P34]; 1 Cor 16:2; 2 Cor 5, 10, 11: acute accent, raised dot, mark of accent or breathing [like spiritus asper] but a dot rather than stroke); Objekt 38 (Tafel XXXIV) (0101 [G 39780; John 1]: low dot, diaeresis, ekthesis, clearly demarcated paragraphs).

Part One: Music and Interpretation in the Early Church

A TENTH-CENTURY MANUSCRIPT

It is the tenth-century manuscript, Objekt 40 in our collection, however, that is both more clearly written and more interesting for its use of ekphonetic notation.[16] The manuscript consists of four pages of a parchment codex, each written on both sides. This codex, along with the previously-mentioned one, is continuous biblical text and has been marked for liturgical use. The extant pages contain almost the full text of chapter 7 of the Gospel of John. The text has been divided into pericopes consisting of about 13–16 verses, and thus consists of four nearly complete pericopes or scenarios. It is worth observing that only three of the four pericopes are notated ekphonetically—that is, the first two and the final one are, but the third one is not. This manuscript appears to have been used in three liturgical contexts. The third pericope, the un-notated one, is also the least visually depictable of the four. The four scenes consist of (1) Jesus going to the Feast of Tabernacles; (2) Jesus teaching at the Feast until someone tries to seize him; (3) a discussion about whether Jesus was the Christ; and (4) Jesus' declaration that, if anyone is thirsty, they should come for living water and the guards' response that they have never heard anyone speak like this.

It is useful to look at one of the pages of this document: folio 3 recto (the plate was included in the original publication), which is the fifth of eight pages of text. The first portion and the final words of the pericope are on the previous and following pages, but this gives an example of the levels of notation. Prosodic marks appear throughout this passage. Those that appear in corresponding pairs include:[17]

1. an oxeia from the previous page combined with the double dots and low teleia that form a unit that includes the first two lines of this page, την δικαίαν κρισιν κρινατε (tēn dikaian krisin krinate)[18]

---

16. Porter and Porter, eds., *New Testament Greek Papyri and Parchments*, Objekt 40. This manuscript is discussed further regarding other details in chapter 12 below.

17. See Engberg, "Greek Ekphonetic Neumes," 38–39, where he describes the "classical" period of the use of ekphonetic notation, in which they are customarily used in pairs.

18. Wellesz's descriptions are useful here (*History of Byzantine Music*, 284–300), where he suggests that it is thought to represent the voice rising to a higher note and remaining there until the end of the phrase.

2. apostrophos at the beginning and ending of Ελεγον οὖν τινὲς (Elegon oun tines)[19]
3. apeso hexo, or double apostrophos combined with oxeia, the double apostrophos below the first omicron and the oxeia stroke above the final syllable: οὐχ οὗτος εστιν (ouk outos estin)
4. hypokrisis, the three strokes stacked vertically before and after the phrase ον ζητοῦσιν αποκτειναι (on zētousin apokteinai)[20]
5. bareia, encompassing the phrase, και ιδε (kai ide)[21]
6. kremaste, the swooping stroke above the first letter and the last two letters of the phrase, μηποτε αληθως εγνωσαν (mēpote alēthōs egnōsan)[22]
7. kentemata, in this manuscript, a series of four linear dots above the first two letters of the first word and the two letters of the final word of the phrase, αλλ εστιν ἀληθινὸς ο πεμψας με (all estin alēthinos o pempsas me)[23]

We can see also, however, the layout of the page, with letters that are ekthetic protruding to the left of the column of text. Some of these correspond with modern verse beginnings and some do not. For instance, v. 25 begins with the word ελεγον (elegon) and the beginning epsilon is ekthesis.[24] The beginning of v. 26 is not marked in this way,[25] but the beginning of the word μήποτε (mēpote) in the middle of the verse is demarcated in this way.[26] Again, the beginning of v. 27 is not ekthesis, which begins with the words αλλα τούτον (alla touton),[27] but the beginning of the next three verses, that is, 28, 29, and 30, are all ekthesis: v. 28 (ἔκραξεν [ekraksen]);[28] v. 29 (ἐγῶ οἶδα [egō oida]);[29] and v. 30 (ἐζήτουν

---

19. It is thought to be a lower pitch of voice, without emphasis.
20. This probably indicates emphasis with a full stop.
21. This probably indicates a lowering of the voice but with emphasis.
22. This probably indicates a rising of the voice, with accentuation.
23. This is thought to be an ascending third.
24. See the third line in the first column.
25. Verse 26 begins at the beginning of line 10 in the first column.
26. See this in line 14 in the first column.
27. This is in the twentieth line of the first column (the fifth line from the bottom).
28. See the fourth line in the second column.
29. See the seventh line from the bottom in the second column.

[ezētoun]).[30] It is notable that each verse on this page that begins with an epsilon is given pronounced treatment. In all cases on this page, a teleia marks the end of a unit preceding these large decorated letters, although these are not the only uses of teleia in this passage.

CONCLUSION

Obviously, many questions about both the musical and interpretive qualities of these ekphonetic markings still exist, and a number of issues should be pursued further. One issue is simply whether or not to include these markings in editions of New Testament manuscripts. We have thought it is important to represent these, and therefore we have included them in our new editions, as indications of living use. The question of whether ekphonetic notation represents something other than music and whether real music is only indicated by syllabic symbols and traditional musical notation probably merits further discussion. I think the definition of music may need to be expanded. The question of why non-biblical texts, such as P.Oxy. XV 1786, use musical notation and why biblical texts use ekphonetic notation might still be pursued. Questions of how the development throughout these New Testament manuscripts in their use of various levels of notation might relate to the development of the early Christian church also could provide some insights. Certainly the question of Greek versus Semitic or other influence has not been solved.[31] And, finally, it might be instructive to discover why Carsten Høeg's book on ekphonetic notation sat unread for well over sixty years in the Institute for Classical Studies.

REFERENCES AND FURTHER READING

Barker, Andrew, ed. *Greek Musical Writings 1: The Musician and His Art*. Cambridge Readings in the Literature of Music. Cambridge: Cambridge University Press, 1984.
Comotti, Giovanni. *Music in Greek and Roman Culture*. Translated by Rosaria V. Munson. Baltimore: Johns Hopkins University Press, 1989.

---

30. This is in the second from the last (penultimate) line in the second column.

31. Werner, "The Conflict between Hellenism and Judaism," 457; Idelsohn, *Jewish Music*. Various other studies have also called into question the notion of a predominantly Jewish influence, e.g., Smith, "The Ancient Synagogue," 1–16; McKinnon, "On the Question of Psalmody," 159–91; and McKinnon, ed., *Music in Early Christian Literature*; see also West, "Analecta Musica," 47–54. See discussion in chapter 7 below, as well as in chapters 2 and 3 above.

Cosgrove, Charles. H. *An Ancient Christian Hymn with Musical Notation: Papyrus Oxyrhynchus 1786. Text and Commentary.* Studien und Texte zu Antike und Christentum 65. Tübingen: Mohr Siebeck, 2011

Engberg, Gudrun. "Greek Ekphonetic Neumes and Masoretic Accents." In *Studies in Eastern Chant I*, edited by Miloš Velimirović and Egon Wellesz, 37–49. Oxford: Oxford University Press, 1966.

Gamberini, Leopoldo. *La Parola e la Musica Nell'antichità: Confronto fra Documenti Musicali Antichi e dei Primi Secoli del Medio Evo.* Florence: L. S. Olschki, 1962.

Georgiades, Thrasybulos. *Musik und Rhythmus bei den Griechen: Zum Ursprung der Abendländischen Musik.* Hamburg: Rowohlt, 1958.

Hunt, Arthur S., and H. Stuart Jones. "1786. Christian Hymn with Musical Notation." In *The Oxyrhynchus Papyri XV*, edited by Bernard P. Grenfell and Arthur S. Hunt, 21–25. Egypt Exploration Society Graeco-Roman Memoirs. London: Egypt Exploration Fund, 1922.

Hannick, Christian. "Les Lectionnaires Grecs de L'apostolos avec Notation Ekphonetique." In *Studies in Eastern Chant IV*, edited by Miloš Velimirović and Egon Wellesz, 76–80. Crestwood, NY: St Vladimir's Seminary Press, 1979.

Høeg, Carsten. *La Notation Ekphonétique.* Monumenta Musicae Byzantinae Subsidia 1.2. Copenhagen: Levin and Munksgaard, 1935.

Hunger, Herbert, and Christian Hannick. *Katalog der Griechischen Handschriften der Osterreichischen Nationalbibliothek*: Part 4. Vienna: Osterreichischen Nationalbibliothek, 1994.

Jourdan-Hemmerdinger, Denise. "Nouveaux Fragments Musicaux sur Papyrus (Une Notation Antique par Points)." In *Studies in Eastern Chant IV*, edited by Miloš Velimirović and Egon Wellesz, 81–111. Crestwood, NY: St. Vladimir's Seminary Press, 1979.

Landels, John G. *Music in Ancient Greece and Rome.* London: Routledge, 1999.

Mathiesen, Thomas J. *A Bibliography of Sources for the Study of Ancient Greek Music.* Music Indexes and Bibliographies 10. Hackensack, NJ: J. Boonin, 1974.

Mountford, James Frederick. "The Cairo Musical Fragment." In *New Chapters in the History of Greek Literature 3: Some Recent Discoveries in Greek Poetry and Prose of the Classical and Later Periods*, edited by J. U. Powell and Eric A. Barber, 260–61. Oxford: Clarendon, 1933.

———. "Greek Music in the Papyri and Inscriptions." In *New Chapters in the History of Greek Literature 2: Some Recent Discoveries in Greek Poetry and Prose, Chiefly of the Fourth Century BC, and Later Times*, edited by J. U. Powell and Eric A. Barber, 146–83. Oxford: Clarendon, 1929.

Pöhlmann, Egert, and Martin L. West, eds. *Documents of Ancient Greek Music: The Extant Melodies and Fragments Edited and Transcribed with Commentary.* Oxford: Clarendon, 2001.

Porter, Stanley E., and Wendy J. Porter, eds. *New Testament Greek Papyri and Parchments: New Editions.* Mitteilungen aus der Papyrussammlung der Österreichischen Nationalbibliothek (Papyrus Erzherzog Rainer) Neue Serie XXIX, XXX. Folge (MPER XXIX, XXX). Berlin: de Gruyter, 2008.

Reinach, Théodore. *La Musique Grecque.* Paris: Editions d'Aujourd'hui, 1926.

Wellesz, Egon. *A History of Byzantine Music and Hymnography.* 2nd ed. Oxford: Clarendon, 1998 [1961].

PART ONE: MUSIC AND INTERPRETATION IN THE EARLY CHURCH

Werner, Eric. "Music." In *The Interpreter's Dictionary of the Bible*, edited by George Arthur Buttrick, 3:457–69. 4 vols. Nashville: Abingdon, 1962.

———. "The Oldest Sources of Synagogical Chant." *Proceedings of the American Academy for Jewish Research* 16 (1947) 225–32.

———. *The Sacred Bridge: The Interdependence of Liturgy and Music in Synagogue and Church During the First Millennium*. 2 vols. New York: Columbia University Press, 1959; New York: Ktav, 1984.

West, Martin L. *Ancient Greek Music*. Oxford: Clarendon, 1992.

7

Is Early Christian Music Jewish or Greco-Roman?

INTRODUCTION

THE WORD "MISSAL" AND its homophone "missile" serve here as a point of observation.[1] First, "missal," the book that contains all the texts that are said or sung at Mass for the entire year,[2] was not developed until the tenth to the thirteenth centuries[3] but is used here in a broad sense as an authoritative document that identifies the words and musical texts of even the earliest Christian liturgy, the theoretical canon that concerns musicologists and liturgists. "Misguided" missals in this sense suggests the possibility that church tradition has not accurately reflected the music of the early church in its canon of music for the liturgy. For instance, while scholars are dependent on early sources—writings from the Jewish or the Greco-Roman perspective—there is always a question of accurate interpretation of these sources. Similarly, documents that have actual musical notation of any sort are extremely limited in number,

---

1. Original publication of this chapter included the phrase "Misguided Missals."

2. Willi Apel writes that the missal contains "the complete liturgical texts, of the musical items as well as of the prayers, lessons from Scriptures, psalms, etc.," with the Missal (or *Missale*) being specifically for the Mass. Its companion book, the Gradual (or *Graduale*), contains the actual chants for the Mass (see *Gregorian Chant*, 15).

3. See, e.g., Hope, "Liturgical Books," 67, and Howell, "From Trent to Vatican II." See also a brief historical summary, including introduction to the liturgical books, in Sandon, ed., *Use of Salisbury*, vi, and Dickinson, ed., *Missale*, iii, where he writes in the preface that "the Missal is the most important book," although it "is not complete without . . . the Gradual, giving the ancient music of the Missal."

and it is entirely possible that none existed in the earliest period of the Christian churches.

Secondly, "missile," a twenty-first century weapon of war, has perhaps entered the equation in attempts to define the elusive parameters of what may have existed musically in the early Christian church. "Misguided" missiles in this sense suggests that scholars who concentrate on discrediting the opposing view as to influences on early Christian music may be misdirecting their energies, for undoubtedly both Jewish and Greco-Roman influences must be acknowledged.

For my purposes, homophonic words that can provide musical reference to the early church and simultaneously conjure up imagery of twenty-first-century disputes are useful. The debate—is early Christian music Jewish or is it Greco-Roman?[4]—perhaps has more overtones of the second kind of missile than the first, for prejudices sometimes have interfered with a judicious approach to the subject. The twentieth- to twenty-first-century discussion of music of the early church has often consisted of scholars presenting views that they perhaps *wish* to be true, for particular theological or religious reasons, although exclusive positions frequently cannot be substantiated. The current view sees the influence on the music of the early Christian church as Jewish, with a majority of New Testament scholars promoting this view, and I would agree that it is futile to argue that there was no influence of Jewish culture and belief on early Christianity, for it grew to some degree directly out of Judaism. On the other hand, to argue against Greek influence is equally unfounded, for the young church was situated fully within the Hellenized culture of the Greco-Roman world. Several scholars through musical and liturgical investigation have gone against the consensus and have reintroduced the influence of Greco-Roman culture. To my mind, there is some disparity between those who focus on the arguments and those who are inclined to take adamant positions or aggressive postures, rather than addressing the data and the arguments. Similarly, there is some question as to whether the direction of the present-day discussion is misguided, for the evidence suggests neither one single influence nor the other, but, rather, an uncomfortable mix of at least these two musical cultures.[5]

---

4. For an introduction to this discussion within a wider context, see chapter 3 above.

5. A third element of this discussion could include the dichotomy of the term "Greco-Roman" itself, where the Greek side of things is often treated. This is in part because there has been little known about Roman music, and, further, a perception

DIFFICULTIES IN INVESTIGATING EARLY CHRISTIAN MUSIC

While the prevailing perception of the early Christian church is that it was a singing church, references in the New Testament to music are not numerous.[6] There is virtually nothing to indicate the actual notation or sound of the music and many inferences must be drawn by the reader who is particularly interested in the music of the early church. This lack of material is sometimes the basis for unfounded assumptions, because although there is little to substantiate them, there is also little to disprove them. Edwin Hatch summarizes the problems associated with this kind of inquiry, by identifying two of the most significant problems; he writes, "The one is the tendency to overrate the value of the evidence that has survived . . . The other is the tendency to under-estimate the importance of the opinions that have disappeared from sight, or which we know only in the form and to the extent of their quotation by their opponents."[7]

For instance, many scholars have accepted the idea that musical instruments were banned both from the early church and from the Jewish synagogue on account of their "worldly nature." Some believe they were banned throughout the first century; others, that they were banned only after the destruction of the Jewish temple as a way of expressing disapproval. Eric Werner writes,

> Rabbinic sources explain the strict prohibition of any instrumental music in the Synagogue as an expression of mourning for the loss of the Temple and land, but the present writer has been able to show that a certain animosity against all instrumental music existed well before the fall of the Temple . . . It seems that this enmity towards instrumental music was a defence against the musical and orgiastic mystery cults in which Syrian and Mesopotamian Jews not infrequently participated . . . The primitive Christian community held the same view, as we know

---

that it was fairly barbaric, which may represent simply a lack of information. See, e.g., Scott, "Roman Music."

6. See a summary in Smith, *Musical Aspects*, 59–65.

7. Hatch, *Influence of Greek Ideas*, 10. Although these comments were part of lectures first given in 1888, the fact that they were deemed important enough to reprint in 1957 and still stand as sound judgments for historical inquiry says much about the quality of Hatch's contribution to scholarship.

Part One: Music and Interpretation in the Early Church

from apostolic and post-apostolic literature: instrumental music was thought unfit for religious services.[8]

One of the difficulties with the latter part of this statement is that most of the literature that expresses a view against instrumental music was written several centuries later than the early period of Christianity and may not express the views that were held in the first or second century. The lack of early documents is a problem that is common to the period, but assertions that are made on much later evidence must be subjected to some scrutiny.

There is evident animosity between some Jews and non-Jews in the first centuries after Jesus Christ that can be seen in various writings. Werner writes that "Concerning the music of Hellenism, the Rabbinic position was unequivocal: they viewed it with the greatest suspicion, rightly connecting it with the orgiastic cults of Asia Minor . . . The early Church held, at least in the first two centuries, exactly the same principles as normative Judaism."[9] Werner cites ecclesial authorities that provide evidence of an anti-Jewish position; for instance, Diodorus of Tarsus "complained bitterly that the Church was imitating Jewish songs and asked of what use the many Hebrew words and Psalmodies could be."[10] However, Diodorus lived in the fourth century CE (died ca. 390), so this is not a definite indication of the trend in the earliest days of the Christian church. Similarly, Chrysostom "warned Christians against imitating Jewish practices and customs" and is stingingly anti-Jewish and sarcastic in his perspective, citing Matt 9:23–24 first to make his point:

> And when Jesus came to the ruler's house, and saw the aulos players, and the crowd making a tumult, he said, "Depart; for the girl is not dead but sleeping." And they laughed at him. Noble tokens, these, of the rulers of the synagogue—auloi and cymbals raising a dirge in the hour of her death.[11]

But, again, Chrysostom lived in the fourth century (ca. 347–407), so it is difficult to ascertain whether fourth-century patterns duplicate or even represent those of the earliest two centuries.[12]

---

8. Werner, "Music of Post-Biblical Judaism," 315.

9. Werner, "Conflict," 457.

10. Werner, "Conflict," 458.

11. Chrysostom, *Matt. Hom.* 11.7 (cited in McKinnon, ed., *Music in Early Christian Literature*, 84n178).

12. Werner, "Conflict," 459.

IS EARLY CHRISTIAN MUSIC JEWISH OR GRECO-ROMAN?

Undoubtedly there was reciprocal antagonism between at least some of the Jews and non-Jews, but these statements do not necessarily represent all those involved in the discussion in the first century, again, because what is thought to be known about both the sentiments of the people involved and the actual music of the early Christian church can be read back only from much later documents. Werner, for example, speaks of tenth-century documents in referring to the Jewish musical traditions, which means that they are removed from the period of interest here by almost 1,000 years. While it can reasonably be argued that music did not change much in the first millennium, this is still a very long period of time. In his defence of the Jewish tradition found in the music of the church, but the lack of sources until the tenth or even eleventh centuries, Werner poses the question that the reader might ask:

> How is it possible that we possess 14 fully written pieces of ancient Greek music, and not a scratch of Hebrew? The explanation is simple: The Greeks had a system of notation, based upon the alphabet, which identified each tone with a letter—hence our naming of tones after letters, a, b, c, d, e, and so on. We Jews did not use symbols for each tone, but for each whole phrase. Indeed it would have been rather difficult to break up one of those florid, richly embellished Hebrew melodies into single tones. Thus, from the practical point of view the cantillation marks of Jews, Syrians, Armenians, Byzantines, and those of the early Roman Church were more practical, more appropriate to the style of the music, which they symbolized, but alas, much less faithful than the comparatively clumsy Greek characters.[13]

The explanation may be simple, as Werner says, but it does not entirely solve the problem of the lack of documentation to support his hypotheses for the dominant influence of Hebrew music on the music of the early Christian church—that problem remains.

An example from a biblical scholar that shows the course of the discussion is found in Clifford W. Dugmore's preface to the 1964 reprint of his 1944 book, *The Influence of the Synagogue upon the Divine Office*. He includes revealing statements that have a bearing on the development of the discussion of this essay:

> The original preface was necessarily "dated" and has been omitted. The "Introduction," which has also been omitted, drew attention to the older emphasis on the influence of the Mystery

---

13. Werner, "Oldest Sources," 225–26.

Religions and of Hellenism upon the worship and theology of the primitive Church, and sought to redress the balance of this nineteenth-century approach (whilst recognizing the contribution of Greece) by stressing the influence of Judaism and, especially, of the Synagogue to the development of early Christian worship. This view has found increasing support in the intervening years.[14]

While genuine attempts have been made to counterbalance the bias of some past scholars regarding the music of the church,[15] nonetheless, the attempt cannot be a substitute for genuine investigation on either side of the equation. Dugmore himself mentions factors that show the influences of both cultures, even if not always directly related to music. For example, he speaks of "the pre-Christian elements of the liturgy of the Synagogue" being the reading and exposition of the Scriptures, and the reference in Acts 17:2 to the Berean Jews who had daily access to them, saying that this "suggests that in the synagogues of the Dispersion access could be had to the rolls of Scripture (Greek) at any time, just as, presumably, was the case in the synagogues in Palestine."[16]

In another vein, a factor that contributes to the difficulties of studying early Christian music is summarized by Alec Harman. He describes the beginning of the fourth century, with the division of the Roman Empire into East and West, and further liturgical divisions that resulted in five main groups of the Christian church. In the east, these were Syrian, Byzantine, and Egyptian, all retaining the Greek language, and in the west, Roman and Gallican, using the Latin language.[17]

Tracing these five, with their various offshoots, back to their earliest roots has been something only recently engaged in with any great success, by the collaboration of scholars from various related areas of study, including musicology, theology, historiography, and linguistics. The focus in the twentieth century was on discovering the Jewish roots of the music of the early church. Harman states,

---

14. Dugmore, *Influence*, v.

15. Several offenders are conveniently identified by Werner, *Sacred Bridge*, 2:262n92, where he commends the efforts of one scholar whose "approach does not, fortunately, hark back to Wellhausen's, Lagarde's, or Baumstark's willful and one-sided neglect of the contemporary Judaistic scholarship."

16. Dugmore, *Influence*, 71.

17. Harman, *Medieval and Early Renaissance Music*, 4–5.

We do not know who composed these melodies, but some of them were certainly adapted from Greek and Jewish sources and possibly from folksong also. Which had the greater influence, Greek or Jewish music, was a bone of contention until recently, but although Greek was the accepted language in most of the churches during the early years—hence the words "eucharist" and "kyrie eleison" ("Lord have mercy"—originally a hymn to the Greek sun-god!), which were retained even after the Roman Church had changed over to Latin—and although the church fathers were greatly influenced by Greek thought, it now seems certain that Christian chant owes more to the Jewish synagogue than to the Greek temple. For one thing, the chant melodies as they have come down to us are much more closely allied to Jewish than to Greek music, and as the texts are nearly all taken from the psalms (which are of course Jewish, not Christian) it seems very probable that many of the psalm melodies themselves were adapted from those used in the synagogue. In fact, it has been shown that many such tunes sung today by Jewish communities who have been completely isolated since pre-Christian times are strikingly similar to those of the Christian Church. Furthermore, the different ways of singing the psalms were the same in both church and synagogue: these are now called direct, responsorial, and antiphonal psalmody.[18]

This statement may well summarize the current view, but it raises questions as it answers others. For instance, what examples of Greek chant does he refer to for comparison? What corpus does he use that defines that "the texts are nearly all taken from the psalms (which are of course Jewish, not Christian)," and does he mean in the latter, "Jewish not *Greek*"? How can it be determined that it is (1) "very probable that many of the psalm melodies themselves were adapted from those used in the synagogue" and (2) "the different ways of singing the psalms were the same in both church and synagogue"?[19] Harman states that "Another important type of chant was the hymn, also of Jewish origin but influenced to some extent by Greek models. The first Christian hymns were written (in Greek) for the eastern churches..."[20] The first statement, that the hymn was of Jewish origin, is hard to substantiate, as the term itself is a Greek word, with Greek hymns well known for hundreds of years before

[18]. Harman, *Medieval and Early Renaissance Music*, 5. His parenthetical comments.

[19]. See discussion below on psalmody in the ancient and first-century synagogue.

[20]. Harman, *Medieval and Early Renaissance Music*, 6.

the time of Jesus Christ. Similarly, the second statement, that the "first Christian hymns were written (in Greek)," raises some questions in this regard, especially noting that Harman places "in Greek" in parentheses.

Questions also arise as a result of statements by Alfred Sendrey on the Jewish writer, Philo (ca. 20 BCE—40 CE), whose life would have spanned the life of Jesus Christ. Sendrey says,

> His numerous historical and philosophical essays, both large and small, reveal, on the whole, a good understanding of the general musical culture of his time. But his treatment of the subject is completely under the spell of the musical theory and philosophy of the Hellenes. Facts concerning the music of his own people are almost entirely missing in his writings.[21]

While Sendrey's concern is that Philo, as a Jewish writer, discusses little of the Jewish heritage of music, what is perhaps more significant is that three of Sendrey's own statements in his summary underline the predominance of Greek influence on music at that time. First, Sendrey admits that Philo has a good understanding of the general musical culture of his time. Second, he assumes that Philo Judaeus's writing is "under the spell" of the Hellenes, which suggests that Hellenistic music and musical theory were in fact the most dominant or compelling at the time. Third, he states that facts about the Jewish music "are almost entirely missing in his writings," which again supports the case for a largely Hellenistic approach to music at the time of Philo's writing. The three statements that Sendrey has commented on in fact indicate that Philo is quite consistent in his representation of the music at the turn of the millennium and during the life of Jesus Christ; therefore, Philo's statements may in fact support the case for the Greek or Greco-Roman influence on the soon-to-be-formed Christian church.

These are only a few of the problems faced when dealing with the material related to the music of the early Christian church. More could be mentioned, but these should suffice to show the nature of the inquiry and the difficulties that scholars of either persuasion must or should face. At the very least, it is difficult, perhaps impossible, to ascertain which influence was the very first, although this seems to be at the heart of the debate.

---

21. Sendrey, *Music in Ancient Israel*, 62.

IS EARLY CHRISTIAN MUSIC JEWISH?

Over the last one hundred or so years, there has been a tremendous increase in scholarly writing about the heritage of Judaism in the music of the early Christian church, most notably and comprehensively by Werner in two volumes, both entitled *The Sacred Bridge: The Interdependence of Liturgy and Music in Synagogue and Church during the First Millennium*, as well as numerous articles.[22] Werner's work is monumental and impossible to ignore—he presents intuitive hypotheses that have gained credibility as more information has come to light, as well as assimilating data in a way that has revolutionized this area of inquiry. However, his work is sometimes coloured by emotive language and backlashing tendencies (not that they are without some provocation against earlier studies of scholars who ignored Jewish influences and contemporary Jewish scholarship). Roger T. Beckwith reminds the readers that "At its origin, Christianity was a Jewish religion. Jesus Christ was a Jew, and his first followers were Jews."[23] It should come as no surprise to find an overlap of Judaism with Christianity and numerous imprints of a Jewish heritage in the musical traditions of the Christian church.

In the preface to the first volume of *The Sacred Bridge*, Werner freely admits that in the study of liturgy, liturgical music, and the necessary accompanying interpretation of historical documents, "Prejudice cannot be fully avoided, it being an intrinsic part of genuine religious conviction."[24] This prejudice shows itself in his own article on "Music" in *The Interpreter's Dictionary of the Bible*, where he writes, "Indeed, all evidence points to the chant and music of the primitive church as practically identical with the customs and traditions of the synagogue,"[25] making it seem very clear-cut, which it is not.[26] Numerous biblical scholars state with confidence that the tradition of the synagogue was carried on into the Christian church, but there is an increasing number of questions in this regard. One scholar writes that from the earliest times people sang psalms "following the practice of the synagogue,"[27] but what this practice may have been is unknown, as there is no record of psalm-singing, at

---

22. Some of which are reprinted in Werner, *Three Ages*.
23. Beckwith, "Jewish Background," 39.
24. Werner, *Sacred Bridge*, 1:xv.
25. Werner, "Music," 466.
26. See McKinnon, "On the Question of Psalmody"; Smith, "Ancient Synagogue."
27. Robertson, "Psalmody."

least in the ancient synagogue.[28] Ralph P. Martin says that the "Church was cradled in Judaism, and borrowed many of its forms of worship from the Temple and synagogue," although he says he must "admit that there is some doubt as to the extent to which the singing of divine praises had developed in the Palestinian synagogues of the first century."[29] Another writer refers to the "natural continuity of responsorial psalmody from synagogue to church."[30] Again, this assumption is possible but undocumented. Dom Gregory Dix gives an outline of the Christian synaxis (order of liturgy to precede the Eucharist), stating that it was followed everywhere.[31] Specifically included in his list is psalmody, but Paul F. Bradshaw points out that these elements of the Christian synaxis are found only with certainty in fourth-century documents, and it is unknown if the fourth-century practices reflected the primitive practices of the early church.[32] In contrast to the outline referred to by Dix, Bo Reicke's reconstruction of the normal worship on a sabbath makes no mention of music.[33] Evidence that Werner compiles throughout his two volumes of *The Sacred Bridge* serves only to verify that the earliest traditions that are known seem to correspond to *later* Jewish chant, but there is little knowledge of how those came to be interwoven in the early centuries of the Christian church, or of what influences Jewish chant may have absorbed.[34]

Judging from these various statements, it appears that many scholars have followed the assumption that the solitary source for the

---

28. See McKinnon, "On the Question of Psalmody"; Smith, "Ancient Synagogue."

29. Martin, *Worship*, 40.

30. Connolly, "Responsorial Psalmody."

31. Dix, *Shape of the Liturgy*, 38.

32. Bradshaw, *Search*, 137–38.

33. Reicke, *New Testament Era*. Ulrich and Pisk, *History of Music and Musical Style*, 39, writing from a musical perspective, take a much more conservative view than do biblical scholars, proposing that "As early as the third century, psalm-singing was a well-established part—perhaps the main element—of the Christian ritual."

34. Smith (*Musical Aspects*, 7), for example, writes, "Jewish musical practice, of course, did not escape the syncretistic influences of Oriental and Hellenic cultures in the centuries preceding the Christian era. The liturgy of the dispersion synagogues especially was affected. The mere fact that the texts were sung in Greek language must have brought about some modification of the traditional music. Also, if analogy with later processes is of any value at this point, it is well known that the music of more recent Jews has been strongly colored by the music native to the lands in which they were living."

musical-liturgical traditions of the Christian church is the Jewish synagogue and/or temple. However, just as Werner denounces those who have in the past come from an "all-Hellenistic approach,"[35] so he himself virtually excludes reference to, or acknowledgment of, influences other than Jewish in what clearly was a period of multiple influences. Werner clearly denounces scholars who do not follow his own presuppositions. There is no mincing of words for those who have not cited his own work favourably,[36] although he clearly rejects the work of James McKinnon, who presents evidence that calls into question the viability of a strictly Jewish position on early Christian music.[37] Werner rarely makes reference to such works and certainly never in a positive light.

In Werner's discussion about the languages of prayer in the synagogues, he admits that

> In the Jewish Church at least three idioms were considered: Hebrew, Aramaic, and Greek. Hebrew was then, in the second

---

35. Werner, *Sacred Bridge*, 1:28.

36. See, e.g., Werner, *Sacred Bridge*, 2:219n69, who refers to "Mr. McKinnon's study, *The Church Fathers and Musical Instruments*," saying the following: "The author had limited himself to a few selected Fathers, mostly of the Western Church; also his knowledge is rather limited. The Syrian, Armenian, and most of the Byzantine Fathers have—luckily—escaped his attention, not to mention the rabbinic authorities. So has my study, 'If I Speak in the Voices of Angels . . .' [actually Werner's article is entitled "If I Speak in the Tongues of Men"] escaped his attention, where St. Paul's hostile attitude to all instruments is shown and explained, although this occurs in a document *before* the fall of the Temple. Nor has the author taken cognizance of my study, 'The Conflict between Hellenism and Judaism . . .'" Later in the same volume, it appears to be McKinnon again who receives attention, although not by name this time. Werner writes that there is evidence that "seems to demonstrate the well-established function of a number of synagogues in Palestine at least a century before Christ. If certain scholars have more recently overlooked these facts in order to be 'news-worthy,' and claim that there is no evidence of a synagogue before the fall of the Temple (in 70 CE), they are either ignorant, or less than honest, or both" (Werner, *Sacred Bridge*, 2:236n119). If it is McKinnon who is the recipient of the latter criticism, which it seems to be, it is a bit puzzling, for I have seen no reference in his work to the idea that there was no synagogue, nor even well-established synagogues, before 70 CE, rather, that there is some question as to the role that music had in them until this time. McKinnon's documentation implies that the synagogue remained a place for study of the Scriptures, but not for services that included a full liturgy with psalmody.

37. It should be noted that McKinnon's work addresses the argumentation or lack of documentation for a particular position, but I have not found instances of him attacking the person who represents the argument. This, however, is not to say that Werner may not be accurate in his criticism of McKinnon's selective evidence and possibly limited broader scope of knowledge of the subject.

century A.D., all but a dead language. Its use was confined to religious and legal discussions, to scholarly expositions, and to prayer . . . [I]n the apostolic and post-apostolic centuries Aramaic prayers were at least used as often as were Hebrew. This, however, does not hold true for all of Palestine; in Caesarea, for example, the language of the Synagogue was Greek . . . In the entire Diaspora the language of the synagogues was Greek.[38]

Here he freely acknowledges the predominance of the Greek language, and yet elsewhere denies that there could have been Greek influence of any significance on the music of the early church. Werner further states:

> Moreover, we must not forget that there was a Greek synagogue in Jerusalem itself, where most of the prayers were recited in the Koine (Greek vernacular). These regional synagogues in Jerusalem contributed much to the uniformity of liturgical tradition throughout the Diaspora, since their authority was unquestionable.[39]

He points out that

> In no way different was the attitude of the early Church toward the language of prayer. The Apostles used all three languages according to their respective environments, and if one interprets in a rationalistic manner I Cor. 14:16 (". . . Wherefore let him that speaketh in an unknown tongue pray that he may interpret . . ."), one may regard the entire passage as a plea for the unlimited use of the Greek vernacular in worship. This principle was generally accepted . . .[40]

Here he freely recognizes the predominance of the Greek language in both the Jewish synagogue and the Christian church, yet he refuses to permit the possibility of its influence.

Again, Werner writes, "The entire terminology of the Synagogue, whether referring to its dignitaries or to the conduct of the service, is familiarly understood in the New Testament; the original Hebrew terms were simply translated into Greek."[41] But the wording of this sentence within which Werner places his premise that the Christian liturgy and

---

38. Werner, *Sacred Bridge*, 1:28.
39. Werner, *Sacred Bridge*, 1:29.
40. Werner, *Sacred Bridge*, 1:29.
41. Werner, *Sacred Bridge*, 1:2.

ultimately its music are almost exclusively Jewish in origin is belied by the fact that the institution within which these forms were said to originate is itself called by a Greek term, "synagogue." Although this is well known by every New Testament scholar, and certainly by any person who attended the early synagogues, Werner ignores that even within the confines of a Jewish institution there is evidence that the Greco-Roman environment had an influence on it. Interestingly, at this point Werner admits that "Our knowledge of the Synagogue liturgy at the time of Jesus is very limited, since most of the descriptive sources originated in the following centuries."[42] Later changes in the synagogue seem to have been implemented to counteract the creeping influence of Greco-Roman culture, a sure acknowledgment of the intensity of its influence.

Without question, Werner brings his own unique perspicacity to the discussion of vocal music versus instrumental music in the early church. He comments that the primacy of vocal music over instrumental music is so completely established that it is not often realized that this position was not a consistent one throughout the history of the early Christian church. Equally, he points out that "it would be a bold inference if we were to assume that there was no instrumental music in the liturgy of the Early Church. Quite to the contrary! Why all these outbursts, why all this frenzied searching for all kinds of reasons to justify the prohibition of instrumental music, if there was actually no violation of these injunctions?"[43] Werner cites two of the main reasons commonly given for the Christian avoidance of instrumental music: first, its association with pagan cults and, second, its association with Jewish sacrificial rites. However, if the synagogue banished instrumental music after the destruction of the temple in 70 CE, and if the Christian church avoided use of them for the above-mentioned reasons, it is interesting to note that Christian and Jewish practices coincided exactly, but for entirely different reasons. Regarding musical instruments, Werner says, "Rabbinic and patristic literature should be used only with great caution; while the texts deal mainly with the music of the temple—in an idealizing fashion—they

---

42. Werner, *Sacred Bridge*, 1:2–3.

43. Werner, *Sacred Bridge*, 1:316–17 (317); it is a good point. However, see also his article, "If I Speak in the Tongues of Men . . ." in which he argues that it is clearly evident that Paul despised musical instruments; I find his arguments unconvincing on this point, but intriguing, nonetheless.

were written at least 150 years after the temple's destruction. Many, if not all, of them rely upon hearsay."[44]

An example of the selective nature by which certain kinds of evidence can be presented and biases maintained can be seen in the work of a respected scholar in the field of Jewish music, in particular, Sendrey. Sendrey discusses several of the early attestations to Jewish instruments during the time of the early Christian church, including reference to a coin of Bar Kokhba. His explanation of the instruments depicted on this coin is not entirely convincing, for he tries to show that what looks like the *aulos*,[45] an instrument that is not viewed favourably by the Jewish leaders,[46] is actually a pair of trumpets. He begins by saying that the coin "shows a pair of trumpets; they are designed in such a shortened and clumsy fashion that it is somewhat difficult to reconstruct their original shape." He continues:

> Nevertheless, we maintain that they are reproductions of the sacred trumpets of the Temple. In these numismatic designs the exact shape of the depicted instruments was only of a secondary importance; the main objective must have been a patriotic demonstration, on coins issued by the victorious national hero, of a sacred symbol of the Jewish religion. The oboe (*halil*) was far from having the same symbolic meaning for the Jews as the *hazozerot* (sacred trumpets), the use of which was instituted by the commandment of the Lord Himself (Num. 10:2) . . . The fact that on the coins *two* instruments are represented, is an unmistakable sign that they are the sacred trumpets.[47]

Sendrey briefly refers to Curt Sachs, mentioning but downplaying that Sachs thinks that they do not represent trumpets, but oboes. Sachs's own words are:

> Among the Jewish coins stamped during Bar Kokba's revolt against Emperor Hadrian (132–35 A.D.), some show pairs of wind instruments. Numismaticians call them trumpets, or even

---

44. Werner, "Musical Instruments," 370.

45. For description and discussion of the aulos, a reedpipe or oboe that is played in pairs, see McKinnon and Anderson, "Aulos"; and Michaelides, "Aulos."

46. See Werner, "If I Speak in the Tongues of Men," 19, who writes, "The rabbis held a particularly low opinion of certain instruments: the *halil* (a primitive clarinet, or a kind of αὐλός)." For discussion of the *aulos* in relation to the New Testament church at Corinth, see chapter 5 above.

47. Sendrey, *Music in Ancient Israel*, 64–65.

trombones; but this is incorrect. The stout shape, the reedlike top, the disk that supports the lips, and the bell are all features of the modern Arabian oboe *zamr* and its relatives. Consequently, this oboe existed in Jewish Palestine at the beginning of the second century A.D.[48]

What the coin seems to represent, therefore, is not the sacred trumpets that Sendrey would like them to represent, but more likely that ubiquitous instrument with the questionable reputation, the Greek-named *aulos*.[49]

The difficulty that Sendrey has in accepting that something other than the sacred trumpets could be represented on these coins, and the assumption that he makes in determining that they "must be" the sacred instruments, may call into question other statements and assumptions in this discussion. More significantly, it shows the nature of the problem of determining facts when prior assumptions are in place. Some of these same tendencies have been seen in the arguments of Werner, who, although he admits to the predominance of the Greek language in the synagogue and further admits that little is known of the liturgy of the synagogue in the first few centuries and little of the Jewish music, still asserts the dominance of Jewish influence on early Christian music. He seems to have almost single-handedly taken upon himself to engage in a battle of Judaism over Hellenism, not entirely unlike the one he describes in his article, "The Conflict between Hellenism and Judaism in the Music of the Early Christian Church." Few scholars have made such an impact upon the study of Jewish origins of early Christian music, but perhaps no one has seen it so clearly as a battle, either. The question of what comprised the music of the early church is still open to dispute; perhaps more questionable are some of the assertions or assumptions made by Werner in particular, as well as some others who hold the same positions, in his aggressive posture to influence the view we have of early Christian music.

---

48. Sachs, *History*, 120 (see also 248).

49. Having referred to the instrument by its Greek name, however, is not to suggest that the Jewish musical tradition does not have its own early reference to a similar instrument. Sendrey includes in his own book a reference to (and photograph of) a bronze figurine (ca. 1300–1200 BCE) of a Jewish flute-girl playing a double oboe (see *Music in Ancient Israel*, 310 and 68 [illustration no. 36]).

Part One: Music and Interpretation in the Early Church

IS EARLY CHRISTIAN MUSIC GRECO-ROMAN?

As I have mentioned in the section above, several recent scholars have opposed the idea that there has simply been an ongoing tradition from Jewish synagogue to Christian church. In McKinnon's research into the early rabbinical writings and other contemporaneous literature, he, for instance, found no evidence to support the idea that instruments were banned in the synagogue. However, he similarly found no positive information to suggest that musical instruments were ever employed in the ancient synagogue. As a result of his research, he further concluded that the central element of the service, the simple declamation of Scripture, had no call for the use of instruments in any case.[50] In other research into the perspectives of the church fathers, McKinnon clearly shows the prejudice that is evident in someone such as John Chrysostom, but also shows that too much has been made of this in some ways. For instance, he introduces the example of Chrysostom's polemic against musical instruments that shows an "extravagant manner" of expression: "John Chrysostom . . . refers to musical instruments along with dancing and obscene songs as the 'devil's garbage,' and on another occasion declares that, 'Where the aulos is, there, by no means, is Christ.'"[51] However, regarding the relationship of musical instruments to singing, McKinnon points out that

> Music historians have tended to assume that there is a direct connection, that is, that ecclesiastical authorities consciously strove to maintain their music free from incursion of musical instruments. There is little evidence of this in the sources however. What one observes is that there are two separate phenomena: a consistent condemnation of instruments in the contexts cited above, and an ecclesiastical psalmody obviously free of instrumental involvement . . . The truth remains that the polemic against musical instruments and the vocal performance of early Christian psalmody were—for whatever reasons—unrelated in the minds of the church fathers.[52]

McKinnon's approach to the literature is to raise questions in areas that are considered certainties by others. This is seen in his opinion that, in regard to Christianity, the destruction of the temple happened too late

---

50. McKinnon, "Exclusion."
51. McKinnon, ed., *Music in Early Christian Literature*, 1.
52. McKinnon, ed., *Music in Early Christian Literature*, 3.

to have influenced synagogal music and hence to have any real bearing on the early history of Christian music, although there would have been a parallel in the history of the music of both Judaism and Christianity. He suggests that by the end of antiquity, there would have been two equal factors in the music of the Christian church: "the Hebraic inheritance of psalmody and the Hellenic inheritance of musical theory."[53]

In 1984, John A. Smith published an article in which he raised the question prior to the one that asks if there was instrumental accompaniment to the singing in the synagogue: that is, was there *singing* in the ancient synagogue? And if not, is there any reason to assume that the music of the early church was simply an extension of that of the synagogue? Smith speaks disparagingly of the scholar who "stretches historical credibility to absurd limits by reading back elements of fourth-century Christian practice into the first century and then assuming their synagogal origin."[54] He states: "The result of such speculative retrojection ... has been to give the false impression that the first-century synagogue service was more highly developed than the evidence from the contemporary sources suggests."[55] Smith points out that there have been recent studies, namely that of McKinnon, that call into question the long-held assumption that there was singing in the ancient synagogue, and that there was any formal psalmody in the first-century synagogue. McKinnon writes that the notion that "psalmody flourished in the ancient synagogue is a notion created primarily by Christian liturgical and musical historians,"[56] and that there is only one group of scholars who have "failed to claim an important role for psalmody in the ancient synagogue: Jewish liturgical historians. They have little to say on the matter for the simple reason that the primary sources provide no occasion to discuss it."[57] Bradshaw, also, says,

> Liturgical and musical historians have tended to assert confidently that psalmody was a standard part of the early synagogue ... There is, however, an almost total lack of documentary

---

53. McKinnon, "Early Western Civilization," esp. 1–12.
54. Smith, "Ancient Synagogue," 2.
55. Smith, "Ancient Synagogue," 2.
56. McKinnon, "On the Question of Psalmody," 180.
57. McKinnon, "On the Question of Psalmody," 182. But see also Smith, *Musical Aspects*, 10, who writes, "The convertible usage of 'sing' and 'say' is not uncommon to the O.T.," and that the "same lack of precision" can be found in dealing with the New Testament.

evidence for the inclusion of psalms in synagogue worship. The Mishnah lists a psalm for each of the seven days of the week (24, 48, 82, 94, 81, 93, 92) which was sung by the Levites at the Temple sacrifices (*Tamid* 7.4), and at the important festivals the *Hallel* (Pss. 113–18) accompanied the sacrifices. But while the *Hallel* seems to have been taken over into the domestic Passover meal at an early date, and apparently also into the festal synagogue liturgy, the first mention of the adoption of the daily psalms in the synagogue is not until the eighth century.[58]

At this juncture, McKinnon's investigation reminds us that, according to Jewish writings, the Hallel was not sung, as is often thought, but it was recited.[59]

It is noteworthy that these three scholars are not suggesting that early Christian music was not influenced by Jewish culture and religious practice but are calling into question assumptions that have made it into the mainstream of current thinking, assumptions that are possibly unfounded. An example of these kinds of assumptions can be seen in the article on "Music" in *The Anchor Bible Dictionary*, for if even *some* of the observations of the above-mentioned scholars are accurate, this article would need to be reassessed as to whether it accurately represents the state of the discussion. While such dictionary articles do not claim to represent original research, they are often used as the source of basic information for biblical scholars who work in related areas, but who are not necessarily specialists in music or liturgy. Opinions that may be totally unfounded are thus introduced into the mainstream of the subject. In the article mentioned, the writer makes statements such as (1) "It was in the synagogue, however, that music continued to flourish and serve as an emotional and didactic aid to the maintenance of Judaism"; (2) "the writers of the NT and the founders of the new Christian movement very likely adopted what they knew of synagogue music to their own worship"; and (3) "The borrowing from synagogue worship of both hymn

---

58. Bradshaw, *Search*, 22–23. See also McKinnon, ed., *Music in Early Christian Literature*, who presents the texts in chronological order.

59. McKinnon, "On the Question of Psalmody," 184–85. In McKinnon ("Early Western Civilization," 10), he suggests that in "Judaism the psalmody that accompanied sacrifice in the late Temple was music in the fullest sense, but the psalms recited in the synagogues, and in the early Christian gatherings as well, were more scripture than song. They were no doubt recited with some sort of cantillation, but so was all scripture; it would take several centuries in each of the religions before psalmody became music in a selfconscious sense." Cf. again Smith, *Musical Aspects*, 10n38.

and chorus singing added the emotional, communal feeling needed to help build the new movement."[60] While these statements are obviously couched in tentative language, there is some question whether they can be substantiated at all. Nonetheless, they seem to represent a common (mis?)perception of music in the New Testament.

However, at the beginning of the twentieth century, there were the opposite kinds of assumptions being made to those just cited. For instance, in the first volume of *The Oxford History of Music* (1901), Harry Ellis Wooldridge made the kind of statement that could be seen to justify Werner's aggressive stance. Wooldridge spoke of "expecting" the music of the Christian ritual to resemble Greco-Roman practice and immediately followed these words with the statement: "we find these expectations fully justified."[61] If one were to use Wooldridge's statement as the gauge for the general state of the discussion, it would seem that there was little warranted investigation into anything besides a Greco-Roman perspective in the late nineteenth century and the early part of the twentieth century. When the volume was published in 1901, Bernard P. Grenfell's and Arthur S. Hunt's edition of the earliest Christian hymn, P.Oxy. XV 1786, published in 1922, was still some years away. As it is still the earliest known fragment of a Christian hymn with musical notation,[62] it is difficult to know what material would have constituted a study of the music of the early Christian church to justify Wooldridge's remarks.

Here, again, it must be pointed out that Werner himself participates in the same kind of presentation but from the opposite stance. For instance, in his thirteen-page article on "Music" in *The Interpreter's Dictionary of the Bible*, one-half of one page deals with how the music of the New Testament has fused with Hellenistic music, and even under that heading the bulk of the material is an argument for the Semitic influence seen in the music; in his bibliography, there is little mention of those

---

60. Matthews, "Music in the Bible."

61. Wooldridge, *Polyphonic Period*, 25.

62. Hunt and Jones, "1786. Christian Hymn"; Pöhlmann and West, eds., *Documents*, 190–94; and Cosgrove, *Ancient Christian Hymn*, 12, who writes, "But for now, P.Oxy. 1786 is our only example of pre-Gregorian Christian music." More detailed treatment is offered below in chapter 9, with references elsewhere through this volume. There is now the possibility that the newly edited fragments of P.Oxy. LXV 4462, which are dated to the second century, could fit in this category. See West, "Texts with Musical Notation," 88, where he writes, "It looks as if these verses may have been of a philosophical or religious cast," and remarks on similarities to Gregory of Nazianzus, Carm. 2.2.4.55.

works that would represent a Greco-Roman influence on this music.[63] While obviously much discussion has taken place about the music of the Jewish synagogue and its influence on the early Christian church, with advocates of the Jewish heritage not infrequently citing evidence of synagogal practice as an indication of the Jewish influence, it must be acknowledged, as mentioned earlier, that the very fact that the word for these Jewish gathering-places is Greek in origin—"synagogue"—suggests an environment where boundaries are not as distinct as many would like them to be, nor influences as definite as their various proponents might wish to present them. There can be little doubt that there were Hellenistic or Greco-Roman influences on both the Jewish synagogue and the early Christian church, as well as Jewish influences.

New Testament "hymns" also provoke discussion along these lines. Whether they were actually hymns to be sung is not part of my discussion in this chapter, but the hymn-like or poetic nature of some of these passages allows for a brief inclusion of them here. Ralph P. Martin holds to the common position that the early church took over from the temple and synagogue the use of hymns and psalms.[64] However, he also refers to Jewish-Christian fragments of hymnic praise in 1 Tim 1:17 and identifies a mix of influences here; he describes the phrase "King of the ages" as an exact phrase used at Jewish table prayers and in synagogue praise, but he views "for ever and ever" as a Greek phrase.[65] Both phrases are significant in the terminology of the Christian church and are still used in this context. Joachim Jeremias refers to the latter as "a Greek expression which helps to anchor the doxology of 1 Timothy in the Church life of some Greek-speaking Hebrew Christian community,"[66] again an acknowledgment of a confluence of cultures. Carl Kraeling and Lucetta Mowry, in their discussion of the "confessional hymn" in 1 Tim 3:16, say that they think the structure is oriental (and they think the music must have been oriental), but admit that the parallelism is Hellenistic in its rhetorical construction.[67] While those who might argue for an Aramaic background for texts such as these—based apparently on the ease with which they can be re-translated into Aramaic, although constructing a hypothetical

---

63. Werner, "Music," 469.

64. Martin, *Worship*, 45.

65. Martin, *Worship*, 45.

66. Jeremias, *Die Briefe an Timotheus und Titus*, 13 (cited in translation in Martin, *Worship*, 46).

67. Kraeling and Mowry, "Music in the Bible," 308.

Aramaic text from which to work seems to introduce numerous dubious factors and difficulties—also seem to argue for the strictly Jewish influence on the music, there is an undeniable tendency in these (potentially) musical texts to have characteristics that are also Hellenistic. Here one can see the difficulty in maintaining that a single influence shaped the music of early Christianity. Similarly, Kraeling and Mowry discuss the nature of the hymn in Phil 2:6–11 and suggest that the construction is completely remote from Jewish psalmody; the text, which is a hymn to Christ, is entirely out of keeping with Jewish tradition, while the rhythm is not quantitative but accentual, suggesting an oriental melody and not a Greek mode.[68] Whether they are right or wrong, they acknowledge that the evidence does not point to a single pure tradition, but to a mix of traditions, Jewish and non-Jewish. To ignore one or the other is to ignore a great number of important details and facts.

IS THE EARLIEST NOTATED CHRISTIAN HYMN JEWISH OR GRECO-ROMAN?

One final example, P.Oxy. XV 1786, continues to be one of the most fascinating documents for the study of music in the early centuries of the Christian church, which is why it is mentioned at points throughout this volume. Greek hymns of music in the era of the early church were commonly known, being sung to a god or gods, but this is the first known hymn with musical notation to make reference to the Christ of Christianity.[69] Of this hymn, Martin West writes,

> This hymn . . . is perhaps the latest in date of the known texts recorded in the ancient Greek notation. At the same time it is by a considerable interval the oldest surviving example of music used in Christian worship. It is therefore a matter of some interest to determine, if possible, to what musical tradition it belongs . . . Egon Wellesz . . . denied that the music of the hymn was of genuinely Greek character, and stated decisively that it represented a new ecclesiastical music modelled on patterns deriving

---

68. Kraeling and Mowry, "Music in the Bible," 309.

69. Music at the time of Jesus Christ is thought by many to have consisted mainly of unaccompanied melody, which has later come to be known as plainsong or plainchant. Three styles characterized this vocal music: (1) syllabic, usually with one note per syllable; (2) neumatic or group, with two or three notes per syllable; and (3) melismatic, with more notes or groups of notes per syllable (see Ulrich and Pisk, *History of Music and Musical Style*, 27).

from Jewish or Syriac hymnody. He thought that the hymn might even be a translation from a Jewish or Syriac original.[70]

West argues that Egon Wellesz's position is mistaken "and that those who see the hymn as eminently a product of Greek tradition are on altogether stronger ground."[71] Werner writes,

> Hellenistic chant, as we know from its remnants, limited itself to a strictly syllabic relation of word and tone. Thus, one syllable corresponded to one and only one tone, a principle which naturally excludes any melismatic nonsyllabic motifs. The Oxyrhynchus Hymn breaks with this principle, especially in the four Amens, which are placed at the end of verses. Thus, the Semitic element of so-called "punctuating melismata" has entered into a basically Hellenistic structure. A Hebrew heritage, the melismatic formulas, is recognizable in a hymn of the Gentile church...[72]

Werner's statement at this point is not an unreasonable proposal; however, A. W. J. Holleman, following Werner, believes that the papyrus was simply a failed exercise in applying Greek musical notation to an already existing hymn. He says that the papyrus is "a demonstration of the inadequacy, and at least as regards the rhythmical signs, of the fundamental error of using the existing Greek notation for Christian music."[73] Again, however, it must be added that there is no documentation for the early notation of Jewish music at this time, the earliest documents coming from around the tenth century CE.

West says, "The fact that the hymn is expertly recorded in the Greek notation itself suggests a composer with a Greek musical education, which had probably included the study of Mesomedes's works. He is a Christian, but his religious outlook may have been formed in a syncretistic atmosphere..."[74] West further argues for the Greco-Roman relationship of this fragment of music based on the poet's use of a Homeric expression, adapted by Callimachus to Zeus, later used by Clement and

---

70. West, "Analecta Musica," 47. One of Wellesz's statements along this line is in Wellesz, "Interpretation," 347, where he speaks of "Christian chant, which is of Syro-Palestinian origin and was in no way connected with Greek or Roman music."

71. West, "Analecta Musica," 47.

72. Werner, "Music," 467–68.

73. Holleman, "Oxyrhynchus Papyrus 1786," 11.

74. West, "Analecta Musica," 50. For brief introductory discussion on Mesomedes, see Leichtentritt, *Music, History, and Ideas*, 20–21.

Origen to apply to the Christian God.⁷⁵ West says, "It was this Alexandrian confluence of Christian doctrine with Hellenic culture that put the title at our hymnodist's disposal. The continuing influence of Greek poetic tradition betrays itself" in his use of forms of the words.⁷⁶

West argues that scholars who claim that the music stems from oriental principles of composition both downplay the anapaestic character of the music and elevate the fact that a syllable is set to two or three notes.⁷⁷ West points out that there are several texts

> from the Roman period such as the Oslo and Michigan papyri... and the Oxyrhynchus papyri 2436... and 3161, which show that Greek music in the second and third centuries was becoming increasingly florid. If this tendency is slightly more developed in the Christian hymn than in the other texts, it is no more so than might be expected in view of the hymn's date. Individually the melisms it contains are no more extravagant than those seen in the Michigan papyrus, which is dated to the second century.⁷⁸

Elsewhere, he similarly states: "I can see no feature of the music that cannot be illustrated from the foregoing documents of the art as it existed in the second- and third-century Empire. It is only a little further along the path towards ever greater ornament, as might be expected from its date."⁷⁹

West, therefore, refutes the assertion of Wellesz that, because the music consists of a series of melodic formulas, which Wellesz states are unknown in Greek music, it must be from the Middle East. West responds that in fact melodic formulas were well known in Greek music, as evidenced by several musical fragments, and that knowledge of the melodies of the Middle East is not nearly as well documented. In most cases where there is any kind of documentation, it is by reconstructed melodies from "widely separated Jewish communities in the modern era."⁸⁰ Rather than simply asserting a single line of influence, however, West writes that "whatever Byzantine ecclesiastical music may have owed

75. The reconstructed title to which West refers is δωτὴρ μόνος πάντων ἀγαθῶν (dōtēr monos pantōn agathōn).
76. West, "Analecta Musica," 50–51.
77. West, "Analecta Musica," 52.
78. West, "Analecta Musica," 52.
79. West, *Ancient Greek Music*, 325.
80. West, "Analecta Musica," 52.

Part One: Music and Interpretation in the Early Church

to liturgical tradition going back to the Primitive Church (and ultimately to Jewish chant), there is nothing implausible in its also owing something to earlier Greek music."[81] This is the point at which many biblical scholars depart, for at present it seems—according to my reading of the state of the discussion—that those who argue for a Jewish influence feel compelled to argue that it is an exclusive influence, while those who argue for a Greco-Roman influence acknowledge that there are at least these two significant influences on the music of the early church, that is, both Jewish and Greco-Roman. William Sheppard Smith's balanced conclusion is that there is "one obvious and certain lesson to be learned from the extant data—the fact of variety."[82] The clear picture seems to be that there is no clear picture; instead, there is an intermingling of cultural and religious influences on the music of the early Christian church.

CONCLUSION

In looking at the general state of the research into whether the music of the early church was Jewish or Greco-Roman, there does seem to be a sense of misguided effort, and possibly some lack of genuine inquiry. This is particularly apparent on the part of those who either adamantly argue for or unquestioningly assume a single influence on early Christian music. From my analysis of the research into this subject, it seems that few scholars accept the less clearly defined categories of multiple influences; the majority are not willing to concede that overlapping forces were at work on this aspect of the early church. Some scholars admit at one point that there was more than one force shaping the music, but then ignore those statements when it is convenient to do so. After looking at these various examples, I think it would be an overstatement to say that there is a genuine battle over the canon of musical texts that comprise early Christian music and the dominant influences that shaped it, but it

---

81. West, "Analecta Musica," 53, whose position is followed in the most recent full study by Cosgrove, *Ancient Christian Hymn*, 11–12. Reese writes that the "famous Oxyrhynchos hymn . . . has been held to show traits linking Christian Chant with the music of Greek paganism, both through its stylistic features and through the Greek notation in which it survives," and he admits that the "rarity of ancient melodies makes it impossible to determine whether the Hebrew influence or the Greco-Roman was the stronger," and "that both influences were at work" (*Music in the Middle Ages*, 114, 115n4). His position here supports the one that is most tenable—that both perspectives must be represented.

82. Smith, *Musical Aspects*, 58.

would not be an overstatement to say that the direction of the discussion seems to be aimed more at other scholars than at their arguments. There is resistance to acknowledging multiple influences, perhaps inversely proportionate to the resistance that Werner felt in the past towards Jewish influences and Jewish scholarship. This field of study is highly complex, enough to require every informed contribution and contributor. I think it is clear that both Jewish and Greco-Roman culture had an influence on the music of the early Christian church, which is one of the reasons that its study has been so difficult—one must be expert in many areas at once. Certainly Werner has raised the level of inquiry; he has both engaged in and called for comprehensive comparative approaches that have revolutionized the discipline. However, in spite of a desire on the parts of some to find a true lineage in one direction or another, it seems that in order for scholarship in this area to really move forward, biblical scholars, musicologists, historians, and liturgists must accept that the relationship of at least these two cultures—Jewish and Greco-Roman—resulted in a synthesis that was neither exactly one culture nor the other, but incorporated aspects of both in a new approach to music that corresponded to the new faith of Christianity itself.

REFERENCES AND FURTHER READING

Apel, Willi. *Gregorian Chant*. Bloomington: Indiana University Press, 1990.

Beckwith, Roger T. "The Jewish Background to Christian Worship." In *The Study of Liturgy*, edited by Cheslyn Jones, Geoffrey Wainwright, and Edward Yarnold, 39–51. Revised ed. London: SPCK, 1992.

Bradshaw, Paul F. *The Search for the Origins of Christian Worship: Sources and Methods for the Study of Early Liturgy*. Oxford: Oxford University Press, 1992.

Connolly, Thomas H. "Responsorial Psalmody." In *The New Grove Dictionary of Music and Musicians*, edited by Stanley Sadie, 15:759. 20 vols. London: Macmillan, 1980.

Cosgrove, Charles H. *An Ancient Christian Hymn with Musical Notation: Papyrus Oxyrhynchus 1786. Text and Commentary*. Studien und Texte zu Antike und Christentum 65. Tübingen: Mohr Siebeck, 2011.

Dickinson, Francis Henry, ed. *Missale ad usum insignis et praeclarae ecclesiae Sarum*. Oxford: J. Parker, 1861–1883.

Dix, Gregory. *The Shape of the Liturgy*. Westminster: Dacre, 1954.

Dugmore, Clifford W. *The Influence of the Synagogue upon the Divine Office*. London: Faith, 1964 [1944].

Harman, Alec. *Man and his Music: The Story of Musical Experience in the West. Volume 1. Medieval and Early Renaissance Music (up to ca. 1525)*. London: Barrie and Jenkins, 1962.

Hatch, Edwin. *The Influence of Greek Ideas on Christianity*. New York: Harper and Brothers, 1957.

PART ONE: MUSIC AND INTERPRETATION IN THE EARLY CHURCH

Holleman, A. W. J. "The Oxyrhynchus Papyrus 1786 and the Relationship between Ancient Greek and Early Christian Music." *Vigiliae Christianae* 26 (1972) 1–17.

Hope, David Michael. "Liturgical Books." In *The Study of Liturgy*, edited by Cheslyn Jones, Geoffrey Wainwright, and Edward Yarnold, 65–69. 1978. Reprint, London: SPCK, 1983.

Howell, Clifford. "From Trent to Vatican II." In *The Study of Liturgy*, edited by Cheslyn Jones, Geoffrey Wainwright, and Edward Yarnold, 241–48. 1978. Reprint, London: SPCK, 1983.

Hunt, Arthur S., and H. Stuart Jones. "1786. Christian Hymn with Musical Notation." In *The Oxyrhynchus Papyri XV*, edited by Bernard P. Grenfell and Arthur S. Hunt, 21–25. Egypt Exploration Society Graeco-Roman Memoirs. London: Egypt Exploration Fund, 1922.

Jeremias, Joachim. *Die Briefe an Timotheus und Titus*. Göttingen: Vandenhoeck and Ruprecht, 1953.

Kraeling, Carl H., and Lucetta Mowry. "Music in the Bible." In *Ancient and Oriental Music*, edited by Egon Wellesz, 283–312. New Oxford History of Music 1. London: Oxford University Press, 1966 [1957].

Leichtentritt, Hugo. *Music, History, and Ideas*. Cambridge, MA: Harvard University Press, 1938.

Martin, Ralph P. *Worship in the Early Church*. 2nd ed. Grand Rapids: Eerdmans, 1978.

Matthews, Victor H. "Music in the Bible." In *Anchor Bible Dictionary*, edited by David Noel Freedman, 4:934. 6 vols. New York: Doubleday, 1992.

McKinnon, James W. "Early Western Civilization." In *Antiquity and the Middle Ages: From Ancient Greece to the Fifteenth Century*, edited by James W. McKinnon, 1–44. Man and Music. Basingstoke, UK: Macmillan, 1990.

———. "The Exclusion of Musical Instruments from the Ancient Synagogue." *Proceedings of the Royal Musical Association* 106 (1979–1980) 77–87.

———. "On the Question of Psalmody in the Ancient Synagogue." *Early Music History* 6 (1986) 159–91.

McKinnon, James W., ed. *Music in Early Christian Literature*. Cambridge Studies in the Literature of Music. Cambridge: Cambridge University Press, 1987.

McKinnon, James W., and Robert Anderson. "Aulos." In *The New Grove Dictionary of Musical Instruments*, edited by Stanley Sadie, 1:85–87. London: Macmillan, 1980.

Michaelides, Solon. "Aulos." In *The Music of Ancient Greece: An Encyclopedia*, edited by Michaelides Solon, 42–46. London: Faber and Faber, 1978.

Pöhlmann, Egert, and Martin L. West, eds. *Documents of Ancient Greek Music: The Extant Melodies and Fragments Edited and Transcribed with Commentary*. Oxford: Clarendon, 2001.

Reicke, Bo. *The New Testament Era: The World of the Bible from 500 B.C. to A.D. 100*. Translated by David E. Green. Philadelphia: Fortress, 1968.

Reese, Gustave. *Music in the Middle Ages: With an Introduction on the Music of Ancient Times*. New York: Norton, 1940.

Robertson, Alec. "Psalmody." In *A Dictionary of Liturgy and Worship*, edited by John G. Davies, 326. London: SCM, 1972.

Sachs, Curt. *The History of Musical Instruments*. New York: Norton, 1940. Reprint, London: J. M. Dent and Sons, 1942.

Sandon, Nick, ed. *The Use of Salisbury: The Ordinary of the Mass*. Antico Church Music. Newton Abbot, UK: Tabitha Phillips, 1984.

Scott, J. E. "Roman Music." In *Ancient and Oriental Music*, edited by Egon Wellesz, 404–20. New Oxford History of Music 1. London: Oxford University Press, 1966 [1957].

Sendrey, Alfred. *Music in Ancient Israel*. New York: Philosophical Library, 1969.

Smith, John A. "The Ancient Synagogue, the Early Church and Singing." *Music & Letters* 65 (1984) 1–16.

Smith, William Sheppard. *Musical Aspects of the New Testament*. Amsterdam: W. Ten Have, 1962.

Ulrich, Homer, and Paul Amadeus Pisk. *A History of Music and Musical Style*. New York: Harcourt, 1963.

Wellesz, Egon. "The Interpretation of Plainchant." *Music & Letters* 44 (1963) 343–49.

Werner, Eric. "The Conflict between Hellenism and Judaism in the Music of the Early Christian Church." *Hebrew Union College Annual* 20 (1947) 407–70.

———. "'If I Speak in the Tongues of Men . . .': St. Paul's Attitude to Music." *Journal of the American Musicological Society* 13 (1960) 18–23.

———. "Music." In *The Interpreter's Dictionary of the Bible*, edited by George Arthur Buttrick, 3:457–69. 4 vols. Nashville: Abingdon, 1962.

———. "The Music of Post-Biblical Judaism." In *Ancient and Oriental Music*, edited by Egon Wellesz, 313–35. New Oxford History of Music 1. London: Oxford University Press, 1966 [1957].

———. "Musical Instruments." In *The Interpreter's Dictionary of the Bible*, edited by George Arthur Buttrick et al., 3:349–76. 4 vols. New York, Abingdon, 1962.

———. "The Oldest Sources of Synagogical Chant." *Proceedings of the American Academy for Jewish Research* 16 (1947) 225–32.

———. *The Sacred Bridge: The Interdependence of Liturgy and Music in Synagogue and Church During the First Millennium*. 2 vols. New York: Columbia University Press, 1959; New York: Ktav, 1984.

———. *Three Ages of Musical Thought: Essays on Ethics and Aesthetics*. New York: Da Capo, 1981.

West, Martin L. "Analecta Musica." *Zeitschrift für Papyrologie und Epigraphik* 92 (1992) 1–54.

———. *Ancient Greek Music*. Oxford: Clarendon, 1992.

———. "Texts with Musical Notation." In *Oxyrhynchus Papyri LXV*, edited by Michael W. Haslam et al., 81–102. Egypt Exploration Society Graeco-Roman Memoirs 85. London: Egypt Exploration Society, 1998.

Wooldridge, Harry Ellis. *The Oxford History of Music Vol 1: The Polyphonic Period. Part I—Method of Musical Art, 330–1330*. Oxford: Clarendon, 1901.

8

Romanos Melodus and the Ancient Christian Musical Tradition

INTRODUCTION

THIS CHAPTER PROVIDES A discussion of the sixth-century Christian poet Romanos Melodus as the context for presentation of an edition of a fragment of one of his *kontakia*, or poetic and singable sermons. This fragment, discovered in the sands of Egypt and now housed in the Austrian National Library's collection of papyri in Vienna, is only the fourth such fragment identified as containing one of Romanos's sermonic poems (at the time of the original publication). Editing the poem for publication raises several questions regarding the origins and development of music within the early church, besides raising a few questions regarding the textual traditions of Romanos.

ROMANOS MELODUS AND HIS WRITINGS

Discoveries of papyri and parchments of the major Christian Greek poet of the sixth century, Romanos Melodus, have been few. Little is known of Romanos's life, apart from the fact that he lived in the sixth century. It appears to have been established that he was born at the end of the fifth century in Emesa in Syria, was deacon in the Church of the Resurrection in Beirut, and then came to Constantinople, where he died and was buried in the Church of the Virgin, sometime after 555 CE, since he refers to earthquakes in that city, the last occurring at this time (but before 565 CE).[1] Romanos was known to write what in the ninth century came to

---

1. See Maas and Trypanis, eds., *Sancti Romani Melodi Cantica*, xv–xvii;

be called cantica (*kontakia*). These are versified sermons set to music, each with a number of metrically identical acrostic stanzas using a common refrain, preceded by a prelude in a different metre.[2] The metre is not classical but relies upon accentuation, with its rhythm established through the number of syllables in each metrical unit.[3] There are various theories on how the *kontakia* were delivered, but musical notation does not survive on any of the papyri found to date, only on manuscripts from the thirteenth century and later.[4] According to Paul Maas and Constantine Trypanis, eighty-five of Romanos's *kontakia* have survived, although it is not certain how many of these are authentic and how many are spurious.[5]

To date, there have been three papyrus/parchment manuscripts of Romanos identified, to which P.Vindob. G 26225 should be added as a fourth. Interestingly, all four of the papyrus/parchment manuscripts belong to the Austrian National Library, which also houses one of the important medieval codices with Romanos's *kontakia* in it (Cod. Vind. Suppl. gr. 96 [twelfth century]).[6] The first papyrus of Romanos published was P.Vindob. G 29430 recto,[7] a sixth- or seventh-century papyrus later identified as a small portion of canticle 46 stanza 6 (Maas and Trypanis).[8] The second Romanos papyrus to be published was P.Amst. I 24 (= P.Amst. inv. no. 198) = P.Vindob. G 26216,[9] later identified for the recto as a small sixth- or seventh-century papyrus portion of canticle 2 stanzas 6 and 8 (Maas and Trypanis).[10] The third manuscript is

---

Romanus Melodus, *Romanos le Mélode: Hymnes*, 1:13–14. Trypanis suggests a date before 562 CE (see *Fourteen Early Byzantine Cantica*, 10).

2. Maas and Trypanis, eds., *Sancti Romani Melodi Cantica*, xi. Cf. Romanus Melodus, *Romanos le Mélode: Hymnes*, 1:15–18.

3. Maas and Trypanis, eds., *Sancti Romani Melodi Cantica*, 511.

4. Maas and Trypanis, eds., *Sancti Romani Melodi Cantica*, xi–xii.

5. Maas and Trypanis, eds., *Sancti Romani Melodi Cantica*, xvii.

6. On the manuscripts, see Maas and Trypanis, eds., *Sancti Romani Melodi Cantica*, xxv–xxviii; Romanus Melodus, *Romanos le Mélode: Hymnes*, 1:24–33.

7. See no. 41 in Oellacher et al., *Griechische Literarische Papyri II*, 68–69.

8. Maas, "Romanos auf Papyrus"; Zuntz, "Romanos Papyrus." On dating, see KV 85 in Aland and Rosenbaum, *Repertorium*, 561.

9. See no. 24 in Salomons et al., *Die Amsterdamer Papyri* I, 48–49. This papyrus, although published in the Amsterdam collection, is actually part of the Vienna collection, and is now housed there again.

10. Brunner, "'P. Amst.' I 24." Brunner contended that one could not match the verso with any known text of Romanos (185). However, Aland and Rosenbaum claim

a parchment of Romanos, P.Vindob. G 26068 flesh side,[11] again later identified as a small seventh- or eighth-century parchment portion of canticle 14 prooemium and stanza 1 (Maas and Trypanis).[12] The fragmentary nature and limited size of these papyri parchments means that our identification of P.Vindob. G 26225 as part of canticle 16 stanzas 6–10 (Maas and Trypanis) of the writings of Romanos Melodus, as described below, is apparently the first time that publication and identification of his work have gone hand-in-hand. This is also the single largest papyrus/parchment manuscript of Romanos so far to be discovered and published. Examination of all the papyri confirms that they are all from different manuscripts.

P.VINDOB. G 26225: AN EDITION

P.Vindob. G 26225 is a light-coloured papyrus with dark black ink on the recto of the papyrus where the ink is still visible (the verso is blank, which can be explained along several lines, including its being a single selection, possibly for private or liturgical use). Unfortunately, the papyrus has been abraded in a large number of places (especially lines 1–6, 13–16, and 20), with only the merest traces of ink to be found on a number of lines, as well as there being apparent but undecipherable marks of ink between a number of these lines. As a result, in some instances letters can only be deciphered by close first-hand observation of impressions made by the letters when they were written on the papyrus, a feature not easily seen on the photograph (in our original publication). The papyrus is also broken away in numerous places, with holes in a number of lines and a ragged left-hand side, compared to the relatively straight right-hand side. Since this is the right-hand side of what was at one time a large page, there are a number of blank lines, probably resulting from shorter lines at the ends of cola. There are also a number of lines where the lettering ends short of the right edge, indicating that this is the end of the line and the beginning of the right margin. The hand is a small, neat, and squarish sloping majuscule, with only a few instances of the letters being connected (e.g.,

---

to have identified the small parts of the lines with parts of stanzas 12 and 13, although they must read a number of letters differently than in the *editio princeps*. Aland and Rosenbaum, *Repertorium*, 566. On dating, see see KV 86 in Aland and Rosenbaum, *Repertorium*, 563.

11. See no. 41 in Treu and Diethart, *Griechische Literarische Papyri*, 77–78.

12. Römer, "Romanus Melodus."

ψι). Most of the letters are written on their line, apart from descending verticals of such letters as υ and ψ. The υ is particularly elegant, with a long sweeping tail. The strokes are consistently written, without varying thickness between verticals and horizontals. There are no accentuation marks or other marks of punctuation, apart from one instance of diaeresis over υ in line 8. The scribe used nomina sacra in a number of places, as indicated below. According to the records of the Papyrus Collection of the Austrian National Library the piece of papyrus was examined by Carl Wessely, who dated it to the seventh century. Examination of the hand in comparison with others seems to indicate to us a date of the sixth to seventh centuries.[13] The hand is the most delicate and smallest of those used on any of the Romanos papyri discovered to date.

Due to the fragmentary nature of this papyrus, and the textual variants that it seems to include, we provide (1) a diplomatic transcription, (2) a reconstructed reading text of this portion, and then (3) an attempted reconstruction of stanzas 6–10 of the canticle.[14]

Diplomatic Transcription

Recto:

Lines	
1	].ρισ.υ.μουνομ.ς [
2	]κσδαδ[ ]//////ημεν[
3	] φαιδροσμεν[
4	]////////////////////// υν///[
5	]///////////////////////////[
6	]υ.δ.[ ]χομενος.[
	>———————
7	].ωκαθισαισεαλλως [
8	].υκρατουσσουοϋμνος [
9	]νυψιστοισσωσον. [
10	].υμ.ν.ικινησου [
11	]

---

13. See the discussion in Cavallo and Maehler, *Greek Bookhands*, nos. 46 and 53.

14. For text-critical comments, we rely upon no. 16 in Maas and Trypanis, eds., *Sancti Romani Melodi Cantica*, 116–22; and no. 32 in Romanus Melodus, *Romanos le Mélode: Hymnes*, 4:13–53.

PART ONE: MUSIC AND INTERPRETATION IN THE EARLY CHURCH

12   ].μεροναπα[ ]τọυ [
13   ]ạυτọυ [
14   ] παν.ε [ ]ε̣ι̣δ̣.ς [
15   ] . . . ọ.νọ.νạ . . . ε̣ [
16   ]/////////////////////////[
17   ]τọνδ̣ικα[ ]ọν̣σε [
18   ]νομονλυτρωτην [
19   ]π̣ιδιημ̣α̣σ̣αφη [
20   ] . . . . . . .ε̣λησọν̣ [

P.Vindob. G 26225 (7.2 cm × 18.2 cm; provenance unknown; 6th–7th century)

1–6: Lines 1–6 are heavily abraded, so much so that in many, if not most, places there are only faint bits of ink visible. However, at places it is possible to decipher letters on the basis of the impression left on the papyrus by the pen stroke.

1: The left-hand edge of the papyrus is broken away, but traces of two letters before ρ and ι are visible, and what could be σ following them, a clue to why there is a curve in the ink stroke. There is then space for about five letters, before the remaining visible letters. In the midst of this abraded section, there is a descending stroke, probably indicating υ. The length of this section indicates that a nomen sacrum, ι(ησο)υ, was probably used in this line (see the reading text below).

1–2: There are what appear to be some marks of ink between lines 1 and 2, but these do not seem to be indications of another line of text, since there is not enough space in the relatively well-ordered lines of this manuscript. The papyrus has a number of stray ink marks on it elsewhere.

2: The first several letters are partially broken away due to the condition of the papyrus, but are still identifiable, and there are the faint signs of the horizontal strokes over the two nomina sacra, κ(υριο)ς δα(υι)δ. The space following has a hole and then a severely abraded section, in which it is difficult to know how many letters were written. There are then the faint markings of four letters. The ε seems clearer than the others, but these last four are all far from certain.

3: This line is both short due to the breaking away of the papyrus at the beginning of the line and abraded. Four of the letters are clear, ο, σ, ε, and ν. The α and ι are also relatively clear, although far from certain.

4: This line is heavily abraded, with only part of what looks like the vertical stroke of an υ and the bottom right-hand corner of a ν to be seen. Other letters are also conceivable on the basis of these markings.

5: This line is completely abraded, although it appears to have had lettering at one time.

6: The initial letter is on the edge of the broken away papyrus and looks like an υ. However, it may simply be a right-hand vertical stroke of a number of other letters (see the reading text below). A nomen sacrum is apparently used for αδ(αμ). The first letter has only a part of the lower left, but the δ is clear. It also has a faint stroke over it. The two letters that follow this nomen sacrum are highly contentious. Both are very rounded, and both seem to have cross-bars, indicating such possible letters as θ, ε, or possibly a small σ. The last letter of the line has a small part of a left-hand hook, such as is found with α, σ, or ε in this scribe's hand.

6–7: There is a clear stroke drawn between these lines of letters, with what looks like a diple at the beginning.

7: The initial ω curves around a break in the left-hand side of the papyrus. There is some abrasion of the papyrus in the middle of this line, although sufficient ink and pressure marks on the papyrus are present to decipher the lettering.

8: There is diaeresis with trema over the υ in υμος.

9: The first letter of the line is clearly a ν. See the relevant discussion below in the reading text.

10: There is the faintest bit of ink that indicates a letter before the υ. Most of the letter after the μ is gone because of a hole in the papyrus, although there is the bottom of a vertical stroke. The letter after the first ν is abraded.

11: There is no writing visible on this line (see the reading text below).

12: Although the tops of the first six letters and of the last five letters of the line are broken away, there is enough of most of them to make some identification, apart from the initial letter, which simply has a small stroke.

13: Most of this line is missing due to the condition of the papyrus. The initial letter resembles an α or a δ, due to the triangular shape of the strokes.

14: After the first three letters, which are clearly decipherable, the papyrus is abraded and broken away. Only the last of the letters, σ, is clear.

15: Due to severe abrasion, this line is very difficult to decipher. The letters that are partially decipherable consist mostly of curved strokes and the combination of vertical and slanting strokes of the letters ο and ν (see the reading text below for discussion of the readings of these letters). The final letter has the roundedness of probably an ε, although a σ or α is also a possibility.

16: This line is abraded, but there does not seem to be any writing on it (see reading text below).

17: After the first ν, there are several large holes and severe abrading of the line. The bottom part of the δ is visible, as are parts of the vertical and sloping strokes of the ι and κ. Abrasion makes decipherment of ους difficult, but the final ε is clear (see the reading text below).

19: Abrasion makes decipherment of five of the last six letters difficult, although the bottom part of the μ, the curves of the two αs, and part of the φ are present.

20: This line is broken away and abraded for the first half, making it impossible to suggest letters on the basis of the faint ink markings. However, five of the final six letters, though very faint, are decipherable on the basis of the impression of the letters on the papyrus, with not much ink present.

Partial Reading Text

No doubt due to the state of textual studies at the time, Maas and Trypanis state in their introduction that "The transmission of the text [of Romanos] is therefore 'contaminated,' and no subdivision or grouping into families of manuscripts is possible. The single Romanos papyrus (P.Vindob. G 29430) shows that variants found in the codices are very old, many probably going back to the days of the poet himself."[15] However, this verdict has been questioned by both Günther Zuntz and Theodore Brunner. After editing P.Vindob. G 29430, Zuntz in response to Maas and Trypanis states, "this statement in the new Romanos edition . . . will have to be reversed on examining the wording of the papyrus in its relation to the evidence of the codices . . ." He concludes that the papyrus, though it has blunders, "contains a text superior to that of the later codices."[16] Brunner also has shown in his recent discussion of P.Amst. I 24 = P.Vindob. G 26216 that the variants of that papyrus merit further consideration

---

15. Maas and Trypanis, eds., *Sancti Romani Melodi Cantica*, xxvii–xxviii.
16. Zuntz, "Romanos Papyrus," 465–66.

for their importance in the textual transmission.[17] As we shall see below, the same is true of P.Vindob. G 26225. Some of the readings may represent corruptions, but others may well indicate an earlier text, since the papyri predate the medieval manuscripts by at least four centuries, and are much closer to the original date of composition, perhaps even within one hundred years of the poet's own lifetime. Variants from the medieval tradition are noted below. It appears that the average complete line length of P.Vindob. G 26225 was 74–78 characters on a complete page, although about 19 characters is the largest number visible on this manuscript on the longest extant line. This number is fairly consistently maintained from lines 1–3 and 7–20. Thus, the scribe essentially wrote each stanza not colometrically but continuously, although apparently he did indicate the break between stanzas 7 and 8 with a clear stroke, but not any others. There are no signs of punctuation (such as the raised dot) to indicate the ends of cola. There appear to have been a number of places where this text varies from the later medieval codices. These include having a shorter text, especially in lines 4–6, since there does not appear to have been enough space for the wording as found in the later medieval manuscripts. The most likely explanation (see below) is that one or more of the lines of stanza 7 was not written, either inadvertently or intentionally, by the scribe. It is impossible to recover what happened now. There are also apparent variants in words, and some alterations in word order, including variation in the refrain that slightly alters the metrical pattern. We follow the medieval manuscripts as recorded in Maas and Trypanis and José Grosdidier de Matons (see *Romanos le Mélode: Hymnes*) in the following reading text.

1 ἡ] χάρις σοῦ Ἰ(ησο)ῦ μου ὁ νόμος
2 ὁ] κ(ύριο)ς δα(υὶ)δ[ ]εὐλογημέν[ος
3]φαιδρὸς μὲν[
4]///// προσκυνῶ////[
5]///////////////////////[
6 τὸ]ν ἀδ(ὰμ) ὁ ἐ[ρ]χόμερος ἀ[νακα | λέσασθαι
7 πώ]λῳ καθίσαι σε ἀλλ' ὡς
8]τοῦ κράτους σου ὁ ὕμνος
9 ἐ]ν ὑψίστοις σῶσον

17. Brunner, "P. Amst.' I 24," 189.

PART ONE: MUSIC AND INTERPRETATION IN THE EARLY CHURCH

10   δον]ούμενοι κινήσου-
11   vacat
12   σ]ήμερον ἀπα[ι]τρύ-
13   ]αὐτοῦ
14   ]πάντε[ς] εἰδὼς
15   ]ἐρχόμενος ἀνακαλέ-
16   vacat
17   πραότα]τον δίκα[ι]όν τε
18   ]νόμον λυτρωτὴν
19   ἐλ]πίδι ἡμᾶς ἀφῆ-
20   ταπεινω]θέντας θέλησον

1: The spacing requires that the nomen sacrum for ἰησοῦ was used on this line, but no supralinear stroke is now present. Codex Athous Laurae Γ 27 (D, eleventh century) reads σύ and codex Mosquensis Synod. 437 (M, twelfth century) reads τοῦ instead of σοῦ. σύ does not seem likely at all due to the amount of space. τοῦ is a possibility in terms of length but looks more like a corruption. So, we have chosen to follow the other codices, Athous Batopediou 1041 (A, tenth–eleventh century), Corsinianus 366 (C, eleventh century), Patmiacus 213 (P for Maas and Trypanis, Q for Grosdidier de Matons, eleventh century), Taurinensis B. iv. 34 (T, eleventh century), and Vind. Suppl. gr 96 (Δ for Maas and Trypanis, V for Grosdidier de Matons, twelfth century).[18]

2: The spacing makes it tempting to believe a raised dot was used after δα(υί)δ to divide the cola, but since there are no other punctuation marks on the papyrus, ευλογ, written in an abraded part of the papyrus, probably filled the entire abraded space. Grosdidier de Matons notes a number of variants in the medieval manuscripts at this point. This manuscript clearly has the two nomina sacra, κ(ύριο)ς δα(υί)δ, together, with codices A D M P/Q T Δ/V. However, it is difficult to know what wording follows, since the decipherable lettering could also be compatible with ὁ ἐρχόμενος following directly after the nomina sacra, as read in M or Δ/V. The spacing of the line, as well as that of the following four lines, seems to require the longer reading as written here.

3: The letters that are clear, ο, σ, ε, and ν, seem to indicate the reading above. This section, φαιδρὸς μὲν εἰς ὄχημα, is questionable for metrical and text-critical reasons, but is found in A D M P/Q T and Δ/V, rather

---

18. See Romanus Melodus, *Romanos le Mélode: Hymnes*, 4:38.

than [φ]αιδρὸν γ]ὰρ τὸ ὄχ(ημα) found in the margin of P/Q.[19] Neither this nor the alternative reading solves the metrical inconsistencies of this line noted by Maas and Trypanis.[20] The letters that can be seen could conceivably match with some of those in the following phrase, καὶ οὗτος ὑπόκειται, but this does not seem as likely as the above reading.

4: This reconstruction is highly uncertain, since it is based upon parts of only two letters, but it seems to fit the medieval textual tradition. Codex T reads προσκυνῶν, but the lack of clearly written letters makes it impossible to tell whether the next letter in this line was ν.[21]

6: The nomen sacrum for ἀδάμ was used here. The preceding letter, although it looks like an υ, may well be the right vertical of a ν, which is used here in the reconstruction. No other variant is suggested in the textual tradition. On the basis of the lettering after the hole in the papyrus, it appears that the two letters before the hole should be read as ο and ε. If this reconstruction is correct, with the colon reading εὐλογημένος εἶ τὸν Ἀδ(αμ) ὁ ἐρχόμενος ἀνακα | λέσασθαι, this represents a variation in the word order of the refrain (see line 15 also) from εὐλογημένος εἶ ὁ ἐρχόμενος τὸν Ἀδ(ὰμ) ἀνακαλέσασθαι. This variant is not noted by Maas and Trypanis or Grosdidier de Matons as appearing in any other of the medieval manuscripts. The shift in the metrical pattern is minimal, however. Maas and Trypanis give the following pattern for the refrain:

᷉ ᷉ ᷉ — ᷉ ᷉ ᷉ — ᷉ ᷉ — ᷉ ᷉ — ᷉ ᷉ ᷉ — ᷉ ᷉

The pattern of the line as we read it only varies in one syllable (the fourteenth):

᷉ ᷉ ᷉ — ᷉ ᷉ ᷉ — ᷉ ᷉ — ᷉ ᷉ ᷉ ᷉ — ᷉ ᷉ ᷉ — ᷉ ᷉

There does not appear to have been enough room on line 6 for ἀνακαλέσασθαι to have finished here. Perhaps the word finished between lines 6 and 7 before the start of the stroke dividing the stanzas (note that the diple is present on the papyrus near the right side of the line), or the word finished at the beginning of line 7.

7: The drawn line between lines 6 and 7 of the manuscript indicates a break between stanzas 7 and 8. Stanza 8 probably began at the beginning of line 7, unless the completion of ἀνακαλέσασθαι started the line

---

19. See Maas and Trypanis, eds., *Sancti Romani Melodi Cantica*, 118; Romanus Melodus, *Romanos le Mélode: Hymnes*, 4:38.

20. Maas and Trypanis, eds., *Sancti Romani Melodi Cantica*, 118.

21. See Romanus Melodus, *Romanos le Mélode: Hymnes*, 4:38.

(see comments on line 6, above). This manuscript reads καθίσαι, with A C D P/Q Δ/V, rather than καθῆσαι with M or καθήσεσθαι with D or T.²²

8: The manuscript reads τοῦ κράτους σου, with A D M P/Q T, rather than σοι ἔνδοξος with C and Δ/V.²³

9: The clear ν at the beginning of the line indicates that the article τοῖς was not used before ὑψίστοις, with C and Δ/V, whereas the article is found in A D M P/Q and T.²⁴

10: The papyrus agrees with codexes A P/Q and T, which read κλῶνες οἱ δονούμενοι κινήσουσι τὰ σπλάγχνα σου, rather than βλέψον εἰς τοὺς κράζοντας πρός σέ in C and Δ/V, or κλόναι οἱ δοξούμενοι Βοᾶν in D.²⁵

11: The last colon of stanza 8 probably finished at the beginning of this line, leaving the rest of it vacant.

12: Stanza 9 probably began at the beginning of line 12.

13: The manuscript reads αὐτοῦ, with A D M P/Q, although τούτου may be the reading in C V and T.²⁶

15: The letters partially decipherable on this line are roughly compatible with the refrain as written in the medieval manuscripts (see on line 6 above, and the reconstruction in the next section, where line length seems to indicate a shorter refrain). However, the letters are also compatible with the variant form used above. The abraded condition of the papyrus renders the reading here less than certain. Nevertheless, we have reconstructed here with the variant refrain used above.

16: Stanza 9 probably ended at the beginning of this line, leaving the rest of it vacant.

17: The papyrus appears to read δίκαιόν τε καί, with C and Δ/V, rather than δίκαιον τὸν καί, with D M, or δίκαιον καί, with A P/Q.²⁷ The reading of this manuscript, as well as the variant in codex D and M, adds a syllable necessary for the metrical pattern. We have read what looks like a σ above, but the condition of the papyrus means that τ is also possible, with the left part of the crossbar being abraded.

---

22. See Romanus Melodus, *Romanos le Mélode: Hymnes*, 4:40.

23. See Romanus Melodus, *Romanos le Mélode: Hymnes*, 4:40.

24. See Romanus Melodus, *Romanos le Mélode: Hymnes*, 4:40.

25. See Maas and Trypanis, eds., *Sancti Romani Melodi Cantica*, 119; Romanus Melodus, *Romanos le Mélode: Hymnes*, 4:40.

26. See Romanus Melodus, *Romanos le Mélode: Hymnes*, 4:42.

27. See Maas and Trypanis, eds., *Sancti Romani Melodi Cantica*, 120; Romanus Melodus, *Romanos le Mélode: Hymnes*, 4:42.

19: The manuscript has ἡμᾶς ἀφη, which we have reconstructed as ἡμᾶς ἀφῆ | καν, with C M P/Q Δ/V, although the lettering here could be reconstructed as ἡμᾶς ἀφ' | ἡμῶν, with A and several minuscules. D reads ἀφ' ἡμῶν ἡμᾶς.[28]

CANTICLE 16, STANZAS 6–10

We offer here a reconstruction of the stanzas and cola (separated by a single vertical stroke) in which this papyrus fragment is found according to the medieval manuscripts.[29] We have used nomina sacra in those places indicated by usage elsewhere, but not where there is no indication from the papyrus itself. We have not added punctuation and have kept text-critical marks to a minimum. The parts of the lines on the right-hand side of the reconstruction represent the papyrus fragment. Square brackets are used in the standard fashion in conjunction with the diplomatic transcription and reading texts above. A double vertical stroke marks the end of what is probable on line 6.

1   (6) ἡ] χάρις σοῦ Ἰ(ησο)ῦ μου | ὁ νόμος

2   ἣν Σαοὺλ φθονῶν καὶ διώκων | Δα(υὶ)δ δὲ διωχθεὶς

      τὴν χάριν βλαστάνει | σὺ γὰρ εἶ ὁ κ(ύριο)ς Δα(υὶ)δ | εὐλογημέν[ος

3   εἶ τὸν Ἀδ(ὰμ) ὁ ἐρχόμενος ἀνακαλέσασθαι |

      (7) ἅρμα φωτὸς ὁ ἥλιος καὶ οὗτος σοι δεδούλωται] φαιδρὸς μὲν [εἰς

4   ὄχημα | καὶ οὗτος ὑπόκειται τῇ κελεύσει σου

      ὡς πλάστου καὶ θ(εο)ῦ | καὶ πῶλος σε νῦν ἔτερψε προσκ]υν[ῶ σου

5   [τὸ εὔσπλαγχνον . . .]

6   . . . εὐλογημένος εἶ] τὸν Ἀδ(ὰμ) ὁ ἐρχόμενος ἀ[νακα || λέσασθαι |

7   (8) ἰσχὺν τὴν σὴν ἐνδείκνυσαι τὰ εὐτελῆ

      αἱρούμενος πτωχείας γὰρ εἶδος ἦν | ἐν πώ]λῳ καθίσαι σε ἀλλ' ὡς

8   ἔνδοξος σαλεύεις τὴν Σιὼν | εὐτέλειαν

      ἐσήμαινε μαθητῶν τὰ ἱμάτια | ἀλλ' ἦν] τοῦ κράτους σου ὁ ὕμνος

9   τῶν παίδων καὶ ἡ τοῦ ὄχλου

      συνδρομή | ὡσαννὰ κραζόντων ὅ ἐστι σῶσον δὴ ἐ]ν ὑψίστοις | σῶσον

---

28. See Romanus Melodus, *Romanos le Mélode: Hymnes*, 4:40.

29. See Maas and Trypanis, eds., *Sancti Romani Melodi Cantica*, 118–20, for the cola divisions generally followed, although with some adaptations. *Romanos le Mélode: Hymnes* (4:38–45) divides the cola differently in a number of places. For a critical response to our readings and the resultant reconstructions, see Kroder, "Anmerkungen."

10 ὁ ὑψηλὸς τοὺς ταπεινωθέντας | ἐλέησον
ἡμᾶς τοῖς κλάδοις προσέχων | κλῶνες οἱ δον]ούμενοι κινήσου-
11 σι τὰ σπλάγχνα σου | τὸν Ἀδ(ὰμ) ὁ ἐρχόμενος ἀνακαλέσασθαι |
12 (9) Ἀδ(ὰμ) ἡμῖν ἐποίησε τὸ χρέος ὃ
ὀφείλομεν φαγὼν ὃ οὐκ ὤφειλε | καὶ μέχρι τῆς σ]ήμερον ἀπα[ι]τού-
13 μεθα ἀντ᾽ αὐτοῦ οἱ αὐτοῦ | οὐκ ἤρκεσε
τῷ χρήσαντι ἔχειν τὸν χρεωστήσαντα | ἀλλὰ καὶ τοῖς] αὐτοῦ
14 ἐφίσταται τέκνοις πατρῷον χρέος ἀπαιτῶν | καὶ κενοῖ τὸν οἶκον
ἁπλῶς τοῦ ὀφειλέτου
πάντας ἐκσύρων | διὸ ὡς δυνατῷ προσφεύγωμεν] πάντε[ς] | εἰδὼς
15 ὅτι ἡμεῖς πτωχεύομεν σφόδρα |
σὺ αὐτὸς ἀπόδος ἃ ὀφείλομεν | τὸν Ἀδ(ὰμ) ὁ] ἐρχόμενος ἀνακαλέ-
16 σασθαι |
17 (10) ῥύσασθαι πάντας ἤλυθας καὶ
μάρτυς ὁ προφήτης σου ὁ οὕτως καλέσας σε | πραότα]τον δίκαιόν τε
18 καὶ σώζοντα Ζαχαρίας ποτὲ | ἐκάμομεν
ἡττήθημεν πανταχόθεν ἐξεβλήθημεν | τὸν] νόμον λυτρωτὴν
19 ἐδόξαμεν ἔχειν καὶ κατεδούλωσεν
ἡμᾶς | τοὺς προφήτας πάλιν καὶ οὗτοι ἐπ᾽ ἐλ]πίδι ἡμᾶς ἀφῆ-
20 καν |διὸ μετὰ βρεφῶν σὲ
γονυπετοῦμεν | ἐλέησον ἡμᾶς τοὺς ταπεινω]θέντας | θέλησον

2: Σαούλ may have been treated as a nomen sacrum on the papyrus, due to line length.

5–6: There are far too many words in the medieval tradition for the number of lines on the papyrus, so it is conceivable that one of the lines of the stanza was omitted. We have omitted the following wording presented virtually identically in Maas and Trypanis and Grosdidier de Matons (*Romanos le Mélode: Hymnes*), without significant textual variants (cola 4–8 of the stanza are divided): ποτὲ γάρ δι᾽ ἐμὲ ἐτέθης ἐν φάτνῃ ἐν τοῖς σπαργάνοις εἰληθεὶς | καὶ νυνὶ τῷ πώλῳ ἐπέβης οὐ||ρανὸν θρόνον κεκτημένος | οἱ ἄγγελοι ἐκεῖ τὴν φάτνην ἐκύκλουν | ἐνταῦθα μαθηταὶ τὸν πῶλον συνεῖχον | δόξα τότε ἤκουες καὶ νῦν.[30] A possible, though entirely hypothetical, explanation is that the scribe deleted the material after σου in line 4 (see reconstructed text above) down to the σου just before the

---

30. Maas and Trypanis, eds., *Sancti Romani Melodi Cantica*, 118–19; Romanus Melodus, *Romanos le Mélode: Hymnes*, 4:39–40.

two vertical strokes inserted above, and then continued with the remaining text. This instance of haplography would delete roughly the amount of material required to leave two lines of text for lines 5 and 6 of the papyrus. Of course, there are a number of other variants that may have been contained in this papyrus that are now no longer recoverable.

6–7: We have included the completion of ἀνακαλέσασθαι at the end of line 6, even though there is not enough room for the entire word. It may have finished between lines 6 and 7, before the drawn dividing line, which only seems to have begun about halfway across the papyrus, or at the beginning of line 7.

8: Σιών may have been treated as a nomen sacrum.

11: This is a short line, since it is the end of stanza 8. The fact that line 11 on the manuscript is empty indicates that the line did not have εὐλογημένος εἶ at the beginning of the last colon, with Grosdidier de Matons, rather than including it, with Maas and Trypanis.[31]

14: This line is longer than the others by approximately 40 characters. The only major textual variant in the medieval manuscripts, apparently, is deletion by codex A of πάντας ἐκσύρων. These words may not have been in this manuscript, but these twelve letters alone are not enough to explain the spacing difficulties. It is possible that an instance of haplography occurred with the ων endings of ἀπαιτῶν and εκσύρων, resulting in deletion by the scribe of approximately the necessary number of letters. For this reason, we have left the text as it is in the majority of manuscripts (C D M P/Q T Δ/V).[32]

15: The length of this line indicates that the words εὐλογημένος εἶ were not included at the beginning of the last colon, with Grosdidier de Matons, contra Maas and Trypanis.[33]

16: Line 16 is a short line of only a few letters, since line 15 appears to end without having completed the word ἀνακαλέσασθαι.

19–20: See the partial reading text above for explanation of the reading adopted here.

---

31. See Romanus Melodus, *Romanos le Mélode: Hymnes*, 4:40; Maas and Trypanis, eds., *Sancti Romani Melodi Cantica*, 119

32. See Romanus Melodus, *Romanos le Mélode: Hymnes*, 4:42.

33. See Romanus Melodus, *Romanos le Mélode: Hymnes*, 4:12; Maas and Trypanis, eds., *Sancti Romani Melodi Cantica*, 119.

20: The reading with θέλησον seems secure in this manuscript, providing early evidence for this metrically irregular line, noted by Maas and Trypanis.[34]

CONCLUSION

The *kontakia* of Romanos Melodus illustrate well the development of the musical tradition within the Christian church, along with the sermonic tradition, especially in the diverse Eastern church that includes Greek and Syrian influences. By the time of the sixth century, there was a flourishing musical tradition, so much so that music had become fundamental to sermonic delivery, as illustrated by Romanos Melodus's versified musical sermons. The level of sophistication is indicated by both the words and the musical elements as indicated by the poetic features of rhythm and structure that were designed to engage the hearers by means of various means. Romanos Melodus presented a number of important Christian themes to his congregation, as is illustrated in the example presented in this kontakion edited above.[35] The importance of the tradition is indicated by the vibrant medieval manuscript tradition, which provides a number of differing religious traditions as shown by the sets of variants. The tradition had obviously continued as a living tradition that was transmitted into the medieval period, as these sermons were used within the Eastern church. The ability to understand these versified musical sermons depends upon a variety of factors, including knowledge of the Christian Scriptures, appreciation of the Greek poetic tradition, knowledge of varied Christian theological traditions, rudiments of early Christian music, and Greek textual criticism.

REFERENCES AND FURTHER READING

Aland, Kurt, and Hans-Udo Rosenbaum. *Repertorium der Griechischen Christlichen Papyri II: Kirchenväter-Papyri*. Patristische Texte und Studien 42. Berlin: de Gruyter, 1995.
Brunner, Theodore F. "'P. Amst.' I 24: A Romanus Melodus Papyrus." *Zeitschrift für Papyrologie und Epigraphik* 96 (1993) 185–89.
Gador-Whyte, Sarah. *Theology and Poetry in Early Byzantium: The Kontakia of Romanos the Melodist*. Cambridge: Cambridge University Press, 2017.
Koder, Johannes. "Anmerkungen zu dem Romanos-Papyrus Vindob. G 26225." *Jahrbuch der österreichischen Byzantinistik* 53 (2003) 23–26.

---

34. Maas and Trypanis, eds., *Sancti Romani Melodi Cantica*, 120.
35. See Gador-Whyte, *Theology and Poetry*.

Maas, Paul. "Romanos auf Papyrus." *Byzantion* 14 (1939) 381.

Maas, Paul, and Constantine A. Trypanis, eds. *Sancti Romani Melodi Cantica: Cantica Genuina*. 1963. Reprint, Oxford: Clarendon, 1997.

Oellacher, Hans, et al. *Griechische Literarische Papyri II*. Mitteilungen aus der Papyrussammlung der Nationalbibliothek in Wien NS 3. Baden bei Wien: R. M. Rohrer, 1939.

Römer, Cornelia E. "Romanus Melodus auf einem Wiener Pergament." *Zeitschrift für Papyrologie und Epigraphik* 109 (1995) 298–300.

Romanus Melodus. *Romanos le Mélode: Hymnes*. Translated by José Grosdidier de Matons. 5 vols. Sources Chrétiennes 99, 110, 114, 128, 283. Paris: Editions du Cerf, 1964–1981.

Salomons, Robert Paul, et al. *Die Amsterdamer Papyri I: P. Amst. I*. Studia Amstelodamensia ad Epigraphicam, ius Antiquum et Papyrologicam Pertinentia 14. Zutphen, Holland: Terra, 1980.

Treu, Kurt, and Johannes M. Diethart. *Griechische Literarische Papyri Christlichen Inhaltes II (MPER N.S. XVII)*. Papyrus Erzherzog Rainer 17. Vienna: Österreichische Nationalbibliothek, 1993.

Trypanis, Constantine A. *Fourteen Early Byzantine Cantica*. Wiener Byzantinistische Studien 5. Vienna: Böhlau in Kommission, 1968.

Zuntz, Günther. "The Romanos Papyrus." *The Journal of Theological Studies* 16 (1965) 463–68.

Part Two

Musical Traditions and Interpretations

9

The Composer as Interpreter of the Bible

INTRODUCTION

THE ROLE OF THE composer of sacred music as an interpreter of the Bible is one yet to be fully explored. The musical settings of biblical texts can provide not only insights into the composer's interpretation of the passage itself but also a window into the history of interpretation as it is represented at the time of the composition. Approaches that a composer may have taken include altering a biblical passage, juxtaposing several biblical passages with each other, using a non-biblical text to provide commentary on a biblical one, or specifically setting individual words or phrases in a way that highlights them.

This chapter provides a transition from Part One of this volume, concerned with ancient biblical and early Christian music, to the later musical traditions and innovations of the church. To make that transition, I begin with two ancient texts before moving to later texts of the Christian church. I will comment briefly on five specific works that span the two millennia of Christianity. Each one contributes uniquely to the corpus of sacred music, in that the composer has interpreted some aspect of the Bible. The first two are not works that can easily be performed—the first, because there is no musical notation, and the second, because both the text and the music are fragmentary and the musical notation itself can only be read with some difficulty. The first of these two is in Greek, is found in the New Testament, and has sometimes been referred to as "the earliest Christian hymn";[1] the second is also in Greek, but is written on

---

1. Barrett, *Earliest Christian Hymn*, 6. Of course, other passages in the New Testament might also have this claim made about them, such as Phil 2:6–11 (on which

a scrap of papyrus (P.Oxy. XV 1786) and is the earliest known example of a Christian hymn with musical notation. The final three examples are readily available in recorded form: the first of these is a Latin work by an English composer of the Reformation period in Britain, John Sheppard; the second is a German motet by Johann Sebastian Bach; and the final work is a Latin motet by the twentieth-century French composer, Francis Poulenc.

What do these five disparate works—separated by centuries or even millennia—have in common that could possibly draw them into the same discussion? In some respects, very little; yet each one has a specific relationship to the New Testament and to the Christian church. This is the common thread that I would like to follow throughout this grouping, by presenting the text, introducing the composer, identifying some features about the work, and, finally, discussing one or more aspects about the composer's role in interpreting the biblical passage found within the work. In each case, the composer has contributed some form of interpretation of the biblical passage.

1 TIMOTHY 3:16: AN EARLY CHRISTIAN HYMN (FIRST CENTURY)

The first composition, if that is the right term, that I treat is found in the New Testament, in one of the letters traditionally attributed to Paul the apostle, 1 Tim 3:16.

The Text

Greek	Transliteration	English translation
Καὶ ὁμολογουμένως μέγα ἐστὶν τὸ τῆς εὐσεβείας μυστήριον·	kai homologoumenōs mega estin to tēs eusebeias mustērion	And beyond all question, the mystery of godliness is great:
ὅς	hos	Who
ἐφανερώθη ἐν σαρκί,	ephanerōthē en sarki	was manifested in a body,
ἐδικαιώθη ἐν πνεύματι,	edikaiōthē en pneumati	was vindicated by the Spirit,

see chapter 12 below) (see Barrett, *Earliest Christian Hymn*, 623–24). For discussion of the implications of authorship, see Porter, "Pauline Authorship"; cf. Guthrie, *Pastoral Epistles*, 224–40.

ὤφθη ἀγγέλοις,	ōphthē angelois	was seen by angels,
ἐκηρύχθη ἐν ἔθνεσιν,	ekēruchthē en ethnesin	was preached among the nations,
ἐπιστεύθη ἐν κόσμῳ,	episteuthē en kosmō	was believed on in the world,
ἀνελήμφθη ἐν δόξῃ.	anelēmphthē en doksē	was taken up in glory.

The Composer

Paul the apostle has traditionally been thought to be the author of 1 Timothy, which would date the letter to about 62–63 CE.[2] However, following recent trends, many scholars now think that the letter is pseudepigraphal and was written later than the time of Paul, with proposals ranging from the end of the first century to as late as mid-second century. There is still significant evidence for Pauline authorship of 1 Timothy, which I tend to accept, but it will be seen that the present discussion is not necessarily dependent on this view.

There is a similar lack of consensus regarding who wrote the specific passage found in 1 Tim 3:16. Since the beginning of the twentieth century, the view that has found increasing acceptance is that the writer of 1 Timothy, whether Paul or a later writer, quoted an early Christian hymn or creedal statement.[3] Nonetheless, assuming that Paul did write the letter, it remains entirely possible that he also wrote the passage in 3:16. First, it is early in the history of the Christian church for there to have existed such a theologically developed Christian hymn to quote if Paul did not write it himself. Secondly, we know of no other writer besides Paul who could have written this hymnic passage so early in the period. If there was someone else, we would surely have heard the name of this person or at least of their fame, and would have some indication of other writing of theirs.[4] Thirdly, the shift in the style of writing of the verse is frequently cited as evidence for a quotation of another writer, but this shift can be accounted for by the fact that this is a different genre of

---

2. For a brief overview of the various positions on dating and authorship, see Guthrie, *New Testament Introduction*, 607–49; Porter, *Apostle Paul*, 419–31. This passage is also treated in chapter 4 above.

3. Norden, *Agnostos Theos*, 250–63. See more recent analysis and critique of this subject in Fowl, *The Story of Christ*, 37–45.

4. This would also make Paul the likely candidate as author of v. 16 even if he did not write the letter.

writing than the surrounding letter.[5] Whether or not Paul had written the section earlier than the time of writing the letter, so that he is quoting himself, is not particularly relevant here. It seems to me that Paul is the reasonable choice for the author of the passage in v. 16.

The Passage and Features of its Interpretation

Here we encounter the question of whether this passage is a hymn or a creedal statement. In Ralph Martin's outlining of characteristics of a creed compared with those that would define a hymn,[6] it is apparent that the categories are not exclusive. In fact, in Martin's article on the topic, 1 Tim 3:16 fits with some of the criteria of a creed, but, in even more cases, with those of a hymn. Some of the features that are known to be characteristics of ancient hymns are worth noting. For instance, the Greek word ὕμνος (humnos) was used for many centuries in Greek classical culture before Christianity's inception. For instance, at least since the time of Homer, a hymn was a song of adoration to a god. This can be seen in the Homeric hymns,[7] but also in a later example, such as Cleanthes's *Hymn to Zeus*.[8] Performance of a hymn addressed to a god was even the focus of competitions in the ancient world.[9] In Stephen Fowl's investigation of New Testament hymns, he discusses perspectives that early Christians may have had of hymns. Although the word they used was the same, there are differences in usage that must be considered. When the hymn was introduced into New Testament literature, the sense was radically altered from its previous usage. For instance, although the Greek meaning of hymn was

---

5. The argument that the first word, ὅς (*hos*), is an indication that the "quotation" is drawn from a larger text could also be evidence for Paul's role as an interpreter in his use of language. Paul may refer to the neuter word "mystery" in the opening statement by using the masculine relative pronoun ὅς, *hos* since a similar shift from neuter to masculine is found in Col 2:2 ("in order that they may know the mystery of God, namely Christ") where the author *personifies* the mystery as the person of Christ.

6. Martin, "Aspects of Worship," 14–17. For much more recent treatments, see Fowl, *The Story of Christ*, 31–45; and Gordley, *New Testament Christological Hymns*, esp. 7–37.

7. Allen and Sikes, *Homeric Hymns*.

8. See no. 537 in von Arnim, ed., *Stoicorum veterum fragmenta*.

9. See Henderson, "Ancient Greek Music," 363, who says, "'The First Delphic Hymn' or paean to Apollo . . . was composed almost certainly in the later second century BC and written in the 'vocal' notation on stone at Delphi, where it must have won a prize in the Pythian festival." For a recent treatment of this subject, see West, *Ancient Greek Music*, 14–21.

a song of adoration *to a god*, the passage in 1 Timothy is not addressed *to God* but is written in such a way that it is specifically *about Christ*. From the perspective of a Greek-speaking Jew, a hymn might represent what is found in the headings of some of the Psalms that are not songs of praise but are nonetheless addressed *to God*. Here again the same distinction must be made, and that is that the 1 Timothy passage is not addressed *to God* but is *about Christ*.[10] Using these Greek and Jewish definitions, 1 Tim 3:16 would not strictly be considered a hymn. However, Fowl comments that the term hymn can still be used for what we find in 3:16, for the definition is "the construction of a later, critical community, and not a straightforward translation of ὕμνος in either its specific or generic sense."[11] As a result, the passage in 3:16 might still be called a hymn, but a hymn in a new sense. This hymn is perhaps one of the early templates for Christian hymns, a pattern that can be seen in hymns of the Christian faith throughout the centuries to follow.[12]

The structure and language of this hymn are also indicators of the interpretive role in which the writer is engaged, for 1 Tim 3:16 uses a different style of writing that sets it apart from the rest of the letter.[13] The writing is extremely compact, using a total of eighteen words in six lines. Some commentators divide these lines into three groups of two lines each, and some divide it into two groups of three lines each, but in either case, the writing is distinctly poetical.[14] However, the content of these six lines is expansive, summarizing six events in which Christ is central. The use of the six verbs in the passive voice are a means by which Christ is understood as the grammatical subject of each phrase. This may be a new way of writing a hymn, that is, using language to poignantly highlight important events that are focused on Christ but are not written as though addressed to him. Paul may have reinvented the procedure of hymn writing as he interpreted the story of Christ in these six brief and memorable lines.

Finally, the context of 1 Timothy in which this hymn is placed has implications for the role of Paul as an interpreter. The simple fact that this hymn was placed within the letter provides not only an insight into the

10. Fowl, *The Story of Christ*, 31–34.

11. Fowl, *The Story of Christ*, 33.

12. See also chapter 12 below. Cf. Gordley, *New Testament Christological Hymns*, 183–90 (esp. 184–85).

13. See Norden, *Agnostos Theos*, 250–63.

14. See Martin, "Aspects of Worship," 22–26.

author's view of the story of Christ, but also how he saw it functioning within the larger context of the letter.[15] For the sake of brevity, I will mention just one point. Throughout 1 Timothy, a recurring subject is that of negative forms of speech, such as "meaningless talk" (1:6), "malicious talkers" (3:11), "godless myths and old wives' tales" (4:7), "gossips and busybodies" (5:13), "unhealthy interest in controversies and quarrels about words . . . malicious talk" (6:4–5), and "godless chatter" (6:20). The emphasis here seems to prompt Paul to invoke not only several "trustworthy sayings," which may stem from earlier sources,[16] but also the hymn in 3:16, which may well be his own. The hymn can be seen as a means to oppose the then current hold that asceticism had on the church, as well as the generally destructive effects of negative speech among its members.[17] The succinct and poetical nature of the words of the hymn, particularly apparent in its Greek form with its six passive verbs, makes it a hymn that is highly memorable and easy to say (or sing), even though the content of the hymn still engages scholars 2000 years later.

P.OXY. XV 1786: A CHRISTIAN HYMN WITH MUSICAL NOTATION (THIRD CENTURY)

The second example is the oldest Christian hymn with musical notation, a papyrus fragment that initially generated significant scholarly discussion and now has re-emerged as an important text for consideration in the development of the early church.[18]

The Text

```
1        ]ομου πασσι τε θεου λογιμοι δε[.].[.]αι. . .ν[
2        ο]υ ταν ηω σιγατω μηδ' αστρα φαεσφορα χ[.]ζε
3  [σ]θων [εx]ολειπ[οντων] ρ[ιπαι πνοιων πηγαι] ποταμων ροθιων
                                πασαι υμνουντων δ' ημων
4  [π]ατερα χυιον χαγιον πνευμα πασαι δυναμεις επιφωνουντων
                                αμην αμην κρατος αινος
5  [αει και δοξα θεωι] δ[ωτ]η[ρι] μονωι παντων αγαθων αμην
                                                    αμην[19]
```

15. Fowl, *The Story of Christ*, 175–94.
16. See the discussion in Knight, *Faithful Sayings*, 148–52.
17. See Guthrie, *Pastoral Epistles*, 39–43, esp. 42–43.
18. See "P.Oxy. XV 1786."
19. This reading of the text, visually representing the lines as they are on the

Martin L. West's translation, supplemented with the first line provided by Charles H. Cosgrove, is as follows:

> ... together all the eminent ones of God ... Let it be silent, let the luminous stars not shine, let the winds(?) and all the noisy rivers die down; and as we hymn the Father, the Son, and the Holy Spirit, let all the powers add 'Amen, amen.' Empire, praise always, and glory to God, the sole giver of all good things. Amen, amen.[20]

Eric Werner translates it,

> ... all splendid creations of God ... must not keep silent, nor shall the light-bearing stars remain behind. . . . All waves of thundering streams shall praise our Father and Son, and Holy Ghost, all powers shall join in: Amen, Amen! Rule and Praise (and Glory) to the sole Giver of all Good. Amen, Amen."[21]

The Composer

It is unknown who originally wrote this hymn or who wrote it down with its musical notation, but it is dated to the latter part of the third century.[22] The fact that the hymn was written down may suggest that it had been known previously, for the passing on of music was largely by means of

---

papyrus fragment, is largely that of Pöhlmann and West, eds., *Documents*, 191, and substantially the same in most regards with Cosgrove, *Ancient Christian Hymn*, 37. The major areas of difference between their two editions, understandably, are at the ends of lines 1 and 2 (reconstructions are included within square brackets). I use a more recent edition here than was originally presented in West, "Analecta Musica," 47, who followed Egert Pöhlmann, due to subsequent examination and analysis by the authors involved. Pöhlmann, ed. (*Denkmäler altgriechischer Musik*, 106–9) includes a reconstruction of the first two lines of the text, with translation, as follows:

[Σὲ πατὲρ κόσμων, πατὲρ αἰώνων, μέλπωμεν] ὁμοῦ πᾶσαί τε θεοῦ λόγμοι δο[ῦλα]ι. [ὅσ]α κ[όσμος]
  [ἔχει πρὸς ἐπουρανίωνι ἁγίῳ σελάων πρ]υτανήῳ, σιγάτω, μηδ' ἄαστρα φαεσφόρα λ[αμπ]έ-
  ... [Father of the world, Father eternal, celebrate with song and dance as one all creatures of God, notable slaves. As far as the world has toward the holy heaven shine to the president(?), be not silent stars shine ...]

20. West, *Ancient Greek Music*, 325; Cosgrove, *Ancient Christian Hymn*, 37.

21. Werner, "Music," 467–68.

22. See the original edition of this papyrus in Hunt and Jones, "1786. Christian Hymn," 21, which has been reaffirmed in the latest edition by Cosgrove, *Ancient Christian Hymn*, v.

oral tradition and this would have been the means to preserve the hymn. In that case, it may represent beliefs and musical practices of the church from some time earlier than the late third century. There is also some reason to believe, however, that the hymn was a new composition.[23] In either case, the hymn is representative of at least some aspects of the music of the Christian church in the latter part of the third century.

The Work

This musical fragment was found written on the back of a papyrus that had earlier been used to record an account for purchase of corn. The fragment was analyzed and first published in 1922 in one of the volumes by two of the great early papyrologists, Bernard P. Grenfell and Arthur S. Hunt, with this particular fragment edited by Hunt and another classicist, H. Stuart Jones. Hunt and Jones called it a "Christian Hymn with Musical Notation" in that first publication and, to this day, this particular fragment, known as P.Oxy. XV 1786,[24] remains the earliest known Christian hymn with musical notation (although some recently edited documents may have some bearing on this particular claim).[25]

There is much discussion about the foundations of the hymn itself. Scholars such as Hunt and Jones came from a classical background and commented on the Greek influence that they saw in the text and in the notation of the hymn. They provided some clues as to its environment (found as it was in Oxyrhynchus, Egypt), its function, and even its possible sound. The papyrus with its musical notation was thought to give insight into hymns and hymn writing of the third-century Christian church, and possibly earlier. However, a question that must be raised is how the text of the hymn fits with statements by some scholars that nonbiblical texts were not used in the Christian church at this time. Was this, perhaps, considered a "biblical" text at the time?[26]

---

23. West suggests this by his reference to the composer having studied the works of the composer Mesomedes (see "Analecta Musica," 50).

24. Hunt and Jones, "1786. Christian Hymn," 21–25.

25. There is now the possibility that the newly edited fragments of P.Oxy. LXV 4462, which are dated to the second century, could fit in this category. See West, "Texts with Musical Notation," 88, where he writes, "It looks as if these verses may have been of a philosophical or religious cast," and remarks on similarities to Gregory of Nazianzus, Carm. 2.2.4.55.

26. Massey H. Shepherd writes about "the reaction in orthodox circles, about the turn of the third century, against the use in the liturgy of all nonbiblical psalms and

Towards the middle of the twentieth century, scholars such as Eric Werner began to argue for an almost exclusively Jewish background to, and influence on, the hymn. Werner posited that the formulaic "Amen, Amen" found near the end and again at the very end of the musical fragment had been taken over almost directly from Jewish chant. He based his statement on the melismatic characteristics of the music on the words "Amen, Amen" and on the corresponding melismatic nature of Jewish chant."[27] However, in West's more recently published editions of new fragments of texts with musical notation, he writes that two of the new texts "reveal that the evolution of the melisma had gone further by the third century than we were aware."[28] In other words, the use of more than one note for a syllable, found on the "amen, amen" of P.Oxy. XV 1786, is now thought to have been used much earlier in Greek music than was previously thought. Cosgrove provides a chart that records statistics for use of melisma in manuscripts from the second to fourth centuries and concludes that "These figures suggest an increasing tendency toward the use of melisma with the passage of time."[29] This calls into question the positions of both Werner, who, based on the use of melismatic formulas or several notes per syllable in Jewish music, posited that this was a specifically Jewish feature,[30] and Egon Wellesz, who argued that the hymn must be specifically Syrian in background, also because of the melismatic nature of Syrian music.[31]

The system of notation used in this hymn is generally agreed to be Greek. The notes are roughly equivalent to a modern tenor part, ranging an octave from F below middle C to F above middle C.[32] The symbols

---

hymns. It was not until the middle of the fourth century that Christian hymnody once more blossomed in the church's worship" ("Hymns," 668). This does raise some questions as to what status this particular hymn had in the context of the Christian church: was it acceptable in the church liturgy or was it perhaps only used in a private context?

27. Werner, "Music," 467. Melisma refers to the use of multiple notes per syllable of text, as compared with the restrictive use of one note to each syllable.

28. West, "Texts with Musical Notation," 81.

29. Cosgrove, *Ancient Musical Hymn*, 103.

30. Various other studies have also called into question the notion of a predominantly Jewish influence, e.g., Smith, "Ancient Synagogue"; McKinnon, "On the Question of Psalmody"; and addressed in McKinnon, ed., *Music in Early Christian Literature*; see also West, "Analecta Musica," 47–54.

31. Wellesz, *History of Byzantine Music*, 152–56 (esp. 155–56).

32. Cosgrove, *Ancient Christian Hymn*, 88, 117, who argues for the equivalent of a baritone voice, with an octave range of C# before middle C to C# above middle C,

used for vocal notation, at least in this range of the voice, are taken basically from the Greek alphabet, with increasing adaptation of the letters as one moves further away from the middle range, either higher or lower.[33] The symbols used in P.Oxy. XV 1786 are written above the words and are recognizable letters, such as: R Φ C O ξ I Z E (they are written in majuscule letters approximating to the appearance of those used here). The rough equivalent of these notes to modern ones are R = F; Φ = G; C = A; O = B; ξ = C; I = D; Z = E; E = F (these correspondences would need to be adjusted if Cosgrove is correct). Other signs that are found indicate rests, lengthening of notes, and legato. Because of the lacunae, scholars have offered various reconstructions and readings of both the text and the musical notation.[34]

Questions of Interpretation

Hunt and Jones summarized the contents of the hymn as the following: "Creation at large is called upon to join in a chorus of praise to Father, Son, and Holy Spirit, and the concluding passage is the usual ascription of power and glory to the 'only giver of all good gifts.'"[35] Similarly, Cosgrove states the following:

> The natural elements are summoned to silence in preparation for the church's offering of praise to the Trinity. The angelic powers are called upon to respond to this praise with amens and a doxology. The call for the natural elements (including stars) to be still and the command that the angelic powers answer with a doxology give the church's praise of the Trinity a cosmic scope.[36]

A doxology, such as this "usual ascription" might be termed, was already well established in the Christian church by this time. M. Alfred Bichsel writes that the lesser doxologies, such as the Latin *Gloria Patri*

---

while acknowledging that pitch would have varied according to performance without use of a fixed pitch instrument. See also Pöhlmann and West, eds., *Documents*, 191, who place the melody upon the treble clef.

33. West, "Analecta Musica," 36–42.

34. Besides those mentioned above, see, e.g., Reinach, *La Musique Grecque*, 207–8; Mountford, "Greek Music," 177; Pöhlmann, *Denkmäler altgriechischer Musik*, 106–9; and for discussion of the origin or adaptation of the musical notation, see West, "Analecta Musica," 36–46.

35. Hunt and Jones, "1786. Christian Hymn," 22.

36. Cosgrove, *Ancient Christian Hymn*, 63.

("Glory be to the Father, and to the Son, and to the Holy Spirit: as it was in the beginning is now, and ever shall be, world without end. Amen"), were already in use in Rome at the time of Clement (ca. 91), and that in later centuries a doxology was used after each psalm.[37] It is possible that this is how the doxology at the end of the hymn fragment is being formulaically used but it also suggests that the writer was integrating the Old Testament-like sections (see below) with the doxology, but clearly placing the hymn within the Christian tradition by referring to "the Father, the Son, and the Holy Spirit."

Werner states that the "scriptural influence upon this composition is undeniable,"[38] and mentions three psalms whose influence can be seen: Pss 93:3–4; 148:4; and 19:1–2.[39]

Ps 93:3–4	LXX (92:3–4)
The seas have lifted up, Lord,	ἐπῆραν οἱ ποταμοί, Κύριε,
The seas have lifted up their voice;	ἐπῆραν οἱ ποταμοὶ φωνὰς αὐτῶν.
The seas have lifted up their pounding waves	ἀπὸ φωνῶν ὑδάτων πολλῶν θαυμαστοὶ
Mightier than the thunder of the great waters	οἱ μετεωρισμοὶ τῆς θαλάσσης·
Mightier than the breakers of the sea— the Lord on high is mighty.	θαυμαστὸς ἐν ὑψηλοῖς ὁ κύριος.

Ps 148:4	LXX (148:4)
Praise him, you highest heavens	Αἰνεῖτε αὐτόν, οἱ οὐρανοὶ τῶν οὐρανῶν,
and you waters above the skies.	καὶ τὸ ὕδωρ τὸ ὑπεράνω τῶν οὐρανῶν.

Ps 19:1–2	LXX (18:2–3)
The heavens declare the glory of God;	Οἱ οὐρανοὶ διηγοῦνται δόξαν θεοῦ,

37. Bichsel, "Hymns, Early Christian," 351.
38. Werner, "Music," 467.
39. But here it must be remembered that this perceived influence is particularly dependent upon his translation, as opposed to West's and Cosgrove's, and that West is a classicist and a specialist in ancient Greek musical documents and Cosgrove is a specialist in the New Testament and music. Both West's and Cosgrove's translations, which negate the participation of all the elements, have quite a different focus than that found in these psalms. Cosgrove, *An Ancient Christian Hymn*, 39, recognizes that Pss 19 and 148, along with 47, 69, and 96, suggest the idea of the praise of nature; 50, as well as Ps 148:2 LXX indicating heavenly beings as powers.

the skies proclaim the work of his hands.	ποίησιν δὲ χειρῶν αὐτοῦ ἀναγγέλλει τὸ στερέωμα.
Day after day they pour forth speech;	ἡμέρα τῇ ἡμέρᾳ ἐρεύγεται ῥῆμα,
night after night they display knowledge.	καὶ νὺξ νυκτὶ ἀναγγέλλει γνῶσιν.

Several influences that Werner does not mention, however, are, for instance, Rev 5:13, which includes part of the doxology:

> Then I heard every creature in heaven and on earth and under the earth and on the sea, and all that is in them, singing, "To him who sits on the throne and to the Lamb be praise and honor and glory and *power, for ever* and ever!"
>
> καὶ πᾶν κτίσμα ὃ ἐν τῷ οὐρανῷ καὶ ἐπὶ τῆς γῆς καὶ ὑποκάτω τῆς γῆς καὶ ἐπὶ τῆς θαλάσσης καὶ τὰ ἐν αὐτοῖς πάντα ἤκουσα λέγοντας,
> Τῷ καθημένῳ ἐπὶ τῷ θρόνῳ καὶ τῷ ἀρνίῳ
> ἡ εὐλογία καὶ ἡ τιμὴ καὶ ἡ δόξα καὶ τὸ κράτος
> εἰς τοὺς αἰῶνας τῶν αἰώνων.

and Rev 7:11b–12:

> They fell down on their faces before the throne and worshiped God, saying: "*Amen*! Praise and *glory* and wisdom and thanks and honor and *power* and strength be *to our God* for ever and ever. *Amen*!"
>
> καὶ ἔπεσαν ἐνώπιον τοῦ θρόνου ἐπὶ τὰ πρόσωπα αὐτῶν καὶ προσεκύνησαν τῷ θεῷ λέγοντες,
> Ἀμήν, ἡ εὐλογία καὶ ἡ δόξα καὶ ἡ σοφία καὶ ἡ εὐχαριστία καὶ ἡ τιμὴ καὶ ἡ δύναμις καὶ ἡ ἰσχὺς τῷ θεῷ ἡμῶν εἰς τοὺς αἰῶνας τῶν αἰώνων · ἀμήν.

There are also some echoes of 1 Tim 1:17:

> Now to the King *eternal*, immortal, invisible, *the only God*, be honor and *glory for ever* and ever. *Amen*.
>
> Τῷ δὲ βασιλεῖ τῶν αἰώνων, ἀφθάρτῳ ἀοράτῳ μόνῳ θεῷ, τιμὴ καὶ δόξα εἰς τοὺς αἰῶνας τῶν αἰώνων, ἀμήν

While there are only six examples of the use of some lexical form of the word ὑμνέω in the Greek New Testament (Matt 26:30; Mark 14:26; Acts 16:25; Eph 5:19; Col 3:16; Heb 2:12), there are many examples of it in the Septuagint. However, it is unclear whether there is significant influence from the Septuagint on this hymn, or whether the hymn reflects the later writings of the New Testament and perhaps other writings of the period. There is certainly some similarity with other hymn-like writing that precedes or is roughly contemporary with P.Oxy. XV 1786, such as where Clement of Alexandria writes of Terpander's hymn to Zeus: "Zeus, beginning of all, ruler of all, Zeus, to you I send this beginning of hymns."[40]

That textual criticism is a significant factor in determining even the basic reading of this text is seen in the different glosses of West/Cosgrove and Werner. In West's and Cosgrove's versions, the created elements are commanded to cease their normal activity while the created beings "hymn" God, a common use of the term in Greek hymns.[41] In contrast, in Werner's version, the created elements are commanded to marshal their forces in the acclamation of praise to God. If West's and Cosgrove's translations of the fragmentary text are more accurate, then the Old Testament influence is less obvious at this point, since there are very few prayers in the Old Testament that command silence (but see Hab 2:20, "But the Lord is in his holy temple; let all the earth be silent before him"). However, in Cleanthes's *Hymn to Zeus*, the statement in lines 38-39, "For neither men nor gods have any greater privilege than this: to sing for ever in righteousness of the universal law,"[42] suggests by inference that only humans and gods have this privilege of hymning God.[43] Conversely, the reading of Werner, or of Hunt and Jones's original summary of "Creation at large" being "called upon to join in a chorus of praise to Father, Son, and Holy Spirit" brings the Old Testament influence more to the forefront; for instance, Ps 148:5 calls upon all creation to "praise the name of the Lord," with all manner of created beings and heavenly bodies and elements called upon to praise the name of the Lord.

---

40. See no. 59 in McKinnon, ed., *Music in Early Christian Literature*, 35, citing Clement of Alexandria, *Str.* 6.11.88. Cf. Cosgrove, *Ancient Christian Hymn*, who cites some but not all of the above, along with drawing attention to a number of other reference, although usually not sustained passages.

41. For phrasing similar to "hymn God," see Thom, *Cleanthes' Hymn to Zeus*, line 6 (See no. 537 in von Arnim, ed. *Stoicorum veterum fragmenta*): "Therefore I shall hymn you and sing forever of your might" (translation taken from Long and Sedley, *Hellenistic Philosophers*, 2:54).

42. See no. 537 in von Arnim, ed. *Stoicorum veterum fragmenta* (translation taken from Long and Sedley, *Hellenistic Philosophers*, 2:54).

43. In contrast, the powers in P.Oxy. XV 1786 are commanded only to add "Amen, Amen."

PART TWO: MUSICAL TRADITIONS AND INTERPRETATIONS

In either case, this hymn seems to have some roots in the words of a psalm, some in verses such as are found in Revelation, and some in the language of Greek hymn writers. There are three distinct elements that distinguish the final form of this hymn. First, the composer in his interpretation of his sources, has changed reference from "the Lord," which is found in the psalms of the Hebrew Bible or Old Testament, to "the Father, Son and Holy Spirit," which incorporates a distinctly Christian element into this hymn. Secondly, he has integrated the Old and New Testaments rather than simply citing the Old Testament. Thirdly, he has incorporated language that is characteristic of sources such as Cleanthes's *Hymn to Zeus*. The result is that the composer of this hymn seems to have synthesized and reinterpreted earlier documents in an unprecedented way.

JOHN SHEPPARD: *VERBUM CARO FACTUM EST* ("THE WORD WAS MADE FLESH") (SIXTEENTH CENTURY)

I now turn from the third century to the height of sixteenth-century English music at the time of the English Reformation, with a selection by the composer John Sheppard.

The Text[44]

Verbum caro factum est	The word was made flesh
et habitavit in nobis:	and dwelt among us:
cuius gloriam vidimus	and we beheld his glory
quasi unigeniti a patre,	as of the only Son of the Father,
plenum gratae et veritatis (John 1:14)	full of grace and truth (John 1:14)
In principio erat verbum	In the beginning was the Word,
et verbum erat apud Deum,	and the Word was with God,
et Deus erat Verbum (John 1:1)	and the Word was God (John 1:1)
Gloria Patri et Filio et Spiritui Sancto (Doxology).	Glory be to the Father and to the Son and to the Holy Spirit (Doxology).

---

44. A similar but not identical form of this text can be found in the Catholic Church's *Liber Usualis Missae et Officii*, 357. The text reads as follows (with repetitions not indicated here): *Verbum caro factus est, et habitavit in nobis: et vidimus gloriam ejus, gloriam quasi Unigeniti a Patre, plenum gratiae et veritatis. Omnia per ipsum facto sunt, et sine ipso factum est nihil. Gloria Patri, et Filio, et Spiritui Sancto.* The John 1:1 text of the second part of Sheppard's setting is found in the first verse of Lesson IX, which follows the respond.

The Composer

John Sheppard was born as early as 1512,[45] or as late as 1520,[46] and died ca. 1559/60. He composed his music during the shift from Latin to the English vernacular in the Reformation in Britain. There is little documented about his life, but he is known to have been Master of the Choristers at Magdalen College, Oxford, in 1542.[47] As far as his musical output, however, Peter le Huray says that "In terms of sheer quantity Shepherd has no mid sixteenth-century rival."[48] Because much of his music has only been systematically published in more recent years, little has been known about it.[49] Today, Sheppard's music is increasingly being included in the standard repertoire of cathedral, church, and college choirs.

The Work

Sheppard's settings of responsories are a significant part of his oeuvre. Hugh Benham writes that the responds of Sheppard "contain some of his most impressive writing,"[50] part of the significance being in the fact that of the 16 choral responds, 12 of them are settings of texts that had not previously been set.[51] In the setting of *Verbum caro factum est*, we have one of those early settings.[52] The manuscript that includes this Latin respond-motet is housed at Christ Church, Oxford,[53] and the work is set for six voice-parts: treble, mean, alto 1, alto 2, tenor, and bass.[54] The

---

45. Sheppard, *John Sheppard I*, ix–xi (esp. ix).

46. Benham, *Latin Church Music*, 195.

47. Le Huray, *Music and the Reformation*, 208.

48. Le Huray, *Music and the Reformation*, 208.

49. This is largely due to the fact that entire parts of his music are missing, a common problem in music of this period, partly because of the practice of writing separate parts in separate books and, it is thought, partly because of the destruction that took place in the sixteenth century in English churches and cathedrals during the turmoil of the Reformation.

50. Benham, *Latin Church Music*, 197.

51. Benham, *Latin Church Music*, 197; see also Harrison, *Music in Medieval Britain*, 366–81 (esp. 370–72).

52. See Hofman and Morehen, eds., *Latin Music*, 174, who list only two settings of this Latin text known in British sources at this time, citing Sheppard's as the earliest setting, followed by only one other, that of (Edward?) Blancks (ca. 1550–633).

53. See Christ Church Mus 979, Christ Church, University of Oxford.

54. The tenor part of this setting is lost, but Harrison writes that "thanks to the monorhythmic method of writing the plainsong . . . it is possible to reconstruct with

setting is for Christmas Day, the ninth respond at Matins[55] (or the third respond of the third nocturn), and the processional respond at Mass.

There is a long history of responsorial psalmody, of which the responsory is a later development and variation. St Augustine, for instance, describes a psalm that is sung by a soloist, and mentions that the congregation responds with a short interjection, although the exact nature of this interjection is not known. It is thought that, at this time, an entire psalm was sung. Later, the psalm became abbreviated, until eventually a single verse of a psalm was used. Dom Gregory Murray writes that "the regular form of a responsorial chant is that after the whole has been sung, the first section is repeated as far as the beginning of the verse."[56] However, he also observes that "the Roman method was to repeat the whole of the first part of a responsory, while the Gallican method (which now prevails in the Divine Office) was to repeat only the last clause of the R[esponse] after the V[erse]."[57] Later, texts other than the Psalms were treated in a similar way. Benham defines a respond during the fifteenth and sixteenth centuries as

> a chant which followed a lesson, often commenting on it in some way . . . Every respond consisted of two main parts, the "response" (begun by a soloist or small group of soloists and continued by the choir) and the verse or verses (solo throughout). At its simplest the pattern was response, verse, latter part of response repeated . . . The third, sixth and ninth responds at Matins, and those at Vespers normally had the first part of the Gloria Patri as a second verse sung to the same melody as the first, after the repeat of the response; this was followed by a second, often shorter repeat . . .[58]

---

certainty those responds in which the cantus firmus was in the tenor," and lists *Verbum caro factum est* as being one of those responds that has been reconstructed in this way (see *Music in Medieval Britain*, 370–71).

55. Note that in the *Liber Usualis Missae et Officii*, 357, it is indicated as "Resp. 8."
56. Murray, *Choral Chants*, 16.
57. Murray, *Choral Chants*, 16.
58. Benham, *Latin Church Music*, 17–18. See also Hughes, *Medieval Manuscripts*, 26–33; Apel, *Gregorian Chant*, 95–96, 182. See also Harrison, *Music in Medieval Britain*, 61, where he writes the following description: "Though the antiphon and the respond both had their origin in the early forms of psalmody, they had, in general, distinct forms and ritual functions in the Middle Ages. While the antiphons were choral chants sung with a psalm the responds were more elaborate chants sung after lessons. Hence Matins with nine lessons had also nine responds. In its normal form a respond was begun by one or a few singers and continued by the choir; then the verse was sung

This corresponds to the pattern that we see in Sheppard's setting. However, he sets the text in such a way that the reading of it is significant. This is in contrast to some settings where the common use of the style of the responsory or respond in Psalm texts progressively abbreviated the response of the choir until the text was unintelligible as a whole.[59]

The Interpretation

The text of Sheppard's responsory is short and comes from two verses in the New Testament as well as part of a traditional doxology of the Christian church, known as the Lesser Doxology, which is included here in its traditional manner for the third respond of a nocturn (see above). The verses are quoted from the Latin Vulgate, the first being John 1:14, and the second John 1:1. The third is the doxology, which is not unlike the text of the baptismal command in Matt 28:19. As mentioned above, one of Sheppard's significant contributions is that of setting to polyphonic music texts that had not otherwise been set in this manner. This particular setting represents one of those contributions, and the very nature of its setting contributes to a new way of reading the text, for even though it follows a familiar pattern, the pattern would have existed in the form of chant and not in a combination of polyphony and chant. The setting of John 1:14 and John 1:1 alternates between a single chant line, sung by three soloists in unison, and the polyphonic setting of all six voices, with the plainchant as *cantus firmus*. The use of this alternating pattern of chant and polyphony can also be seen, for instance, in the works of Sheppard's contemporary, Thomas Tallis. Benham's description of a responsory above corresponds basically with Sheppard's setting of this passage, but Benham continues:

> The earliest settings of responds, as of Alleluias, had polyphony for the solo sections. Choral treatment began much later than in the case of Alleluias, in Taverner's day . . . It is almost certain that Taverner's *Dum transisset* I and II are the first choral responds; but Tallis and Sheppard made the major contributions to the type, treating some sixteen new texts between them.[60]

---

by the soloist or soloists and the respond was repeated from mid-point by the chorus. The third, sixth and ninth responds at Matins, i.e., the third respond of each nocturn, were distinguished by the singing of the first half of the *Gloria patri* (to the same music as the verse) after the repeat, followed by the same or a still shorter repeat."

59. See Hughes, *Medieval Manuscripts*, 27, who mentions that this practice of abbreviation occurred already in the ninth century.

60. Benham, *Latin Church Music*, 18.

Paul Doe writes that, before the first half of the sixteenth century, "Earlier Responsory settings had been limited to a very small number of texts, mostly for Compline or certain ceremonies, in which only the solo parts of the plainsong were set in polyphony. These new festal Responsories, however, are fundamentally different in that they set the choral part of the chant," referring specifically to the "transfer of polyphony from solo to choral chant, and the clear presentation of the plainsong as an equal-note *cantus firmus*."[61] Sheppard's use of this new distribution of polyphony and plainchant between the parts, and his setting of the John passage, are the means by which he takes traditional elements and very subtly reworks them into a new interpretive work.

Within the individual lines of the polyphonic section of this work, Sheppard makes use of the highest note of each voice range to set up a formal and symmetrical pattern of emphasis.[62] This use of the highest note in the upper four voices is clearly symmetrical between the three sections of the John 1:14 text: the highest note in the treble is used four times in section I, once in section II, and four times in section III; the highest note in the mean is used three times in section I, five times in section II, and three times in section III; in the first alto part, the usage of the highest note is three times in section I, four times in section II, and three times in section III; and in the second alto part, the usage is evenly divided between the three sections, being used three times in each. The specific plan in evidence here is further supplemented in that each of these four upper voices uses the upper note of its range the same number of times: thirteen in each. In the lowest two voices, tenor and bass, the use of the highest note is heard only three times, and in this case, the division is spread between the two voices: the bass uses it in section I, the tenor in section II, and the bass again in section III. It is difficult to determine the exact meaning of this structure, but it certainly suggests that Sheppard worked out his presentation of music and this text with great care and attention to detail. The combination of the use of the highest notes of the individual six lines with the corresponding syllables of the words (where at least in three instances the highest note is used) gives a reading of the text that is emphasized or highlighted as follows:

---

61. Doe, "Latin Polyphony," 93–94.

62. See Porter, *Early English Composers and the Credo*, for more detailed treatment of emphasis and interpretation in the settings of composers John Taverner, Christopher Tye, Thomas Tallis, John Sheppard, and William Byrd.

I	Verbum caro factum est et habi*ta*vit in *n*obis; (The *word* was made flesh and *dwelt* among *us*)
II	*cui*us *glori*am vidimus *qua*si unigeniti a *pat*re, (and *we* his *glory* beheld *as of* the only Son of the *Father*)
III	plenum *gra*tiae et veritatis. (full of *grace* and *truth*)

A fairly natural reading of the text can be seen to be held in high esteem, although at this late stage in the development of Latin polyphony one might expect to see more focus simply on musical elaboration and perhaps even a disregard for the text.

There are also several elements of Sheppard's setting that make use of the unique features of responsories in order to reshape these particular texts. John 1:14 is the verse that is treated polyphonically, while the other two verses are sung in chant by the three designated soloists.[63] The pattern of repetition in the text is as follows:

> The word was made flesh and dwelt among us
>   and dwelt among us
>   and dwelt among us
> We beheld his glory as of the only Son
> as of the only Son
> as of the only Son of the Father
> of the Father
> Full of grace and truth
> and truth and truth and truth
> and truth and truth.
>
> *In the beginning was the word and the word was with God and the word was God.*
>
> We beheld his glory as of the only Son
> as of the only Son
> as of the only Son of the Father
> of the Father
> Full of grace and truth
> and truth and truth and truth
> and truth and truth.
>
> *Glory be to the Father and to the Son and to the Holy Spirit.*

---

63. As mentioned above, this is in contrast to the standard practice of setting the soloists' parts in polyphony and the response part in plainchant.

Full of grace and truth
and truth and truth and truth
and truth and truth.

Sheppard, using the techniques of a responsory, gives increasing prominence to the second and third parts of John 1:14. By giving this text a polyphonic setting and inverting the traditional choral pattern, Sheppard has given increasing prominence to the penultimate phrase that is sung by the choir in full polyphony—"full of grace"—and even more prominence to the final phrase, "of truth," by its many repetitions. In John 1:14, the words "we beheld his glory as of the only Son of the Father" follow directly after the preceding phrase "the word was made flesh and dwelt among us," but in the second setting, a new context is set up that reads, "In the beginning was the word and the word was with God and the word was God / we beheld his glory as of the only Son of the Father." This is then taken one further step in the last section, where "and we beheld his glory as of the only Son of the Father / full of grace and truth" now reads "Glory be to the Father and to the Son and to the Holy Spirit / full of grace and truth." Similarly, this drawing of attention back to the text of John 1:14 is a means of giving full focus to this verse as fundamental to the reading of the other two texts. Sheppard has taken a liturgical practice and applied it to a text that had not been set polyphonically in this way. In doing so, he has provided a new perspective on this New Testament text.

J. S. BACH: *DER GEIST HILFT UNSER SCHWACHHEIT AUF* ("THE SPIRIT HELPS US IN OUR WEAKNESS," BWV 226) (EIGHTEENTH CENTURY)

I now move to the eighteenth century and the great German composer, Johann Sebastian Bach, and examine briefly one of his motets.

The Text

Der Geist hilft unser Schwachheit auf	The Spirit helps us in our weakness.
denn wir wissen nicht, was wir beten sollen, wie sichs gebühret;	We do not know what we ought to pray
sondern der Geist selbst vertritt uns aufs beste	but the Spirit himself intercedes for us
mit unaussprechlichem Seufzen (Rom 8:26).	with groans that words cannot express (Rom 8:26).

Der aber die Herzen forschet,	And he who searches our hearts
der weiß, was des Geistes Sinn sei;	knows the mind of the Spirit,
denn er vertritt die Heiligen nach dem,	because the Spirit intercedes for the saints
das Gott gefallet (Rom 8:27).	in accordance with God's will (Rom 8:27).
Du heilige Brunst, süßer Trost,	Look down, Holy Dove, Spirit bow;
nun hilf uns, frohlich und getrost	Descend from heav'n and help us now:
in deinem Dienst beständig bleiben,	Inspire our hearts while humbly kneeling,
die Trübsal uns nicht abtreiben.	To pray with zeal and contrite feeling!
O Herr, durch dein Kraft uns bereit	Prepare us, through Thy cleansing pow'r
und stärk des Fleisches Blödigkeit	For death, at life's expiring hour:
daß wir hie ritterlich ringen,	That we may find the grave a portal
durch Tod und Leben zu dir dringen	To Thee in heav'n, and life immortal!
Halleluja, halleluja (Martin Luther).	Hallelujah! Hallelujah! (Martin Luther).

The Composer

The name Johann Sebastian Bach seems to be universally known. In fact, it would be surprising to meet someone who had not heard of Johann Sebastian Bach and did not know something about him, and yet this composer's work still merits further study and exploration. This man, who lived from 1685 to 1750 and was not the first choice for the position of choirmaster at the Thomasschule in Leipzig, is today revered simply as one of the greatest, if not *the* greatest, of composers. As incomprehensible as it seems today, after his death, much of his music was forgotten. Among others, Felix Bartholdy-Mendelssohn can be given credit for re-introducing Bach's *St Matthew Passion*,[64] and thus sparking a revived interest in Bach's choral works. Bach's settings of both the *St Matthew Passion* and the *St John Passion*, as well as his *Mass in B Minor*, are substantial works that, appropriately, are now often performed. His works for

---

64. The performance took place on March 11, 1829, in the Berlin Singakademie (see Schweitzer, *J. S. Bach*, 1:241–43 [esp. 242]). For a very interesting account of the events leading up to the performance and the evening itself, as recounted by Eduard Devrient, who handled the business negotiations and also sang the part of Christ in the performance, see David and Mendel, eds., *Bach Reader*, 376–86.

organ are part of the standard repertoire of the great organists. His cantatas, although perhaps infrequently used in liturgical settings outside the Lutheran context, nonetheless are included in many choral repertoires and performed as part of sacred or secular musical concerts. Pianists like Edwin Fischer in the early part of the twentieth century reintroduced the concertos for keyboard by performing them in several concerts (and recording them) in 1933–1938 in Berlin,[65] and Claudio Arrau, in a series of 12 recitals in 1935–1936, also in Berlin, performed all of Bach's keyboard works, introducing some if not most of them for the first time to the general public of the twentieth century. Glenn Gould, arguably one of the most remarkable and intellectual pianists of the twentieth century, can be heard using a concert venue as the platform from which to present a pianistic treatise on the fundamental supremacy of Bach's *Goldberg Variations*, with works by Sweelinck, Schönberg, and Mozart as foils.[66] But simultaneously, there is continued and revived interest in the levels of interpretation that Bach brought to the texts of his music, whether they be passions, masses, cantatas, or, as in this case, motets. Study has been done on the notations that Bach wrote alongside Bible passages,[67] and certainly, in his music, there seems always to be either musical commentary on the texts of the works that he presents, or an indirect commentary based on the compilation of the texts themselves.

The Work

Bach's contribution to the history of interpreting the New Testament by means of his musical-textual settings includes his motet, *Der Geist Hilft unser Schwachheit auf*. This is one of Bach's six known motets.[68] In contrast with the several hundred cantatas of Bach, six of anything, especially works this short, seems unexpected. However, they were not settings that had a regular place in the Lutheran service of Leipzig in the eighteenth century, apart from being specially commissioned works for specific occasions. This motet is the only one that has an autograph registering its intended purpose. It was written, "for the burial of the late

65. Bach, *Well-Tempered Clavier*.
66. Gould, *Salzburg Recital*.
67. See Cox, ed., *Calov Bible*; and Leaver, *Bach and Scripture*.
68. There is some discussion about this number. In the past, there were several other motets attributed to J. S. Bach, which are no longer considered authentic, and there are at present some possibilities of others being attributed to him that until now have not been.

professor and rector Ernesti,"[69] which dates it to October 1729. Johann Heinrich Ernesti was rector of St Thomas School as well as professor of poetry in the University.[70] The main part of the text comes from Rom 8:26–27 (In the same way, the Spirit helps us in our weakness. We do not know what we ought to pray, but the Spirit himself intercedes for us with groans that words cannot express. And he who searches our hearts knows the mind of the Spirit, because the Spirit intercedes for the saints in accordance with God's will [NIV]).

The remainder of the text is from the third stanza of Martin Luther's hymn, *Kamm, Heiliger Geist, Herre Gott* (1524); the choral arrangement that forms the third part of this motet is based on the melody of this same hymn.[71]

There are three main sections in this work, which in its entirety lasts approximately eight minutes in performance. The first section uses the first of the two verses from Rom 8. This section is entirely set for double choir of soprano, alto, tenor, and bass. The second section uses the second verse of the Romans text, v. 27, which is marked "Alla breve" in the score. Here the two choirs are merged into one four-part choir. The third and final section is again for the combined voices of the two choirs and is in the style of the chorale that would normally be found at the end of a cantata.

The Interpretation

In this work, the word *Geist* ("Spirit") is frequently set to a long fluctuating or undulating line; in Bach's language of setting text to music, this seems to symbolize the nature of the word "ghost" or "spirit" by its movement of the line. Later in the first section, the word that is given a long melismatic line is the final word of the phrase *mit unaussprechlichem Seufzen* ("with inexpressible *groanings*"). Here Bach uses more chromatic notes and angular intervals than in the rest of the work, a means of expressing the anguish of the text; for instance, in the highest voice of the first choir (measure 130) at the word *Seufzen*, the soprano sings an ascending diminished fifth or tritone, and finishes the word on the same

---

69. "Bey Beerdigung des seel. fin. Prof. und Rectoris Ernesti" (cited by Klaus Hofmann in his preface in Ameln, ed., *Johann Sebastian Bach Motets*, 2, 4).

70. Terry, "Johann Sebastian Bach," 306. This Ernesti is not to be confused with Johann August Ernesti, who later also became rector of the St. Thomas School, who was instrumental in development of the higher critical method, and who had a well-known conflict with Bach resolved in Bach's favour (see Baird, *History*, 108–14).

71. This hymn comes from the fourth edition of the *Gesangbuch Eisleben* (1598).

interval, but descending this time. This interval is notoriously difficult to sing and, at least in the seventeenth and eighteenth centuries, was generally avoided in good voice leading. Here, however, Bach seems to use it specifically because of these properties. Similarly, he uses minor seconds and the outline of a diminished seventh chord to emphasize the text and its accompanying expression.

Another example is in the alto voice in Choir I (measures 132–33), which begins the word *Seufzen* on the notes A, Ab-G, Ab-G. These intervals of minor seconds are sometimes used by Bach to signify sorrow or pain, and here the repetition of Ab-G seems to accentuate this factor. Many such examples of this use of chromatic notes and difficult intervals in the individual voices can be found in this section. From the extended passages of this particular word-setting, it seems clear that Bach intended the music and the text to fully reflect each other, and in fact, for the music to elucidate the text at this point.

This first section of the motet is the longest of the three sections and presents the part of the text that speaks of suffering in its most extended passages (although this is not readily captured by the choirs that perform it). In the second section, where the biblical text shifts its emphasis more from the personal dimension to that of the "mind of the Spirit" and "God's will," the music becomes more straightforward and less densely written. Removing the antiphonal aspect of two choirs by merging them into one and changing the style of the section to "alla breve" results in a more spacious sense, which seems to underline the more pragmatic and cerebral aspect of this second verse, a characteristic underlined also by its fugal setting.

The third section is the most brief and straightforward and brings the listener, at least presumably the traditional church person of Bach's day and location, back to the familiarity of Luther's hymn. The writing is in the familiar chorale style, and the verse, selected specifically for its appropriateness to the situation, speaks of help from the Holy Spirit—in keeping with the earlier text from the book of Romans—of preparation for death, finding the grave a door or portal to God in heaven, and to life immortal. The concluding "Hallelujah, hallelujah" at this point seems oddly fitting and provides a victorious if brief conclusion to the work.

By means of Bach's setting of two verses in the book of Romans and their juxtaposition with Luther's hymn, one journeys through a text illustrating suffering and pain to one that moves to the mind of God and ultimately to the hymn that speaks of life immortal. Bach's interpretation of Rom 8:26 and 27 in this context certainly gives an insight into the spirit of the passage.

FRANCIS POULENC: *TENEBRAE FACTAE SUNT* ("IT BECAME DARK") (TWENTIETH CENTURY)

The last example I discuss is by the twentieth-century composer, Francis Poulenc, a composer who was unlikely to be considered among the significant sacred music composers.

The Text

Tenebrae factae sunt	It became dark
dum crucifixissent Jesum Judaei,	when the Jews had crucified Jesus,
et circa horam nonam	and around the ninth hour
exclamavit Jesus voce magna.	Jesus exclaimed in a loud voice:
Deus meus, ut quid me dereliquisti?	"My God, why have you forsaken me?"
Et inclinato capite,	and with inclined head
emisit spiritism.	He gave up the spirit.
Exclamans Jesus magna ait.	Crying out, Jesus with a loud voice said:
Pater, in manus tuas	"Father, into your hands
commendo spiritism meum.	I commend my spirit."
Et inclinato capite,	and with inclined head
emisit spiritum.[72]	He gave up the spirit.

The Composer

Francis Poulenc (1899–1962), known as one of the French *Les Six* ("The Six"), was not a likely candidate to be a serious composer of sacred music, but around 1936 he did turn seriously to the art of composing sacred choral music.[73] Poulenc himself said that he hoped that when his sacred works were better known that the public would see he was not just a "frivolous author."[74] Henri Hell's statement that the "predominantly sober

---

72. This text can be found in *Liber Usualis, Feria VI* in *Parasceve, Nocturn* II, *Lectio* V, 597–98.

73. Daniel, *Francis Poulenc*, 199. See chapter 2 above for discussion of this example as well.

74. See Poulenc, *Entretiens* (taken from the publication of radio interviews

aspect of Poulenc's choral works is one of the most interesting features of his art"[75] suggests that Poulenc's desire was fulfilled. His sacred choral works indeed became a solid part of the choral repertory of the twentieth century.

The Work

Although Wilfred Mellers characterizes Poulenc as "all sentimentality and nostalgia,"[76] the piece considered here, one of *Quatre motets pour le temps de penitence* ("Four Motets for a Time of Penitence") is not about sentiment and nostalgia. Nevertheless, the motets are "personally expressive," as Mellers later writes in his biography of the composer.[77] Poulenc's own comment about setting texts to music in songs is, "I find myself able to compose music only to poetry with which I feel total contact—a contact transcending mere admiration."[78] While this motet is not in the category of "song," one's impression is that Poulenc experiences that same sense of connectedness or contact with the text of this work as he did with songs, and places himself within the environment of the event that it depicts. Keith Daniel writes, "Controlled, sustained dramatic effect is the key aspect of these motets . . . and examining the means Poulenc uses to achieve this . . . reveals their true beauty,"[79] while Henri Hell writes that this work for *a cappella* choir "is a work of the standing of the Mass with the difference that the choral writing is less subtle and the religious message rather more dramatically conveyed."[80] Mellers describes the motets as "powerfully subjective, even 'expressionist,' pieces while being also devotional music that may function as an act of worship in church."[81] All three authors concur that *Tenebrae factae sunt* is a highly significant work.

The text is the key to this powerful motet, which was written with the other three motets in 1938–1939. The text that forms the basis of

---

between Poulenc and Rostand).

75. Hell, *Francis Poulenc*, 44.

76. Mellers, *Man and his Music*, 4:227.

77. Mellers, *Francis Poulenc*, 152.

78. Cited in Machlis, *Introduction*, 207–8.

79. Daniel, *Francis Poulenc*, 227. He also writes that he thinks *Tenebrae factae sunt* "is the most striking of the pieces."

80. Hell, *Francis Poulenc*, 59, where he also comments on the "tragic note in the sombre *Tenebrae factae sunt*, remarkable for its violent climaxes and its skilful use of the varied registers of the voices."

81. Mellers, *Francis Poulenc*, 79.

Poulenc's third of *Tenebrae factae sunt* ("Four Motets for a Time of Penitence") is a standard text for Holy Week[82] (but it is by no means a standard musical interpretation of it, for brief discussion of which, see below). This composite of the four Gospel accounts of the Crucifixion of Christ is as follows. The first phrase of the text, "It became dark when the Jews had crucified Jesus," is paraphrased from the three Synoptic Gospel accounts of Matt 27:45, Mark 15:33, and Luke 23:44. These opening words are the least similar to the biblical text, for the Gospel accounts do not state that "it became dark *when the Jews had crucified Jesus*," only that it became dark. The second portion of the text, "and around the ninth hour Jesus exclaimed in a loud voice: 'My God, why have you forsaken me?,'" follows closely the passages from Matt 27:46 and Mark 15:34. The next section, "and with inclined head, he gave up his spirit," although it seems to follow on directly from the preceding line, is not as closely connected in the New Testament texts. This can be seen in John 19:30 ("When he had received the drink, Jesus said, 'It is finished.' *With that, he bowed his head and gave up his spirit*") and in Matt 27:50 ("And when Jesus had cried out again in a loud voice, *he gave up his spirit*").[83] The lines, "Crying out, Jesus with a loud voice said: 'Father, into your hands I commend my spirit,'" are found only in Luke 23:46 ("*Jesus called out with a loud voice, 'Father, into your hands I commit my spirit.'* When he had said this, he breathed his last").

The Interpretation

Poulenc himself stated that he "wrote four motets for Holy Week which are as realistic and as tragic as a Mantegna painting,"[84] and that "Mantegna . . . correspond[s] very closely, in fact, to my religious ideal," that of "mystical realism."[85] Ernst H. Gombrich writes that Andrea Mantegna (1431–1506) tried "to imagine quite clearly what the scene must have looked like in reality," including both the inner meaning of the story, as evidenced in earlier painters, but also its outward circumstances.[86] The text of *Tenebrae factae sunt*, with its inclusion of two of Jesus' statements,

---

82. It is used in the second Nocturn of Matins on Friday.
83. There is only a slight similarity to the Markan passage (Mark 15:37).
84. Cited by Daniel, *Francis Poulenc*, 225, from Poulenc's *Entretiens*.
85. Poulenc, *My Friends and Myself*, 58.
86. Gombrich, *Story of Art*, 256–60 (esp. 259). Gombrich refers to Mantegna's paintings as being much like scenes in a play (260).

one according to Matthew and Mark, and one according to Luke, provides the kind of detail, even drama, that Poulenc wished for this depiction of the grief and sorrow of the final moments of Jesus' life before he died.

Poulenc mixes features of old with new in his writing of this work, and, in so doing, brings about a metamorphosis of the text and the scene that it depicts. Mellers, for instance, writes that "Poulenc's techniques are . . . orthodox in musical terms, for the vocal lines start from the rhythms of the words, and grow from, if they do not always adhere to, vocal modality."[87] Later, he writes that the vocal lines in the motet do not "deny Renaissance principles," but involve "a progressive degree of 'humanization' from medieval spirituality to Renaissance physicality: which becomes overt at the fluctuating harmonies on the 'ninth hour' and at Christ's frenzied chromatics and dotted rhythms in his appeal, 'voce magna,' to his Father."[88] Here we can see the evidence of the change that is wrought by Poulenc.

The first muted notes of the motet give an impression of darkness and foreboding, setting the scene of the crucifixion. One distinctive feature that I wish to draw attention to is the point in the text where Jesus exclaims in a loud voice *Deus meus, ut quid me dereliquisti?* ("My God, my God, why have you forsaken me?"). It is poignant that only the first two words are sung in "a loud voice." These words are then echoed very quietly, with the following words of the statement also sung quietly. In a dramatic reading of this passage, one might well expect to hear the entire line spoken loudly, even increasing in volume: "My God, my God, WHY HAVE YOU FORSAKEN ME?" However, Poulenc's depiction of this cry, in which only the first two words are a loud cry, and all the following words are quiet, vividly presents Jesus having used all the breath he could muster to speak out the first two words. The echo of these words is very much like the sound of a desperate, dying, and forsaken man: "MY GOD . . . my God . . . why have you forsaken me . . . ?" Poulenc's choice of the upper voices and upper notes to sing *Deus meus* ("My God") further suggests a strained sound, a sound that cannot be sustained and drops off to a lower range as well as dynamics. This portrayal of physical exhaustion that made even breathing difficult corresponds to the image of the Crucifixion that is depicted in the Gospel accounts, as well as other historical accounts of those who have been crucified. The physical reality

---

87. Mellers, *Francis Poulenc*, 80.
88. Mellers, *Francis Poulenc*, 82.

of a crucifixion[89] bears out Poulenc's interpretation of the scene of Jesus on the cross.

CONCLUSION

This chapter has attempted to form a bridge from the first part of this volume on ancient biblical music to the Christian church and its musical tradition, by selecting and illustrating examples in which biblical interpretation occurs through musical form. While this chapter has merely touched on these five works, a New Testament hymn, a third-century hymn, a sixteenth-century liturgical piece by John Sheppard, an eighteenth-century motet by Johann Sebastian Bach, and a twentieth-century motet by Francis Poulenc, nonetheless I think that it is evident that each one unveils and interprets unique facets of the biblical text by means of its musical setting. There are features in each work that reveal the composer's role as an interpreter of the Bible. Although the composition of sacred music often has been seen as a less creative role than that of writing music for its own sake, it seems to me that, in fact, the composer who writes sacred music has the unique opportunity of engaging with the text at a theological level by composing a musical work that recreates the text in a new form. In this new form, the composer has set out for performance and for evaluation a personal interpretation of the biblical text.

REFERENCES AND FURTHER READING

Allen, Thomas W., and Edward Ernest Sikes. *The Homeric Hymns*. London: Macmillan, 1904.

Ameln, Konrad, ed. *Johann Sebastian Bach Motets BWV 225–230*. Kassel: Bärenreiter-Verlag, 1995.

Apel, Willi. *Gregorian Chant*. Bloomington: Indiana University Press, 1990.

Arnim, Hans Friedrich August von, ed. *Stoicorum veterum fragmenta: Vol. 1*. Stuttgart: B.G. Teubner, 1964.

Bach, Johann Sebastian. *The Well-Tempered Clavier*. Performed by Edwin Fischer. CD Recording. EMI, 1989.

Baird, William. *History of New Testament Research: Volume One. From Deism to Tübingen*. Minneapolis: Fortress. 1992.

Barrett, G. S. *The Earliest Christian Hymn*. London: James Clarke, 1897.

Benham, Hugh. *Latin Church Music in England, c. 1460–575*. London: Barrie and Jenkins, 1977.

---

89. For extensive discussion of crucifixion, see Hengel, *Cross of the Son of God*, esp. 93–185.

Part Two: Musical Traditions and Interpretations

Cosgrove, Charles. H. *An Ancient Christian Hymn with Musical Notation: Papyrus Oxyrhynchus 1786. Text and Commentary*. Studien und Texte zu Antike und Christentum 65. Tübingen: Mohr Siebeck, 2011

Cox, Howard H., ed. *The Calov Bible of J. S. Bach*. Ann Arbor, MI: UMI Research, 1985.

Daniel, Keith W. *Francis Poulenc: His Artistic Development and Musical Style*. Studies in Musicology 52. Ann Arbor, MI: UMI Research, 1980, 1982.

David, Hans T., and Arthur Mendel, eds. *The Bach Reader: A Life of Johann Sebastian Bach in Letters and Documents*. New York: W. W. Norton, 1945.

Doe, Paul. "Latin Polyphony under Henry VIII." *Proceedings of the Royal Musical Association* 95 (1968) 81–96.

Fowl, Stephen E. *The Story of Christ in the Ethics of Paul: An Analysis of the Function of the Hymnic Material in the Pauline Corpus*. Journal for the Study of the New Testament Supplement Series 36. Sheffield: JSOT, 1990.

Gombrich, Ernst H. *The Story of Art*. 16th ed. London: Phaidon, 1995.

Gordley, Matthew E. *New Testament Christological Hymns: Exploring Texts, Contexts, and Significance*. Downers Grove, IL: InterVarsity, 2018.

Gould, Glenn. *Salzburg Recital 25. August 1959: Bach, Mozart, Sweelinck, Schönberg*. CD Recording. Sony, 1994.

Guthrie, Donald. *New Testament Introduction*. Rev. ed. Downers Grove, IL: InterVarsity, 1970.

———. *The Pastoral Epistles: An Introductory and Commentary*. Rev. ed. Tyndale New Testament Commentaries. Leicester, UK: InterVarsity, 1990.

Harrison, Frank Llewellyn. *Music in Medieval Britain*. Bruen, The Netherlands: Fritz Knuf, 1980.

Hell, Henri. *Francis Poulenc*. Translated by Edward Lockspeiser. London: John Calder, 1959.

Henderson, Isobel. "Ancient Greek Music." In *Ancient and Oriental Music*, edited by Egon Wellesz, 336–403. New Oxford History of Music 1. London: Oxford University Press, 1966 [1957].

Hengel, Martin. *The Cross of the Son of God: Containing the Son of God, Crucifixion, the Atonement*. Translated by J. Bowden. London: SCM, 1986.

Hofman, May, and John Morehen, eds. *Latin Music in British Sources c. 1485—c. 1610*. Early English Church Music Supplementary 2. London: Stainer and Bell, 1987.

Hughes, Andrew. *Medieval Manuscripts for Mass and Office: A Guide to their Organization and Terminology*. Toronto: University of Toronto Press, 1982.

Hunt, Arthur S., and H. Stuart Jones. "1786. Christian Hymn with Musical Notation." In *The Oxyrhynchus Papyri XV*, edited by Bernard P. Grenfell and Arthur S. Hunt, 21–25. Egypt Exploration Society Graeco-Roman Memoirs. London: Egypt Exploration Fund, 1922.

Knight, George W., III. *The Faithful Sayings in the Pastoral Letters*. Kampen: Kok, 1968.

Le Huray, Peter. *Music and the Reformation in England 1549–1660*. Cambridge Studies in Music. Cambridge: Cambridge University Press, 1978.

Leaver, Robin A. *Bach and Scripture: Glosses from the Calov Bible Commentary*. St. Louis, MO: Concordia, 1985.

Liber Usualis Missae et Officii pro Dominicis et Festis I. vel II. Classis cum Cantu Gregoriano ex Editione Vaticana Adamussim Excerpto et Rhythmicis Signis in Subsidium Cantorum a Solesmensibus Monachis Diligenter Ornato. Typis Societatis S. Joannis Evang. Paris: Desclee and Sons, 1929.

Long, Anthony A., and David N. Sedley. *The Hellenistic Philosophers*. 2 vols. Cambridge: Cambridge University Press, 1977.

Machlis, Joseph. *Introduction to Contemporary Music*. New York: W. W. Norton, 1979.

Martin, Ralph P. "Aspects of Worship in the New Testament Church." *Vox Evangelica* 2 (1963) 6–32.

McKinnon, James W. "On the Question of Psalmody in the Ancient Synagogue." *Early Music History* 6 (1986) 159–91.

McKinnon, James W., ed. *Music in Early Christian Literature*. Cambridge Studies in the Literature of Music. Cambridge: Cambridge University Press, 1987.

Mellers, Wilfrid. *Francis Poulenc*. Oxford: Oxford University Press, 1993.

———. *Man and his Music: The Story of Musical Experience in the West. Romanticism and the Twentieth Century*. 4 vols. 1962. Reprint, London: Barrie and Jenkins, 1977.

Mountford, James Frederick. "Greek Music in the Papyri and Inscriptions." In *New Chapters in the History of Greek Literature 2: Some Recent Discoveries in Greek Poetry and Prose, Chiefly of the Fourth Century BC, and Later Times*, edited by J. U. Powell and Eric A. Barber, 146–83. Oxford: Clarendon, 1929.

Murray, Dom Gregory. *The Choral Chants of the Mass*. The Society of St Gregory 7. Bristol: Burleigh, 1947.

Norden, Eduard. *Agnostos Theos: Untersuchungen zur Formengeschichte religiöser Rede*. 1913. Reprint, Darmstadt: Wissenschaftliche Buchgesellschaft, 1956.

"P.Oxy. XV 1786. Christian Hymn with Musical Notation." *University of Oxford*. Online: https://portal.sds.ox.ac.uk/articles/online_resource/P_Oxy_XV_1786_Christian_Hymn_with_Musical_Notation/21132973.

Pöhlmann, Egert, ed. *Denkmäler Altgriechischer Musik: Sammlung, Übertragung und Erläuterung aller Fragmente und Fälschungen*. Nürnberg: Verlag Hans Carl, 1970.

Pöhlmann, Egert, and Martin L. West, eds. *Documents of Ancient Greek Music: The Extant Melodies and Fragments Edited and Transcribed with Commentary*. Oxford: Clarendon, 2001.

Poulenc, Francis. *Entretiens avec Claude Rostand*. Paris: R. Julliard, 1954.

———. *My Friends and Myself: Conversation Assembled by Stephane Audel*. Translated by James Harding. London: Dennis Dobson, 1978.

Porter, Stanley E. *The Apostle Paul: His Life, Thought, and Letters*. Grand Rapids: Eerdmans, 2016.

———. "Pauline Authorship and the Pastoral Epistles: Implications for Canon." *Bulletin for Biblical Research* 5 (1995) 105–23.

Porter, Wendy J. *Early English Composers and the Credo: Emphasis as Interpretation in Sixteenth-Century Music*. Routledge Research in Music Series. London: Routledge, 2022.

Reinach, Théodore. *La Musique Grecque*. Les introuvables. Paris: Editions d'Aujourd'hui, 1926.

Schweitzer, Albert. *J. S. Bach*. Translated by E. Newman. 2 vols. London: Breitkopf and Härtel, 1911.

Shepherd, Massey H., Jr. "Hymns." In *The Interpreter's Dictionary of the Bible*, edited by George Arthur Buttrick, 2:667–68. 4 vols. New York: Abingdon, 1962.

Sheppard, John. *John Sheppard 1: Responsorial Music*. Translated and edited by David Chadd. London: Stainer and Bell, 1977.

Smith, John A. "The Ancient Synagogue, the Early Church and Singing." *Music & Letters* 65 (1984) 1–16.

Terry, Charles Sanford. "Johann Sebastian Bach." In *Grove's Dictionary of Music and Musicians*, edited by Eric Blom, 1:293–321. 10 vols. 5th ed. New York: St. Martin's, 1954.

Thom, Johan C. *Cleanthes' Hymn to Zeus: Text, Translation, and Commentary*. Studien und Texte zu Antike und Christentum 33. Tübingen: Mohr Siebeck, 2005.

Wellesz, Egon. *A History of Byzantine Music and Hymnography*. 2nd ed. Oxford: Clarendon, 1998 [1961].

Werner, Eric. "Music." In *The Interpreter's Dictionary of the Bible*, edited by George Arthur Buttrick, 3:457–69. 4 vols. Nashville: Abingdon, 1962.

West, Martin L. "Analecta Musica." *Zeitschrift für Papyrologie und Epigraphik* 92 (1992) 1–54.

———. *Ancient Greek Music*. Oxford: Clarendon, 1992.

———. "Texts with Musical Notation." In *Oxyrhynchus Papyri LXV*, edited by Michael W. Haslam et al., 81–102. Egypt Exploration Society Graeco-Roman Memoirs 85. London: Egypt Exploration Society, 1998.

10

Resurrection in the Western Wind Credos of Taverner, Sheppard, and Tye

INTRODUCTION

ALTHOUGH IT MAY SEEM that sixteenth-century English composers of sacred music almost formulaically set the text of the Latin Credo (or Creed) to music, on closer examination, it can be seen that they did more than simply provide a musical background for these words—they engaged in a form of musical commentary on and musical interpretation of the theological text.[1] In this chapter, I have chosen to explore briefly this dimension in three works that are related not only by the common text of the creed, but also by the secular melody upon which each composition is based. The three settings of the mass are from the first half of the sixteenth century and each bears the title, *Western Wind*. These *cantus firmus* masses,[2] by John Taverner, John Sheppard, and Christopher Tye, are so described because they use the *Western Wind* melody as the foundation upon which the musical setting is built, and are based on "the love lyric, 'Westron wynde when wylle thow blow.'"[3] An extant version of

---

1. For a fuller development of this notion in the context of treating the Latin Credo settings by Taverner, Tye, Tallis, Sheppard, and Byrd, see Porter, *Early English Composers and the Credo*.

2. The term *cantus firmus* refers to polyphonic settings of the mass from the fifteenth century onwards that were based on melodies or tunes that were *fixed*. The melody initially was found in the lowest voice, but in the sixteenth century became associated with the tenor voice.

3. Petti, *John Taverner*, iii.

these lyrics with an accompanying melody is held in the British Library,[4] but most scholars do not accept that these three mass settings are actually based on the melody that is found in this manuscript, for it bears little resemblance to the recognizable melody that each composer uses in his mass setting. In the preface to his edition and arrangement of Taverner's setting of the mass for liturgical use, Henry B. Collins comments, "Of the beautiful melody on which the Mass is founded, nothing appears to be known."[5] Hugh Benham sums it up by saying, "No source . . . has been traced" and that the melody in the British Library "bears few similarities to the melody in the Mass."[6] Regarding the discrepancy between the *Western Wind* melody in the British Library and the one that is used in each of the three mass settings, Paul Doe thinks that the musical style of the version used by the three composers "ill accords with the forthright monosyllabic vocabulary of the verse."[7] Further to this, Benham writes, "Paul Doe has put forward some ingenious, but probably not very convincing, theories about this."[8] The most common suggestion, and probably the most logical conclusion, is that the lyrics could well have been set more than once, as this practice was not unknown in the sixteenth century,[9] and that the melody that is available is not the one that the three composers used. A further suggestion about the unknown source of the melody is the likelihood that the love lyric was popular at the court of Henry VIII. Based on knowledge of Taverner's own composition of secular songs in his early years at Henry VIII's court, Peter Phillips proposes that Taverner himself may have written the melody.[10] In reference to the nature and original context of the secular love lyric and melody, Collins in the 1920s hastens to assure the potential performer of the work that it "has of course no secular associations at the present day which might make it unsuitable for liturgical use."[11]

4. Found in the tenor part book held in the British Library, MS Royal, App. 58, f. 5.

5. Collins, "Introduction," 3.

6. Benham, *Latin Church Music*, 150.

7. Doe, "Introduction," xi.

8. Benham, *Latin Church Music*, 150 (he refers to Doe, "Latin Polyphony," 81).

9. Petti, *John Taverner*, iii.

10. See *Commemorating*. However, for fuller discussion of this melody and an alternative view of its origin, see Davison, "Western Wind Masses," esp. 428–34.

11. Collins, "Introduction," 3.

The main source of the three masses is the document usually known as the "Gyffard Part-Books," where "All three *Western Wind* masses are... transcribed together in the order of seniority of the composers, and the authorship of each is clearly identified in every part in the main hand of the manuscript."[12] Of this "seniority of the composers," Phillips refers to Taverner:

> It has long been assumed that Taverner's setting came first and that the ones by Tye and Sheppard were written to complement it. There are a number of good reasons for believing this, though none puts the matter beyond all doubt. Taverner was the senior figure both in reputation and age... the Taverner setting was placed first in the main source, followed by Tye and Sheppard in that order.[13]

It is customary to arrange these three masses in the order described by Phillips: Taverner, Tye, and then Sheppard. However, in this chapter, although Taverner's version will remain first in the order, I will place Sheppard's in second position and Tye's as the final one, for reasons which I will clarify.

The masses have some noticeable similarities, such as each being scored for four voices and each using the technique of variation by means of the secular melody being repeated throughout the work. But while they share several characteristics, each is remarkably individual as well. Doe remarks, "All three composers mark the traditional structural divisions of English Masses by reducing the texture at such points as... 'Et incarnatus' in the Credo."[14] What Doe does not say is that apart from that structural division in the Credo, all three treat the potential divisions in the text quite differently, bringing a unique approach to various sections and highlighting ideas in the text in distinctly individual ways.

In discussing these three settings of the standard text of the Credo, especially pertaining to the phrases *et resurrexit* and *et exspecto resurrectionem mortuorum*, it becomes apparent that there are numerous techniques that composers of this period used to provide variation and interest in setting a text to music. I would contend that some of these techniques are consistently used to highlight or bring to the foreground certain ideas in the text, while others are used to relegate ideas more to

---

12. Petti, *John Taverner*, 3.
13. Phillips, "Liner Notes," 3–4.
14. Doe, "Introduction," xii.

the background. How the three composers used these devices in the two short sections here studied illustrates the individual casts that are given to the two phrases of the text.

JOHN TAVERNER (CA. 1495–1545)

John Taverner's *Western Wind* Mass, along with that of both John Sheppard and Christopher Tye, is set for four voice-parts: treble, mean, tenor, and bass. Taverner's is set in the Dorian mode or first mode, transposed up a fourth.

Several scholars have argued that this must be a later work of Taverner, on account of "the prevalence of binary rhythm, as well as the masterly freedom of the counterpoint."[15] This might place it in the early 1540s. Petti concludes that the most likely date from his point of view is around 1525, while Colin Hand thinks that it could be as early as 1510–1520, although later he says that the construction of the work suggests that the composer was in his mature years, which could conceivably place it much later.[16]

Taverner's use of the *Western Wind* melody to set the mass has been cited as "Arguably the most poignant example of Taverner's influence on his successors."[17] Certainly, this use of a *cantus firmus* from a secular source is the first-known instance of this kind of composition by an English composer, although it was already an established practice on the continent.[18] Taverner's use of the secular tune as the basis of the mass is, in effect, a series of variations, each variation based on the melody, which he places in various voices. Based on the variety of method, Frank Harrison considers it "a notable demonstration of the art of variation by contrapuntal addition."[19]

In the Credo, Taverner sets the *Western Wind* melody first in the tenor voice, where it is most traditionally placed, but where it is not necessarily the most apparent to the listener. He begins the Credo with

15. Collins, "Introduction," 3.
16. Petti, *John Taverner*, 11; Hand, *John Taverner*, 58–60.
17. See *Commemorating*, 2.
18. Harrison, *Music in Medieval Britain*, 283; Brown, *Music in the Renaissance*, 248.
19. The techniques he refers to are "homorhythm, differentiated counterpoint, points of imitation derived from and independent of the theme, counterpoint in sequential ostinato ... and counterpoint in strict ostinato" (Harrison, *Music in Medieval Britain*, 284).

the highest voice, the treble, singing the opening interval of the melody, which is a rising perfect fifth. For the listener who has already heard the first section of the mass, it would seem that the treble is about to sing the familiar melody, but the melody is actually heard in the tenor voice two measures later. Taverner repeats the tune throughout the text, making use of it nine times in the course of the Credo. The order in which the melody appears in the various voices is as follows:

1. in the tenor at *Patrem omnipotentem*
2. in the treble at *et in unum Dominum Jesum Christum*
3. in the treble at *Deum de Deo*
4. in the tenor at *qui propter nos homines*
5. in the treble at *et incarnatus*
6. in the bass at *crucifixus*
7. in the tenor at *et resurrexit*
8. in the treble at *et iterum venturus est*
9. and finally in the treble at *et exspecto resurrectionem mortuorum*.

For this particular study, the two phrases that I focus on are *et resurrexit* and *et exspecto resurrectionem mortuorum*. I contend that how the composers treat them within the context of the overall structure is significant. Taverner has used the beginning of the melody to identify nine sections of the text, creating a balanced structure.[20] At *et resurrexit*, the first time that "resurrection" is mentioned in the text of the creed, the tune of the *Western Wind* melody is in the tenor voice, but the tenor is not the first voice-part to introduce the words of the text. Nor is it the upper voice, so the initial rendition of the melody of the *Western Wind* melody is submerged beneath the treble and mean parts. Taverner matches the initial rising interval of the familiar tune by beginning the treble part with an ascending leap of a fifth; however, the treble does not go on to sing the melody line, which gives a kind of false start to the melody. Immediately after the first two notes of the treble, the tenor begins with the actual tune, providing a kind of imitation between the two initial voices and also a sense of familiarity, for the melody has already

---

20. Throughout the entire mass, Taverner uses a systematic and well-planned overall structure, of which this symmetry is only a part. Both Harrison (*Music in Medieval Britain*, 282–83) and Reese (*Music in the Renaissance*, 779) make a note of this large-scale plan. For a close examination of Taverner's technique, see Messenger, "Texture."

been used extensively throughout the previous section of the mass, prior to the Credo. This anticipation of the melody in the opening interval of the treble and then the tenor taking the lead line is reminiscent of the opening of the Credo, *Patrem omnipotentem*, where the same pattern of false start and then the following voice actually singing the melody is suggestive of a link between the two sections. Musically, it reminds the listener of the opening; ideologically, it links the phrase "resurrection of Jesus" with the initial phrase "the omnipotent Father." It could be argued that the composer has drawn a subtle theological connection of the resurrection of Jesus back to the power of the Father. After the first note of the tenor, the bass enters with an ascending interval, not of a fifth, but of a third. The effect of these three entries is that of a slight compression and building of tension, in that the third entry follows more closely after the second than the second does the first. Similarly, the interval of the third is slightly smaller than the interval of the second and first. Taverner reserves *et resurrexit* largely for three voices only, for the mean only comes in at the following phrase, *tertia die*. In each of the three voices, the nature of the leap from *et* up to *re-surrexit* places emphasis on the first syllable of *et re-surrexit*. At the same time, the leap upwards builds an anticipatory tension into the phrase and may be seen to represent musically the upward motion or leap of "resurrection."

There are several differences that occur at the second "resurrection" phrase, *et exspecto resurrectionem mortuorum*. First, Taverner switches the metre to three beats, rather than two or four, an approach to this final section of the Credo text that all three composers implement. This shift in metre is a technique that builds at least a perceived acceleration in tempo, which in turn creates a rise in intensity and, in this case, even anticipation. Whether the anticipation is related to the theological subject of looking forward to the potential resurrection of the dead—or simply the nearing arrival of the end of the piece—is difficult to ascertain. Perhaps there is an element of both.

Secondly, in comparing *et resurrexit* and *et exspecto resurrectionem*, the melody in the latter is in the treble, rather than in the tenor, and therefore is more audible to the listener. Third, throughout most of the preceding sections from *et incarnatus* to the end of *non erit finis* (which just precedes *et exspecto resurrectionem*), there have been mainly three voices singing at any one time. *Et exspecto resurrectionem* marks the return to the full four voices, which remain to the end of the Credo. Fourth, at *et exspecto*, the voices move in fairly closely matched rhythm, shifting to more individual lines as they approach the word *resurrectionem*. Taverner matches the prescribed melody very aptly to the words at this point, giving emphasis by the two distinct upward leaps in the tune to the words in the following manner: *et ex-spe-cto resur-re-ctionem mortuorum*. The shape of the melody with these words brings a life and energy to the phrase and moves the text into what may be called a foreground position, in that it moves the words to the forefront of the listener's perception.

JOHN SHEPPARD (D. 1559/60?)

John Sheppard's *Western Wind* Mass for four voices, as with Taverner's setting, is in the Dorian mode transposed up a fourth. Sheppard's setting of the overall mass is significantly shorter than the other two. Nicholas Sandon, in the preface to his edition of the Sheppard masses, describes this mass in particular as "an example of the type of shorter mass which became more prominent during the later years of Henry VIII."[21]

Phillips comments on the brevity of the setting by writing that Sheppard "regularly omitted the third phrase of the tune (partly a repeat of the second [phrase]). He also made the most substantial cuts of the three from the text of the Mass."[22] This is not true of the Credo, however. He goes on to say,

> But the most significant reason for the brevity of the Sheppard is its musical language, which shows every sign of having been fashioned some time after that of Taverner and Tye. Although there are passages which pay homage to the melismatic, rhythmically complex style of the early 16th century, a good deal of this setting is more or less syllabic, possibly influenced, consciously or unconsciously, by the new Protestant ideal of textual clarity.[23]

There are other features of this setting, however, that ideologically, if not chronologically, place Tye's mass later than Sheppard's setting, on which I will say more below.

Sheppard uses the *Western Wind* melody seven times in the Credo; six out of the seven times, it is placed in the treble voice. The only deviation from this straightforward pattern is at *crucifixus*, where the voice that sings the *Western Wind* melody is the tenor. The pattern is as follows:

---

21. Sandon, ed., *John Sheppard II*, x.
22. Phillips, "Liner Notes," 5.
23. Phillips, "Liner Notes," 5.

1. the melody is in the treble at *Patrem omnipotentem*
2. it is in the treble at *et ex Patre*
3. and in the treble at *et incarnatus*
4. the melody shifts to the tenor at *crucifixus*
5. it returns to the treble at *et resurrexit*
6. it remains in the treble at *et iterum*
7. and is still in the treble for the final time at *et exspecto*.

The balanced scheme around which Sheppard weaves his setting of the creed is similar to that of Taverner's version. However, where Taverner has used the *Western Wind* melody three times (between *Patrem* and *et incarnatus*), Sheppard reduces its use to a single time, thus tightening up the first "half" of the text to place the *crucifixus* in the central position. Sheppard has, however, used other devices to give prominence to *et resurrexit* and *et exspecto resurrectionem*. Five out of seven times the melody begins in an imitative style, one voice entering after another, sometimes rather closely, and sometimes with more independent lines. Only twice is the entry with all four voices singing at the same time and basically singing the same rhythm—at *et resurrexit* and at *et exspecto resurrectionem*. In fact, the first time in the whole setting of the Credo where the voices sing in a homophonic style is at *et resurrexit*. Sheppard appears to have reserved this particular technique to highlight this phrase.

Similarly, Sheppard's placement of the melody in the treble in the first three sections of the Credo gives it a prominence that is significantly more noticeable to the listener than if it had been placed in a lower part with other parts written above it, parts that are perhaps related to the shape of the melody, but not the melody itself. Sheppard's movement of the melody line down to the tenor voice in the *crucifixus* and then his bringing it back to the treble at *et resurrexit* gives these later words added impetus, as the reminder of the melody that has been so prominent in the first three sections and then somewhat submerged. This simple technique not only brilliantly articulates a sense of the death and burial of Christ but gives added impetus to the idea of resurrection in the following section.

As in Taverner's setting of this melody, the metre changes at *et exspecto*, a not unusual marking point for the change,[24] the shift in metre

---

24. Sandon, ed. (*John Sheppard II*) introduces a 6/8 marking in his edition at this point, whereas previously the standard has been 4/4 with a couple of 5/4 bars fitted in.

giving a sense of increased tempo. The *Western Wind* melody begins again in the treble voice and, as mentioned above, is joined by the three other voices in a homophonic entry, with all four voices singing the same rhythm on the first three syllables and then developing slightly independent lines. Both Taverner and Sheppard shape the melody, which is in the treble voice, to the syllables of *et exspecto resurrectionem mortuorum* in an almost identical manner in this section, with the upward leap on *et ex*-spe-*cto* and *resur*-re-*ctionum*. Both composers also write the part for mean or alto in such a way that both upper voices sing almost the same rhythm to the end of *et exspecto resurrectionem*, shifting at *mortuorum*.

CHRISTOPHER TYE (CA. 1500–1572/73)

The third setting of the *Western Wind* mass, this time by Christopher Tye, is again set for treble, mean, tenor, and bass. Tye's setting is in the Dorian mode, but is not transposed, as are Taverner's and Sheppard's versions. A main distinction in comparing Tye's setting with those of Taverner and Sheppard is that Tye does not move the *Western Wind* melody from part to part, as Taverner does extensively in his setting of the Credo and Sheppard does more sparingly in his; instead, Tye keeps it exclusively in one voice. Furthermore, Tye chooses the one voice that neither Taverner nor Sheppard uses for this purpose: Tye sets the melody-bearing voice as the mean (or alto) part.

Phillips describes Tye's setting as "more through-composed than either of the others,"[25] but part of that feature of being through-composed is the result of Tye's decision to keep the melody always resting slightly below the surface—apart from when he strips away the upper voice completely—so that the most audible melody in the highest voice must be somewhat different from the familiar *Western Wind* melody, but neither a dominant melody nor one that is recognizably repeated. The alternative would have been to construct the setting in such a way that the treble voice is constantly singing a second melody contrasting with the mean, thus having two melodies vying for attention; the most reasonable choice, and the one that provides Tye with the most musical scope while remaining true to the intention of using the *Western Wind* melody as a basis, is to create a more through-composed style. Tye does allow the melody of the various parts to be quite imitative of the melody of the *Western Wind* tune without giving it the prominence of being in

25. Phillips, "Liner Notes," 4.

the upper-most audible voice. Again, Phillips writes, "A rather striking difference between the two treatments [Taverner's and Tye's], however, is Tye's addition of an extra beat between the second and third phrases of the melody, which neatly disturbs its otherwise regular duple time. Sheppard made this addition as well, though not so consistently."[26] Here, Tye has used a single beat to create a unique facet to his composition. Where Taverner uses the melody nine times in his setting of the Credo and Sheppard uses the melody seven times, Tye chooses eight, which does not have the symmetrical shape or the central high point of the other two. Therefore, he throws the balance off just slightly, giving the Credo a feeling of slight unpredictability. The points at which the familiar melody begins, always in the mean, are at:

1. *Patrem*
2. *et in unum*
3. *et ex Patre*
4. *genitum*
5. *et incarnatus*
6. *crucifixus*
7. *et resurrexit*
8. *et exspecto resurrectionem mortuorum.*

Again, a distinction in the three composers' choices of which points to begin the melody is in evidence: both Taverner and Tye begin the melody five times before *crucifixus*, but the third and fourth in Tye's setting are at different parts in the text than in the third and fourth of Taverner's setting; and where Sheppard begins the melody three times before *crucifixus*, Tye's version inserts the melody once between Sheppard's first and second, and once between his second and third. The contrariness of Tye's pattern would seem to indicate that Tye might also use the melody more times after *crucifixus*, but in fact, he reduces the number: where Taverner and Sheppard both begin the melody on *et resurrexit*, on *et iterum,* and finally on *et exspecto resurrectionem*, Tye begins it only at *et resurrexit* and *et exspecto resurrectionem*. But not only does he reduce the number of times that one hears the *Western Wind* melody, he actually deletes the section in between *et resurrexit* and *et exspecto resurrectionem*, so that the two sections that refer to resurrection are now side by side in the text

---

26. Phillips, "Liner Notes," 4.

and in the musical setting. Contrary to some opinions on deletions in the Credo, I would argue that deletion is a conscious decision by the composer to move something in the text to the background.[27] This abrupt shift from *et resurrexit* to *et exspecto resurrectionem* is a clever excision that unexpectedly catapults the listener to the end of the text, giving a somewhat ironic twist to the statement *et exspecto* "and I expect," for the end arrives much sooner than one expects. Is Tye giving a personal viewpoint on the unexpectedness of the future resurrection of the dead? Is he giving it an ironic twist that highlights the difference between reciting a statement of belief and the possibility of its actual occurrence? Based on the manner in which Tye sets various aspects of the music, the latter is a possibility; irony is certainly not limited to written discourse only, but is an inherent possibility in musical composition as well.

The beginning of the *Western Wind* melody is the upward leap of a fifth, but at *et resurrexit*, rather than use the fifth exclusively, Tye, again in his own predictably unpredictable manner, uses four different ascending jumps. The tenor introduces the text *et resurrexit* with a leap of a third, the treble follows with a leap of a sixth, the mean brings in the *Western Wind* melody with the leap of a fifth, and the bass enters on a leap of a fourth. All four represent the idea of upward motion, but each with an individuality that prevents this section from sounding too formulaic, while still retaining the characteristic of being somewhat imitative.

When he reaches the final section of text to be cast into the *Western Wind* tune, *et exspecto resurrectionem*, Tye gives it a fairly lengthy "false" start. First, the tenor begins the section with an upward leap of a third and then sings a melody line that resembles the tune but is not exactly it. Secondly, immediately following the tenor's entry, the bass enters with the ascending fifth leap of the opening of the *Western Wind* melody and then continues on for another six or seven notes of what seems to be the familiar melody, but then moves away from the pattern. Thirdly, the treble voice enters with the same melody line as the tenor voice has previously introduced, now an octave higher. Only after all three parts have presented something representative of the melody does Tye bring in the fourth voice, the mean, with the actual complete melody line. In

---

27. Cf. Hand, *John Taverner*, 41, where he argues unconvincingly against the conclusion of Ruth Hannas in her classic article, Hannas, "Concerning Deletions." While Hand may have valid reasons for disregarding Hannas's opinion that cuts in the Credo were based on contemporary religious and political beliefs, he does not actually present these reasons in support of his case.

each case, there is a sense of having arrived at the melody and then a building tension as it becomes apparent that, in actuality, the first three voices have each been given a melody line that is not quite the genuine tune. There is a sophistication and wit in this aspect that is lacking in the other settings, a building of expectation and then delayed fulfilment. Doe's description of one of the techniques used by both Sheppard and Tye in the *Western Wind* settings of the mass is that "Sheppard and Tye usually drop the Treble, which in Tye's Mass has the effect of 'uncovering' the tune (always in the Mean) and giving it sudden prominence as the highest voice."[28] However, in this particular instance Tye has appeared to "uncover" the tune to the listener, only for the listener to discover that it isn't the real thing. By the time the *Western Wind* melody does appear, it is by far the most delayed of any of the renderings of the tune in the entire Credo setting. Tye's use of this technique to build anticipation and delayed actuality may be seen as a means by which he has theologically interpreted the text: he has not only used musical techniques to bring the concept of "resurrection of the dead" to the foreground but has played out the sense of raised hope with which believers might look forward to this potential resurrection of the dead.

SYNOPSIS AND CONCLUSIONS

While English composers in the sixteenth century often deleted sections of the Credo text, there is an interesting progression in the kind of deletions that these three composers made in their versions of the *Western Wind* Credo settings, particularly if one places Tye's version as chronologically the last one. All three composers deleted everything to do with the Spirit, the Church, and baptism—which can be accomplished in a single excision. Apart from that, Taverner included everything else. Sheppard excluded the section *deum de deo, lumen de lumine, deum verum de deo vero* ("God of God, light of light, very God of very God"). Tye, however, did not exclude that section, but he did, as described above, exclude an entirely different section that affects the reading here: *et iterum venturus est cum gloria judicare vivos et mortuos, cujus regni non erit finis* ("and he shall come again with glory to judge both the quick and the dead, whose kingdom shall have no end"). By removing this section, he elevates the final section of text by placing it next to *et resurrexit*, and in so doing, gives unprecedented weight to *et exspecto resurrectionem mortuorum* ("and I

---

28. Doe, "Introduction," xii.

expect/look forward to the resurrection of the dead"). While "resurrection of the dead" appears to be highlighted in all three Credo settings over mention of Jesus' resurrection, of the three, Tye brings "resurrection of the dead" more to the foreground of his setting than does either Taverner or Sheppard. These factors suggest a development in Tye's version of the Credo that would seem to place it later than Taverner's and Sheppard's settings. Some of the features in Tye's setting seem to be written in response to the two preceding settings of the *Western Wind* and, certainly in regard to these two phrases, there is a more fully developed sense of personal interpretation of the text than is found in the other two. Even with such an apparently straightforward text as the Credo, these three composers reveal themselves as conscious interpreters of this text.

REFERENCES AND FURTHER READING

Benham, Hugh. *Latin Church Music in England, c. 1460–575*. London: Barrie and Jenkins, 1977.

Brown, Howard Mayer. *Music in the Renaissance*. Prentice-Hall History of Music Series. Englewood Cliffs, NJ: Prentice-Hall, 1976.

Collins, H. B. "Introduction." In Taverner, John. *The Western Wynde: Mass for Four Voices*, edited by H. B. Collins, 1–4 (n.p.) London: J. & W. Chester, 1924.

Commemorating the 450th Anniversary of his Death: John Taverner c. 1490–545. Directed by Peter Phillips. CD Recording. Gimell, 1995.

Davison, Nigel. "The Western Wind Masses." *The Musical Quarterly* 57 (1971) 427–43.

Doe, Paul. "Introduction." In *Christopher Tye II: Masses*, edited by Paul Doe, ix–xv. Early English Church Music 24. London: Stainer and Bell, 1980.

———. "Latin Polyphony under Henry VIII." *Proceedings of the Royal Musical Association* 95 (1968) 81–96.

Hand, Colin. *John Taverner: His Life and Music*. London: Eulenburg, 1978.

Hannas, Ruth. "Concerning Deletions in the Polyphonic Mass Credo." *Journal of the American Musicological Society* 5 (1952) 155–86.

Harrison, Frank Llewellyn. *Music in Medieval Britain*. Studies in the History of Music. 4th ed. Buren, The Netherlands: Fritz Knuf, 1980.

Messenger, Thomas. "Texture and Form in Taverner's 'Western Wind' Mass." *Journal of the American Musicological Society* 22 (1969) 504–8.

Petti, Anthony G., ed. *John Taverner (c. 1490–1545): The Western Wind Mass for Four Voices*. London: Chester Music, 1982.

Phillips, Peter. "Liner Notes." In *Western Wind Masses* by John Taverner, Christopher Tye, and John Sheppard. Directed by Peter Phillips. CD Recording. Gimell, 1993.

Porter, Wendy J. *Early English Composers and the Credo: Emphasis as Interpretation in Sixteenth-Century Music*. Routledge Research in Music Series. London: Routledge, 2022.

Reese, Gustave. *Music in the Renaissance*. Rev. ed. New York: Norton, 1959.

Sandon, Nick, ed. *John Sheppard II: Masses*. Translated by Nick Sandon. Early English Church Music 18. London: Stainer and Bell, 1976.

11

Images of Christ in Credos of Bach, Beethoven, and Stravinsky

INTRODUCTION

IN THE PREVIOUS CHAPTER, I treated three Reformation era composers in their interpretation of the Latin Credo in relation to *resurrection*. In this chapter, I turn to three later composers to examine their treatment of the same text but concentrate upon their images of Christ within the Credo. These three composers, Bach, Beethoven, and Stravinsky, each deviated from their normal patterns of compositional scope to use the Latin text of the Mass. Bach normally wrote compositions in German, Beethoven did not write religious music as a rule, and Stravinsky might reasonably have been expected to use Russian. Each set the mass in a way that depicts a unique image of Christ. This image becomes apparent in a comparison of the Credo sections of Bach's *Mass in B Minor*, Beethoven's *Missa Solemnis*, and Stravinsky's *Mass*. By focusing briefly on the overall structure of each mass, and then specifically on the central Credo sections as they relate to the Christ figure, some instructive observations can be made. Without using the works to speculate on each composer's religious faith, certain personal details of each composer and his known intentions for the mass do shed light on the particular image of Christ that is created, as do the musical and textual details of each composition.

In an attempt to draw theological characteristics out of sacred musical compositions there is a tendency to read into the music and text insights that may well not be there. As a case in point, Martin Cooper uses the opening bars of Beethoven's Credo to caricature theological speculation:

> Is the orchestra's initial leap . . . a leap of faith? and are the rugged entries of the first theme, with its suspensions and ascents into the void symbolical of Beethoven's battle against doubt? are the suspensions, as it were, suspensions of disbelief? and when the bass line in bar 8 climbs towards an E flat that is in fact sung by the sopranos while the basses break off prematurely, are we to believe that Beethoven dispatched the basses to the heights in search for a God that they never found, and that the sopranos take up the search instead—to discover a God whose omnipotence keeps them, twelve bars later, on a top B flat for the best part of five bars? It is difficult to believe in detailed symbolism of this kind.[1]

I agree—this is difficult to believe. As fascinating as such speculation might be, there is little in the music or in Beethoven's life that allows us to make such correlations of music and biography. However, apart from this kind of biographical interpretive reading, how the composer emphasizes certain words or phrases of the text or selects keys or musical motifs to indicate related sections all combine to form a certain picture or image of the subject. As Robert L. Marshall says, "the text of the Mass Ordinary—at least in the two lengthy sections, the *Gloria* and the *Credo*—does not unambiguously suggest any particular subdivision or formal ordering. The design is therefore up to the composer."[2] Rather than use the works to try to view the *composer*, I will show how certain choices the composer has made in setting the Credo section of each of the following masses allows for a certain way of viewing the *subject*, in this case the image of Christ.

BACH'S *MASS IN B MINOR*

I begin my study with Bach's well-known *Mass in B Minor*, a major work that has been compelling for scholarly examination and still merits a few further probings here.

Background to Bach's Mass in B Minor

Johann Sebastian Bach (1685–1750) wrote—or compiled and re-wrote—the *Mass in B Minor* (1749) near the end of his life.[3] There are two is-

---

1. Cooper, *Beethoven*, 241–42.
2. Marshall, *Music of Johann Sebastian Bach*, 182.
3. This discussion expands upon my discussion of Bach's *Mass in B Minor* in

sues that continually emerge in establishing the proper background for understanding this mass. The first is its composite nature. The issue of parody is continually raised in discussion about the *Mass in B Minor*. The practice of using past material or borrowing music and reworking it into new compositions was a common one in Bach's day.[4] Today this borrowing might be viewed unfavourably, but it is in large part what makes the *Mass in B Minor* enduring.[5] The majority of these earlier sources are Bach's own religious works. The works used span the years 1714 to 1749, most of Bach's career as a composer.[6] When Bach used movements from his earlier church cantatas, he did not take them over as they were, but rewrote them to a higher degree of perfection than the model.[7] Bach often took sections of his own secular work, for example, music written for a one-time occasion such as a coronation, and rewrote such work into his sacred music—but never the reverse. Whether secular or sacred in its original form—perhaps an instrumental line rewritten for voices or a chorus rewritten to fit a slightly different text—the setting of the *Mass in B Minor* became the final form. Wolff comments that, in Bach's work, "as the result of further compositional refinements, the Mass movements whose parody models are known invariably surpass the pieces on which they are based."[8]

The second issue is the theological implications of Bach's *Mass in B Minor*. The work has caused much speculation and debate, partly because, although Bach had set the mass several times, for this, his greatest and final sacred work, he again chose the Latin text rather than the customary German of his cantatas. Therefore, musicians and theologians question why he chose to compose the work and why he did so in a language that appears to be in some conflict with both the theology and practices of the German Lutheran Church. Some suggest that Bach was leaning towards Catholicism, although even in post-Reformation Germany there were certain Protestant cities and churches, including Leipzig where Bach lived for the last twenty-five years or so of his life, where the

---

chapter 2 above.

4. Marshall, *Music of Johann Sebastian Bach*, 32.

5. Butt, *Bach*, 42; cf. Butt, "Mass in B Minor," 285–86.

6. Leaver, "Mature Vocal Works," 116. It has been suggested that Bach's major source was the Dresden Mass tradition, on which, see Stauffer, *Bach*.

7. Geiringer, *Johann Sebastian Bach*, 207.

8. Wolff, *Bach*, 333.

mass was celebrated in ways identical to the Catholic mass,[9] and the use of the Latin texts in Leipzig was "in keeping with its liturgy, which had continuously employed the language of medieval Christendom for these parts of public worship."[10] In any case, there are numerous hypotheses regarding how this work fits with the rest of Bach's sacred compositions. Wolff calls it a "political move . . . with the aim of obtaining the title of court composer,"[11] but Schweitzer states about the mass: "It is as if Bach had here tried to write a really *Catholic* Mass; he endeavours to present faith under its larger and more objective aspects."[12]

Despite all of this speculation regarding his motives, we can reasonably conclude that Bach probably did not expect the work as a whole to be performed in church, particularly as the music alone can take over two hours to perform. John Butt writes: "The conclusion which many writers . . . are reluctant to reach is that Bach may have compiled the work with no specific practical end in mind, an act which would clearly be more appropriate for a composer of a later age, when music had become an 'autonomous' art." However, Butt goes on to say, ". . . perhaps the most useful means of summing up its meaning and content is to consider its 'universality,' with regard both to its place in Bach's oeuvre and [to] its apparent ecumenicism . . . he seems to have had one aim in mind: the summation and perfection of his entire lifework."[13] Although it is difficult to prove what Bach may have thought, an argument can be made that the mass is in fact a summative and emblematic work of Bach's musical career, certainly of his sacred vocal music.

Although there is still doubt regarding Bach's intentions for the complete mass, the five main sections of the mass—Kyrie, Gloria, Credo, Sanctus, and Agnus Dei—are well-suited to Bach's sense of proportion and balance. Within these five sections, the Credo is situated in the middle of the text as the theological centre and the "intellectual formulation," as Barry Cooper calls it.[14] It is probable that Bach wrote at least the Credo, or what he himself titles as the *Symbolum Nicenum* (Nicene

---

9. Spitta, *Johann Sebastian Bach*, 2:263.

10. Terry, *Music of Bach*, 88.

11. See Wolff, *Bach*, 35, where he further comments that the "choice of this 'interdenominational' subject was precisely because of the conversion of the reigning electoral house to Catholicism . . ."

12. Schweitzer, *J. S. Bach*, 2:314.

13. Butt, *Bach*, 24.

14. Cooper, *Beethoven*, 240.

Creed), to be used in its entirety for the liturgy. The manuscript of the *Symbolum Nicenum* has its own title page, which suggests that it was designed to exist on its own and marks its potential use as a separate work.[15] Bach's musical treatment of the words of the Credo shows the significance of this central movement and how he focuses it on the image of the crucified Christ.

An Image of the Crucified Christ

Bach divides the Credo text into nine sections with the *crucifixus* at the centre. He uses this division along with the relationships of time signatures and keys, the musical forms of the sections, and the choice of choir versus soloists to frame the middle movement, the *crucifixus*. Ultimately, the image of the crucified Christ emerges as the most significant image of Bach's Credo. His use of archaic elements gives a sense of continuity with a past tradition that also focuses on the *crucifixus*. The various elements that Bach uses leave little ambiguity as to the centrality of the crucified Christ.

The nine sections into which Bach divides the Credo are as follows:

1. *credo in unum deum*	1. I believe in one God
2. *credo in unum deum, patrem omnipotentem, factorem coeli et terrae, visibilium omnium et invisibilium*	2. I believe in one God, the Father Almighty, maker of heaven and earth and of all things visible and invisible[16]
3. *et in unum dominum Jesum Christum, filium dei unigenitum, et ex patre natum ante omnia saecula, deum de deo, lumen de lumine, deum verum de deo vero: genitum, non factum, consubstantialem patri per quem omnia facta sunt qui propter nos homines et propter nostram salutem descendit de coelis*	3. and in one Lord Jesus Christ, the only begotten son of God, begotten of his Father before all worlds, God of God, light of light, very God of very God, begotten, not made, being of one substance with the Father by whom all things were made who for us men [sic] and for our salvation came down from heaven
4. *et incarnatus est de spiritu sancto ex Maria virgine et homo factus est*	4. and was incarnate by the Holy Spirit of the virgin Mary and was made man
5. *crucifixus etiam pro nobis sub Pontio Pilato passus et sepultus est*	5. was crucified also for us under Pontius Pilate, he suffered and was buried

15. Butt, *Bach*, 15.
16. Bach repeats the phrase from the first chorus in this section.

6. et resurrexit tertia die secundum scripturas et ascendit in coelum sedet ad dexteram dei patris et iterum venturus est cum gloria judicare vivos et mortuos cujus regni non erit finis	6. and rose again the third day according to the Scriptures and ascended into heaven and sitteth on the right hand of God the Father, and he shall come again with glory to judge both the quick and the dead, whose kingdom shall have no end
7. et in spiritum sanctum dominum et vivificantem qui ex patre filioque procedit qui cum patre et filio simul adoratur et conglorificatur qui locutus est per prophetas et unam sanctam catholicam et apostolicam ecclesiam	7. and in the Holy Spirit, the Lord and giver of life, who from the Father and the Son proceedeth, who with the Father and the Son together is worshipped and glorified, who spake by the Prophets; and in one holy catholic and apostolic Church
8. confiteor unum baptisma in remissionem peccatorum et expecto resurrectionem mortuorum	8. I acknowledge one baptism for the remission of sins and I look for the resurrection of the dead
9. et expecto resurrectionem mortuorum et vitam venturi saeculi. amen.	9. and I look for the resurrection of the dead and the life of the world to come. Amen.

Nos. 1 and 2 are linked ideologically in expressing belief in God the Father and nos. 8 and 9 are linked in dealing with the Christian church. Nos. 3 and 7 are linked by each being about one other member of the Trinity. The middle three—nos. 4, 5, and 6—relate to the details of Christ's life and are the central focus of the text on which Bach builds the symmetry of his work. Of these three—incarnation, crucifixion, and resurrection—he places the crucifixion at the heart of the Credo.

Bach uses the time signatures of these nine sections to reinforce the central placement of the *crucifixus*:

Part Two: Musical Traditions and Interpretations

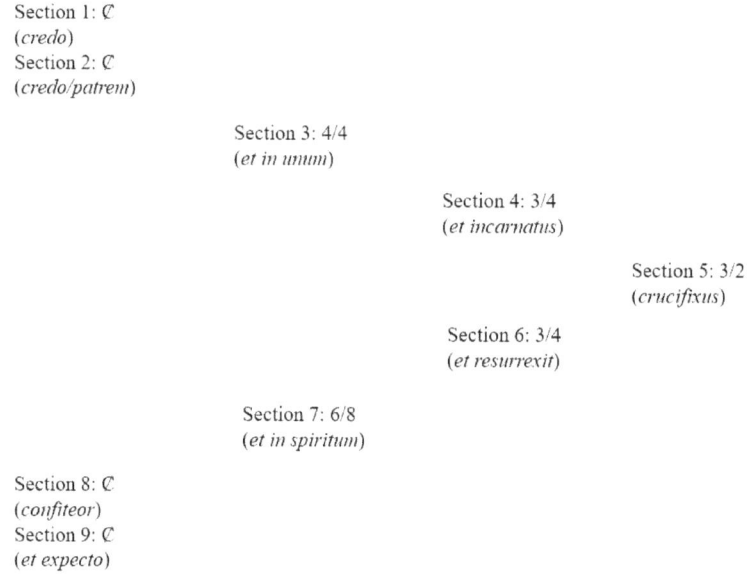

Figure 1. Placement of the *Crucifixus* in the Credo by Time Signature

The two outer movements at the beginning and at the end of the Credo are all marked ₵ ("cut-time"); the three central movements are all set in three beats to the bar. Of the three middle movements, the two outer ones are in 3/4, giving three quarter notes to the measure. Only the *crucifixus* in the centre is set in 3/2. The 3/2 setting of the *crucifixus*, which gives three half-notes to each measure, allows the central section to move at a slower pace to accommodate the slowly repeated descending bass line. The third section, *et in unum dominum*, is the only section in 4/4 and deals with the subject of Jesus as the second person of the Trinity, while the seventh section, *et in spiritum*, is the only setting written in 6/8 and is about the Spirit. Perhaps the 4/4 as a multiple of two can be seen to represent the second person of the Trinity and the 6/8 as a more complex multiple of three than 3/4, for instance, can be seen to represent the third person of the Trinity. Obviously too much can be—and has at times been—made of this symbolism, but the structural and theological correlates do seem to exist.

The relationship of the keys focuses on the *crucifixus* as central as well. Although the work is referred to as the B minor mass, the predominant key in the Credo (and in fact the entire mass) is that of D major. The first two sections of the Credo are in D major, although technically the first movement is in the archaic Mixolydian mode. This is in keeping with Bach's use of an archaic Gregorian chant melody in this first section. The last two sections also have this kind of integral relationship, making use of an archaic mode and a Gregorian melody in the first of the two sections. The duet that deals with the second person of the Trinity, section 3, is in the key of G major, which is closely related to D major by being built on the subdominant of the D scale. The key of A major is the other major key most closely related to D major, built on the dominant, and it is no surprise to discover that Bach set the solo in section 7, which deals with the third person of the Trinity, in A major. These two movements, the duet and the solo, surround the three middle choruses that focus on Christ's birth, death, and resurrection. The setting of the *crucifixus* is in E minor. Figure 2 shows the arrangement of the keys. The key of E minor is somewhat unusual for the Credo, or at least a less predictable key for D major than the rest of the Credo. As the relative minor of G major, it relates most closely to the duet, *et in unum dominum*, which expresses belief in the Lord Jesus Christ.

Section 1: D mode
(*credo*)
Section 2: D major
(*patrem*)
   Section 3: G major
   (*et in unum*)
      Section 4: B minor
      (*et incarnatus*)
         Section 5: E minor
         (*crucifixus*)
      Section 6: D major
      (*et resurrexit*)
   Section 7: A major
   (*et in spiritum*)
Section 8: F# mode
(*confiteor*)
Section 9: D major
(*et expecto*)

Figure 2. Placement of the *Crucifixus* in the Credo by Key

This is not an unexpected relationship, as Bach has placed great emphasis on the complexity of the second person of the Trinity in the *et in unum dominum* (mentioned below) and shows the connection of the person of the *et in unum dominum* with the person of the *crucifixus* as fundamental to the significance of the crucifixion.

Bach uses soloists in the Credo only to depict the second and third persons of the Trinity.[17] For instance, Bach chooses a duet for *et in unum dominum* as a way of describing the internal relationship of Father and Son. Here Bach writes for two independent voices, soprano and alto soloists, to portray the difficult concept of the oneness of Jesus and God, yet the separateness of Jesus as Son and second person of the Trinity. The *et in unum dominum* was originally music from a love song by Bach, which quite naturally was set as a duet. The "two-in-oneness" of this setting is appropriate for a text depicting the second person of the Trinity, Jesus Christ. Written as a strict canon, with one part closely imitating the other, the notes are separated by a fourth and each musical statement is echoed by the other as if to emphasize how one follows the other.[18] It is not always the same voice that leads, suggesting the intertwining of the two-in-one. Evidence of this symbolism comes from Bach's own words on the manuscript, where he wrote "Two voices express 2."[19] The only other section to be written as a solo is *et in spiritum*, which is about the Holy Spirit. Otherwise, all the main sections of the Credo are sung by the choir, perhaps to keep extraneous personalities out of the picture and to more closely align it with the actual corporate confession of the Credo by a church congregation.

While Bach emphasizes this two-in-one image, it is not his main focus; nor is the *et incarnatus*, as lovely as it is. The *et incarnatus* and the *et resurrexit* on either side contrast with the *crucifixus*. There is a strong sense of progression through the three events—from the incarnation through the crucifixion to the resurrection. But the focus that Bach presents as central to interpretation of the Credo text is that of the crucifixion. By the very manner in which Bach lays out the entire *Mass in B Minor*, there is a sense of orderliness and symmetry. This holds true not only for the musical ideas, but also for the textual ideas. Everything is presented within the boundaries of this symmetry and especially the words of the

---

17. Spitta notes that the solos "assume a less personal character than is usual even with Bach," which is perhaps in keeping with depicting persons of the Trinity (see *Johann Sebastian Bach*, 3:46).

18. See Spitta, *Johann Sebastian Bach*, 3:31, where he says that the "intention is unmistakable, since the musical scheme allows of the canonic imitation on the fourth below from the very beginning."

19. Butt, *Bach*, 52.

Credo are laid out with great attention to detail and overall form. As a result of this orderliness and logic, the image of the crucifixion of the living Christ that Bach depicts forms the apex of the work but is also portrayed as part of a greater plan and *not* simply as an extremely emotional image.[20] Grief is represented through recognized musical symbolism without being trivialized. The passacaglia, a slowly descending bass line that moves chromatically, is a well-recognized Baroque musical symbol used to depict grief.[21] Stephen Daw's comment is that "the bass-line of the great 'Crucifixus' has the universally understood poignancy of the lament."[22]

Although Bach had implemented this particular musical idiom in various ways periodically throughout his life, it is noteworthy that, for one of his most significant and enduring musical images, he chose what for him was already thirty-five years old: the opening chorus of the cantata no. 12, *Weinen, Klagen, Sorgen, Zagen*. To this he adds an introduction, changes some of the instrumentation, intensifies the pulse of the passacaglia bass line, and adds "a textually motivated a cappella concluding phrase ('... passus et sepultus est') that modulates from E minor to G major,"[23] but it is familiar nonetheless.[24]

However, drawing from much further back than even his own early writing, Bach based his Credo on archaic traditions in several ways. First, Bach used the archaic language of the Credo, as mentioned above. Alfred Mann remarks that "Bach's remarkable use of the entire Catholic Mass text linked his work to that of the great composers of the past; the B Minor Mass may be considered a conscious contribution that Bach made to that genre of composition which had been the noblest musical form since the days of Dufay, Josquin, and Palestrina."[25] Secondly, he used ancient modes and Gregorian melodies or chants to form the basis of several sections (i.e., sections 1 and 8). Christoph Wolff comments on Bach's use of two pairs of opening and ending choruses that incorporate "a *stile antico* movement, with liturgical *cantus firmus*..." followed by a full chorus

---

20. Contrast Bach's and Beethoven's approaches in McCaldin, "Choral Music," esp. 405.

21. Geiringer, *Johann Sebastian Bach*, 261–62.

22. Daw, *Music of Johann Sebastian Bach*, 161.

23. Wolff, *Bach*, 333.

24. It would be useful here to listen to a recording of the *crucifixus* of Bach's *Mass in B Minor*, noting especially his use of the underlying passacaglia, the repeated bass line.

25. Mann, *Bach Studies*, 8.

movement. Wolff further identifies how inside these framing choruses, the arias further frame the central three choruses "whose texts, in turn, mark the Christological center of the Nicene dogma. In this chiastic-symmetrical form . . . the *stile antico* emerges as a palpable architectonic unit."[26] Mann also comments that chant "had served through the ages as thematic material upon which composers based their compositions in more and more complex structures. Bach had used chant melodies on various occasions, but they became of primary importance to him when he turned his full attention to the composition of the Mass text."[27] Thirdly, Bach also refers to earlier practices by his use of five parts in the choir, rather than the customary four parts.[28] For instance, where there would normally be soprano, alto, tenor, and bass, he has written two soprano parts as well as alto, tenor, and bass. "This may seem to be a small difference, but in reality it signifies a different orientation of style; the five-part texture was prevalent in the century before Bach, not in his own . . ."[29] In Bach's later years he devoted serious study to the compositional techniques and styles of Italian composers, such as Palestrina (ca. 1525–1594), who wrote for these same five parts for choir, and here we see Bach drawing on that earlier tradition.

Bach's integration of archaic elements both stylistically and structurally into the *Mass in B Minor* connects it with much earlier church practice and results in a sacred work that establishes continuity with a long history of church music. His division of the text, his use of various elements to identify chiastic, symmetrical structure and focal point such as the pattern of time signatures and key signatures, and the use of soloists to frame central choruses, all unerringly point to the Christ figure in the *crucifixus* as central to Bach's setting of the Credo, and ultimately of his setting of the mass. All of these factors contribute to Bach's setting of the Credo image of Christ having an archaic and timeless sense, and, perhaps, a universal and ecumenical one.

---

26. Wolff, *Bach*, 102. He also says, ". . . traditional vocal polyphony was almost entirely bound to liturgical practice, predominantly in works with Latin texts; it became the *stile antico*" (87).

27. Mann, *Bach Studies*, 29–30.

28. Geiringer, *Johann Sebastian Bach*, 208.

29. Mann, *Bach Studies*, 21.

BEETHOVEN'S *MISSA SOLEMNIS*

From Bach's Mass, we now turn to Beethoven's *Missa Solemnis*, written by another of the great musical composers but one not known for embracing sacred music. Nevertheless, the *Missa Solemnis* offers interesting interpretations of this text.

Background to the Missa Solemnis

Ludwig van Beethoven (1770-1827) intended his *Missa Solemnis* or Mass in D Major for the occasion of the enthronement of Archduke Rudolph as Archbishop in 1820.[30] Beethoven started on the work in 1819 but continued working on it until 1823 and, needless to say, missed the intended occasion. The work was first performed on April 7, 1824, in St. Petersburg, and was published in 1827, soon after the composer's death.

There have been numerous theories regarding the origins of Beethoven's *Missa Solemnis*. A common theory is that it depicts Beethoven's personal religious experience and beliefs.[31] For example, Paul Bekker relates the entire composition of the Mass as growing out of a spiritual crisis Beethoven had in 1819.[32] Warren Kirkendale proposes that the *Missa Solemnis* directly conforms to the rules and accepted forms of religious music of the day.[33] According to Barry Cooper, who takes a slightly jaundiced view of Beethoven and his reasons for composition, the three motivating forces for Beethoven's creativity were performance, publication, and payment, as some of his shrewd business dealings even for the *Missa Solemnis* suggest.[34] However, as pragmatic as Beethoven may have been, there is no doubting the depth of emotion he explores or the level of creativity he displays in this work. In a letter of 1824, Beethoven writes about the *Missa Solemnis*, "it was my chief aim to awaken, and to render lasting, religious feeling as well in the singers as in the hearers."[35] Cooper comments that Beethoven "... used in his setting every means of musical imagery to enhance the meaning of the

---

30. This expands upon my comments in chapter 2 above on Beethoven's *Missa Solemnis*.
31. Solomon, *Beethoven Essays*, 227-28.
32. Bekker, *Beethoven*, 269-70.
33. Kirkendale, "New Roads," 676-77, 699-700.
34. Cooper, *Beethoven and the Creative Process*, 30.
35. Beethoven, *Beethoven's Letters*, 331.

text and make it more intelligible to the listener."[36] Without attempting or presuming to understand Beethoven's intentions or his theological preferences, there is one aspect of the Christ figure that he makes very visible—the humanity of Christ.

An Image of the Humanity of Christ

An image that Beethoven focuses on and develops throughout his Credo in the *Missa Solemnis* is the human aspect of Christ. Although it is common to associate the *Missa Solemnis* with Beethoven's own experience and to presume that the work is an expression of his own emotions,[37] what is more pertinent to my particular study is that he depicts an image of Christ with a pronounced emphasis on Christ's human characteristics. This human side is developed by attention first of all to the statement that he is human, and second to the exploration of human emotion that Christ experiences, especially the suffering of his death by crucifixion. While settings of the Credo text naturally include *et homo factus est* ("and was made man"), Beethoven sets this statement in a new way. He uses various elements to identify *et homo factus est* as central to the Christ-figure as seen in the Credo, such as his division of the text, his use of tempos and keys and their interrelationships to identify the structural layout of the work, his attention to certain words and ideas in the various sections, and his integration and contrast of soloists and chorus.

Beethoven's division of the text is a significant factor in determining his image of Christ. He creates fifteen independent sections of the words of the Credo, dividing the text as follows:

1. *credo in unum deum, patrem omnipotentem, factorem coeli et terrae, visibilium omnium et invisibilium*	1. I believe in one God, the Father Almighty, maker of heaven and earth and of all things visible and invisible
2. *[credo] in unum dominum Jesum Christum, filium dei unigenitum, et ex patre natum ante omnia saecula*	2. [I believe] in one Lord Jesus Christ, the only begotten son of God, begotten of his Father before all worlds[38]

---

36. Cooper, *Beethoven and the Creative Process*, 57.

37. Bekker, *Beethoven*, 273.

38. Here, as well as in nos. 11 and 12, Beethoven substitutes the word Credo, "I believe" (noted in square brackets), for the customary word *et*, "and."

3. *deum de deo, lumen de lumine, deum verum de deo vero: genitum, non factum, consubstantialem patri per quem omnia facta sunt*	3. God of God, light of light, very God of very God, begotten not made, being of one substance with the Father by whom all things were made
4. *qui propter nos homines et propter nostram salutem descendit de coelis*	4. who for us men [sic] and for our salvation came down from heaven
5. *et incarnatus est de spiritu sancto ex Maria virgine*	5. and was incarnate by the Holy Spirit of the virgin Mary
6. *et homo factus est*	6. and was made man
7. *crucifixus etiam pro nobis sub Pontio Pilato passus et sepultus est*	7. was crucified also for us under Pontius Pilate, he suffered and was buried
8. *et resurrexit tertia die secundum scripturas*	8. and rose again the third day according to the Scriptures
9. *et ascendit in coelum sedet ad dexteram dei patris et iterum venturus est cum gloria*	9. and ascended into heaven and sitteth on the right hand of God the Father and he shall come again with glory
10. *judicare vivos et mortuos cujus regni non erit finis*	10. to judge both the quick and the dead whose kingdom shall have no end
11. [*credo*] *in spiritum sanctum dominum et vivificantem qui ex patre filioque procedit qui cum patre et filio simul adoratur et conglorificatur qui locutus est per prophetas*	11. [I believe] in the Holy Spirit, the Lord and Giver of life, who from the Father and the Son proceedeth, who with the Father and the Son together is worshipped and glorified, who spake by the Prophets
12. [*credo*] *in unam sanctam catholicam et apostolicam ecclesiam confiteor unum baptisma in remissionem peccatorum et expecto resurrectionem mortuorum et vitam venturi saeculi. amen.*	12. [I believe] in one holy catholic and apostolic Church; I acknowledge one baptism for the remission of sins and I look for the resurrection of the dead and the life of the world to come. Amen.[39]
13. *et vitam venturi saeculi. amen.*	13. And the life of the world to come. Amen.
14. *et vitam venturi saeculi. amen.*	14. And the life of the world to come. Amen.
15. *et vitam venturi saeculi. amen.*	15. And the life of the world to come. Amen.

39. The entire Credo text is completely stated in the first twelve divisions that Beethoven has made, with the last line repeated in each of the final three sections. For the purpose of identifying the main focus of the body of the text and musical work, these last three sections will be left on their own as an appended musical unit, functioning separately as the closing fugue of the work.

Part Two: Musical Traditions and Interpretations

In dividing the sections as he does, Beethoven identifies several phrases as distinctive that Bach, for instance, does not. For example, Beethoven sets *et homo factus est* separately, rather than including it with *et incarnatus est*. The separation of the phrase "and was made man" from the previous words that began "and was incarnate" gives a new emphasis to Jesus Christ becoming human. Where typically the statement is: "and was incarnate by the Holy Spirit of the virgin Mary and was made man," here "and was made man" becomes an entirely separate statement.

There is ambiguity on several levels as to whether the central focus of Beethoven's Credo consists of three or four sections. If there are three, *et homo factus est* is placed in the middle of the three sections. If there are four, then even if the more complex and weighty movement of the *crucifixus* is central by intention, the symmetrical balance does not fully support this arrangement. The question relates partly to the passage that follows immediately after the *crucifixus*—the *et resurrexit*. In some ways *et resurrexit* seems to belong to the previous group and in some ways to the following group. Undoubtedly, this ambivalence is not entirely unintentional nor is it particularly inappropriate. In either instance, Beethoven uniquely emphasizes the humanity of Christ by giving special attention to the announcement: *et homo factus est*.

The tempos of the first twelve sections give an indication of inner groupings within the work, as well. Roger Fiske says,

> the Viennese Credo was almost always in three sections:
> Fast: Credo in unum Deum, etc.
> Slow: Et incarnatus est, etc.; in a contrasting key
> Fast: Et resurrexit tertia die, etc.
> Often the Credo ended with a fugue to the words "et vitam venturi saeculi. Amen". . . Beethoven was content to write in the usual three main sections and to end conventionally with a fugue . . .[40]

Indeed, sections 1–4 are at a fairly fast tempo, sections 5–7 are at slow tempos, and the following five sections, 8–12, are again at fast tempos, followed by the massive closing fugue. If these tempos indicate divisions, as they seem to, they first of all identify the traditional middle section of the Credo text but then secondarily identify the middle section of nos. 5–7 as the pivotal point of those three, which places *et homo factus est* at the centre. Although the *crucifixus* is the more traditional

---

40. Fiske, *Beethoven's Missa Solemnis*, 11.

place of focus, Beethoven draws our attention instead first to the phrase "and was made man."

The keys and their relationships throughout the Credo and particularly in the central section also bring a pronounced emphasis to the phrase *et homo factus est*, rather than focusing entirely on the *crucifixus*. While the *Missa Solemnis* is also known as the Mass in D, the Credo itself is structured around the key not of D major but of B flat major, as the two beginning and two ending sections of the Credo are all in B flat major. The central section of the Credo is set in various keys around the tonality of D. The *et incarnatus* is in an archaic mode, centred on D and sounding somewhat like D minor, and the *crucifixus* is in D minor, although frequently sounding like it is trying to move away from the key. The only section in the Credo that is set in the home key of the Mass, D major, is *et homo factus est*. In William Drabkin's commentary on the key for this section he puts it in the context of the entire Mass: "It is sometimes remarked that this passage helps unify the Mass by recapitulating its home key, thus linking the one movement not in D major—the Credo—to the rest of the work."[41] But he suggests that D major is a sidetrack from the "quasi-minor" Dorian mode of the *et incarnatus* as a way of setting up the D minor of the *crucifixus*, which implies the centrality of the *crucifixus*.[42] However, perhaps this one instance of D major in the Credo is better understood as a clue to Beethoven's own perspective on the significance of *et homo factus est*. This section does not involve the complexity of writing that is found in the *crucifixus*, but it does accentuate and dramatize a high point of tension and release in the work. This isolated return to the home key of the entire work perhaps indicates that Beethoven has shifted the balance slightly from the traditional focus of the *crucifixus* to give tremendous import to the words preceding it, *et homo factus est*.

Beethoven places the following section, *et resurrexit*, in the archaic Mixolydian mode. It is difficult to determine whether by this he intended it to be linked to the earlier section, *et incarnatus*, which is also set in an archaic mode, as this would frame the inner sections of *et homo factus est* and *crucifixus*, or merely as an archaic way of making a pronouncement before entering into the following section, *et ascendit*. The ambiguity and lack of schematized symmetry in Beethoven's setting of the Credo mark a

---

41. Drabkin, *Beethoven*, 107.
42. Drabkin, *Beethoven*, 107.

shift in focus from the icon-like predictability of the Christ figure to one that has more evolving human dimensions.

Even the words that Beethoven chooses to emphasize contribute to a certain image of Christ in this work. In the second movement, he uses *fortissimos* on the word *dominum* ("Lord"), and then later on the word *natum* ("born" or "begotten"). In the fourth movement, the hymn-like *qui propter*, he vividly highlights the words *descendit de coelis*, using familiar word-painting that makes use of descending scales to depict descending from heaven. By commanding attention to the words *dominum*, *natum* and then *descendit de coelis*, he sets up an image that is later revealed, that of the humanity of Christ in *et homo factus est*. Here the word that is dwelt upon and developed is *homo* ("man"). The concept of humanity is further developed in the *crucifixus*, where the word explored to the greatest degree is *passus* ("suffered"). Here Beethoven gives each soloist a specific role to play in bringing out the individual and human quality of Christ's suffering.[43]

The interaction and contrast of the soloists and the chorus directs yet more attention to the human image that Beethoven dwells on in *et incarnatus*, *et homo*, and *crucifixus*. All four soloists are used in *et incarnatus*, singing in a *mezza-voce* or semi-spoken style. The chorus enters about half-way through this section, *pianissimo*, in a semi-spoken style of chant. Fiske describes the combination of "the unusual simplicity of two-part counterpoint with modalism" as "mysterious and awesome."[44] The combination does create a sense of mystery that underlines the text at this point: the inexplicable concept of how God could in some way become human. Fiske gives a further impression of this section: "When these same words are intoned on one note, *pianissimo*, by the whole chorus, the effect is for a brief moment like the murmured undertones of the congregation at a normal church service."[45] From this quiet and intense chanting section the tenor emerges singing the word *et* on the high note E, the same note all the upper voices of the choir have been chanting. As

---

43. Two words that are not given prolonged emphasis in the *et resurrexit* are the very words, *et resurrexit*. Compared with Bach's use of all the voices of the choir in a fairly lengthy section of the *et resurrexit* in his mass, Beethoven's use of one voice to make the solitary statement of *et resurrexit* in less than two measures is short indeed. Whether this is for dramatic effect—a bold quick pronouncement—or because the concept of resurrection is difficult to believe and Beethoven chose to move as quickly through it as possible, is difficult to say.

44. Fiske, *Beethoven's Missa Solemnis*, 58.

45. Fiske, *Beethoven's Missa Solemnis*, 59.

the music abruptly changes from the archaic mode into D major the tenor note moves up a tone to F# to begin the full phrase, *et homo factus est*.[46] In this shift to D major and to the higher tone, Beethoven has used the *tierce de picardie*, the sudden and rather unexpected change from ending on a minor chord to a major chord, to make a dramatic transition from high suppressed tension to bold release, as vivid as the first breaking through of sunlight in a sunrise. The tenor at this point depicts *et homo factus est* as though he himself were surprised and utterly delighted to discover that he is human and truly alive.[47] Beethoven sets the next repetitions of *homo* and *et homo factus est* as an exchange back and forth between tenor and chorus, both of whom treat the words with tenderness, even awe, yet in a manner of conversation. Here Beethoven develops the central image of his Mass—the humanity of the Christ figure—with tremendous emotion and sensitivity. The single voice of the tenor conversing with the chorus allows one to imagine the Christ figure represented as one who has a natural and earthly relationship with humanity because of his own humanity.[48] In the *crucifixus* that follows, the human-ness of this figure is treated in greater detail. Here Beethoven returns to using all four soloists. Each one separately emphasizes *passus*, drawing out the sense of human emotion and human suffering. This contributes to Beethoven's Christ image by filling in the depth of his humanity.

Beethoven's approach to the text, sometimes giving more than one perspective, emphasizes an unwillingness to force every detail into a pre-set mould, giving a human dimension to his image that perfect symmetry would not. He uses archaic features in a way that seems to underline that he is *not* conforming to ancient patterns but creating new ones, and, in this case, giving a new perspective on the humanness of Christ. The way one section musically grows out of the previous one, as in *et homo factus est* moving right out of *et incarnatus*, gives Beethoven's image of Christ a depth and warmth that may not be found in a truly liturgical setting of the text. Perhaps as a result there is a sense of three dimensions

---

46. McCaldin, "Choral Music," 404.

47. See Matthews, *Beethoven*, 204, where he comments on the tenor as he "breaks into the warm D major harmony of 'et homo factus est.' This is surely one of the Mass's most inspired moments, coming as it does before the agonised D minor of the 'Crucifixus' . . ."

48. At this point, it would be helpful to listen to an excerpt of a recording of Beethoven's *Missa Solemnis*, beginning in the *et incarnatus* to hear the contrast of the tenor line in *et homo factus est*.

in his image of Christ that is not typical of earlier settings of the Mass. The image of Christ that Beethoven depicts seems to live and breathe, and even seems quite modern.[49]

STRAVINSKY'S *MASS*

The last example to consider is the *Mass* by a composer who is rarely identified with sacred music, but who had firm convictions about it.

Background to the Mass

Igor Stravinsky (1882–1971), who is probably still most well-known to the general public for his unprecedented use of rhythm and percussion in his ballet of 1911, *The Rite of Spring*, had moved an incredible distance from that work by the time he composed the *Mass* in the mid-1940s.[50] Stravinsky wrote his *Mass* (1944–1948) for mixed chorus and double wind quintet in the latter part of what some term his neo-classical period (Stravinsky himself would not necessarily have agreed with this designation). The first public performance of the *Mass* was at La Scala, Milan, on October 27, 1948, although this was not his choice of venues. Stravinsky wrote the Mass with the intention that it be used liturgically, not as a concert performance piece.[51] Stravinsky's often-quoted comment is that his *Mass* "was partly provoked by some Masses of Mozart that I found in a second-hand music store in Los Angeles in 1942 or 1943. As I played through these rococo-operatic sweets-of-sin, I knew I had to write a Mass of my own, but a real one."[52] This is one of Stravinsky's few uncommissioned works, which suggests that he wrote out of genuine piety, as opposed to simply writing for a business contract.

The *Mass* is not long, especially when compared to Bach's *Mass in B Minor* and Beethoven's *Missa Solemnis*. The score indicates 17 minutes, although Stravinsky actually intended it to take longer—but only by six minutes. Within these small parameters, Stravinsky uses the classical

---

49. Although I disagree with much in Adorno ("Alienated Masterpiece"), I believe that he has articulated in some ways what I have arrived at musically regarding the humanness of Beethoven's work.

50. This discussion expands upon my comments in chapter 2 above on Stravinsky's *Mass*.

51. Stravinsky and Craft, *Igor Stravinsky*, 76.

52. Stravinsky and Craft, *Igor Stravinsky*, 77.

element of symmetry, shaping the *Mass* as a formal arch, with the longest movement being the Credo.

Stravinsky chose the Latin text of the Mass, having gained experience with the language in *Oedipus Rex* (1927),[53] although the natural choice of language would seem to have been his native Russian, particularly as he had rejoined the Russian Orthodox Church in the late 1920s. Stravinsky's own practical reason for writing for the Catholic Mass as opposed to the Russian Church was that, as Stravinsky himself says, ". . . Orthodox tradition proscribes musical instruments in its services . . ." And he was not prepared to write a Mass for unaccompanied voices.[54]

The *Mass* is written for trebles and altos (both upper parts designated for children's voices), tenors and basses. Although since the earliest performances of the *Mass* women's voices have frequently been used, Stravinsky's explicit direction was that the upper parts be sung by children. In one of his letters he writes that for a New York recording of the *Mass* he used children who were "not at all first-rate," but he chose them, nevertheless, "because the presence of women in the music of the Mass, no matter how perfect they might be, would be a more serious mistake for the sense and spirit of this music than the imperfection of a chorus of children." A woman's voice, he claimed, "is always too passionate for liturgical chant."[55] Along with one of his numerous strong and now politically unacceptable opinions we also see his intended use for the *Mass*—the liturgy.

A Symbolic Image of the Crucified Christ

The image Stravinsky creates is a somewhat flat symbolic figure of the crucified Christ. As Gilbert Amy points out, one would have difficulty in finding sentimentalism in any of Stravinsky's portrayal of the sacred,[56] and this is particularly true of his *Mass*. Stravinsky identifies significant elements but does not particularly develop or interpret them. This is evident in the length of the entire *Mass*, as well as in the length of the Credo within the Mass. Since the Credo lasts only about four minutes in performance, there is little time with a text of this length and complexity to develop any one phrase either musically or textually. This is obviously

53. Amy, "Aspects," esp. 196.
54. Stravinsky and Craft, *Igor Stravinsky*, 77.
55. Craft, ed., *Stravinsky*, 1:246–47.
56. Amy, "Aspects of the Religious Music," 195.

Stravinsky's intention. The Credo is written in one movement and is scored for voices to sing in a semi-chanted style. The first phrase is sung by the priest, reinforcing that the proper setting be the liturgy.

Apart from the priest's intonation, the setting is one long, practically unbroken chant. The instrumentation is an unusual combination of two oboes, cor anglais, two bassoons, two trumpets, and three trombones, which creates a sound not unlike that of an organ. This also marks the Credo's suitability for the traditional liturgy. The dynamics of the Credo rarely vary from the *piano* marking. The dynamic range is narrow, and the vocal range is also quite limited. There are few, if any, dramatic effects or ornamentation. In fact, there is little that draws attention to itself. Further evidence of this is that Stravinsky uses no soloists in the Credo—no one individual emerges in this section at all. Stravinsky focuses attention on the function of the text. He draws attention to several textual details that are essential to the Christ of the Credo but does not elaborate them or interpret them. As a result, Stravinsky creates in this section of his Mass an image of Christ that is almost featureless and flat. The Credo has few elements of dramatic contrast and practically no emotion that would suggest the warmth of a living Christ. The image is a symbolic one that does not seem intended to display a natural life-likeness or an ethereal otherworldliness, but a functional image. Stephen Walsh notes that Stravinsky avoids "elaborately evolved musical structures . . . that do not have to do with a straightforward declamation of the words."[57] Stravinsky himself gives us the key to his Credo: "In making a musical setting of the Credo I wished only to preserve the text in a special way. One composes a march to facilitate marching men, so with my Credo I hope to provide an aid to the text. The Credo is the longest movement. There is much to believe."[58] Since a march is not written for contemplation and interpretation but rather as a functional tool to allow the marchers to move systematically and rhythmically forward, so Stravinsky has created a setting of the Credo—and ultimately an image of Christ—that is to be used functionally to move one along in liturgical worship.

Stravinsky makes use of forms that are classical or baroque in nature, emphasizing for instance the symmetrical features of some of these early works. He also uses a more severe or unornamented style. Mikhail Druskin calls it "an anticipation of the strictness and austerity of the

---

57. Walsh, *Music of Stravinsky*, 193.
58. Craft, "Stravinsky's *Mass*" (cited in White, *Stravinsky*, 447).

IMAGES OF CHRIST IN CREDOS OF BACH, BEETHOVEN, AND STRAVINSKY

composer's 'late' manner."[59] Robert Siohan emphasizes that the "austere polyphony of this score harks back to the past, and in some of its passages to an almost medieval hieraticism."[60] The *Mass* uses Gregorian chant as well as polyphony and counterpoint with more emphasis than previous works of Stravinsky, contributing to its archaic nature.[61] The use of features such as plainsong and syllabic word-setting, among others, points to the *Mass* being based on traditional church idioms.[62]

Contributing to the symbolic image of Christ is Stravinsky's use of symmetry in dividing the text into sections. After the priest's intonation, the work can be divided into three nearly equal-length sections of 52 measures, 49 measures, and 52 measures. The first section begins at *patrem* (cf. Bach nos. 2–3; Beethoven nos. 1–4), the second section at *et incarnatus est* (Bach nos. 4–6; Beethoven nos. 5–10), and the third section at *et in spiritum sanctum* (Bach nos. 7–9; Beethoven nos. 11–12). These are fairly consistent with traditional divisions of the text. The text that is given the most unusual rhythmic treatment is *et homo factus est* ("and was made man"). The rhythm of the voices and text at this point and the pulling of the instruments—notably the two trumpets—against the voices distinguish it from the rest of the work. But there is little here to suggest that Stravinsky is trying to interpret this phrase in any particular way or to give any indication of his own personal view of the meaning of the text. The only place where there is more than one measure of rest in the voices—in this case there are five measures in a row—is just following *et homo factus est* and just prior to *crucifixus*. Again, without giving much elaboration to the phrases, Stravinsky presents them in such a way that the traditional heart of the Credo text, the *crucifixus*, is definitely identified. Stravinsky has thus drawn attention to the phrase "and was made man" but has not amplified it. He then sets up the phrase dealing with the crucifixion by using the five measures of rest. The *crucifixus*—written for five voices, with the tenor in two parts—is distinct from the four voice parts of the rest of the Credo. The only instruments at this point are the cor anglais and bassoons until the words *passus et sepultus est*, where the oboes dispassionately enter. Stravinsky has highlighted the recognizable and significant details of the image of Christ, especially his being made

---

59. Druskin, *Igor Stravinsky*, 26.
60. Siohan, *Stravinsky*, 129.
61. White, *Stravinsky*, 100.
62. Walsh, *Music of Stravinsky*, 193.

human and then his resurrection, but the composer has not tried to fill in any kind of meaning around them. The words of the crucifixion are prepared and presented but not given emotional expression of any kind. The *crucifixus, et resurrexit,* and *et ascendit* are all delivered in the semi-chant of the earlier sections of the Credo with little variation.[63]

The first and only crescendo in the Credo begins at *cujus regni* ("whose reign"), increasing in pitch and volume on the *non erit finis* ("will never end"), with a *fermata* or pause on the second syllable of *finis*. The tenor line moves upward where one might expect a unison octave but results in a major ninth instead. The unison is reached at the next sentence of the text, when the voices move back to semi-chant on an E major chord at *et in spiritum sanctum*. The next words that are emphasized are done so in several ways. Stravinsky marks these words *poco più f* ("a little louder") and changes from using eighth notes and combinations of eighth notes and quarter notes to using four straight quarter notes on the words *ecclesiam, peccatorum,* and *mortuorum*. The corresponding marking in the score for the instruments is *marcato*. Although these words may have been marked simply to make them more interesting or to aid the memory or the ear, their emphasis contributes to the functional image of Christ that is depicted in relationship to the words highlighted—"church," "sin," and "death." The whole movement ends with an unexpectedly lovely *amen* written for voices without accompaniment, marking the end of Stravinsky's aid to the text of the Credo.

In this setting of the Mass, there is an element of timelessness. André Boucourechliev comments that the *Mass*'s "ascetic character, the attempt to achieve a timeless language and the instrumentation ... places it outside chronological considerations."[64] I think that Stravinsky was attempting to do just that—to write a setting of the Credo in particular that would transcend normal time boundaries. These elements also contribute to the *Mass*'s symbolic function, a function that links what André Souris calls "consecrated musical forms" and the traditions and nature of the church.[65] By setting the Credo in this manner, Stravinsky showed himself to belong, at least in this instance, to the long historical

---

63. At this point, it would be helpful to listen to a recording of the Credo of Stravinsky's *Mass*, particularly noting the rhythmic interest in *et homo factus est*, the several measures of instruments only that follow it, and then the chant-like nature of the *crucifixus*.

64. Boucourechliev, *Stravinsky*, 228.

65. Souris, "Le Sons du Sacré," 49.

line of church composers. He captured the essence of the church dogma and presented it in a form that could be equated with the tradition of the great icon painters of the Orthodox Church, always basing this work on a traditional form and preserving the sense of the archaic, but not without giving it somewhat of a personal stamp.

CONCLUSION

Both Bach and Stravinsky allow the traditions of the church and the Credo to determine how they portray their images of Christ. All three composers use archaic elements in their works, but Bach and Stravinsky use them to draw lines of connection to the church and church composers of the past, while Beethoven uses them to emphasize that he is trying to develop a completely new view of the subject. Where Bach and Stravinsky use symmetry, for instance, as an integral means of shaping their work and ultimately their forms of the image of Christ, Beethoven uses elements of symmetry only to move away from them. Beethoven's image seems to be set very much in the present, requiring little effort on the part of the listener to gain its moving emotional impact. Bach's and Stravinsky's images seem to be set in antiquity, requiring a certain amount of effort to understand the larger significance of them, and perhaps resulting in a more cerebral perception of the image of Christ. Where Bach tries to elucidate elements that are inexplicable, like the concept of the second person of the Trinity, Beethoven elaborates on the elements that are humanly understandable and passes rather superficially over things that are difficult to understand. Beethoven does not concentrate on *how* Christ could be human but brings out the human emotions that simply emphasize his humanity. Stravinsky does not stop to evaluate any one area but creates a measured rhythmic setting by which one can move efficiently through the words of the Credo. The composers have obviously used the techniques of their individual periods to create these compositions, but they have also drawn from a wide range of compositional elements from earlier and contemporary periods in providing new ways of interpreting—or not interpreting—the text. Each has demonstrated that the image of Christ that is created is altered by the weight, development, and placement of a phrase or section of the text, especially dealing specifically with Christ. Each has given us a perspective on the intrinsic meaning of the Credo and, more specifically, a particular view of the image of Christ.

PART TWO: MUSICAL TRADITIONS AND INTERPRETATIONS

REFERENCES AND FURTHER READING

Adorno, Theodor W. "Alienated Masterpiece: The *Missa Solemnis*." In *Essays on Music*, ed. Richard Leppert, 569–83. Translated by Susan H. Gillespie. Berkeley: University of California Press, 2002.

Amy, Gilbert. "Aspects of the Religious Music of Igor Stravinsky." In *Confronting Stravinsky: Man, Musician, and Modernist*, edited by Jann Pasler, 195–206. Berkeley: University of California Press, 1986.

Beethoven, Ludwig van. *Beethoven's Letters*, edited by Arthur Eaglefield-Hull and Alfred C. Kalischer. Translated by John S. Shedlock. New York: Dover, 1972 [1926].

Bekker, Paul. *Beethoven*. Translated by Mildred Mary Bozman. London: Dent, 1925.

Boucourechliev, André. *Stravinsky*. Translated by Martin Cooper. London: Victor Gollancz, 1987.

Butt, John. *Bach: Mass in B Minor*. Cambridge: Cambridge University Press, 1991.

———. "Mass in B Minor." In *J. S. Bach*, edited by Malcolm Boyd, 284–89. Oxford Composer Companions. Oxford: Oxford University Press, 1999.

Cooper, Barry. *Beethoven and the Creative Process*. Oxford: Clarendon, 1990.

Cooper, Martin. *Beethoven: The Last Decade 1817–1827*. London: Oxford University Press, 1970.

Craft, Robert, ed. *Stravinsky: Selected Correspondence*. 3 vols. London: Faber and Faber, 1982.

———. "Stravinsky's *Mass*: A Notebook." In *Igor Stravinsky*, edited by Edwin Corle, 201–6. New York: Duell, Sloan and Pearce, 1949.

Daw, Stephen. *The Music of Johann Sebastian Bach: The Choral Works*. East Brunswick, NJ: Fairleigh Dickinson University Press, 1981.

Drabkin, William. *Beethoven: Missa Solemnis*. Cambridge: Cambridge University Press, 1991.

Druskin, Mikhail. *Igor Stravinsky: His Life, Works and Views*. Translated by Martin Cooper. Cambridge: Cambridge University Press, 1983.

Fiske, Roger. *Beethoven's Missa Solemnis*. London: Paul Elek, 1979.

Geiringer, Karl. *Johann Sebastian Bach: The Culmination of an Era*. London: George Allen and Unwin, 1967.

Kirkendale, Warren. "New Roads to Old Ideas in Beethoven's *Missa Solemnis*." *Musical Quarterly* 56 (1970) 665–701.

Leaver, Robin A. "The Mature Vocal Works and their Theological and Liturgical Context." In *The Cambridge Companion to Bach*, edited by John Butt, 86–122. Cambridge: Cambridge University Press, 1997.

Mann, Alfred. *Bach Studies: Approaches to the B Minor Mass*. American Choral Review 27.1. New York: American Choral Foundation, 1985.

Marshall, Robert L. *The Music of Johann Sebastian Bach: The Sources, the Style, the Significance*. New York: Schirmer, 1989.

Matthews, Denis. *Beethoven*. London: Dent, 1985.

McCaldin, Denis. "The Choral Music." In *The Beethoven Companion*, edited by Denis Arnold and Nigel Fortune, 387–410. London: Faber and Faber, 1971.

Schweitzer, Albert. *J. S. Bach*. Translated by E. Newman. 2 vols. London: Breitkopf and Härtel, 1911.

Siohan, Robert. *Stravinsky*. Translated by Eric W. White. London: Calder and Boyars, 1965.

Solomon, Maynard. *Beethoven Essays*. Cambridge, MA: Harvard University Press, 1988.
Souris, André. "Le Sons du Sacré dans la Musique de Stravinsky." In *Conditions de la Musique, et Autres Écrits*. Brussells: Éditions de l'Université; Paris: Éditions du Centre National de la Recherche Scientifique, 1976.
Spitta, Philipp. *Johann Sebastian Bach: His Work and Influence on the Music of Germany, 1685–1750*. Translated by Clara Bell and John Alexander Fuller-Maitland. 3 vols. 1889. Reprint, New York: Dover, 1951.
Stauffer, George B. *Bach: The Mass in B Minor. The Great Catholic Mass*. New Haven: Yale University Press, 2003.
Stravinsky, Igor, and Robert Craft. *Igor Stravinsky: Expositions and Developments*. London: Faber and Faber, 1959.
Terry, Charles Sanford. *The Music of Bach: An Introduction*. London: Oxford University Press, 1933.
Walsh, Stephen. *The Music of Stravinsky*. Oxford: Clarendon, 1993.
White, Eric Walter. *Stravinsky: The Composer and His Works*. London: Faber and Faber, 1979.
Wolff, Christoph. *Bach: Essays on His Life and Music*. Cambridge: MA: Harvard University Press, 1991.

12

Sacred Music at the Turn of the Millennia

INTRODUCTION

It is common to approach music historically by seeing a work in the context of its immediate surroundings, including the music that immediately precedes and follows it, in order to discern the advances or innovations that a particular composer or period brought to the development of music. But is there something to be gained by comparing three widely disparate points in the history of sacred music? Can these points in history provide windows of access into or illumination of the Christian faith that is represented through its music? I think that indeed they can provide these very things—an opportunity to see the changing elements of faith over the span of two millennia. Obviously, these brief glimpses in no way give a full or complete picture of the given time period, but they do provide some details that ultimately contribute to a more comprehensive view of the history of sacred music within the tradition of the Christian church.

The three historical points that I have selected occur roughly at the beginning, middle, and end of two millennia. The span of time is from the first century after Christ to the end of the twentieth century. I focus first on what is considered by many to be the earliest Christian hymn in the New Testament, and which was undoubtedly written in the first century. Second, I look at a tenth-century manuscript that is representative of New Testament passages, preserved by scribes and marked with ekphonetic notation for some sort of liturgical chant or cantillation of the text. Third, I discuss a choral work that is based on New Testament texts, and which was published in 1990. These three works represent different strands of the history of sacred music, and yet also have some common foundations. They also show a certain shifting in the history of interpretation as it is seen through the hand of the composer. All three works are intricately connected with the New Testament, and each represents at least some aspect of the faith of the time in which it was written. In chapter 9, I followed a specific trajectory from the ancient world up to the present. Emphasis in this chapter is focused on the beginning, middle, and conclusion of two millennia, a slice of history that we know as the history of the Christian church, so far.

A NEW HYMN IN PHILIPPIANS (FIRST CENTURY)

Philippians 2:6–11 is often referred to as an early Christian hymn. What is usually meant by "early" is that it is a quotation from something written earlier than the writing of the epistle;[1] I will discuss this briefly below. The decision about whether it is technically a hymn has not reached a consensus,[2] but most would certainly agree that the writing style of these six verses is very different from the style that precedes and follows them.

ὃς ἐν μορφῇ θεοῦ	hos en morphē theou	who, being in very nature God,
ὑπάρχων οὐχ ἁρπαγμὸν	huparchōn ouch harpagmon	did not consider equality
ἡγήσατο τὸ εἶναι ἴσα θεῷ,	hēgēsato to einai isa theō,	with God something to be grasped,
ἀλλ' ἑαυτὸν ἐκένωσεν μορφὴν δούλου λαβών,	alla heauton ekenōsen morphēn doulou labōn,	but made himself nothing, taking the very nature of a servant,
ἐν ὁμοιώματι ἀνθρώπων γενόμενος·	en homoiōmati anthrōpōn genomenos.	being made in human likeness.
καὶ σχήματι εὑρεθεὶς ὡς ἄνθρωπος ἐταπείνωσεν ἑαυτὸν	kai schēmati heuretheis hōs anthrōpos etapeinōsen heauton	And being found in appearance as a man, he humbled himself

1. For example, see Martin, *Carmen Christi*, xxxiv, who says, "We are on firm ground in stating that Philippians ii.6–11 represents a hymnic specimen, taken over by Paul as a *paradosis* from some early Christian source with a Jewish background." For recent discussion, see Fewster, "Philippians 'Christ Hymn'"; and Gordley, *New Testament Christological Hymns*, 79–110.

2. See, e.g., Fee, "Philippians 2:5–11," 30, where he states, "primarily I want to call into question the whole matter of the passage as a hymn, which, despite most scholarship to the contrary, it almost certainly is not."

PART TWO: MUSICAL TRADITIONS AND INTERPRETATIONS

γενόμενος ὑπήκοος μέχρι θανάτου,	genomenos hupēkoos mechri thanatou,	and became obedient to death—
θανάτου δὲ σταυροῦ.	thanatou de staurou.	even death on a cross!
διὸ καὶ ὁ θεὸς αὐτὸν ὑπερύψωσεν	dio kai ho theos auton huperupsōsen	Therefore, God exalted him to the highest place
καὶ ἐχαρίσατο αὐτῷ τὸ ὄνομα τὸ ὑπὲρ πᾶν ὄνομα,	kai echarisato auto to onoma to huper pan onoma,	and gave him the name that is above every name,
ἵνα ἐν τῷ ὀνόματι Ἰησοῦ πᾶν γόνυ κάμψῃ	hina en tō onomati Iēsou pan gonu kampsē	that at the name of Jesus every knee should bow,
ἐπουρανίων καὶ ἐπιγείων καὶ καταχθονίων,	epouraniōn kai epigeiōn kai katachthoniōn,	in heaven and on earth and under the earth,
καὶ πᾶσα γλῶσσα ἐξομολογήσηται	kai pasa glōssa eksomologēsētai	and every tongue confess
ὅτι κύριος Ἰησοῦς Χριστὸς	hoti kurios Iēsous Christos	that Jesus Christ is Lord,
εἰς δόξαν θεοῦ πατρός.	eis doksan theou patros.	to the glory of God the Father (NIV)

The understanding of the word "hymn" (ὕμνος, humnos) from the perspective of Greek classical culture is a song of praise addressed to a god or gods. However, as with the passage in 1 Tim 3:16,[3] the Philippians hymn is not addressed to God but is specifically *about Christ*.[4] An alternate sense for the term "hymn" from the context of a Greek-speaking Jew would distinguish a second kind of hymn—and that would be of the kind referred to in the headings of some of the Psalms, which are not songs of praise, but are nonetheless addressed to God.[5] Here again, the distinction is that the Philippians passage is not addressed *to God* but is *about Christ*.[6] In neither sense can this Philippians passage be considered a hymn.[7]

---

3. For similar discussion on 1 Tim 3:16, see chapter 9 above, as well as chapter 3.

4. See discussion in Martin, "Aspects of Worship," 8–9, although Martin writes that both Greek and Christian hymnody as "songs of praise were addressed to the Deity," which does not seem to be the case here (8).

5. See Fowl, *The Story of Christ*, 31–33; see also Smith, *Musical Aspects*, 20, who says, "The word 'hymn' was in common use in the pre-Christian Orient, being used to indicate a general song of praise to the divine being(s), a usage well known to the Jews."

6. See discussion in Hengel, *Between Jesus and Paul*, 78–96 and passim.

7. See Trench, *Synonyms*, 299, who observes that, apart from Paul's use, the noun ὕμνος (*humnos*) is not used in the Apostolic Fathers, not in the writings of Justin Martyr, nor in the *Apostolic Constitutions*. He provides the possible explanation that the

However, Stephen Fowl's comment on this problem of terminology is that it "in no way invalidates the use of the term hymn ... Rather, it means that in calling these passages hymns we are using a term that is the construction of a later, critical community, and not a straightforward translation of ὕμνος in either its specific or generic sense."[8]

I would suggest that this passage was later recognized as a new kind of hymn. After seeing that Phil 2:6–11 does not fit within these early definitions of "hymn," a second grey area of categorization is the understanding of the traditions of music that may have been used in the early church. Scholars frequently write that the music of the early Christian church came directly from the ancient synagogue. Paul Bradshaw points to the widespread influence of Gregory Dix, especially his *The Shape of the Liturgy*, and says, "Dix shared the standard scholarly consensus that the first half of the rite was 'in its Shape simply a continuation of the jewish [sic] synagogue service of our Lord's time.'"[9] Dix's statement has specific implications for music, as he includes psalmody in his reconstruction of the synaxis,[10] and there has been widespread acceptance of his view. His own further statement is that this early part of the rite "was carried straight over into the christian [sic] Church by its jewish [sic] nucleus in the decade after the passion,"[11] later referring to its "original unchanging outline" as it was found "everywhere."[12] However, recent study from musicological, liturgical, and Jewish historical perspectives has not only called into question the thought that the early church simply took over the music of the synagogue,[13] but also raises questions about

---

word "was for the early Christians so steeped in heathenism, so lined with profane associations, and desecrated by them, there were so many hymns to Zeus, to Hermes, to Aphrodite, and to the other deities of the heathen pantheon, that the early Christians shrunk [sic] instinctively from the word." If Trench is correct in his assessment, it also provides an interesting insight into the mind of Paul, who is obviously undeterred by these associations, and seeks to redefine the word by employing it on two occasions as a noun. Its use as a verb, as in P.Oxy. XV 1786, is found not only in the parallels of Matt 26:30 and Mark 14:26, but also in Acts 16:25 and Heb 2:12.

8. Fowl, *The Story of Christ*, 33.

9. Bradshaw, *Search*, 137–38.

10. Grisbrooke, "Synaxis," 353, who says, "The name synaxis ... is today normally used only of that service which is the most ancient and archetypal of them all, the office of readings and prayers which precedes the celebration of the eucharist."

11. Dix, *Shape of the Liturgy*, 36.

12. Dix, *Shape of the Liturgy*, 38.

13. Note that earlier biblical scholarship did refer to this possibility, i.e., Martin,

whether there was an established synagogue liturgy existing in such a precise form before the destruction of the Jewish temple in 70 CE.[14] This research has cast some doubt, for instance, on whether there was established and formal psalmody in the synagogue at this point. There seems to be no documentary evidence for believing that psalmody existed in any kind of structured form in the synagogue that Jesus would have known. This does not mean that the early Christian church did not carry on Jewish patterns of singing psalmody as it was practised in the temple, but it does leave the much larger question of what is meant by the statement that the music of the early church was taken over from the synagogue, because we seem to know nothing about music in the synagogue. Some have thought that psalmody would have been less like song and much more in the nature of chant or cantillation.[15] What is largely accepted, at least about the psalmody of the early Christians, is that it would have incorporated a type of responsorial singing,[16] and it

---

Worship, who, although he writes that the "Church was cradled in Judaism, and borrowed many of its forms of worship from the Temple and synagogue" (40) also mentions that "we admit that there is some doubt as to the extent to which the singing of divine praises had developed in the Palestinian synagogues of the first century" (41). See also Hengel, *Between Jesus and Paul*, 90, where he says that "so-called 'official' Pharisaic Judaism did not have any singing of hymns in its synagogue services, leaving aside say the recitation of the hallel psalms on certain feast days."

14. For discussion of this point, see McKinnon, "Christian Antiquity," 69, who writes that it "is unlikely that there was already in place a formal service of the word that could be adopted en bloc by the first Christians. Such a synagogue service began to take shape only after the destruction of the Temple by the Romans in AD 70." See also Bradshaw, *Search*, 18–19, who questions a formal synagogue liturgy in the entire first century.

15. However, see Augustine, *Conf.* 10.33.49–50, where he refers to the practice of Athanasius, "who required the reader of the psalm to perform it with so little inflexion (*flexu*) of voice that it was closer to speaking (*pronuntianti*) than to singing (*canenti*)" (cited in McKinnon, ed., *Music in Early Christian Literature*, 155). Based on Athanasius's requirement, the "readings" were too musical, otherwise there would have been no need for this guideline. A question this raises is, was this a characteristic even in the earliest days of the Christian church or a development much closer to the time of Athanasius? In either case, whether the earliest forms were more along the lines of chant or of song, this does not exclude either classification from discussions of "music"—on the contrary, they are critical to discussion of music in the early church. It is likely that most readings were done in some manner of chant or cantillation, e.g., see McKinnon, "Early Western Civilization," 10, and Hengel, *Between Jesus and Paul*, 189.

16. See Smith, *Musical Aspects*, 16–17, who gives some of the historical background to this thought: "It seems that in general among the ancient Jews, the extent of the congregation's participation in the musical part of the worship service was

would likely have been monophony, that is, sung in unison (or in octaves, given the different voice ranges).[17]

The subject of music in the early Christian church has provoked a century of lively, even heated, debate.[18] Many pieces of the puzzle have been found for later periods of liturgical music[19] and many clues are still being pieced together to answer numerous questions regarding the particularly cloudy part of the earliest musical history of the Christian church.[20] Documents have been found over the last hundred or so years that have added greatly to the corpus of musical knowledge about the first few centuries after Christ, such as the Oxyrhynchus papyrus known as P.Oxy. XV 1786, the earliest known fragment of a Christian hymn with musical notation, dating to the late third century.[21] Based on it,

---

relatively slight. The burden for the musical part of the service, apart from any help from a choir, seems to have rested upon an individual cantor or precentor. The share of the congregation was apparently in large part merely the answering of the solo voice of the precentor at appropriate places with short responses as 'Amen,' 'Hallelujah,' or 'Hosanna,' or at greater length, participating responsively in the *Shema*, the *Shemoneh 'Esreh*, the *Hallel*, and other Psalms and parts of the liturgy chanted responsively. The simple musical *response* (of a group to an individual) is of very ancient origin and was in general use among the nations of antiquity."

17. Westermeyer, *Te Deum*, 62, writes that "[h]owever diffuse the practice of the early church, it included the ideal of singing 'with one voice,'" which is thought to mean unison singing. Westermeyer points to two first-century sources that may indicate this, first, that of Clement, who flourished ca. 96: "Let us, therefore . . . cry out earnestly to him as if *with one voice*" (1 Clem. 34.5-7 [translations in McKinnon, ed., *Music in Early Christian Literature*, 18]); and Ignatius (ca. 35–107): ". . . you might sing in one voice through Jesus Christ to the Father" (Ign. *Eph.* 4.1-2 [translations in McKinnon, ed., *Music in Early Christian Literature*, 19]).

18. For some discussion of the twentieth-century debate, see chapter 7 above.

19. For instance, a document that explained much of Byzantine musical notation was discovered in the 1880s, virtually unlocking a thousand or more years' worth of musical secrets. See the brief synopsis of the discovery of the most important clues to the deciphering of Byzantine music in Høeg, *La notation ekphonétique*, 18–19, and chapter 6 above for further discussion.

20. See, e.g., Smith, *Musical Aspects*; Werner, *Sacred Bridge*; McKinnon, "On the Question of Psalmody"; West, *Ancient Greek Music*; Scott, "Roman Music."

21. Grenfell and Hunt, eds., "1786. Christian Hymn," 21; Pöhlmann and West, eds., *Documents*, 191–94; and Cosgrove, *Ancient Christian Hymn*. There is now the possibility that the newly edited fragments of P.Oxy. LXV 4462, which are dated to the second century, could fit in this category. See West, "Texts with Musical Notation," 88, where he writes, "It looks as if these verses may have been of a philosophical or religious cast," and remarks on similarities to Gregory of Nazianzen, *Carm.* 2.2.4.55. For further discussion of this important text, see especially chapter 9 above.

questions have been raised as to whether the roots of Christian music are to be found in the ancient Greek modes and notation,[22] or, as some have thought, whether this papyrus is simply the attempt of someone who knew Greek notation to try to record a hymn that would otherwise not be found with this notation.[23] Meanwhile, there has been ongoing questioning about the music of the earliest Christian church, going back to basic questions, such as the one mentioned above: did the music of the early church actually come directly from the synagogue, and would it have included formal psalmody if it did not come from the synagogue? Furthermore, what kind of music was there? Was it all vocal (the most common opinion) or were there instruments to accompany the singing? The church fathers, for instance, have much to say about the evils of musical instruments, but do their statements also represent the opinions or practices of the Christian church in the first century? Eric Werner argues that the apostle Paul detested musical instruments, although his case is not entirely convincing on this point.[24] These and numerous other questions have created a lively discussion, to say the least. Obviously, simple answers to these questions will not be found in this chapter.

Leaving aside the question of what the music may have sounded like, I return to the possibility that Phil 2:6–11 can qualify as a hymn, not because it was already being sung in the early church, but because it had just been written and was therefore incorporated into the developing Christian liturgy as a new hymn.

Many scholars think that this passage is a quotation of some sort, and many would say that it is a quotation by Paul of someone else.[25] I find it less and less convincing that Paul quoted a hymn that was previously known to the early Christians or even that he quoted some poetic passage from a contemporary,[26] partly because of the difficulty of re-

---

22. E.g., P.Oxy. XV 1786 "testifies to the fact that the educated Christian Greeks accepted and transplanted the musical system of their ancestors" (see Lang, *Music in Western Civilization*, 23).

23. See discussion of this in West, "Analecta Musica," 36–46.

24. Werner, "'If I Speak in the Tongues of Men.'"

25. Although there are several who argue that Paul may have written it. See discussion along this line in Wright, "Ἁρπαγμός," 352: "[I]f someone were to take it upon themselves to argue, on the basis of my conclusions, that the 'hymn' was originally written by Paul himself . . . I for one should find it hard to produce convincing counter-arguments." See also Silva, *Philippians*, 92–93; and Martin, *Carmen Christi*, 42–62.

26. See Gundry, "Style and Substance," esp. 288, who writes, "[T]he concentricity, chiasms, and related other parallels in Phil 2:6–11 rather favor the view that this

constructing who this writer may have been. It seems increasingly more likely that Paul wrote the passage himself. For one thing, casual reference is sometimes made to the "hymns" of the early Christian church, but the church had only existed for about thirty years by the time of Paul's writing; this is very early for the church to have had an established set of hymns of this nature. Furthermore, who besides Paul is known to have written at this developed theological level by this time? Surely if there was someone who was writing new hymns, this person would be known by name, at least, if not by the writings.

Fowl argues that the primary focus of the discussion of the hymn should be its function within the argumentation of Paul in Philippians, rather than where the hymnic material originated. Fowl discusses the use of hymns as concrete entities or exemplars, which could be "extended by analogy to offer solutions to particular problems" being experienced by the Christian community—in this case, persecution of the church.[27] Fowl clarifies that it can only be called an exemplar in retrospect, after it has been used to solve a problem. The possibility this raises, however, is that in this case Paul has composed and introduced in his letter a hymn—not one that has been known previously and used in the Christian community, but one that will become known and used as a result of his having introduced it. Just as Fowl's exemplar can be used by analogy to solve current problems, so the use of this hymnic passage as an actual hymn, not simply something to be read aloud in a letter format but sung by the community in whatever form it may have taken musically, results in a hymn that can be of use to all those who perform or hear its vocalization. This hymn then may have become the heart of the message to the church at Philippi, that is, the model of Christ's obedience even to death, rather than simply being a reminder of something that they already knew.

In sum, the Philippians hymn may not be the earliest Christian hymn by virtue of its citing a previously-known hymn in the church at Philippi, or already being used in the Christian church at large, but it may nevertheless represent the very beginning stages of creating formal Christological hymns of the Christian church. It does not neatly fit the Greek definition of the word "hymn," nor does it fit the theological concepts of either the Greek hymn or the Jewish psalm of praise to God. What it does do is represent a template for Christian theology and

---

passage represents Paul's own exalted prose (a view gradually regaining favor) rather than an early Christian hymn."

27. Fowl, *The Story of Christ*, 93.

hymn-writing, one that reflects a ternary pattern of Christology, that is, Christ's pre-existence, his incarnation and death on a cross, and his resurrection and ultimate exaltation. In this hymn, we see the newness of the Christian faith and the establishment of a corresponding new hymn. The newness of both the faith and the hymn is evidenced in the new way that the ideals of a hymn are presented and in its new interpretation of the characteristics of God as manifested in Christ Jesus. This pattern came to be transmitted within the hymnic tradition of the Christian church to the present.

A NEW TESTAMENT LECTIONARY WITH EKPHONETIC NOTATION (TENTH CENTURY)

This tenth-century document is comprised of four folios, or eight pages, from a parchment codex.[28] The biblical text of this parchment is John 6:71—7:46. The pages are part of a gathering, the first page beginning in the middle of a pericope or scenario. The pages are of roughly equal size, about 24 × 31.5 cm (10 × 13 in). The manuscript has been damaged by having been folded in half, which makes reading certain letters and marks of notation difficult on the middle line, particularly on the fourth or outer sheet. There are many indications that this text was originally used in a liturgical context, including the headings that divide the units according to a liturgical calendar. *Nomina sacra* include IC (*IS*), XC (*CHS*), ΠΝΑ (*PNA*), ΠΝ (*PN*), ANON (*ANON*), shortened forms for "Jesus," "Christ," "Spirit" (two forms), and "man."

Caspar René Gregory speculated that the manuscript originated in eastern Asia Minor or perhaps Armenia,[29] while Herbert Hunger thought on the basis of the decoration that it originated in Egypt.[30] The provenance remains unknown. The hand is in a pronounced Coptic style or Alexandrian majuscule, which is identifiable by thick horizontal and thin vertical strokes. The letters are formed in a very regular, upright fashion. Each line averages 10 characters and the columns are approximately 24 lines long, with an average of 3 verses per column, 6 verses per

---

28. "GA 0105." This codex is located at the Austrian National Library (Suppl. Gr. 121), and its Gregory-Aland numbering is 0105 (see Gregory, *Textkritik*, 3:1066–74; Hunger and Hannick, *Katalog*, 208). See also a newer edition of this parchment in Porter and Porter, eds., *New Testament Greek Papyri and Parchments*, Objekt 40. This document is discussed from a different perspective in chapter 6 above.

29. Gregory, *Textkritik*, 3:1066.

30. Hunger and Hannick, *Katalog*, 208.

page.³¹ This parchment, with its 8 pages, comprises just over 46 verses. Decoration of the manuscript, which is typical of the period, includes large decorated letters, which are the first letter of a section and are much larger in size than the regular lettering of the text. These letters are written ekthesis, that is, extending well into the margin to the left of the column.

Two of the common marks written on this manuscript are marks of punctuation: the most common is a small cross, the *teleia*; a second is a combination of two dots that looks much like the present-day colon. These signs usually occur at the ends of short or long units. Marks of punctuation also include a raised dot and low dot. It is these, in conjunction with the diacritical marks known as ekphonetic notation, that are of interest to me here. The markings are musical-rhetorical, as first speculated by Gregory.³² Some of the ekphonetic notation includes signs called *oxeia, apostrophos, apeso exo, kentemata, bareia, hypokrisis,* and *kremaste,* which will be explained briefly below.³³

It is likely that the ekphonetic markings, except the small crosses or *teleia,* have been added by one or more later hands, through the course of the manuscript being used in a liturgical context over a number of years, although the markings are very consistent throughout. Abbreviations for ἀρχή (*archē*, "beginning") and τέλος (*telos*, "end") are written beside the columns to mark the beginning and ending of reading units, which consist of about 13–16 verses. Egon Wellesz writes that "hardly any two codices containing the same pericopes have exactly the same ecphonetic notation throughout the text: there are many divergencies to be found, but only in small details. In the main there must have been, from the beginning, a single tradition for chanting the pericopes."³⁴

This is one of the reasons that scholars think that the signs represent known melodies or melodic formulas prescribed for certain kinds of phrases and to be used at certain points in the musical-reading.³⁵ In the

---

31. The text is divided into two columns on each page as follows: Page 1 (John 6:71—7:3, 7:3–6); Page 2 (7:7–10, 7:10–13); Page 3 (7:13–16, 7:16–18); Page 4 (7:18–22, 7:22–24); Page 5 (7:24–27, 7:27–30); Page 6 (7:30–32, 7:32–35); Page 7 (7:35–37, 7:37–39); Page 8 (7:40–42, 7:43–46).

32. Gregory, *Textkritik,* 3:1066; see Wellesz, *History of Byzantine Music,* 284–300.

33. See Engberg, "Greek Ekphonetic Neumes," 38–39, where he describes the "classical" period of the use of ekphonetic notation, in which they are customarily used in pairs.

34. Wellesz, *History of Byzantine Music,* 256; cf. Tillyard, *Handbook,* 13, who writes, "Byzantine Hymnody is more like recitative than melody."

35. See the useful discussion of melodic formulas in a related context in

four folios or eight pages that are preserved in this particular gathering, the text is divided into four pericopes or scenarios, only three of which are notated ekphonetically. The first pericope is that of Jesus going to the Feast of Tabernacles; the second is Jesus teaching at the Feast (up to the point where someone tried to seize him); the third is further discussion about whether Jesus was the Christ, but this pericope is not notated ekphonetically. The fourth is Jesus' declaration that, if anyone is thirsty, he should come to him for living water, ending with the guards saying that they have never heard anyone speak like this, although the page following this last one of the parchments would have had further verses to complete the pericope. Wellesz writes that normally there is a formulaic introduction to a reading from the Gospel, delivered in a narrative style without accentuation (*kathiste*) and consisting of the words τῷ καιρῷ ἐκείνῳ (*tō kairō ekeinō*, "at that time")[36] although this does not appear to be the case in this manuscript. Similarly, at the end of a reading, there would often be increased variety in the notation, which is in evidence in this manuscript, although not following exactly the formula described by Carsten Høeg.[37] This coincides with at least two kinds of liturgical factors, one being the possible climax of the reading itself and the other being the musical or non-musical elements of the liturgy that are to follow, where the implementation and realization of the ekphonetic notation would provide clues to those who would follow the reading, perhaps providing pitch and opening formulas for music that is to follow.

For the sake of brevity, my remarks are confined to one pericope, which falls almost entirely on page five of the eight. It contains a representative sampling of the markings of ekphonetic notation. The text begins midway through John 7:24 and ends at v. 30:

> ... make a right judgment. 25 At that point some of the people of Jerusalem began to ask, "Isn't this the man they are trying to kill? 26 Here he is, speaking publicly, and they are not saying a word to him. Have the authorities really concluded that he is the Christ? 27 But we know where this man is from: when the Christ comes, no one will know where he is from." 28 Then Jesus, still teaching in the temple courts, cried out: "Yes, you

---

Velimirović, *Byzantine Elements*, 61–67.

36. Wellesz, *History of Byzantine Music*, 253.

37. For description of a normal formula at the end of a pericope, see Høeg, *La notation ekphonétique*, 22–23, who includes markings that one finds in pairs in these manuscripts, such as // ... // (or) \\ ... \\ (or) ```` ... ````, etc.

know me, and you know where I am from. I am not here on my own, but he who sent me is true. You do not know him, 29 but I know him because I am from him and he sent me." 30 At this point they tried to seize him, but no one laid a hand on him, because his time had not yet come (NIV).

The full realization or understanding of these markings is not entirely certain yet, although much progress was made last century in determining various features of them, as mentioned above.[38] Following the identifications as Wellesz has outlined them, the reading has the following characteristics.[39]

> (oxeia) ... MAKE A RIGHT JUDGMENT. (teleia and colon) (= the voice rises to a higher note and remains there until the end of the phrase)
> 25. (apostrophos) AT THAT POINT WERE ASKING (apostrophos) (= a lower pitch of voice but spoken without emphasis; it can also indicate taking a breath, which delineates shorter phrases in a way that it does not with longer ones)
> (oxeia) SOME OF THOSE FROM JERUSALEM, (teleia)
> (double apostrophos) "ISN'T THIS THE MAN (oxeia) (= apeso exo, as with the single apostrophos, indicating a rise from the beginning of the phrase to the end of the phrase)
> (hypokrisis) THEY ARE TRYING TO KILL? (hypokrisis) (= a full stop according to Wellesz)
> 26 (bareia) AND HERE HE IS, (bareia) (= indicates lowering the voice on the words between the encompassing marks, but lowering in such a way as to give emphasis)
> (apostrophos) SPEAKING PUBLICLY, (apostrophos)
> (oxeia) AND THEY ARE NOT SAYING A WORD TO HIM. (teleia)
> (kremaste) THEY DON'T REALLY KNOW, DO THEY (kremaste) (= the voice rises and gives slight accentuation to the words)
> (apostrophos) THE AUTHORITIES (apostrophos)

---

38. For a more complete treatment of the signs and how they are used, see Høeg, *La notation ekphonétique*, 43–70.

39. For greater ease of reading I have aligned the text to correspond with the notation, as opposed to keeping it in its original columns; for plates and diplomatic and reconstructed texts, see Porter and Porter, eds., *New Testament Greek Papyri and Parchments*, Objekt 40. I have also used a fairly literal word-for-word translation in order to keep the comparison of the notation straightforward.

(kathiste) THAT HE IS THE CHRIST? (kathiste) (= a narrative style without emphasis, although this does not seem appropriate at this point in the text)

27 (bareia) BUT THIS MAN (bareia)
(apostrophos) WE KNOW (apostrophos)
(oxeia) WHERE HE IS FROM: (teleia)
(kathiste) BUT WHENEVER THE CHRIST MAY COME, (kathiste) (= a narrative style without emphasis, but again, it does not seem to match the sense of the text at this point)
(oxeia) NO ONE WILL KNOW (oxeia) (= the voice rises to a higher note and remains there until the end of the phrase)
(oxeia) WHERE HE IS FROM." (oxeia)
28 (apostrophos) THEREFORE CRIED OUT IN THE TEMPLE COURTS, (oxeia) (= apeso exo, indicating a rise from the beginning of the phrase to the end of the phrase)
(apostrophos) JESUS WHO WAS TEACHING (apostrophos)
(oxeia) AND SAYING: (teleia)
(bareia) "YOU KNOW ME (bareia)
(kremaste) AND YOU KNOW WHERE I AM FROM. (kremaste)
(apostrophos) I HAVE NOT COME OF MYSELF, (apostrophos)
(kentemata) BUT HE WHO SENT ME IS TRUE. (kentemata) (= a form of an ascending third)
(oxeia) WHOM YOU DO NOT KNOW. (teleia)
29 (kremaste) I KNOW HIM (kremaste)
(apostrophos) BECAUSE I AM FROM HIM (apostrophos)
(oxeia) AND HE SENT ME." (teleia)
30 (bareia) AT THIS POINT THEY TRIED TO SEIZE HIM (bareia)
(bareia) AND NO ONE LAID A HAND ON HIM (bareia)
(apostrophos) FOR IT HAD NOT YET ARRIVED (apostrophos)
(kentemata) THE HOUR (kentemata)
(apostrophos) OF HIM. (apostrophos)

Some of these phrases clearly are paralleled with that of a present-day reading. For instance, the use of the *apeso exo*, rising from the beginning of the sentence to the ending, occurs on the following statement: "Isn't this the man?" (οὐχ οὗός ἐστιν [*ouch houos estin*]). The rising motion throughout the phrase is indicated visually by a mark below the first letter (*apostrophos*) upwards to the mark above the final letter (*oxeia*);

this matches the natural rising intonation of a question. A second statement that uses this combination of *apostrophos* below the first letter and *oxeia* above the final letter (*apeso exo*) is "Therefore [Jesus] cried out in the temple courts" (ἔκραξεν οὖν ἐν τῷ ἱερῷ [*ekraksen oun en tō hierō*]). Here the rising intonation also matches the sense of this phrase, with a rise in intensity as Jesus prepares to make his announcement.

The *oxeia* is one of the most common forms of ekphonetic notation and can encompass many kinds of statements. The fact that the voice is elevated does not necessarily imply heightened accentuation, but rather may be seen as the equivalent of a voice required for a public audience, one that naturally is more elevated than the voice one uses in one-to-one dialogue. *Hypokrisis* seems to mean a lengthy separation of words, a pause that delineates the section. The phrase found within two hypokrisis signs is "the one they are trying to kill" (ὃν ζητοῦσιν ἀποκτεῖναι [*hon zētousin apokteinai*]). The combination of its preceding phrase (see above, with the use of *apeso exo*) and this one is that of rising intonation on "isn't this the man . . . ," followed by a significant pause separating it from the completing phrase ". . . they are trying to kill?"

Use of the *bareia* in this passage is also interesting and seems appropriate to the sense of the words. The phrases that are found within sets of *bareiai* are: "And here he is" (καὶ ἴδε [*kai ide*]); "but this one [man]" (ἀλλὰ τοῦτον [*alla touton*]); "(and) you know me" (κἀμὲ οἴδατε [*kame oidate*]); and "at this point they tried to seize him" (ἐζήτουν οὖν αὐτὸν πιάσαι [*ezētoun oun auton piasai*]). In each of these cases, the phrase gains a degree of intensification by dropping the pitch, giving added emphasis to the words in the process. All four instances of the use of *bareia* in this particular pericope are appropriately placed on phrases that are significant factors in the story.

The final mark that I will call attention to is the *kremaste*, which indicates that the voice rises and gives slight accentuation to the words. The two phrases that use this form of notation are "and you know where I am from" (καὶ οἴδατε πόθεν εἰμί [*kai oidate pothen eimi*]) and "I know him" (ἐγὼ οἶδα αὐτόν, [*egō oida auton*]). Again, these are short phrases, but pivotal in the context of this particular pericope.

Even without knowing the exact sound of these musical-ekphonetic units, it can be recognized that the markings are not random but that there is a very specific plan.[40] Some of it is formulaic, and formulas that

---

40. See, again, Wellesz, *History of Byzantine Music*, 256.

PART TWO: MUSICAL TRADITIONS AND INTERPRETATIONS

can often be found at the endings of pericopes or lectionary readings are in evidence in this manuscript. There are varying degrees of accuracy in manuscripts of this nature, but in this particular parchment, the markings are consistent and occur in logical divisions, if not always identical to the ones a modern-day interpreter would use. The shape of the text is clear, and it becomes increasingly obvious that both the text itself and the meaning of the text are held in high regard, with the text elucidated by its notation. The particular focus on single words or groups of two words often gives an indication of emphases that were considered important, perhaps giving more clarity to the text than the longer phrases one might commonly use today.[41] In either case, there is evidence of very close readings of the text[42] and an expectation that the person who was to deliver these musical readings would accurately interpret and deliver the text as the ekphonetic notation prescribed.[43]

At this point in the history of sacred music, we see tremendous adherence to the biblical text, with it providing the foundation on which musical delivery was based. Musically, there may have been much more freedom than the notation and the idea of musical formulas suggests, and some freedom of interpretation may well have been common within the confines of the formulas and textual fidelity. The ekphonetic notation, as it is written in this manuscript, indicates that while there are some obvious correlations with modern speech, it does not correspond exactly with modern-day emphases, particularly in that very small phrases are treated independently and with great attention to detail, not making use of the longer phrases that we would delineate today.

---

41. This is in contrast to later Byzantine notation, where the meaning of the text and the words themselves sometimes become more obscure as melodic embellishment or ornamentation reaches its highest proportions; this is a feature similar to what occurred at the height of the development of Latin Renaissance polyphony.

42. See Wellesz's statement, "The cantillation followed the syntactical structure of the phrase in every detail" (*History of Byzantine Music*, 251).

43. Or "reminded," for there is still further speculation as to how much was specifically indicated in this notation and how much was simply a reminder or clue to the formulas that were already familiar to those who would deliver these lectionary readings.

JOHN TAVENER: "WE SHALL SEE HIM AS HE IS" (TWENTIETH CENTURY)

The leap to this late twentieth-century choral work is large, to say the least, and yet some of the features of this composition fit closely with that of the preceding discussion. The particular composition, John Tavener's hour-long choral work entitled "We Shall See Him as He Is," was published in 1990.[44] Tavener's sacred choral works have incorporated representations of Byzantine musical idioms and theological ideas of the Eastern Christian church, and presented them to an unusually receptive Western Christian church.[45] He depicts—and note that in discussing his own music, he intentionally uses language that has a visual characteristic—some of the features of an ancient practice of worship, but in a form of music that sounds new to the contemporary listener. In a review of a live performance of this work, Richard Langham Smith writes that it "evoked an hour's devotion in the various chapels of a basilica."[46] Tavener definitely attempts to present an element of the visual symbols and visual forms of ritual in his music. Smith's review further describes Tavener's manner of alternating "between the powdery thirds of Anglican church music and the inflections of Byzantium,"[47] with recognition of an intermingling of East and West. David Wright, in his review, writes that the complex problem of reception that this work presents "tends to be glossed over because of the approachability of its surface."[48] The lack of musical development and the imagery can seem simplistic and perhaps too easily accessible. Wright goes on to say, however, that explicit in this work "is a musical and conceptual disdain for the easy-listening apparatus of post-modernity" and that it "demands an act of concentrated listening by its audience," in part because there are such small changes over such a long period of time.[49] So, what seems simple in one respect is perhaps more difficult in another.

44. This discussion expands upon my treatment of Tavener's "We Shall See Him as He Is" in chapter 2 above. Note again that this John Tavener is not to be confused with the sixteenth century, John Taverner, whose name is similar.

45. See discussion of the dichotomy of Eastern and Western perspectives on Christianity and Tavener's own contribution to this discussion in Wilson-Dickson, *Story of Christian Music*, 166–67.

46. Smith, "A Winning Path."

47. Smith, "A Winning Path," 475.

48. Wright, "1992 Prom Premieres (2)," 34.

49. Wright, "1992 Prom Premieres (2)," 34.

The work is scored for a main tenor soloist, as well as additional tenor and soprano soloists, a chorus, and an orchestra consisting of strings, organ, two trumpets, and two sets of timpani. Andrew Burn writes, "With these forces Tavener creates a score of idiosyncratic timbres for each principal idea, a process which may be likened to the different mosaics or paints that make up the colours of an ikon."[50] It should be mentioned here that the idea of a mosaic is not only found in the musical timbres, but also in the compilation of the text, as will be discussed below. Tavener has made much use of the term "ikons" in his music, and his own discussion of it, reflecting his interest in the painted ikons of the Orthodox church. The settings in this work are often deceptively simple, as noted above, although often extreme in vocal and instrumental range, using single changes in orchestration, ornamentation, or dynamics. Burn describes it thus: "There is little development in terms of the 'Classical' western music tradition; the ideas are static and ritualistic, varied primarily through subtle changes of instrumental or choral scoring."[51]

It is interesting to see that what Tavener calls ikons would in most liturgical settings be called pericopes or readings. Having said that, the text is both straightforward and not-so-straightforward as it seems, based largely on the way in which Mother Thekla, the compiler of the text, has arranged it. Features of her contribution to this choral work are noteworthy, for the text itself and the combination of the words and music are important features of the present discussion. For instance, there is no question that the text comes from the New Testament. However, while she has not exactly rewritten it, Mother Thekla has seriously reduced it, to the point of being extremely sparse, even minimalistic. While it appears at first that the text is simply from the Gospel of John, she has actually conflated several books of the New Testament—three books that are traditionally thought to be written by the same author, but which have very different styles of writing and very different roles in the New Testament. These three books include not only the Gospel of John, but the First Epistle of John and the book of Revelation or the Apocalypse of John. Obviously, John is the perceived author, and, in fact, he is the main character of this musical work. The interesting textual merging of these three books, however, can be observed first in the two phrases that comprise the refrain. The first phrase, which forms the title of this

---

50. Burn, "Liner Notes," 3.
51. Burn, "Liner Notes," 3.

work, is "we shall see him as he is." This comes from 1 John 3:2 ("Dear friends, now we are children of God, and what we will be has not yet been made known. But we know that when he appears, we shall be like him, *for we shall see him as he is*"). This, however, is the only part of the text that comes specifically from First John (although the first lines of Ikon 1 have some resemblances). The second phrase of the refrain, "Amen, come Lord Jesus," comes from the penultimate verse in Rev 22:20 ("He who testifies to these things says, 'Yes, I am coming soon.' Amen, come Lord Jesus"). Interestingly, however, the refrain is sung only in Greek throughout the piece until the very last line of the work, where it is sung in English. The rest of the text is all in English and comes almost entirely from the Gospel of John, in reduced form, and, apart from the final section, is chronological as it appears in the Gospel. Again, it is evident that the text is not completely straightforward, for although it at first glance appears simple to the point of being extreme, it in essence gives the full outline of a portrait without filling in the details.

The work, set out in eleven "ikons" or pericopes from the Gospel of John, follows this pattern: Refrain, Ikons 1–3, Refrain, Ikons 4–5, Refrain, Ikons 6–7, Refrain, Ikons 8–9, then a Refrain integrated within Ikon 10, and finally Ikon 11 (a modified version of the refrain, but in English instead of Greek). In Ikon 1, for example, the text is, "I heard: Before time was. Time within. Time beyond. Created. Uncreated. Bodiless Body."[52] The words for Ikon 9 are "I saw: The cross. His body crucified. The Blood. The Water. Linen clothes. Napkin."[53]

As I mentioned, the text of the ikons or pericopes is almost entirely from the Gospel of John. However, the introductory phrases with which each pericope or ikon is opened—either "I saw" or "I heard"—are not a noticeable feature of the Gospel of John. They are, instead, very visible phrases in the book of Revelation; in fact, these two phrases in one form or another appear about 75 times throughout the book, as opening formulas for various visions or audible events that John introduces. It is intriguing that this form of presentation has been used to introduce each ikon in the musical work, for the style of presentation in the Gospel is quite different from that of Revelation. One thing this style provides, however, which is essential to the idea of an ikon depicted in music, is that of an easily recognizable formula. The opening phrase, "I saw" or

---

52. The biblical text for this ikon is taken from John 1:1–4 and 1 John 1:1–2.

53. This is from John 19:16, 17–20:9. The other ikons are largely from John 2–6 and 19.

PART TWO: MUSICAL TRADITIONS AND INTERPRETATIONS

"I heard," has that quality of familiarity both in its brief wording and in the repetition of the musical formula with slight variations or decorations. These give a stylized form of development but do not detract from a recognizable similarity.

It is also noteworthy that the text only gives the outline of each pericope or so-called ikon. The descriptive words, though sparse, are not obscure (see examples given above of Ikons 1 and 9). They serve as succinct, even poignant, reminders for the reader who is familiar with these stories; by their brief symbolic words they allow one fully to recall the events that are depicted. These features are in keeping with the idea of a musical depiction of the visual form of the ikon: representation of the form with familiar style and familiar techniques, never full detail, never life-like recreation of the image, never innovation to draw attention to the innovation itself.

There are many levels at which this work is symbolic and picks up the mannerisms of certain formulas of Byzantine music and eastern Christianity. The declamation of the phrase "I saw" or "I heard" is formulaic. It provides what one might expect if the same ekphonetic sign were written above the phrase every time it occurred in a sacred text, such as was explored above in the portions of John with ekphonetic notation. However, the form of the delivery also has some similarities to the setting of Bach's St John Passion. Both use the pattern of a tenor narrator, extra soloists who act as specific individuals, and a chameleon-like choir that can be the crowd at a marriage feast and can also provide the ambience of a musical halo, an effect that occurs at the entrance of certain ikons in this work.

Does Tavener's work, "We Shall See Him as He Is," give us some insight into faith at the turning of this millennium? Although it can at first hearing strike the listener as contrived, its features provide us with valuable insights into the Christian faith at the beginning of the twentieth-first century and, perhaps, views into similar practices of faith nearly a millennium ago. For instance, Tavener has chosen simple lines, lines that are frequently set to be sung in unison, which is reminiscent of an ancient practice of singing. Although Mother Thekla has provided a text that has been highly edited, streamlined, and compiled in a mosaic-like way, it does not deviate from the actual depiction of the pericope or ikon, in its own way reflecting the ancient practice of holding the text in high regard. This cleanness of line, both in the music and in the text, projects an image of timelessness, which is undoubtedly what Tavener was hoping to achieve. Similarly, the use of the Greek language as the refrain and title is another feature that draws this modern-day work back to the inception of Christianity, and certainly to the height of Byzantine chant. In a stylized way, through means that some might call simplistic or mannered, Tavener has nonetheless drawn a full circle that brings the end of a millennium back to its beginning. By bringing it back to the biblical text and unison singing, which characterized the music of the Christian church for most of that first millennium, he has also provided a larger full circle that brings us back to the very inception of Christianity. Tavener has certainly given us insight into the present-day penchant to reread and reinterpret old texts, rearranging then in new kaleidoscopic ways. By taking on ancient forms, or at least modern representations of ancient forms, he has reworked the old in such a way as to present a work that seems quite new.

CONCLUSION

The three points in the history of sacred music that have briefly been discussed here are in no way representative of the greatest works in sacred music, for the parameters of this discussion have completely bypassed all of those compositions that would traditionally be considered the greatest choral works, including those of Palestrina, Tallis, Byrd, Mozart, Bach, Beethoven, Schubert, and so on. Nonetheless, these three works represent significant characteristics of sacred music at the beginning, middle, and end of two millennia. The first, as one of the most highly discussed passages in the New Testament and one that many have thought may be an older hymn, has created great interest for those scholars who have tried to determine of what the music of the New Testament may have consisted. Most of all, the Philippians hymn represents aspects of the newness that was inherent at the inception of the Christian faith and church, both newness in defining what a hymn is and newness in presenting Jesus Christ. The second, the Gospel of John passage, by means of its ekphonetic notation, gives us some clues to its musical presentation in a liturgical setting. It is a stage in Byzantine chant that is foundational for later developments in sacred chant, providing insights into the musical practices of the Byzantine church and other Christian churches in the ninth to thirteenth centuries. This notated text also gives us a view of the church at a point when faithfulness to the text was perhaps more straightforward than in later periods, where individuality has been developed to a great extent. Having said this, there is no definite indication that there was not some degree of spontaneity involved or some level of personal interpretation by the performer within the confines of the formulas of the notation. Nonetheless, the formulas also show us that the text was revered and preserved, perhaps giving us some idea of the ideals of faith in the Christian church at the time. The third work, Tavener's choral composition, written at the end of the second millennium after Christ, represents the continuing musical and liturgical need to reinterpret a fundamental text of the Christian church, the story as presented in the Gospel of John. By taking on some characteristics of ancient musical formulas, trying to imbue them with visual characteristics, and redefining and reshaping the basic text, this work provides some direct ties to the Byzantine church and to the early Christian church, providing a window into these earlier cultures. At the same time, the work stands on its own as a window into faith at the end of a millennium, a work in which some features of the faith of East and West are merged through a collage or mosaic of text fragments and musical-formulaic fragments. Perhaps in this work, in which something new is created out of those things that are most ancient, we see a recent example of a genuine attempt to describe the faith of today that is trying fully to exist in the present but to not lose hold of the most valuable things of its history. In this way, Tavener's work successfully completes a millennium by bringing modern-day faith back to the practices of one thousand years ago and back to the precepts of the beginning of Christianity.

REFERENCES AND FURTHER READING

Bradshaw, Paul F. *The Search for the Origins of Christian Worship: Sources and Methods for the Study of Early Liturgy.* Oxford: Oxford University Press, 1992.

Burn, Andrew. "Liner Notes." In *We Shall See Him as He Is* by John Tavener. Performed by BBC Welsh Symphony Orchestra. Directed by Richard Hickox. CD Recording. Colchester, UK: Chandos, 1992.

Cosgrove, Charles. H. *An Ancient Christian Hymn with Musical Notation: Papyrus Oxyrhynchus 1786. Text and Commentary.* Studien und Texte zu Antike und Christentum 65. Tübingen: Mohr Siebeck, 2011.

Dix, Gregory. *The Shape of the Liturgy.* Westminster: Dacre, 1954.

Engberg, Gudrun. "Greek Ekphonetic Neumes and Masoretic Accents." In *Studies in Eastern Chant I*, edited by Miloš Velimirović and Egon Wellesz, 37–49. Oxford: Oxford University Press, 1966.

Fee, Gordon D. "Philippians 2:5–11: Hymn or Exalted Pauline Prose?" *Bulletin for Biblical Research* 2 (1992) 29–46.

Fewster, Gregory P. "The Philippians 'Christ Hymn': Trends in Critical Scholarship." *Currents in Biblical Research* 13 (2015) 191–206.

Fowl, Stephen E. *The Story of Christ in the Ethics of Paul: An Analysis of the Function of the Hymnic Material in the Pauline Corpus*. Journal for the Study of the New Testament Supplement Series 36. Sheffield: JSOT, 1990.

"GA 0105." *The Center for the Study of New Testament Manuscripts*. Online: https://manuscripts.csntm.org/manuscript/Group/GA_0105.

Gordley, Matthew E. *New Testament Christological Hymns: Exploring Texts, Contexts, and Significance*. Downers Grove, IL: InterVarsity, 2018.

Gregory, Caspar René. *Textkritik des Neuen Testaments*. 3 vols. Leipzig: Teubner, 1909.

Hunt, Arthur S., and H. Stuart Jones. "1786. Christian Hymn with Musical Notation." In *The Oxyrhynchus Papyri XV*, edited by Bernard P. Grenfell and Arthur S. Hunt, 21–25. Egypt Exploration Society Graeco-Roman Memoirs. London: Egypt Exploration Fund, 1922.

Grisbrooke, W. Jardine. "Synaxis." In *A Dictionary of Liturgy and Worship*, edited by John G. Davies, 353–54. London: SCM, 1972.

Gundry, Robert H. "Style and Substance in 'The Myth of God Incarnate' according to Philippians 2:6–11." In *Crossing the Boundaries: Essays in Biblical Interpretation in Honour of Michael D. Goulder*, edited by Stanley E. Porter, Paul Joyce, and David E. Orton, 271–93. Leiden: Brill, 1994.

Hengel, Martin. *Between Jesus and Paul: Studies in the Earliest History of Christianity*. London: SCM, 1983.

Høeg, Carsten. *La Notation Ekphonétique*. Monumenta Musicae Byzantinae Subsidia 1.2. Copenhagen: Levin and Munksgaard, 1935.

Hunger, Herbert, and Christian Hannick. *Katalog der Griechischen Handschriften der Osterreichischen Nationalbibliothek*: Part 4. Vienna: Osterreichischen Nationalbibliothek, 1994.

Lang, Paul H. *Music in Western Civilization*. London: Dent, 1963 [1941].

Martin, Ralph P. "Aspects of Worship in the New Testament Church." *Vox Evangelica* 2 (1963) 6–32.

———. *Carmen Christi: Philippians 2:5–11 in Recent Interpretation and in the Setting of Early Christian Worship*. Society for New Testament Studies Monograph Series 4. 1967. Reprint, Grand Rapids: Eerdmans, 1983.

———. *Worship in the Early Church*. 2nd ed. Grand Rapids: Eerdmans, 1978.

McKinnon, James W. "Christian Antiquity." In *Antiquity and the Middle Ages: From Ancient Greece to the 15th Century*, edited by James W. McKinnon, 68–87. Man and Music 1. London: Granada Group and Macmillan, 1990.

———. "Early Western Civilization." In *Antiquity and the Middle Ages: From Ancient Greece to the Fifteenth Century*, edited by James W. McKinnon, 1–44. Man and Music. Basingstoke, UK: Macmillan, 1990.

———. "On the Question of Psalmody in the Ancient Synagogue." *Early Music History* 6 (1986) 159–91.

McKinnon, James W., ed. *Music in Early Christian Literature*. Cambridge Studies in the Literature of Music. Cambridge: Cambridge University Press, 1987.

Pöhlmann, Egert, and Martin L. West, eds. *Documents of Ancient Greek Music: The Extant Melodies and Fragments Edited and Transcribed with Commentary*. Oxford: Clarendon, 2001.

PART TWO: MUSICAL TRADITIONS AND INTERPRETATIONS

Porter, Stanley E., and Wendy J. Porter, eds. *New Testament Greek Papyri and Parchments: New Editions*. Mitteilungen aus der Papyrussammlung der Österreichischen Nationalbibliothek (Papyrus Erzherzog Rainer) Neue Serie XXIX, XXX. Folge (MPER XXIX, XXX). Berlin: de Gruyter, 2008.

Scott, J. E. "Roman Music." In *Ancient and Oriental Music*, edited by Egon Wellesz, 404–20. New Oxford History of Music 1. London: Oxford University Press, 1966 [1957].

Silva, Moisés. *Philippians*. Baker Exegetical Commentary on the New Testament. 2nd ed. Grand Rapids: Baker, 2005.

Smith, R. L. "A Winning Path." *Musical Times* 133 (1992) 475–76.

Smith, William Sheppard. *Musical Aspects of the New Testament*. Amsterdam: W. Ten Have, 1962.

Tillyard, Henry J. W. *Handbook of the Middle Byzantine Musical Notation*. Monumenta Musicae Byzantinae Subsidia 1/1. Copenhagen: Levin and Mundsgaard, 1935.

Trench, Richard C. *Synonyms of the New Testament*. 9th ed. London: Macmillan, 1880.

Velimirović, Miloš. M. *Byzantine Elements in Early Slavic Chant*. Monumenta Musicae Byzantinae Subsidia 4. Copenhagen: Munksgaard, 1960.

Wellesz, Egon. *A History of Byzantine Music and Hymnography*. 2nd ed. Oxford: Clarendon, 1998 [1961].

Werner, Eric. "'If I Speak in the Tongues of Men . . .': St. Paul's Attitude to Music." *Journal of the American Musicological Society* 13 (1960) 18–23.

———. *The Sacred Bridge: The Interdependence of Liturgy and Music in Synagogue and Church During the First Millennium*. 2 vols. New York: Columbia University Press, 1959; New York: Ktav, 1984.

West, Martin L. "Analecta Musica." *Zeitschrift für Papyrologie und Epigraphik* 92 (1992) 1–54.

———. *Ancient Greek Music*. Oxford: Clarendon, 1992.

———. "Texts with Musical Notation." In *Oxyrhynchus Papyri LXV*, edited by Michael W. Haslam et al., 81–102. Egypt Exploration Society Graeco-Roman Memoirs 85. London: Egypt Exploration Society, 1998.

Westermeyer, Paul. *Te Deum: The Church and Music*. Minneapolis: Fortress, 1998.

Wilson-Dickson, Andrew. *The Story of Christian Music: From Gregorian Chant to Black Gospel: An Authoritative Illustrated Guide to All the Major Traditions of Music for Worship*. Oxford: Lion, 1992.

Wright, David. "1992 Prom Premieres (2)." *Tempo* 183 (1992) 33–34.

Wright, N. T. "Ἁρπαγμός and the Meaning of Philippians 2:5–11." *The Journal of Theological Studies* 37 (1986) 321–52. Republished in revised form in Wright, *The Climax of the Covenant: Christ and the Law in Pauline Theology*, 56–98. Edinburgh: T. & T. Clark, 1991.

13

Contemporary Worship Songs and Suffering

INTRODUCTION

IN HIS TREATMENT OF pain, C. S. Lewis implies that what we normally think of as pain or suffering is not, in fact, the greatest problem we face; the deeper problem is trying to understand why God does not *do* something about it![1] Does not he *want* his creatures to be happy? Worse yet, what if God *cannot* do anything about it? What if he does not have the power? And if I mention these thoughts out loud, will God punish me and make my life even more miserable?

Songwriter and author Michael Card draws attention to the missing role of lament in our worship today and what role it played in the lives of major biblical characters.[2] In Ps 13, for instance, the psalmist cries out, "How long, O LORD? Will you forget me forever? / How long will you hide your face from me? / How long must I wrestle with my thoughts and every day have sorrow in my heart? / How long will my enemy triumph over me?" Many of the psalms interweave joyful praise with cries of utter despair, anguish, and even anger at God's willful silence and apparent impotence; some of them include an almost shockingly honest expression of pain and suffering.[3] The book of Job lays out the "unfair deal" that Job receives.[4] His immense pain and suffering begin with the physical devastation of his possessions and livelihood and family, and continue on

---

1. Lewis, *Problem of Pain*, 26
2. Card, *Sacred Sorrow*.
3. Lewis, *Reflections*; see also Brueggemann, *Praying the Psalms*, 20, on "disorientation" and "orientation" as the driving power of the Psalms.
4. Brueggemann, *Message of the Psalms*, 169, on getting a "fair deal" from God.

to even greater depths with the dubious assistance of his friends, further aided by his own mental torment and physical ailments.

The New Testament also contains a surprising and astonishing range of expressions of pain and suffering. Jesus teaches his disciples that, just as he must suffer, they must suffer, too: "Whoever wants to be my disciple must deny themselves and take up their cross and follow me. For whoever wants to save their life will lose it, but whoever loses their life for me and for the gospel will save it" (Mark 8:34–35, TNIV). Jesus lets them know that there *will* be pain and suffering for his true followers. His words in John 16:20 are clear: "Very truly I tell you, you will weep and mourn while the world rejoices. You will grieve, but your grief will turn to joy." It is Paul, however, who teaches us most directly about the importance of pain and suffering within the worshiping community, and about the need to *share* it with the community. He writes to the Philippians that it is their duty to "suffer for him [Christ]," and that Paul is going through the same struggles that they are (Phil 1:29–30). He is not ashamed to share Christ's suffering with Christ's fellow believers.

Together, Old and New Testament observations suggest that vibrant worshiping communities must have a place for genuine expressions of pain and suffering. More important, perhaps, our musical worship is one place where such expressions should take place.

In light of the foregoing, in this chapter, I focus on whether or not there is a place within the current canon of the 77 most frequently sung worship songs[5] to voice our questions, our pain, our sorrow, and our suffering. In other words, do we have current worship music that assists us to worship God in the darkness—something more substantial than just a "whistling in the dark" that superficially props up our courage? I wanted to know which of the most frequently used 77 songs actually express something about pain and suffering, and which ones might contribute meaningfully to worship.

METHOD OF ANALYSIS

With these observations about the presence of pain and suffering in worship in mind, in order to determine if the 77 most frequent worship

---

5. My task in writing this chapter was to address my comments to a specific canon of songs that was in use in churches at the time of writing. The canon has changed in the meantime, but I think that the general observations I made then still have relevance for later musical choices of the church in its worship.

songs express aspects of pain and suffering, I start with a definition and then specify three levels of analysis.

Definition of Pain and Suffering

To begin, how can "pain and suffering" be defined? Definitions of "pain" include the word "suffering" or distress, while definitions of "suffering" refer to it as the bearing of "pain" or distress, so it is reasonable to group pain and suffering here as a single category.[6] Although "pain and suffering" may refer simply to physical distress, I also use the term with regard to the kind of mental, emotional, or spiritual distress that Christians may endure. This distress may be brought about by an event, such as the physical disability or death of a loved one through a car accident, disease, or war. It may be brought about through broken or troubled relationships, through internal stresses that are difficult to identify, or through the person's own actions.

Levels of Analysis

As noted above, I was interested in how many songs in the top 77 not only express pain and suffering, but how many do so in meaningful and focused ways. On this basis, I gathered songs among the 77 that do more than simply use words or phrases that refer to pain and suffering, although such words and phrases were a necessary first step in selecting songs for analysis. My method of analysis thus included three levels: (1) the lyrics, (2) the lyrical-musical interchange, and (3) the context in which the song focused on pain and suffering is performed.

The first level of analysis focused on (1) *the lyrics*. At this level I looked for lyrics that made some reference to pain and suffering in each song before examining the meaningfulness of such expression. Some of the words I considered were "affliction," "agony," "bewilderment," "condemned," "crucified," "crushed," "crying," "cut off," "darkness," "desert," "despair," "despised," "forsaken," "hurting," "pain," "persecuted," "pressed," "shame," "shedding his blood," "sorrow," "suffering," "the cross," "the crown of thorns," "troubled," "weeping," "wilderness," and "wound."

As for meaningfulness of lyrical expression, this is necessarily subjective. However, as a practicing worship leader I must make the decision regarding meaningfulness since a simple word or phrase that refers to

---

6. Easily accessible websites that discussed definitions of pain and suffering included answers.com, laborlawtalk.com, and legaldictionary.thefreedictionary.com.

pain or suffering may not be enough to establish a song as meaningfully expressing pain and suffering. To help consider how meaningful the lyrics related to pain and suffering are, I looked primarily at (a) whether pain and suffering is the overt focus (central theme) of the song; (b) if the expression is not overt, whether there is a strong underlying or implicit expression of pain and suffering that calls out to God; and (c) whether the lyrics are theologically appropriate when it comes to expressing pain and suffering.

In the second level of analysis, I looked at (2) *the lyrical-musical interchange*, which assesses the sound of the music in combination with the lyrics. This level helped explore further the meaningfulness of the songs identified at the first level. After my first level of analysis of the lyrics helped me to formulate a list of worship songs that could potentially allow for meaningful expression of pain and suffering, the second level focused on (a) the music itself and (b) how the music fits with the lyrics. In terms of the music itself, I asked, does the music *sound* musical and could a congregation sing it? When it comes to how the music fits with the lyrics, I observed whether the music supports the *meaning* of the words and aids in their *expression*.

Finally, the most important practical question (or level) for any worship leader follows from the first two levels and focuses upon (3) *the context*, that is, "Is this song meaningful in my context?" I need to determine if the worship song that identifies or expresses pain and suffering fits with my congregation. Without this final step, the overall discussion of lyrics or lyrical-musical interchange is not particularly useful. It is in making this third decision that I would say many worship leaders struggle.

RESULTS AND DISCUSSION

In this section, I present the results of my method of analysis described above and discuss the results in the context of my central research question.

The Lyrics

I begin with the lyrics of the songs, before turning to the other two elements.

Which Songs Have Lyrics That Express Pain and Suffering?

The first level of analysis looked at the lyrics in two stages. Applying the list of words and phrases dealing with pain and suffering described above in the method of analysis section, I identified 22 songs that make some reference to pain and suffering. See table 1 below for this list of songs and relevant words or phrases I considered.

Song Title	Relevant Words or Phrases	Comments
1. *Above All*	"like a rose trampled on the ground / You took the fall . . ."[7]	Pain and suffering (P/S) of Jesus
2. *Awesome God*	"it wasn't for no reason that He shed his blood"	P/S of Jesus Christ ("shed his blood"; "at the cross"); possibly P/S of God in relation to Adam and Eve in Garden of Eden, and in relation to Sodom.
	"mercy and grace He gave us at the cross"	
3. *Because He Lives*	"face tomorrow / fear is gone, because I know He holds the future"	Implied personal emotional, physical, psychological P/S
	"life is worth the living just because He lives"	Implied personal spiritual P/S requiring healing, forgiveness, pardon
	"Son . . . came to love, heal and forgive / he bled and died to buy my pardon"	
	"child can face uncertain days"	Personal P/S of parent(s)
	"fight life's final war with pain"	Personal physical P/S
	"death give way to victory"	
4. *Better Is One Day*	"for my soul longs and even faints for You"	Personal spiritual P/S
	"my heart and flesh cry out for You, the living God / Your Spirit's water for my soul"	

---

7. Other language and imagery of the crucifixion are also used in this song.

PART TWO: MUSICAL TRADITIONS AND INTERPRETATIONS

Song Title	Relevant Words or Phrases	Comments
5. *Blessed Be your Name*	"when the darkness closes in Lord still I will say / blessed be the name of the Lord"	Personal P/S
	"when I'm found in the desert place / though I walk through the wilderness"	Personal P/S
	"on the road marked with suffering / though there's pain in the offering"	Personal P/S
	"You give and take away / You give and take away / my heart will choose to say, Lord, blessed be Your name"	Personal P/S and cost of choosing to bless the name of the Lord
6. *Breathe*	"I'm desperate for You, and I'm lost without You"	Personal spiritual P/S
7. *God of Wonders*	"and as I stumble in the darkness, I will call your name by night"	Implied personal P/S
8. *Here I Am to Worship*	"Light of the world, You stepped down into darkness"	Implied P/S of Christ
	"and I'll never know how much it cost to see my sin upon that cross"	A quality of personal spiritual P/S in recognition of P/S of Christ
9. *I Could Sing of your Love Forever*	"and let the Healer set me free"	Personal physical or spiritual P/S
10. *I Stand in Awe*	"yet God crushed You for my sin . . . You are beautiful beyond description" (e.g., for your compassionate and merciful act of dying for me on the cross)	A quality of personal spiritual P/S corresponding to seeing P/S of Christ
11. *Lord, I Lift your Name on High*	"from the earth to the cross my debt to pay, from the cross to the grave"	A quality of personal spiritual P/S corresponding to seeing P/S of Christ
12. *Lord, Reign in Me*	"Lord, reign in me, reign in Your power / over all my dreams in my darkest hour"	Personal P/S

Song Title	Relevant Words or Phrases	Comments
13. *Oh How He Loves You and Me*	"what He did there brought hope from despair"	Personal P/S
14. *Our God Reigns*	"He was despised / and we took no account of Him"; "our sin and guilt that bruised and wounded Him"; "on His shoulders bore our shame"; "Meek as a lamb that's led out to the slaughterhouse . . . His life ran down upon the ground like pouring rain"	Mostly identifying the P/S of Christ; corresponding corporate P/S
	"Waste places of Jerusalem break forth with joy . . . the Lord has saved and comforted His people"	P/S in these places, people needing to be saved and comforted
15. *Praise the Name of Jesus*	"He's my Rock, He's my Fortress, He's my Deliverer, in Him will I trust"	Implication of personal P/S: in need of a rock, fortress, deliverer
16. *Shine, Jesus, Shine*	"consume all my darkness"	Personal P/S
17. *The Heart of Worship*	"I'm sorry, Lord, for the thing I've made it / when it's all about You, all about You, Jesus"	Personal spiritual P/S
18. *The Wonderful Cross*	"cross, bids me come and die"	A call to personal and spiritual P/S
	"When I survey the wondrous cross / on which the Prince of Glory died / my richest gain I count but loss / and pour contempt on all my pride"	P/S of Jesus on the cross; corresponding personal P/S as response
	"See from His head, His hands, His feet / sorrow and love flow mingled down / Did e'er such love and sorrow meet / or thorns compose so rich a crown?"	P/S of Jesus on the cross

PART TWO: MUSICAL TRADITIONS AND INTERPRETATIONS

Song Title	Relevant Words or Phrases	Comments
	"Were the whole realm of nature mine / that were an offering far too small / love so amazing so divine / demands my soul, my life, my all"	Corresponding recognition of personal P/S as response
19. *Trading my Sorrows*	". . . my shame"	Personal P/S
	(the worshiper describes being in different types of pain—both physical and emotional)	
20. *Turn your Eyes upon Jesus*	"O soul, are you weary and troubled / no light in the darkness you see?"	Question about P/S spiritual/physical
	"then go to a world that is dying"	P/S of world at large
21. *You Are my All in All*	"taking my sin, my cross, my shame"	Implied spiritual P/S?
22. *You Are my King (Amazing Love)*	"You, my King, would die for me"; "You were forsaken / You were condemned"	P/S of Jesus on our behalf

Table 1. Songs with Reference to Pain and Suffering

DO THE LYRICS MEANINGFULLY EXPRESS PAIN AND SUFFERING?

Of these 22 songs, I then asked the important qualitative question, *Do the lyrics meaningfully express pain and suffering?* To answer this, I used the additional criteria presented above—that is, overt focus, strong implicit expression, and theological appropriateness.

As for the main focus or central theme, nine of the 22 listed in table 1 above have words or phrases that refer briefly to Jesus' pain and suffering, or to one's own, but do not make pain and suffering their focus. These nine songs include *Awesome God*; *God of Wonders*; *I Could Sing of your Love Forever*; *Lord, I Lift your Name on High*; *Lord, Reign in Me*; *O How He Loves You and Me*; *Praise the Name of Jesus*; *Shine, Jesus, Shine*; and *You Are my All in All*. For instance, Rich Mullins's *Awesome God* uses the phrase "he shed his blood" and mentions "the cross," but these are used as points of reference to outline a narrative of biblical events. *I Could Sing of your Love Forever* refers to letting the healer set us free, but this phrase is not its focus. *God of Wonders* mentions stumbling in the darkness and calling out God's name by night but does not focus on this aspect.

After I eliminated the nine songs identified above, 13 songs remained: *Above All*; *Because He Lives*; *Better Is One Day*; *Blessed Be your Name*; *Breathe*; *Here I Am to Worship*; *I Stand in Awe*; *Our God Reigns*; *The Heart of Worship*; *The Wonderful Cross*; *Trading my Sorrows*; *Turn your Eyes upon Jesus*; and *You Are my King (Amazing Love)*.

Several of these remaining 13 songs are more overtly about *our* pain and suffering, two of which I will mention here. One (*Because He Lives*) focuses on the pain and suffering of life experiences. Although the lyrics imply a sense of victory, they actually name some of the very issues that can cause the most pain and suffering. The chorus acknowledges that there has been fear, but "because he lives, all fear is gone," and alludes to a contemplation of not going on with life, but that "life is worth the living just because he lives." The second song, *The Heart of Worship*, focuses more on a spiritual form of pain and suffering. It deals almost exclusively with a personal and spiritual pain and suffering, recognizing a person's own sinfulness and self-preoccupation. This is seen especially in the lines, "I'm sorry, Lord, for the thing I've made it / when it's all about You, all about You, Jesus."

One of the 13 songs that deals almost exclusively with the pain and suffering of Jesus Christ is *The Wonderful Cross*, although much of this is within the traditional hymn by Isaac Watts, *When I Survey the Wondrous Cross*. Notice, however, that the much-more-recently written chorus makes use of the New Testament model of intentionally suffering for the sake of Christ: "O the wonderful cross bids me come and die and find that I might truly live." This alone sets this song in a unique category of worship songs that express pain and suffering.

Overall, I found these 13 songs to have some meaningful expression of pain and suffering, although some have a subtle underlying expression that is not immediately evident just through vocabulary. For instance, *Better Is One Day* speaks of a person's soul longing and even fainting for God, and of one's heart and flesh crying out for Him, the living God. The words themselves do not use direct language of pain and suffering, but the underlying sense concerns a suffering that can only be alleviated by God's Spirit.

Finally, regarding the theological appropriateness of the lyrics, there will never be one answer to this question, but it must be considered. One very important reason for this consideration is that for many churchgoers, especially those without previous theological foundation and spiritual formation, the songs that they leave church singing may well be the main foundation of their theology, that is, their understanding of the Bible and of God and their relationship to God. If the theology of a song is not biblically supportable, it is questionable whether it should be included in congregational worship.[8] This concern is an essential part of being a responsible worship leader.

There are two of the 13 songs identified above that express some level of pain and suffering but should be removed from the list for theological (or literary) reasons. One is very popular and beautiful in almost every way: *Above All*. It offers a window into the suffering of Jesus, especially with the chorus. But the imagery and analogy get confused once we get to the "rose" and talk about "taking the fall." The latter phrase also seems to trivialize the imagery here. More troubling is the theological concern about the concluding statement—that Jesus thought of *me* above everything. It is not, after all, *all* about me, no matter how much I may want it to be.

The second song among the 13 that I would remove for theological reasons is *Breathe*. Even though the words "I'm desperate for you and I'm lost without you" do have an underlying sense of personal and spiritual pain and suffering, the nebulousness of the lyrics (that is, God is not mentioned) and the inescapable sense of girlish love-sickness are not what I consider theologically appropriate for corporate worship today. (I recognize that many would have disagreed with me, especially those for whom this song was personally meaningful.)

After subtracting two for theological reasons, that leaves 11 songs on my list: *Because He Lives*; *Better Is One Day*; *Blessed Be your Name*; *I Stand in Awe*; *Our God Reigns*; *The Heart of Worship*; *The Wonderful Cross*; *Trading my Sorrows*; *Turn your Eyes Upon Jesus*; *You Are my King* (*Amazing Love*).

---

8. This is a discussion that would merit further attention and could benefit greatly from the involvement of theologians and pastors who are interested in how the musical expression of pain and suffering plays a formative role in our corporate worship, regardless of whether they themselves are musicians or not.

The Musical-Lyrical Interchange

I admit that it is difficult to reduce musical evaluation to a step-by-step linear procedure. There is always potential for a song with poor, or perhaps inadequate, music to be eliminated from any potential list on the very first hearing, even if the words *might* be excellent. And for the purpose of this assignment, it is the words that must primarily express pain and suffering in the context of worship, because it is the lyrics that are at the heart of worshipful expression (however, I mention the neglected or unrealized importance of music alone as a vehicle for worship, even corporate worship, in my discussion in chapter 15 below).

THE MUSIC ITSELF

My initial question here is simply, Does the music *sound* musical? In practical terms, that means, if I play the song without focusing on any lyrics, does it have a melody that I and others want to sing? Do the chords of the song carry it along in a creative yet logical way, with harmonies that are potentially expressive of pain and suffering? This by no means suggests that the chords must be minor chords, but the harmonies combined with the melody will have an inherent expressiveness. A good example is the chorus of *Draw Me Close* ("You're all I want / You're all I've ever needed / You're all I want / help me know You are near"). The song—though not about pain and suffering—has a particular sound and feel to it that would make it excellent for this purpose.

There is no set formula, however, to determine whether the music sounds musical. The study of why the sounds of a musical composition are perceived by their listeners the way they are is at least as old as the Greek philosophers. Musical background and worship experience work together to determine which worship songs have music that may help express pain and suffering to the listeners in a specific subculture. In some cases, the "fit" of text and music is so obviously mismatched that the average layperson can sense it immediately. In other cases, evaluating whether a given musical setting is helpful or harmful to communicating a message of pain and suffering may require significant musical training on the part of the evaluator.[9] If the music seems ill-fitting, then as a

---

9. Older excellent words could be set to new music, but this is not always legally possible. If the music is not conducive to congregational singing, good words will not redeem it.

worship planner I will usually eliminate it from my prospective worship song list.

In the final analysis, I did not eliminate any of the 11 remaining songs strictly on the basis of the music, although there are two that have musical problems: *Blessed Be your Name* and *You Are my King* (*Amazing Love*).

The more problematic of the two is *Blessed Be your Name*. In my experience, this song is not easy for a congregation to sing. Apart from some tricky syncopation and a couple of instances where there are too many word-syllables for the musical phrase, the main problem is that the melody begins very low and ends quite high. If one adjusts the key up to accommodate the low notes at the beginning, one ends up with a song that is uncomfortably, even piercingly, high in the chorus; conversely, if one gears the song to accommodate an average vocal range for the chorus, the verse is too low for most to sing. One common solution is to have the opening lines of the verses sung by a soloist or small group, with the congregation joining later. The irony that I have observed and experienced with this song, however, is that although the musical difficulty is rarely totally overcome, congregations still want to sing the song, and they want to *sing it all*!

Another song that has been difficult for the average congregation to sing is *You Are my King* (*Amazing Love*). The syncopation of this song makes it very tricky for a large group to sing well, and most congregational singers do not succeed in articulating many of the notes. Interestingly again, it is a song that congregations have warmed to, no matter how many of the tricky notes they do or do not sing.

How the Music Fits with the Lyrics

There used to be some choice about what music went with what hymn text. The poetry of the hymn texts was frequently written independently and without reference to a particular tune. As long as the metre of the poem matched that of a given tune (that is, the number of syllables of the lyrics matched the notes of the melody line), tunes and poems could be mixed and matched by the worship leader.[10] This allowed for flexibility

---

10. A current example of this is Robin Mark's use of the hymn, *I Will Sing the Wondrous Story*, in contemporary worship gatherings. Some North American hymnals print these hymn lyrics with the tune written by Peter P. Hilhorn (1865–1936), so this has become the *normal* tune for many churchgoers who have used these hymnals. To hear this tune (Tune 1), go to "I Will Sing." However, Mark uses the alternate

and often provided performance options. If one tune did not seem to match the sense of the words, one could choose another tune that did! Contemporary worship music, however, locks music and text together, and they are not easily interchangeable. The music and texts of contemporary worship songs usually are written together from the beginning and incorporate short or unique sections that do not conform to the exact shape of another song.[11] The way that worship leaders often learn a song first is by hearing it from a recording, possibly performed by the very person who wrote both the words and music.

Therefore, it becomes increasingly important to determine whether the music supports the *meaning* of the words and aids in the *expressiveness* of those words. Professional musicians and experienced worship leaders instinctively make these assessments; even if these kinds of questions are rarely explicitly formulated, they are underlying questions nonetheless. Examples of problematic music with lyrics might include a melody that sounds mournful with words that seem to be cheerful and uplifting. Or there is the song that sounds joyful while we are singing of despair. Part of my role as worship leader is providing music that allows and encourages the congregation to sing the words. I am not leading a congregation of professional musicians; I am giving laypeople in the church an opportunity to contribute their own voice in corporate worship that can express pain and suffering. If I have chosen a song to aid a community of worshipers in expressing pain and suffering, then I want it to be simple (though not simplistic) enough that people can sing the music and get to the heart of that pain and suffering, without the music becoming a hindrance.

Of the remaining 11 songs on my list, I would remove one on the basis of what I consider to be a mismatch of text and music, and that is *Our God Reigns*. The music hinders it from effectively contributing

---

melody, known as HYFRYDOL (Rowland H. Prichard, 1811–1887) (Tune 2). This tune is often printed with the hymn lyrics of *Jesus, What a Friend for Sinners* (words by J. Wilbur Chapman, 1859–1918). Mark's use of Tune 2 makes it sound fresh to those more familiar with Tune 1. And Tune 2 is also more worship band-friendly (e.g., the chord structure works well on guitar), as well as having a melody that falls on contemporary ears as more current.

11. Contemporary worship songwriters with a gift for writing lyrics do not always have an equal gift for writing a melody that is intuitively singable. An interesting possible future study would be, for example, to compare the tunefulness or "singability" of melodies written by vocalists, pianists, and guitarists to see if there is a discernible difference.

to worship that is expressive of pain and suffering. Three of the verses clearly speak of the pain and suffering of Christ (see the lyrics in Table 1). The words themselves are from Isaiah, but the music does not adequately support the sense of the words. The song *should* allow us to focus on the immensity of Jesus' pain and suffering on our account, but the rhythm and shape of the musical line does not fit with the nuances in the text and the normal accenting of the syllables, which results in making the words sound superficial and unimportant.

After I removed *Our God Reigns* from the list, all of the remaining 10 songs are excellent examples of good lyrical and musical *fit*. The 10 songs that remain are *Because He Lives*; *Better Is One Day*; *Blessed Be your Name*; *Here I Am to Worship*; *I Stand in Awe*; *The Heart of Worship*; *The Wonderful Cross*; *Trading my Sorrows*; *Turn your Eyes upon Jesus*; and *You Are my King* (*Amazing Love*).

Of these 10, some that stand out musically and lyrically focus on the pain and suffering of Jesus: *Here I Am to Worship* ("glorious in heaven above / humbly You came to the earth You created / all for love's sake became poor"; "and I'll never know how much it cost to see my sin upon that cross"); *I Stand in Awe* ("yet God crushed You for my sin . . ."); and *You Are my King* (*Amazing Love*) ("How can it be that You, my King, would die for me? / I'm forgiven because You were forsaken / I'm accepted, You were condemned").[12]

One song that I already mentioned above has an especially apt musical and lyrical interchange. It focuses almost exclusively on the suffering of Jesus and forces our attention to the cross. It is the combination of hymn and "chorus" (an appropriate use of this term), *The Wonderful Cross*. The most eloquent words are those of Isaac Watts, in the hymn *When I Survey the Wondrous Cross*, but the marriage of the music with this hymn text is exquisite. Not only is the combination beautiful but the original hymn is also extremely user-friendly because almost anyone can sing its melodic range that consists of only five notes. The chorus, now woven with this hymn, takes us back to the New Testament imagery of the suffering of dying to self in order to follow Christ: "O the wonderful cross, bids me come and die and find that I may truly live," which also corresponds with the third verse of Watts's classic hymn. This song

---

12. It is not possible here to demonstrate how the music and lyrics fit together in a meaningful way. This is something I would do in a seminar or workshop for worship teams and interested laypeople. It is best explored in a live setting with musical demonstration and participation.

stands alone as one that focuses our attention on the suffering of Jesus on the cross and the appropriate response to that suffering in our own commitment to him.

Two other songs in my final list of 10 have a wonderful interchange of music and text, and although pain and suffering is not their overt subject, it is the strong underlying thread. The first is *The Heart of Worship*, which voices a spiritual pain and suffering resulting from a broken or half-hearted relationship with God, but it is not only the lyrics that contribute to the song's expressiveness, it is the combination of the music with those words. The second is *Turn your Eyes upon Jesus*, whose opening lines speak directly to the sufferer: "O soul, are you weary and troubled, no light in the darkness you see?" It clearly reminds us what we are to do in the darkness: "turn your eyes upon Jesus." When we cannot hear or see God, when we cannot find answers to our "whys," when we cannot find relief from the pain—we must turn our eyes upon Jesus, the Light of the world. I have been interested to see this refrain used in numerous live worship settings and worship recordings.

The Context

The final level of analysis is determining the context or determining how the worship song (or songs) of pain and suffering fits with *my* or *your* congregation. I could argue that we have already determined which songs are *about* and meaningfully *express* pain and suffering, and that that is enough, but I would find it troubling to leave things there.

It is in this final level of analysis where the decision is made about whether the song is incorporated into *my* (or *your*) worshiping community. If the song is on the CCLI list but it does not belong on the list of songs for *my* own church, then the previous categories are of little value to me, except as an academic exercise. One of the most important questions that the discerning worship leader must answer—and I believe that discernment is absolutely crucial for a serious worship leader—is this: *Does the song give voice to the people in my own congregation, or are the words and/or musical style mismatched with my own worshiping community?* Just because the church down the street uses a song or I find it on a list of top songs does not mean that it is the right choice for my church.

The one song that stands out for its unique role in helping my context of worshipers voice their own pain and suffering is Beth and Matt

Redman's *Blessed Be your Name*.[13] I mentioned earlier that I initially had reservations about the music, but I also noted my experience with this song—that people want to sing it! (And interestingly, this is still true years later.)

The opening words of the song give both sides of the life story. At first, we sing, "Blessed be your name in the land that is plentiful where Your streams of abundance flow / blessed be Your name." This sounds archaic, and it would be easy to dismiss this song as disconnected from contemporary life. The second line has a surprising twist: "Blessed be Your name when I'm found in the desert place, though I walk through the wilderness / blessed be Your name." Who in their right mind is going to take desert/wilderness experiences as the occasion to bless the name of the Lord? But the song does not say that I will *feel* like blessing the Lord. What it does is give me the words to say—perhaps with increasing faith—when things seem very dark around me.

The title, *Blessed Be your Name*, comes from Job's incredible words in the first chapter of the book of Job. We look in on a conversation between the Lord and Satan about Job: the Lord says, "There is no one on earth like him; he is blameless and upright, a man who fears God and shuns evil." Then, Satan negotiates the right to take away Job's great blessings, and we see a series of events that deprives Job of almost everything. The result of this devastation is amazing. Job gets up, tears his robe, shaves his head, falls to the ground, and says this: "Naked I came from my mother's womb, / and naked I will depart. / The LORD gave and the LORD has taken away; / may the name of the LORD be praised" (Job 1:20–21). Wow—what an amazing response!

The chorus of *Blessed Be your Name* begins positively, "Every blessing You pour out I'll turn back to praise," but then ventures into uncomfortable territory: "When the darkness closes in, Lord, still I will say, 'Blessed be the name of the Lord.'" Repetition in the chorus plays a vital role in reminding us of our need to continually repeat these words, even when we do not know *where* God is in the midst of our pain and suffering. We may not understand God's ways; we simply affirm that we will continue to worship him even in our darkness.

---

13. It should be noted here, however, that there are numerous songs that are not on the CCLI list being considered here that are excellent examples. One example would be Tim Hughes's *When the Tears Fall* (2003), included on his recording, *When Silence Falls* (2004).

The second verse is similar to the first. We bless his name when the "sun's shining down on me, when the world's all as it should be," and we bless his name "on the road marked with suffering, though there's pain in the offering." We are reminded that the "road marked with suffering" is normal. We also can admit that there is genuine pain in offering up our trust to God when we do not understand what is happening or why, when we are clearly so crippled by pain and suffering that we can hardly even croak out the words, let alone say them with confidence and joy.

The bridge of this song brings us back to the unfathomable ways of God and the fact that we are called to trust him anyway: "You give and take away, You give and take away / my heart will choose to say, Lord, blessed be Your name." This song is a profound gift to the church: It feels real, rings true, and strongly lays out for us the mandate of blessing and worshiping God, regardless of circumstances. This song provides an excellent aid to genuine worship. Warm feelings may or may not come as a result of singing it, but the affirmations of this song are a legitimate tool for Christians to use to learn how to worship God in the genuinely bad times of life.

Many people are aware of the story of personal heartache in the Redmans' lives that led to composing this song, that of losing a baby. Their story can make this song even more meaningful, but the back story alone cannot account for why the song has become so well-used and loved. The song captures the essence of the struggle between good and bad things happening to us as God's children and the unanswered questions about why God does not seem to intervene. The lyrics, with the full support of the music, bring us back to the determined, even passionate response that we will *choose* to trust and bless God in every situation, regardless of those missing explanations. Even those who struggle with singing the music of the verses or articulating all the syllables in the opening lines can join in with fervour as the music of the chorus lifts us to join together as a congregation to sing, "Blessed be the name of the Lord."

But I come back to the need of determining whether a song fits my congregation. This is difficult. For instance, my own musical experience is fairly broad, so I cannot use this experience alone as the criterion for making decisions for my congregation or chapel. I come from an evangelical tradition, and I like many things about contemporary worship music; I write songs to be used in church and chapel and I lead them with my worship teams. I love working with worship bands. My studies, however, focused on early Anglican musical traditions of sixteenth-century

England, and I experienced the beauty of some of this music in churches and cathedrals in England for several years. My work on ancient Greek musical papyri fragments and early musical notation in lectionaries has opened my eyes and ears to the vast distance between worshipers that span centuries. I have enjoyed participation in a "Gregorian" chant choir, a Bach cantata, and a gospel choir that sang backup for a leading pop musician in a live concert. I found it meaningful to lead worship at casual family camps but also to do solo work for an audience of 10,000. I read and play classical music or improvise on a melodic theme that comes into my head. I love to creatively integrate contemporary worship songs with classic hymns. But my musical experience does not necessarily represent the worshiping communities that I lead. Many of the members of my church congregation and even seminary chapel have little exposure to this range of musical styles. So, one of my goals for these two communities has been to develop a musical language and biblical grounding for our music that expresses the cries of our hearts and voices our meaningful worship back to God. Whether it is the musical literature of the earliest hymns, the most recent of worship songs, or an integration of Scripture texts with song, a worship leader has the opportunity to provide avenues for worshipers to sing meaningful words and prayers.

So, how does a discerning worship leader choose music for our congregation that helps *us* meaningfully express pain and suffering in *our* worship? It is the "us" and "our" here that are important. We need to enter into this kind of worship ourselves, and, as we lead a congregation into this kind of worship, we must enter the very space that we are asking others to enter. There is always a risk in this kind of leading. We can't just point down a path and say, "Go down there." We walk there ourselves and ask them to follow. Meanwhile, we may be experiencing a pain and suffering ourselves at the time. So, we must be wholehearted worshipers ourselves, whether we are simply choosing music and leading it in a service, or whether we have written a song and offer it to others as a vehicle for this unknown journey. But this discussion is one that would require more time and space and probably personal interaction. It will have to be saved for another day.

CONCLUSION

The bottom line is that, of the 77 CCLI songs on the original list that was provided for me to work with, only a few songs—10 at most—lyrically and musically seemed to contribute at an appropriate level to meaningful expression of pain and suffering. Many of the songs that might initially be selected reveal themselves to be inadequate for a variety of reasons, and of the remaining few, only a couple (*Blessed Be your Name*, which focuses on personal pain and suffering, and *The Wonderful Cross*, which focuses on the pain and suffering of Jesus on the cross) rise to the surface as outstanding. So, if meaningful expression of pain and suffering is a vital part of corporate worship, where do we go from here?

I think there are a number of things that we still need to learn about this kind of honest worship, and several ways that we could contribute to it. The Redmans' song provides some guidance. It is honest and it does not avoid the fact that our understanding of God is not laid out in black and white. At the same time, it turns us back to praising God in the midst of very dark times. We could benefit from these points. We do need to be honest about our suffering. We do not need to make complex things simplistic. We do need to find a way of continuing to worship God even when we are feeble. And we do need to be willing to admit that there is no guarantee that the pain and suffering will be removed just because we have great faith in God. But honest worship will teach us how to worship God *through* our pain, in the *middle* of our suffering, in those lonely places of isolation, and in the ambiguity of all the questions that begin with "why."

We know that everybody experiences physical, mental, or spiritual pain and suffering to some degree at some time. Often this is what first brings people into our worshiping communities. What we cannot rely on is a list of popular worship songs to be our sole guide to finding music that gives expression to that pain and suffering in our *own* worshiping community.

The ongoing life of contemporary worshiping communities demands that worship leaders and songwriters contribute intentionally to the meaningful worship life of those communities. I need to have the pulse of my own church, so that I have some idea of the experiences represented by this gathered group of God's people, and those still journeying toward God. It is this kind of knowledge, coming out of my own congregation's experience, that prompted me to write a particular song for them, and us, to sing. This simple song has expressed pain and suffering for a wide range of people—even, in one case, for a woman who had suffered so deeply that she had not cried for twenty years until she began to sing it. No one knows if a song that he or she writes will be a vehicle for others to also worship but let me explain some of the things that go through my mind when I am trying to contribute to this particular aspect of worship services that I lead.

First, I need lyrics that are accessible to others and meaningful to me. The words can be simple, but they need to speak to the deepest parts of my own heart in order for them to potentially speak to others; I can never be sure that they will speak to anyone else, but they must at least be meaningful to me. Secondly, they need to be words that come out of a life deeply in touch with God's Spirit and immersed in his Word, whether anyone else knows that or not. Thirdly, the melody needs to be easily sung, so that it does not become the obstacle that prevents a congregation from participating. Fourthly, if possible, the harmonies need to be relatively straightforward, so that those who do sing by ear can find them.

I think that part of the way forward is to begin writing our own songs for our own worshiping communities. Pastors, youth leaders, teachers, musicians, and laypeople who work with each of the four elements just described can all contribute to the content of these songs. We need to bring the sound of our own voices together to sing about our deepest needs. We need to understand that God knows all about those darkest moments, and that this is why Jesus came to earth in the first place. The reason we can worship God in the darkness is because Christ went there first, on our behalf: "'By his wounds you have been healed'" (1 Pet 2:24).

REFERENCES AND FURTHER READING

Brueggemann, Walter. *The Message of the Psalms: A Theological Commentary.* Minneapolis: Augsburg, 1984.

———. *Praying the Psalms.* Winona, MN: Saint Mary's, 1982.

Card, Michael. *A Sacred Sorrow: Reaching Out to God in the Lost Language of Lament.* Colorado Springs, CO: NavPress, 2005.

"I Will Sing the Wondrous Story Robin Mark with Lyrics (4K)." *YouTube.* https://www.youtube.com/watch?v=egnSK7yz_90.

Lewis, C. S. *The Problem of Pain.* New York: Macmillan, 1962.

———. *Reflections on the Psalms.* New York: Harcourt, Brace and World, 1958.

14

Christian Worship and the Toronto Blessing

INTRODUCTION

THIS ESSAY WAS FIRST written when the Toronto Blessing—an extreme charismatic expression of the Christian faith—was having a huge impact upon churches in North America and the United Kingdom. Beginning at the Toronto Airport Vineyard (as it was then, although the church has apparently left the Vineyard association since that time), the movement spread quickly to a variety of other churches, especially those with charismatic forms of worship. Almost immediately, there was reaction to the movement, as its expression in terms of various outward phenomena was intense. This led to a variety of responses by biblical scholars, theologians, sociologists, church historians, worship leaders, and many others.[1] Some of these reactions are contained within the book in which this chapter first appeared. I wrote the chapter on the worship and music of the Toronto Blessing based upon both study of the movement and first-hand witness to its practices specifically in London, England. Although the Toronto Blessing itself has now faded, as have many similar movements in the past, I think that it is important for us to assess such movements and have criteria for evaluation of them. I attempt to provide these criteria in this chapter by examining the specific instance of the Toronto Blessing.

---

1. See Porter and Richter, eds., *Toronto Blessing*, with a variety of experts writing on the movement.

Part Two: Musical Traditions and Interpretations

THE CONCEPT OF WORSHIP

I begin with a discussion of the concept of worship itself as the appropriate context for evaluating the Toronto Blessing or any other movement that makes similar claims regarding the work of the Holy Spirit.

Setting the Framework for Worship

The churches of the Toronto Blessing herald themselves as "word and spirit" churches, that is, churches where the word is as important as the manifestations of the Spirit.[2] Therefore, it would seem reasonable in discussing the subject of worship that Toronto Blessing churches would be concerned to exemplify a worship that is biblically based and that allows for the proper expression of the gifts of the Spirit. They have said as much—but is this in fact the case? In order to decide, perhaps there is a need to begin with establishing fundamental precepts regarding the biblical basis of Christian worship. But with all the books and articles that have been written in recent years on the subject of worship, is there a possibility of addressing the issue in a few pages? There is no space to refer to something like David Peterson's detailed study of biblical words translated into English as "worship,"[3] but there is still one significant factor that he highlights that can be singled out and addressed here. When the central focus of biblical worship is established, it points in all aspects to Jesus Christ as Lord and God at work through Christ's birth, death, and resurrection. According to D. Gerhard Delling, the well-known New Testament scholar, "it is no longer God who 'builds' this Church, but Jesus. That corresponds exactly to the way in which Jesus elsewhere took statements made in the Old Testament about God and applied them to Himself. He is the One who not only carries out the commission of God but in whom God Himself acts."[4] The Old Testament continually points toward the life and work of the coming Christ; the New Testament presents the story of his birth, his ministry, and ultimately his death and resurrection and then shows how the different authors and early believers worked out their theology based on Jesus Christ as Lord. Worship of the God of the Old Testament points to Christ; worship of the living Christ of the New Testament points back to God. The Holy Spirit, given

2. On the biblical basis of the Toronto Blessing, see Porter, "Shaking the Biblical Foundations?"

3. See Peterson, *Engaging with God*.

4. Delling, *Worship*, 19–20.

as the ongoing substitute for Christ's physical presence (John 16:7), also continually directs attention towards Christ.

Having this understanding of the centrality of Jesus Christ as the key to biblical worship helps to put some things in perspective. There will always be debate about worship, but however the term is used, and regardless of how broad or narrow the use, if it is to be biblical, Christ must be central. If "worship" is used in the context of worship service, worship team, worship leader, the bottom line in determining the role and the validity of that role must be the centrality of Christ. Frederick Herzog rightly states, "Unmistakably Christian worship points to Jesus of Nazareth."[5] Although it would be far too simple to say that this focus eliminates the problems faced in contemporary worship and the differing understandings and practical expressions of it, it does however set a biblical framework and a standard by which to evaluate, a criterion for assessment of some of the things which may uncritically be called worship.

With this mark of Christ-centredness as the standard of biblical worship, Christ-centredness should be evident in the various practical expressions of worship. In contemporary Christian worship, perhaps no area consistently arouses more controversy than music. Nevertheless, without prejudging the specific kinds of music that are to be encouraged in the church, there are some biblical precepts that emerge, and they are surprisingly consistent with the pattern of Christ-centredness established above.

Although there is little idea what the music of the Old or New Testaments would have sounded like, it can be seen that it was an important part of the worship of the church. Some of the terms in the New Testament for the music of the believers are "psalms, hymns, and spiritual songs" (Eph 5:19; Col 3:16).[6] Without knowing exactly what these may have referred to in the early church, it is quite certain that they at least indicate that music was a vital part of their gatherings.

When it comes to establishing the content of early Christian music many scholars look to several New Testament prayers that may well have been early Christian hymns. There is a noticeable consistency in their focus. Luke 1:46–55, Mary's song, *praises God for the Son* she would soon bear; later in the same chapter (Luke 1:68–79), Zechariah's song *praises God* for the fulfillment of his promises to his people, a God who would

---

5. Herzog, "Norm and Freedom," 133.

6. Biblical quotations are from the NIV. These terms are discussed in chapters 2 and 3 above.

through Christ "give his people the knowledge of salvation through the forgiveness of their sins" (1:77). In Luke 2:29–32 Simeon *praises God for Jesus*, the salvation for the people. Philippians 2:6–11, probably the most important early Christian confession, powerfully *depicts Christ*, obedient to death on a cross, but exalted to the highest place, "that at the name of Jesus every knee should bow . . . and every tongue *confess that Jesus Christ is Lord* . . ." (Phil 2:10, 11). Finally, Col 1:15–20 vividly describes Jesus as pre-eminently "the head of the body, the church." These examples "can legitimately be seen as reflecting the sort of liturgical material which early Christians would have used."[7] Regardless of the sound or style of these songs, if indeed they were songs, there is one evident pattern—they all have Christ as their central focus. By now the pattern should be evident that early Christian worship focused upon Christ, as the pertinent biblical texts clearly reveal. This may come as a surprise to some, who are accustomed to separating emotional from cerebral elements in worship. The fact that the music of the early church had a clear focus upon Christ indicates that worship requires an engagement of both heart and mind with God. As Paul says in 1 Cor 14:13b, 14, "For if I pray in a tongue, my spirit prays, but my mind is unfruitful. So, what shall I do? I will pray with my spirit, but I will also pray with my mind; I will sing with my spirit, but I will also sing with my mind." It is crucial that this quality be present for worship to become more than simply empty words, motions, or emotions.

Elements of biblical worship are not restricted to the church-gathering but can and should become an integral part of everyday life to really become the worship portrayed in the New Testament. C. F. D. Moule writes, "All Christian life is worship, 'liturgy' means service, all believers share Christ's priesthood, and the whole Christian Church is the house of God (1 Cor 3:16; Eph 2:22)."[8] However, for the subject at hand the practice as it takes place in formal church gatherings will be considered.

What the Liturgy and Worship of a Church Indicate

The above discussion may seem rather academic. In a sense it is, except that it is important to note that ideas motivate practice. As John Barkley comments,

---

7. Bradshaw, *Search*, 44. Many of the examples above are discussed in this volume at various places, especially chapter 4.

8. Moule, *Worship*, 84.

we see how doctrine or dogma determines worship. The character of worship springs from the nature and character of the God who is believed in. Our concept of God and the way we manifest and expound his relation to man [sic] determine our worship . . . just as theology influences liturgy, so liturgy influences theology, because it brings theological statements before the bar of experience.[9]

Thus, the order of a church service, the time given to various elements of it, elements included or excluded all serve as indicators of the priorities of a particular church. From these it can be seen which things are considered important and which are not. Delling says, "In many respects the essence of a religion is more directly intelligible in its worship than in statements of its basic principles or even in descriptions of its sentiments."[10] Therefore, it is worthwhile to note some of the contrasts of various churches and identify what may be indicated by a single element: a church that emphasizes mostly the spontaneous expressions of individuals compared with a church that keeps to a written congregational response; one where a priest's role is highly revered compared with one that subscribes only to the "priesthood" of the believers; the use of formal individual hymns at various times in the service compared with twenty to thirty minutes of sustained singing of contemporary songs; the antiquity of an order of service contrasted with the recent copyright dates of all materials used in a service; exuberant clapping and dancing in one church building contrasted with a hushed silence in another; the use of the creeds compared with the ever-changing "word of knowledge"; the formal written-out prayer in one, the extemporaneous prayer in another, etc. Without making judgments on any of these particular items, it can be agreed that the actual practices illustrate something of the nature or focus of a given church. By taking a closer look at the way these elements of corporate worship are all worked together in a church, however, some definite assessments can be made of the priorities and character of that church. If the practices of individual churches carry out the beliefs and practices of a movement, then it is possible by logical extension to make some valid statements about the movement as well.

What becomes increasingly apparent is that the manner of worship and the patterns of a particular group may point quite clearly in directions that are not at all what that group had intended or realized. Here

9. Barkley, "Theology of Liturgy," 7.
10. Delling, *Worship*, xi.

some disturbing things emerge about the nature of the worship that is taking place in the churches that are involved in the phenomena of the Toronto Blessing. In taking up the concept of worship, looking at it from several angles in the light of the churches participating in the Toronto Blessing in London and against the background of their biblical roots and traditions, it is possible to draw some conclusions and indicate some signs that should perhaps be heeded.

Specific Historical Church Models and Their Practices

Churches have historically had various ways of coming to terms with the biblical concept of the Christ-centredness of worship. Not everyone is agreed that the historical practices of a church are to be kept at all costs, nor that they necessarily continue to signify biblical precepts and practices. However, it seems that history must be acknowledged as a major participant in the discussion, based on the fact that Christians for generations have debated similar kinds of issues. Practices that have been preserved may have more to say than present generations would like to admit. Looking very briefly at four models of churches, all claiming to be trying to maintain significant features of New Testament practice and Christian history, will provide necessary background. The categories used are not ironclad, since there are numerous churches that emphasize more than one of the models below. But the characterizations can be useful for instructive purposes.

Baptist—Baptism

In Baptist churches, as is evident by the name, one of the central focuses is upon water baptism, usually defined as believer's baptism. There are numerous examples and commands in the New Testament that give credence to the biblical basis of this practice and hence the legitimacy of its occupying a central place in the worship of churches persuaded by these examples (e.g., Matt 28:16–20 [esp. v. 19]; John 3:22, 23; Acts 2:38, 41; 8:38; 12:30, 31; 10:48; 16:31–33). The examples are all of new believers being obedient to the command to believe or repent and be baptized, and, as a result, going through some sort of water baptism as an integral part of their belief in Christ. Without debating the modes of baptism at this point, it can be seen that the New Testament gives substantial background and basis for the practice observed by baptists. For many of these churches, baptism occupies a special place in worship services, or may even constitute a separate service dedicated to the practice.

Charismatic—Tongues

Charismatic churches, including Pentecostals, along with various denominations that may be considered charismatic, believe that there are certain signs of being filled with the Holy Spirit, having received a second work of the Spirit, or being baptized in the Spirit. These signs have traditionally been evidenced by the gift of speaking in tongues and secondarily by the gift of interpretation of tongues. Other gifts of the Spirit have also been highlighted, but these two are the distinctive ones. There are numerous references to both the practice and problems of speaking in tongues and interpretation of tongues in the early church (e.g., 1 Cor 12–14; Acts 2:4, 15). It is interesting to note that Peter used the presence of the phenomena as a way of pointing people to Jesus of Nazareth and presenting his story (Acts 2:22–24). Regardless of the other issues that this topic raises, it is enough at this point to note that tongues were a genuine part of the New Testament accounts of at least some early Christian churches. The manifestation of the charismatic gifts, including especially the gift of tongues, has continued to occupy a significant place in various charismatic worship services. This can be seen in times devoted to speaking or singing in tongues, either individually or as a corporate exercise.

Evangelical—The Preached Word

For many years, in the typical evangelical Protestant church, the preacher's sermon, or exposition of the word and proclamation of the gospel, has been considered the core of the service, with other elements pointing towards it and generally seen as less important. This stems from a belief in the word of God as foundational to one's faith, and therefore necessarily preached and taught for the people to learn from and to obey (2 Tim 3:16). For example, in Luke 4:15–30, Jesus reads from Isa 61:1–2 and proclaims the day of the Lord to be at hand. In Paul's numerous trips to the synagogue, it says that he showed how Christ had fulfilled the Old Testament Scriptures. Biblical proclamation has continued to occupy a place of prime importance in numerous churches. Of course, the sermon has gone through an evolution in recent years and in many cases has become less substantive and more superficial, speaking to the felt needs of the moment, but not necessarily to the long-term needs of the listener. Nevertheless, the sermon's importance continues.

Sacramental—Eucharist

In sacramentalist churches, including such churches as the Anglican or the Church of England, the Eucharist is the focal point. As a near-weekly observance it is not difficult to pinpoint the central role it plays in the worship and liturgy. The death and resurrection of Christ are pivotal to the entire New Testament and therefore crucial for the worship priorities of sacramental churches. The biblical and historical precedents for this practice are substantial. During the last supper with the disciples, Jesus broke bread, representing his body, and offered the cup as his "blood of the covenant, which is poured out for many for the forgiveness of sins" (Matt 26:26–28). In 1 Cor 11:26, following the account of the last supper, it says that this act serves to "proclaim the Lord's death until he comes." Just as these events were important in the early church, so they have traditionally been significant parts of much Christian worship. It is not necessary to observe many sacramental services to realize that the Eucharist often takes half the time of any given service and is placed in the latter half to give predominance to it. The formal liturgy moves unhesitatingly towards the celebration of the Eucharist and culminates in it.

Summary of the Churches

As with any church or denomination, practices are adapted with time and boundaries between denominations become somewhat blurred or changed, but it can be agreed, I think, that each of the four church orientations above represents a distinctive set of church practices endorsed by biblical precedent and agreed upon by previous generations of Christians of each denominational type as central to their theology and their worship. Each distinctive practice is focused in some significant way on Jesus Christ. Each has a biblical basis and early church practice as its foundation, as well as a long line of historical tradition to give credence to it. Finally, each is normally evident by its prominence in the service in the individual church.

CONTEMPORARY PRACTICES IN CHURCHES EXPERIENCING THE TORONTO BLESSING

On the basis of the characterizations of major church models, I now turn specifically to the practices of the Toronto Blessing.

Introduction

There are probably few churches of any description that could stand up to objective scrutiny without revealing some inadequacy or some failure to keep priorities, order, and balance. Nonetheless, the purpose here is to determine the nature of the worship that takes place specifically in the Toronto Blessing churches (in London) by observing some of their practices and measuring them against the standards described earlier as the basis for determining biblical worship. This exercise could certainly be used not only in churches that are experiencing the Toronto Blessing, but also in any church willing to take stock of what its worship services may suggest compared to what its own perceptions, ideals, or official statements may indicate.

Vineyard Roots of the Toronto Blessing

One thing that seems to be consistent in this movement of the Toronto Blessing is that it has strong ties to the Vineyard movement, with the phenomenon of the Blessing said to stem from an outbreaking of the Spirit at the Toronto Airport Vineyard in Toronto, Canada (as mentioned above, the church is apparently no longer a part of this movement). Churches participating in this experience of the Blessing have not necessarily been connected with the Vineyard previously but have come into contact as a result.

One feature of the Vineyard movement has been the way its leaders have picked up on the genuine desire of many individuals to have a more personal element in their worship services. The leaders have been creative and diligent in disseminating their teachings, music, and various other materials reflecting this desire for personal worship, both to those within the movement and also to others who are interested. But it appears that individuals and churches who have not aligned themselves previously with the Vineyard may have proceeded to buy a product of the Vineyard without necessarily investigating the background or potential outcome of it. Perhaps without consciously accepting the theology and practices of the Vineyard movement, many have adopted them without realizing it. There is legitimate debate about some of these, and regardless of where a person may end up at the end of the discussion, it seems important at least to know the issues. Two such issues can make the point adequately. The first concerns the fact that many of the churches displaying the Toronto Blessing align themselves with a movement that has had trouble with establishing the validity of its so-called prophets' messages. The second issue is that of an open canon, that is, that God's revelation extends beyond the confines of the revelation of the Bible. The issue of the open canon is one that not all Christians, perhaps not even all members of the Vineyard, would be willing to accept. If the biblical canon is still open for additions (and deletions?) and any individual can be a receiver of additional revelations, this raises the serious question of who then determines which things are really biblical. Yet this openness is apparently an underlying foundation of the theology of the Vineyard. For this present study and its analysis of biblical worship, in order to agree upon a basis for what constitutes biblical worship, "biblical" must remain that which is already in the written Bible, with tradition, historical factors, and contemporary society definitely coming into play but not accepted as constituting that which is biblical.

Several churches in Britain that have experienced the Blessing have apparently flown individuals to Toronto to learn more about the phenomenon, evidently gathering biblical texts to provide their bases, learning techniques of administering or facilitating the Blessing, and generally gaining more experience of the Blessing themselves.[11] One woman described her experience of being in a room full of pastors or ministers who, during a time of the Blessing, began to make various loud noises, many of them "animal-like." She also felt herself about to "roar" and, in fact, did "roar." But simply because there are many pastors or ministers present does not in itself make something biblical, so this cannot count as evidence in the search for the signs of biblical worship. Another factor which cannot be used as evidence of something being biblical is that of the success of some churches, either in their use of a particular technique or in the manifestation of some fascinating phenomena. Success of these kinds cannot serve as a criterion for what is biblical.

Others, with great enthusiasm, have flown to various countries to teach churches how to experience the Blessing in their own churches

---

11. See Dixon, *Signs of Revival*.

where it had not already reached them. It appears that, for some, simply duplicating the effect of the Blessing is primary, rather than one actually knowing its biblical basis or status. The Blessing may indeed be all that everyone experiencing it hoped it was, but so far, few who have defended it have been able to articulate their defense clearly and scripturally. While one would not want to miss the outpouring of the Holy Spirit purely on academic grounds, equally it would seem foolish to ignore the evidence if it does end up pointing in some other direction.

Elements of Worship in the Churches of the Toronto Blessing

In the light of what has been said above, and using the discussion above as a model, it is important now to describe and evaluate actual practices of Toronto Blessing churches. The following picture emerges from having read many descriptions of the worship services and having attended a number of different kinds of services. I cannot claim to have anything representing a complete picture, but several patterns nevertheless emerged. Before describing those practices that were evidenced, it is worth noting that in the services I observed there was no use of the Lord's Prayer, no recited creed of any sort, no celebration of the Eucharist, no singing of hymns, and little reading of the Bible. This does not indicate that they are never included in these various churches, but it is a point of interest.

Tongues were used, but never just two or three people speaking in tongues in orderly fashion, and there was no interpretation (1 Cor 14:27–28). "Words of knowledge" and "prophecy" were terms used in some services, with individuals using these as a means of speaking words of encouragement to other individuals or the group as a whole. These will not be dwelt upon, however, since they are part of more widespread charismatic phenomena and did not appear to be used in a way that highly influenced the manifestation of the Toronto Blessing.

Music

Although music was discussed above in terms of its biblical foundations, it is now appropriate to apply what was said to the use of music in Toronto Blessing churches. The musicians in the various services observed were of varying calibre and proficiency, but the style of music and its presentation were similar, using the worship band or team. The model was that of an individual song or worship leader, several vocalists, and a small ensemble of instrumentalists, generally including piano or electronic keyboard, guitar, bass, electric guitar, drums, and one or two other instruments. The singing was not exceptional in any case, neither in the leader, in the assisting vocalists, nor in the congregation, but some was noticeably better than others.

The actual songs in every case observed were contemporary. In at least 90 per cent of the songs used where copyright information was included and presented legibly, the copyright dates were from the last two years. None of the services included anything that could be mistaken for a hymn, although one incorporated a contemporary setting to words of a prayer from the Anglican Alternative Service Book. The majority of the songs referred to personal needs and were addressed to the Spirit or were requests of God for "more" of the Spirit.

Perhaps one of the main underlying causes of the widespread movement towards the use of worship teams in contemporary churches is reaction to old models of church that have seemed to become impersonal and irrelevant for present-day people and culture. Part of the effort of those working towards both the implementation of newer songs and the concept of the worship team, therefore, has been to personalize (or humanize) the worship service. Many contemporary songs are written in the first person, with a strong sense of personal and intimate relationship with God, and the worship team, though a group in appearance, is often very individualistic in nature. However, in evaluating the songs in terms of the biblical criteria listed above, something is lost in utilizing only contemporary songs that tend to focus on "me" and "how I feel about God," and the worship team without careful direction sometimes fosters a contrived individuality that often accompanies a stage performance and draws more attention to itself. There seems to be a lack of responsibility and maturity evident in some of these groups or on the part of their leader. Another problem that current worship groups tend to bring to the forefront is an insatiable need for what is "new" and "contemporary" without a bridge to the traditional teaching and historical practices of that church. Of course, simply because something has been done for dozens or hundreds of years does not make it good, but one must wonder whether those making decisions about music and other elements of a worship service are aware of the implications of their practices, especially those that seem to show a disregard for biblical and historical precedent. In general, comparing the lyrics and melodies of the songs that were used in these services with other songs of a similar genre, most were not, in my opinion, of exceptional quality or musicality, that is, they were not songs that I would expect still to hear in a year or two. More importantly, few if any of the songs were about Christ or things foundational to the Christian faith; the songs were consistently about "me" as an individual and were apparently used to focus the individual on furthering the effects of the Blessing.

Prayer

The use of prayer merits similar evaluation. The prayers were sometimes focused on aspects of the current phenomena, calling on God to bring "more, more"; at other times the prayers were addressed to the Spirit and focused on a particular individual, apparently with the goal of that person falling to the floor. These prayers appeared to become quite urgent and repetitive, even forced, when the individual did not fall quickly or at all. Various people were called up at different times to be prayed for or to participate in the praying. In one instance, several who were visiting to learn about the phenomena but who were not known by name were invited up in the morning service to be prayed for but were the ones asked to do the praying in the evening service. Their experience of the Blessing in the morning apparently qualified them to administer it in the evening. It appeared that, as with the songs, the Blessing or some manifestation of the Spirit was usually the actual focus of the prayers, rather than God and his work through Christ.

Sermon

The sermon or "talk" continues to be used in Toronto Blessing churches. At one church, one short message was used as a means of establishing the validity of the Toronto Blessing. There was no actual evidence given from the Bible apart from single verses taken at random and an Old Testament story used as a contemporary allegory of the Toronto Blessing, accompanied by numerous warnings to those who may be skeptical about the Blessing. This evidently was to set the stage for what was to follow, which was a testimony about the Blessing and then the "ministry time." In another church, the message was directed to the people of that church, addressing an issue that had seemed to become pertinent in their church regarding the Blessing. It appears that sermons, rather than being concerned to deepen the biblical or spiritual understanding of the congregation, are often being used apologetically to substantiate and reinforce credibility for the Blessing.

Testimonies

Testimonies, long a staple of more informal and often evangelical churches, continue to be used in Toronto Blessing churches. In several of the services, personal testimonies were given about the experience of the Blessing or something related and were used as preparation for the "ministry time" that followed. Some testimonies were also used as an opportunity to pray for the person who had given the testimony, with the intent of allowing that person to fall publicly under the power of the Spirit or the Blessing, but with no mention of Jesus. This practice of praying for the person who has just testified is apparently recommended in Vineyard materials.[12]

Ministry Time

"Ministry time" is the term that is used to describe the dedicated time in the service when the manifestations of the Spirit are expected to be present. During ministry time, attenders were typically instructed to stack their chairs around the edges of the room (one may realistically wonder if the Blessing could fall upon a church with fixed pews). In one service, no one could remain seated for this time unless they made their way through the crowd to the balcony. This ministry time was not a case of individuals coming forward for prayer or taking the initiative in order to receive some sort of ministry or experience of the Blessing; instead, it was an experience en masse. For someone who may not have been prepared for the experience, it required actively moving away from the crowd. Immediately people were groaning, lying on the floor, laughing, flapping their hands and arms, making indiscernible noises that may have been animal-like, while others were more orgiastic in nature. Some were shaking violently, others were weeping. Some discreetly looked around them after a time and then began their particular noise or action again. Ministry team members—apparently those who have experienced the Blessing's outward manifestations—actively moved from person to person, raising a hand above the individual's forehead or behind their back and apparently praying for or speaking with them, clearing things from behind the person before the person fell, or actually helping them on to

---

12. Dixon, *Signs of Revival*, 325.

the floor. The fact that everything began on cue raises some questions, although further reports indicate that where the church leader has led the way in allowing these signs earlier in the service, the eruptions have become more frequent at different times throughout a service. Other churches have begun including the ministry time in various sections of the service, as well as having a more concentrated time at one particular point, usually near the end of the service. However, it also appears that the Blessing can be timed, planned, or re-enacted whenever it is wanted or needed, whether it be a morning, evening, second service, or the like.

In one service, throughout the ministry time, the pastor kept control of the environment by repeatedly speaking to those who were not evidencing outward signs and reiterating that this was acceptable and not to worry, praying at times, directing ministry team members to other individuals, calling for more members to help, and eventually closing the service down. In another, the pastor continually gave signs to the people, by his actions and personal responses to what was going on in the general part of the service, indicating that responding throughout the service in the varying ways of the Blessing was acceptable, even desirable. At no point was there any specific mention of Christ, no direction given for the person who wanted to know about Christ, and no gospel preached. It appeared in each case that as far as the pastor was concerned, the obvious manifestations of the Spirit or the Blessing (and apparently these were equated) were the central focus. And it seems to be assumed that whatever state one gets into during the ministry time is "of God."

Perhaps something that would be worth considering for a moment is if indeed God did not choose to act in a particular ministry time, if the Holy Spirit did not come upon anyone at the specific time, would anyone notice? Or would the phenomena still be present? Would it simply be a case of the "show must go on," and the ministry time would continue as usual?

The above description gives a brief evaluation of the major features of a typical Toronto Blessing worship service. From the criteria established above, their relation to the Christ-centredness of Christian worship has been mentioned. This effort has been characterized by evaluation in terms of what the Blessing churches themselves do. But it seems important that their overall pattern of worship must also be evaluated in terms of the major models of church worship as well.

Part Two: Musical Traditions and Interpretations

Four Church Models for Comparison

Although the Toronto Blessing churches are distinguished by their common manifestations of the phenomena of the Blessing in their worship services, these churches have much longer-standing ties to the traditional models briefly discussed above. When these general patterns of worship are compared with what is taking place in the Toronto Blessing churches some noteworthy patterns emerge, including some significant changes of focus. It is perhaps worthwhile to note these, if for no other reason than many connected with the Blessing may not be aware of the implications of the shifts in emphasis.

Baptist

What seems to have become dominant in Baptist churches that experience the Toronto Blessing is not that people come to Christ and are baptized, as one might expect, but that believers come for the Blessing or "ministry time." In one church, other church members came from neighbouring churches to participate, not in the service but only in the ministry time. While this may be beneficial in some respects, the question must be raised: has the Blessing or ministry time become more important than people coming to faith and being baptized, even though baptism is a central focus in the New Testament and one woven throughout the tradition and theology of the baptistic churches? While it is admirable that one pastor admitted that ironically people are not coming to Christ and being baptized, and urged his people not to forget baptism and not to let the ministry time become focal in their minds, it seemed evident that indeed that had happened in at least one Baptist church experiencing the Blessing.

Charismatic

In the charismatic tradition, where tongues is the evidence of being Spirit-filled, the Toronto Blessing can be seen usurping the place of tongues and becoming the new evidence of the Spirit's work. Whether one agrees or not with the basis for tongues as the sign of being Spirit-filled, a sudden change of signs does raise questions. In the words of one well-known charismatic theologian, Clifford Hill, "loud, uncontrollable, hysterical laughter has no precedent in scripture as a manifestation of the Spirit of God."[13] The Toronto Blessing is a recent phenomenon with far less bibli-

---

13. Hill, "'Toronto Blessing,'" 10.

cal basis to substantiate it than tongues, yet charismatics have been quick to accept it as a new sign. If charismatics are concerned about the biblical and historical basis for their practices and beliefs, then this element of their worship must also fall under scrutiny.

Evangelical

In churches with a heritage of the word or gospel message being predominant, the Blessing seems to have upstaged the message and become the climax of the service. The message is used as a means of asserting that the Blessing is valid or as a time for talking about the Blessing, but not apparently as a time to present the claims of Christ. This replacement of one main emphasis with another needs to be questioned. This is not simply a case of exchanging one hymn for a contemporary song, nor of adjusting the order of the service; this is substituting a major historical emphasis on teaching or preaching the Bible—a cognitive dimension of the Christian life—for a completely different emphasis: one on outward emotive manifestations.

Sacramental

In looking at a sacramental liturgical model, such as the Anglican or Church of England, in terms of the Toronto Blessing, another major substitution has occurred. The corporate breaking of the bread and the sharing of the cup has been a traditional link to the biblical account of the Last Supper, instituting the bread and wine as remembrances of Jesus' death and resurrection and the forgiveness of sins available as a result. In sacramental churches, the Blessing has apparently superseded the Eucharist as the high point and focus of liturgical practice. Rob Warner makes the enthusiastic comment regarding the presence of the Blessing that on one occasion "So overwhelming was the response that a planned communion service had to be cancelled."[14] The remembrance of Christ's death and resurrection, the observance of them certainly at the heart of the sacramental liturgy, has been, if not literally removed from the liturgy, certainly replaced in importance.

Summary of the Four Churches

Perhaps these substitutions have only occurred in those churches where their traditional focus no longer has meaning for the people. If this is the

14. Warner, *Prepare for Revival*, 16.

case, then several questions should be raised. When there is an emptiness in worship, might it not be easier to begin to worship an ephemeral experience that feels good or temporarily appeases, rather than worshipping the risen Christ as Lord? Does the Blessing fill in wherever there is a void of some sort in the liturgy? If so, shouldn't it be investigated thoroughly before being accepted? Since many Toronto Blessing churches claim to be "word and spirit" churches, shouldn't they be searching the Bible at least as diligently as they seek the manifestations of the Spirit? Shouldn't they consult biblical beliefs and historical practices of the church thoroughly before discarding what has been the heart of their Christian worship? The solution to empty worship might well be to return to the traditional biblical and historical basis of worship rather than abandoning it for a spectacular current phenomenon.

GENERAL EVALUATION

Having established the foundation and commented upon the practice of Toronto Blessing churches, I now wish to provide an evaluation along three lines.

Loss of Traditional Focus of Worship

Living in a day and age when traditional values are suspect, historical ways of doing things are discarded as *passé*, family ties are increasingly broken and rewoven into different patterns, and more and more products on the market are instantly gratifying and constantly changing shape and colour, it is perhaps not surprising to find the church also trying to establish new ways of doing things and looking for more exciting and fascinating elements to liven up worship services and make them relevant and to address the countless needs of the contemporary individual and family. But in the craze to find new and exciting elements, or in getting caught up in the latest thing, churches run the greatest risk of losing what is of proven worth and value. Each of the kinds of churches mentioned above—baptistic, charismatic, evangelical, and sacramental—stands to lose a significant element of the traditional focus of its worship under the influence of the Toronto Blessing. These churches may, consciously or unconsciously, be trading in a traditional focus for one that has little biblical basis, was not apparently endorsed by the practice of the early church and may very well be short-lived. Horn makes some insightful comments regarding the phenomena recorded in the opening chapters of Acts: "How did the apostles react to these occurrences? Did they . . . dwell on them or seek to reproduce them?" He shows what Peter's response was:

> What he did was to move rapidly from the external signs to the essential message. From bewildering events to the truths that made clear his hearers' relation to God. From what they saw to what they needed to hear. In other words, he wanted them to listen to the truths about how they stood before God, about their guilt for the crucifixion, about the rising and exaltation of Jesus, about their need to repent and be baptized.[15]

Perhaps Peter's example of holding on to his original purpose, regardless of events that could easily have diverted him or even have been exploited, is the example most needed in relation to the Toronto Blessing.

Loss of Christ-Centred Worship

Although the phenomena of the Toronto Blessing spread from church to church, city to city, and one continent to another, and while the enthusiasm of church leaders steadily mounted and more and more individuals personally experienced the Blessing, the foundations for it in Christ-centred worship remain weak and insubstantial. It is important to remember that this discussion is not about whether or not these phenomena exist; the question is whether the current patterns of worship retain their "Christian" focus. What has been seen so far in the Blessing churches is the phenomena being given top priority, while significant biblical elements of worship are being cast aside, treated as less important, or even used as a vehicle to promote the Blessing. Perhaps Col 3:16–17 speaks to the point:

> Let the word of Christ dwell in you richly as you teach and admonish one another with all wisdom, and as you sing psalms, hymns and spiritual songs with gratitude in your hearts to God. And whatever you do, whether in word or deed, do it all in the name of the Lord Jesus, giving thanks to God the Father through him.

It seems that Paul has indeed captured the appropriate balance regarding Christian worship in the blending of teaching and instruction, music and praise, all in the name of the Lord Jesus, with thanks to God.

---

15. Horn, "Some Reflections."

Part Two: Musical Traditions and Interpretations

Self-Centred Worship of the Blessing

James Bell says that "Christian worship is never meant to be an end in itself, nor does it exist to simply meet our personal and selfish needs."[16] In the churches that experience the Toronto Blessing, it seems that the Blessing becomes an end in itself, satisfying personal needs. The focus appears to have shifted from God or Christ-centredness and has instead become preoccupation with self and its gratification. The Blessing has taken the place of things that have historically, biblically, and theologically been central and foundational to the Christian faith. The lyrics of the songs used are not about Jesus Christ, the message is not the redemptive message of Christ, testimonies are not typically about Jesus, the celebration of the Eucharist has been replaced by "ministry time," people are not coming to Christ and being baptized, and the congregation is not talking about Jesus. In fact, the primary thing people seem to be talking about is the Blessing. In a generation of "me"-centredness, in this instance many in the church may have fallen prey to the very thing that the church is meant to oppose, the exaltation of the individual over the exaltation of Christ. The Blessing or "ministry time" has taken the central role in the services and is the drawing card for those who attend. If church attendance alone is the bottom line, then this may be acceptable; if biblical worship is more important, then it is unacceptable. In looking at the actual practices of these churches, the visible evidence seems to indicate that the Blessing itself and its effect on the individual has become the thing worshipped.

CONCLUSION

If nothing else, perhaps this brief analysis of worship associated with the Toronto Blessing will encourage churches or individuals to look at their own beliefs and check their practices against what they say that they believe. There is no question that there is something missing in many churches, that many have lost their vitality, and that the form of worship has become so dominating in some that it has practically eliminated the expressive life of the church. But perhaps in addressing this need something else is lost. The Toronto Blessing churches adopted a very informal nature, perhaps as a reaction to the old models of church that have emphasized form over expression. Peterson says something worth

---

16. Bell, *Bridge over Troubled Water*, 172.

considering on this point, addressing both sides of the issue: "Formality may be the expression of a very narrow and inadequate view of worship and informality may be an excuse for lack of preparation or any serious attempt to engage collectively with God."[17] Perhaps there is a need to look for something less sensational and more substantial in worship. One's emotions may easily be drawn to worship the Toronto Blessing, but it requires determination of the mind and heart to worship the risen Christ. The story of Jesus may be very old, but it becomes new in the retelling and living of it. Regardless of how a person feels about worship (and the Bible has very little to say about one's feelings about worship), in order to worship in a biblical sense, the Lordship of Christ must be pre-eminent, and it requires the mind as well as the heart to be actively participating.

REFERENCES AND FURTHER READING

Barkley, John M. "The Theology of Liturgy." *Liturgical Review* 3 (1973) 1–15.

Bell, James L. *Bridge over Troubled Water: Ministry to Baby Boomers—A Generation Adrift*. Wheaton, IL: Victor, 1993.

Bradshaw, Paul F. *The Search for the Origins of Christian Worship: Sources and Methods for the Study of Early Liturgy*. Oxford: Oxford University Press, 1992.

Delling, D. Gerhard. *Worship in the New Testament*. Translated by Percy Scott. London: Darton, Longman and Todd, 1962.

Dixon, Patrick. *Signs of Revival*. Eastbourne: Kingsway, 1994.

Herzog, F. W. "The Norm and Freedom of Christian Worship." In *Worship in Scripture and Tradition*, edited by Massey H. Shepherd, Jr., 98–133. New York: Oxford University Press, 1973.

Hill, Clifford. "'Toronto Blessing'—True or False?" *Prophecy Today* 10 (1994) 10–13.

Horn, B. "Some Reflections on the Toronto Blessing." Leicester: Universities and Colleges Christian Fellowship, 1995.

Moule, Charles F. D. *Worship in the New Testament*. London: Lutterworth, 1961.

Peterson, David. *Engaging with God: A Biblical Theology of Worship*. Grand Rapids: Eerdmans, 1992.

Porter, Stanley E. "Shaking the Biblical Foundations? The Biblical Basis for the Toronto Blessing." In *The Toronto Blessing, or Is It?* edited by Stanley E. Porter and Philip J. Richter, 38–65. London: Darton, Longman and Todd, 1995.

Porter, Stanley E., and Philip J. Richter, eds. *The Toronto Blessing, or Is It?* London: Darton, Longman and Todd, 1995.

Warner, Rob. *Prepare for Revival*. London: Hodder and Stoughton, 1995.

---

17. Peterson, *Engaging with God*, 160.

15

William Byrd, Reformation Liturgy, and Contemporary Worship

INTRODUCTION

WILLIAM BYRD LIVED AND worked as a composer in the chaotic liturgical world of sixteenth-century Reformation England. The Reformation in England seems less well-defined than on the continent, and it came with many ambiguities, although Robin Leaver contends that "there was an essential unity in the basic theological concerns and activities that spanned England and the Continent."[1] Leaver cites G. E. Duffield's preface to a facsimile of the first English psalter, who says, "study of the actual documents suggests that the idea of English isolation in the Reformation period, invented at the end of the nineteenth century, is only a myth. The closest contact was maintained between the English Reformers and those on the Continent."[2] However, Chiara Bertoglio aptly notes that for the English there were "several important spiritual leaders instead of a single charismatic figure," and that "the practical implementation of theological theories often depended on the reigning sovereigns (who did have religious authority but seldom could be considered as theological guides)."[3] Whether or not the experience in England mirrored that on the continent, it must have seemed very much like a post-Christian world to those who lived in England in the middle of it, especially those for whom worship was radically disrupted and uprooted.

---

1. Leaver, *"Goostly Psalmes,"* 1.
2. Leaver, *"Goostly Psalmes,"* 1.
3. Bertoglio, *Reforming Music*, 225.

Byrd lived in a world of worship wars, some of which resulted in fellow believers being put to death.[4] Philip Brett describes Byrd as "a tenacious Catholic in a Protestant country whose governments were increasingly (if unwillingly) committed to punitive action against 'recusants,' those who refused to attend services in the reformed church."[5] Byrd was not willing to betray important theological beliefs even though he had the most significant musical appointment in England, for he worked directly for the Queen of England. He sometimes risked that role by holding to his original liturgical practices and beliefs. At the same time, he provided some of the finest music for worshipers on both sides of this liturgical-theological divide. He created musical expressions of heartfelt worship and beauty for those who worshiped in the Church of England, and he played a major role in musically reshaping the liturgy for this corporate worship that was authorized. However, he also did this for small unauthorized gatherings of worshipers, those who were not in the safe environs of the Church of England. His work, perhaps surprisingly, has relevance for contemporary worship songwriters, leaders, and worshipers in the North American church today.

BYRD'S EARLY YEARS

Byrd was born around 1540[6] and grew up during the height of King Henry VIII's efforts to wield power and to acquire more land and property. William was born into a devout Catholic home. No effort to destroy monasteries or their art or sacred liturgical books or music manuscripts and hand-copied partbooks of choral music—all of which took place under Henry VIII's direction and watchful eye—would have gone unnoticed in that home. The young Byrd lived in a world that had received word, through the Act of Supremacy of 1534, that the King was "the only supreme head in earth of the Church of England."[7] In Peter le Huray's words,

---

4. See, e.g., Williams, *Later Tudors*, 289–91, on the Jesuit Edmund Campion who was executed in 1581 for attempting to restore Catholic faith and worship among those who had become Protestant.

5. Brett, "Liner Notes," 1.

6. For years, scholarly literature represented Byrd's birth year as 1543. But Harley (*William Byrd*, 14) showed how 1540 (or possibly 1539) was a more viable date. Unfortunately, we know little of the young William's childhood or youth, but see Harley, *William Byrd's Modal Practice*, 1. Byrd died in 1623.

7. See a digital reproduction at the UK Parliament website (parliament.uk) and

Part Two: Musical Traditions and Interpretations

One of the most striking manifestations of that new power was to be seen in the whole-sale redistribution of church property, a process that began in 1536 and which continued in various guises for fifty years or more. The first and most spectacular stage was over within the space of four years. During that short time well over eight hundred monastic foundations were dissolved.[8]

The idea that a monastery might be "dissolved" seems so much more innocuous than the physical reality. A. G. Dickens writes, "The religious, cultural and social issues which [the English Reformation] raised remain to this day both profound and inexhaustible."[9] It is tempting to view the Reformation in England like a series of movie clips that capture the swishing of royal robes of one monarch to the next as they each ascend and then descend the throne—from Henry VIII to Edward VI to Mary to Elizabeth I. With those boldly coloured and lavish robes, it is easy to overlook the rustle of dark clerical robes passing by in the background in discreet ways, and the whispers and gasps of everyday churchgoers in the background. The sounds of the English Reformation include the violent crash of falling bricks and toppling statues of the so-called dissolving of those monasteries, as well as the echoes of stinging words of conflict over prayers and rubrics and music within the stone walls of a cathedral.

Interestingly, the Dutch Christian humanist, Erasmus, whose life was over before Byrd's began, took notice of the musical practices in England. Clement Miller writes, "While personally acquainted with popes, kings, and princes, and a frequent visitor to their courts and chapels throughout Europe, Erasmus seemed particularly concerned with the music he heard in England."[10] In one of his comments on music, Erasmus wrote, "In some countries the whole day is now spent in endless singing, yet one worthwhile sermon exciting true piety is hardly heard in six months . . . not to mention the kind of music that has been brought into divine worship, in which not a single word can be clearly understood. Nor is there a free moment for singers to contemplate what they are singing."[11]

Elsewhere, Erasmus expressed further issues with the nature of music in the churches, including their "meaningless sound" and "a certain

---

a modern transcription at the Tudor History website (tudorhistory.org).

8. le Huray, *Music and the Reformation in England*, 2.
9. Dickens, *English Reformation*, v.
10. Miller, "Erasmus on Music," 338.
11. Miller, "Erasmus on Music," 338 (citing Erasmus, *Opera omnia*, 6:73).

elaborate and theatrical music," decrying that people "flock to church as to a theater for aural delight" and bemoaning the fact that "children spend every summer in practicing such warblings." Especially pertaining to English monks, he added, "Their song should be mourned; they think God is pleased with ornamental neighings and agile throats."[12] Miller notes, "In a revealing comment on improvised music in England, Erasmus speaks of a kind of music 'among the English, in which many sing together, but none of the singers produce sounds which the notes on the page indicate.'"[13] Miller thinks it likely that Erasmus heard this improvisational style personally, during one of his stays in England. Truly, England was a place of musical expertise, and improvisation was clearly one area in which they excelled. Contemporary musicians who have developed the skill and expertise of improvisation may find surprising resonance with English church musicians of the early-sixteenth century.

By the time that Byrd was in full form as a musician, there were at least three general perceptions about and approaches to music in the church. Christopher Marsh writes that "England's leading Protestants all agreed on the need to leave behind forever the supposedly obscurantist musical traditions of the late medieval church, but they were permanently divided on the question of what precisely this should entail in practical terms."[14] He describes "moderate Protestants" who shared Luther's view that music was a vital tool of persuasion and should be given a full role in the "service of God," while "Protestants of a hotter sort often looked to continental Calvinism . . . and consequently developed a more suspicious attitude to church music." In a third group "were those on the more radical wing of English Protestantism who denied the validity of virtually all music in the public praise of God."[15] In the wake of the Reformation, both the use of choirs and of organ was under scrutiny, as well as the use of other instruments; meanwhile, at the other end of the spectrum was a rise in the practice of vernacular psalm-singing, at least in parish churches.

Dickens, cited above, mentioned kings, prelates, monasteries, and prayer books. There is no question that there is much to notice about the radical rulings of monarchs, the disrupted lives of church dignitaries, the remains of monasteries, and the prayer books of Edward's reign that

12. Miller, "Erasmus on Music," 339.
13. Miller, "Erasmus on Music," 341.
14. Marsh, *Music and Society*, 392.
15. Marsh, *Music and Society*, 392–94.

reflected the newly-constructed liturgy and subsequent prayer books to come.[16] But Dickens is right to notice the ordinary women and men, in this case, the ones who came to worship God, who longed to worship God, who were the real story when it came to William Byrd's most important music, even if we do not know their personal details or their stories. Byrd's life and work give us glimpses into his heart for God and for the worshiper around him. They also reveal some relevant insights for the church of the twenty-first century, especially for the contemporary songwriter and worship leader. Byrd shows us what it means to write worship music that is meaningful and connects to diverse worshipers. He shows us what it means to be involved in a small disenfranchised group, both empowering them and participating with them, at great personal risk. Byrd's world must have seemed post-Christian, but his work speaks to the fact that he viewed the Christian part to be very much alive and well.

MUSICAL-LITURGICAL BACKGROUND

Late in the 1400s, prior to the Reformation, there was what came to be known as a "rebirth" of music in England, captured especially well in the music of the Eton Choirbooks.[17] Music at the time was hand-copied and contained either in choirbooks or partbooks. Choirbooks contained all the parts for the entire choir in a single book, but in multiple copies, while partbooks contained the separate voice parts in separate books. This meant that each partbook must be available in order for the work to be performed (for example, one book would contain only the bass part, another would contain only the tenor part, etc.). These books were tremendously valuable to the institutions themselves as well as containing part of the nation's cultural heritage. England's music was considered the height of musical achievement in all the surrounding countries at the time. Hugh Benham describes the music in the Eton Choirbook as

---

16. See the content of the Edwardian 1549 Book of Common Prayer in Ketley, ed., *Two Liturgies*, 16–158. Bowers ("Chapel Royal") describes Elizabeth's hesitant shift from Edward's Prayer Book of 1549 to a restoration of the 1552 version with additional rubrics in the 1559 Prayer Book. Her Injunctions from that same year also provided some brief guidance on music and worship.

17. See Benham, *Latin Church Music*, 21, and later in the book where he writes, "The Eton Choirbook . . . is unquestionably one of the greatest monuments of English music in any age" (58). For a fascinating introduction to the rediscovery of the Eton Choirbook and its music, which was heard first in the early 1950s after a 400-year hiatus, see Harrison, *Eton Choirbook*, as well as discussion in his *Music in Medieval Britain*, 307–28.

having been written on a much broader scale than music of preceding eras. Where earlier works were written for three voice-parts, now they were for five parts, which resulted in music that was far more complex and that required larger and more sophisticated resources. The vocal range of the voices was extended both higher and lower, which placed it well beyond the range of what would have been heard on the continent—and the continent was always the point of comparison. Hugh Benham describes the Eton Choirbook music as "complex, elaborate and florid," and how the pieces were known for their very long phrases on a single syllable and for their great rhythmic complexity, such that, "in the words of Erasmus, 'the congregation cannot hear one distinct word.'"[18] But Benham describes the music of the Eton composer as "God-centred, a vehicle for devotion." In his judgment, it aided worship, it was important to worship services, it reflected a divine order, and it was not just for entertainment or merely to display or evoke emotion.[19]

David Wulstan writes that, in the early 1500s, "The resplendent and complex style of polyphony developed by British composers . . . [was] without parallel on the Continent."[20] The music of John Taverner, who lived from 1490 to 1545 (just barely overlapping Byrd's life), reflected the complexity and floridity of Eton's music. The musical range of Taverner's vocalists was wide, with parts written for boy sopranos to sing exceptionally high pitches with some frequency. Wulstan has contended for some time that the music would have been sung up to a minor third higher than what the written sources indicate,[21] so both the ability and the expectations for music and musicians was exceptionally high.

The changes that resulted in England's church music after the rise of Lutheranism on the continent were not received well by those who loved England's church music. Perhaps a hymn like Luther's own interpretation of Psalm 46, which for subsequent generations has epitomized the essence of the Lutheran Reformation, *Ein feste Burg ist unser Gott*, may have been welcomed,[22] but most of the changes resulted in skilled and talented

18. Benham, *Latin Church Music*, 3.
19. Benham, *Latin Church Music*, 3–4.
20. Wulstan, "Vocal Colour," 19.
21. See the full range of this discussion in Wulstan, "Vocal Colour," as well as Bowers, "Performing Pitch," "Further Thought," and "Vocal Scoring."
22. Leaver, *Whole Church Sings*, 158, 149. Leaver refers to how the hymn undoubtedly appeared first as a "broadside" in 1529 (158), which, along with pamphlets and small booklets, could be "relatively quickly set, printed, and sold cheaply" (82),

musicians now being displaced. Benham writes that these changes "had profound effects on the extent and character of church music. If Erasmus had been alive to visit England in Edward VI's reign or in Elizabeth's he would have been delighted to find a major reduction in musical activity, for like him many Reformers considered that far too much time, talent and money had formerly been spent on church music."[23]

The Chantries Act of 1547 had disbanded many choral foundations, with the result that full choral services were only heard in a few cathedrals and chapels now.[24] Reformers may have thought that this was a good change, but, in retrospect, was that really the case?

Byrd's musical education would have begun early. He may have been a student of the English composer Thomas Tallis, and therefore one of the young choristers with the Chapel Royal, or possibly a chorister at St. Paul's Cathedral, along with two brothers.[25] Either way, his musical education would have been excellent. Following the pattern of the best church or cathedral schools in training young choristers during that era, Byrd would have started with learning to sing chants, first from memory and then from musical notation. Then he would have learned to sing parallel lines around a chant, called "faburden," and then to sing descants, where you improvise a counter-melody above a choral piece. Some young choristers learned to play the "viol," an instrument much like a guitar, but played upright. Some learned to play the virginals, a smaller version of a harpsichord. Some learned the organ. Byrd learned and played them all. Improvising descants, singing parallel lines to a chant, and knowing how to play the instruments were all superb training for the improvisation required in actual musical composition.[26] These were critical skills for someone who would become the leading Gentleman of the Chapel Royal.[27] The Gentlemen of the Chapel Royal were the monarch's appointed musicians of the royal entourage, the highest musical appointment available.

---

so it would have been distributed widely. See also Lenti, "Earliest Lutheran Hymn Tradition."

23. Benham, *Latin Church Music*, 6.
24. Benham, *Latin Church Music*, 6.
25. Harley, *William Byrd's Modal Practice*, 1.
26. Harley, *William Byrd's Modal Practice*, 1.
27. See, e.g., le Huray's chapter on the Chapel Royal in *Music and the Reformation in England*, 57–89.

With this training as his own background, it would be interesting to hear what Byrd would have to say to churches in North America who have distanced themselves from trained and educated musicians and moved more towards those who are untrained or uneducated in an effort to embody "authenticity." It is not that there is no room for the educated and trained musician in the contemporary church, but there seems to be far less room than there was. Byrd would surely protest. After all, he poured his life into creating musical art for worship that was at the highest musical level, work that required the very best of his skill, talent, and effort. As a mentor, he would surely expect something similar from a twenty-first-century protegé or student. He would also certainly argue that there must be a place in the church in which that skill, talent, and effort is cultivated and honoured.

This was the context within which Byrd lived and worked, with cataclysmic shifts taking place in the liturgy. He was to write music for an English-language liturgy, instead of Latin, although Latin was still largely the language both of the church and of the academy, which included a musician's training and education. English must have seemed like a foreign language, but the English text was to be transparent and audible, which meant a drastically simplified approach to musical composition.

Thomas Cranmer, Archbishop of Canterbury, created an English Litany in 1544, the first vernacular liturgical book for the public.[28] He followed the principle that he had articulated in a letter to Henry VIII that "in myne opinion, the song that shalbe made thereunto, wolde not be full of notes, but, as nere as may be, for every sillable, a note; so that it may be songe distinctly and devoutly."[29] These instructions actually pertained to monody or chant, not to polyphony as often was mistakenly claimed, but it became a mantra for the rest of the century in one way or another. The often-cited Royal Injunctions of Queen Elizabeth I of 1559, Item 49, was relaxed from earlier articulations but still adhered to the principle of intelligibility of each word in singing:

> that there be a modest and distinct song, so used in all parts of the Common Prayers in the Church, that the same may be as plainly understood, as if it were read without singing. And yet, nevertheless, for the comforting of such that delight in music, it may be permitted, that in the beginning, or in the end of Common Prayer, either at morning or evening, there may be

28. Wulstan, *Tudor Music*, 279–80.
29. *State Papers*, 760–61.

Part Two: Musical Traditions and Interpretations

sung an hymn, or such-like song, to the praise of Almighty God, in the best sort of melody and music that may be conveniently devised, having respect that the sentence of the hymn may be understood and perceived.[30]

For a superb composer such as Byrd, even in his young twenties, this must have seemed restrictive, but although he was not convinced by this approach to liturgy, he approached the challenge with talent and skill and creativity. His work to develop new directions in music for worship is an overlooked area of the impact of the English Reformation on subsequent generations of churches that continue to worship in the English language. While the English-speaking church at large may have known some of the Reformers' music, such as a German hymn from Luther or Psalm-singing in French, it was English-speaking musicians and hymn writers who most directly influenced the development of music and worship in England and, subsequently, in North America. Some of this was through the metrical vernacular psalms developed by those who fled to Switzerland during Mary's brief reign. But it was an English Byrd who implemented approaches to musical worship that still resonate with today's worshipers and whose innovations still have a place in the practices of today.

Byrd's first major position was as organist and master of the choristers at Lincoln Cathedral, at the age of twenty-three. He was the lead musician in a very prestigious cathedral, one that had survived the early days of the Reformation when much to do with music was destroyed, but Lincoln Cathedral's musical resources somehow survived without significant damage. The cathedral still had a choir, consisting of twelve adult singers and nine choristers, young boys.[31] This was an outstanding location to begin a career, to develop as a composer, and to learn the ropes of being the lead worshiper and lead musician. Kerry McCarthy reminds us that we do not really know how Byrd spent his apprentice years, but, even at such a young age, "they left him qualified to run a large musical establishment and compose new works for it,"[32] and compose he did. Later in his life he was "a well-educated man, fluent in the humanistic Latin of the Renaissance, a reader and collector of books."[33] We do not

---

30. Frere and Kennedy, eds., *Visitation Articles*, 23.
31. McCarthy, *Byrd*, 22.
32. McCarthy, *Byrd*, 23.
33. McCarthy, *Byrd*, 23.

know if he studied at a university or traveled abroad in his early years, but there is an educational college with close ties to Lincoln and perhaps Byrd received some of his education in these years.[34]

The prospect of being one of the Gentlemen of the Chapel Royal must have been high in the young Byrd's hopes, and his appointment as one while still in his twenties, while he was the lead musician at Lincoln Cathedral, must have been one of the greatest achievements imaginable for a promising young composer. However, while it would provide opportunities of which few musicians could even dream, it would also provide nearly insurmountable challenges.[35] In that respect, Craig Monson describes the radical changes of music within the Chapel Royal as one monarch followed another, but how it "set the standard for the realm in sacred music."[36] He says, "With the return of the puritan faction after the demise of Mary Tudor, the Chapel Royal remained the most important bastion of elaborate ritual amid the intense and abiding attack on church music by Genevan reformers."[37]

As noted above, Byrd composed at a time when musical composition was at an exceptionally high level, even if there was a major effort to eliminate it from the church or at least reduce its importance. His compositions stood out, even against that backdrop. He was prolific and creative. He was also deeply attuned to the significance of how music embodies the texts that it frames. This was in a period when paying attention to lyrics was not thought to be a high priority, yet Byrd's music shows evidence that he was highly attuned to the words.[38] Today's worship songwriters and leaders are accustomed to the necessity of paying attention to lyrics, and yet, sometimes either the music or the lyrics, or both, seem to be lacklustre, shallow, even trite. Byrd provides a model of paying attention and working diligently and artistically to write, or at least choose, music that emulates this standard of musical and lyrical integrity.

---

34. McCarthy, *Byrd*, 23.
35. McCarthy, *Byrd*, especially her chapter titled "Lincoln Cathedral" (22–37).
36. Monson, "Elizabethan London," 306–7.
37. Monson, "Elizabethan London," 307.
38. Brett ("Word-Setting," 53) writes in reference to Byrd's secular music that Byrd "generally extracts deeper feeling from a poem than composers more dependent for their effects on vivid images or on elaborate parallels."

Part Two: Musical Traditions and Interpretations

PUBLIC WORSHIP

The Church of England was the authorized form of Christian worship and Byrd wrote music especially for this new theological institution. He set the new English language liturgy in his Short Service,[39] a setting that uses simple and accessible musical resources. He also composed a Great Service,[40] a large complex work that provided the church with a musical setting of the liturgy that had a place for many skilled and talented musicians, effectively giving them a voice.

Some of his individual songs, such as his "Sing Joyfully," were very popular.[41] Although there are no longer any extant sixteenth-century sources of this piece, there are about a hundred printed or manuscript versions of it from the early seventeenth century,[42] which provide clear evidence of its continued use. It is interesting to consider the fact that popularity of certain new worship songs is not a unique phenomenon of the twenty-first-century church, after all. Of course, the evidence of popularity in Byrd's day was not found through the number of times a song is accessed through CCLI, or viewed on YouTube, but through the number of copies that were made—potentially hand-copied—in order to keep it in print and in use.[43] Popularity shows us something about what is included in a church's musical canon, and, while not necessarily a reliable form of evaluation of the quality of a piece, it certainly says something about its use in public worship, both in the sixteenth century and in the twenty-first. This gives us a window into a congregation's actual musical practice of worship, a glimpse of a congregation at worship.

Meanwhile, developing in the churches of England was a form of metrical vernacular psalm singing, an influence from the continent. Beth Quitslund writes that the "Prayer Book congregations of the Marian diaspora adopted metrical psalmody as a part of their confessional identity... English writers in Geneva created a hymnal that could articulate a range of godly prayers and affirmations."[44] Interestingly, "the Church

---

39. Monson, ed., *English Services*.

40. See the full setting in Monson, ed., *English Services II*.

41. Monson, ed., *English Anthems*, 82–90.

42. See "Sing Joyfully" (No. 29) in Morris, *Oxford Book of Tudor Anthems*, 287–97, where the source notes are provided by John Morehen (see 287). The lyrics of the piece are from Ps 81:1–4.

43. See discussion of the nature of music printing in the Appendix entitled "Elizabethan Music and Music Publishing" in Kerman, *Elizabethan Madrigal*, 257–67.

44. Quitslund, *Reformation in Rhyme*, 155.

never officially sanctioned it as part of the liturgy."[45] Nonetheless, as Timothy Duguid writes, although "the psalms' only official place in the Prayer Book was in reading and reciting them in prose, some churches began nonetheless to sing metrical psalms both before and after the sermon."[46] Marsh contends that in understanding the Reformation's success in forging new personal identities in England, one of the "most convincing explanations for the transformation will be a musical one."[47] He continues, "Ordinary parishioners may not always have welcomed lengthy sermons, but they loved to sing psalms."[48] Oddly enough, the Queen's Injunctions of 1559 had made room for this, although surely that was not her intention.

Quitslund describes the anomaly of printer John Day's fortune in getting the metrical Psalms into print, "which became the most printed book in England during the early modern period," and asks, "what was everyone doing with all those books? And, as importantly, what did people think about them?"[49] She acknowledges recent studies that emphasize the significance of their popularity and how, in contrast, "later seventeenth-century criticism of the metrical psalms—as puritan, vulgar, and poetically crude—has continued to colour the discussion of their reception in the Elizabethan period. In addition, among literary critics the history of psalm-singing has been influenced by one late Elizabethan and early Jacobean writer who seldom ventures into explicit comments on religion: William Shakespeare. Yet Shakespeare's references to the psalms are unusual and potentially quite misleading. What a closer look at Elizabethan sources shows is a book that was embraced by virtually all of the English church, in marked contrast with its devaluation among the cutting-edge churchmen and literati of the Stuart period."[50] She estimates that "approximately 220,000 copies had been produced by the end of Elizabeth's reign—more than one for each 18 inhabitants of England and Wales in 1600."[51] This was a major grass roots movement that permeated

---

45. Duguid, *Metrical Psalmody*, n.p. See extended discussion in Zim, *English Metrical Psalms*, and the critical edition of the lyrics and melodies in the two volumes by Quitslund and Temperley, *Whole Book of Psalms*.

46. Duguid, *Metrical Psalmody*, n.p.

47. Marsh, *Music and Society*, 391.

48. Marsh, *Music and Society*, 391–92.

49. Quitslund, *Reformation in Rhyme*, 239.

50. Quitslund, *Reformation in Rhyme*, 239.

51. Quitslund, *Reformation in Rhyme*, 242.

the church en masse, and for highly accomplished musician-artists, it must have been devastating to have been replaced so easily and quickly by simple tunes for an entire book of psalms with sing-song poetry that sounded much like these first lines of Ps 23: "The Lord is only my support, and he that doth me feed: How can I then lack anything whereof I stand in need? He doth me fold in cotes [sheds] most safe, the tender grass fast by; And after drives me to the streams which run most pleasantly."[52]

Unsurprisingly, Byrd did not favour these "Genevan jigs," a term considered a contemptuous reference by critics, and one known to be shared by Elizabeth herself.[53] Some scholars suggest that early performance style of the metrical psalms may have been at a lively tempo, but most think that the term "purposefully mocked a singing style which was grave and solemn from the outset."[54] Duguid describes the nature of the derogatory and somewhat sarcastic tone of the phrase:

> an English jig was a burlesque that combined drama, music and dance. It joined improvised popular songs from the past with traditional ritual dances . . . the descriptions of Genevan psalm tunes as "Genevan jigs" refer to their appeal to the peasantry and their use of popular tune styles. Since psalm tunes were to be sung with "weight and majesty," the term was probably also a sarcastic jab at the slower speeds of psalm singing.[55]

It certainly is hard to imagine Byrd, as a master composer, finding something redeemable in these songs, although he did not object to setting the Psalms to be sung in more refined ways. He wrote some fairly expansive five-part settings of psalms for festive occasions, often set as "a simple dialogue between the two sides of the choir," including, for example, "Teach Me O Lord" that made use of solo voices.[56] McCarthy

52. Quitslund and Temperley, *Whole Book of Psalms*, 104.
53. See, e.g., Davies, *Worship and Theology*, 377–404 (esp. 387).
54. Bertoglio, *Reforming Music*, 356.
55. Duguid, *Metrical Psalmody*, n.p. Nicholas Temperley outlines how they originated with Thomas Sternhold's collection of psalm paraphrases for the young King Edward, how John Hopkins added to them after Sternhold died, and then how this small book was printed as "devotional recreation." He says, "when several thousand English Protestants took refuge in Frankfurt, Geneva, and other Continental centres to escape Mary Tudor's return to the Roman rite, its texts became the nucleus of a new development of congregational singing on the French model, represented by the first English metrical psalter with tunes, published at Geneva in 1556." See Temperley, Review of *Metrical Psalmody*, 269.
56. McCarthy, *Byrd*, 34.

writes that the "underlying aesthetic of his liturgical psalm settings . . . is not unlike that of his earliest secular songs: clarity, decorum, and moments of quiet but distinctive beauty."[57]

Bertoglio writes,

> Even among those who, in the Church of England, were closer to the Calvinist positions, music was rarely denied its symbolic dimension and its capacity to move; there was awareness, however that—precisely by virtue of this power—music could be either very useful or potentially very dangerous. The "godly" (i.e. those who fostered a Calvinist orientation in the Anglican Church, frequently in consequence of their experience of Reformed worship during the Marian exile) could sometimes oppose even the chanting of liturgy, let alone the complex polyphony or instrumental music in church, while, of course, metrical psalmody was not only admired but actively encouraged.[58]

There are those in the church of today who have been protesting for years against what they perceive as the equivalent of metrical psalms in contemporary worship. Byrd would urge today's worship songwriter or leader not to waste time on meaningless, frivolous, or mundane songs that do not do justice to the lyrics or the music itself, to say nothing of being worthy of worship to God. He poured himself into developing the very best music possible; he would expect the songwriter of today to do the same. However, a songwriter who does make this investment may not be well-known, and their work can be overlooked in the crowd that is lined up for the next song from songwriters who have become household names in the circles of worship leaders and contemporary worshipers.

Byrd's work took place in an era when there was huge disruption in worship, cataclysmic shifts in everything from style to the language of worship to whether the music could be complex or, of necessity, must be extremely simple. Perhaps it is not surprising to discover that in later years in his life, he committed a good deal of time and artistic effort in assembling music and his own thoughts and observations about it in his *Gradualia* cycle, reflecting "his commitment to well ordered worship."[59] At the time when he was doing this work, recusant worship, that is, illegal worship of Catholics in a legally-Protestant nation, "was elaborate in some places, but also, by its very nature, ephemeral; it was something that

---

57. McCarthy, *Byrd*, 34.
58. Bertoglio, *Reforming Music*, 226.
59. McCarthy, *Liturgy and Contemplation*, 71.

could physically vanish in moments if discovered or hijacked ... English Catholics were accustomed to this sort of surprise. It was a realistic possibility every time they met for worship, even at well-hidden locations deep in the countryside."[60]

For evangelicals and other Protestants today who may be accustomed to viewing Catholics as the "other" in terms of faithful Christian worship, it may seem surprising to think that someday they could find themselves in similar circumstances in their own nations where Christianity has been an accepted religion, but perhaps will not be the case indefinitely. Ironically, they may find themselves identifying more with recusant Catholics in England than those within their own historical church denominational lines of descent. It is interesting to consider that recusants who were not permitted to worship freely, or even at all, "were eager even for detailed descriptions of elaborate worship, being generally unable to participate in it themselves."[61] Will there come a day of longing to just hear about the opportunity of others to engage in full-voiced, free and open Christian worship?

As a composer, Byrd was willing to take risks in his compositions, even in his instrumental works.[62] But as a composer of songs for worship, he was willing to take even greater risks. Meanwhile, Byrd took a creative approach to the traditions and resources that were available to him. For instance, at Lincoln Cathedral, and elsewhere in Elizabethan England, choirs were divided into two separate choirs, one on each side of the chancel, with almost everything alternating back and forth between the two choirs (any visit to an English cathedral or many of the college chapels today will reveal this same pattern still in evidence). Byrd used this given as an opportunity to compose some pieces that would add extra parts at some point in the work, and then return to the original number. He would use these antiphonal resources to the highest level in his Great Service, with up to ten parts in various sections of this extensive English-language setting.[63]

To a worship leader and worship songwriter of today, he—and other great composers, such as Bach—would strongly encourage taking pre-existing restrictions and to use them creatively and well. Buildings

---

60. McCarthy, *Liturgy and Contemplation*, 72.
61. McCarthy, *Liturgy and Contemplation*, 73.
62. McCarthy, *Byrd*, 30–31.
63. McCarthy, *Byrd*, 33.

that provide obstacles, lack of musical resources, inadequate numbers or quality of musicians, all provide an opportunity to be more creative as an artist. Sometimes artists need restrictive challenges to open up new ways of creating and crafting their art, and to give the local church new ways of engaging in worship that are uniquely suited to them.

CONCEALED WORSHIP

Byrd's Latin motets were musical gems, and they captured the heart of the people.[64] Meanwhile, his three Latin Masses are among some of his most important contributions to the worship of the church,[65] not only for their musical value and for their contribution to worship contexts at the time, but also for what they can teach us today. As McCarthy describes it, when Byrd began setting the mass to music in the early 1590s,

> he was doing something that no English composer had done for thirty years. Given the political and cultural risks involved, it is surprising that he managed to do it at all. The 1559 Act of Uniformity strictly forbade the celebration of the old Catholic liturgy in England. Those who went on cultivating it could be punished with fines, imprisonment, or, in exceptional cases, even death. What had taken place daily at every pre-Reformation altar, from the humblest parish church to the greatest cathedral, was now a rare and dangerous luxury.[66]

To slip ever so briefly into the musical world of William Byrd at this point, listen to the opening segment of his Mass for Five Voices, the Kyrie.[67] It is a beautiful setting of this eloquent prayer for mercy, set for a small group of believers that would have included some highly skilled musicians, composed by a musician who had the acclaim and authority to write for the Chapel Royal itself, but who dedicated some of his most beautiful work for these tiny enclaves of worship.

While his Latin motets involved some "expressions of Catholic protest and explicit Catholic solidarity," his Latin Masses were designed

---

64. See, e.g., Kerman, "On William Byrd's Emendemus in melius," as well as Kerman, "Byrd's Motets."

65. The primary source for this is Kerman, *Masses and Motets*. See also the chapter on the three masses in McCarthy, *Byrd*, 133–50.

66. McCarthy, *Byrd*, 134.

67. Listen, for instance, to recordings of the Masses by The Tallis Scholars (thetallisscholars.co.uk) or The Sixteen (thesixteen.com).

simply to enable his fellow Catholic worshipers to worship.[68] These were nothing like the extremely simple Mass setting by John Merbecke in 1550, who was modelling how to set the liturgy along the lines of "for every syllable a note."[69] Instead, they were appreciated by private patrons, such as the Petres, who were active Catholics who also loved music, and small communities that grew up around this family. Byrd and his family found a safe community there in later years when Byrd no longer worked for the Queen.[70] However, there were also Protestant patrons, some who were remarkably eclectic and tolerant in this period, "typified by the Queen's own willingness to employ the Catholic Byrd in the Chapel Royal."[71] Elizabeth is known to have been intentionally blind towards Byrd's Catholic affinities and she herself still apparently loved the music, even the liturgy itself.[72] But it was a fine line for Byrd to walk, guessing at how much would be tolerated and when this would no longer be the case.

Later in life, as already noted, Byrd compiled a collection of some of his music in two books called *Gradualia*, carefully constructed to aid Catholic worshipers in the entirety of their worship services. It is remarkable that both books were published, and even reissued in 1610, all during a time when Catholic worship was illegal and those who were in possession of such books were punishable by law.[73] In his preface to the first volume of *Gradualia*, Byrd spoke eloquently of his belief about the value of his art as a composer in setting texts that are used to worship God. He writes, "For even as among artisans it is shameful in a craftsman to make a rude piece of work from some precious metal, so indeed to sacred words in which the praises of God and of the Heavenly host are sung, none but some celestial harmony (so far as our powers avail) will be proper."[74] He addresses "the True Lovers of Music" as "most highminded and righteous, who delight at times to sing to God in hymns and spiritual songs."[75] In these two volumes, he provided resources so that his fellow worshipers could worship throughout the church year. Even

68. Kerman, "Byrd's Settings," 410.

69. Fellowes, *Office*, 11.

70. In 1594, Byrd moved to Stondon Massey, where other Catholic worshipers also met within the safety of the Petres' residence.

71. Williams, *Later Tudors*, 402.

72. Williams, *Later Tudors*, 401.

73. Kerman, *Masses and Motets*, 224.

74. Strunk, ed., *Source Readings*, 137–38.

75. Strunk, ed., *Source Readings*, 139.

if they were forbidden to meet in churches, they now had the musical and liturgical materials that they needed. North Americans do not know much about this issue (yet), but in some parts of the world, this is a familiar and troubling challenge.

In contemporary church life of the twenty-first century, at least in the evangelical church, the idea of being a *true lover of music* seems to be viewed with some skepticism. Perhaps loving music seems to conflict with loving God. However, for those who truly love music, who find in music great creative and spiritual expression, to say nothing of soul-stirring beauty and a place in which to encounter God's Spirit, for those within whom God has created this capacity, there must be a place for them within the realm of corporate worship, even today.

In the era of Catholic recusant worship, to worship in the manner of a Catholic was dangerous. McCarthy writes, "When recalcitrant English Catholics were jailed or executed, the official charge was treason, claiming the authority of the pope over that of the monarch."[76] It would be tempting to imagine that worship services in these hidden locations with such potential cost would have employed a sparse, bare-bones approach to worship. Interesting details in a recusant commentary by Laurence Vaux, published in 1568, indirectly reveal something of the manner of worship in these secret services. McCarthy notes that "The musical evidence of these passages is slim but compelling."[77] Vaux refers to the gradual and alleluia as "songs," not just allegorically, suggesting that these parts of the service were, indeed, sung. He describes the priest either saying or intoning the *Kyrie*, as well as the *Gloria*. He writes, "all the people, or such as supply their place" actually sing the *Sanctus and Benedictus*. Meanwhile, at the point in the service of the Agnus Dei ("Lamb of God"), Vaux observes that the faithful are present and pray for mercy and peace to be delivered by the hands of the lamb of God. McCarthy observes that the kind of polyphonic settings that Byrd wrote for the Latin Mass for this kind of context would be totally at home here.[78]

These details suggest that worship in these hidden locations looked like a full worship service, complete with sung segments, a priest functioning fully in leading the service, the people responding at the right times with prayers and supplications to God. The reason this is an

---

76. McCarthy, *Liturgy and Contemplation*, 103.
77. McCarthy, *Liturgy and Contemplation*, 77.
78. McCarthy, *Liturgy and Contemplation*, 77.

important window on recusant worship is that in a post-Christian world, where Christian worship in the future may not always be welcomed or tolerated, it is interesting to take note of the fact that worshippers then did not step back from fully engaging in worship, and that a composer such as Byrd still thought it worthwhile to contribute the best of his craftsmanship, his art, his work, to worship that might only take place in these small discreet locations. In a contemporary culture that thrives on megachurches, and where small churches try to emulate what they think they see in a megachurch environment, the idea of a gifted songwriter or worship leader devoting great effort to creating rich resources in order to facilitate worship expressions for a tiny congregation, perhaps one that meets only in a home, and which may never be uploaded to YouTube for millions of others to watch and copy, may seem like an undesirable scenario. However, with Byrd as a model, this option needs to be weighed seriously. Is a musical or worship contribution only valuable if it can be seen and experienced by large crowds or congregations? What if this small group is really the sum total of the worship experience and exposure? Is there still a willingness to pour one's best work into it? And if not, what does that suggest about who it was for in the first place?

One other detail in some of Byrd's compositions merits mention in light of the controversies of his time and potential controversies in a present post-Christian culture. Certain words were the locus of dispute and dissension; for instance, the word "merit" in relation to a "Catholic doctrine of holiness by individual merit" was "one of the teachings most despised by the Reformers."[79] In one motet,[80] Byrd sets the Latin text of a Christmas song that was well known, though not a biblical text. In his setting, he skips over the actual word for "merit" in the text when it shows up in a part, although he leaves exactly the right number of notes that would correspond to its Latin syllables in the music. Was this a casual mistake or oversight? It seems unlikely, because the music and text are meticulously presented in every other way. What seems more probable is that he intentionally did not include the single word that all the controversy was about,[81] counting on the singers to know exactly what word went there and to sing it regardless of it being printed in the

---

79. McCarthy, *Liturgy and Contemplation*, 103.

80. See interesting perspectives on the creative process of composers and songwriters of the time, including how someone like Byrd may have composed at either the organ or with a lute, in Owens, *Composers at Work*, 73.

81. McCarthy, *Liturgy and Contemplation*, 103.

text. Technically, he did not use the "problem" word. Perhaps Christians today in politically sensitive times will find that sometimes they need to be creative at stepping over and around words that could blow up, especially when there are more important things to attend to. Every generation seems to have these touchstones, but they may not be the most important ones to include in songs of worship.

INNOVATION IN WORSHIP

Byrd's music may seem anachronistic to some; that is, it may seem to have no relevance for the contemporary church today. The style is not what a contemporary church uses. Many churchgoers in today's church may not even appreciate a concert of his music, although that perhaps suggests a need for a vastly increased knowledge of and appreciation for great music. Notwithstanding that, Byrd introduced a number of things in his music and into the church that are at least historically relevant.

He developed a kind of choral piece called the "verse anthem," which was designed to have instrumental accompaniment. Liturgical music of the day was choral, so it was designed for a group of skilled singers. It was likely performed without an instrument, or the instrument would have doubled the sung parts. Byrd's "Teach Me, O Lord" is "one of the earliest examples in English church music of the use of a solo voice," not just designed for the whole choir. It also has an independent organ part, not just a doubling of choral lines.[82] So, the piece begins with the organ playing alone, and then a solo voice begins to sing the opening lines, "Teach me, O Lord, the way of thy statutes: and I shall keep it unto the end."[83] Both of these details would surely have made people look up and take notice when they first heard them.

When churches use instrumental accompaniment in songs of worship for the church, as most do for the majority of worship songs today, Byrd had a part in bringing that practice into play. When worship teams use solo voices set apart from the rest of the group, as contemporary worship music—and choral music—frequently does, Byrd had a role in bringing that into church music. These were not part of the familiar mode of the day, so he inaugurated them or rediscovered them and gave them a place

---

82. See "Preface" in Morris, ed. *Oxford Book of Tudor Anthems*, n.p.

83. See "Teach Me, O Lord" (No. 30) in Morris, ed., *Oxford Book of Tudor Anthems*, 298–306; the piece is edited by John Morehen. The Scripture text is from Ps 119:33–38.

in the music of the church. What is now so familiar as to not even merit notice, was at one time, in Byrd's day, innovations in musical worship.

Remember the viol mentioned above? The viol was an instrument for secular music, that is, for consort music. So, what did Byrd do? He brought the viol into choral music in the church; that is, he brought an overtly "secular" instrument into a "sacred" place.[84] He made no apologies for this. There was a period in the twentieth century when the saxophone was not considered appropriate for church music. The "sax" was a "secular" instrument, a "sexy" instrument, not suitable for "sacred music." Eventually, it became apparent to many that a sax could make an outstanding contribution to musical worship in the church. Byrd spoke into that sacred-secular dichotomy back in the sixteenth century by selecting an instrument for sacred worship from a range of instruments that were not normally considered appropriate for worship.

Byrd was a prolific composer of instrumental works, although instrumental composition was still a new field. He published very little of his instrumental music, partly because it was very challenging for printers of the day to set it and print it. Besides that, faith was his prime objective, which, writes Oliver Neighbour, "he could serve most directly by setting sacred texts."[85] But his instrumental music is of the highest order. Neighbour describes how Byrd "brought the same intelligence, energy and certainty of purpose to his instrumental music as to the rest of his output; it shows the working of his genius no less clearly, and is no less remarkable for its qualities of personal expression. No composer, whether English or continental, working without the guidance of a sung text, had hitherto encompassed so wide a range of character or of structural invention."[86] Byrd did not reserve his talent and energies only for the most acceptable elements of worship, but also for his other compositional work that surely was a form of worship but that would not have a place in the liturgy and worship of the day.

In many churches of today, there is little space for instrumental music, apart from functional music that acts as a transition or as a filler or background while something else is taking place. There was little place (one could argue, "no" place) in the continental Reformation for such abstract and non-text-based music in the church, and it is doubtful that

---

84. Consider the idea of sacred places in light of John Inge's thoughtful work, *Christian Theology of Place*.

85. Neighbour, *Consort and Keyboard Music*, 19.

86. Neighbour, *Consort and Keyboard Music*, 19.

there was space in the liturgy in Byrd's locale, either, but the fact that he wrote it is worth noting. Must there be a panoply of words for every moment of our worship? Must our time of worship be totally crammed with words, or could there be space for instrumental compositions in the church today that invite quiet reflection and room to simply be in the presence of God? Must the church always be "working" in order to be a church at worship? Protestant worship practices are grounded in a movement that tried to move away from works-related salvation, and yet, corporate worship often seems to be built upon our "work." What would it be like to have spaces of "rest" in corporate worship? As a rest is what makes sense of spoken sentences, and of musical phrases, perhaps the introduction of "rests" into corporate worship would also bring a greater measure of sense, and of beauty. Perhaps Erasmus's outrage that there is no "free moment for singers to contemplate what they are singing" is relevant for corporate worship today.[87]

One other small off-beat detail worth noting is the impact of the notion of "syncopation," in this case, beginning with more recent generations and then looking at Byrd's day. There were strong opinions in the twentieth century against the introduction of syncopation into music in the church, even in music in general.[88] Syncopation was thought to be a "secular" practice. But, ironically, syncopation had been in use in the church off and on since at least the sixteenth century. Byrd certainly used it in his compositions, including in his sacred works. Even Luther would surely raise an eyebrow over this one, because his early form of "A Mighty Fortress" involves syncopation that still is unsettling to the unwary first-time participant.[89]

ART AND EMOTION IN THE CHURCH

Byrd lived and worked in an era where art was still valued in the church, at least by his royal patron. Howard Mayer Brown summarizes Byrd's gifts as an artist-composer when he writes that Byrd shared with virtuoso Franco-Flemish composer, Orlando Lasso,

---

87. Miller, "Erasmus on Music," 338.

88. See, e.g., Faulkner, "Does Jazz Put the Sin in Syncopation?" which gives some sense of early twentieth-century concerns.

89. See discussion about this hymn and images of 1530 and 1533 versions of the printed music in Fenner, "*Ein feste Burg ist Unser Gott.*"

the astounding fluency to command every technique and genre of his time, but [Byrd] differs from his great contemporaries in at least two important ways: his music reflects the English independence from developments on the continent; and he . . . stands at the beginning as well as at the end of a period of history, for he not only incorporated into his own music the achievements of his predecessors, but he also ushered in the most brilliant musical era his country had ever known, during the later years of Elizabeth I and the reigns of James I and Charles I.[90]

A contemporary of Byrd's, Thomas Morley, also acknowledged the composer's status as a gifted musician, "whoso can, upon any plainsong whatsoever, make such another way as that of Mr. Byrd . . . may with great reason be termed a great master in music."[91]

For Byrd, the hard work of cultivating and refining his art was still prized. This was not exactly true on the continent at the time or in parish churches in England, and it is not exactly true in the church of today. There is among some a reticence about working hard (or admitting that we have worked hard) to create art at the highest level. It would rather be said that "it was nothing," in the interests of an assumed modesty and a more spiritual-sounding humility. Coupled with this is an ambivalence about, perhaps even outright disregard for, the place of art in the church at all. Byrd understood that he was a musical *artist*, and his work was to create *worship art*. He was educated and trained to do this. He was gifted to do this. He was motivated to do this. And he was employed to do this, which was certainly a bonus. But he also did a lot of this on his own time, especially in later years, without hope of payment or recognition for his artistic works.

Added to the dubious role of the arts in the church is the question about the suitability of emotion in music for worship. Criticism against contemporary musical worship in the church sometimes centres on this issue of emotion, and whether such use of emotions is appropriate (beyond its potentially manipulative use). Interestingly, Byrd wrote music that was emotionally evocative. Some of it is exuberantly joyful, such as "Sing Joyfully," mentioned above. Some of it encompasses deep lament for great losses in the church as he knew it and for the people who were now ostracized and forbidden to worship in public places.[92]

90. Brown, *Music in the Renaissance*, 283.

91. Morley, *Plain & Easy Introduction*, 201.

92. See, e.g., Kerman, on an earlier motet in "On William Byrd's Emendemus in melius."

Byrd's motets particularly capture this intense degree of emotion. In fact, in some ways, Byrd's motets functioned for the recusant Catholic worshipers in the way that African American spirituals functioned for a people who were stranded somewhere between God and humanity, in a liminal region that was relegated to being sub- or non-human. The music and words of spirituals embodied deep emotion, and a heartfelt call to God. Catholic worshipers in Byrd's time could be captured and killed. They were separated from familiar places and ways to worship God. They understood what it was to be in exile. Byrd gave them a voice, a means to express this sorrow and anger and fear. Byrd's songs were not an effort to manipulate worshipers, but to give them a voice.

Does the contemporary worship song capture the best of this? Perhaps not. Are the lyrics thoughtfully constructed and well-articulated texts with theological integrity, set to music that eloquently expresses these? Not necessarily, or at least not always. But Byrd might point out that emotion itself is not the problem. I think he would say that the cry has not been matched by the skill to give it voice. In that case, investing in developing the skill and artistry of the artist to do so is well worth pursuing.

Byrd knew the pain of deep loss in his life, loss of beloved forms of worship, loss of artistic freedom in some cases, but, even more, the loss of life of fellow Catholic worshipers. At times, persecution of Catholics was the "fiercest and bloodiest of the century."[93] In 1581, Oxford witnessed the public martyrdom of the Jesuit, St. Edmund Campion, and his fellows (Alexander Briant and Ralph Sherwin), out on one of the main streets of the city, not far from the famous pub where C. S. Lewis and his literary companions later spent many hours. Byrd used his compositional skills to give voice to the outrage and grief that this caused him and others, including both a consort song (that would have been performed in a secular context such as at the monarch's royal residence) and a motet (that would have been used in private Catholic services but also perhaps elsewhere). For this motet, *Deus, venerunt gentes*, he chose the first verses of Ps 79, the very verses that English martyrs frequently spoke as their final prayer, and also considered the official text to use in prayer to request that Catholic faith be returned to full and free expression in England.[94]

---

93. Bertoglio, *Reforming Music*, 528.
94. Bertoglio, *Reforming Music*, 528.

Grief and pain at the situation that Catholic worshipers were experiencing in England gave rise to music that had multiple levels of meaning, both linguistically and musically. As Bertoglio describes it,

> Many of such compositions are of an almost shocking beauty and succeed in blending a touching emotionality with an otherworldly serenity. Though these musicians were suffering themselves for the divisions brought by confessionalization, and were expressing the pain of the members of their community, their music somehow unites them.[95]

She suggests that grief in music can be shared across denominational and confessional boundaries, and writes,

> It is as if the very fact of suffering for one's faith was actually much more important, crucial and meaningful than which confession they represented and which confession was persecuting them. Suffering for Christ, in short, and expressing this suffering through music was the means by which the persecuted were truly in communion.[96]

In the contemporary context of Christian worship, we could learn much about the value of giving voice to grief and pain, both within our own places of worship, and beyond them. Post-Christian worship could learn a lot from Byrd about giving voice to fellow-believers to cry with the psalmist, "How long, Lord?"

THE BUSINESS OF SONGWRITING AND PUBLISHING

Joseph Kerman describes Byrd as "the first English musician to profit from the printing press."[97] Byrd, along with Thomas Tallis, who was a mentor as well as a colleague to Byrd, approached Queen Elizabeth for a patent to print a collection of music, the first of its kind. The patent was granted to them, for more than just this single work. Byrd and Tallis set to work to produce a volume of printed music that included eight of each of their compositions, the collection called *Cantiones Sacrae* ("Sacred Songs").[98] Byrd had to choose the right pieces, prepare music for print,

---

95. Bertoglio, *Reforming Music*, 565–66.
96. Bertoglio, *Reforming Music*, 566.
97. Kerman, "Byrd's Motets," 359.
98. See Milsom, ed., *Thomas Tallis and William Byrd*.

work with a publisher,[99] and he showed that he even understood marketing. Every contemporary church songwriter understands something about this challenge or issue. Regardless of the range of opinion on this aspect of Christian worship songs, that is, whether writing songs of worship should also be about business, most would agree that as a topic, it is pertinent to the church today. Byrd had something to say, for he was at the forefront of it as a practice.[100]

Calvin Miller writes an intentionally provocative piece to describe the troubled intersection of the Reformation and the arts in the evangelical church. I quote him extensively here in the hopes that although his bold style might elicit some smiles, that it also might prompt some thoughtful reflection. He writes,

> the church—particularly the evangelical church—has traditionally been a little schizoid over whether or not the arts are a sanctified way to go about praising God. [On January 1, 1519,] on the eve of the Swiss Reformation, Huldrych Zwingli became the "people's priest" at Grossmünster in Zurich. Incensed over what he considered to be the "pagan icons" of the church, he swept through the building, ripping down the paintings and casting the religious statues to the floor, shattering them.[101]

One might wonder whether Henry VIII took lessons from Zwingli. Miller describes how the Swiss Reformer went on to purge the church of many images, instruments, priestly garments, and so on. In 1531, Zwingli

> was slain in a war for religious liberty. By then, however, he had widely established Reformation sentiments against religious art.... [But] Zwingli's dash through the cathedral ended oddly. There stands in Zurich a well-sculpted statue of the old statue-smasher, Bible in one hand and a sword in the other. If he were alive today, this statue of himself would be too big for him to push over.[102]

Miller probes contemporary practice when he writes, "Evangelical sermons and sanctuaries have been void both of art and interest ... Our

---

99. See insights into the world of sixteenth-century music publishing in Clulow, "Publication."

100. He also understood the need for outside sources of income, and he invested a lot of time in learning about and actively working towards winning legal disputes over property that could help to fund his artistic work.

101. Miller, *Into the Depths of God*, 64.

102. Miller, *Into the Depths of God*, 64–65.

many words produce a dullness of soul, a dead litany of boredom." He suggests that "Art doesn't become idolatry until our praise of God dies and all that is left is our praise for the art form. Idols are born when artists quit worshiping God and begin singing *te deums* to their own genius."[103] There is something in this to ponder for those who are deeply immersed in worship practices in the twenty-first century.

CONCLUSION

Byrd and his fellow Catholic worshipers must have believed that they lived in a post-Christian world. In similar manner, many in the West live in a world where leaders can no longer expect everyone to know the hymns and worship songs being sung or to know or understand the traditions of corporate Christian worship. Perhaps the contemporary context is more like early Christianity.

For Byrd and his fellow-worshipers, their worship became costly. It also became more fervent, more ardent, more intense, and it essentially went underground—or, at least, out of town. They met in secret places, and they were at risk in doing so. Were there problems in Catholic understanding of faith and worship that needed to be addressed? Yes. Were there genuine believers and followers of God within this group? Undoubtedly.

Evangelicals still have things to learn from Catholic worshipers. Evangelicals often admit that they do not recall moments of transcendent worship while sitting in the pew of an evangelical service, but they do catch glimpses of such experiences in a Catholic cathedral, where monks might still chant part of the service, where skilled musicians might still sing some of Byrd's motets and masses.

What would Byrd say to those who live and worship today in a post-Christian culture? He would urge Christians to keep bringing their very best to those who are committed worshipers of God. He modelled the efforts that he thought were merited to provide worship resources for people to engage in meaningful worship. He would surely push to provide the relevant resources that are needed now to give God's people a voice to participate.[104] He would encourage taking some risks in order

---

103. Miller, *Into the Depths of God*, 65.

104. See Kreider and Kreider, *Worship and Mission*, 116–18, who speak of a lost understanding of 1 Cor 14 as a model for worship that has been overshadowed by theological disputes that miss the point. What they call "multi-voiced" worship, and

to offer the very best works of art and artistry and craftsmanship to God, and to his people, even if the group of people who use and appreciate these is small.

Many of Byrd's motets were musical masterpieces designed for these small gatherings of worshipers, possibly gathered around a kitchen table, with only a few musical manuscripts available and a handful of musicians engaged together in singing the liturgy. Byrd's three Masses are pinnacles of his compositional work, but they were not composed to be used for large congregations in the authorized church, only for small, secret gatherings. The later part of Byrd's life was devoted to shaping and preparing his *Gradualia* as a complex of works with all the detailed parts of the liturgy that were needed by the worshipers but were not available to them otherwise. Byrd designed all this for these secret worshippers.

It was not that Byrd did not know how to make something commercial, marketable, income-generating, and valuable for posterity. It was just that he had something more important to do, to provide the very best musical-liturgical resources for those who met to worship in secret. He cared about these worshipers and their needs, and he cared about offering his best work as his own worship to God. But he also poured energy and creativity into musical worship for the official church of the land, for worshipers who met in public places.

There is much to learn from this master composer who functioned on two sides of a theological divide, but who did not sacrifice his integrity, his faith, or his art. Byrd had a creative hand in reshaping the musical liturgy for his fellow English worshipers in the Church of England. He certainly had a major role to play in reshaping the musical liturgy of his fellow Catholic worshipers who met in places of secrecy and were in danger. Both groups still owe him a debt of gratitude. His music is still sung in churches of both traditions. But for those willing to consider it, Byrd has modeled some ways forward for the competing liturgies and practices and values of the North American evangelical church, now also beginning to meet in a post-Christian world.

---

which they believe to be a model worthy of emulation, showed up in various ways during the Reformation, in Luther, in the Swiss Brethren, in the Anabaptists, in early Baptists, and especially among Quakers. Kreider and Kreider suggest that it is time to recover that idea of everyone's participation in worship, making space for the variety of gifts and voices that are present in the group, not just professional leaders at the front.

Part Two: Musical Traditions and Interpretations

REFERENCES AND FURTHER READING

Benham, Hugh. *Latin Church Music in England, c. 1460-575*. London: Barrie and Jenkins, 1977.

Bertoglio, Chiara. *Reforming Music: Music and the Religious Reformations of the Sixteenth Century*. Berlin: de Gruyter, 2017.

Bowers, Roger. "The Chapel Royal, The First Edwardian Prayer Book, and Elizabeth's Settlement of Religion, 1559." *The Historical Journal* 43 (2000) 317-44.

———. "Further Thought on Early Tudor Pitch." *Early Music* 8 (1980) 368-75.

———. "The Performing Pitch of English 15th-Century Church Polyphony." *Early Music* 8 (1980) 21-28.

———. "The Vocal Scoring, Choral Balance and Performing Pitch of Latin Church Polyphony in England, c. 1500-58." *Journal of the Royal Musical Association* 112 (1986-1987) 38-76.

Brett, Philip. "Liner notes." In *Byrd: Missa in tempore paschali*. Performed by Chanticleer. Recorded at St. Ignatius Church, San Francisco, 1986. CD Recording. Arles, Germany: Harmonia Mundi, 1987.

———. "Word-Setting in the Songs of Byrd." *Proceedings of the Royal Musical Association* 98 (1971-1972) 47-64.

Brown, Howard Mayer. *Music in the Renaissance*. Prentice Hall History of Music. Englewood Cliffs, NJ: Prentice-Hall, 1976.

Clulow, Peter. "Publication Dates for Byrd's Latin Masses." *Music and Letters* 47 (1966) 1-9.

Davies, Horton. *Worship and Theology in England: I. From Cranmer to Hooker, 1534-1603; II. From Andrews to Baxter and Fox, 1603-1690*. Grand Rapids: Eerdmans, 1996.

Dickens, A. G. *The English Reformation*. New York: Schocken, 1969 [1964].

Duguid, Timothy. *Metrical Psalmody in Print and Practice: English "Singing Psalms" and Scottish "Psalm Buiks," c. 1540-1640*. St Andrews Studies in Reformation History. Farnham, UK, and Burlington, VT: Ashgate, 2014.

Erasmus, Desiderius. *Opera Omnia Desiderii Erasmi*, edited by J. Clericus. Leiden: Elsevier, 1703-1706.

Faulkner, Anne Shaw. "Does Jazz Put the Sin in Syncopation?" *Ladies Home Journal* (1921) 16-34.

Fellowes, Edmund H. *The Office of the Holy Communion as Set by John Merbecke*. Oxford: Oxford University Press, 1949.

Fenner, Chris. "Ein feste Burg ist unser Gott." *Hymnology Archive*. No pages. Online: https://www.hymnologyarchive.com/ein-feste-burg.

Frere, Walter Howard, and William P. McClure Kennedy, eds. *Visitation Articles and Injunctions: Volume 3: 1559-1575*. Alcuin Club Collections, 16. London: Longman, Greens, 1910.

Harley, John. *William Byrd: Gentleman of the Chapel Royal*. Aldershot, UK: Ashgate, 1997. Amended reprint, 1999.

———. *William Byrd's Modal Practice*. Aldershot, UK, and Burlington, VT: Ashgate, 2005.

Harrison, Frank Llewellyn. *Music in Medieval Britain*. Studies in the History of Music. 4th ed. Buren, The Netherlands: Fritz Knuf, 1980.

Harrison, Frank Llewellyn, ed. *The Eton Choirbook: I*. Musica Brittanica: A National Collection of Music 10. 2nd ed. London: Stainer and Bell, for the Royal Musical Association, 1967.

Huray, Peter le. *Music and the Reformation in England, 1549–1660*. Cambridge Studies in Music. Cambridge: Cambridge University Press, 1978.

Inge, John. *A Christian Theology of Place: Explorations in Practical, Pastoral and Empirical Theology*. New York: Routledge, 2003.

Kerman, Joseph. "Byrd's Motets: Chronology and Canon." *Journal of the American Musicological Society* 14 (1961) 359–82.

———. "Byrd's Settings of the Ordinary of the Mass." *Journal of the American Musicological Society* 32 (1979) 408–39.

———. *The Elizabethan Madrigal: A Comparative Study*. New York: American Musicological Society, 1962.

———. *The Masses and Motets of William Byrd*. The Music of William Byrd 1. London: Faber and Faber, 1981.

———. "On William Byrd's Emendemus in melius." *The Musical Quarterly* 49 (1963) 431–49.

Ketley, Joseph, ed. *The Two Liturgies, A.D. 1549, and A.D. 1552, with Other Documents Set Forth by Authority in the Reign of King Edward VI*. Cambridge: Cambridge University Press, 1844.

Kreider, Alan, and Eleanor Kreider. *Worship and Mission after Christendom*. Harrison, VA: Herald, 2011.

Leaver, Robin A. *"Goostly Psalmes and Spiritual Songs": English and Dutch Metrical Psalms from Coverdale to Utenhove, 1535–1566*. Oxford: Clarendon, 1991.

———. *The Whole Church Sings: Congregational Singing in Luther's Wittenberg*. Grand Rapids: Eerdmans, 2017.

Lenti, Vincent A. "The Earliest Lutheran Hymn Tradition as Illustrated by Two Classic Sixteenth-Century German Chorales." *The Hymn* 50 (1999) 17–25.

Marsh, Christopher. *Music and Society in Early Modern England*. Cambridge: Cambridge University Press, 2010.

McCarthy, Kerry. *Byrd*. Oxford: Oxford University Press, 2013.

———. *Liturgy and Contemplation in Byrd's Gradualia*. New York: Routledge, 2007.

Miller, Calvin. *Into the Depths of God: Where Eyes See the Invisible, Ears Hear the Inaudible, and Minds Conceive the Inconceivable*. Minneapolis: Bethany House, 2000.

Miller, Clement. "Erasmus on Music." *The Musical Quarterly* 52 (1966) 332–49.

Milsom, John, ed. *Thomas Tallis and William Byrd: Cantiones Sacrae 1575*. Early English Church Music 56. London: Stainer and Bell, 2014.

Monson, Craig. "Elizabethan London." In *The Renaissance: From the 1470s to the End of the 16th Century*, edited by Iain Fenlon, 304–40. Englewood Cliffs, NJ: Prentice Hall, 1989.

Monson, Craig, ed. *The English Anthems*. The Byrd Edition 11. London: Stainer and Bell, 1983.

———, ed. *The English Services*. The Byrd Edition 10a. London: Stainer and Bell, 1980.

———, ed. *The English Services II (The Great Service)*. The Byrd Edition 10b. London: Stainer and Bell, 1982.

Morley, Thomas. *A Plain & Easy Introduction to Practical Music (1597)*, edited by R. Alec Harman. New York: Norton, 1952.

Morris, Christopher, ed. *The Oxford Book of Tudor Anthems: 34 Anthems for Mixed Voices*. Oxford: Oxford University Press, 1978.
Neighbour, Oliver. *The Consort and Keyboard Music of William Byrd*. The Music of William Byrd 3. London: Faber and Faber, 1978.
Owens, Jessie Ann. *Composers at Work: The Craft of Musical Composition 1450–1600*. New York: Oxford University Press, 1997.
Quitslund, Beth. *The Reformation in Rhyme: Sternhold, Hopkins and the English Metrical Psalter, 1547–1603*. Burlington, VT: Ashgate, 2008.
Quitslund, Beth, and Nicholas Temperley. *The Whole Book of Psalms: Collected into English Metre by Thomas Sternhold, John Hopkins, and Others*. A Critical Edition of the Texts and Tunes. 2 vols. Renaissance English Text Society. Temple, AZ: Arizona Center for Medieval & Renaissance Studies, 2018.
State Papers Published under the Authority of His Majesty's Commission: Volume 1: King Henry the Eighth: Parts 1 and 2. London: John Murray, 1831.
Strunk, Oliver, ed. *Source Readings in Music History: The Renaissance*. New York: W. W. Norton, 1965.
Temperley, Nicholas. Review of *Metrical Psalmody in Print and Practice*, by Timothy Duguid. *Music & Letters* 96 (2015) 269–71.
Williams, Penry. *The Later Tudors: England 1547–1603*. The New Oxford History of England. Oxford: Clarendon, 1995.
Wulstan, David. *Tudor Music*. London: J. M. Dent, 1985.
———. "Vocal Colour in English Sixteenth-Century Polyphony." *Journal of the Plainsong and Medieval Music* 2 (1979) 19–60.
Zim, Rivkah. *English Metrical Psalms: Poetry as Praise and Prayer, 1535–1601*. Cambridge: Cambridge University Press, 1987.

Part Three

The Past and Present of
Music and Worship

16

New Songs in Biblical and Christian History

INTRODUCTION

"SING TO THE LORD a new song." The Psalms (33:3; 40:3, 96:1, 98:1, 149:1), Isaiah (42:10), and John's Revelation (5:9 and 14:3) all refer to a new song of worship, and yet, the contemporary worship song is often represented as a recent phenomenon, as though it was introduced in the twentieth century. Nothing could be further from the truth. The Old Testament, the New Testament, and the span of church history all reveal that the contemporary worship song has always been an essential component in the life and worship of believers.

The first musician in the Old Testament, John's vision at the end of the New Testament, Johann Sebastian Bach from the eighteenth century, and Hillsong beginning in the late twentieth century all have this in common: they all have something to do with the contemporary worship song. Perhaps we think that the Bible and people throughout history have nothing to teach us about contemporary worship songs, because they are from the past and can know nothing about what is "contemporary." The meaning of the word "contemporary" is notoriously difficult to pin down because it always represents a changing background. What is contemporary now is soon dated. The word "new" provides similar challenges. Our New Testament is in contrast to and in conjunction with the Old Testament. The word "new" always implies a relationship to something that is old, or, at least, older. For example, one of the thirty-nine colleges that currently constitutes Oxford University is called "New College." In 1379, when it was founded by William of Wykeham, it was new. New College is no longer new, but it retains the name. It is not difficult to find numerous examples of this muddying of meaning where the word "new" or "contemporary" is used.

These words have relative or contextual values. This is one reason why the development and use of markedness theory in linguistic and musical-linguistic studies is so significant, because the fluctuation of background in a given work is studied as a context for establishing what is marked or brought into prominence in the foreground of that particular work.[1] When musicologists look at the musical styles of an era, what emerges as the standard practice in that era is the context against which new compositions or compositional techniques stand out. In music in the church, certain kinds of songs or styles of music become the background against which new forms of song are perceived as "new" or "contemporary," without making judgments about whether they are considered good or bad. In each case, what is new or contemporary today may be perceived as old tomorrow.

Nonetheless, there is something important about these words, "contemporary" and "new." Worship needs to be current and relevant, even if it uses historical liturgies or formulas. Worship is something like manna that could not be saved for another day, apart from on the Sabbath. It was either fresh or it was stale. So it is with worship. Even if the components of worship are historical and traditional, they must be infused with a freshness, perhaps new appreciation and insight, a new energy and delight, or a new tempo or rhythm or perspective that reorients the worshiper towards a living and eternal God whose compassionate love is new every morning.

The nature of music is that it exists "in the moment," unlike some of the other arts. You can look at a printed piece of music, you may be able to imagine it in your head, but the music exists in real time. You can listen to a recording of a performance, but you can still only listen to it as it is aurally passing. You cannot listen to it apart from some kind of performance (live, electronic, mental). Sculpture and painting, however, often exist as stationary objects to be observed and appreciated at will and at length. No one has to turn them on or perform them. You may be able to walk around them or towards them and step back from them. But music must move note by note through a song in order for it to be heard and appreciated.

---

1. See, e.g., Battistella, *Markedness*, and his later work, *Logic of Markedness*. This is explored further in relation to music in the opening chapters of Porter, *Early English Composers and the Credo*.

Many believers seem to be sure about what constitutes appropriate worship music. This perspective may be influenced by that person's worship culture, whether that is geographical or ethnic or historical or experiential or denominational. The spectrum of expectations is considerable: songs that capture heartfelt expression vs. songs that present clear theological statements; songs with structured musical parts vs. those with free harmonization; musical styles with historical precedence vs. styles that are more recent; the use of choirs and classically trained musicians versus singers and instrumentalists who improvise; music with space for display of skill and ability vs. music and style that preclude any show of ability, etc.

However, even those who contend that historical precedence is of utmost importance in choosing music for worship must recognize that believers have not always worshiped using the same worship songs or musical forms that we use now. New songs and forms of worship music have been an integral component of Christian worship since the inception of Christian faith,[2] and, prior to that, in the worship of believers throughout the Old Testament.

CONTEMPORARY WORSHIP MUSIC IN THE OLD TESTAMENT

Early in Genesis, we are introduced to Jubal, the first named musician, "the father of all who play stringed instruments (kinnor)[3] and pipes

---

2. See debate about whether there was music in the early synagogue and the question of its relationship to music in the early church, in McKinnon, "On the Question of Psalmody," and Smith, "Ancient Synagogue."

3. The NIV's use of "stringed instruments" corresponds well with Braun's description of the *kinnor*. The *kinnor* appears about forty-two times in the Old Testament, an instrument used for secular celebrations, for lament or mourning, for praise, and it was played during the transport of the ark. But it was also an instrument used by prostitutes and the wicked, connected with miraculous healings and with prophetic ecstasies (see Braun, *Music in Ancient Israel/Palestine*, 16–19 [17]). Clearly it was not just a "holy" instrument but an instrument used for a wide variety of purposes and occasions. The LXX uses several terms in translating this word: *kithara, kinyra, psalterion,* and *organon*. The Vulgate uses *cithara, lyra, psalterium,* and *organum*. Regardless of the uncertainty, scholars are quite convinced that it was a lyre, although the form of this instrument undoubtedly changed significantly over the years. A wood that remains unknown to us, called almugwood, was used in its construction, as well as in the related instrument, the *nebel*. Josephus tells us that the instrument had ten strings (*Ant.* 7.12.3), Jerome said six (*PL* 26.969), and b. 'Arak 13b says seven. It was played with a plectrum but could be played by hand for a more soothing sound. You

('ugab)."[4] The kinnor is commonly believed to be a kind of small harp,[5] and the 'ugab, though still without scholarly consensus, is probably a long flute-like instrument, which we know from Egypt and Sumeria, and later in the Near East.

Jubal, as the first named musician in the Old Testament, must have had a major role in creating music, writing new songs for these instruments, perhaps inventing the instruments themselves, and certainly shaping the line of musicians who would play these instruments and who would sing these songs or write new ones. It is intriguing that Jubal's music-making is apparently one of the components of normal work life, for we see him situated between brother Jabal's agricultural work and cousin Tubal-Cain's work as a forger of bronze and iron. This raises some interesting and surprisingly early perspectives on the intersection of faith, work, and worship: a farmer, a musician, and an ironsmith, each representing a line of work that apparently are not incongruous.

There are about twelve instruments mentioned in the Old Testament (apart from the group of instruments mentioned in Daniel, perhaps from around 167–64 BCE). Some of these instruments are still a mystery to archaeologists and musicologists, for even the early translations of their

---

can imagine this somewhat in the way that a guitar may be played with a pick but can also be played with just the fingers—although the instrument itself was handled very differently, and was more like a small harp, some of which were symmetrical and others asymmetrical in shape and design (Braun, *Music in Ancient Israel/Palestine*, 17–19).

4. The NIV uses "pipe" to translate '*ugab* in this verse. The term is found four times in the Old Testament (Gen 4:21; Ps 150:4; Job 21:12; 30:31). It is still not entirely clear what this instrument was. Its root word may associate it with "ardor, sensual desire, lust." The LXX uses *kithara*, *organon*, and *psalmos* to translate it, while the Vulgate uses '*abbuba*, an oboe-like instrument, and *organum* (see Braun, *Music in Ancient Israel/Palestine*, 31–32 [31]). Clearly, it was already somewhat unclear what this instrument really was! Its use was varied: it was used for lament, as an instrument of the wicked, and also used in the concluding doxology of the Psalms (although this was performed outside the Temple, and in combination with other instruments). It has been thought to be some kind of water organ, which is an instrument with a hydraulic device, or a kind of pipe that was often associated with prostitutes. Curt Sachs offers a plausible interpretation as a long flute-like instrument, with its name being somewhat onomatopoeic (vowels u-u), and because this instrument is attested in neighbouring cultures of the time, Egypt and Sumeria, and later in the Near East (Israel/Palestine) (see Braun, *Music in Ancient Israel/Palestine*, 32). See also the early work of Sachs (*History*), especially chapters on instruments in antiquity, including Sumer and Babylonia, Egypt, and Israel (67–127).

5. It may have been either a symmetrical or asymmetrical harp, with six, seven, or ten strings.

names are inconsistent, while the artifacts are limited, and of course there are no recordings of how they sounded.[6] However, the world's oldest fragment of a song with preserved musical notation was discovered in the mid 1990s in Ugarit, now Ras Shamra, on the Mediterranean coast of Syria, a "hymn" to a spiritual being. It was written in cuneiform, from about 1400 BCE, making it approximately 3400/3200 years old.[7] Surprisingly, we are still learning new things about the ancient world, in which the Old Testament was embedded.

There are songs in the Old Testament that are specifically related to individuals or events, so they represent some kind of new song at the time. The Song of Moses and Miriam celebrated the miraculous safe crossing through the parted waters of the Red Sea. Miriam led the women in song and dance with percussion instruments, providing early evidence of a woman worship leader, and evidence that worship included percussion as well as singing and dance. The song of Deborah in the book

---

6. These instruments are (1) *'aseberosim*, a kind of clapper made of cyprus wood; (2) *halil*, a pipe or oboe-clarinet-type instrument—not "flute," as many translations use; (3) *hasosera*, a trumpet made of beaten or hammered silver, about 40-cm long (as per Josephus, *Ant.* 3.12.6); (4) *kinnor*, a lyre with 10, 6, or 7 strings; (5) *mena'an'im*, probably a clay rattle; (6) *mesiltayim, selselim*, ceremonial cultic instruments, considered instruments of the guild of Levites, never played by women in the Bible, some kind of struck metal idiophone, a kind of cymbals, with the *selselim* seeming to be more in use by the people at large and the *mesiltayim* as reserved for ceremonial and liturgical use by the Levitical guild; (7) *nebel, nebel 'asor*, an instrument specific to Levitical guilds, most scholars consider it a harp, although there is no archaeological evidence for this kind of instrument at the time. According to Josephus, the *nebel* had 12 strings (contrasting with the *kinnor*'s 10, 6, or 7), while the *nebel 'asor* seems to have had 10 strings; (8) *pa'amon* refers to the bells at the bottom of the priest's robe, possibly providing apotropaic and prophylactic functions connected with exorcisms; (9) *qeren hayyobel*, a ram's horn; (10) *sopar* and *soperot hayyobelim*, the most-frequently mentioned instrument in the Old Testament, also survived in Jewish liturgy, generally believed to have been a naturally-occurring horn, of a goat or a ram; (11) *top*, an onomatopoeic word representing a drum, most commonly believed to be a round frame of wood, about 25–30 cm. in diameter and looking much like a tambourine, minus the metal jingles; (12) *'ugab*, likely a flute-like instrument. Modern musicology classifies these instruments into four groups: idiophones (percussion instruments made from resonating material), membranophones (percussion instruments, usually a hollow cylinder with membranes stretched across each end), chordophones (stringed instruments) and aerophones (wind instruments) (see Braun, *Music in Ancient Israel/Palestine*, 11–12).

7. It is addressed to the moon god's wife, Nikkal. The tonal sounds are apparently familiar-sounding to a Western ear, equivalent to a do-re-mi scale. See, also, Draffkorn Kilmer, "Cult Song," who claims to have discovered harmony coded in the musical notation, something not thought to exist in the ancient world.

of Judges celebrated the defeat of her people's enemies, including Jael and her deadly use of a tent-peg (we would likely hesitate to include such detail in a worship song today). The song of Hannah, in 1 Samuel, arose after years of infertility when she finally received an answer to her prayer to have a son. As part of her worship, although perhaps not a song as we know it (did she sing it?), she dedicated him back to the Lord. David sang a moving lament in Second Samuel over the death of his best friend, Jonathan. In each of these, the song on the lips of the character was specific to the event and their own involvement in it, which means that it was a very "contemporary" song at the time. In the case of David's lament, his words were not just about general sadness or sorrow, but they were specifically about the loss of this friend, and how that loss affected him at the time. In fact, lament is often very specific, urgent, immediate. Real lament seems to be, by nature, "contemporary," as modelled by David himself.[8]

Meanwhile, there were several large-scale events that generated new expressions of worship through song, especially those connected with one of three men: Jehoshaphat, Hezekiah, or Nehemiah. In Second Chronicles, Jehoshaphat's enemies were coming to make war on him (2 Chr 26). He was nervous. He gathered the people of Judah together, and they met at the temple of the Lord in the front of the new courtyard (v. 5), including not only the men, but their wives, children, and babies (v. 13). Jehoshaphat stood up and cried out to God, reminding God of his previous acts of mercy and power, reminding him of the current emergency. He closed with, "We do not know what to do, but our eyes are on you." The Lord told him through Asaph (of psalm fame, I believe) that God himself would fight the battle, though they would still need to march. They fell down and worshiped God, undoubtedly with renewed fervour. The next day, they set out, and Jehoshaphat appointed men to sing to the Lord, to praise him for the splendour of his holiness. They were given a musical refrain: "Give thanks to the Lord, for his love endures forever" (cf. Pss 118 and 136). As they began to sing and praise, the Lord did what he said he would do. When the men re-entered Jerusalem, they headed to the temple of the Lord with harps and lyres and trumpets to celebrate in song. Surely each of these was a "new" song, or at the very least, a song sung with new fervour.

---

8. See discussion of lament in Brown and Miller, eds., *Lament*; Waltke et al., *Psalms*; Witvliet, *Worship*, 39–63; and Wolterstorff, *Lament*.

In 2 Chr 29:25–30 (see also 2 Kgs 18:3–4), Hezekiah was purifying the Temple, not only by re-instating its musical procedures, but by ensuring that the people understood worship and who it was that they were worshiping. He challenged them to worship the Lord from the heart. The Levites were stationed with cymbals, harps, and lyres, the priests were ready with their trumpets, and as the offering to the Lord began, so did singing to the Lord, accompanied by the temple worship band. They sang praises with gladness and bowed down and worshiped. What a "new song" this must have been. Had the music been archived and re-found? Had it been lost forever, due to a breakdown in oral tradition, and new songs written in their stead? It is unlikely that printed music was available, so unless someone had kept the oral tradition alive, or perhaps etched the words and musical notation on a rock, it was lost. Whatever the actual music used on this occasion, it must have been the most "contemporary" worship service that the participants could have ever imagined or experienced. Of course, this is both the beauty and the challenge of worship music. It calls on its creators to find new ways to make the old fresh and relevant and dynamic, as well as to incorporate entirely new expressions.

In Nehemiah, repentance and worship were interwoven. The Israelites were gathered together, fasting, wearing sackcloth, and putting dust on their heads as signs of their contrition. They stood to confess their own sins and their ancestors' sins. They continued to stand for another quarter of the day to read from the Book of the Law of the Lord their God. They spent another quarter of the day in confession and in worshiping the Lord their God. They cried out with loud voices to the Lord. And then the Levites said: "Stand up and praise the Lord your God, who is from everlasting to everlasting." After this followed the Levites' prayer, which must have had some form of musical expression, because they were the musicians, after all. The intensity and fervour of their refrain, "Praise the Lord, our God, from everlasting to everlasting!," must have been a resounding "new" song of worship to God on that day.

Meanwhile, interspersed throughout the Psalms is a persistent reiteration of and call for a "new" song of worship. When the Lord had delivered David from all his enemies, David sang a "new" song to the Lord, recorded in 2 Sam 22 and in Ps 18. In Ps 40:3, the psalmist acknowledged his desperation and helplessness, how God saved him and "puts a new song in my mouth, a hymn of praise to our God." This "new" song came from God himself. Psalm 96:1 calls on the people to "sing to the Lord a new song." In fact, it calls on all the earth to sing to the Lord, to sing to the Lord and praise his name. The penultimate psalm (Ps 149) is a call to "sing to the Lord a new song" (v. 1), to sing it as praise in the assembly of God's faithful people. The psalmist calls on the people to "rejoice in their Maker, to be glad in their King, to praise his name with dancing, to make music to him with timbrel and harp. For the Lord takes delight in his people." And then the psalmist instructs them "to sing for joy on their beds," that this should be the last thing to pass their lips and fill their minds as they lie down to sleep for the night, ready with a new song of praise to God as they face a new day.

The Psalms remind us that music is integral to heart-felt worship, and the term "song" seems to imply heart-engagement:

- "Come before him with joyful songs" (100:2)
- "Sing the praises of the Lord, you his faithful people; praise his holy name. For his anger lasts only a moment, but his favour lasts a lifetime; weeping may remain for a night, but rejoicing comes in the morning" (30:4; surely this is a call for a new song)
- "Clap your hands, all you nations; shout to God with cries of joy . . . Sing praises to God . . . For God is the King of all the earth; sing to him a psalm of praise" (47:6)
- "But I will sing of your strength, in the morning I will sing of your love; for you are my fortress, my refuge in times of trouble" (59:16; these are all reasons to give voice to a new song of praise to God)
- "I will sing of the Lord's great love forever; with my mouth will I make your faithfulness known through all generations" (89:1)
- "I will sing of your love and justice; to you, Lord, I will sing praise" (101:1)
- "With singing lips my mouth will praise you" (63:5)
- "Sing and make music to the Lord" (27:6)
- "Extol him with music and song" (95:2)
- "Burst into jubilant song with music" (98:4)
- "Sing and make music with all my soul" (108:1)

These psalms leave little doubt that a new song or new musical and heart-felt expression is called for when responding to God's being and his works.

In another of the psalms, although it does not refer to it as "song," Ps 107 gives reason for worshipers and worship-song writers to tell their stories. In four different scenarios, the refrain, "Let the redeemed of the Lord tell their story," invites participants who have been redeemed by God in four different ways to tell their story of redemption. Each has a refrain that celebrates the salvation of the Lord. Everyone has a new story of their own salvation to tell, and what better way to remember and tell (and re-tell) a story than through music.

The prophet Isaiah makes specific reference to a new song. In response to the Lord's words of promise, Isa 42:10 says, "Sing to the Lord a new song, his praise from the ends of the earth, you who go down to the sea, and all that is in it, you islands, and all who live in them." Again, in response to the Lord's words about past faithfulness and future promise, Isaiah says, "Sing for joy, you heavens, for the Lord has done this; shout aloud, you earth beneath. Burst into song, you mountains, you forests and all you trees, for the Lord has redeemed Jacob, he displays his glory in Israel" (Isa 44:23).

In Isa 49:13, the heavens are called on to shout for joy, the earth to rejoice, the mountains to burst into song! This seems to imply that something so new and so tremendous is taking place that the mountains are to burst into song. Having never seen or heard mountains burst into song before, I am not exactly sure what this means, but that does not mean I don't believe it could happen. It certainly would seem like a new expression of praise to God to be present for such an outburst. I do not know of any song of the mountains that already exists, but surely this would be a new song of worship to God. At the very least, this would be a new setting of a song of worship, orchestrated for a mountain chorus.[9]

Finally, Isa 55:12 depicts a new song being created right before the eyes of those going out in joy, those who are being led in peace. The accompaniment to this celebratory parade is the mountains and the hills erupting into song before their eyes, and the trees of the field clapping their hands. Again, having never seen such a performance, it is unclear what the song might sound like or how it would appear in performance,

---

9. See also Isa 52:9 ("Burst into songs of joy together, you ruins of Jerusalem, for the Lord has comforted his people, he has redeemed Jerusalem") and 54:1 ("'Sing, barren woman, you who never bore a child; burst into song, shout for joy, you who were never in labor; because more are the children of the desolate woman than of her who has a husband,' says the Lord"). These provide solid reasons to engage in a new song, or at the very least, a new expression of worship through song.

but I expect it would be spectacular, a musical sound and a visual manifestation unlike any that we currently know. Does it just mean that there would be a small volcano and a big wind that causes the trees to blow around a lot? Perhaps. But why couldn't God provide a way for mountains and hills to actually burst out into a song of worship for the God who created them? Why couldn't the trees work together like a rhythm section or dance troupe to accompany the singing of the hills and mountains? Why not?[10]

It is interesting that Ezra (2:64–67) documents that two hundred singers returned from exile, but note also that they are listed right there after the male and female slaves and right before the list of animals (horses, mules, camels, and donkeys). Lest musicians get too high an impression of themselves, this perhaps provides an antidote.

The Old Testament records at least two strong views that the Lord has on certain "worship" music. Amos records that the Lord has his own lament and Amos uses this lament to propel a call to repentance. The Lord's lament uses words like "I hate, I despise your religious festivals" and "I cannot stand your assemblies... Away with the noise of your songs! I will not listen to the music of your harps. But let justice roll on like a river, righteousness like a never-failing stream!" He minces no words. Music can accompany the most shallow and unholy of expressions, and apparently that was what was going on in these festivals. These pretenses at being festivals of worship to the Lord were something that he would not tolerate, that he, in fact, abhorred.

However, in Isa 29, the Lord speaks of a day when the people of Zion, who live in Jerusalem, will weep no more. This is a day when the Lord binds up the bruises of his people and heals the wounds he inflicted. He says, "And you will sing as on the night you celebrate a holy festival; your hearts will rejoice as when people playing pipes go up to the mountain of the Lord, to the Rock of Israel." When the Lord is really being worshiped, heart-felt music is in order, and the Lord endorses it.[11]

---

10. Other Old Testament references that could be noted include Jer 30:19 ("From them will come songs of thanksgiving and the sound of rejoicing"). Note that there is a different kind of new song in Lamentations, with reference to being mocked with songs, mocked all day long (3:14, 63). These are new songs, perhaps, but not songs of worship. In Amos 8:3, the Lord declares that the songs in the temple will turn to wailing, and Mic 2:4 talks about being taunted with a mournful song of ruin.

11. Oddly, a musical ensemble is called into the Lord's service in the following passage. The Lord brings his arm down with raging anger and consuming fire, with cloudburst and thunderstorm and hail. The voice of the Lord shatters Assyria, striking

At various points throughout the Old Testament, worshipers are called to sing new songs of praise to the Lord. Not once do we read, "Sing an old song to the Lord." Of course, the people must have sung old songs, but somehow these songs had to be new in their heart-felt expression in order to qualify as appropriate songs for the Lord. In each of these examples, contemporary expressions of worship are exactly what was required.

THE CONTEMPORARY WORSHIP SONG IN THE NEW TESTAMENT

Liturgists, church musicians, and many worship leaders wish that the New Testament had more to say about music and worship than it does. It certainly does not come with printed music, chord charts, or recordings. But those brief passages that exist do tell us something. Although there were no electronic media in the New Testament era, there was, in fact, something much better. There was a lively culture of music-making in the musical-cultural environment of the New Testament, where people actually participated in and created the music that was occurring. As recently as the early twentieth century, this was still a viable part of many communities, but by the twenty-first, this has largely been lost, at least in Western culture. We can turn music on, but most of us no longer know how to "make" music.

In the Gospels, both Matthew (11:17) and Luke (7:32) give us a colloquial glimpse into the children in the market who were singing their kid-songs, and referring to playing instruments of some sort to go along with them, as they called out to each other: "We played the aulos, and you didn't dance; we sang a dirge, and you didn't cry." In Matthew, we glimpse a musical ensemble that had been employed to entertain in a wealthy man's house, a house that Jesus himself entered. Jesus saw the aulos players (note that this should be translated "pipe" or "oboe" not "flute" as some translations use) and the noisy crowd that were assembled for this gathering (Matt 9:23). Through the perspective of an older son returning from a field, we get a glimpse of a celebratory party in a home, a place full of music and dancing (Luke 15:25). So, we get a sense of music as an integral part of life: children singing in the marketplace, social occasions

---

them down with his rod, and then, "Every stroke the Lord lays on them with his punishing club will be to the music of timbrels and harps, as he fights them in battle with the blows of his arm." The Lord apparently *orchestrates* his massive and explosive event of judgment!

that included hired musicians in a wealthy ruler's home, and celebration through music and dancing in a family home.

Somehow it seems odd to realize that we know that Jesus actually sang.[12] Was he a tenor, a bass, a baritone? What was it like to listen to Jesus singing, and to be one of his small group singing with him? It is interesting to imagine a group of guys, fishermen and from other walks of life, singing a hymn with Jesus. Then, "when they had sung a hymn, they went out to the Mount of Olives" (Matt 26:30; Mark 14:26). Scholars generally assume that this was the great Passover hymn, consisting of Pss 113–18, known as the Great Hallel.[13] It was Passover, so this is a reasonable conclusion, but it is interesting that the Gospels do not specifically say this, when they could have. Was it a different hymn, instead, or a new hymn, or an old hymn sung in a different way?

We also know that Paul sang. What did he sound like? Did he have a big low voice, or maybe a raspy kind of voice? Did he sound like Josh Groban or Bryan Adams or Bono or Bob Dylan? Whatever he sounded like, he was a public speaker and communicator in a day when you had to be loud to be heard—not required, perhaps, in an acoustically-brilliant design like an amphitheatre such as one finds in Ephesus, but certainly to be heard out in the general crowds in the markets. It would not have required loud singing, however, to penetrate the jail cells where he and Silas worked on their worship song repertoire in the late hours of the night. There they were, singing "hymns" in jail. What hymns? Were they psalms? Were they new "hymns," as in Phil 2? Were they hymns that Paul had written? One thing we know is that "hymns" in ancient times did not have four lines that rhyme, as they are found in standard hymn collections today. The sound of their singing would undoubtedly sound unusual to our ears today. But Paul and Silas were actively singing (and praying) at midnight, "and the other prisoners were listening to them" (Acts 16:25). Maybe this was just because the other prisoners were all trying to sleep, but they must have been very curious about this musical duo. We might think of worship songs in a church, but worship songs in jail should prompt us to think differently about what those worship songs entail. Whatever Paul and Silas were singing, old or new, their songs of worship must have had a fresh urgency and fervour to them in this context.

12. O'Connor, "Singing of Jesus."

13. See O'Connor, "Singing of Jesus," 437–38, who reviews the perspectives on this.

Liturgists and musicologists imagine that singing in the period of the New Testament would have been more like chant than singing as we know it today. This might seem to imply that there would not be a recognizable melody or tune (at least to our ears), perhaps just intonation formulas at the beginnings and ends of lines of text. But Paul's own words tell us that "melody" was an important component of song, even then. He writes to the Corinthians (1 Cor 14:7): "Even in the case of lifeless things that make sounds, such as the aulos or harp, how will anyone know what tune is being played unless there is a distinction in the notes?"[14] Paul expects his readers to find in his example of "recognizing a tune" a useful analogy for the need for interpretation of tongues.[15] Clearly, melody in song was an important feature then as now.

In Paul's letter to the church at Ephesus (Eph 5:18–19), he writes: "be filled with the Spirit, speaking to one another with psalms, hymns and songs from the Spirit." Paul contrasts the creative effects of wine that leads to debauchery with the completely opposite creative effects of being filled with the Spirit. Paul directs the believers to speak to one another with psalms, hymns, and songs from the Spirit. There is no need for him to use three forms of a single word here to communicate what he is saying, if he only means one thing. There is reason to conclude that they refer to three different forms of song.[16] These words may well refer to psalms that were already known to the (previously Jewish) Christians,

---

14. Note that the *aulos* is found in several places in the New Testament (1 Cor 14:7; Matt 9:23; Rev 18:22). It was either a single- or double-reed instrument, known from the Roman period, and represented in many archaeological artifacts. It was an instrument that was used for laments for the dead, but it was also used at weddings. This instrument had a complex reputation, for it was used in erotic festivals, and was known as an instrument used by prostitutes. Professional mourners used it in the New Testament and the children in the market refer to that same use in Matthew and Luke. A contemporary instrument such as the saxophone, which was used in jazz and dance bands, seems to have such a reputation. It was not readily accepted in orchestras (even though Gershwin specifically wrote for it in orchestral works), and even late in the twentieth century, there were universities in North America that did not accept saxophone as a legitimate musical instrument in a music degree program, so study and performance had to be done with another instrument. Two-thousand years earlier, the *aulos* was an instrument with a disreputable reputation. This makes it all the more fascinating that Paul uses it for his example of appropriate interpretive use of tongues in the church, with attention to careful articulation of notes so that you can recognize a melody. The appropriation of this instrument for spiritual application seems to redeem its negative associations.

15. See some discussion in chapter 5 above.

16. See, e.g., Wellesz, *History of Byzantine Music*, 33–35.

to hymns that had already become part of the repertoire of Christian worship music, and to new songs or expressions of worship music. Paul's following sentence, "Sing and make music from your heart to the Lord" in Eph 5:19 suggests that there is an aspect of spiritual music-making that comes directly from the heart. Perhaps Paul is just directing the believers to sing with feeling, but these words could imply something more creative and generative.

Paul uses similar words to the church at Colossae (Col 3:16) where he says: "Let the message of Christ dwell among you richly as you teach and admonish one another with all wisdom through psalms, hymns and songs from the Spirit, singing to God with gratitude in your hearts." The final member of this triad of musical song-types seems to stand outside the canon of familiar psalms and hymns of worship. Perhaps we deny the true nature of the Spirit if we eliminate the creation of new songs of worship.

Paul includes another reference to a hymn that is intriguing. He says to the Corinthians: "What then shall we say, brothers and sisters? When you come together, each of you has a hymn, or a word of instruction, a revelation, a tongue or an interpretation. Everything must be done so that the church may be built up" (1 Cor 14:26). At first glance, this does not appear to be a reference to a new song, and yet, the last three in his list are likely references to spontaneous utterances that are inspired by the Spirit. A revelation implies something relevant right now, tongues occurs in the moment, and interpretation takes place immediately after what is spoken in tongues. If these three elements are contemporary components of the church gathering, perhaps the first two are also. A word of instruction must be relevant, current, and applicable to the body of believers at the time. It is reasonable to consider Paul's use of "hymn" to refer to a song that is fresh and current. Paul himself may have been the writer of the hymn in Phil 2, even if scholars have doubts about it.[17] If so, Paul sets the direction for writing new hymns for Christian worship.

John recounts a conversation that Jesus has with a woman. From it, we learn a great deal about the role of the contemporary worship song in worship. Interestingly, this is Jesus' main teaching on worship,

---

17. The evidence against Paul as writer of this passage is unconvincing. Who was the writer, if it was not Paul? Is it likely to have been a great Christian poet or musician of the New Testament era whose name was never recorded, or who faded into oblivion? Paul cites his sources elsewhere, including philosophers and poets of the time, so it is unlikely that he used someone else's hymn here without mentioning whose it was.

communicated to this woman (although at least one disciple must have been present, or we would not have the account). In this conversation, Jesus turns previous notions of worship upside down. The crazy thing about it is that the person who the Father is seeking as an appropriate worshiper—the person who receives this instruction and is the first communicator/teacher of Jesus' information about worship—is a person we would barely welcome into our churches today in a leadership position, in a day and age when we Christians consider ourselves quite accepting and welcoming. First of all, she was a woman. This is still thought to be unacceptable in some churches. Second, she had had numerous husbands and was currently living common-law with her most recent boyfriend. Would we hire her as our worship leader? Not likely. Yet, this is the woman that Jesus was on his way to locate, in order to communicate what God the Father was looking for in a worshiper. And in his message to her about worship, Spirit and truth were the two main components. Truth seems to represent all that is foundational and unchanging about God's word, his laws, his character, the one we are to worship. The Spirit seems to represent all that is new and fresh and unpredictable and life-giving that is built on that established truth. God the Father is true, unchanging, everlasting, eternal. God the Spirit is as unpredictable and uncontainable as the wind blows where it will, and no one knows where it comes from or where it goes. Jesus makes this new understanding of worship known to the world through this woman at a well. God is spirit and his worshipers must worship in Spirit and truth. A new song is in order.

The book of Hebrews calls on us to worship with reverence and awe. The writer reminds us in Heb 9:1 that "the first covenant had regulations for worship and also an earthly sanctuary," in contrast with the later one. Further (in 10:1), on Christ's sacrifice once for all, we are reminded that "the same sacrifices repeated endlessly year after year, [cannot] make perfect those who draw near to worship." If we are to fulfill the mandate of Heb 12:28, "Therefore, since we are receiving a kingdom that cannot be shaken, let us be thankful, and so worship God acceptably with reverence and awe," then our sacrifice and our songs must call for some form of new expression.

John has a vision of worship and a new song that challenges us all. In John's revelation of the ultimate never-ending worship service, we read about an experience unlike anything John could have imagined on his own. Even with his description, it remains almost unimaginable. What we do know is that, at the heart of it, is a new song (Rev 5:9), a new song that draws on something as archaic as the song of God's servant Moses (Rev 15:3) and at the same time is an entirely new interpretation of song and even of "sound" itself. Revelation 14:2 says, "And I heard a sound from heaven like the roar of rushing waters and like a loud peal of thunder. The sound I heard was like that of harpists playing their harps." What kind of sound is this that combines rushing waters and thunder and harps? We get a tiny hint of what the voice of the One we worship sounds like (Rev 1:15): "his voice was like the sound of rushing waters." But what does that mean? When we hear it in that day, will the sound of that voice be both brand new and yet heartrendingly familiar, where the forever past and forever future are captured in the voice of the one who called everything into being? This is cause for every worshiper to sing a new song.

CONTEMPORARY WORSHIP MUSIC IN THE HISTORY OF THE CHURCH

From the mere scraps of information that we have about the music of early Christian worship, we try to extrapolate what worship may have looked and sounded like in those early years. A second-century letter from the Roman official, Pliny the Younger, to Trajan, is critical to our understanding. It tells us that Christians were singing hymns "to Christ as to a god."[18] This was seen as something new and extraordinary in a culture that had many gods and may have sung hymns to any number of them, but never before to this person named "Christ." Singing a new hymn to Christ could cost the singers their lives.

We have lyrics of a late third-century or early fourth-century hymn referred to as the "Candlelight Hymn,"[19] as well as one attributed to Clement of Alexandria (ca. 170–220).[20] Meanwhile, the discovery of the earliest Christian hymn with musical notation was one of the most

---

18. Pliny the Younger, *Ep. Tra.* 10.96 (Melmoth, Loeb Classical Library).

19. One of our oldest hymns "Hail, Gladdening Light" was in use in the late third or early fourth century. It was called the "Candlelight Hymn" and used while the lamps were being lit for the evening service. The hymn begins, "Hail, gladdening Light, of his pure glory poured, Who is the immortal Father, heavenly, blest." This Greek text is still used in the Orthodox church. But we have no music for the lyrics of this hymn from this period, nor for many that follow. The music most known to worshipers is likely the setting by Louis Bourgeois from the sixteenth century.

20. Houghton, *Christian Hymn-Writers*, 8 (translation by Henry M. Dexter [1853] and music by Felice de Giardini [1769]).

monumental discoveries for the study of early Christian worship music, written in Greek letters and notation on a papyrus fragment from Oxyrhynchus, identified as P.Oxy. XV 1786.[21] Discovered in the late 1800s by archaeologists Bernard Grenfell and Arthur Hunt, it was located in the dry desert climate of Egypt in the city or area of Oxyrhynchus, a perfect environment that preserved thousands of documents because of its dry climate. The papyrus is a wide strip of a fragment of papyrus that used to be housed in the Ashmolean Museum in Oxford, where I had the privilege of examining it.[22]

There are some questions about the translation, because what we have is a fragment, not an entire page. Martin West translates:

> ... Let it be silent
> Let the Luminous stars not shine,
> Let the winds (?) and all the noisy rivers die down;
> And as we hymn the Father, the Son and the Holy Spirit,
> Let all the powers add "Amen Amen."
> Empire, praise always, and glory to God,
> The sole giver of good things, Amen Amen.[23]

Notice that the words do not sound quite like our familiar hymns of today or recent generations. There are several reasons why this document is significant. In the first place, the fact that it exists at all and that we know about it is significant, for so far nothing like it has ever been discovered. The words are unique, that is, they are not a direct quotation of a biblical text. The phrase "Father, Son, and Holy Spirit" shows us that

---

21. Hunt and Jones, "1786. Christian Hymn." See also Pöhlmann and West, *Documents*, 190–94.

22. It has been held in the Papyrology Rooms of the Sackler Library, Oxford. Note that the earliest fragment we have of any notated Greek music (i.e., lyrics with some kind of musical notation) is a Greek secular fragment from about 200 BCE. The secular fragment is about 5-cm or 2-in square, a small dark papyrus fragment with very dark ink writing. It uses Greek majuscules (i.e., capital letters) written above the Greek text, to indicate what the notes of melody are to the specific syllable of a word. The oldest complete song is the *Seikilos* Epitaph, found on a tombstone near Aidin, Turkey, not far from Ephesus. It is variously dated from 200 BCE to 100 CE. Older fragments, recently discovered, exist of notated music in other languages, such as Assyrian.

23. West, *Ancient Greek Music*; cf. Cosgrove, *Ancient Christian Hymn*, 37. Eric Werner reads these lyrics differently, with his translation representing the resources of the earth actually bursting forth into song, *accompanied* by human voices, instead of being silent while we sing our worship to the Father, Son, and Holy Spirit. This hymn is highly significant and is discussed in more detail in chapter 9 above and referenced elsewhere in this volume.

trinitarian theology was already being expressed in a Christian worship song in the third century. This suggests that new songs were being written that reflected the recent impact of theological developments taking place in that era, such as in the Councils that began to meet. Furthermore, a hymn with musical notation shows that innovation in the musical culture was being used in the Christian sphere. The fact that musical notation is included tells us that there was value placed on the preservation of a specific melody line for this hymn. The notation uses Greek letter names, placed in several positions above the appropriate syllable of text, which is remarkably similar to what a chord chart looks like today. Two sets of "Amen" at the end of the song include additional notation, that is, extra notes, which reveals an elaboration at this point in the song, something that seems more improvisational, and therefore requires more notes for one syllable or word. This was surely a "new" song of worship in the church.

The fourth to sixth centuries provide us with lyrics of songs that became formalized in the liturgy, such as Gloria in excelsis Deo and Te Deum (Laudamus). Te Deum ("we praise you, God") is a hymn commonly attributed to Ambrose and Augustine.[24] The Kyrie Eleison ("Lord, have mercy") is perhaps the most "contemporary" of all sung prayers for all time, because it always has the capacity to express one's current need for God's mercy.[25] Thanks are due to nineteenth-century John Mason Neale (1818–1866), Anglican author, historian, and hymnwriter himself, educated at Trinity College, Cambridge, for his translations into English of many hymns of these early centuries.

A figure who led in an era of creative hymn-writing was Romanos Melodus, or St. Romanos the Melodist, a unique figure in the history of Christian song and worship. I was privileged to be part of the discovery, with my husband, Stan, of the fourth fragment ever identified from this sixth-century Christian hymnwriter, an example that we have written about in more detail.[26] Known as "the most famous liturgical poet of the

---

24. This hymn follows the outline of the Apostles' Creeds and uses some psalms at the end.

25. The words capture the simplest of heart-felt prayers to God: *Kyrie eleison, Christe eleison, Kyrie eleison* ("Lord, have mercy; Christ, have mercy; Lord, have mercy"). We find the heart of this prayer in the publican's prayer in Luke 18:9–14, an honest prayer from a sinner to a holy God. Again, this song comes down with no original music, but because of its inclusion in the Mass, it has prompted many musical settings.

26. See chapter 8 above.

Orthodox Church" and "the greatest poet of the Greek middle ages,"[27] Romanos attributed his gift to a vision of the Virgin Mother of God who gave him a scroll to swallow (compare Ezekiel's and John's similar accounts).[28] Romanos came from Syria, but lived most of his life in Constantinople.[29] His life spanned the rebuilding of the Great Church of Holy Wisdom that we know as Hagia Sophia, a magnificent church that must be seen to fully appreciate. Once an awe-inspiring place of Christian worship, now it is a public museum-site for tourists visiting Turkey. We know little about Romanos's personal life, but we have the legacy of *kontakia*, the chanted sermons that he composed.[30] Romanos brought a form of chanted sermon to its highest development, where brief stanzas were followed by a repeated refrain. It is thought that the verse was chanted from the pulpit and that the choir, and likely the congregation, joined in the refrain.[31] This is a more participatory mode of preaching than many churches would have even today, and certainly a more musical form of preaching. Romanos used this as a form of liturgical storytelling or a form of "narrative preaching," which provided the means for the congregation to be involved in the story.[32]

27. Louth, "Invitation," xv.

28. See Ezek 2:8—3:3 and Rev 10:9–11.

29. He was born in the late fifth century CE and probably died in 565. He lived during the reign of Emperor Justinian (527–65) and through the destruction of Constantinople in the Nika riot of 532.

30. The word *kontakion* is not found until the ninth century. Sixth-century Byzantine poets used words such as υμνος, ερος, ωδη, φαλμος, and δεησις (see n. 1 in Maas and Trypanis, eds., *Sancti Romani Melodi Cantica*, xi).

31. A *kontakion* consisted of a short prelude (some of these by Romanos have become hymns in themselves), called *koukoulion* (or *kontakian*), followed by longer stanzas (or verses), perhaps between 18 and 24, all in identical metre called *ikoi*. Later versions of a *kontakion* may have different preludes for specific occasions. Initial letters of each stanza often formed an acrostic, like "of the humble Romanos," or additional words like "hymn," "poem," or "chant." The music of these was set in one of the eight musical tones of the Orthodox Church, four of which are "authentic" and four of which are "plagal." The last line of the prelude was matched by the last line of the stanza, which was the part likely repeated by singers or even the whole congregation after the solo singer, or *melodus*, had chanted the stanza. Romanos's *kontakia* often used dialogue in order to fully present them, so there may have been more than one chanter present for the stanzas.

32. The actual music of all of these has long been lost. Byzantine scholar Trypanis writes that Romanos, in conjunction with several other sixth-century poets like him "succeeded in combining the solemnity and dignity of the sermon with the delicacy and liveliness of lyric and dramatic poetry and . . . created some of the most vivid and

Part Three: The Past and Present of Music and Worship

From the eighth and ninth centuries, some will recognize the important Latin hymn, VENI CREATOR SPIRITUS.[33] However, many believers know one hymn from this era that captures the hearts of contemporary worshipers, although it was only translated into English in the early part of the twentieth century: "Be Thou My Vision."[34] There are several twenty-first-century "new" versions of this hymn that attest to the value of new expressions of old songs.

Lectionaries with ekphonetic notation were significant by the tenth century. These manuscripts contained the Scripture readings for corporate worship with small markings interspersed within the texts, called ekphonetic notation, that provided clues to how to vocally handle and present the text during worship. For centuries, oral tradition was how most music in the church was handed down, where one generation of musicians taught the next the patterns and techniques of the musical world of chant.[35] The code for these particular markings was only broken in the early part of the twentieth century, while many mysteries about it still remain.[36] What we see in the documents that I have handled and transcribed is a more interpretive handling of the text than one might expect.[37] Although these are formulas, there is something about each

---

yet impersonal masterpieces written in the Greek language ... the kontakion remains the one and only great original achievement of Byzantine literature" (Maas and Trypanis, eds., *Sancti Romani Melodi Cantica*, xiv). Apparently, it "is well attested that in the reign of Anastasios the singing by rival choirs during the Divine Liturgy in the Great Church of different versions of the Thrice Holy Hymn caused a popular riot of such seriousness that it almost resulted in the abdication of the Emperor." This tells us something not only about the nature of theology hanging in the balance at this time, but also something about the nature of Christian formal worship, with competitive simultaneous choirs (see St. Romanos the Melodist, *Kontakia*, xxv).

33. The English is "O Holy Spirit, by whose breath" (translated by John W. Grant [1968]; music: Mechlin plainsong [Mode 8]; harmony by Healey Willan [1995]; tune: VENI CREATOR SPIRITUS).

34. "Be Thou my Vision" (words: Irish [eighth century]; translated by Mary E. Byrne [1905]; versification by Eleanor H. Hull [1912]; music: traditional Irish folk melody; harmony by Jack Schrader [1989]; tune: SLANE).

35. A few ancient cultures still preserve their ancient melodic formulas and melodies, such as an Ashkenazy community in Spain, and these have given scholars windows into this practice.

36. Høeg, *La Notation Ekphonétique*.

37. By including two of these in our publication of New Testament manuscripts in the Austrian National Library, complete with identification of all of the ekphonetic markings, we set a new standard in publication of these documents. Most publications tend to ignore paratextual markings, although they are visible in photographs, for

one that exemplifies a "new" song of worship, a "new" interpretation or presentation of the text, to be handled with the unique voice of each new articulation or vocalization. No matter how perfectly one memorizes and presents something—sung or spoken—there is always interpretation, always a uniqueness to the voice, and always something individual that takes place in the execution and performance of it. This means that even chant, and other forms of liturgical intonation, although meticulously handed down through oral tradition, still had room for interpretation, however slight.

In the twelfth century, a remarkable woman composer, Hildegard von Bingen (1098–1179), was a devout believer from her youngest years and a writer of new songs of worship. Her music displays a deep and mystical spirituality.[38] One piece that captures something of her imagery is *Columba aspexit*. The evocative language of this song depicts the priest going about his regular duties of worship. But there is a holy witness to this scene: a dove representing the Holy Spirit looks from a high window down onto the dim setting in this cathedral scenario. The quintessential recording of this song is moving and beautiful, inviting the heart to soar up to that Spirit that rests above.[39] This song is truly a "new song" of worship.

Also in the twelfth century were increasing numbers of hymn lyrics, such as *Veni, Veni Immanuel*, familiar to many as the great Advent hymn, "O Come, O Come, Immanuel."[40] Some hymns were from Bernard of Clairvaux,[41] who is thought to have penned the lyrics for "Jesus, the Very

---

which, see Porter and Porter, eds., *New Testament Greek Papyri and Parchments*. See discussion in chapter 6 above.

38. See, e.g., Porter, "Hildegard of Bingen."

39. The recording I refer to is the rendering by Emma Kirkby (see *Feather on the Breath of God*).

40. Music: *Processionale*, 15th C.; adapt. Thomas Helmore, 1854, tune: VENI IMMANUEL.

41. Bernard of Clairvaux (1091–1153) was born in Burgundy to nobility, was also a monk, and an illustrious and powerful person. Luther spoke of him with great respect. He was considered something of a saint even while he lived. Political rulers and leaders would seek his advice, although he was never officially more than the Abbot of Clairvaux (see, Houghton, *Christian Hymn-Writers*, 13–14).

Thought of Thee"[42] and "O Sacred Head, Now Wounded."[43] The latter was made new again to a later generation when Bach added his harmonization, which is how it is usually heard today. A new hymn from the thirteenth century that is still sung by Christian worshipers today comes from St. Francis of Assisi, "All Creatures of our God and King."[44] This is the hymn that most closely aligns with the words of P.Oxy. XV 1786, the earliest-known Christian hymn with musical notation (noted above).

In the sixteenth century in Europe, much of what had become familiar in the church was brought into question. Once that door was opened, it would never be completely shut again. What that means is that someone like Martin Luther had something to do with why we have drums and electric guitars in the church today. Suddenly musicians, employed by monarchs or wealthy patrons to write music for the church, were no longer setting the Latin Mass. In England, for example, composers were setting the service in English language for the first time. Psalmody arose on the continent, which was an attempt to transform the psalms into simple rhymes and simple melodies for congregations to sing, a practice that also made its way to England and elsewhere.[45]

Meanwhile, William Byrd brought radically interpretive moves to interpreting the Mass in his musical settings and writing of other new songs of worship. Although Byrd worked for Queen Elizabeth, the head of the Church of England, he used his own musical genius and a great deal of courage and blatant disregard for politics to approach the Latin Mass with three new settings for the reclusive Catholic community that explored levels of musical and linguistic interpretation that were unprecedented. Worshiping as a Catholic was strictly illegal at the time, and his heartfelt settings of the Mass and other newly expressive songs of worship are some of his most monumental works, and illustrative of new

---

42. "Jesus, the Very Thought of Thee" (Latin; ca. 1150; attributed to Bernard of Clairvaux [without proof]; translator: Edward Caswall [1849]; music: John B. Dykes [1866]).

43. "Herzlich tut mich" (from Latin *Salve Caput Cruentatum*; medieval; Latin poem attributed to Bernard of Clairvaux [but also to Arnulf von Loewen (1200–1251)]; German translator: Paul Gerhardt [1656]; English translator: James W. Alexander [1830]; music: Hans L. Hassler [1601]; adaptation and harmony: Johann S. Bach [1729]).

44. Words: Francis of Assisi, 1225; trans. William H. Draper, c. 1910; Music: *Auserlesen Catholische Geistliche Kirchengësange*, Cologne, 1623; adapt. / harm. Ralph Vaughan Williams, 1906, tune: LASST UNS ERFREUEN.

45. See, e.g., Quitslund and Temperley, *Whole Book of Psalms.*

songs of worship.[46] Also writing in the sixteenth century was Palestrina in Italy,[47] considered the benchmark of polyphony-writing. Philosopher Karl Popper wrote that he considered sixteenth-century polyphony the great accomplishment in the Western world,[48] certainly an era of magnificent new songs of worship.

The upheaval of the sixteenth century in Europe provided an impetus for new developments in contemporary sacred music in the congregational hymn. The hymn was all about congregational participation and expression. If you worship for some length of time in a formal liturgical church that relies primarily on professional choirs and soloists, you notice the lack of congregational involvement in worship through hymn-singing. This may give a glimpse into how unusual it must have been for congregations to be singing hymns in corporate worship. Beautiful historic buildings of worship are the perfect setting for great choirs to present musical renditions of praise, as written by some of the greatest composers. However, choral masterpieces do not invite the local parishioner to join in. Should a lay worshiper in the pew be tempted to do so, they would meet with active disapproval. The result is that congregations come to expect the choir and soloists to perform the music, while they remain mute. When the congregation is invited to sing a single hymn in this context, it becomes evident that the people either are not comfortable with singing in public or simply do not know how. Congregational song has lost out in these professional environments. At one time, the choral settings were "new songs" of worship to God, while simpler hymns were also "new songs" of worship. Pieces that remain in the repertoire much later often indicate that the piece was new and relevant in its day and retain some of their initial vitality. So, we begin to see the hymn as we know it today: four to six lines forming rhyming stanzas or verses, perhaps followed by a refrain or chorus.

In the seventeenth century, there were two broadening trajectories, one of formal classically trained composers writing works that required professional musicians to perform them, and the other of simple creations for the average congregational singer. The hymns were heartfelt, and often the lyrics and the music were written in the same era, which speaks of a more collaborative approach to hymn-writing. In the

---

46. See discussion in chapter 15 above.

47. See, e.g., his *Missa Papae Marcelli*. The Spanish composer Victoria (ca. 1548–1611) was remarkable for his heart-felt *Tenebrae Responsories*.

48. Popper, *Unended Quest*, 56.

eighteenth century, some of the world's most renowned and prolific composers were at work. George Frideric Handel (1685–1759) is famous for his Messiah, truly a "new song" of worship that takes Scripture directly from his translation and re-interprets it for the listeners, through instrumentation, melodies, solo arias and recitatives, and choral responses to his passionate presentation of Scripture. Handel had already developed a style of setting biblical scenarios, perhaps not always with altruistic motives, but nonetheless, setting biblical stories in a manner that brought people to see them—a not insignificant accomplishment. The fact that he devised some of these in response to London's rule that you could not perform opera during the season of Lent suggests that he was partly devious, partly resourceful, and partly brilliant to come up with the plan. The otherwise silent halls of London during Lent were opened to present biblical stories to the people, without the distraction of costumes and sets. For many still today, his Messiah is a work of excellent soul-lifting and inspiring songs of worship to the Lord.

In Johann Sebastian Bach (1685–1750) we see a master composer at work, often weaving old and new together for the church's contemporary and meaningful worship. Although one of his greatest works, the Mass in B Minor, was a setting for the Latin Mass, which does not as obviously fit within the bounds of his own Lutheran church traditions (although the formal Latin Mass was still used on occasion in Lutheran churches of the time), most of his church worship music is in the language of the people, German. Bach wove together the music of the professional musician with the capability of the local parishioner for congregational worship. He took music of previous songwriters and hymn-writers, and recast them for his own context,[49] giving them newness and freshness. He used songs that the congregation would know and gave them newly harmonized settings to sing. He placed these congregational songs or chorales within the Lutheran liturgy in the form of a cantata, where the congregation was invited to participate with the choir and orchestra. Part of the genius of Bach was to reinvent the old as new and vibrant. In many cases, this was through his new musical settings of lyrics that captured heart-felt expression of response to God, much of which is still unparalleled in its intensity and imagery.

---

49. Bach's harmonizations for earlier songs are often how we know them today. One example is the familiar setting of Martin Luther's "A Mighty Fortress Is Our God," changed from its original lively rhythms to an isometric and more singable setting and harmonized by Bach (see note to hymn #48 in "Hymns for Worship").

NEW SONGS IN BIBLICAL AND CHRISTIAN HISTORY

Increasing numbers of hymn-writers and their hymns emerged in the eighteenth century. Isaac Watts (1674–1748) described what he saw as the deplorable condition of psalmody in the seventeenth century as one full of "dull indifference," and how a "negligent and thoughtless air... sits upon their faces." These worshipers seemed to desire that no innovation would disturb this unhappy state of affairs. Watts's hymns became an "assault on the unreasoning immobility of those who presented a stone wall of opposition to any change in the old psalmody."[50]

Those who think that the issue of contemporary worship music is a modern-day phenomenon are greatly mistaken. Watts faced the issue of how to teach new songs to the people, many who would have been illiterate. These new songs had to be presented in a way that they could be taught and sung back by the congregation, line by line. Watts tried to make his hymns faithful to Scripture. He chose one main theme, rather than trying to tell the whole gospel story in a single hymn. He began with a bold opening line and progressed to a final climax. He believed that a hymn should be short. His reputation as the founder of English hymnody is not without reason. Although there had been many hymn-writers before him, his main achievement seems to have been that he was the first to convince the church to accept this "new" form of worship song, the "hymn," in its worship. The exclusive use of metrical psalmody was now opened up, however unwillingly, for the "contemporary worship song." In this case, that new song was "the hymn."

Charles Wesley (1708–1788) and his older brother John Wesley (1703–1791) both had moving encounters with Christ. They were tireless in their efforts to influence the people in London for Christ. John was well-known for translating hymns for use in evangelization and spiritual instruction. Charles was the brother that could supply seemingly endless numbers of new hymns. Many expressed the sense of revival that was filling the air. Prior to this, there was little hymn-singing in the Anglican church, because metrical psalms were still being enforced in many congregations. While a few Dissenting congregations may have started to include the hymns of Watts, it was Charles Wesley's hymns that began to make their way into the singing of Methodists, Anglicans, and Dissenters alike. Although classically trained, Charles chose plain speech for his hymns, but he used words and imagery that were rich in doctrine and theology. He chose mostly to write about the great objective truths of

---

50. Houghton, *Christian Hymn-Writers*, 54.

Part Three: The Past and Present of Music and Worship

God—Father, Son, and Holy Spirit—and how faith impacted these doctrines in his own life and the lives of others.[51] Meanwhile, another single hymn from the eighteenth century is John Newton's "Amazing Grace" (1779). This song voices Newton's contemporary worship experience and response to God, and it still rings true for many today. In some cases, this is the one song that a person from outside the church today recognizes as a Christian song of worship.

In the nineteenth and twentieth centuries, "new" songs or "hymns" increased almost exponentially. A hymn like "When Peace Like a River (It Is Well)," with its well-known story of grief and loss, found a place in corporate worship,[52] while African American spirituals brought a freshness and urgency to congregational singing.

Elsewhere, I tell the story of a black Canadian woman whose name was Harriett ("Hattie") Rhue Hatchett (1863–1958). Her father reached safety in southern Ontario by means of the Underground Railway. As a hymn-writer, Hattie wrote both lyrics and music. Even today, not all hymn-writers contribute both lyrics and music. Many of her songs were lost in fires, but she did publish several of them. Her first, "The Sacred Spot," was apparently chosen as a marching hymn for Canadian troops. I wonder whether Canadians realized that it was a black Baptist woman who called them to remember not just other soldiers and the nurses who gave their lives, but also called their attention back to a holy and kind Father who, she contended, would guard each grave and would ultimately welcome his people into a place where his will is done, and where there is peace, love, and unity?[53]

In the twentieth century,[54] some of the "new" songs/hymns or "contemporary worship songs" were powerful expressions of worship for

---

51. Houghton, *Christian Hymn-Writers*, 96.

52. Words: Horatio G. Spafford, 1873; Music: Philip P. Bliss, 1876.

53. See Porter, "Quartet," 102.

54. New songs of worship music in the twentieth century surely must also include the world of classical composition, whether they are a part of congregational singing or not. Some of these were profound creations that were deeply spiritual and thoughtfully challenging. Traditional liturgical pieces were set in new ways, such as Igor Stravinsky's (1882–1971) *Mass* and *Pater Noster* (The "Lord's Prayer") and Sergei Rachmaninov's (1873–1943) *Vespers* for the Russian Orthodox Church. John Tavener's (1944–2013) "Icons of Light" and "We Shall See Him as He Is" bring the Byzantine era together with the contemporary Greek Orthodox Church. Gustav Faure's (1845–1924) *Requiem* is a work of beautiful and spiritual expression. Lili Boulanger (1893–1918) wrote with an unparalleled depth of spiritual cry and anguish, yet unwavering trust. She was dead

people who may be our parents or grandparents. For instance, the hymn "How Great Thou Art" was new when those who are elderly seniors now were young. Just because it was in hymnbooks early on did not mean that it was ancient. In fact, these same seniors can remember when the song was first introduced, and how it allowed them to sing praise to God with heartfelt expression that was previously unknown to them (as my own mother described it to me). In my own work with congregations and individual worshipers, I have learned that for many older believers, it is the songs that were being sung at the time of their conversion or at the point of their most intense spiritual awareness and sensitivity, often from their youth or early adult years, that remain for them the most important songs of worship—no matter what they sound like now. So, it isn't always that older people simply like "old" better than "new," but it is that those songs somehow captured the "contemporary" essence of their most moving and dynamic times or perceptions of God in worship, the "newness" of those spiritual experiences. With those songs still come the memories of freshness in their spiritual lives. This, however, can make a person deaf to the quality or content in a new song of worship. For example, in one church where I led a communion service, we sang several moving and powerful songs about the cross and the blood of Jesus. An elderly woman came up to me afterward to vociferously complain that we "never sings songs about the cross and about the blood anymore." We had, in fact, sung several in that very service, but I think that what she meant was that we had not sung the song that captured her own experience of a "new" song of worship. For her, that song was "The Old Rugged Cross." And, no, we had not sung it in that service.

THE CONTEMPORARY WORSHIP SONG NOW

In looking back on the twentieth century, it seems that when it came to worship music in the church, all hell broke loose. Or, perhaps, in retrospect, it was all heaven that broke loose. Constraints that had been firmly in place were shifting. People accustomed to patterns of musical worship in their own churches were suddenly floundering, and they often

---

by her mid 20s but wrote profound settings of psalms (*Du fond de l'abime, Psalume 24, Psaume 129*). Francis Poulenc's (1899–1963) "Four Motets for a Time of Penitence" (*Quatre motets pour un temps du penitence*) is a thought-provoking work. These provide different kinds of new songs of worship, not designed for congregational singing, but certainly designed to prompt members of worshiping congregations to think deeply and experience richly from other realms of worship music.

responded with anger, indignation, even rage. This is a familiar response in times of crisis when all that seems to be right and good—or at least familiar—is undermined. Groups like Love Song started to shake up the music of the church.[55] Songs about a deep desire for deeper Christian spirituality challenged complacency in worship.

Andrae Crouch was a highly gifted songwriter and powerful performer who could fill a concert hall with thousands of people, and essentially, through his music, preach and present an extended altar call. His songs were outside the norm of Christian music found in the hymnbooks of the time. Ironically, one or more of his songs is found in almost every hymnbook created in recent years. His song "My Tribute" is the most-recorded Christian song ever written. His passion for the gospel and for expounding Christian truth and calling people to commitment was unique, and he did this through "new" songs of worship. Keith Green, too, was a passionate songwriter and performer, calling the church to wake up. His message was a call to obedience, faithfulness, and Christian commitment. One short song of his has practically become a universal classic, "Create in Me a Clean Heart."

Since those early days of breaking out of traditional hymn-singing and into something that called for the instrumentation and rhythm sections of the bands of local culture, there has been an ongoing struggle to find where all these different expressions of worship to God really belong. There has been much in the so-called "Christian" music and worship song writing industry that has been driven by commercialism and ego. Yet, there are still those who, with great integrity and deep commitment to Christ, challenge us all through their new songs. These songs express in new ways for a new generation the truths that all Christians need to encounter and be challenged with: namely, a call to worship God wholeheartedly, a call to deep commitment, to live lives of faith and service to Christ, a call to live in the empowerment of the ever-new breath of the Holy Spirit.

Note that at no point am I saying that every contemporary worship song is good, or inspired, or worth using or keeping—not in this generation, and not in any generation. Many contemporary worship songs are ephemeral, some are poorly written, and many will not stand the test of time. This has always been true. Of the thousands of hymns written by the most well-known hymn-writers over the last few centuries, in an

---

55. See Powell, *Encyclopedia of Contemporary Christian Music*, for comprehensive coverage of the century in this regard.

average hymnbook (if you remember the hymnbook), there may be between 400 to 700. Of those, any given congregation may actually know or sing only a small fraction of these, and many of them could arguably have been left out.

Meanwhile, the level of musicianship in churches seems to have suffered. Members of church choirs usually could read music and sing notated parts. Some congregations were known for their four-part hymn-singing, whether they had printed music or not. These levels of musicianship have been lost in many congregations. In many churches today, members of worship teams do not read music or sing harmony, and what they learn, they learn from a recording. At the same time, the congregation isn't waiting for the choir to perform for them—congregations must do the singing themselves.

Over the years that I have led worship services, I have introduced many new songs. Some were completely new, some were new ones that I wrote myself, some were new to our community, some were old but placed in new settings, some were combined in new ways with other songs or interwoven with Scripture. Still others were just so old that they seemed new by virtue of their unfamiliarity. A "new" song can be new on a range of different planes, and being new just for the sake of being new is not quite the same as "singing a new song to the Lord."

My brief summary of biblical examples and the unfolding of Christian history has shown that there has always been a place or a need for a new song of worship. The Holy Spirit can move through things that are ancient and established, breathing freshness into these forms. But the Holy Spirit surely is not constrained to using only songs of worship that were penned hundreds of years ago. If God's compassionate love is something that we can experience new every morning, we should be able to write an occasional new song about that.

The writers of new songs of worship from the late twentieth and early twenty-first century are familiar names to many, such as Twila Paris, Andrae Crouch, Keith Green, Stuart Townend, Matt Redman, Tim Hughes, Chris Tomlin, Keith Getty, and so on. And, as noted in my original title, there was an outpouring of new songs of worship from Hillsong and its sub-groups in Australia, first noticed through the songs of Darlene Zschech and Ruben Morgan, and Joel Houston and Brooke Fraser Ligertwood, as well as from other song-writing communities and individuals. Some of their contributions are superb, while others will disappear fast. This is always part of the culling that reveals the gems of musical worship that can speak in new ways even on repetition.

CONCLUSION

From the very first mention of music and song in the Old Testament to this moment today we have always needed expressions of worship through "new songs." Each song that we have recorded in some form, we did so because it was new and relevant to somebody at the time. Some of these songs have become fresh and meaningful to later generations as well.

Sometimes the Psalms and other passages in the biblical text have been the source of our new songs. In the New Testament, Jesus himself provided the key that unlocked the notion that worship was about a radical combination of truth and the Spirit, steadfast and yet ever-new. Perhaps these two notions reveal the mysterious balance between what is unchanging and what is always moving like the wind, or between what is solid and tangible with what is intangible and untouchable. We recognize that God and his Word are steadfast, consistent, unchanging. But through the Spirit we see limitless potential for new insights that are as fresh as the dew in the morning.

Psalms, hymns, and songs from the Spirit that have carried our worship to God through the centuries have always included fresh expressions of this worship. Sometimes songwriters explored God's truth or attributes or deeds in new ways, while others tried to describe new experiences of the Spirit, or levels of commitment to Christ. Each of these involved new uses of language and imagery, or new modes of melody, harmony, rhythm, instrumentation, or all of these. Each generation has had its contributions to the "new song" of worship, although sometimes these have been lost or have become impenetrable or irrelevant in the passing of time. In the future, someone else will pen a new song of worship that may be more beautiful or expressive than those we have known before, and it will find a place in the broad repertory of Christian worship songs.

If we thought that "contemporary worship music" was created in the twentieth century and carried into the twenty-first, clearly this was not the case. Nor was it created in the century before that, or the one before that. I believe that the "contemporary worship song" was dreamed up by God himself. It was called for and modeled throughout the Old Testament, not only in the Psalms, but certainly highlighted there. It was communicated by Jesus to a thirsty woman at a well, who would have been glad to receive the magic water that he seemed to promise, but instead became the bearer of something much better. It permeated worship in the Early Church, though the documents of its musical history are scarce, and carried on right through to the most recent song of worship you sang in church (or via an online gathering) this last week. It may have been part of the worship song that you heard for the first time last week, or that you wrote yourself the other day.

If we think that this will all change when we reach heaven, and we can finally just sit back and listen to all our old favourites—like stepping into a restaurant that plays all the songs we knew in our teens—I don't think it's going to happen. I think the best of the best will be there—and probably sounding a lot better than it does here. But there will be a "new song," one that somehow combines all our voices together into a sound and song that echoes the roar of rushing waters and a loud peal of thunder and harpists playing their harps. It may remind us of the music of songwriters we have not yet met, like Jubal and David and John, or like Hildegard and Johann, or others who are writing songs of worship today. This song of worship will be everlastingly new, combining all our voices and languages and melodies and harmonies and rhythms and instruments, to sing a song worthy of the God who created us, sustained us, and has welcomed us into his presence. We will sing to the Lord a new song that will no longer go out of date or become unfashionable, because there, contemporary and new will be words that are always in the present.

REFERENCE AND FURTHER READING

Battistella, Edwin L. *The Logic of Markedness*. New York: Oxford University Press, 1996.

———. *Markedness: The Evaluative Superstructure of Language*. New York: State University of New York Press, 1990.

Braun, Joachim. *Music in Ancient Israel/Palestine: Archaeological, Written, and Comparative Sources*. Translated by Douglas W. Stott. Grand Rapids: Eerdmans, 2002.

Brown, Sally A., and Patrick D. Miller, eds. *Lament: Reclaiming Practices in Pulpit, Pew, and Public Square*. Louisville: Westminster John Knox, 2005.

Cosgrove, Charles. H. *An Ancient Christian Hymn with Musical Notation: Papyrus Oxyrhynchus 1786. Text and Commentary*. Studien und Texte zu Antike und Christentum 65. Tübingen: Mohr Siebeck, 2011.

Draffkorn Kilmer, Anne. "The Cult Song with Music from Ancient Ugarit: Another Interpretation." *Revue d'Assyriologie et d'archéologie orientale* 68 (1974) 69–82.

A Feather on the Breath of God: Sequences and Hymns by Abbess Hildegard of Bingen (†1179). Performed by Gothic Voices with Emma Kirkby. Directed by Christopher Page. CD Recording. London: Hyperion, 1984.

Part Three: The Past and Present of Music and Worship

Høeg, Carsten. *La Notation Ekphonétique*. Monumenta Musicae Byzantinae Subsidia 1.2. Copenhagen: Levin and Munksgaard, 1935.

Houghton, Elsie. *Christian Hymn-Writers*. Wales: Evangelical Press of Wales, 1982.

Hunt, Arthur S., and H. Stuart Jones. "1786. Christian Hymn with Musical Notation." In *The Oxyrhynchus Papyri XV*, edited by Bernard P. Grenfell and Arthur S. Hunt, 21–25. Egypt Exploration Society Graeco-Roman Memoirs. London: Egypt Exploration Fund, 1922.

"Hymns for Worship." Calvin Institute of Christian Worship and Faith Alive Christian Resources (2010). Online: https://www.faithaliveresources.org/Content/Site135/FilesSamples/49583pdf_00000007260.pdf.

Louth, Andrew. "An Invitation to the Christian Mystery." In St. Romanos the Melodist, *Kontakia: On the Life of Christ*. Translated by Archimandrite Ephrem Lash, xv–xxii. London: HarperCollins, 1998.

Maas, Paul, and Constantine A. Trypanis, eds. *Sancti Romani Melodi Cantica: Cantica Genuina*. 1963. Reprint, Oxford: Clarendon, 1997.

McKinnon, James W. "On the Question of Psalmody in the Ancient Synagogue." *Early Music History* 6 (1986) 159–91.

O'Connor, Michael. "The Singing of Jesus." In *Resonant Witness: Conversations between Music and Theology*, edited by Jeremy S. Begbie and Steven R. Guthrie, 434–53. Grand Rapids: Eerdmans, 2011.

Pöhlmann, Egert, and Martin L. West, eds. *Documents of Ancient Greek Music: The Extant Melodies and Fragments Edited and Transcribed with Commentary*. Oxford: Clarendon, 2001.

Popper, Karl. *Unended Quest: An Intellectual Autobiography*. London: Fontana, 1976. First published as "Autobiography of K. Popper." In *The Philosophy of Karl Popper*. The Library of Living Philosophers 14, edited by Paul Arthur Schilpp. Chicago: Open Court, 1974.

Porter, Stanley E., and Wendy J. Porter, eds. *New Testament Greek Papyri and Parchments: New Editions*. Mitteilungen aus der Papyrussammlung der Österreichischen Nationalbibliothek (Papyrus Erzherzog Rainer) Neue Serie XXIX, XXX. Folge (MPER XXIX, XXX). Berlin: de Gruyter, 2008.

Porter, Wendy J. *Early English Composers and the Credo: Emphasis as Interpretation in Sixteenth-Century Music*. Routledge Research in Music Series. London: Routledge, 2022.

———. "Hildegard of Bingen, the Breath of God, and a Musical Prophetic Voice." In *The Arts and the Bible*, edited by Stanley E. Porter and Wendy J. Porter, 62–88. McMaster New Testament Studies 10. Eugene, OR: Pickwick, 2024.

———. "A Quartet and an Anonymous Choir: The Remarkable Lives and Ministries of Four Black Baptist Women in Late Nineteenth-Century Ontario." In *Canadian Baptist Women*, edited by Sharon M. Bowler, 89–112. McMaster General Studies Series 8. Eugene, OR: Pickwick, 2016.

Powell, Mark Allan. *Encyclopedia of Contemporary Christian Music*. Peabody, MA: Hendrickson, 2002.

Quitslund, Beth, and Nicholas Temperley. *The Whole Book of Psalms: Collected into English Metre by Thomas Sternhold, John Hopkins, and Others. A Critical Edition of the Texts and Tunes*. 2 vols. Renaissance English Text Society. Temple, AZ: Arizona Center for Medieval & Renaissance Studies, 2018.

Sachs, Curt. *The History of Musical Instruments*. New York: Norton, 1940. Reprint, London: J. M. Dent and Sons, 1942.

Smith, John A. "The Ancient Synagogue, the Early Church and Singing." *Music & Letters* 65 (1984) 1–16.

St. Romanos the Melodist. *Kontakia: On the Life of Christ*. Translated by Archimandrite Ephrem Lash. London: HarperCollins, 1998.

Waltke, Bruce K., James M. Houston, and Erika Moore. *The Psalms as Christian Lament: A Historical Commentary*. Grand Rapids: Eerdmans, 2014.

Wellesz, Egon. *A History of Byzantine Music and Hymnography*. 2nd ed. Oxford: Clarendon, 1998 [1961].

West, Martin L. *Ancient Greek Music*. Oxford: Clarendon, 1992.

Witvliet, John D. *Worship Seeking Understanding: Windows into Christian Practice*. Grand Rapids: Baker Academic, 2003.

Wolterstorff, Nicholas. *Lament for a Son*. Grand Rapids Eerdmans, 1987

17

Theological Reflections on the History of Christian Worship

INTRODUCTION

How often do we as Christians, on our two-thousand-year journey of Christian worship so far, stop to reflect theologically on where we are, how we got here, and where we are going? An honest look at our history suggests that we have not always made the best choices in the past. An honest look at our present should prevent us from developing what C. S. Lewis calls "chronological snobbery."[1] The practice of Christian worship—then and now—is humbling testimony to the fact that we rarely get it all right.

Not long before the conference at which this chapter was first presented, I returned from a journey to the *Holy Land*, a journey that took us to modern-day Israel and to places where we could see, imagine, and experience the land of the Old and New Testaments, as other Christians have done throughout the centuries. We saw the land. We walked in places where Abraham and Isaac and Moses and Joshua and David walked. We

---

1. Lewis (*Surprised by Joy*, 167) writes, "Barfield . . . made short work of what I have called my 'chronological snobbery,' the uncritical acceptance of the intellectual climate common to our own age and the assumption that whatever has gone out of date is on that account discredited. You must find out why it went out of date. Was it ever refuted (and if so by whom, where, and how conclusively) or did it merely die away as fashions do? If the latter, this tells us nothing about its truth or falsehood. From seeing this, one passes to the realization that our own age is also 'a period,' and certainly has, like all periods, its own characteristic illusions. They are likeliest to lurk in those wide-spread assumptions which are so ingrained in the age that no one dares to attack or feels it necessary to defend them."

walked in places where Jesus walked with his disciples, and saw hills and valleys, lakes and a river that formed the backdrop to his life and ministry on earth. Sometimes we could barely peer through the layers of civilization—and of ecclesial cultures—to catch an ephemeral glimpse of Jesus' world. In some places, we could vaguely "get back" to that original site and catch a feeling of stepping into the history of two-thousand years ago, as on the Sea of Galilee, or of several thousands of years ago, as on Tel Dan or Tel Hazor, or seeing Mount Hermon off in the distance. Sometimes we sensed that "wrinkle in time," to quote Madeleine L'Engle's award-winning novel and trilology, transported from a current era into another one. And sometimes we felt despair over those who had worked so hard to preserve something holy, since, in the end, any sense of holiness was lost.

All of us on the journey rode on the same bus, had the same guide, and saw the same sites and sights, but each had a slightly different agenda; one thing captured one person's interest while others were exploring elsewhere. So, it is with this historical journey of theological reflection and Christian worship. Christian worshipers of God are part of the same journey, but not always traveling exactly together or with the same interests or observations.

I think of a childhood story that still prompts my own theological reflection. It was a story in a church youth magazine. I probably read it in church (during my father's sermon?), but I cannot say for sure. It went something like this: A group of young boys were playing on a sandy beach. One of them challenged the rest to see who could walk the straightest line in the sand, setting the destination at a big rock some distance down the beach. This did not seem like an intimidating challenge, and each confidently set out to win this easy competition. When they had all reached the big rock, they eagerly looked back to check on their footprints and were stunned to see that only one set of prints was straight. The rest seemed to be all over the place. How could this be? They asked the boy who had walked a straight path how he did it. He replied that he just kept his eyes on the big rock, he did not look down at his feet.

So, I decided to try my own variation on this challenge. We lived in a very small village in the Canadian province of Alberta, and it was late fall. We had just had our first snow, and no one had yet driven or even walked on the snow-covered road. The streetlights were on, and I set out to determine whether I could walk straight or not. I headed towards the distant streetlight. For the first half of the distance, I kept my eyes on the road, trying to walk as straight as I could by carefully watching my feet.

Then, at one point, I changed tactics, looked up at the streetlight and just kept my eyes on it, without looking down at my feet at all. I reached the streetlight, looked back, and was astounded at the difference. The first half of my footprint path formed a line that was a complete mess, though I had been careful to walk as straight as I possibly could. The second portion of my footprint path was absolutely straight. Amazing. This experiment has always captured my theological imagination of what it means to follow Christ. My own efforts at walking a straight line are impossible unless I am focused on the One I am following. But even on a purely pragmatic level, it reminds me that walking a straight path requires a clearly focused destination point.

If we could view from above this worship journey of ours since the time of Christ, I think it would look a lot more like the Israelites wandering in the wilderness for forty years than we would like to admit, and a lot more like my crooked footprints when I was trying to do my best.

Admittedly, it is only as we look back behind us that we can see the trajectories that have led from an initial point of departure to the ultimate goal of a journey or to some other point, whether that journey is one of physical travel or intellectual pursuit or seeking after the heart of God. While we are on the journey, it can be difficult to get our bearings, to know exactly where we are going and how we are doing. In the journey of Christian worship, the quality of our theological reflection will be what determines where, how, and whom we worship. As Harold Best writes, "nobody does not worship," that is, everyone "is bowing down and serving something or someone—an artifact, a person, an institution, an idea, a spirit, or God through Christ."[2] If we are just watching our feet, it is easy to lose our bearings, get off track, double back without realizing it, or get mired in a muddy stretch.

Karen Westerfield Tucker observes,

> A survey of the history of Christian liturgy shows that movements to revitalize worship are typically accompanied by an examination—and sometimes a retrieval—of what is deemed exemplary and vital from previous periods. Such an approach was taken, for example, in the mid-twentieth century by theologians and liturgical scholars who advocated for a 're-turn to the sources' (*retour aux sources*) or what they termed *ressourcement*.[3]

---

2. Best, *Unceasing Worship*, 17.
3. Westerfield Tucker, "Wesley's Emphases on Worship," 227.

Here we see some of the roots of what became known as an "ancient-future" worship paradigm.

It is important to work with the biblical text, and the insights that biblical scholars can bring, in order to "get our bearings," to look back at specific points in the Old and New Testaments that depict worship or instruct us about worship then. And then it is critical that we consider what implications these texts, stories, and instructions have for us today, and to explore how we have or have not implemented those insights, or how our perspectives have changed on them. In light of this, I invite you to travel with me through numerous "wrinkles in time," to view from a bird's-eye perspective the historical journey of theological reflection and Christian worship that has brought us to where we are today. Perhaps we will also learn something about what is needed for faithful and meaningful worship tomorrow.[4]

To facilitate our reflection, I will periodically draw on some of the resources or voices of theological reflection. Sometimes the voice will be that of Scripture, sometimes specific voices from Christian history, sometimes the voice of someone from the contemporary culture or the voice of personal experience, sometimes it will be the voice of logical evaluation, and sometimes we may recognize the voice of wisdom and discernment, the voice of the Holy Spirit. Any one of these voices can prompt us to greater insights.

For instance, it is easy to argue that we should just "go back to Scripture," but our journey will show us many missteps made by those who thought they were doing just that. There is still debate about how key passages translate into present practices of Christian worship. Some would argue that Christian history is all we need, but we are reminded that many mistakes have been made, and so we approach our historical predecessors as wise, but not infallible, teachers. Sometimes the wisdom

---

4. Although admittedly presumptuous, I take as license to present such an audacious survey the comments by scholar and historian F. Donald Logan, Professor Emeritus of History at Emmanuel College, Boston, in his *History* (note that Logan's "Middle Ages" are more comprehensive in scope than most). Logan notes in his preface that writing a book that is so broad is not something he would earlier have done, but in later years, he found it compelling to engage in the task, in the hope that it would inspire readers to investigate those areas within it that capture their interest. I offer this chapter in that same spirit, in the hope that it will inspire the reader to pick up on one, several, or even many of the various areas that are of personal interest and pursue them in their own explorations. Each one could be rewarding, worthwhile, even life changing.

we gain from their teaching is to avoid what they did. We need to hear the voice of the contemporary culture and what it is telling us about worship, then or now, and how to respond appropriately. We need the voices of real personal experience then and the voices of real experience now. When we no longer personally engage in worship, we know we have lost something essential. We need the voice of reason and logic that helps us to weigh and evaluate the other voices and to make good decisions to address problems or deal with issues. Finally, we need the voice of wisdom and discernment, that of the Holy Spirit, especially audible when we have an attitude of prayer that permeates all of our theological reflection.

So, let us step into our journey, recognizing that believers throughout the centuries have already been engaged in theological reflection, regardless of what they called it. Sometimes Scripture alone is the dominant voice, sometimes church tradition speaks out loudly, sometimes culture wins—or loses—the day, sometimes personal experience is influential, sometimes good logical evaluation is pursued or ignored, and sometimes we see the Holy Spirit move in an intangible way that cannot be denied.

Throughout this journey, I will use the historic present tense in an attempt to invite us into each century as though we are really entering into it and looking around, not just looking back from our historical perspective. Regularly throughout this narrative I will interject a question or thought to prompt our own theological reflection on something about our own worship today. The possibilities of theological reflection on each of these eras and episodes and the worshipers themselves could provide a lifetime of fruitful discussion and learning. I trust that just an occasional prompting will be sufficient to spark the reader's own ongoing theological reflection.[5]

JOURNEY OF WORSHIP PART 1: THE FIRST FIVE CENTURIES AFTER CHRIST

The first five centuries of the Christian era were formative for subsequent Christian worship practice and bear diligent scrutiny, even if the sources are at times limited.

---

5. The reader is encouraged to begin a journal of theological reflection on Christian worship, a place to note historical events that you would like to explore more fully, sites that you would like to visit, artifacts that you would like to see, questions and thoughts about any of them, and insights you gain (for brief answers to questions about terminology to do with liturgy and worship, see Bradshaw, ed., *New Westminster Dictionary*).

First Century

In order to begin at the beginning of Christianity, we have to "begin before the beginning." This is not referring to the long history of worship of God in the Old Testament, although that would also be an appropriate starting point for this journey. No, this refers to the birth of Christ, which happens "before Christ," so to speak, at least using the system by which we may refer to dates (BC ["before Christ"] and AD [*Anno Domini*, "in the year of our Lord"]). Jesus is born *before* the so-called "year of our Lord," that is A.D."[6] when our new era begins.

Imagine the conversations that are going on in homes, in synagogues, on street corners, and in the markets in these early days. Initially they are about an unusual birth. Later they are about this teacher, Jesus, and the events of his life. And then the circumstances of his death hit the marketplace conversations. Finally, there is the silly news that he has been seen alive, "risen from the dead," they say. Right. But friends and acquaintances report that they have actually seen him after his death. Imagine the mystified dialogues, the heated arguments, and the silent musings of theological reflection and theological wrestling as Jesus' friends, followers, neighbours, or enemies try to sort out what has just taken place. And where do the friends and followers go now? The church, set up by Jesus during his time on earth, is "emerging." There is no such thing as the New Testament Scriptures yet. But there is a lot to think about, a lot to consider, a lot to weigh.

There aren't that many believers at the time; in fact, few enough that it is a wonder that they create anything of that early church. Rabbi Gamaliel instructs the Sanhedrin, who are fearful of this upstart group, on how they should view them: "Leave these men alone!" (although, in fact, there are a significant number of women in that original group). "Let them go! For if their purpose or activity is of human origin, it will fail. But if it is from God, you will not be able to stop these men; you will only find yourselves fighting against God" (Acts 5:38-39, NIV). And, yes, the

6. Logan (*History*, 3) writes, "Enigmatic as it may sound, Christ was born Before Christ. When in the sixth century Dionysius Ixiguus used the birth of Christ to date the beginning of the Christian era, he mistakenly believed that Christ was born in the Roman year 754 *ab urbe condita* ('from the founding of the city'), and that year is called the first year of the Christian era: AD 1. In fact, King Herod, during whose reign Christ was born, died in the Roman year 750, and the date given by modern scholars for Christ's birth generally falls between 8 and 4 BC. The date of Christ's death—and, indeed, his age at the time of his death—are not known for certain, but he was probably executed in the year AD 30."

Part Three: The Past and Present of Music and Worship

church in the first century grows despite persecution, not least because it is willing to include all social classes, including slaves.[7]

The records of early Christian worship are scanty at best.[8] Musicologists, liturgists, and archaeologists of this period all agree. The tiny bits of early Christian worship that we know about include the earliest simple creedal statements possibly connected with the act of baptism,[9] reference to psalms, hymns, and spiritual songs that are used by the earliest Christians in the New Testament,[10] and words spoken by Jesus when the believers share in the Lord's Supper together, which Paul cites in 1 Cor 11:24–25. Paul's use of poetic passages—thought by many scholars to be quotations, but it is surely probable, even likely, that he writes them himself—must be at the heart of many of the earliest worship gatherings of the new believers.[11]

Imagine how tender their hearts are in these earliest days, receptive and responsive to Christ's message, and to his call on their lives to worship him with all their heart and soul and mind and strength and to minister to one another with Christ-like love. It is easy to imagine that it is all quite wonderful.

But these believers, first called Christians at the city of Antioch (Acts 11:26) that still exists in present-day Turkey, are also real every-day people. We know something of the successes and failures of the early Christian worshiping communities from the letters of Paul.[12] Even in Paul's time and during his ministry, faithful believers cannot always work together. Is it any surprise that fellow-believers and Christian worshipers struggle throughout the centuries?

These early days of Christianity are no walk in the park, no matter how compelling and lovely the notion of that fledgling church. By the

---

7. Collinge, *Historical Dictionary of Catholicism*, 4.

8. A foundational volume for research on the first centuries of Christian worship is Bradshaw, *Search*. See some discussion of musical influences in chapter 7 above, as well as chapter 3.

9. See, e.g., chapter 3 above.

10. See the compelling if controversial discussion of "psalms, hymns, and spiritual songs" in Wellesz, *History of Byzantine Music*, 33–35.

11. See some suggestions about Paul and the earliest hymn in chapter 12 above, as well as chapter 9.

12. See one exploration of some of the complexities in chapter 5 in this volume.

third quarter of the first century, Christians are being persecuted by the likes of Nero,[13] and others to follow.

Second Century

By the early part of the second century, we see that it is established that Christians meet on the first day of the week, "the Lord's Day,"[14] and this sets the pattern for the next two millennia.[15]

Also, early in this century (ca. 112), regular correspondence between a Roman official, Governor Pliny the Younger,[16] and Emperor Trajan (53–117 CE),[17] reminds us of the newness of Christianity and the potential personal costs of this new faith. Pliny, a senator and literary man, has been appointed by Trajan to handle a province previously poorly administered, and these letters show how Pliny is obligated to discuss with the Emperor many small issues of administration. One of these is the issue of the new Christians. Pliny admits that he has not previously been present at any of the legal examinations of the Christians and does not really know the parameters of the penalties assessed to them or how searching his inquiry should be. He wonders whether age and robustness should be a factor and whether someone who recants is treated differently.

13. In 64 CE, Nero blames and punishes Christians for the burning of Rome, and this persecution lasts three years. Note also that there are specific times and locations of ongoing persecution of Christians throughout the first two centuries (Logan, *History*, 8).

14. Note that the Lord's Day is not known as "Sunday" until mid-second century. See Buxton, "Sunday"; Wegman, *Christian Worship*, 26–28; and White, *Introduction to Christian Worship*, 50–53. The classic monograph on this topic is Rordorf, *Sunday*, esp. 177–237, which is well worth reading.

15. Early sources that refer to the Christian day of worship include Did. 14.1; Pliny the Younger, *Ep. Tra.* 10.96 (Melmoth, Loeb Classical Library); and Justin Martyr, *1 Apol.* 65–67.

16. Pliny the Younger (61–112 CE) was a lawyer, an author, and the magistrate of Rome. Hundreds of his letters exist, many to emperors or to the historian Tacitus. He worked as a magistrate under the Emperor Trajan. He was born in what is now northern Italy. Of his many letters, there are two regarded as particularly significant: one is the one referred to above; the other is his description of the eruption of Mount Vesuvius in August 79 CE, where he and his uncle were located, and in which his uncle died (see Pliny the Younger, *Ep.* 6.16 [Radice, Loeb Classical Library]).

17. Trajan, more fully, Marcus Ulpius Nerva Traianus, was Roman Emperor while the Empire had its largest territory. He ruled 98–117 CE. He was born in the area we now know as Spain. As Emperor, he is known for his public building program, influencing the shape of Rome, and seen in buildings such as the Forum, the Market, and the Column, all known by his name being attached to them.

He wonders whether just carrying the name "Christian" should be punished if the person really is innocent of any other crime.[18]

Pliny's procedure is this: he asks potential "Christians" if they are, in fact, Christian. If they say "yes," he asks a second and then a third time, adding the threat of capital punishment if they continue to say "yes." If they do keep saying yes, then he orders them to be executed (and we know that Pliny does execute some Christians in 112 CE). Pliny's questioning seems to make clear which persons really are Christians or not. Those who deny being Christians, who repeat an invocation to the gods, who offer adoration with wine and incense to the emperor's image, and who finally curse Christ (all set up by Pliny as tests), are the ones that Pliny knows cannot really be Christians, because he has heard it said that those who are really Christians cannot be coerced into doing any of these things.[19]

How would *we* do in this context? When was the last time we personally or corporately faced serious punishment or physical cost, to say nothing of losing our lives, for claiming to be a Christian? How important *is* our faith in Christ to us? Would we be tempted to try to fit in with the crowd, a crowd that gets to walk away unscathed (well, at least, by all appearances)?

In Pliny's experience, some initially claim to be Christians and then, well, they change their minds! Some say they have recanted "long before." Interestingly, it is from the description of these recanters that we know something further about Christian gatherings, because it explains that "they were in the habit of meeting on a certain fixed day before it was light, when they sang in alternate verses a hymn to Christ, as to a god."[20] We will come back to this below. But notice something else they do in these meetings: they also bind themselves "by a solemn oath, not to any wicked deeds, but never to commit any fraud, theft or adultery, never to falsify their word, nor deny a trust when they should be called upon to deliver it."[21] That's quite a commitment. This clearly harmless ceremony over, they meet again to eat together.

Now, in order to more fully investigate the nature of what these previous Christians have described, Pliny has two women, called "deaconesses," tortured in order to get at the truth, but these women will not deny

---

18. Pliny the Younger, *Ep. Tra.* 10.96 (Melmoth, Loeb Classical Library).
19. Pliny the Younger, *Ep. Tra.* 10.96 (Melmoth, Loeb Classical Library).
20. Pliny the Younger, *Ep. Tra.* 10.96 (Melmoth, Loeb Classical Library).
21. Pliny the Younger, *Ep. Tra.* 10.96 (Melmoth, Loeb Classical Library).

their faith. Through his investigation he decides that it is really just some superstition taken to great lengths. He is concerned, however, about how many people may be endangered by this superstition, because people of all ages and both sexes will be subjected to the prosecution. Not only has this "Christian" phenomenon spread to people throughout the city, but to those in the villages and rural districts as well.[22]

On the so-called positive side, Pliny observes to Trajan that his investigations and punishment have successfully persuaded some of those who initially called themselves Christians to change their minds. He is glad to report that the previously empty (pagan) temples are beginning to be filled with worshipers again, the sacred festivals are being revived, and there is an increased demand for sacrificial animals, a business that was in something of a recession![23]

It should be noted that the observation that Christians who are singing a hymn "to Christ as to a god" (cited above) are doing this in the context of a pluralistic society that has multiple "gods." So far, however, no other groups would have worshiped "Christ" as a god in this way, so this is seen as unusual, but also the reason that Pliny can subsume it under the notion of superstition. The evidence of this statement also indicates that from the earliest century after Christ, music has been integral to Christian worship.[24] Pliny's letter also makes clear (although this larger reference is often not included when the passage is cited) that there is a terrific price to pay for being a Christ-follower, a "Christian."

When we think longingly about the notion that early Christians had a "simple faith" or dream of getting back to the "simplicity" of the early believers, we might have missed that these early Christians faced potential imprisonment, punishment, torture, and execution for their faith, including not only adult men but youths and women. The story of the two deaconesses reminds us also that there was a greater equality between women and men in the New Testament and early Christian times than people from the twenty-first century might expect.

One of the most significant biblical artifacts from the second century, copied around 125 CE, is what we know as $\mathfrak{P}^{52}$ or P.Ryl. Gk. 457 (Papyrus Rylands Greek 457), one of our earliest Greek papyrus fragments

---

22. Pliny the Younger, *Ep. Tra.* 10.96 (Melmoth, Loeb Classical Library).

23. Pliny the Younger, *Ep. Tra.* 10.96 (Melmoth, Loeb Classical Library).

24. See some of the debate about music in the synagogue, and the question of its relationship to music in the early church, in McKinnon, "On the Question of Psalmody," and Smith, "Ancient Synagogue."

from the New Testament. This fragment of a couple of inches of papyrus contains sections of John 18. The artifact is on display at the Rylands Library in Manchester, UK, only discovered in Egypt in 1920 by Bernard Grenfell, and subsequently published by Colin Roberts in 1935.[25] It is from fragments like these, as well as larger more complete documents, that we have our New Testament as we know it today, each small and large fragment helping to verify the oldest and most authentic tradition of the text that is known to us.[26] This fragment bears testimony to the fact that in the earliest days after Christ, someone recognized that it was critical to preserve the documents of Christianity, especially records of the life and words of Jesus. Because our first full biblical texts are only from the fourth century (e.g., Codex Sinaiticus, held in the British Library), earlier small fragments like $\mathfrak{P}^{52}$ are crucial to biblical scholarship, and to those who hold Scripture as the inspired word of God himself and want to see the earliest and most reliable texts possible.

Imagine, however, that we only had these tiny fragments. How important *is* Scripture to us in our Christian worship? Do we really value the Bible, when most of us who live in the twenty-first century have never experienced a day in our lives when it was not available in multiple convenient sizes and translations, with our choice of favourite covers? How can we begin to understand its value?

Mid-way through the second century, Justin Martyr (ca. 100–165) provides a defense for Christianity in his address to Emperor Antoninus Pius, in hopes that the emperor will personally attend to the Christians' case.[27] He describes how the Christians meet: "And on the day which is called Sunday, all who live in the cities or in the country gather together to one place and the memoirs of the apostles and the writings of the prophets are read *as long as time permits*."[28] As we read this description, do we find ourselves somewhat chastened as we consider whether we are eager to hear Scripture read or not? How long is "as long as time

---

25. See the original publication in Roberts, ed., *Unpublished Fragment*. Excellent images of this papyrus are available online by searching "P. Rylands Greek 457" or, as it is also known, Rylands papyrus "$\mathfrak{P}^{52}$," the latter being the number assigned in the Gregory-Aland catalogue of New Testament manuscripts. There has been recent controversy on the dating of this papyrus, on which see Porter, *John*, 13–36.

26. See, e.g., Porter, *How We Got the New Testament*.

27. Quasten, *Patrology: Volume I*, 199 (see 196–219 for an introduction to Justin Martyr and his writings).

28. Justin Martyr, *1 Apol.* 62 (cited in Quasten, *Patrology: Volume I*, 216 [emphasis mine]).

permits"? What if we could hear the words of Scripture as a life-altering communication from God, given to us through his apostles and prophets? Would it change our approach to corporate worship, or not? Would it alter our personal private times of worship, or not?

Justin Martyr continues, "Then the reader concludes, and the president verbally instructs and exhorts . . . then we all rise together and offer up our prayers . . . bread is brought and wine and water; and the president in like manner offers up prayers and thanksgivings according to his ability, and the people give their assent by saying, 'Amen.'"[29] (Interesting! What does it mean that the president "offers up prayers and thanksgivings according to his ability"?) And then they share in the bread and wine and water. He adds, "But Sunday is the day on which we hold our common assembly because it is the first day on which God, when he changed darkness and matter, made the world, and Jesus Christ our Savior on the same day rose from the dead."[30]

So we see how some of the believers celebrate the Lord's Supper and we again observe that they meet on Sunday for their gatherings.[31] In fact, there is compelling argument that they first meet on Sunday evenings, not Sunday mornings, as many Christians today might assume.[32] Meanwhile, having recently returned from Jerusalem where I experienced some of the city-wide influence of Shabbat, which is our Saturday, I am more conscious of the distinctive identity of these new Christians and the significance of their earliest celebrations taking place on Sundays instead. How unusual and counter-cultural it must have been. And, as Willy Rordorf observes, how inconvenient, because Sunday was a working day![33]

One further practical instruction on the Lord's Day meeting from the Didache (a late first or probably second-century book of instructions to Christians) outlines:

---

29. Justin Martyr, *1 Apol.* 67 (cited in Quasten, *Patrology: Volume I*, 216–17).

30. Justin Martyr, *1 Apol.* 62 (cited in Quasten, *Patrology: Volume I*, 217).

31. Baldovin, "Christian Worship," 162. See some discussion of the issues in identifying when Sunday worship comes about, in Bradshaw, *Search*, 39, 92–93; Jungmann, *Early Liturgy*, 19–28.

32. Rordorf, *Sunday*, 175–237.

33. Rordorf (*Sunday*, 203) writes, "It would have been quite impossible for Christians to have assembled for a second time in the course of the day on Sunday; they had to work."

> On the Lord's own day, assemble in common to break bread and offer thanks; but first confess your sins, so that your sacrifice may be pure. However, no one quarreling with his brother may join your meeting until they are reconciled; your sacrifice must not be defiled. For here we have the saying of the Lord: "In every place and time offer me a pure sacrifice; for I am a mighty King, says the Lord; and my name spreads terror among the nations" (*Did.* 14).[34]

As I reflect on these words, I distantly recall a Lord's Supper where an emphasis was made on fellow-believers making things right with one another before they participated in the Lord's Supper together. More than one person walked across the aisle to talk to someone in another pew before they participated in eating and drinking at the Lord's Table. What would it be like if we always followed this instruction (see Matt 5)? Would worship in the church of today be transformed? Would we see revival breaking out everywhere? Or would it just become one more rote, or superficially pious, action?

Third Century

Theology gets lots of airtime in the third century. We meet Tertullian (ca. 160–220), a North African author, often referred to as the "father of the Latin church." Johannes Quasten notes that "Tertullian was the first person to use the Latin word *trinitas* for the three divine persons," and also the one who applied the term *persona* to the Holy Spirit.[35] Christian worshipers now are familiar with the notion and persons of the Trinity, and we readily think of the Holy Spirit as a person, but these early theological discussions about the Trinity and the Holy Spirit must have been challenging and troubling to early worshipers.

One of the most significant pieces of artifactual evidence of the early Christian worshiping community from the third century is the papyrus fragment, P.Oxy. (or Papyrus from Oxyrhynchus) XV 1786, officially published by Arthur Hunt and Stuart Jones in 1922 as "Christian Hymn with Musical Notation."[36] To date, there has been nothing that compares with this particular fragment of a hymn. Not only is it the first known

---

34. Quasten, *Patrology: Volume I*, 33 (citing the translation from Quasten and Plumpe, ed., *Ancient Christian Writers*).

35. Quasten, *Patrology: Volume II*, 324–25.

36. Grenfell and Hunt, eds., "1786. Christian Hymn." See also Pöhlmann and West, eds., *Documents*, 190–94.

Christian hymn that has musical notation connected with it (which reads much like a modern-day chord chart), but its text is remarkable and unique, certainly not what one might expect from such an early fragment. Theologically, it is interpretive, not just a quotation of another text, and it refers to the Trinity,[37] although how that connects to Tertullian is difficult to say. It does show us, however, that contemporary Christian worship music of the time is keeping up with cutting-edge theological developments. The hymn has a musically developed "Amen," which suggests that by this time, there are some significant musical components of worship. Twenty-first century scholarship is coming to agreement that in this text, non-human creation is being called to silence so that humans (and angels) can sing praise to God, a notion also seen in other kinds of religious song in the same time-period.[38] The fact that it exists as a document with lyrics and musical notation at all suggests that someone, possibly living in Oxyrhynchus, which is not too far from the big city of Alexandria, recognizes a need for more than just oral tradition.[39]

Fourth Century

In the fourth century, the nations of Armenia, Georgia, and Ethiopia all adopt Christianity.[40] The Edict of Milan is signed by the believing Roman Emperor in the East (Constantine, 272–337), and the pagan Roman Emperor in the West (Licinius, 263–325), who agree to proclaim religious toleration in the Roman Empire. They specifically cite Christianity as a religion to be tolerated, that is, that Christians are no longer to be persecuted, and people have the freedom to choose the Christian religion if they wish. As Donald Logan writes about the time, "The emergence of Christianity into the full light of day provided the opportunity and, indeed, the necessity for Christians to reflect on the nature of their

---

37. See the extensive and provocative treatment of this hymn in the excellent monograph by Cosgrove, *Ancient Christian Hymn*.

38. Cosgrove, *Ancient Christian Hymn*, 35–47. For my own discussion of P.Oxy. XV 1786, see other chapters in this volume, especially chapters 7 and 9.

39. Today there is increasing interest in the role of oral tradition; for an introduction to the subject, see, e.g., Lord, *Singer of Tales*; Lord, *Epic Singers*; Finnegan, *Literacy and Orality*.

40. See, e.g., Metzger, *Early Versions*, 153–57 (esp. 153), on Armenia's claim to the "honour of being the first kingdom to accept Christianity as its official religion"; and the introduction of Christianity into Georgia (182–85) and Ethiopia (215–23). See some description in Stringer, *Sociological History*, 92–95 (Armenia), 141–42 (Georgia), and 143–44 (Ethiopia).

religion."[41] In other words, Christians are forced into some kind of theological reflection, whether they are intending such or not. Questions about the divinity of Christ and what the Godhead really is are troubling and difficult to ascertain. Can we even comprehend the ambiguity that surrounds early Christian worshipers as they face these questions for the first time?

Intense theological debates result in the Councils of the fourth century, especially to do with the divinity of Jesus, the specific relationship of Jesus to God the Father, and the nature of the Trinity. One of the results of these debates is the Nicene Creed. Note that the Orthodox Church still holds the Nicene-Constantinopolitan Creed as their classical statement of belief, without the later changes.[42] It is determined that Jesus is equal to the Father, that he is one with the Father, and that he is of the *same* substance as the Father. At the following Council, it is determined that Jesus was also truly human.[43]

As we look back at these Councils, especially if we grew up with the results of them as part of our own Christian beliefs, they seem almost superfluous, the results being virtually self-evident. But if we each had to arrive at these conclusions ourselves without a prior framework for them, it would become apparent that the issues are far more difficult to sort out than we might expect. What the people are doing is theological reflection on a grand scale in a very public venue.

Soon Byzantium is renamed "Constantinople" and becomes the capital of the Byzantine Empire. This city (present-day Istanbul) is important in Christianity, not least for its spectacular church, Hagia Sophia, built by the Emperor Justinian, and (at that time) home to vibrant Christian worship.[44] By this time in the fourth century, there are now

---

41. Logan, *History*, 9. He also notes that Christians comprise about 10 percent of the empire at this time. See extensive discussion that explores the rising numbers of Christians in the first few centuries in Stark, *Rise of Christianity*, 3–27.

42. See, e.g., Prokurat et al., "Introduction," 1. See also discussion in Payton, *Light from the Christian East*, 69–71.

43. For older introductions to the development of the Creeds, see Badcock, *History*; Kelly, *Early Christian Creeds*; Warren, *Liturgy and Ritual*. For more recent discussion about their content and relevance, see Johnson, *Creed*.

44. Hagia Sophia now officially has "museum" status and does not function as a church. Thoughtful visitors to this previous Christian church will find plenty of scope for theological reflection as they see the remains of Christian worship in a building that has also been the home of non-Christian worship and now is simply an official state building, a relic of worship.

four great Catholic (read: orthodox, authentic) churches: Rome, Constantinople, Alexandria, and Antioch.

Also in the fourth century, two further significant churches are built on important sites for Christians: the Church of the Nativity in Bethlehem and the Jerusalem Church of the Holy Sepulchre. These are important if somewhat confusing sites for pilgrims to the Holy Land, then and now. Perhaps one of the greatest services they present to a twenty-first-century visitor is to prompt serious theological reflection on what it means to "preserve" a "holy" site. If you've been there, you understand this; if you have not, you should go.

The "book" is vital to Christianity, and Christianity is largely responsible for the move towards the "book" as we know it.[45] Our earliest complete Christian Bible, Codex Sinaiticus (held in the British Library, as noted above),[46] and the nearly complete Codex Vaticanus (held in the Vatican), come from the middle of the fourth century (350 CE). I recall my own early theological reflection on how dependent the biblical text was on regular people and their faithfulness in transcribing it. This reflection was prompted on my first trip to England, before my husband and I moved there. We visited the British Museum. One of the things we saw was Codex Sinaiticus, sitting in a glass case, its pages open to one of the Gospels. As I saw the beautifully written text, I also noted all the markings in the margins, places where a scribe had corrected or added something. I believe I counted 28 marginal notations on the two pages that were open. I began to realize that my simple faith rested on more potential for human intervention than just Moses breaking the Tablets with the Ten Commandments! It was disturbing. As I have thought about this many times over the years, I have come to realize what an incredible trust God has placed in human beings, to give them—to give us—the responsibility to faithfully pass on what is true and important.

The fourth century also brings with it a new aroma, as incense becomes associated with Christian worship, especially during the celebration of the Eucharist.[47] As I reflect on the combination of aromas with worship, I try to imagine the woody aroma of the cedar-wood used in

---

45. See, e.g., Metzger, *Text of the New Testament*, 3–35.

46. The majority of the codex is held by the British Library. The Codex Sinaiticus website is worth exploring and makes available downloadable images (codexsinaiticus.org). See also Porter, *How We Got the New Testament*, 125–27.

47. Pierce, "Vestments and Objects," 850.

the construction of Israel's temple.[48] The cedar fragrance inside must have been remarkable—surely deeply imprinted on the memory of every person who ever worshiped there. I imagine the savory aromas of its char-grilled sacrifices. Although the Old Testament rarely describes the aromas of these sacrifices, the smell of cooking meat on an open fire must literally have permeated the worship environment. I smell the smoking perfume of the priest's censer.[49] I catch a heady whiff of the fragrance of expensive perfume poured onto Jesus' feet.[50] I am sobered by the intense smell of spices prepared for his body in the tomb.[51] As I think of Paul's description of Christ's life given for us as a fragrant offering and sacrifice to God (Eph 5:2), I consider how much of our twenty-first century fragrance-free evangelical worship misses out on this potent sensory portion of worship. For instance, what evangelical thinks of a fragrant cedar-lined closet when they think of worship? Or of the aromas of barbecuing meat integrated into their place of worship? Or of specially mixed holy perfumes that are reserved only for the place of worship? Even if burnt offerings and incense are no longer required for our worship, must we eliminate all savory aromas that remind us of sacrifice, and the memory-prompting fragrances of holy worship space?

Fifth Century

The Bible comes into focus in the fifth century in a new way, with increasing numbers of translations of the Bible, or at least of the New Testament, into various languages of the Orthodox Church, including the

---

48. See Solomon's use of cedar in the temple in 1 Kgs 6:9 ("So he built the temple and completed it, roofing it with beams and cedar planks," NIV) and 6:15–18 ("He lined its interior walls with cedar boards, paneling them from the floor of the temple to the ceiling, and covered the floor of the temple with planks of juniper. He partitioned off twenty cubits at the rear of the temple with cedar boards from floor to ceiling to form within the temple an inner sanctuary, the Most Holy Place . . . The inside of the temple was cedar . . . Everything was cedar; no stone was to be seen," NIV).

49. See Lev 16:12 ("He [Aaron] is to take a censer full of burning coals from the altar before the Lord and two handfuls of finely ground fragrant incense and take them behind the curtain," NIV).

50. Matt 26:7; Mark 14:3; Luke 7:38; John 12:3.

51. John 19:39 describes Nicodemus accompanying Joseph of Arimathea to prepare Jesus' body for burial, taking a mixture of myrrh and aloes weighing about seventy-five pounds. Luke 23:55–56 says, "The women who had come with Jesus from Galilee followed Joseph and saw the tomb and how his body was laid in it. Then they went home and prepared spices and perfumes" (NIV).

Ethiopian Orthodox (is it significant that the Ethiopian eunuch was one of the first persons mentioned in the New Testament to be interested in an understandable translation of the text?), the Syriac (or Syrian) Orthodox, and the Armenian Orthodox.[52] There is already a Gothic version,[53] and Jerome is the man "destined to fix the literary form of the Bible of the entire Western Church" in the Latin Vulgate.[54] Does it prompt some humble theological reflection when we note that each of these cultures is already served by a Bible in its own language more than a thousand years before the Reformation?

The councils in the fifth century make further decisions on the human and divine nature of Jesus. Philip Schaff's translation of the Symbol (or Creed) of Chalcedon reads:

> We, then, following the holy Fathers, all with one consent, teach men to confess one and the same Son, our Lord Jesus Christ, the same perfect in Godhead and also perfect in manhood; truly God and truly man, of a reasonable [rational] soul and body; consubstantial [coessential] with the Father according to the Godhead, and consubstantial with us according to the Manhood; in all things like unto us, without sin; begotten before all ages of the Father according to the Godhead, and in these latter days, for us and for our salvation, born of the Virgin Mary, the Mother of God, according to the Manhood; one and the same Christ, Son, Lord, Only-begotten, to be acknowledged in two natures, *inconfusedly, unchangeably, indivisibly, inseparably*; the distinction of natures being by no means taken away by the union, but rather the property of each nature being preserved, and concurring in one Person and one Subsistence, not parted or divided into two persons, but one and the same Son, and only begotten, God the Word, the Lord Jesus Christ; as the prophets

---

52. See Metzger, *Early Versions*, on the early Eastern versions (Syriac, Armenian, Georgian, Ethiopic, and minor Eastern versions) as well as the early Western versions (Latin, Gothic, Old Church Slavonic, and minor Western versions). See, e.g., Porter, *How We Got the New Testament*, 153-60, on the history of Syriac, Latin, and Coptic translations.

53. Metzger, *Early Versions*, 376-77. Logan (*History*, 18) describes Ulfilas (ca. 311-83; of Greek and Goth heritage, Christian on the Greek side) who is made a bishop at Constantinople in 341 with the mission to convert his fellow Goths. He is bilingual and "accomplished two remarkable feats: he created the written Gothic language by inventing its alphabet and then he translated the Greek Bible into Gothic." When the Visigoths enter the empire in 376, the Bible and their religious services are all in their language.

54. Metzger, *Early Versions*, 332.

from the beginning [have declared] concerning him, and the Lord Jesus Christ himself has taught us, and the Creed of the holy Fathers has handed down to us.[55]

What would Christianity look like today if these councils had not taken place, I wonder?

A significant missionary movement begins in the fifth century. Patrick (ca. 387–493) is credited with beginning the missionary work in Ireland. Although he comes as pastor to Christians who are already there, he plays an important role in the conversion of the Irish and speaks of baptizing thousands.[56] Sometimes those of us who live in the twenty-first century think that missions are a recent innovation. We forget that missions have been around since Jesus initiated it, and since Paul acted on it and brought Christianity to Europe, and since people like Patrick (so much more than green shamrocks) took up the mantle.

JOURNEY OF WORSHIP PART 2: THE SIXTH TO THE TENTH CENTURY

In this next period, we turn to a church that has expanded to many other parts of the world and is becoming an established entity with its own traditions of worship in place.

Sixth Century

During the rule of Pope Gregory the Great (540–604), much reform of the church structure takes place,[57] and his name becomes connected with monastic and cathedral music known as Gregorian Chant, although chant or plainchant exist long before the time of Gregory.[58] In some ways, chant cannot be surpassed for its association with liturgy and ritual and mystery; the sounds of it heard in an ancient place of Christian worship

---

55. Schaff, *Creeds*, 62–63 (square brackets and italics are original).

56. Logan, *History*, 23; Latourette, *History of Christianity*, 102; Bainton, *Christendom*, 143–44.

57. See Driscoll, "Conversion of the Nations," 185–88; and Thibodeau, "Western Christendom," 226–27, 244–45.

58. See brief introduction in Dowley, *Christian Music*, 50–61; and Wilson-Dickson, *Story of Christian Music*, 30–32. See more through discussion in McKinnon, "Emergence of Gregorian Chant," and Hiley, "Plainchant Transfigured." A classic work is Apel, *Gregorian Chant*; a more recent monograph is Levy, *Gregorian Chant and the Carolingians*.

THEOLOGICAL REFLECTIONS ON THE HISTORY OF CHRISTIAN WORSHIP

are inexplicably evocative, its choral echoes circling round and round before they fade away into a numinous distance.[59] The sound seems to transport you to a previous century of worshipers gathered in this same location, hearing the same sounds, standing on the same stone floor, perhaps sitting on the same hard seats as later generations (because congregational seating is not part of most ancient churches). For those of us who worship in places and styles that have a very short history, worshiping in ancient cathedrals, churches, or chapels in other parts of the world helps to re-orient our historical worship perspective.

In the sixth century, we are introduced to an innovation in the church, a dramatic interconnection between music and preaching, demonstrated by the famous hymnwriter, Romanos Melodus (ca. 485–562). He brings what is known as the "song-sermon" to its apex. In this song-sermon, the cantor-hymnwriter-preacher chants the verses of the sermon from the pulpit, and the choir and congregation join in the refrain.[60] As I consider this mode of delivery, and the artistry involved in creating these interactive sermon pieces, I wonder whether modern-day approaches to preaching and worship are really more innovative than this. Surely ours is the most creative generation ever. Or is it? However, the song-sermon style of Romanos Melodus relies on the giftedness and energies of the writer and presenter, to say nothing of the ability and training of choir and congregation, so it is not a preaching and worship mode that can last long—and nor does it. It is a reminder that high creativity and artistry in worship forms are not confined to the current generation, and also a reminder that they cannot always be sustained.

Seventh to Ninth Centuries

The seventh century brings a surprising religious development to the world, which originates in Arabia. A man named Mohammed is born in about 570 at Mecca and dies in 632. In a hundred years, his followers are evident from the Atlantic to the Indian Ocean to the interior of Asia. From then on, Christians are compelled to take note.

---

59. Oddly, it is only more recently that many of these institutions rediscovered chant, and re-inserted it into their liturgy, having left it behind for a long period of time.

60. See discussion of Romanos and his works in Maas and Trypanis, eds., *Sancti Romani Melodi Cantica*, xi–xxxi; and the introductory material in St. Romanos the Melodist, *Kontakia*, xv–xxxii. See also chapter 8 above.

Part Three: The Past and Present of Music and Worship

In the eighth century, visual and tactile images, "icons," come to the forefront of the Christian church and its conversations. Early in the century they are banned; later in the century they are re-approved, by the Seventh Ecumenical Council (787).[61] It is intriguing that there are two instances of icons formally brought back into the church after previously being banned. In both cases, a woman Empress makes the compelling case for visual imagery in the church. Icons, like those found in the Oriental (or Orthodox) churches, are not familiar in most evangelical forms of worship. As I think about the sparse and somewhat blank interior of my own formative church experience, I consider how minimal a role beautiful art and objects played. Strictly functional church interiors often are not places of great beauty. Although sometimes their homely simplicity has a kind of beauty, sometimes they are simply homely. It is not that one cannot worship God there, but there is something rich and complex and rewarding in worship connected to locations and works of beauty. Do we still substitute icons for God in our worship? Undoubtedly. But by removing all works of art, do we unwittingly substitute a God that is too familiar, too homey, too small, too plain?

From the eighth century we retain the Latin hymn lyrics, *Veni Creator Spiritus* (Come, Holy Spirit, Creator, Come),[62] and that most-loved Irish hymn, *Be Thou My Vision*.[63] Although tunes will be married to these texts much later, it is interesting that the latter is one that contemporary worshipers and worship leaders love and use regularly, not just as a "token" hymn sung to appease an older generation.

Tenth Century

Lectionaries in the tenth century now take prominence in our historical journey of theological reflection and worship because they are at the heart of corporate worship, and they begin to show developed markings

---

61. Prokurat et al., "Introduction," 7–8. The Byzantine church here is focused on iconoclasm (726–843), although ultimately favouring the use of images. Interestingly, monks are the leading opponents of iconoclasm, and this helps to secure the monks' position in the church (7–8). For an introduction to icons, as well as numerous full-colour plates, see Babic, *Icons*. For enlightening and thoughtful reflection on icons, then and now, see Jensen, *Substance of Things Seen*, 51–74.

62. Latin lyrics are attributed to Rhabanus Maurus (776–856; English translation by John Cosin, 1627); see Westermeyer, *Let the People Sing*, 28.

63. The text is ancient Irish: *Rob tum o bhoile, a Comdi cride*. For its translation, see Byrne, "Prayer." See also Westermeyer, *Let the People Sing*, 340.

called ekphonetic notation. These small notations within the scriptural text indicate to the reader or cantor how to divide the text and how to modulate their voice to most adequately—-and artistically?—present these words.[64] There still is much that is not known about ekphonetic notation, especially because it is a kind of code that is not unlike our modern-day chord charts. A contemporary chord chart means nothing if you do not already know the melody and the timing and rhythm and overall sound of the song, because it is a kind of musical shorthand or code for those who already know the music. I have reflected frequently on this interesting correlation between the tenth and twenty-first centuries and remain intrigued that so much of current worship practice functions similarly to the way that oral tradition functioned in the past—although we may presume that we live in an entirely literate society.

JOURNEY OF WORSHIP PART 3: THE ELEVENTH TO THE FIFTEENTH CENTURY

The third period in our journey encompasses an established church that is a world entity. With its widespread influence come tensions that lead to division.

Eleventh Century

Not unlike today, Christians in the eleventh century make pilgrimages through the Middle East to the Holy Land. Theirs is a dangerous journey of potential persecution. They experience a brief period of safety for their travels, and then persecution of Christians on pilgrimage begins again. Thousands of churches are destroyed, including the Church of the Holy Sepulchre, thought to be built over the tomb of Jesus in Jerusalem.[65] Having seen this church in its most recent form, with more than one Christian faith tradition simultaneously in evidence, each asking to be noticed and revered, I grasp an inkling of the struggle that must exist over this site in the eleventh century, and on through the centuries to follow. However, as a North American with only a few generations behind me in my Western land of immigrants, the power of ancient historical rootedness can elude me.

---

64. The most important early introduction to this subject is Høeg, *La notation ekphonétique*. See also chapters 6 and 12 above.

65. See Armstrong, *Jerusalem*, 259, for part of the complex narrative that surrounds this and many other events in Jerusalem.

Part Three: The Past and Present of Music and Worship

Eastern and western churches formally split in the eleventh century.[66] James Payton writes:

> There were occasional rifts . . . and ecclesiastical communion was periodically broken. Each of these, however, was eventually healed. Consequently, the mutual denunciations and excommunications in 1054 occasioned no particular anxiety at the time: people expected that, as before, there would be an eventual restoration of that communion. Nevertheless, the division lingered; indeed, it has never been officially healed.[67]

The Crusades follow (1069–1099, 1144–1155, 1187–1192, 1202–1204).[68] As with all hindsight, it is easy to "know" what is right, and to believe that what we would have done would have been better, but I wonder. What would we have determined to be right, and how would we have responded if we had been there?

As with all of life, beginnings and endings co-exist. In England, Westminster Abbey is consecrated in 1065;[69] only a year later the Normans conquer Britain, and that is the beginning of "1066 and All That."[70] The Holy Roman Emperor, Henry IV, argues for clerical celibacy,[71] surely an end to other beginnings.

However, another beginning worth noting is the founding of the first university, in Bologna, Italy, in 1088.[72] How can someone born in twentieth-century North America even comprehend a world before universities? Even as I think of Paul the Apostle and his official study with Gamaliel, I wonder about the years that are unaccounted for after his conversion on the Damascus Road. What was he doing during those years, and where was he? Was he studying at the feet of the risen Christ somewhere, in a

---

66. Collinge, *Historical Dictionary of Catholicism*, 8.

67. Payton, *Light from the Christian East*, 33. He notes, however, that it was the event in 1205, the fourth Crusade, that assured this ongoing division. See below on the thirteenth century.

68. See Logan, *History*, 118, on the temptation to overemphasize the role of the crusades in the life of the church in the Middle Ages. See also Johns, "Christianity and Islam," 171–74; Morris, "Christian Civilization," 209–10, 224–25.

69. For Westminster Abbey's history as a place of worship, see "History."

70. Sellar and Yeatman's *1066 and All That* is lighthearted and comical but also provocative and insightful.

71. See, e.g., Thibodeau, "Western Christendom," 216, 219–20, on the universal ban on clerical marriage or "concubinage" and efforts at reform in this regard.

72. See some of the fascinating discussion of the history of universities in Carpenter, *Music in the Medieval and Renaissance Universities*.

private university? Was he being taught by the Holy Spirit, in a place that we know nothing about? And what would university education be like if it was designed and implemented by the Great Teacher himself or the one who "will guide you into all the truth" (John 16:13)?

Just a few years later, in 1096, the University of Oxford is in operation, with Cambridge beginning a few years after that, founded by scholars who leave Oxford after a series of tragic events and several deaths. Rivalry between these two institutions continues through the centuries.

Theology and worship in much of the western world is influenced both directly and indirectly by several of these earliest educational institutions, as colleges and universities are founded elsewhere. Logan writes:

> A line of descent can be drawn from the medieval universities at Bologna and Paris to almost every college and university in the Western world. A line can be seen reaching from Paris to Oxford to Cambridge to Harvard and another line from Paris to Germany to the United States in the nineteenth century. . . the essence of the university as an institution has remained unchanged: the meeting of teachers and students around books.[73]

The liberal arts are to be studied first, and then, afterwards, theology, law, or medicine. The liberal arts cover seven areas, the *trivium*: grammar, rhetoric, and logic (which comes to mean philosophy), and the *quadrivium*: arithmetic, geometry, astronomy, and music, some of which is outlined already by Boethius (ca. 475/77–525/26) in the sixth century.[74] Perhaps of interest to seminarians today is that *after* this initial education, a person can move on to study theology. Theology at the time begins with formal study of the Bible, followed by systematic theology, followed by a series of academic exercises in order to become a master of theology—a course of study of about twelve years.[75]

Poignant still today is Boethius's concern, as expressed by Henry Chadwick:

> It is [Boethius's] great fear that amid the general collapse of higher studies in his time, the knowledge acquired by the

---

73. Logan, *History*, 225.

74. See Chadwick, *Boethius*, 70–107, on the quadrivium. See also, e.g., Thibodeau, "Western Christendom," 244–45. Wilson (*Music of the Middle Ages*, 4) writes, "the study of the trivium and quadrivium encompasses an attempt to see the various phenomena of the world not as separate entities, but as part of one interrelated world order."

75. Logan, *History*, 233–34.

philosophers and scientists of classical Greece may simply be obliterated by a failure in transmission. Books may lie in libraries but, if they are to survive for more than a generation, they need users who understand and value their contents or they will rapidly suffer from neglect, and the valuable space they occupy will be applied to other purposes.[76]

As I notice the amount of library space now dedicated to coffee and conversation (although I enjoy both), the permanent removal of books from library shelves by librarians themselves, the shift in priorities of students from purchasing books for research to simply purchasing more technology, and the permanent closure of some of the most important used-book stores in the world, I wonder if Boethius isn't still relevant, not only as a prophet for the eleventh century, but for the twenty-first. Does our approach to worship parallel this trend?

Twelfth Century

In the twelfth century, Anselm (1033–1109) pioneers arguments for the existence of God and tries to understand the atonement and the nature of faith.[77] Meanwhile, Hildegard von Bingen (1098–1179) explores deep spirituality, becoming the first composer—not just the first woman composer—of written music to be known by the composer's name.[78] Much about her life and work is intriguing, not least that her "music is not drawn from plainchant and is in some respects highly individual,"[79] and that it is written in a manner that fosters *rumination*, "chewing on," "a special Hildegardian facet of contemplative medieval practice."[80] Both Anselm and Hildegard are doing—and providing us with models and tools for doing—theological reflection on worship.

To visit the ruins of a monumental place of worship used in the twelfth century should prompt reflection on worship. Tintern Abbey, situated on the River Wye in Wales, is such a place (ruined as the result of Henry VIII's Dissolution of the Monasteries in 1540). It is still breathtakingly beautiful (and definitely worth writing a poem about,

---

76. Chadwick, *Boethius*, 69.
77. Richardson, ed., *Dictionary*, 10, 18–24.
78. See, e.g., Dowley, *Christian Music*, 62–63; and Porter, "Hildegard of Bingen."
79. Bent and Pfau, "Hildegard of Bingen," 494.
80. Bent and Pfau, "Hildegard of Bingen," 495. They also note that her morality play is the earliest by more than a century.

although the famous poem by Wordsworth, known by its name, disappointingly has nothing to do with Tintern Abbey itself).[81] But how do we process the notion of a beautiful building—designed for worship of God—that ends up in ruins, and just stays that way? What happens to worship there? Where do the worshipers go? Does this destruction hinder God's plan? Or facilitate it? And why does this empty monument still prompt deep reflection on God, and even ongoing communion with him? Meanwhile in the twelfth century, work begins on the great Notre Dame Cathedral in Paris. It, too, is a marvelous church, and is still standing, even if recently badly damaged by fire. But I find something more deeply and spiritually compelling in the architectural frame that is open to the sky at Tintern Abbey.

During the twelfth century, the question about what the central event of Christian worship—the Eucharist celebration or Mass—signifies begins to turn towards the crucifixion rather than the Last Supper. More congregations find themselves watching the event of the Eucharist, rather than participating in it, because it is now being done on behalf of those watching. The raising of the elements becomes crucial for the faithful attendants to "see" the event of bread and wine being "turned into Christ's body and blood,"[82] a spectacle perhaps hovering between mystery and magic. As I consider the evolving celebrations of the Eucharist (and their competing theologies), I also ponder how much of the mystery and beauty of this event seems to be irretrievably lost to the contemporary evangelical church. Are we all really so sure that we know exactly what is going on when we participate in the bread and the wine? Would a bit more uncertainty and a greater wonder serve us better?

A great Bernard comes from this century, Bernard of Clairvaux (1090–1153), especially known for the Mary-hymn, *Ave maris stella* ("Hail, Star of the Sea").[83] A great hymn of the faith is also known from this period, although its author is not: *Veni, Veni Immanuel* ("O Come, O Come, Emmanuel").[84] The text of "O Sacred Head, Now Wounded" possibly also comes from this century[85] (to which Bach later brings his

81. Wordsworth, "Lines Composed a Few Miles above Tintern Abbey."
82. Logan, *History*, 146.
83. Kelly, ed., *Plainsong*, 205–6.
84. The familiar music for this text is later, from the fifteenth century, drawn from a requiem mass in a French Franciscan collection of chants (see, e.g., "Hymns for Worship," 37).
85. This Latin hymn-text is sometimes attributed to Bernard of Clairvaux (ca.

touch of musical genius: he arranges Hans Hassler's musical setting and then incorporates it into his own Passion music).[86] In these three hymn lyrics, we see an interesting diversity in Christian worship in the twelfth century: the rise of Mary-worship, a focus on the Old Testament and the heritage of the Jews, and a focus on the suffering of Jesus on the cross.

Thirteenth to Fifteenth Centuries

The beginning of the thirteenth century brings the sack of Constantinople (1204) by Christian Crusaders and the final breach between eastern and western Christendom. A first-hand account compels us to recognize the violence of this scene:

> Then the streets, squares, two storied and three-storied houses, holy places, convents, houses of monks and nuns, holy churches (even God's Great Church), the imperial palace, were filled with the enemy, all war-maddened swordsmen, breathing murder, iron-clad and spear-bearing, sword-bearers and lance-bearers, bowmen, horsemen, boasting dreadfully, baying like Cerberus and breathing like Charon, pillaging the holy places, trampling on divine things, running riot over holy things, casting down to the floor the holy images (on walls or on panels) of Christ and His holy Mother and of the holy men who from eternity have been pleasing to the Lord God, uttering calumnies and profanities, and in addition tearing children from mothers and mothers from children, treating the virgin with wanton shame in holy chapels, viewing with fear neither the wrath of God nor the vengeance of men.[87]

This account by Nicholas Mesarites goes on to depict the further indecencies and horrors of the scene, adding, "Such was the reverence for holy things of those who bore the Lord's Cross on their shoulders."

1091–1153), as well as to Arnulf von Lowen (1200–1251) (see "Hymns for Worship," 39).

86. Bach uses various harmonizations for this hymn in his St. Matthew Passion, as well as incorporating it twice in the Christmas Oratorio. See, e.g., the entry for "Passion Chorale" in Boyd, ed., *J. S. Bach*, 361, and brief discussion of the adaptation of this hymn with musical excerpts in Grout and Palisca, *History of Western Music*, 253–54. See a general introduction to Bach and his music in Emery and Wolff, *Bach*, and Wolff, "Bach."

87. This translation of the account of the sack of Constantinople in 1204 as recorded by Nicholas Mesarites, a Funeral Oration, "Epitaphius," is found in Brand, ed., *Icon and Minaret*, 131–32.

Somehow, referring to it in the historian's terminology as "the sack of Constantinople" sounds so much more remote than seeing it through an onlooker's eyes. How *did* a Christian deal with the destruction and violation of their house of God—by other Christians?

We are introduced to St. Francis of Assisi (1181/82–1226), who is "among the most admired Christians after the apostles" and who is noted for crossing enemy lines during the fifth Crusade (1219) to speak to the Sultan.[88] Tradition says that St. Francis of Assisi penned "All Creatures of Our God and King."[89] This hymn reminds us of, but also contrasts with, the third-century hymn from Oxyrhynchus (P.Oxy. XV 1786), noted above. The twelfth-century one calls on all creation to lift up their voices and sing, while the earlier one appears to call on all creation except for humans to be silent, so that God's people can sing praises to him.

In the fourteenth century, the widening division between eastern and western churches becomes a final separation.[90] Only in more recent years has there been much serious interest on the part of western Christians in exploring and understanding more about their previous fellow-worshipers in the East.[91]

Back in the West, an Oxford theologian, John Wycliffe (ca. 1330–1384), after significant deep personal theological reflection, tackles the developing notions of the sacraments, challenges the finances of the clergy and ultimately the role of popes, and works with a colleague to translate the Bible into Middle English.[92] The English-speaking world is forever altered by this early move to translate the Bible into English.

The fifteenth century is dominated by the invention of the movable-type printing press, which changes not only the world at large but also worship in the local church. The printed word is a major influence throughout Christianity, a faith that relies on the faithful handing down

---

88. Marty, *Christian World*, 93, writes of how "Francis turned his back on family wealth and took on oaths of poverty, even as he tried to start peaceful conversations with Muslims."

89. The editors of "Hymns for Worship" describe the piece thus: "Francis' 'Canticle of the Sun' is a catalogue hymn in which various facets of creation are urged to praise the Lord with their 'Alleluias'" (41).

90. Latourette (*History of Christianity*, 564–97) brings some insight into this widening gulf and ultimate divide.

91. Payton, *Light from the Christian East*, 13–14.

92. See a brief overview of Wycliffe's life in Estep, *Renaissance and Reformation*, 58–68.

of the Word.⁹³ Now individuals can read it for themselves—well, eventually. There are some deaths before that occurs. One is of the Czech, Jan Hus (ca. 1370–415), who follows in Wycliffe's footsteps, and eventually is burned at the stake for it.⁹⁴ The very first printed Bible, the Gutenberg Bible (ca. 1454),⁹⁵ makes its appearance in Germany, and the Bible in book form as we know it begins to take physical shape.

Meanwhile, in Italy, the Sistine Chapel is built (1473–1481),⁹⁶ an Inquisition seeks to eliminate non-Christians from Spain by strongly "encouraging" them to be baptized,⁹⁷ and a baby is born in Eisleben, Germany, who will further change Christendom: a child named Martin Luther (1483–1546).

JOURNEY OF WORSHIP PART 4: THE SIXTEENTH TO THE NINETEENTH CENTURY

The fourth part of this journey of worship focuses on a select few significant events and people in a time that was filled with many more important occurrences than can be addressed here. This was an age of dissent on many fronts. Nevertheless, this was an important period especially in the life of what came to be the Protestant church.

Sixteenth Century

Although bringing with it the artistic fulfillment and magnificent musical strands of polyphony, the sixteenth century also brings a cacophony

---

93. Porter (*How We Got the New Testament*, 147) writes that, at the time, "only thirty-three languages had a portion or more of the Bible," although for those who have thought that the Reformation was the beginning of translation into the vernacular, this may be surprising news.

94. See, e.g., Estep, *Renaissance and Reformation*, 69–77, on Jan's life and death, and some of the outcomes.

95. See "Gutenberg Bible." For digital pages of the entire Bible (from ca. 1454), see "Gutenberg Digital."

96. The Vatican makes a spectacular navigable 360-degree view of the Sistine Chapel available online (see "Sistine Chapel"). Two-finger scrolling will allow for a view of all corners, including floor, walls, and ceiling, and zooming in to see details at any point. The opportunity to see the Sistine Chapel without hundreds of people around is rare, although I admit that I had that opportunity while attending a special conference held in the Vatican in October 2013. Palestrina's music appropriately fills the aural space online.

97. Latourette (*History of Christianity*, 657) notes that thousands of Jews were baptized as a result.

of people and events that rock and split Christianity into shards and splinters, each seeming to take on a life of its own, almost all of it connected to "worship."[98]

Michelangelo's masterpiece in the Sistine Chapel becomes one of the world's best-known and revered works of sacred art, although he includes much that is earthy and seemingly not-so-sacred. This place of worship becomes the destination of many a pilgrimage from then onwards until today, best experienced with Palestrina's polyphony as the musical tapestry around its perimeter.[99]

A simple paper nailed on a university noticeboard in 1517 by Martin Luther heralds the beginning of the German Protestant Reformation,[100] and becomes a catalyst for the entire Protestant Reformation. The Anabaptist movement also begins (1525).[101] Luther's *Deutsche Messe* (1526) alters the liturgy of the Mass.[102] Heinrich Zwingli's (1484-1531) simple theology seems appealing (if not everything about his approach does): if it is in Scripture, it should be followed; if it is not in Scripture, it should not be followed.[103]

---

98. See, e.g., Estep, *Renaissance and Reformation*; Noll, *Confessions and Catechisms*; and relevant chapters throughout McManners, ed., *Oxford Illustrated History of Christianity*; Latourette, *History of Christianity*; and Wainwright and Westerfield Tucker, eds., *Oxford History of Christian Worship*.

99. Listen, for example, to Palestrina, *Missa Papae Marcelli*. See Lockwood et al., "Palestrina."

100. Elton (*Reformation Europe*, 15) notes that there "was nothing unusual about" Luther's nailing of a paper to the door of the Castle Church in Wittenberg: "Any scholar who wished to defend any propositions of law or doctrine could invite learned debate by putting forth such theses, and church doors were the customary place for medieval publicity." Collinge (*Historical Dictionary of Catholicism*, 13) notes that although the reformation movement looks different in each place (e.g., Switzerland, the Low Countries, England), they are all arguing against the way the medieval church has developed the system by which spiritual mediation is thought to take place. Collinge contends that Luther's issue with indulgences is typical of this position, and that reformers believe in God's sovereignty, his freedom to give the grace of salvation, the importance of God's word through Scripture (i.e., not church tradition), and direct participation of believers in their relationship with God that is not dependent on church hierarchy.

101. Estep, *Anabaptist Story*, 9-28.

102. See the brief summary in Elton, *Reformation Europe*, 54; see also Leaver, *Luther's Liturgical Music*.

103. See, e.g., Elton, *Reformation Europe*, 66-74; Noll, *Confessions and Catechisms*, 37-46.

Part Three: The Past and Present of Music and Worship

Henry VIII (1491–1547) creates an independent Church of England (1534), Thomas More (1478–1535) is executed for objecting,[104] and many Roman Catholics in England are killed in the next 40 years.[105] Henry orders the destruction ("dissolution") of Catholic monasteries (1536–1540), and eliminates 800 institutions in four years, mostly for the cash and property.[106] One can still today see statues that are missing their heads as a result of this period. Some of these monasteries are re-invented as Church of England abbeys and cathedrals, others are simply destroyed or abandoned.

William Tyndale (ca. 1494–1536) is the reformer who provides what is arguably the greatest English translation of the New Testament, much of which surprisingly shows up verbatim in the later Authorized Version (King James Version). However, Parliament bans Tyndale's translation,[107] a friend betrays Tyndale's ongoing work, and he is executed.[108] How can a twenty-first century Christian look into the events of the Reformation and not be deeply troubled by the needless deaths? At the same time, are we not also somewhat chastened by the passion with which believers believe, and live and die for what they believe, in the sixteenth century?

John Calvin (1509–1564) produces his *Institutes of the Christian Religion* (Latin, 1536; French, 1541). Jacob Hutter (ca. 1500–1536) founds an Anabaptist group called the Hutterites.[109] I think of the Hutterites who live in the general area where I grew up, and wonder about the challenges for groups of people who try to locate themselves permanently in a particular point in history and attempt to maintain that lifestyle in later centuries and cultures. But then, how different are we who locate our

---

104. See ch. 1 "Catholics and Protestants in Controversy (1534–1568)" in Davies, *Worship and Theology in England*.

105. One outspoken Catholic who is not killed is one of England's greatest composers, William Byrd, whose longevity is due to some very favourable royal *blindness* on the part of the Queen. See an introduction to Byrd and his music, written by leading Byrd scholar, Kerman, "Byrd, William"; see also chapter 15 above. See esp. ch. 6 on Byrd in Porter, *Early English Composers and the Credo*.

106. Elton, *Reform and Reformation*, 234. Elton depicts Henry VIII's motives for the dissolution as being little more than "greed for places he liked" and "passion for developing his country palaces" (202). See discussion by Dickens, *English Reformation*, 147–54.

107. See Dickens, *English Reformation*, 129–32.

108. See, e.g., Porter, *How We Got the New Testament*, 161–63. See also Dickens, *English Reformation*, 70–75; and Estep, *Renaissance and Reformation*, 250–55.

109. Estep, *Anabaptist Story*, 131–49.

worship in a specific era, including—or maybe especially—those of us whose roots are in the Protestant Reformation?

Another inquisition begins (under Pope Paul III, 1542). The Council of Trent, the counter-reformation against Protestantism, defines its own official theology (1545–1563).[110] The Church of England creates the Book of Common Prayer (1549).[111] Queen Mary reverts England to Roman Catholicism (1553–1558) and has over 250 Protestant Reformers burned at the stake.[112]

The Geneva Bible (1560) is the first Bible to include chapter and verse numbers,[113] which may come as a surprise to some modern-day Christians who assume that these have always been part of the original texts.

The Anabaptist Menno Simons (1496–1561) begins the now well-known Mennonites.[114] Simons, an ordained Roman Catholic Priest (in Friesland), is first exposed to the term "rebaptism" in his 30s when he hears of someone being beheaded for holding to this belief. He subsequently becomes suspicious of the biblical foundation for infant baptism and later meets some Anabaptists who practice a "believer's baptism."[115] This is an important foundational point for all later Baptists and Free Churches whose theology and practice is based on believer's baptism.

Also around this time, the English discover "a new term of abuse—'Puritan.'" Initially an insult against nonconformist clergy, that is, zealous protestants who won't wear the required liturgical vestments, it soon becomes a term used by anyone against pious people.[116]

Great composers of this century include Palestrina of Italy (ca. 1525–1594),[117] mentioned above, and William Byrd of England (ca. 1540–1623).[118] In England, the shift from Latin to the vernacular gives

---

110. Mitchell, "Reforms," 333–43.

111. See Ratcliff, *Booke of Common Prayer*, and comparisons by Swete, *Church Services and Service-Books*. See also Ketley, *Two Liturgies*.

112. Estep, *Renaissance and Reformation*, 262–65.

113. Dickens, *English Reformation*, 288.

114. See, e.g., Estep, *Anabaptist Story*, 151–76.

115. See Estep, *Anabaptist Story*, 13–15, regarding a night in 1525 when Conrad Grebel initiates believer's baptism.

116. Coffey and Lim, "Introduction," 1.

117. See, e.g., Grout, *History of Western Music*, 261–70; Sadie and Latham, eds., *Cambridge Music Guide*, 120–25. See also Lockwood et al., "Palestrina."

118. See, e.g., Grout, *History of Western Music*, 273–75; Sadie and Latham, eds., *Cambridge Music Guide*, 129–33; and dedicated monographs by Kerman (*Masses and Motets*), and Harley, *William Byrd*.

rise to a new kind of ultra-simplified service music in English, in part so that all the words can be understood.[119] While this seems like a very reasonable move, it spells the end of one of the heights of musical composition and artistry. Of the era of polyphonic composition, philosopher Karl Popper writes, "it is possibly the most unprecedented, original, indeed miraculous achievement of our Western civilization, not excluding science."[120]

In Germany, Luther's own musical setting of the German Lutheran Mass influences worship in the vernacular.[121] Worship in the new German Lutheran form is more congregationally based and begins a new involvement of the people in music for worship. Luther's hymn, "A Mighty Fortress," is the quintessential Reformation song, with words and music both credited to Luther himself (1529), although many twenty-first century congregations would find the original version of the music surprisingly challenging to sing. During this century, those countries that continue to use either the Roman Catholic rite or the new Church of England liturgy (although it looks much like the Roman Catholic) still have professional choirs with very little participation by congregations, although congregants are likely to understand the words for the first time.

Many facets of the Protestant Reformation require our ongoing thoughtful and honest theological reflection, such as the question of the roles of art and music—and beauty—for worship. Is simple accessibility and mere functionality sufficient for creatures who have been designed by a Creator, whose capacity to imagine and create artistic works is immense and unfathomable?

Seventeenth Century

Early in the seventeenth century, John Smyth (d. 1612) founds the Baptist Church (1609), objects to infant baptism,[122] and demands church-state

---

119. Compare the complexity of Latin works dealt with in Benham, *Latin Church Music*, with the new note-per-syllable English setting in Fellowes, ed., *Office*.

120. Popper, *Unended Quest*, 56.

121. Westermeyer (*Te Deum*, 141–49) insightfully discusses Luther's views on theology and music, and his concern to facilitate congregational singing. Luther believes that the discipline of studying music follows immediately after theology, and that music deserves the highest praise next to the Word of God (see 144). For thorough discussion, see Leaver, *Luther's Liturgical Music*.

122. White (*Protestant Worship*, 120–22) describes the origins of the Separatists, how John Smyth moves to Amsterdam and famously baptizes himself, distancing

separation. Meanwhile, the King James Version or Authorized Version of the Bible is released in England (1611),[123] much of which is verbatim from Wycliffe's translation, as noted above.

Attention is drawn to the New World, where fledgling movements and religious institutions are being established. The most famous separatists, known as the Pilgrim Fathers, leave England for the Netherlands and then sail the Atlantic to begin the Plymouth Colony (1620).[124] Puritan John Winthrop (1587/88–1649) delivers the highly-quoted sermon, "A Model of Christian Charity," with his now famous reference to their future existence as a "City upon a Hill" (1630).[125] The sermon is still worth reading. Puritans at first remain part of the Anglican Church, but eventually are removed from the Church of England as "Nonconformists."[126]

One of the great American educational institutions is founded in 1636 with 16 students and one master. It is known as Harvard College. I think about how it was a place initially designed to train ministers. How many of our educational institutions began with that initial vision of ministerial training?

An English dissenter, George Fox (1624–1691), experiences Inner Light (1646) and establishes the Society of Friends or the Quaker movement, which is especially concerned with communing with God without the aid of clergy, symbols, or even words.[127] John Bunyan (1628–1688) writes *Pilgrim's Progress* (1678).[128] Is it possible to read this book, including Part II, without engaging in deep personal theological reflection? This allegory is evidence of a man who thought deeply about his life of faith and worship.

New hymns begin to appear in the first half of the century—and they are not welcome. In fact, churches are splitting over the notion of introducing "hymns" into public worship! Russel Squire tells of the struggle to introduce hymns into English worship, and he notes how difficult it is for us to realize that such a prejudice ever existed.[129] He writes of a Baptist

---

himself from the notion of infant baptism. After Smyth's death, his friend, Thomas Helwys, returns to England to begin the first Baptist congregation in England.

123. See a summary in Porter, *How We Got the New Testament*, 163–65.
124. Coffey and Lim, "Introduction," 5.
125. See "John Winthrop."
126. See White, *Protestant Worship*, 117–34.
127. White, *Protestant Worship*, 135–49.
128. See the fascinating story of his life in Deal, *John Bunyan*.
129. Squire, *Church Music*, 131–35.

church whose minister is Benjamin Keach (and later, Charles Spurgeon), a church that decides to introduce hymn singing into its worship. The result is "a sizable minority who left the worship service and met together elsewhere in a 'songless sanctuary.'"[130] Psalms are considered acceptable for singing, but recently composed "unscriptural" hymns are not![131] As always when I consider this, I am struck by how some things do not change: the music of worship is frequently a source of contention for worshipers, now and then. Some of the radical new hymns of the seventeenth century include: "Now Thank We All our God,"[132] "Jesus, Priceless Treasure,"[133] "Sing Praise to God Who Reigns Above,"[134] and "Praise to the Lord, the Almighty."[135] Can we even imagine a church splitting over the introduction of these hymns, especially troublesome because they are "humanly composed"?

More hymn lyrics are now matched with a hymn tune.[136] This is a reminder that there was a greater fluidity between lyrics and music then than the life-long user of a church hymnbook in later centuries might expect. I recall handling one old hymnbook in which all the pages were divided horizontally. The upper portion of the page had music, the bottom had text, and one could turn to separate upper and lower half-pages to match lyrics with any number of tunes that would fit the syllables. The modern-day hymnal maintains information in the back pages that still allows for this, but when the text is typed right into the music, we come to believe that those lyrics must be sung with that specific tune. How inflexible we have become.

In the latter part of the seventeenth century, we encounter the innovative hymn-writing of Isaac Watts (1674–1748) and his ongoing effort to get his hymns into use in the church to raise the quality of singing and

---

130. Squire, *Church Music*, 131.

131. Squire, *Church Music*, 131–32.

132. Words by Martin Rinkart, 1636; translation by Catherine Winkworth, 1863; music by Johann Crüger, 1647.

133. Words by Johann Franck, 1653; translation Catherine Winkworth, 1863; music by Johann Crüger, 1653.

134. Words by Johann J. Schütz, 1675; translation by Frances Cox, 1864; music from the Bohemian Brethren's *Kirchengesänge*, 1566.

135. Words by Joachim Neander, 1680; translation by Catherine Winkworth, 1863; music from *Ernewerten Gesangbuch*, Stralsund, 1665.

136. See Squire, *Church Music*, 134–38, on Methodist hymnody.

the level of meaningful singing.[137] He writes a lot of hymns—about 750 of them.[138] But psalmody is still the norm of music in the average post-Reformation church of the time,[139] which can be a pretty lifeless form of music—at least, Watts clearly thinks so. He reportedly describes the singing in both Anglican and Nonconformist services in the following way: "The singing of God's praise is the part of worship nighest heaven, and its performance among us is the worst on earth."[140] As a fifteen-year-old complaining to his father about this after a service, he gets this response from his father: "Give us something better, young man."[141] The young Watts sets to work on this immediately, and introduces his first hymn to the Independents' meeting that night through the clerk's "lining out," that is, singing a line and having the congregation repeat it. He recognizes that the issue of how to teach new music to a congregation is important, and this is still true today. Watts writes two kinds of hymns for worship, one a re-casting of the psalms in contemporary language, which makes David sound more "Christian" ("Imitations of the Psalms," as he calls them), and the other, hymns that are of "human composure."[142] Texts of hymns by Watts that many worshipers still sing today include: "When I Survey the Wondrous Cross,"[143] "I Sing the Mighty Power of God,"[144] "Jesus Shall

---

137. White (*Introduction to Christian Worship*, 125) describes Watts's efforts to introduce hymn singing as something that meets with stubborn resistance. It is not really accepted among Puritans (Congregationalists) and Presbyterians until into the nineteenth century.

138. Reynolds and Price (*Survey of Christian Hymnody*, 56) write that his reputation as the "Father of English hymnody" rests not on being the first to write English hymns, but on the fact that he wrote "new songs" that moved away from strict Scripture language and freely expressed biblical truth with poetic expression.

139. Spinks, "Anglicans and Dissenters," 517, writes, "Although sacred songs and poems were not unknown in the English church, the general practice of the Church of England, and of the early independent churches, was to sing metrical psalmody." Davies (*Worship and Theology in England*, 522) describes "the transition from prose psalm to metrical psalm and eventually to hymnody." Lamb (*Psalms in Christian Worship*, 150) comments on how England's "Psalm tunes began to be forgotten in the eighteenth century" and church music receives new impetus from hymns instead.

140. Bailey, *Gospel in Hymns*, 48.

141. Bailey, *Gospel in Hymns*, 48–49.

142. Bailey, *Gospel in Hymns*, 48–49.

143. These lyrics are originally published in his *Hymns and Spiritual Songs* (1707) (see "Hymns for Worship," 74).

144. Watts publishes these lyrics in his *Divine and Moral Songs* (1720) (see "Hymns for Worship," 75).

Reign," "Joy to the World," and "O God, our Help in Ages Past."[145] Who can imagine now that these would have been troubling because they were so modern—and so human? Of course, not all of Watts's hymns are great, and the poorer ones disappear. When we evaluate contemporary song- and hymn-writing for worship, a similar natural culling takes place. Many will disappear, and some will be retained for further generations of vibrant worshipers.

Eighteenth Century

The seeds of Methodism (the term "Methodist" initially being derogatory) are planted in Oxford University through a small group called the Holy Club, initiated in 1729 by brothers John Wesley (1703–1791)[146] and Charles Wesley (1707–1788). The latter soon is famous for his gifted hymn-writing.[147] Interestingly, it is not until some years later, in 1738, that first Charles and then John both experience a new-found quiet confidence and inner peace through a conscious personal trusting in Christ for salvation.[148] Hymn-singing finally begins to take root in England, with Wesley's publication of *Hymns and Sacred Poems* in 1740.[149] Together, the Wesleys begin to include hymns in conjunction with the Lord's Supper, although not yet during the Church of England liturgy.[150]

145. Lyrics for these three of his hymns are from 1719.

146. John Wesley leads a revival known for rigorous spiritual practice, personal piety, and concern for the poor, imprisoned, and uneducated. Maddox and Vickers ("Introduction," 1) write, "What began as a meeting of a few students at Oxford who were seeking accountability has blossomed into a worldwide movement consisting of more than 100 denominations, which minister to more than 75 million people. When one adds to this the Pentecostal and Charismatic churches that trace their heritage from Methodist roots, the number of Christians who can be regarded as Wesley's spiritual or ecclesiastical dependents is staggering." Westerfield Tucker notes that Wesley "observed that 'as long as there are various opinions there will be various ways of worshipping God; seeing a variety of opinion necessarily implies a variety of practice,'" and posited "that mutual respect, not separation or division, should be the response" ("Wesley's Emphases on Worship," 226).

147. Maddox and Vickers ("Introduction," 8) note the "broad areas of agreement between the brothers on matters of doctrine, so that hymns of Charles are often the best illustrations of theological points that John makes in sermons." They also summarize the differences: Charles "was committed to the revival of *the Church of England*, whereas John was committed to the *revival* of the Church of England" (italics original).

148. Latourette, *History of Christianity*, 1023–25.

149. Squire, *Church Music*, 134.

150. Westerfield Tucker, "Wesley's Emphases on Worship," 231.

As with Watts, Wesley writes a lot of hymns, except that he writes over 8,000.[151] (How does one even comprehend this quantity?) Nonetheless, hymn-singing in the Anglican Church is still apparently very bleak. A few dissenting congregations *may* include some hymns of Watts. However, this begins to change more dramatically, and Methodists, Anglicans, and Dissenters all find reasons to sing Wesley's doctrinally rich, theologically sound, and lyrically well-crafted hymns. Nicholas Temperley writes of Wesley's hymns that "They were innovative in their use of the first person, expression of intense personal feeling, and vivid depiction of the suffering of Christ."[152] Today, many of Charles's works remain among the best-loved in the hymn repertoire, such as: "And Can It Be,"[153] "Christ the Lord Is Risen Today,"[154] "Hark the Herald Angels Sing,"[155] "O for a Thousand Tongues to Sing,"[156] "Come Thou Long-Expected Jesus,"[157] and "Rejoice the Lord Is King."[158]

George Whitefield (1714-1770), friend of the Wesleys, plays an important part in the movement initiated by them. Whitefield's itinerant open-air preaching in Bristol brings coal-coated miners to tears, and to faith.[159] The three men at the forefront of this movement try to reform the Church of England through a return to the gospel, but Methodists become a formal separate denomination after John Wesley's death.

Meanwhile, the First Great Awakening breaks out in Massachusetts, under the preaching of Jonathan Edwards (1703-1758). His sermon from 1741, "Sinners in the Hands of an Angry God," might still prompt something of a great awakening if pastors throughout North America

---

151. See discussion of many of these in Kimbrough, ed., *Charles Wesley*.

152. Temperley, "Wesley."

153. Words by Wesley, 1738; music by Thomas Campbell, 1825.

154. Words by Wesley, 1739; music from *Lyrica Davidica*, 1708.

155. Words by Wesley, 1739; music by Felix Mendelssohn, 1840, adapted by William Cummings, 1856.

156. Words by Wesley, 1739; music by Carl G. Gläser, 1828, adapted and arranged by Lowell Mason, 1839.

157. Words by Wesley, 1744; music from Christian F. Witt's *Psalmodia Sacra*, 1715; adapted by Henry J. Gauntlett, 1861.

158. Words by Wesley, 1744; music by John Darwall, 1770. Familiar hymns by others from this century include John Newton's "Amazing Grace," and others such as "There Is a Fountain Filled with Blood," "O Come, All Ye Faithful," "Come Thou Almighty King," "Be Still My Soul," "Come Thou Fount of Every Blessing," "All Hail the Power of Jesus' Name," and "Angels We Have Heard on High."

159. Latourette, *History of Christianity*, 1025.

today all agreed to read it one Sunday instead of preaching their typical message. It certainly pulls no punches. Whitefield, now in America, brings intense feeling and dramatic expressiveness to his own preaching in the Colonies, and thousands, up to 30,000 at a time, gather to hear him and respond to his messages as the Great Awakening develops.[160]

Back in Leipzig, Germany, the music of Johann Sebastian Bach (1685–1750) dramatically influences the history of Christian worship, not only for Lutherans, but for generations of believers of many denominations around the world.[161] His masterful integration of highly-skilled instrumentalists and vocalists, together with simpler settings of songs for participation by the congregation—what we know as chorales, set within the structure of the Lutheran service—sets a benchmark for integrated Christian worship that has never really been reached again. Bach himself is known for his own theological reflection, in part captured in the notes in his Calov Bible. This three-volume Bible is a German translation with commentary by Martin Luther and Wittenberg theology professor Calovius. Bach's copy is discovered in the twentieth century in a home in St. Louis, Missouri, with many markings and notations in it by the great worship-music writer himself. By 1 Chr 25, he notes that this passage is the true foundation of all God-pleasing music.

Handel's *Messiah* (1741) remains *the* choral work to accompany either Christmas or Easter celebrations of the church,[162] although its inception is pragmatic. Opera, full of costumes and pageantry, is not allowed in eighteenth-century performance houses of England during Lent, so Handel (1685–1759) dreams up an alternate form of musical performance that relies on biblical texts and does not require staging. The result is a work that is equally at home in the concert venue and in the church, even today.

---

160. Latourette, *History of Christianity*, 958–60.

161. Every significant history of music textbook includes at least a basic introduction to the life and work of Bach. See, e.g., Sadie and Latham, eds., *Cambridge Music Guide*, 184–204. See also dedicated monographs on some of his monumental works, such as Butt, *Bach*, as well as edited volumes encompassing his life and work, such as Butt, ed., *Cambridge Companion to Bach*. See also chapter 11 above for discussion of Bach.

162. See, e.g., Burrow, *Handel*; Bullard, *Messiah*; Luckett, *Handel's Messiah*.

Nineteenth Century

In the nineteenth century, we encounter the rise of the Sunday School movement in the United States (it started earlier in Britain),[163] the beginning of the Stone-Campbell Movement,[164] and the founding of the Plymouth Brethren (but preferring to be called "Brethren") in which "Ordained clergy were considered superfluous."[165] We hear of the revivals of Charles Finney (1830), and the Second Great Awakening in America.[166] The latter results in Whitefield's introduction of Isaac Watts's hymns to America, soon to become standard in many churches that had mostly been singing the psalms.[167]

The Oxford or Tractarian Movement in England begins with a group of High Church Anglicans concerned to recover more Catholic elements of the Christian faith and reincorporate them into the Anglican liturgy (1833).[168] With this movement comes a return to more symbols and objects, such as candles and censers, and more decorative elements, such as elaborate clerical vestments. Meanwhile, in the Oriental (Orthodox) Churches of the East, music and liturgy maintains its steady and ongoing reverence for the numinous and historical.

Many new movements begin in the nineteenth century, including Mormonism[169] and the Seventh-Day Adventists, the latter founded after the

---

163. Latourette, *History of Christianity*, 1267. Previously, in 1780 in England, Robert Raikes begins a Sunday School in his home city of Gloucester, designed for moral and religious education for very poor children on the one day of the week when they are not working! Although others had made even earlier attempts, it is Raikes whose efforts are eventually emulated throughout the British Empire (see also 1031–32).

164. See Latourette, *History of Christianity*, 1041–43, on two similar movements, led by Barton W. Stone (1772–1844) in Virginia, and Thomas Campbell in Pennsylvania, later joined by his son, Alexander Campbell (1788–1866). Both movements attempt to transcend denominational divisions to try to get back to an ideal of the New Testament church, including calling themselves simply Christians or Disciples of Christ (Stone), or Reformers or Disciples (Campbell) (or restorationists). In 1832, Stone and Alexander Campbell agree to work together.

165. White, *Protestant Worship*, 131.

166. Donakowski, "Age of Revolutions," 372–74.

167. Dowley, *Christian Music*, 120–21.

168. Donakowski, "Age of Revolutions," 365, 369–70. Their publications or "tracts" give rise to the name "Tractarian." They are also called Newmanites and Puseyites after two of their high-profile leaders, Cardinal John Henry Newman and Edward Bouverie Pusey.

169. White, *Protestant Worship*, 186.

Part Three: The Past and Present of Music and Worship

end of the world that they predict does not occur.[170] The Southern Baptist Convention begins (1845) over the issue of slavery, consisting of Baptists in eight slave-holding states that are unwilling to give up their slaves.[171] A Methodist preacher founds the Salvation Army with a vow to bring the gospel into the streets to the most desperate and needy, and vigorously uses tambourine and brass instruments to get their attention (1865).[172]

Bibles again make headlines in the Christian world, with the Revised Version of 1881–1894, brought about by the Church of England.[173] An intentionally non-mainstream Bible Student movement results in the Jehovah's Witnesses (1884),[174] while, in contrast, a group that is dedicated to distributing Bibles far and wide, the Gideons International (1899), becomes known for its free distribution of Bibles. Many fifth-graders receive one in their schools.[175] Meanwhile, Dwight L. Moody founds Moody Bible Institute, designed to train both men and women, especially in instruction of the Bible.[176]

Worship in the nineteenth century warmly welcomes hymns now, including: "Holy, Holy, Holy,"[177] "O Worship the King,"[178] "Just as I Am,"[179] "Silent Night,"[180] "Crown Him with Many Crowns,"[181] "The Church's One Foundation,"[182] "Immortal Invisible,"[183] "Take my Life and Let It

---

170. White, *Protestant Worship*, 186–87.

171. Latourette, *History of Christianity*, 1261.

172. Webber, ed., *Complete Library of Christian Worship*, 2:87–88, 245–46.

173. This version uses a Greek text based upon the major codices and not the Received Text, following the Hebrew Masoretic Text of the Old Testament, and using Greek word order where possible for translation.

174. Latourette, *History of Christianity*, 1260.

175. For their history, see "About Us."

176. See George, ed., *Mr. Moody*.

177. Words by Reginald Heber, 1827; music by John B. Dykes, 1861.

178. Words by Robert Grant, 1833; music by Joseph M. Kraus, ca. 1785, in William Gardiner's *Sacred Melodies*, 1815.

179. Words by Charlotte Elliott, 1836; music by William B. Bradbury, 1849.

180. Words by Joseph Mohr, 1818; music by Franz Grüber, 1818.

181. Words by Matthew Bridges, 1851, and Godfrey Thring, 1874; music by George J. Elvey, 1868.

182. Words by Samuel J. Stone, 1866; music by Samuel S. Wesley, 1864.

183. Words by Walter C. Smith, 1867; music (Welsh) in John Roberts's *Caniadau y Cyssegr*, 1839, adapted from a Welsh ballad (*Hymns for Worship*, 149).

Be,"[184] "Like a River Glorious,"[185] and "O the Deep, Deep Love of Jesus."[186] Spirituals begin to play a significant role in worship, such as: "Were You There?"[187] and "Go, Tell It on the Mountain."[188] New songs of personal expression include: "What a Friend We Have in Jesus,"[189] "My Jesus, I Love Thee,"[190] "Blessed Assurance,"[191] and "When Peace Like a River (It Is Well)," the story of which is familiar and still moving and powerful.[192] Each of these becomes a potential gem of theological insight or personal theological experience.

JOURNEY OF WORSHIP PART 5: THE TWENTIETH CENTURY

In the early years of the twentieth century, the Azusa Street Revival in Los Angeles, California, is where the modern Pentecostal movement begins to take shape,[193] a movement that subsequently influences much of North America and the rest of the world. We see the rise of Dispensationalism,[194] and modern missions gain new impetus.[195] Karl Barth begins a critique of Liberal Christianity and stimulates the onset of the neo-orthodox movement.[196]

---

184. Words by Frances R. Havergal, 1874; music by Henri A. César Malan, 1827.

185. Words by Frances R. Havergal, 1878; music by James Mountain, 1876.

186. Words by Samuel Trevor Francis, ca. 1890; music by Thomas J. Williams, 1890.

187. Words and music: African American spiritual, nineteenth century.

188. Words and music: African American spiritual, nineteenth century.

189. Words by Joseph M. Scriven, 1855; music by Charles C. Converse, 1868.

190. Words by William R. Featherstone, ca. 1862; music by Adoniram J. Gordon, 1876.

191. Words by Fanny Crosby, 1873; music by Phoebe P. Knapp, 1873.

192. Words by Horatio G. Spafford, 1873, after losing his four daughters in a ship collision; music by Philip P. Bliss, 1876, who names the tune "Ville du Havre," after the boat that was destroyed (*Hymns for Worship*, 186).

193. White, *Protestant Worship*, 194–97.

194. Burgess, ed. (*New International Dictionary*, 584–86) notes seven commonly-held dispensations or chronological categories of biblical history: innocence, conscience, civil government, promise, law, grace, and the kingdom.

195. See Burgess, ed., *New International Dictionary*, 885–91, on the Pentecostal missions movement.

196. Latourette (*History of Christianity*, 1382–84) describes the internal religious struggles that result from World War I, especially in Germany, as people search for something more reliable and believable, if they choose to believe at all. Barth "declared

Religious radio is on the rise, and Billy Sunday is at work as an open-air high-energy evangelist in the United States.[197] In a less-welcoming part of the world, Dietrich Bonhoeffer's writings are the result of deep and costly theological reflection. In prison, he lives by the church calendar, not the monthly calendar. On November 21, 1943, he writes, "A prison cell, in which one waits, hopes, does various unessential things, and is completely dependent on the fact that the door of freedom has to be opened *from the outside*, is not a bad picture of Advent."[198] He is executed by the Nazis in 1945.

Still in the 1940s, the Revised Standard Version New Testament is now in print (1947), the Dead Sea Scrolls are discovered (1947),[199] a new State of Israel is declared (1948), and Billy Graham begins his first crusade in a tent in Los Angeles, described as "The Canvas Cathedral with the Steeple of Light."[200] There are two World Wars mixed in behind all this, which raise troubling questions and disturbing doubts for many believers about God's sovereignty and kingdom. The extermination of millions of Jews and others in Hitler's world remains an oozing wound of humanity. A thoughtful day at the Jewish memorial, Yad Vashem (www.yadvashem.org), in Jerusalem, should surely be included in every reflective Christian's life-schedule. The jumbled mound of mismatched, thread-bare, worn-out shoes lying beneath a clear section in the floor is provocative fuel for theological reflection. More challenging yet is trying to interpret what you see in a stark place like an actual concentration camp, such as the one at Sachsenhausen, Germany.[201]

In the 1950s, Mother Teresa inaugurates her Missionaries of Charity, Campus Crusade for Christ starts up at the University of California at Los Angeles (UCLA), and the most widely-used critical edition of the Greek New Testament enters into a new era of editorship with its 21st

---

that what we must do is to heed not what other men say about God, but what God has to say to men" (1383); see also 1420–21 on neo-orthodoxy in the Americas.

197. Latourette (*History of Christianity*, 1419) describes William Ashley "Billy" Sunday, former professional baseball player, noting "his spectacular, informal pulpit mannerisms" and "his 'sawdust trail' along which converts made their way from their seats to the front of the 'tabernacles' which were erected for him."

198. Bonhoeffer, *Letters and Papers*, 416 (emphasis original).

199. Peruse these online at the Leon Levy Dead Sea Scrolls Digital Library at www.deadseascrolls.org.il.

200. See Rasmussen, "Billy Graham's Star," who tells of Graham's Crusades starting in LA in a tent at Washington Boulevard and Hill Street.

201. See "Sachsenhausen."

edition under the editorship of Kurt Aland.²⁰² C. S. Lewis captures the imaginations of readers of all ages in his so-called "Story for Children," *The Lon, the Witch and the Wardrobe*, a story that continues to influence many a grown-up's view of worship, while his entire oeuvre of writings, including his scholarly work, articulates a well-thought-out Christian world view.²⁰³

Note that during this decade, the United States Pledge of Allegiance is changed from "one nation, indivisible" to "one nation under God, indivisible,"²⁰⁴ but in the following decade, the United States Supreme Court makes a decision against school prayer. One might wonder how "one nation under God, indivisible" would come to this conclusion. Meanwhile, the film "The Ten Commandments" is produced.

In the 1960s, the Second Vatican Council is announced,²⁰⁵ Martin Luther King has a dream about civil rights,²⁰⁶ Oral Roberts founds a university, and various unlikely church groups and denominations begin to merge.²⁰⁷

In the 1970s, music in the church begins to be challenged by a shifting cultural norm. Folk music, pop music, and bands like the Beatles give rise to some edgier artists in the Christian world, such as Love Song (often considered *the* most important Christian band).²⁰⁸ Keith Green brings an impassioned challenge to the Christian status quo.²⁰⁹ Andrae Crouch writes and sings songs in such a way that any venue is transformed into an apocalyptic worship service, transforming a generation of worshipers, both black and white. He still influences the church through his music that has been adopted into many standard hymnbooks.²¹⁰ These artists begin to

---

202. Porter (*How We Got the New Testament*, 48) discusses the development of this form of the Greek New Testament from Eberhard Nestle in 1898, to the twenty-first edition with Kurt Aland in 1952, and subsequent editions up to the present (see 48–50).

203. See, e.g., Porter, "Worldview of C. S. Lewis."

204. See "Pledge of Allegiance."

205. Haquin, "Liturgical Movement," 704–6; Overath, ed., *Sacred Music*.

206. See "Martin Luther King."

207. E.g., the United Church bringing Congregationalists, Evangelicals and Reformed—Calvinists and Lutherans—together; and the United Methodist Church bringing Methodists and Evangelical United Brethren together.

208. Powell, *Encyclopedia of Contemporary Christian Music*, 543–47.

209. Powell, *Encyclopedia of Contemporary Christian Music*, 381–86.

210. Powell, *Encyclopedia of Contemporary Christian Music*, 210–14.

cut a new swathe through Christian culture in a way that most musicians and bands that follow can never duplicate. The Jesus Movement is alive and well,[211] and the power and passion of these worshipers-through-song captivate many Christians who wonder if they had previously been sound asleep in their faith and worship. It is a euphoric time that seems to kindle a love for Jesus and a love for one another.

Meanwhile, Hal Lindsey influences everyday Christians to look for the end of the world with his *Late Great Planet Earth*. Another Bible, the New American Standard, is published; Jerry Falwell begins Liberty University; yet another Bible, the New International Version, comes out; Jim Bakker begins his so-called PTL ("Praise the Lord") television ministry; James Dobson launches his *Focus on the Family*; the Chicago Statement on Biblical Inerrancy is crafted;[212] and the most-watched film of all time is released, called simply "Jesus." It would seem that Christian worship has reached some kind of a peak—or is that just an illusion? Only time will tell. And it does.

In the final decades of the twentieth century, we begin to experience what comes to be known as "the worship wars,"[213] although this is clearly not a new phenomenon, since we have seen, through almost each of the preceding centuries, some form or another of worship war. As a new generation dreams of a more passionate and life changing experience of God and Jesus, and longs to experience this in their local church, it becomes noticeable that there is a large crack in the structure of what many think is "the" way of worship. The organ had finally gained its long-fought-for status as the instrument of worship, for it was only "by the end of the nineteenth century, most had accepted organs," so it is interesting that at the end of the twentieth century, only a hundred years later, many churches no longer have, or use, an organ in their musical worship.[214] Meanwhile, that new generation finds more accessible instruments to express their heart-felt tunes of worship. Many of these instruments are introduced by bands in the early days of the Jesus Movement, instruments such as

---

211. See all three previous footnotes for Powell's insights into the Jesus Movement.

212. See "Chicago Statement."

213. See a well-crafted apologetic for this musical expression in Frame, *Contemporary Worship Music*. See also the more colloquial contributions of Hamilton, "Triumph of Praise Songs," and Crouch, "Amplified Versions."

214. Westerfield Tucker ("North America," 615) describes the surprising outcome of the long-lasting heated debates over, and strong resistance to, the introduction of the organ into the church.

acoustic guitars, electric guitars, drums, and keyboards. Oddly, we see the precursor of some of these instruments in various parts of the Old Testament and throughout the Psalms. Hymns, once a radical new form of expressive worship,[215] are now seen as the established and formulaic music of the church. From the opposite perspective, these new forms of music (although surely we see by now that "new" is a meaningless word?) are viewed as sensual, frivolous, and divisive. The drive towards worship music that is in touch with the heart has not abated, but recent years have seen a welcome move towards making the "new" songs of this worship more substantive, theologically grounded, and musically well-crafted.[216]

JOURNEY OF WORSHIP PART 6: THE TWENTY-FIRST CENTURY

This journey of two millennia of changing worship styles, and the music and practices that go with it, has now reached the twenty-first century, our century. Much has happened over the previous almost two thousand years, but there are indications that there is more to come.

Here and Now

As we reflect on how we got here, we also face the question of where *here* actually is. Some divide our basic modes of western Christian worship into six categories: formal-liturgical, traditional hymn-based, contemporary music-driven, charismatic, blended, and emerging.[217] Even these designations should prompt our theological reflection! Within the last stream, *emerging*, there have been attempts to distinguish further categories, identified by whether there is high or low change in message (that is, orthodox or new message) and high or low change in method (that is, orthodox or new method of delivery).[218] The voices of many are in unison on the point that culture and our personal expression has changed and therefore our worship must change to meet or match those shifts,[219] although it is possible that the voices of culture and personal experience

---

215. See, e.g., the above discussion about Isaac Watts.

216. "Newer" hymns, such as "In Christ Alone" by Stuart Townend and Keith Getty (2001) and "How Deep the Father's Love" by Stuart Townend (1995), set a new standard that appealed to a wide range of age-groups in many congregations.

217. Basden, ed., *Exploring the Worship Spectrum*.

218. Sweet, "Introduction," 19.

219. Carson, *Becoming Conversant with the Emerging Church*.

are currently too loud. It is certain that many of the loudest voices speak out of an autobiographical reaction to the church of their youth, which they now view as narrow, inflexible, inauthentic, and possibly deceptive. It is no surprise that this brings a reactionary, if possibly over-reactionary, response. Any new directions in worship practice should compel us to evaluate honestly, without defensiveness, what authentic Christian worship really is. But that is always easier said than accomplished.

We see the historical tendency to react strongly to current troubling ideas and events, and we can see that this worship journey is complicated. We need to look back to how and why it began. We need to consider the journey so far—both the long historical view and our own more localized historical view. And we need a glimpse of the goal of our journey to guide us there. We need that rock to look at down the beach or that streetlight at the end of the road, so we know where we are supposed to be heading, at least for this stretch of the journey. Perhaps at that rock or streetlight we will need to locate the next marker.

In Jesus' conversation with the woman at the well in John 4, he turns some notions of worship upside down in his statement that the Father seeks worshipers (John 4:23–24). He communicates something rather astounding to this woman with his revelation that there is an ongoing quest on the part of the *Father* to find those worshipers who will worship him in Spirit and truth.

Are we a bit surprised that Jesus gives his most critical information about the new Christian worship to a woman? (I consider her the first Christian worship leader). More importantly, are we taken off-guard to realize that God is actually seeking us? In this declaration, Jesus challenges a familiar paradigm of seeker-based worship, far older than a movement in Chicago, but also evident throughout the history of Christian worship. Are we not to seek after God? Yes, of course, we are to seek earnestly after the heart of God with all of our being. But the notion that this is how worship begins is already out of kilter. God is not hiding. According to Jesus, he is actively seeking *us*. In our worship, it is not we who are seeking God, it is the reverse. Our worship is our *responding* to the God who is seeking us—perhaps seeking us since the day he set out to find the newly-clothed Adam and Eve in the Garden. When we confuse this, we get off-track.

God's revelation to us is incredible, unfathomable, humanly incomprehensible, but does it require a complicated response? Apparently not. Angels and shepherds are cast together in one opening scene. Children are welcomed on Jesus' knee. Repentant sinners are forgiven without delay, tax-collectors included. Regular working guys—that is, not priests, not religious authorities—are personally invited to be the first disciples of Jesus. Women are part of that earliest group of followers, in a culture where that was unlikely. A woman is given some of the first and most precious information about the "new" worship. Men and women of dubious moral fibre are included in Jesus' inner circle when they respond to him. And on it goes, in a pattern of invitation and welcome to any and all who will genuinely respond.

True worship is the act of response with heart, soul, mind, and body to the Holy Creator, God. He invites us into communion with him through Jesus Christ. He invites us into his presence through the power of his Holy Spirit. He invites us to respond to him because that is *why* we were created, and *what* we were created to do.

God is seeking after worshipers to come close to him. Many of our predecessors tried to maintain great distance between the worshiper and God, so they missed the intimacy. Now, in over-reaction, we attempt to make God so small and predictable that we miss both the mystery and the majesty.

And so . . .

As I look at the myriad churches and Christian institutions with their criss-crossing pathways, the stops and starts, the detours and doubling back, the Christian wars and church disputes and liturgical fossilizations since the time of Jesus Christ, I am troubled by our worship mess. The Israelites wandering in the wilderness, as depicted in the Old Testament, have nothing on Christians in the past two millennia. Perhaps we have been granted this wandering journey because we have been no more willing and able to trust God than the Israelites were.

In some ways, our worship needs to become simpler, so that our hearts can be fully engaged. At the same time, we are suffering deeply from a pervasive shallowness, and once again, we need our intellects to become fully engaged. We are not currently suffering from too much education in the church, but from too little. Can we take seriously the call to learn all that can be learned of God and his truths, of salvation through Christ, of the work of the Holy Spirit, but also bring our worship response with our hearts fully engaged and open? I hear a call to a simpler genuine expressive worship of heart-felt response, but simultaneously to a more comprehensive worship that aligns our minds with Christ and our hearts in mystery and wonder. The two guiding principles of worship are that we worship in Spirit and truth. "Truth" is not a particularly popular notion right now, but presumably that is irrelevant from God's perspective.

CONCLUSION: WHERE NOW?

Martin Stringer observes the history of Christian worship from a sociological perspective, noting that the relationship between the human and the divine is foundational to God's revelation to the world, and that the possibility for intimacy and devotion are not just twenty-first century notions, but central to Christianity and seen throughout the history of its discourses.[220] He discusses the relevance of its texts, noting not only that the texts that are foundational to Christian worship are the witnesses to God's revelation but also that they are partial, that is, they do not give specific answers to every single question and situation; therefore, they always require some level of interpretation. Sociologically, Stringer would say, they are minimalistic, which means that there is always "the potential for Christians . . . to 'go back,' to 'reform,' to 'simplify,' to get back to the purity of the 'Gospel message.'"[221] He continues: "The potential for reform, with its essentially backward gaze, is . . . built into the fundamental structure of all Christian discourses and will always be present to a greater or lesser extent, even in the history of Christian worship."[222]

But, as I said at the outset, may God prevent us from what C. S. Lewis calls "chronological snobbery,"[223] that is, assuming that we know better than those who have lived in the past just because we live in the present. May God also prevent us from worshiping at the feet of any of our historical predecessors. Perhaps they founded our particular church or inspired us with a way of worshiping, but surely they do not deserve our worship. For instance, when I say that I am a Protestant, what, exactly, am I "protesting"? Am I still living in the sixteenth century, protesting indulgences, and worshiping at the feet of one of the leaders of the Reformation? Perhaps the Calvinist or the Lutheran might ask how Calvin's or Luther's name becomes more significant than Christ. Each of us might have important questions to ask ourselves about these kinds of things.

---

220. Stringer, *Sociological History*, 20–22.
221. Stringer, *Sociological History*, 20–23 (here 23).
222. Stringer, *Sociological History*, 23.
223. Also used by his friend, Owen Barfield.

Sometimes I envision smaller worshiping communities that look more like the early church than we have seen for some time, with simpler forms of worship, creeds that are simple statements of faith in God the Father and his Son, baptism that is a simple event that accompanies the onset of new life and faith, and Scripture that is studied deeply, led by faithful students of Scripture and engaged in by those of all ages and maturity of faith. The mode of delivery could be less important and the substance more critical.

The Lord's Supper could be a simple meal, not shrouded with pomp and ceremony, but eaten in a home-like environment, an act that combines the human with the spiritual in a way never since surpassed—that perfect mixture of matter and mystery—taking us once again to a simple room where Jesus ate and drank with his followers, foreshadowing his great act of love, his death, and future meals together (what about that meal with two of his disciples, who did not even recognize him until he broke that bread and poured that wine? Would *we* recognize Jesus if he was serving?)

Music might once again be a holy and inspired mix of psalms, hymns, and spiritual songs—singing Scripture, honouring the best of previous musical expressions of praise and theology and instruction to one another, and writing our own spiritual expressions for voices and instruments, hearts and minds, guided by and full of the Spirit and truth.

But, then, I remember Pliny and what it was really like for Christians in the second century, back when it was "so simple." I falter in my theological reflection, hesitate in my pursuit of a purer worship, and reconsider the merits of such an attempt.

Nonetheless, how *are* we doing as Christians on our two-thousand-year journey of Christian worship so far? Do we understand how we got here, and where "here" is? Do we know where we are going? More importantly, what does God think about our worship? At the least, this retrospection should illustrate our need to check in with Scripture a bit more often, to learn at the feet of our historical predecessors but not worship at their feet, to wisely assess our current culture, to recognize the genuine need for deep personal engagement with God in our worship, to weigh these voices carefully, and to listen closely for the voice of the Holy Spirit who speaks truth and leads us in discernment. May we not just react to the things immediately around us or just keep doing the same thing unreflectively but may we each take seriously the need to open our hearts and minds to the Father, who, after all, is seeking us.

Part Three: The Past and Present of Music and Worship

REFERENCES AND FURTHER READING

"About Us." *The Gideons International*. No pages. Online: https://www.gideons.org/about.

Apel, Willi. *Gregorian Chant*. Bloomington: Indiana University Press, 1958.

Armstrong, Karen. *Jerusalem: One City, Three Faiths*. New York: Knopf, 1996.

Babic, Gordana. *Icons*. London: Bracken, 1988.

Badcock, Francis J. *The History of the Creeds*. London: SPCK, 1930.

Bailey, Albert E. *The Gospel in Hymns: Backgrounds and Interpretations*. New York: Charles Scribner's Sons, 1950.

Bainton, Roland H. *Christendom: A Short History of Christianity and its Impact on Western Civilization*. New York: Harper and Row, 1964.

Baldovin, John F. "Christian Worship to the Eve of the Reformation." In *The Making of Jewish and Christian Worship*, edited by Paul F. Bradshaw et al., 156-83. Two Liturgical Traditions 1. Notre Dame, IN: University of Notre Dame Press, 1991.

Basden, Paul A., ed. *Exploring the Worship Spectrum: Six Views*. Grand Rapids: Zondervan, 2004.

Benham, Hugh. *Latin Church Music in England, c. 1460-575*. London: Barrie and Jenkins, 1977.

Bent, Ian D., and Marianne Pfau. "Hildegard of Bingen." In *The New Grove Dictionary of Music and Musicians*, edited by Stanley Sadie and John Tyrrell, 11:493-99. 2nd ed. New York: Grove, 2001.

Best, Harold M. *Unceasing Worship: Biblical Perspectives on Worship and the Arts*. Downers Grove, IL: InterVarsity, 2003.

Bonhoeffer, Dietrich. *Letters and Papers from Prison*, edited by Eberhard Bethge. New ed. 1953. Reprint, New York: Macmillan, 1970.

Boyd, Malcolm, ed. *J. S. Bach*. Oxford Composer Companions. Oxford: Oxford University Press, 1999.

Bradshaw, Paul F. *The Search for the Origins of Christian Worship: Sources and Methods for the Study of Early Liturgy*. Oxford: Oxford University Press, 1992.

Bradshaw, Paul F., ed. *The New Westminster Dictionary of Liturgy and Worship*. Louisville: Westminster John Knox, 2002.

Brand, Charles M., ed. *Icon and Minaret: Sources of Byzantine and Islamic Civilization*. Englewood Cliffs, NJ: Prentice-Hall, 1969.

Bullard, Roger A. *Messiah: The Gospel according to Handel's Oratorio*. Grand Rapids: Eerdmans, 1993.

Burgess, Stanley M., ed. *The New International Dictionary of Pentecostal and Charismatic Movements*. Rev. and expanded ed. Grand Rapids: Zondervan, 2002.

Burrows, Donald. *Handel: Messiah*. Cambridge Music Handbooks. Cambridge: Cambridge University Press, 1991.

Butt, John. *Bach: Mass in B Minor*. Cambridge: Cambridge University Press, 1991.

Butt, John, ed. *The Cambridge Companion to Bach*. Cambridge: Cambridge University Press, 1997.

Buxton, Richard F. "Sunday." In *The New Westminster Dictionary of Liturgy and Worship*, edited by Paul F. Bradshaw, 1-52. Louisville: Westminster John Knox, 2002.

Byrne, Mary Elizabeth. "A Prayer." *Ériu: Journal of the School of Irish Learning* 2 (1905) 89-91.

Carpenter, Nan Cooke. *Music in the Medieval and Renaissance Universities*. 1958. Reprint, New York: Da Capo, 1972.

Carson, D. A. *Becoming Conversant with the Emerging Church: Understanding a Movement and Its Implications*. Grand Rapids: Zondervan, 2005.

Chadwick, Henry. *Boethius: The Consolations of Music, Logic, Theology, and Philosophy*. Oxford: Oxford University Press, 1981.

"The Chicago Statement on Biblical Inerrancy." *International Council on Biblical Inerrancy*. Online: https://library.dts.edu/Pages/TL/Special/ICBI-1978-11-07.pdf.

Coffey, John, and Paul C. H. Lim. "Introduction." In *The Cambridge Companion to Puritanism*, edited by John Coffey and Paul C. H. Lim, 1–18. Cambridge: Cambridge University Press, 2008.

Collinge, William J. *Historical Dictionary of Catholicism*. Historical Dictionary of Religions, Philosophies, and Movements 12. Lanham, MD: Scarecrow, 1997.

Cosgrove, Charles. H. *An Ancient Christian Hymn with Musical Notation: Papyrus Oxyrhynchus 1786. Text and Commentary*. Studien und Texte zu Antike und Christentum 65. Tübingen: Mohr Siebeck, 2011.

Crouch, Andy. "Amplified Versions: Worship Wars Come Down to Music and a Power Plug." In *Worship at the Next Level: Insight from Contemporary Voices*, edited by Tim A. Dearborn and Scott Coil, 128–30. Grand Rapids: Baker, 2004.

Davies, Horton. *Worship and Theology in England: I. From Cranmer to Hooker, 1534–1603; II. From Andrews to Baxter and Fox, 1603–1690*. Grand Rapids: Eerdmans, 1996.

Deal, William. *John Bunyan: The Tinker of Bedford*. Westchester, IL: Good News, 1977.

Dickens, A. G. *The English Reformation*. New York: Schocken, 1969 [1964].

Donakowski, Conrad L. "The Age of Revolutions." In *The Oxford History of Christian Worship*, edited by Wainwright and Westerfield Tucker, 351–94. Oxford: Oxford University Press, 2005.

Dowley, Tim. *Christian Music: A Global History*. Minneapolis: Fortress, 2011.

Driscoll, Michael S. "The Conversion of the Nations." In *The Oxford History of Christian Worship*, edited by Wainwright and Westerfield Tucker, 175–215. Oxford: Oxford University Press, 2005.

———. *Reformation Europe 1517–1559*. Fontana History of Europe. London: Fontana/Collins, 1963.

Estep, William R. *The Anabaptist Story: An Introduction to Sixteenth-Century Anabaptism*. 3rd ed. Grand Rapids: Eerdmans, 1996.

———. *Renaissance and Reformation*. Grand Rapids: Eerdmans, 1986.

Fellowes, Edmund H. *The Office of the Holy Communion as Set by John Merbecke*. Oxford: Oxford University Press, 1949.

Finnegan, Ruth. *Literacy and Orality*. Oxford: Basil Blackwell, 1988.

Frame, John M. *Contemporary Worship Music: A Biblical Defense*. Phillipsburg, NJ: P&R, 1997.

George, Timothy, ed. *Mr. Moody and the Evangelical Tradition*. London: T. & T. Clark, 2004.

Grout, Donald J., and Claude V. Palisca. *A History of Western Music*. 3rd ed. New York: W. W. Norton, 1980.

"Gutenberg Bible." *University of Cambridge Digital Library*. Online: https://cudl.lib.cam.ac.uk/view/PR-INC-00001-A-00001-0001-03761/1.

"Gutenberg Digital." *Göttingen Gutenberg Bible*. Online: http://www.gutenbergdigital.de/gudi/start.htm.

PART THREE: THE PAST AND PRESENT OF MUSIC AND WORSHIP

Hamilton, Michael S. "The Triumph of Praise Songs: How Guitars Beat Out the Organ in the Worship Wars." In *Worship at the Next Level: Insight from Contemporary Voices*, edited by Tim A. Dearborn and Scott Coil, 74–85. Grand Rapids: Baker, 2004.

Haquin, André. "The Liturgical Movement and Catholic Ritual Revision." In *The Oxford History of Christian Worship*, edited by Wainwright and Westerfield Tucker, 696–720. Oxford: Oxford University Press, 2005.

Harley, John. *William Byrd: Gentleman of the Chapel Royal*. Aldershot, UK: Ashgate, 1997. Amended reprint, 1999.

Hiley, David. "Plainchant Transfigured: Innovation and Reformation through the Ages." In *Antiquity and the Middle Ages: From Ancient Greece to the 15th Century*, edited by James W. McKinnon, 120–42. Man and Music. London: Macmillan, 1990.

"History of Westminster Abbey." *Westminster Abbey*. No pages. Online: https://www.westminster-abbey.org/history/history-of-westminster-abbey.

Hunt, Arthur S., and H. Stuart Jones. "1786. Christian Hymn with Musical Notation." In *The Oxyrhynchus Papyri XV*, edited by Bernard P. Grenfell and Arthur S. Hunt, 21–25. Egypt Exploration Society Graeco-Roman Memoirs. London: Egypt Exploration Fund, 1922.

"Hymns for Worship." Calvin Institute of Christian Worship and Faith Alive Christian Resources (2010). Online: https://www.faithaliveresources.org/Content/Site135/FilesSamples/49583pdf_00000007260.pdf.

Jensen, Robin M. *The Substance of Things Seen: Art, Faith, and the Christian Community*. Grand Rapids: Eerdmans, 2004.

"John Winthrop, a Modell of Christian Charity (1630)." Collections of the Massachusetts Historical Society. Online: https://history.hanover.edu/texts/winthmod.html.

Johns, Jeremy. "Christianity and Islam." In *The Oxford Illustrated History of Christianity*, edited by John McManners, 163–95. Oxford: Oxford University Press, 1990.

Johnson, Luke Timothy. *The Creed: What Christians Believe and Why It Matters*. New York: Doubleday, 2003.

Jungmann, Josef A. *The Early Liturgy: To the Time of Gregory the Great*. Liturgical Studies 6. Translated by Francis A. Brunner. Notre Dame, IN: University of Notre Dame Press, 1959.

Kelly, John N. D. *Early Christian Creeds*. London: Longmans, 1960.

Kelly, Thomas Forrest, ed. *Plainsong in the Age of Polyphony*. Cambridge Studies in Performance Practice 2. Cambridge: Cambridge University Press, 1992.

Kerman, Joseph. "Byrd, William." In *The New Grove Dictionary of Music and Musicians*, edited by Stanley Sadie and John Tyrrell, 4:714–31. New York: Grove, 1980.

Ketley, Joseph, ed. *The Two Liturgies, A.D. 1549, and A.D. 1552, with Other Documents Set Forth by Authority in the Reign of King Edward VI*. Cambridge: Cambridge University Press, 1844.

Kimbrough, Steven T., Jr., ed. *Charles Wesley: Poet and Theologian*. Nashville: Kingswood, 1992.

Lamb, John A. *The Psalms in Christian Worship*. London: The Faith, 1962.

Latourette, Kenneth S. *A History of Christianity*. New York: Harper and Row, 1953.

Leaver, Robin A. *Luther's Liturgical Music: Principles and Implications*. Lutheran Quarterly Books. Grand Rapids: Eerdmans, 2007.

Levy, Kenneth. *Gregorian Chant and the Carolingians*. Princeton: Princeton University Press, 1998.

Lewis, C. S. *Surprised by Joy*. 1955. Reprint, London: Fount, 1977.

Lockwood, Lewis, et al. "Palestrina, Giovanni Pierluigi da." In *The New Grove Dictionary of Music and Musicians*, edited by Stanley Sadie and John Tyrrell, 18:937–57. New York: Grove, 1980.

Logan, Donald F. *A History of the Church in the Middle Ages*. London: Routledge, 2002.

Lord, Albert B. *Epic Singers and Oral Tradition*. Ithaca, NY: Cornell University Press, 1991.

———. *The Singer of Tales*. Harvard Studies in Comparative Literature 24. Cambridge, MA: Harvard College, 1960. Reprint, New York: Atheneum, 1968.

Luckett, Richard. *Handel's Messiah: A Celebration*. London: Victor Gollanz, 1992.

Maas, Paul, and Constantine A. Trypanis, eds. *Sancti Romani Melodi Cantica: Cantica Genuina*. 1963. Reprint, Oxford: Clarendon, 1997.

Maddox, Randy L., and Jason E. Vickers. "Introduction." In *The Cambridge Companion to John Wesley*, edited by Randy L. Maddox and Jason E. Vickers, 1–12. Cambridge: Cambridge University Press, 2010.

"Martin Luther King—I Have a Dream Speech—August 28, 1963." *YouTube*. https://www.youtube.com/watch?v=smEqnnklfYs.

Marty, Martin E. *The Christian World: A Global History*. New York: Modern Library, 2007.

McKinnon, James W. "The Emergence of Gregorian Chant in the Carolingian Era." In *Antiquity and the Middle Ages: From Ancient Greece to the 15th Century*, edited by James W. McKinnon, 88–119. Man and Music. London: Macmillan, 1990.

———. "On the Question of Psalmody in the Ancient Synagogue." *Early Music History* 6 (1986) 159–91.

McManners, John, ed. *The Oxford Illustrated History of Christianity*. Oxford: Oxford University Press, 1990.

Metzger, Bruce M. *The Early Versions of the New Testament: Their Origin, Transmission and Limitations*. Oxford: Clarendon, 1977.

———. *The Text of the New Testament: Its Transmission, Corruption and Restoration*. New York: Oxford University Press, 1968.

Mitchell, Nathan D. "Reforms, Protestant and Catholic." In *The Oxford History of Christian Worship*, edited by Wainwright and Westerfield Tucker, 307–50. Oxford: Oxford University Press, 2005.

Morris, Colin. "Christian Civilization (1050–1400)." In *The Oxford Illustrated History of Christianity*, edited by John McManners, 196–232. Oxford: Oxford University Press, 1990.

Noll, Mark A. *Confessions and Catechisms of the Reformation*. Leicester, UK: Apollos, 1991.

Overath, Johannes, ed. *Sacred Music and Liturgy Reform after Vatican II*. Rome: Consociatio Internationalis Musicae Sacrae, 1969.

Palestrina. *Missa Papae Marcelli*. The Tallis Scholars. Directed by Peter Phillips. CD Recording. Oxford, UK: Gimell 1980.

Payton, James R., Jr. *Light from the Christian East: An Introduction to the Orthodox Tradition*. Downers Grove, IL: IVP Academic, 2007.

Part Three: The Past and Present of Music and Worship

Pierce, Joanne M. "Vestments and Objects." In *The Oxford History of Christian Worship*, edited by Wainwright and Westerfield Tucker, 841–65. Oxford: Oxford University Press, 2005.

"The Pledge of Allegiance." *Ushistory.org*. No pages. Online: https://www.ushistory.org/documents/pledge.htm.

Pöhlmann, Egert, and Martin L. West, eds. *Documents of Ancient Greek Music: The Extant Melodies and Fragments Edited and Transcribed with Commentary*. Oxford: Clarendon, 2001.

Popper, Karl. *Unended Quest: An Intellectual Autobiography*. London: Fontana, 1976. First published as "Autobiography of K. Popper." In *The Philosophy of Karl Popper*. The Library of Living Philosophers 14, edited by Paul Arthur Schilpp. Chicago: Open Court, 1974.

Porter, Stanley E. *How We Got the New Testament: Text, Transmission, Translation*. Grand Rapids: Baker, 2013.

———. *John, his Gospel, and Jesus: In Pursuit of the Johannine Voice*. Grand Rapids: Eerdmans, 2015.

———. "The Worldview of C. S. Lewis." *McMaster Journal of Theology and Ministry* 16 (2014–2015) 3–50.

Porter, Wendy J. *Early English Composers and the Credo: Emphasis as Interpretation in Sixteenth-Century Music*. Routledge Research in Music Series. London: Routledge, 2022.

———. "Hildegard of Bingen, the Breath of God, and a Musical Prophetic Voice." In *The Arts and the Bible*, edited by Stanley E. Porter and Wendy J. Porter, 62–88. McMaster New Testament Studies 10. Eugene, OR: Pickwick, 2024.

Powell, Mark Allan. *Encyclopedia of Contemporary Christian Music*. Peabody, MA: Hendrickson, 2002.

Prokurat, Michael, et al. "Introduction." In *Historical Dictionary of the Orthodox Church*, edited by Michael Prokurat et al., 1–10. Religions, Philosophies and Movements 9. Lanham, MD: Scarecrow, 1996.

Quasten, Johannes. *Patrology: Volume I. The Beginning of Patristic Literature: From the Apostles Creed to Irenaeus*. Utrecht: Spectrum, 1950.

———. *Patrology: Volume II. The Ante-Nicene Literature: After Irenaeus*. Utrecht: Spectrum, 1953.

Quasten, Johannes, and Joseph C. Plumpe, eds. *Ancient Christian Writers: The Works of the Fathers in Translation*. Westminster, MD: Newman; London: Longmans, Green, 1946.

Rasmussen, Cecilia. "Billy Graham's Star Was Born at his 1949 Revival in Los Angeles." *Los Angeles Times*, September 2, 2007. https://www.latimes.com/archives/la-xpm-2007-sep-02-me-then2-story.html.

Ratcliff, Edward C. *The Booke of Common Prayer of the Churche of England: Its Making and Revisions 1549–1661*. London: SPCK, 1949.

Reynolds, William J., and Milburn Price. *A Survey of Christian Hymnody*. 4th ed. Revised and enlarged by David W. Music and Milburn Price. Carol Stream, IL: Hope, 1999.

Richardson, Alan, ed. *A Dictionary of Christian Theology*. Philadelphia: Westminster, 1969.

Roberts, Colin Henderson, ed. *An Unpublished Fragment of the Fourth Gospel in the Rylands Library*. Manchester: Manchester University Press and the John Rylands Library, 1935.

Rordorf, Willy. *Sunday: The History of the Day of Rest and Worship in the Earliest Centuries of the Christian Church*. Translated by A. A. K. Graham. London: SCM, 1968.

"Sachsenhausen—Oranienburg (Germany)." *JewishGen: The Global Home for Jewish Genealogy*. No pages. Online: https://www.jewishgen.org/forgottencamps/camps/sachsenhauseneng.html.

Sadie, Stanley, and Alison Latham, eds. *The Cambridge Music Guide*. Cambridge: Cambridge University Press, 1985.

Schaff, Philip. *The Creeds of the Greek and Latin Churches, with Translations*. London: Hodder and Stoughton, 1878.

Sellar, Walter Carruthers, and Robert Julian Yeatman. *1066 and All That: A Memorable History of England, Comprising All the Parts You Can Remember, Including 103 Good Things, 5 Bad Kings and 2 Genuine Dates*. 1930. Reprint, London: Mandarin Paperbacks, 1993.

"The Sistine Chapel." *The Vatican*. Online: https://www.vatican.va/various/cappelle/sistina_vr.

Smith, John A. "The Ancient Synagogue, the Early Church and Singing." *Music & Letters* 65 (1984) 1–16.

Spinks, Bryan D. "Anglicans and Dissenters." In *The Oxford History of Christian Worship*, edited by Wainwright and Westerfield Tucker, 492–533. Oxford: Oxford University Press, 2005.

Squire, Russell N. *Church Music: Musical and Hymnological Developments in Western Christianity*. St. Louis: Bethany, 1962.

St. Romanos the Melodist. *Kontakia: On the Life of Christ*. Translated by Archimandrite Ephrem Lash. London: HarperCollins, 1998.

Stark, Rodney. *The Rise of Christianity: A Sociologist Reconsiders History*. Princeton: Princeton University Press, 1996.

Stringer, Martin D. *A Sociological History of Christian Worship*. Cambridge: Cambridge University Press, 2005.

Sweet, Leonard. "Introduction: Garden, Park, Glen, Meadow." In *The Church in Emerging Culture: Five Perspectives*, edited by L. Sweet, 13–41. Grand Rapids: Zondervan, 2003.

Swete, Henry Barclay. *Church Services and Service-Books before the Reformation*. London: SPCK, 1896.

Temperley, Nicholas. "Wesley: (2) Charles Wesley (i)." In *The New Grove Dictionary of Music and Musicians*, edited by Stanley Sadie and John Tyrrell, 27:304, New York: Grove, 1980.

Thibodeau, Timothy. "Western Christendom." In *The Oxford History of Christian Worship*, edited by Wainwright and Westerfield Tucker, 216–53. Oxford: Oxford University Press, 2005.

Wainwright, Geoffrey, and Karen B. Westerfield Tucker, eds. *The Oxford History of Christian Worship*. Oxford: Oxford University Press, 2005.

Warren, Frederick Edward. *The Liturgy and Ritual of the Ante-Nicene Church*. London: SPCK, 1897.

Webber, Robert E., ed. *The Complete Library of Christian Worship*. 8 vols. Peabody, MA: Hendrickson, 1993–1994.

Wegman, Herman A. *Christian Worship in East and West: A Study Guide to Liturgical History*. Translated by Gordon W. Lathrop. New York: Pueblo, 1985.

Wellesz, Egon. *A History of Byzantine Music and Hymnography*. 2nd ed. Oxford: Clarendon, 1998 [1961].
Westerfield Tucker, Karen B. "North America." In *The Oxford History of Christian Worship*, edited by Wainwright and Westerfield Tucker, 586–632. Oxford: Oxford University Press, 2005.
———. "Wesley's Emphases on Worship and the Means of Grace." In *The Cambridge Companion to John Wesley*, edited by Randy L. Maddox and Jason E. Vickers, 225–41. Cambridge: Cambridge University Press, 2010.
Westermeyer, Paul. *Let the People Sing: Hymn Tunes in Perspective*. Chicago: GIA, 2005.
———. *Te Deum: The Church and Music*. Minneapolis: Fortress, 1998.
White, James F. *Introduction to Christian Worship*. 3rd ed. Nashville: Abingdon, 2000.
———. *Protestant Worship: Traditions in Transition*. Louisville: Westminster John Knox, 1989.
Wilson, David Fenwick. *Music of the Middle Ages: Style and Structure*. New York: Schirmer, 1990.
Wilson-Dickson, Andrew. *The Story of Christian Music: From Gregorian Chant to Black Gospel, an Authoritative Illustrated Guide to All the Major Traditions of Music for Worship*. Oxford: Lion, 1992.
Wolff, Christoph. *Bach: Essays on His Life and Music*. Cambridge: MA: Harvard University Press, 1991.
———. "Bach, § III: (7) Johann Sebastian Bach." In *The New Grove Dictionary of Music and Musicians*, edited by Stanley Sadie and John Tyrrell, 2:319–82, New York: Grove, 2001.
Wordsworth, William. "Lines Composed a Few Miles above Tintern Abbey, On Revisiting the Banks of the Wye During a Tour, July 13, 1798." In *William Wordsworth: The Prelude, Selected Poems and Sonnets*, edited by Carlos Baker, 52–57. New York: Rinehart, 1948.

Index of Modern Authors

Abert, Harmann, 45, 50
Achtemeier, Paul J., 64, 66, 68
Adorno, Theodor W., 218, 224
Alan, Kurt, 137, 138, 150, 399
Allen, Thomas W., 54, 68, 158, 183
Ameln, Konrad, 177, 183
Amy, Gilbert, 32, 34, 219, 224
Anderson, Robert, 44, 52, 87, 96, 122, 134
Angus, Samuel, 84, 95
Apel, Willi, 40, 44, 45, 50, 109, 133, 170, 183, 374, 406
Armstrong, Karen, 377, 406
Arnold, Denis, 224
Arnim, Hans Friedrich August von, 55, 68, 158, 167, 183
Aune, David E., 58, 67, 68

Babic, Gordana, 376, 406
Badcock, Francis J., 370, 406
Bailey, Albert E., 391, 406
Bainton, Roland H., 374, 406
Baird, William, 177, 183
Baker, Carlos, 412
Baldovin, John F., 367, 406
Barber, Eric A., 107, 185
Barker, Andrew, 100, 106
Barkley, John M., 272, 273, 389
Barrett, Charles Kingsley, 78, 95
Barrett, G. S., 155, 156, 183
Barton, Stephen C., 94, 95

Basden, Paul A., 401, 406
Battistella, Edwin L., 324, 353
Bauer, Walter, 50, 85, 95
Baxter, Richard, 21
Beale, Gregory K., 67, 68
Beard, Mary, 84, 95
Beckwith, Roger T., 47, 50, 117, 133
Beeck, Frans Jozef van, 43, 50, 67
Begbie, Jeremy S., 354
Bekker, Paul, 211, 212, 224
Bell, James, 288, 289
Benham, Hugh, 169-71, 183, 188, 199, 294-96, 318, 388, 406
Bent, Ian D., 380, 406
Bertoglio, Chiara, 290, 302, 303, 313, 314, 318
Best, Harold M., 358, 406
Blomberg, Craig L., 77, 78, 86, 95
Bonhoeffer, Dietrich, 398, 406
Boyd, Malcolm, 224, 382, 406
Bowers, Roger, 294, 295, 318
Bowler, Sharon M., 354
Bradshaw, Paul F., 40, 48-50, 60, 68, 118, 125, 126, 133, 229, 230, 246, 272, 289, 360, 362, 367, 406
Brand, Charles M., 382, 406
Braun, Joachim, 325-27, 353
Brett, Philip, 291, 299, 318
Brown, Howard Mayer, 190, 199, 311, 312, 318
Brown, Sally A., 328, 353

Brueggemann, Walter, 249, 268
Brunner, Theodore F., 137, 142, 143, 150
Bucer, Martin, 21
Bullard, Roger A., 394, 406
Burgess, Stanley M., 397, 406
Burn, Andrew, 33, 34, 242, 246
Burrows, Donald, 406
Butt, John, 202-4, 208, 224, 394, 406
Buttrick, George Arthur, 35, 53, 108, 135, 185, 186
Buxton, Richard F., 363, 406
Byrne, Mary Elizabeth, 342, 376, 406

Calvin, John, 21, 386, 404
Cannon, George E., 64, 68
Card, Michael, 249, 268
Carpenter, Nan Cooke, 378, 406
Carson, Donald A., 61, 68, 401, 407
Chadwick, Henry, 379, 380, 407
Clericus, J., 318
Clulow, Peter, 315, 318
Coffey, John, 387-89, 407
Coil, Scott, 407, 408
Collinge, William J., 362, 378, 385, 407
Collins, H. B., 188, 190, 199
Comotti, Giovanni, 91, 92, 95, 100, 106
Connolly, Thomas H., 118, 133
Conzelmann, Hans, 62, 68, 75, 95
Cooper, Barry, 203, 211, 212, 224
Cooper, Martin, 200, 201, 224
Cosgrove, Charles H., 26, 27, 34, 45, 50, 55, 69, 101, 107, 127, 132, 133, 161, 163-65, 167, 184, 231, 246, 339, 353, 369, 407
Cox, Howard H., 176, 184, 390
Craft, Robert, 32, 35, 218-20, 224, 225
Cranmer, Thomas, 21, 297
Crawford, Michael, 84, 95
Cross, Frank L., 66, 69
Crouch, Andrae, 350, 351, 399
Crouch, Andy, 400, 407
Culy, Martin M., 76, 97
Cumming, Charles Gordon, 55, 69, 393

Daniel, Keith W., 179-81, 184
David, Hans T., 175, 184
Davids, Peter H., 66, 69
Davies, Horton, 302, 318, 386, 391, 407

Davies, John G., 134, 247
Davison, Archibald T., 45, 50
Davison, Nigel, 188, 199
Daw, Stephen, 209, 224
Deal, William, 389, 407
Dearborn, Tim A., 407, 408
Debrunner, Albert, 85, 96
Deichgräber, Reinhard, 56, 63-65, 69
Delling, D. Gerhard, 270, 273, 289
Dickens, A. G., 292-94, 318, 386, 387, 407
Dickinson, Francis Henry, 109, 133
Dix, Gregory, 48-50, 118, 133, 229, 246
Dixon, Patrick, 278, 282, 289
Doe, Paul, 172, 184, 188, 189, 198, 199
Donakowski, Conrad L., 395, 407
Dowley, Tim, 374, 380, 395, 407
Drabkin, William, 215, 224
Draffkorn Kilmer, Anne, 327, 353
Driscoll, Michael S., 374, 407
Druskin, Mikhail, 32, 35, 220, 221, 224
Dugmore, Clifford W., 48, 51, 113, 114, 133
Duguid, Timothy, 301, 302, 318, 320
Dunn, James D. G., 61, 62, 64-69

Engberg, Gudrun, 104, 107, 235, 246
Erasmus, Desiderius, 292, 293, 295, 296, 311, 318, 319
Estep, William R., 383-87, 407

Farmer, Henry G., 43, 51, 92, 96
Farris, Stephen, 60, 61, 69
Faulkner, Anne Shaw, 311, 318
Fee, Gordon D., 63, 69, 78, 79, 86, 96, 227, 246
Fellowes, Edmund H., 306, 318, 388, 407
Fenlon, Iain, 319
Fenner, Chris, 311, 318
Fewster, Gregory P., 63, 69, 227, 247
Finnegan, Ruth, 369, 407
Fiske, Roger, 214, 216, 224
Fitzmyer, Joseph A., 60, 61, 69
Forbes, Christopher, 75, 96
Fortune, Nigel, 224
Fowl, Stephen E., 59, 63-65, 69, 157-60, 184, 228, 229, 233, 247
Frame, John M., 400, 407

INDEX OF MODERN AUTHORS

Freedman, David Noel, 70, 134
Frere, Walter Howard, 298, 318

Gador-Whyte, Sarah, 150
Galpin, Francis W., 20, 51
Gamberini, Leopoldo, 100, 107
Garland, David E., 74, 96
Gasque, W. Ward, 69
Geiringer, Karl, 202, 209, 210, 224
George, Timothy, 396, 407
Georgiades, Thrasybulos, 100, 107
Gombrich, Ernst H., 181, 184
Goppelt, Leonhard, 66, 69
Gordley, Matthew E., 60, 69, 158, 159, 184, 227, 247
Goudge, Henry Leighton, 76, 96
Gould, Glenn, 176, 184
Gregory, Caspar René, 27, 35, 234, 235, 247
Grenfell, Bernard P., 26, 35, 51, 70, 107, 127, 134, 162, 184, 231, 247, 339, 354, 366, 368, 408
Grisbrooke, W. Jardine, 229, 247
Grout, Donald J., 382, 387, 407
Gundry, Robert H., 59, 63, 69, 232, 247
Guthrie, Donald, 65, 66, 69, 156, 157, 160, 184
Guthrie, Steven R., 354

Hamilton, Michael S., 400, 408
Hand, Colin, 190, 197, 199
Hannas, Ruth, 197, 199
Hannick, Christian, 27, 35, 46, 51, 100–102, 107, 234, 247
Haquin, André, 339, 408
Harley, John, 291, 296, 318, 387, 408
Harman, Alec, 114–16, 133, 319
Harper, John, 19, 35
Harrison, Frank Llewellyn, 169–70, 184, 190, 191, 199, 294, 318, 319
Haslam, Michael W., 53, 135, 186, 248
Hatch, Edwin, 111, 133
Hawthorne, Gerald F., 97
Hell, Henri, 180, 184
Henderson, Isobel, 43, 51, 55, 69, 158, 184
Hengel, Martin, 31, 35, 55, 69, 183, 184, 228, 230, 247

Herzog, F. W., 271, 289
Hickox, Richard, 34, 246
Hiley, David, 374, 408
Hill, Clifford, 284, 289
Hodge, Charles, 77, 96
Høeg, Carsten, 98, 106, 107, 231, 236, 237, 247, 342, 354, 377
Hofman, May, 28, 35, 169, 184
Hofmann, Klaus, 177
Holleman, A. W. J., 45, 49, 60, 70, 130, 134
Hope, David Michael, 109, 134
Horn, B., 286, 287, 289
Horst, Pieter W. van der, 48, 51
Houghton, Elsie, 338, 343, 347, 348, 354
Houston, James M., 355
Howell, Clifford, 109, 134
Howell, Evelyn B., 88, 89, 96
Hucke, Helmut, 47, 51
Hughes, Andrew, 171
Hughes, Dom Anselm, 52, 71
Hunger, Herbert, 170, 171, 184
Hunt, Arthur S., 26, 27, 35, 45, 51, 55, 70, 101, 107, 127, 134, 161, 162, 164, 167, 184, 231, 247, 339, 354, 368, 408
Huray, Peter le, 169, 184, 291, 292, 296, 319
Husmann, Heinrich, 46, 51

Idelsohn, Abraham Z., 46, 47, 51, 106
Inge, John, 310, 319

Jeffery, Peter, 46, 51, 60, 70
Jensen, Robin M., 376, 408
Jeremias, Joachim, 128, 134
Johns, Jeremy, 378, 408
Johnson, Luke Timothy, 370, 408
Jones, Cheslyn, 20, 35, 50, 133–34
Jones, H. Stuart, 26, 27, 35, 45, 51, 55, 70, 96, 101, 107, 127, 134, 161, 162, 164, 167, 184, 247, 339, 354, 368, 408
Joyce, Paul, 69, 247
Jourdan-Hemmerdinger, Denise, 101, 107
Jungmann, Josef A., 367, 408

INDEX OF MODERN AUTHORS

Käsemann, Ernst, 65, 70
Kelly, John N. D., 370, 408
Kelly, Thomas Forrest, 381, 408
Kennedy, William P. McClure, 298, 318
Kerman, Joseph, 300, 305, 306, 312, 314, 319, 386, 387, 408
Ketley, Joseph, 294, 319, 387, 408
Kiefer, Otto, 85, 96
Kimbrough, Steven T., Jr., 393, 408
King, Martin Luther, 399, 409
Kirkendale, Warren, 211, 224
Kirkby, Emma, 343, 353
Klassen, William, 71
Knight, George W., III, 57, 70, 160, 184
Knox, John, 21
Koder, Johannes, 150
Kraeling, Carl H., 62, 64, 70, 128, 129, 134
Kreider, Alan, 316, 317, 319
Kreider, Eleanor, 316, 317, 319

Lamb, John A., 391, 408
Landels, John G., 100, 107
Lang, Paul H., 232, 247
Latham, Alison, 387, 394, 411
Latourette, Kenneth S., 374, 383-85, 392-98, 408
Leaver, Robin A., 176, 184, 202, 224, 290, 295, 319, 385, 388, 408
Leichtentritt, Hugo, 130, 134
Leith, John H., 57, 70
Lenti, Vincent A., 296, 319
Leppert, Richard, 224
Levy, Kenneth, 374, 409
Lewis, C. S., 249, 268, 313, 356, 399, 404, 409, 410
Lewis, Naphtali, 74, 96
Liddell, Henry George, 96
Lim, Paul C. H., 387, 389, 407
Lockwood, Lewis, 385, 387, 409
Logan, Donald F., 359, 361, 363, 369, 370, 373, 374, 378, 379, 381, 409
Long, Anthony A., 167, 185
Longenecker, Richard N., 56, 70
Lord, Albert B., 369, 409
Louth, Andrew, 341, 354
Luckett, Richard, 394, 409

Luther, Martin, 21, 29, 175, 177, 178, 293, 295, 298, 311, 317, 343, 344, 346, 384, 385, 388, 394, 404

Maas, Paul, 136-39, 142-51, 341, 342, 354, 375, 409
Machlis, Joseph, 180, 185
Maddox, Randy L., 392, 409, 412
Mann, Alfred, 209, 210, 224
Marsh, Christopher, 293, 301, 319
Marshall, I. Howard, 61, 65, 70
Marshall, Robert L., 201, 202, 224
Martin, Ralph P., 48, 49, 51, 56, 62, 63, 65, 69, 70, 97, 118, 128, 134, 158, 159, 185, 227-30, 232, 247
Marty, Martin E., 383, 409
Mathiesen, Thomas J., 100, 107
Matthews, Denis, 217, 224
Matthews, Victor H., 127, 134
Maxwell, William D., 47, 51
McCaldin, Denis, 209, 217, 224
McCarthy, Kerry, 298, 299, 302-5, 307, 308, 319
McKay, Heather A., 48, 51
McKinnon, James W., 38, 40-44, 48, 49, 51, 52, 56, 60, 70, 82-84, 87, 91-93, 96, 106, 112, 117-19, 122, 124-26, 134, 163, 167, 185, 230, 231, 247, 325, 354, 365, 374, 408, 409
McManners, John, 385, 408, 409
Meeks, Wayne A., 39, 52, 56, 70
Mellers, Wilfred H., 31, 35, 180, 182, 185
Mendel, Arthur, 175, 184
Messenger, Thomas, 191, 199
Metzger, Bruce M., 369, 371, 373, 409
Meyer, Marvin W., 84, 96
Michaelides, Solon, 87, 96, 122, 134
Miller, Calvin, 315, 316, 319
Miller, Clement, 292, 293, 311, 319
Miller, Patrick D., 328, 353
Milligan, George, 89, 93, 94, 96
Milsom, John, 314, 319
Mitchell, Nathan D., 387, 409
Moffatt, James, 75, 96
Monson, Craig, 299, 300, 319
Moore, Erika, 355

416

INDEX OF MODERN AUTHORS

Morehen, John, 28, 35, 169, 184, 300, 309
Morley, Thomas, 312, 319
Morris, Christopher, 300, 309, 320
Morris, Colin, 378, 409
Moule, Charles F. D., 272, 289
Moulton, James Hope, 89, 93, 94, 96
Mountford, James Frederick, 101, 107, 164, 185
Mowry, Lucetta, 62, 64, 70, 128, 129, 134
Murray, Dom Gregory, 170, 185

Neighbour, Oliver, 310, 320
Noll, Mark A., 385, 409
Norden, Eduard, 56, 58, 65, 70, 157, 159, 185

O'Brien, Peter T., 63, 64, 70
O'Connor, Michael, 334, 354
Oellacher, Hans, 137, 151
Orr, William F., 76, 96
Orton, David E., 69, 247
Overath, Johannes, 399, 409
Owens, Jessie Ann, 308, 320

Palestrina, 209, 210, 245, 345, 384, 385, 387, 409
Palisca, Claude V., 382, 407
Parry, Reginald St John, 74, 96
Pasler, Jann, 34, 224
Payne, Philip Barton, 75, 96
Payton, James R., Jr., 370, 378, 383, 409
Peterson, David, 270, 288, 289
Petti, Anthony G., 187-90, 199
Pfau, Marianne, 380, 406
Phillips, Peter, 188, 189, 193, 195, 196, 199
Pierce, Joanne M., 371, 410
Pisk, Paul Amadeus, 118, 129, 135
Plummer, Alfred, 74, 97
Plumpe, Joseph C., 368, 410
Pöhlmann, Egert, 35, 45, 52, 55, 70, 100, 101, 107, 127, 134, 161, 164, 185, 231, 247, 339, 354, 368, 410
Popper, Karl, 388, 410

Porter, Stanley E., 5, 6, 27, 35, 61, 69, 70, 82, 88, 97, 99-104, 107, 156, 157, 185, 234, 237, 247, 248, 269, 270, 289, 324, 343, 354, 366, 371, 373, 384, 386, 389, 399, 410
Porter, Wendy J., 23, 27, 28, 35, 99, 101-4, 107, 172, 185, 187, 199, 234, 237, 248, 343, 348, 354, 380, 386, 399, 410
Poulenc, Francis, 7, 31, 156, 179-85, 349
Powell, J. U., 107, 185
Powell, Mark Allan, 350, 354, 399, 400, 410
Price, Milburn, 391, 410
Prokurat, Michael, 370, 376, 410

Quast, Kevin, 78, 97
Quasten, Johannes, 38, 39, 43, 45, 52, 60, 70, 366-68, 410
Quitslund, Beth, 300-302, 320, 344, 354

Rasmussen, Cecilia, 398, 410
Ratcliff, Edward C., 387, 410
Reese, Gustave, 132, 134, 191, 199
Reid, Daniel G., 97
Reicke, Bo, 118, 134
Reinach, Théodore, 45, 52, 100, 107, 164, 185
Reynolds, William J., 391, 410
Richardson, Alan, 380, 410
Richter, Philip J., 269, 289
Roberts, Colin Henderson, 366, 410
Robertson, Alec, 117, 134
Robertson, Archibald, 74, 97
Römer, Cornelia E., 138, 151
Romanus Melodus (St. Romanos the Melodist), 6, 7, 136-39, 141-51, 340-42, 354, 355, 375, 411
Rordorf, Willy, 363, 367, 411
Rosenbaum, Hans-Udo, 137, 138, 150

Sachs, Curt, 43, 44, 52, 122, 123, 134, 326, 355
Sadie, Stanley, 51, 52, 96, 133, 134, 387, 394, 406, 408, 409, 411, 412
Salomons, Robert Paul, 137, 151
Sanders, Jack T., 58, 71

INDEX OF MODERN AUTHORS

Sandon, Nick, 109, 134, 193, 194, 199
Schaff, Philip, 373, 374, 411
Schilpp, Paul Arthur, 354, 410
Schlesinger, Kathleen, 44, 52
Schweitzer, Albert, 175, 185, 203, 224
Schweizer, Eduard, 62, 71
Scott, J. E., 44, 52, 111, 135, 231, 248
Scott, Robert, 96
Sedley, David N., 167, 185
Sellar, Walter Carruthers, 378, 411
Sendrey, Alfred, 43, 46, 62, 116, 122, 123, 135
Shepherd, Massey H., Jr., 162, 169, 185, 289
Sheppard, John A., 7, 23, 28, 29, 156, 168, 169, 171–74, 183, 185, 187, 189, 190, 193–96, 198, 199
Sikes, Edward Ernest, 54, 68, 158, 183
Silva, Moisés, 63, 71, 232, 248
Siohan, Robert, 32, 35, 221, 224
Smith, John A., 39, 40, 43, 45, 49, 52, 60, 71, 106, 117, 118, 125, 135, 163, 186, 325, 355, 365, 411
Smith, Richard Langham, 241, 248
Smith, William Sheppard, 60, 71, 111, 118, 125, 126, 132, 135, 228, 230, 231, 248
Snyder, Graydon F., 71
Solomon, Maynard, 211, 225
Souris, André, 222, 225
Spinks, Bryan D., 391, 411
Spitta, Philipp, 203, 208, 225
Squire, Russell N., 389, 390, 392, 411
Stark, Rodney, 97, 411
Stanley, Arthur Penrhyn, 76, 97
Stauffer, George B., 202, 225
Stravinsky, Igor, 8, 29, 32, 34–36, 200, 218–25, 348
Stringer, Martin D., 369, 404, 411
Strunk, W. Oliver, 46, 52, 306, 320
Sweet, Leonard, 401, 411
Swete, Henry Barclay, 387, 411

Talbert, Charles H., 75, 76, 97
Taylor, David, 84, 97
Temperley, Nicholas, 301, 302, 320, 344, 354, 393, 411

Terry, Charles Sanford, 177, 186, 203, 225
Theissen, Gerd, 84, 97
Thibodeau, Timothy, 374, 378, 379, 411
Thiselton, Anthony C., 77, 78, 97
Thom, Johan C., 167, 186
Tillyard, Henry J. W., 27, 35, 235, 248
Treitler, Leo, 46, 52
Trench, Richard C., 228, 229, 248
Trypanis, Constantine A., 136–39, 142–51, 341, 342, 354, 375, 409
Tyrrell, John, 406, 408, 409, 411, 412

Ulrich, Homer, 118, 129, 135

Vanderburgh, Frederick Augustus, 55, 71
Velimirović, Miloš, 27, 35, 107, 236, 246
Vickers, Jason E., 392, 409, 412

Wainwright, Geoffrey, 35, 50, 133, 134, 385, 407–12
Walsh, Stephen, 32, 35, 220, 221, 225
Walther, James A., 76, 96
Waltke, Bruce K., 328, 355
Warner, Rob, 285, 289
Warren, Frederick Edward, 211, 224, 370, 411
Watson, Edward W., 76, 97
Webber, Robert E., 396, 411
Wegman, Herman A., 363, 411
Wellesz, Egon, 27, 35, 39, 43, 45–47, 51–53, 56, 69–71, 96, 98, 104, 107, 129–31, 134, 135, 163, 184, 186, 235–37, 239, 246, 248, 335, 355, 362, 412
Werner, Eric, 27, 35, 38, 39, 41, 43–48, 52, 55, 60, 71, 101, 106, 108, 111–14, 117–23, 127, 128, 130, 133, 135, 161, 163, 165–67, 186, 231, 232, 248, 339
Wesley, Charles, 347, 392, 393
Wesley, John, 21, 347, 392
West, Martin L., 27, 35, 36, 43–45, 49, 52, 53, 55, 70, 71, 100, 101, 106–8, 127, 129–32, 134, 135, 158, 161–65, 167, 185, 186, 231, 232, 248, 339, 354, 355, 368, 369, 410

Westerfield Tucker, Karen B., 358, 385, 392, 400, 407–12
Westermeyer, Paul, 231, 248, 376, 388, 412
White, Eric Walter, 32, 36, 220, 221, 225
White, James F., 20, 36, 363, 388, 389, 391, 395–97, 412
Williams, Penry, 291, 306, 320, 344, 397
Wilson, David Fenwick, 379, 412
Wilson-Dickson, Andrew, 241, 248, 374, 412
Witherington, Ben, III, 84, 97
Witt, Reginald Eldred, 84, 85, 97
Witvliet, John D., 328, 355
Wolff, Christoph, 202, 203, 209, 210, 225, 382, 412

Wolterstorff, Nicholas, 328, 355
Wooldridge, Harry Ellis, 127, 135
Wordsworth, William, 381, 412
Wright, David, 241, 248
Wright, N. T., 59, 63, 71, 232, 248
Wulstan, David, 44, 53, 295, 297, 320

Yarnold, SJ, Edward, 35, 50, 133, 134
Yeatman, Robert Julian, 378, 411

Zim, Rivkah, 301, 320
Zschietzschmann, Willy, 87, 97
Zuntz, Günther, 137, 142, 151
Zwingli, Heinrich, 315, 385
Zwingli, Ulrich, 21

Index of Ancient Sources

OLD TESTAMENT

Genesis
4:21	325, 326

Exodus
12:6–8	18
12:24–27	18
15:20	80

Leviticus
16:12	372

Numbers
6:24–26	24, 25

Judges
4:4	80

1 Samuel
2:1–10	22, 61, 328
10:5	90

2 Samuel
22	329

1 Kings
6:5–18	372
6:9	372

2 Kings
18:3–4	329

1 Chronicles
25	394
29:11	67

2 Chronicles
26	328
26:5	328
26:13	328
29:25–30	329

Ezra
2:64–67	332

Nehemiah
1–13	329

Job
1–42	249
1	264
1:20–21	264
10:12	24
21:12	326
30:31	326

Psalms

13	249
18	329
19	165
19:1–2	165
19:4	89
23	302
24	126
27:6	330
30:4	330
33:3	323
40:3	323, 329
46	295
47	165
47:6	330
48	126
50	165
59:16	330
63:5	330
79	313
69	165
81	126
81:1–4	300
82	126
85:7	24
89:1	330
92	126
93	126
93:3–4	165
94	126
95:2	330
96	165
96:1	323, 329, 330
98:1	323
98:4	330
100:2	330
101:1	330
107	331
108:1	330
110	55
113–18	57, 126, 334
118	328
118:26	24
119:33–38	309
136	60, 328
148	165
148:2	165
148:4	165
148:5	167
149	330
149:1	323, 330
150:4	326

Proverbs

10:24	24

Isaiah

5:12	91
6:3	24, 66
8:3	80
26:19	63
29	332
30:29	91
42:10	323, 331
44:23	331
49:13	331
52:9	331
53	62
55:12	331
60:1	63
60:2	63
61:1–2	275

Jeremiah

30:19	332

Lamentations

3:14	332
3:63	332

Ezekiel

2:8—3:3	341
13:17	80

Daniel

2:37	67

Joel

2:28	80

Amos

8:3	332

Micah

2:4	332

Habakkuk

2:20	167

Zechariah

1:77	271, 272

NEW TESTAMENT

Matthew

5	368
5:9–13	22
9:23–24	44, 112
9:23	333, 335
9:27	23
11:16–17	44
11:17	333
15	103
18	102
18:33	24
21:9	24
26:7	372
26:17–30	18
26:26–28	276
26:30	41, 43, 57, 166, 229, 334
27:45	31, 181
27:46	31, 181
27:50	31, 181
28	101
28:5–19	101, 103
28:16–20	274
28:19	57, 58, 171, 274

Mark

3	102
8	102
8:29	57, 58
8:34–35	250
14:3	372
14:12–26	18
14:26	41, 43, 57, 166, 229, 334
15	102, 103
15:33	31, 181
15:34	31, 181
15:37	181

Luke

1–2	61
1:46–55	22, 58, 60, 61, 271
1:68–79	22, 58, 271
1:77	271, 272
2:14	23, 58
2:29–32	22, 58, 272
2:36	80
4:15–30	275
4:15–16	48
7:32	44
7:38	372
9	102
10	102, 103
12	103
15:25	44, 333
18:9–14	340
19	102
19:38	24
21	103
22:7–22	18
23:44	31, 181
23:46	31, 181
23:55–56	372
24	103

John

1	103
1:1–18	61, 62
1:1–16	58, 61, 62
1:1–4	33, 243
1:1–2	33
1:1	28, 168, 171
1:14	28, 29, 168, 171–74
1:29	23, 24
2–6	243
3:22	274
3:23	274
4	402

John (cont.)

4:23–24	402
6:71—7:46	27, 102, 234
6:71—7:3	235
7	102, 103
7:3–6	235
7:7–10	235
7:10–13	235
7:13–16	235
7:16–18	235
7:18–22	235
7:22–24	235
7:24–30	236, 237
7:24–27	235
7:24	236
7:27–30	235
7:30–32	235
7:32–35	235
7:30	236
7:35–37	235
7:37–39	235
7:40–42	235
7:43–46	235
8	102
9	102
11	102
12	102
12:3	372
16:7	271
16:13	379
16:20	250
18	366
19	243
19:16	243
19:17—20:9	243
19:30	31, 181
19:39	372

Acts

2:4	275
2:15	275
2:17	80
2:22–24	275
2:38	274
2:41	274
2:42	18
2:46	18
4:24–30	58
4:24	58
4:26	58
5:38–39	361
5:42	58
8:38	274
9:20	57, 58
9:22	58
10:36	57, 58
11:20	57, 58
11:26	362
12:9	80
12:30	274
12:31	274
10:36	57
10:48	274
11:20	57
11:26	362
12:9	80
16:25	43, 57, 166, 229, 334
16:31–33	274
17:2	48, 114
17:3	57, 58
18:5	57, 58
18:28	58
22:6	58

Romans

1:3–4	57, 58
3:13–18	58
3:24–26	58
8	29, 177
8:26–27	29, 177
8:26	174, 179
8:27	175, 177, 179
9:33	58
10:9–10	58
10:9	56–58, 62
10:18	89
11:33–36	58
15:5–6	39
16:25–27	57, 58

1 Corinthians

3:16	272
5:4	58

INDEX OF ANCIENT SOURCES

7:14	82
8:6	57, 58
9	103
10:16–17	18
10:21	18
11	74
11:5	73, 74, 76, 80, 85
11:6	93
11:20–29	18
11:23–26	22
11:24–25	362
11:26	57, 58, 276
12–14	275
12:3	58
13	44
13:14	58
14	73, 75, 84–86, 89, 316
14:2a	86
14:2b	86
14:2c	86
14:3	86
14:4	86
14:5a	86
14:5b	86
14:6a	86
14:6b	86
14:7–9	44
14:7	78, 86–89, 335
14:8	89
14:9	86, 89
14:11	86, 89, 90
14:13	86
14:13b	272
14:14	272
14:15	43
14:18	86
14:19	86
14:21	86
14:23	86
14:26	43, 44, 57, 336
14:27–28	279
14:27	86
14:28	86
14:29	86
14:34–35	5, 72–95
14:34	74, 80–82, 89
14:35	89, 93
14:36	76
14:39	86
15:3–5	56–58, 62, 63
16:2	103

2 Corinthians

1	103
1:3–4	58
2	103
5	103
5:18–21	58
6	103
8	103
10	103
11	103
11:12–15	58
13:13	57, 58

Ephesians

1:3–14	58
2:12–19	58
2:14	58
2:16	58
2:22	272
4:4–9	58
4:10	58
5:2	372
5:4	94
5:11–12	93
5:14	58, 63
5:18–19	335, 336
5:19	4, 39, 44, 56, 166, 271, 336

Philippians

1:29–30	250
2	334, 336
2:5–11	8, 57–59
2:6–11	56, 58, 63, 64, 129, 155, 156, 227–29, 232, 233, 272
2:10	272
2:11	272

Colossians

1:12–14	58
1:15–20	56, 58, 59, 64, 65, 272
2:2	158
2:8	58
2:9–15	58
2:13–15	58
3:8	94
3:16–17	287
3:16	4, 39, 44, 56, 166, 271, 336

1 Thessalonians

3	103
4	103

1 Timothy

1:6	160
1:15	57, 58
1:17	57, 58, 128, 166
3:11	160
3:16	7, 56, 58, 59, 62, 65, 66, 128, 156–60, 228
4:7	160
5:13	160
6:4–5	160
6:12	58
6:15–16	57, 58
6:20	160

2 Timothy

1:8–10	58
2:11–13	56, 58
3:16	275

Titus

1:10–11	93
3:4–7	58

Hebrews

1:3	58
2:12	166, 229
9:1	337
10:1	337
12:28	337

James

2:19	57, 58
4:12	58
5:13	44

1 Peter

1:3–12	58
1:3–5	58
1:18–21	58
1:18–20	58
2:4–8	58
2:6–8	57, 58
2:6–7	58
2:21–25	58
2:21–22	58
2:24	268
3:18–22	58, 66
3:18	58

1 John

1:1–2	33, 243
2:2	57, 58
2:22	58
3:2	33, 243
4:2	57, 58
4:10	58
4:15	57, 58
5:1	57, 58
5:5	58

2 John

1:1	171

Jude

24–25	57, 58

Revelation

1:4–8	58
1:15	338
4:8–11	58
4:8	24, 58, 66, 67
4:11	58

5:8	39	**EARLY CHRISTIAN**	
5:9–14	58	**WRITINGS**	
5:9–10	58		
5:9	44, 323, 337	CSEL LXIV, 7–8	84
5:12	44, 58, 67	PG XXXIH, 356	82
5:13	58, 166	PL XIV, 924–45	84
7:9–12	58	PL XXIII, 519	83
7:11b–12	166	PL 26.969	325
7:10	58		
7:12	58	Did. 8.2	22
10:4a	87	Did. 9	19
10:9–11	341	Did. 14	368
11:15–18	58	Did. 14.1	363
11:15	58		
11:17–18	58	**Ambrose**	
12:10–12	58	*Explanatio psalmi* 9	84
14:2	338		
14:3	44, 58, 323	**Augustine**	
15:3–4	58	*Conf.* 10.33.49–50	230
15:3	44, 338		
16:5–7	58	**1 Clement**	
18:22	44, 87, 335	34.5–7	231
19:1–2	58		
19:3	58	**Clement of Alexandria**	
19:5–8	58	*Str.* 6.11.88	167
19:5	58		
19:6–8	58	**Chrysostom**	
19:14	58	*Matt. Hom.* 11.7	112
22:17	58		
22:20	33, 243	**Cyril of Jerusalem**	
		Dialogues contra pelagianos 1.25	83
RABBINIC WRITINGS		*Procatechesis* XIV	82
Tamid 7.4	126	**Gregory of Nazianzus**	
b. 'Arak 13b	325	*Carm.* 2.2.4.55	127, 162, 231
PHILO		**Ignatius**	
		Eph. 4.1–2	231
Contempl. 10.80–81	40		
Ebr. 75	67		
JOSEPHUS			
Ant. 3.12.6	327		
Ant. 7.12.3	325		

Justin Martyr

1 Apol.	19
1 Apol. 62	366, 367
1 Apol. 65–67	363
1 Apol. 67	367

GRECO-ROMAN WRITINGS

Achilles Tatius

Leuc. Clit. 2.14.8	88

Aristotle

Eth. nic. 4.8.6	93

Cassius Dio

Hist. rom. 54.16.2	81

Cleanthes

Hymn to Zeus	27, 55, 158, 167, 168

Hippolytus

Trad. Ap.	21, 22

Homer

Il. 10.12–13	91
Il. 18.495	91

Plato

Tim. 37E	67

Pliny the Younger

Ep. 6.16	363
Ep. Tra.	67
Ep. Tra. 10.96	338, 363–65

Pseudo-Aristotle

[*Aud.*] 801a.29–30	88
[*Aud.*] 801b.1–2	88, 89

PAPYRI

BGU IV.1024.7.20	93

P.Oxy

XV 1786	4, 6, 7, 26, 45, 49, 55, 101, 106, 127, 129, 130, 155, 156, 160–68, 229, 231, 232, 339, 344, 368, 369, 383
XXII 2346	131
XLIV 3161	131
LXV 4462	127, 162, 231

www.ingramcontent.com/pod-product-compliance
Lightning Source LLC
Chambersburg PA
CBHW072116290426
44111CB00012B/1683